Donghyun Jeong
Pauline Baptism among the Mysteries

Beihefte zur Zeitschrift
für die neutestamentliche
Wissenschaft

Edited by
Knut Backhaus, Matthias Konradt, Judith Lieu,
Laura Nasrallah, Jens Schröter, and Gregory E. Sterling

Volume 257

Donghyun Jeong

Pauline Baptism among the Mysteries

Ritual Messages and the Promise of Initiation

DE GRUYTER

ISBN 978-3-11-221420-6
e-ISBN (PDF) 978-3-11-079138-9
e-ISBN (EPUB) 978-3-11-079150-1
ISSN 0171-6441

Library of Congress Control Number: 2023932402

Bibliographic Information published by the Deutsche Nationalbibliothek
The Deutsche Nationalbibliothek lists this publication in the Deutsche Nationalbibliografie;
Detailed bibliographic data are available in the Internet at http://dnb.dnb.de.

© 2025 Walter de Gruyter GmbH, Berlin/Boston
This volume is text- and page-identical with the hardback published in 2023.
Printing and binding: CPI books GmbH, Leck

www.degruyter.com

For my grandmother
(1936 – 2023)

πάντοτε σὺν κυρίῳ ἐσόμεθα

Acknowledgements

This monograph is a revised version of my dissertation. I am grateful for Emory University's generous funding and interdisciplinary academic environment. I also thank the editors of the BZNW series for agreeing to publish my manuscript. I appreciate the anonymous reviewer's critiques and suggestions that helped me refine my arguments, as well as De Gruyter's editorial assistance that facilitated the transition from a dissertation to a book.

I would like to express my sincere gratitude to my dissertation advisor Steven Kraftchick for his invaluable guidance and encouragement. Steve always pushed me to ask critical questions about subject matter, methodologies, and my own writing. I am also indebted to the other members of my committee, Walter Wilson, Susan Hylen, and Sandra Blakely, all of whom helped my project with their profound expertise and critical acumen. I extend my thanks to Vernon Robbins and Carl Holladay, whose methodological creativity and exegetical rigor influenced my scholarship. Carl offered thorough feedback on my manuscript at the initial stages of revision for publication, which I deeply appreciate. I also feel fortunate to have had formative conversations with my NT cohort (Steve M., Ebby, Zane, Jon) and the Korean doctoral students in biblical studies (Hyunju, Hyun Woo, and Gilha).

I have been privileged to work with and learn from several scholars, colleagues, and faith communities beyond Emory. Special thanks go to Adela Yarbro Collins, who has been offering valuable advice at each point of my scholarly journey. I am grateful to Jae Duk Choi, Jin Young Choi, Roger Nam, and Kwok Pui-lan, for their mentorship, and to Bryan Whitfield for his hospitality during my teaching at Mercer in 2021–2022. I had opportunities to present portions of my research at academic conferences—2020 AAR/SBL Annual Meeting and 2021 AAR/SBL Southeastern Regional Meeting—and I appreciate constructive comments from participants. I express my gratitude to Ellen White and Wayne Coppins who read earlier drafts of my manuscript and gave valuable feedback that strengthened my arguments. Support from Pyungkwang Presbyterian Church (Seoul) and Korean Central Presbyterian Church of Atlanta has nourished me and my family spiritually and financially. I extend my appreciation to President José Irizarry, Dean Margaret Aymer, and all the faculty members of Austin Presbyterian Theological Seminary for our formative academic environment.

I owe a special debt of gratitude to wonderful libraries and library staff that supported my research and writing process. Much of this manuscript was written in the midst of the coronavirus pandemic. Emory's Pitts Theology Library and Woodruff Library provided me with necessary resources in a timely manner even when physical spaces were closed. The final stages of revision for publication took place throughout the first academic year of my teaching at Austin Seminary. The seminary's library (Wright Learning and Information Center) has been the ideal place for this work, and I want to acknowledge David Schmersal for his effective assistance.

My family members, both in Korea and in the US, deserve my deepest thanks for their steadfast love and support.

Austin, May 2023   Donghyun Jeong

Contents

List of Figures and Tables —— XIII

Abbreviations —— XIV

1 Introduction —— 1
1.1 Presuppositions —— 2
1.2 An Outline of the Study —— 6
1.3 The Thesis of the Study —— 9

2 Paul and the Mysteries: Retrospective and Prospective —— 11
2.1 The History of Scholarship —— 11
2.1.1 The Inaugurated Quest: Paul/Early Christianity Was Dependent on the Mysteries —— 14
2.1.1.1 Franz Cumont —— 15
2.1.1.2 Alfred Loisy —— 16
2.1.1.3 Richard Reitzenstein —— 18
2.1.2 The Moratorium on the Quest: No Dependency on the Mysteries —— 21
2.1.2.1 Wagner and Wedderburn —— 22
2.1.2.2 "Jewish Backgrounds" —— 25
2.1.2.3 Jonathan Z. Smith —— 27
2.1.3 The Continued Quest —— 28
2.1.3.1 New Testament and Early Christianity Scholars —— 30
2.1.3.2 Classicists and Ancient Historians —— 32
2.1.3.3 Scholars who Focus on Philosophical/Literary Aspects of Mystery Language —— 35
2.1.4 The Need for an Analytical Framework —— 37
2.2 The Analytical Framework of this Study —— 38
2.2.1 Roy Rappaport —— 39
2.2.2 Martin Riesebrodt —— 48
2.2.3 My Integrated Framework —— 56

3 Initiation into the Dionysiac Mysteries —— 66
3.1 The Self-referential Messages, or the Benefits Initiation Promises —— 69
3.1.1 Transformation of One's Religious and Social Self —— 69
3.1.2 Blessed Civic Life —— 73
3.1.3 Ecstasy and Deliverance in the Present —— 76
3.1.4 Deliverance in the Future —— 80

3.2	The Canonical Messages, or the Grounds for the Efficacy of the Initiation's Promises —— 84
3.2.1	Dionysus Established the Initiation Ritual —— 84
3.2.2	Dionysus Suffers and Overcomes —— 85
3.2.3	Dionysus Returns —— 88
3.2.4	Dionysus Is Identified with His Devotees —— 91
3.2.5	Dionysus Is the Intercessor in the Afterlife —— 99
3.3	Beyond Initiation —— 103
3.3.1	Is Initiation Alone Sufficient? —— 103
3.3.2	Religious Virtuosity as Both What is Promised and What Enables Other Benefits —— 106
3.4	Summary —— 107

4 Initiation into the Mysteries of Isis —— 109

4.1	The Self-referential Messages, or the Benefits Initiation Promises —— 111
4.1.1	Transformation of One's Religious and Social Self —— 111
4.1.2	*Sōtēria:* Protection/Deliverance —— 116
4.1.3	Isis's Guardianship: Permanent Relationship with the Goddess —— 120
4.1.4	Blessed Afterlife —— 122
4.1.5	Development of One's Cognitive Capability —— 128
4.2	The Canonical Messages, or the Grounds for the Efficacy of the Initiation's Promises —— 131
4.2.1	Isis Established the Initiation Ritual —— 131
4.2.2	Isis is the All-powerful, Universal Deity —— 133
4.2.3	Isis Sympathizes with Her Devotees —— 134
4.2.4	The Initiates Share the Fate and Suffering of Isis —— 137
4.3	Beyond Initiation —— 146
4.3.1	Is Initiation Alone Sufficient? —— 146
4.3.2	Religious Virtuosity as Both What is Promised and What Enables Other Benefits —— 148
4.4	Summary —— 151

5 Initiation into the Pauline Communities (I): Baptism in 1 Corinthians —— 153

5.1	Preliminary Considerations —— 153
5.2	Discussions of Key Passages —— 159
5.2.1	1 Corinthians 1:10–17 —— 159
5.2.1.1	Exegetical Discussion —— 159
5.2.1.2	The self-referential messages, the canonical messages, and things beyond baptism —— 167

5.2.2	1 Corinthians 1:26–31 —— **168**	
5.2.2.1	Exegetical Discussion —— **168**	
5.2.2.2	The self-referential messages, the canonical messages, and things beyond baptism —— **172**	
5.2.3	1 Corinthians 6:9–11 —— **172**	
5.2.3.1	Exegetical Discussion —— **172**	
5.2.3.2	The self-referential messages, the canonical messages, and things beyond baptism —— **176**	
5.2.4	1 Corinthians 10:1–5 and 1 Corinthians 12:12–13 —— **178**	
5.2.4.1	Exegetical Discussion —— **178**	
5.2.4.2	The self-referential messages, the canonical messages, and things beyond baptism —— **191**	
5.2.5	1 Corinthians 15:18–19 —— **192**	
5.2.5.1	Exegetical Discussion —— **192**	
5.2.5.2	The self-referential messages, the canonical messages, and things beyond baptism —— **195**	

6 "Baptism for the Dead" (1 Cor 15:29): Ritual Blending and Innovation —— 197

6.1	Introductory Remarks —— **197**
6.2	Investigation of the Context in Roman Corinth —— **201**
6.2.1	Rituals for Initiation: focusing on the Mysteries of Melikertes-Palaimon —— **201**
6.2.2	Funerary Rituals and Beyond —— **210**
6.3	Ritual Blending and Innovation —— **222**

7 Initiation into the Pauline Communities (II): Baptism in Galatians and Romans —— 228

7.1	Discussions of Key Passages —— **228**
7.1.1	Galatians 3:25–29 —— **228**
7.1.1.1	Exegetical Discussion —— **228**
7.1.1.2	The self-referential messages, the canonical messages, and things beyond baptism —— **238**
7.1.2	Romans 6:1–14 within Romans 5–8 —— **239**
7.1.2.1	Exegetical Discussion —— **239**
7.1.2.2	The self-referential messages, the canonical messages, and things beyond baptism —— **270**
7.2	Synthesis: Baptism in the Pauline Communities and Paul's Interpretation of Baptism —— **273**

8 Conclusion —— 280

Appendix: References to Baptism in the Undisputed Pauline Letters —— 286

Bibliography —— 292

Index of Names —— 312

Index of Ancient Names —— 318

Index of Subjects —— 319

Index of Ancient Sources —— 321

List of Figures and Tables

Figure 1:	Pelike, art trade, side A, Sotheby's, London 1995, 36 Nr. 72 ——	**89**
Figure 2:	Chous, Meidias Painter, New York, Metropolitan Museum of Art 75.2.11 ——	**90**
Figure 3:	Calyx krater, Polygnotos group, Copenhagen, The National Museum of Denmark ABC 1021, side A —— **90**	
Figure 4:	Apulian krater, Museo Arqueológico Nacional, Madrid, inv. no. 1999/99/124 ——	**95**
Figure 5:	Red jasper, Munich, SMM 2587 ——	**97**
Figure 6:	Red-orange cornelian, Munich, SMM 537 ——	**97**
Figure 7:	Orange cornelian, Munich, SMM 2190 ——	**97**
Figure 8:	Apulian krater, Toledo Museum of Art, Object number: 1994.19 ——	**100**
Figure 9:	Votive altar, Musée du Louvre, inv. no. MA 1544 ——	**124**
Figure 10:	Theseion 140, National Archaeological Museum, Athens ——	**126**
Figure 11:	NAM inv. no. 1244. National Archaeological Museum, Athens ——	**127**
Figure 12:	Sanctuary of Poseidon, Isthmia ——	**206**
Figure 13:	Terracotta votive plaque, drawing ——	**207**
Figure 14:	Roman bronze coin, LA 105, 700 ——	**207**
Figure 15:	Roman bronze coin, LA 105, 752 ——	**207**
Figure 16:	Group from Vari, inv. no. 26747. National Archaeological Museum, Athens ——	**212**
Figure 17:	Map of Corinth ——	**217**
Figure 18:	Graves, the North Cemetery, *Corinth Vol. XIII*, Plate 123 ——	**218**
Figure 19:	Conceptual blending: the basic diagram ——	**223**
Figure 20:	Concentual blending in Romans 6 ——	**224 (n. 97)**
Figure 21:	Conceptual blending: multiple blends ——	**225**
Figure 22:	Baptism for the dead, using multiple blends ——	**225**
Table 1:	1 Corinthians 10:2, 4 and 12:12–13 ——	**187**
Table 2:	The structure of Romans 6:1–14 ——	**240**
Table 3:	Quantitative features of Romans 5–8 ——	**268**

Abbreviations

AA	*American Anthropologist*
AB	Anchor Bible
AHK	Richard S. Ascough, Philip A. Harland, John S. Kloppenborg, *Associations in the Greco-Roman World: A Sourcebook* (Waco 2012)
AJP	*American Journal of Philology*
AN	*Ancient Narrative*
ANRW	*Aufstieg und Niedergang der römischen Welt*
AP3 A	*Archaeological Papers of the American Anthropology Association*
ARG	*Archiv für Religionsgeschichte*
ARS	*Antigüedad, Religiones y Sociedades*
Bib	*Biblica*
BTB	*Biblical Theology Bulletin*
BZNW	Beihefte zur Zeitschrift für die neutestamentliche Wissenschaft
CA	*Cultural Anthropology*
CBQ	*Catholic Biblical Quarterly*
CBR	*Currents in Biblical Research*
CED	Pierre Roussel, *Les cultes égyptiens à Délos du IIIe au Ier siècle av. J. -C.* (Paris 1916)
CGRN	Collection of Greek Ritual Norms
CIL	*Corpus Inscriptionum Latinarum*. 3 vols.
CLE	*Carmina Latina Epigraphica*
EC	*Early Christianity*
EKK	Evangelisch Katholischer Kommentar zum Neuen Testament
ETL	*Ephemerides Theologicae Lovanienses*
GJ	Fritz Graf and Sarah Iles Johnston, *Ritual Texts for the Afterlife* (2nd edition; London 2013)
HABES	Heidelberger Althistorische Beiträge und Epigraphische Studien
HJ	*Hibbert Journal*
HR	*History of Religions*
HSCP	*Harvard Studies in Classical Philology*
ICS	*Illinois Classical Studies*
HTR	*Harvard Theological Review*
IEJ	*Israel Exploration Journal*
IG II^2	Johannes Kirchner (ed.), *Inscriptiones Graecae II et III: Inscriptiones Atticae Euclidis anno posteriores*, 2nd edition
IG IV	Max Fraenkel (ed.), *Inscriptiones Graecae Aeginae, Pityonesi, Cecryphaliae, Argolidis* (Berlin 1902)
IG X,2 1	Charles Edson (ed.), *Inscriptiones Graecae X: Inscriptiones Epiri, Macedoniae, Thraciae, Scythiae. Pars II, fasc. 1: Inscriptiones Thessalonicae et viciniae* (Berlin 1972)
IG XII,5	Friedrich Hiller von Gaertringen (ed.), *Inscriptiones Graecae XII,5. Inscriptiones Cycladum.* 2 vols. (Berlin 1903–1909)
IG XIV	Georg Kaibel (ed.), *Inscriptiones Graecae XIV. Inscriptiones Siciliae et Italiae, additis Galliae, Hispaniae, Britanniae, Germaniae inscriptionibus* (Berlin 1890)
IJPT	*International Journal of Philosophy and Theology*

I.Kyme	Helmut Engelmann, *Die Inschriften von Kyme* (Bonn 1976)
I.Miletos	Donald F. McCabe, *Miletos Inscriptions. Texts and List* (Princeton 1984)
Jaccottet	Anne-Françoise Jaccottet, *Choisir Dionysos: les associations dionysiaques, ou, La face cachée du dionysisme*, 2 vols. (Zürich 2003)
JBL	*Journal of Biblical Literature*
JHS	*Journal of Hellenic Studies*
JR	*Journal of Religion*
JSNT	*Journal for the Study of the New Testament*
JSSR	*Journal for the Scientific Study of Religion*
JTC	*Journal of Theology and the Church*
JTS	*Journal of Theological Studies*
KD	Kerygma und Dogma
KJCS	*Korean Journal of Christian Studies*
LCL	The Loeb Classical Library
LSAM	Franciszek Sokolowski, *Lois sacrées de l'Asie Mineure* (Paris 1955)
MA	*Mediterranean Archaeology*
MH	*Museum Helveticum*
NICNT	The New International Commentary on New Testament
NIGTC	The New International Greek Testament Commentary
NovT	*Novum Testamentum*
NTL	New Testament Library
NTS	*New Testament Studies*
OF	Alberto Bernabé (ed.), *Poetae Epici Graeci.* II *Orphicorum et Orphicis similium testimonia et fragmenta.* Fasc. 1/2
PGM	*Papyri Graecae Magicae*
P.Oxy	*The Oxyrhynchus Papyri*
PP	*Past and Present*
RB	*Revue Biblique*
RBL	*Review of Biblical Literature*
RGRW	Religions in the Graeco-Roman World
RICIS	Laurent Bricault, *Recueil des inscriptions concernant les cultes isiaques*, 3 vols. (Paris 2005)
RPP	*Religion Past and Present*
SBA	*Studies in the Bible and Antiquity*
SEG	Jacob E. Hondius (ed.), *Supplementum Epigraphicum Graecum*
SEÅ	*Svensk exegetisk årsbok*
SIRIS	Ladislav Vidman (ed.), *Sylloge inscriptionum religionis Isiacae et Sarapiacae* (Berlin 1969)
SJOT	*Scandinavian Journal of the Old Testament*
SJT	*Scottish Journal of Theology*
SMM	Staatliche Münzsammlung München
SoR	*Sociology of Religion*
SP	Sacra Pagina
ST	*Studia Theologica*
Syll.³ (=SIG³)	Wilhelm Dittenberger (ed.), *Sylloge inscriptionum graecarum*, 3rd edition. 4 vols.
TAPA	*Transactions of the American Philological Association*
TDNT	*Theological Dictionary of the New Testament*
TJ	*Trinity Journal*

Totti	Maria Totti, *Ausgewählte Texte der Isis- und Sarapis-Religion* (Hildesheim 1985)
TPAPA	*Transactions and Proceedings of the American Philological Association*
TynBul	*Tyndale Bulletin*
WBC	Word Biblical Commentary
WUNT	*Wissenschaftliche Untersuchungen zum Neuen Testament*
ZAC	*Zeitschrift für antikes Christentum*
ZNW	*Zeitschrift für die neutestamentliche Wissenschaft*
ZPE	*Zeitschrift für Papyrologie und Epigraphik*
ZRG	*Zeitschrift für Religions- und Geistesgeschichte*

Note on Translation:

* All English translations of Greek and Latin sources are from LCL unless otherwise noted.
* All English translations of the New Testament and the HB/LXX are my own unless otherwise noted.

1 Introduction

Why did some first-century "pagans" choose to perform Christ-baptism, i.e., the initiation ritual of new cultic groups appropriating the stories of ancient Israel and venerating the recently deified *Christos* alongside the traditional Jewish God?[1] What benefits did they gain from baptism, when compared to rituals devoted to other deities in the ancient Mediterranean world? Additionally, what did baptism mean for their post-baptism life? In an attempt to answer these questions, I compare baptism in the Pauline communities and the initiation rituals of the Greco-Roman mysteries (especially, the Dionysiac mysteries and the mysteries of Isis), focusing on their respective ritual messages.[2] In doing so, I also seek to articulate

---

[1] I use the term "pagan/pagans" in a non-pejorative sense. My use of the term is mainly inspired by Paula Fredriksen, who prefers "pagan" to "gentile" in order to emphasize that "ancient people(s) were intrinsically in relation to their gods." In this regard, those who were usually called "gentile Christians" in previous scholarship are, in her book, called "ex-pagan pagans"—a "deliberately oxymoronic" expression highlighting that "they were non-Jews who, *as* non-Jews, committed themselves to the exclusive worship, in some specifically Jewish ways, of the Jewish god" (italics original). Paula Fredriksen, *Paul: The Pagans' Apostle* (New Haven: Yale University Press, 2017), 34. I do not assume that most (if not all) ex-pagans in Paul's Christ groups were originally pagan sympathizers/god-fearers already attached to Jewish synagogues even before their encounter with Paul's gospel proclamation; perhaps some came into contact with the Jewish God because of their reception of the gospel message (consider, for example, what Paul implies in 1 Thess 1:9–10, 1 Cor 6:11, and 12:2).

[2] Given the great variety of mysteries in the Greco-Roman world, it is hard to form a satisfactory definition of these mysteries (Jan N. Bremmer, *Initiation into the Mysteries of the Ancient World* [Berlin: Walter de Gruyter, 2014], xii). Furthermore, as Klauck points out, "Many of the cultic possibilities which we have already seen [in other cults] are replicated in the mysteries: sacrifices, ritual meals, rites of purification, processions, the veneration of statues of the gods," and "[t]his means the boundaries [between the mysteries and other cults] are imprecise, with a variety of transitional forms" (Hans-Josef Klauck, *The Religious Context of Early Christianity: A Guide to Graeco-Roman Religions*, trans. Brian McNeil [Minneapolis: Fortress, 2003], 86). In this study, I do not provide a fresh definition of the mysteries, but rather follow Walter Burkert's use of the term mysteries in relation to the concept of *initiation*, adding Bremmer's other characteristics (see below). Note that the Greek terms related to mysteries (μυστήρια, μυεῖν, μύησις) were often translated into Latin as *initia, initiare, initiatio*. According to Burkert, "[M]ysteries are initiation ceremonies," that is, "cults in which admission and participation depend upon some personal ritual to be performed on the initiand" (Walter Burkert, *Ancient Mystery Cults* [Cambridge: Harvard University Press, 1987], 7–8). On p. 11, Burkert continues: "Mysteries were initiation rituals of a voluntary, personal, and secret character that aimed at a change of mind through experience of the sacred." Bremmer's description of the general characteristics of the mysteries is also largely similar. Citing recent (more moderate) attempts at definition (e.g., secrecy and impressive initiation rituals), Bremmer adds the "voluntary character," "nocturnal performance," "preliminary purification," "the obliga-

Paul's theology of baptism and his apostolic self-understanding expressed through the pattern of baptism.

In this introduction, I will present a set of presuppositions underlying my comparative task, an outline of the chapters in this book, and my overall thesis. Basic terminological issues are discussed in footnotes 1 to 6.

1.1 Presuppositions

As Jonathan Z. Smith once noted, "there is nothing 'natural' about the enterprise of comparison. Similarity and difference are not 'given.' They are the result of mental operation."[3] This monograph specifically compares "rituals"—namely, baptism in Paul's letters and the initiation rituals of the mysteries.[4] This task presupposes the following:

---

tion to pay for participation," "rewards promised for this life and that of the next," "the fact that the older Mysteries were all situated at varying distances from the nearest city," and their being "open to male and female, slave and free, young and old" (*Initiation*, xii). Of course, the mystery cults were not homogeneous, and therefore, it is not that all those characteristics existed in all the mystery cults to the same degree (thus, it is similar to the task of defining ritual; see footnote 4). It should also be noted that the last part of Burkert's definition ("... a change of mind through experience of the sacred") is criticized by Bremmer: "[N]othing indicates that any such change of mind was involved in the [mysteries] ... Burkert was evidently still under the influence of Cumont at this point. And anyway, what does 'experience' mean in this case? Did people have all and always the same experience? How do we know their experience?" (Bremmer, *Initiation*, xi–xii). Following Burkert and Bremmer, I also prefer the label "mystery cults" (or simply, "the mysteries") over "mystery religions." In the history of scholarship, "mystery religions" often connoted self-contained, comprehensive systems that competed with and/or threated the emerging Christian "religion" (Bremmer, *Initiation*, x–xi and 164). This description does not fully correspond to the reality of the first-century Mediterranean world; it is more reasonable to regard the mysteries as "cults" existing within the overall landscape of Greek and Roman religion with some distinctive features. Similarly, it is hard to speak of Christianity as a full-fledged religion in the context of the mid-first century.

3 Jonathan Z. Smith, *Drudgery Divine: On the Comparison of Early Christianities and the Religions of Late Antiquity* (Chicago: University of Chicago Press, 1990), 51.

4 When I use the term "ritual," I am aware of the criticism that ritual is a modern scholarly construct, especially invented and developed in the Western world ("religion" has also been subject to similar criticism, which I will discuss later). Bell critically notes, "[H]istorically, the whole issue of ritual arose as a discrete phenomenon to the eyes of social observers in that period in which 'reason' and the scientific pursuit of knowledge were defining a particular hegemony in Western intellectual life" (Catherine Bell, *Ritual Theory, Ritual Practice* [Oxford: Oxford University Press, 1992], 6). She admits that ritual activities have existed since the prehistoric era; her point is that only in the modern period did they begin to be perceived as a distinct phenomenon (Catherine

(1) Unlike some scholars in the late nineteenth/early twentieth century, I do not think it feasible to conduct the broader task of comparing Christianity (or Paul) to the mysteries in toto, but particular *rituals* can be compared productively.

(2) I operate upon the premise that the κύριος Χριστός was the cultic deity for Paul's groups largely made up of Christ-devotees from pagan backgrounds.[5] This

---

Bell, *Ritual: Perspectives and Dimensions* [New York: Oxford University Press, 1997], 1). Bell rather focuses on "'ritualization' as a strategic *way* of acting" and examines "how and why this way of acting differentiates itself from other practices" (italics in original, *Ritual Theory*, 7). Yet, I think the internal distinction between ritual behavior and non-ritual behavior was to varying degrees already there in non-Western and/or premodern societies, and thus, the notion of ritual is not an entirely modern invention. Furthermore, the term ritual can be useful as an analytical category for modern scholars and help them identify particular social and behavioral patterns in individuals and groups in the ancient world (including Bell's focus: the process of ritualization). Given that the task of defining "ritual" amounts to an independent project with no consensus, I do not attempt to offer my own definition of ritual. As Grimes puts it, "[D]efining 'ritual' is like defining 'jazz'" (Ronald L. Grimes, *The Craft of Ritual Studies* [New York: Oxford University Press, 2014], 186). Rather than proposing a precise definition, I accept a broad understanding, including several characteristics (e.g., speech acts, collective, repeated, purposeful, etc.) that many scholars have suggested, of a "polythetic" or "fuzzy" category/class of ritual. Examples of such are found in Jan A. M. Snoek, "Defining 'Rituals,'" in *Theorizing Rituals: Issues, Topics, Approaches, Concepts*, ed. Jens Kreinath et al. (Leiden: Brill, 2006), 11. According to Snoek, "Polythetic characteristics are not present in all members of a polythetic class, but each occurs in a majority of them" ("Defining 'Rituals,'" 5). I do not follow Snoek's particular distinctions of ritual, rite, and ceremony because such distinctions make little difference for my project. As for other ways of distinguishing the related terms (e.g., ritual, rite, ceremony), see Ronald L. Grimes, *Ritual Criticism: Case Studies in Its Practice, Essays on Its Theory* (Columbia: University of South Carolina Press, 1990), 9–10; also, Victor Turner's well-known distinction between ritual and ceremony in terms of social function—the former is "transformative" and the latter is "confirmatory"—in *The Forest of Symbols: Aspects of Ndembu Ritual* (Ithaca: Cornell University Press, 1967), 95.

5 Mack questions the use of "Christ cult" (especially "pre-Pauline Christ cult") and argues for replacing it with the term *"christos* associations" (Burton L. Mack, "Rereading the Christ Myth: Paul's Gospel and the Christ Cult Question," in *Redescribing Paul and the Corinthians*, ed. Ron Cameron and Merrill P. Miller [Atlanta: SBL, 2011], 37–38 and 65–72). Mack's tone is definitive when he rhetorically repeats the phrase, "No Christ cult there" ("Rereading the Christ Myth," 65–66). While I take his point that "we be clear about the social climate or atmosphere of such ritual occasions in keeping with customary association practices and interests of the time and not let them take on the aura of later forms of Christian ritual and worship" ("Rereading the Christ Myth," 73), I doubt that the terms "cult" and "association" can be contrasted in the way Mack uses them. In fact, cultic elements were part of most associations, as Kloppenborg notes: "[M]ost associations had cultic dimensions," be it "occupational guilds, cultic associations, and *collegia domestica*" (John S. Kloppenborg, *Christ's Associations: Connecting and Belonging in the Ancient City* [New Haven: Yale University Press, 2019], 107; he nevertheless continues to work with the division). Kloppenborg's conclusion aligns "Christ assemblies" most closely with "cultic associations and occupa-

Christos was perceived as the communities' cultic deity by those who came to know these groups in the first-century Mediterranean world.⁶ It is possible that the pagans Paul encountered understood the stories and ritual activities of this new deity in comparison with, or through the lens of, other deities already familiar to them from their day-to-day experience.⁷

(3) Thus, my working hypothesis is that baptism is an entry ritual practiced among the Christ-cult groups living in this pagan environment, and therefore, the initiation rituals of the mysteries are "good to think with."⁸ In other words, I basically agree with the older scholarly view that early Christian baptism can be seen as a form of initiation ritual.⁹

---

tional guilds" (*Christ's Associations*, 347). If this conclusion is correct, then Mack's sharp distinction between cult and association would not be helpful.

6 I will use "Christ-devotees" and "Christ-believers" (interchangeably) to refer to the members of the communities Paul's letters addressed, rather than using the term "Christians" which could be anachronistic. Admittedly, the term Christ-"believers" is not without problems, because, as Horrell and Adams note, it "emphasiz[es] belief more than is appropriate" (David G. Horrell and Edward Adams, "Introduction: The Scholarly Quest for Paul's Church at Corinth: A Critical Survey," in *Christianity at Corinth: The Quest for the Pauline Church*, ed. Edward Adams and David G. Horrell [Louisville: Westminster John Knox, 2004], 1, n. 1). Yet, I think using "Christ-believers" or "Christ-believing community," etc., can be partly justified by the fact that Paul uses similar terms when addressing his groups (οἱ πιστεύοντες, lit. the believing ones/those who believe). See also Ryan S. Schellenberg, "οἱ πιστεύοντες: An Early Christ-Group Self-Designation and Paul's Rhetoric of Faith," *NTS* (2019): 33–42.

7 This is more clearly the case when one examines material culture. Balch imagines Paul preaching the gospel in a house with paintings and sculptures of other deities from the Greco-Roman world, noting, "Greco-Roman houses, unlike many modern ones, were filled with art, including paintings, mosaics, and sculptures ... My question is: When Paul preached in such houses, or when there was a discussion after a Eucharist, might there have been art in the houses related to the sermon or to the Eucharistic conversations that would have shaped how Paul's audience received his message?" David L. Balch, "The Suffering of Isis/Io and Paul's Portrait of Christ Crucified (Gal. 3:1): Frescoes in Pompeian and Roman Houses and in the Temple of Isis in Pompeii," *JR* 83 (2003): 25.

8 This expression (derived from Lévi-Strauss) has often been applied to the comparison between early Christ groups and Greco-Roman associations. See, for example, Kloppenborg, *Christ's Associations*, 9. The use of this useful expression is found in other comparative studies, too. See, for example, Sandra Blakley, *Myth, Ritual, and Metallurgy in Ancient Greece and Recent Africa* (New York: Cambridge University Press, 2006), 2.

9 DeMaris strongly contests the view that baptism is an initiation ritual; he instead argues that baptism should be understood as a "boundary crossing ritual." Richard E. DeMaris, *The New Testament in its Ritual World* (London; New York: Routledge, 2008), 27. Yet, as Turley astutely points out, DeMaris's later discussion of 1 Cor 15:29 betrays that his view is still based on the assumption that baptism is a rite of passage. Stephen Richard Turley, *The Ritualized Revelation of the Messianic Age: Washings and Meals in Galatia and 1 Corinthians* (New York: T&T Clark, 2015), 20.

This presupposition does not mean that I will attempt to find precise verbal correspondence between mystery initiations and Pauline baptism—for example, trying to find words sharing the βαπτ- root in ancient references to the mysteries or, conversely, to find the technical terminology of the mysteries in the Pauline letters.¹⁰ Rather, the comparative task of this project focuses on the *messages* of ritual, rather than (or not only) the particular medium used in ritual (e.g., water). Scholarly doubts about the validity of this comparative task were often caused by the facile observation about the different use of water between the mysteries and early Christian groups.¹¹ Yet, if initiation is more than just the use of water

---

10 The former (i.e., to find words sharing the βαπτ- root in ancient references to the mysteries) is probably an impossible task. As Ferguson notes in his comprehensive survey, "The usage of [words from the βαπτ- root] in a *religious* sense is rare apart from Judaism and Christianity" (italics mine, Everett Ferguson, *Baptism in the Early Church: History, Theology, and Liturgy in the First Five Centuries* [Grand Rapids: Eerdmans, 2009], 38). See also his helpful survey of this word group used in Greek literature on pages 38–59 (he shows some cases in which this word group is used metaphorically [pp. 52–55] and religiously [pp. 55–56; yet, mostly postdating the NT]). Conversely, to find the technical terminology of the mysteries in the Pauline letters) is not impossible, because Paul, as other ancient authors—Jewish, Christian, and pagan alike—indeed employed terminology reminiscent of the mysteries (this material will be briefly covered in the history of scholarship in Chapter 2). The focus of my work, however, is not diverse uses of mystery language as literary phenomena; I leave this for future research. Also, scholars have pointed out that attempts to find strict "verbal parallels" between the New Testament/early Christian literature and non-Christian writings in antiquity are often fraught with methodological problems and issues. L. Michael White and John T. Fitzgerald, "*Quod Est Comparandum:* The Problem of Parallels," in *Early Christianity and Classical Culture: Comparative Studies in Honor of Abraham J. Malherbe*, ed. John T. Fitzgerald et al. (Leiden: Brill, 2003), 13–39; M. David Litwa, *We Are Being Transformed: Deification in Paul's Soteriology,* BZNW 187 (Berlin: Walter de Gruyter, 2012), 30–31. This is even more true with the present task, which understands the mysteries as *comparanda*.

11 It is customary that scholars criticize any proposal that relates the mystery initiations to baptism by pointing out the fact that Christ-baptism was basically a water-ritual, whereas purification by water in the mysteries was not the initiation proper (which should be performed in secret by definition) but merely a preliminary activity in public. Everett Ferguson in his recent comprehensive monograph on baptism also takes this view: "[S]ome have associated [washings with water in initiation to the mysteries] with the practice of Christian baptism … [but] [t]he washing in the Mysteries was a preliminary preparation for the initiation; in Christianity it was the center of initiation into the church." Ferguson, *Baptism in the Early Church*, 28–29 (note here that even though Ferguson does not consider baptism to be related to mystery initiation, he still considers baptism an *"initiation"* into a Christian community). This is a fair critique if one takes into account the ritual medium only. Kloppenborg also notes that "most cultic associations" did not employ water rituals as their entry rituals (then, baptism in early Christ groups would not have many *comparanda*). Yet, he also states, "[W]hether a group used baptism, a *dokimasia*, some other initiatory rite, or some combination of these, entry into the group needed to be marked." Kloppenborg, *Christ's Associations*, 143–44. That is, what matters for entry rituals is not what medium is used. Comparing

in a certain way, the same is also true for baptism.¹² This is not to say that I understand initiation rituals and baptism as mere theological abstractions; I am taking seriously the embodied nature of rituals. Yet, I believe a more fruitful comparison can be made possible by paying attention to what messages are communicated by such embodied activities, not just by looking at what medium is used in what ways.

(4) Lastly, I do not presuppose any simple genealogical relationship between the initiation rituals of the mysteries and Pauline baptism.¹³ Nor do I undertake the present task primarily in the hope of finding (or denying) that the mysteries contain the "dying and rising deities" type and the pattern of participants' dying and rising with the deities through initiation. This preoccupation of many scholars in previous generations caused a deadlock. Diverse and nuanced messages of rituals, along with their chronological developments, local variants, innovative moments—that is, particularities of each mystery initiation—should be taken into consideration.

1.2 An Outline of the Study

In the first part of Chapter 2, I will survey the history of scholarship on "Paul and the mysteries" according to three stages (the Inaugurated Quest, the Moratorium on the Quest, and the Continued Quest), thereby clarifying the *status quaestionis* on the broader topic. This periodization only serves a heuristic purpose, especially considering overlaps between these periods, as well as diversity within each stage. The Inaugurated Quest refers to the initial stage of inquiry in the late nineteenth and early twentieth century, when the claim that Paul/early Christianity was de-

---

the reconstructed messages communicated by each ritual will open new ways to explore the neglected aspects of how and why rituals—baptism and mystery initiations—worked in their contexts. It would be an interesting task to compare early Christian baptism with some initiation rituals of other Jewish groups in the Second Temple period (especially, appearing in the Dead Sea Scrolls), but that would be left for future research (note that water ritual was not usually part of initiation in other Jewish groups of the Second Temple period; see Jonathan D. Lawrence, *Washing in Water: Trajectories of Ritual Bathing in the Hebrew Bible and Second Temple Literature* [Atlanta: SBL, 2006], 71–77; 135–41).

12 For the latter, see Robin M. Jensen, *Baptismal Imagery in Early Christianity: Ritual, Visual, and Theological Dimensions* (Grand Rapids: Baker Academic, 2012), 2. She notes, "In the early church, the application of water was essential, but it was only one aspect of an elaborate ceremony that had several stages and benefits."

13 Similarly, regarding the question of how to view the relationship between Christ groups and Greco-Roman associations, see Kloppenborg, *Christ's Associations*, 5. Kloppenborg emphasizes that his comparison is heuristic.

pendent on the pagan mysteries was dominant. The Moratorium on the Quest (roughly from the mid-twentieth century onward) followed the Inaugurated Quest. These scholars were intense in their refutation of the dependency theory, and the quest itself was often regarded as an outdated, misguided inquiry. Despite this, some other scholars (especially, since the late twentieth century) continue the quest, ergo, the Continued Quest; I situate my own work in this third stage. While appreciating the achievements of the Continued Quest, my review of literature will also demonstrate the necessity for a better framework to assess and interpret ancient evidence.

In the second half of Chapter 2, therefore, I will set forth my analytical framework, drawing on the theories of two scholars, Roy Rappaport (cultural anthropology) and Martin Riesebrodt (sociology of religion). Employing this integrated analytical framework allows me to compare baptism in the Pauline letters and initiation rituals of the mysteries by focusing on three questions,[14] which provides a structure for the following chapters: 1) What benefits does each initiation ritual promise its participants? 2) What are the underlying messages or structures that guarantee the efficacy of those rituals?[15] 3) How and to what extent is the initiation

---

[14] Chester asks a similar set of questions regarding the mystery cults: "If initiation was voluntary, and did not bring with it any automatic improvement in social status, the question arises of what those being initiated hoped to achieve through it. What were the hoped-for benefits?" and later, "Whatever was hoped for, how was it to be achieved? What was the nature of the relationship between the individual and the deity created by initiation?" Stephen J. Chester, *Conversion at Corinth: Perspectives on Conversion in Paul's Theology and the Corinthian Church* (London; New York: T&T Clark, 2005), 267–75 (here, 272 and 274). Yet, his discussion of the questions is relatively brief, compared to the task of this monograph.

[15] The first two questions are the question an initiate would ask a senior initiate, other authorities, or any other bystander: *What benefits does this initiation have for me? And how can I be sure it will really work?* Based on sociological research on modern religious movements (by sociologists such as Stark and Bainbridge) and social-historical works on Greco-Roman associations (Kloppenborg himself is a scholar of note in this area of research), Kloppenborg draws the conclusion that the "appeal" of early Christ groups is largely related to providing social capital and a sense of security/belonging—i.e., enabling the newcomer to enter into a "network of trust." He notes, "Some of the appeal of Christ assemblies can be surmised: they cultivated strong affective ties, participated in communal dining and other rituals of belonging, adopted fictive family language to describe their members, and operated under the auspices of a deity that 'called' them and was imagined to have agency in transforming humans. The ethics promoted both in Paul of loving one another and outdoing each other in showing honor (Rom 12:10) and in John of mutual love (John 13:35) aimed at producing a strong network of trust that could have had a strong appeal only for subelite city dwellers." Kloppenborg, *Christ's Associations*, 327. I concur with Kloppenborg's observations, but his work only tentatively explores what benefits were (believed to be) provided by cultic deities (cf. p. 326). This aspect should be explored further. My project provides nuance by focusing on

ritual connected to the participants' cognition and ethics beyond initiation itself? The first two questions, which relate to "self-referential messages" and "canonical messages" in Rappaport's theory, are intertwined. One's participation in ritual (this is part of self-referential messages) activates the canonical order and publicizes one's acceptance of it; in turn, the canonical messages underwrite the efficacy of the divine pledges indicated by ritual and create obligations for the ritual participant. The third question, whether initiation extends beyond the ritual enactment, helps one discern ways in which an initiation ritual is embedded into the larger symbolic world in which divine-human and intra-human relationships are formed. The sections of my monograph that address this third question also ask how the notion of "religious virtuosity" (discussed by Riesebrodt, but originally introduced by Weber[16]) is envisioned in relation to initiation, and this virtuosity is connected back to both the self-referential and the canonical messages of the initiation ritual.

This established frame of analysis will guide the discussions in the following chapters. Chapters 3 and 4 will explore the initiation rituals of the Dionysiac mysteries and the mysteries of Isis, respectively, by examining primary sources—ancient literature, inscriptions, papyri, and visual representations. I will pay attention to, and distinguish, the social, cultural, and historical particularities of classical Greece, the Hellenistic period, and the Roman Principate; however, I also provide synthetic discussions to highlight some patterns and characteristics commonly found in the mystery traditions. Baptism in the Pauline communities and Paul's interpretation of baptism will be the focus of Chapters 5–7. These three chapters will be organized slightly differently from Chapters 3 and 4 to allow for a detailed exegesis of Paul's passages. In each chapter subsection, key passages will be discussed in detail first, and these will be followed by a synthetic discussion exploring the self-referential messages, the canonical messages, and how baptism is understood within the broader network of practices and implications. With this organizing principle, Chapter 5 will focus on passages from 1 Corinthians, and Chapter 7 on Galatians and Romans. Chapter 6 functions as a bridge between Chapters 5 and 7 with its exploration of 1 Cor 15:29 which details Paul's distinctive interaction with ritual innovation in his Corinth group. In all these chapters, commonalities and differences between Paul's communities and Paul himself in terms of their views and practice of baptism will be discerned and articulated. Finally, an overall conclusion will be provided (Chapter 8).

---

the moment of initiation and the messages communicated by initiation rituals, including messages pertaining to the symbolically constructed reality of the mystery deities.
16 Max Weber, *Sociology of Religion* (Boston: Beacon, 1963), 162–63.

1.3 The Thesis of the Study

When examining ritual messages in Pauline baptism and mystery initiations, my argument will be centered on the following two, interrelated points.

1) The first point is that baptism in the Pauline communities is basically analogous to the initiation rituals of the mysteries. Both baptism in Paul's Christ groups and the initiation rituals of the mystery cults commence a person's membership into the cultic community, establish new social relationships, grant a newly established or enhanced personal relationship between the deity and her/his devotees, and grant the devotees the deity's deliverance from adverse situations both in the present and future. In both baptism and mystery initiation, the deity's personal characteristics vis-à-vis her/his devotees, the deity's powerful achievements, and a shared identity between the deity and the devotees (usually the deity takes the initiative to come closer) are crucial to the efficacy of the promised benefits. Even faith/trust, which extends beyond the initiation ritual itself and is arguably the most "Christian" form of religiosity, is part of the symbolic network of initiation rituals. When I state that baptism is analogous to the initiation rituals of the mysteries, it might seem that I am simply reaffirming the presupposition from which I start my inquiry. Yet, my thesis is neither tautology nor meant to ignore the differences between baptism and mystery initiations. Rather, this comparative investigation will demonstrate that while Pauline baptism does share an overall pattern of ritual messages with mystery initiations, the distinctive features of baptism can be carefully analyzed and explained in light of these shared messages.

2) When conceptualizing Paul's self-understanding and theology with regard to the baptismal ritual, one should view Paul as an "exegete" (ἐξηγητής), rather than "eisegete" (εἰσηγητής) of the ritual.[17] That is, the figure of Paul appearing in his letters should primarily be understood as an interpreter of the Christ cult and its initiation, rather than a cult founder, whose primary role was to establish a new cult by transferring rituals to a new situation. Despite establishing Christ-cult groups in various places in the Mediterranean world, Paul appears to be less interested in transferring the baptismal ritual per se. Paul's baptismal theology presents a religious-philosophical exposition of what it means to be initiated into this new kind of mystery-cultic group. One can find Paul participating in ancient discursive practice making use of initiation rituals and expanding their epis-

---

[17] For the terms eisegete (initiator/founder) and exegete (interpreter/communicator) in the context of cultic/religious dispersion in antiquity, see Polymnia Athanassiadi and Constantinos Macris, "La philosophisation du religieux," in *Panthée: Religious Transformations in the Graeco-Roman Empire*, ed. Laurent Bricault and Corinne Bonnet (Leiden: Brill, 2013), 70–71.

temological, ethical, and social implications. Paul serves as an innovative ritual interpreter for his communities, not only by communicating baptismal messages already known to him and his audience, but also by developing new messages of baptism that are intelligible to his ex-pagan audience and yet different from those of comparable mysteries in the ancient Mediterranean.

While Paul's ministry is not primarily about transferring the ritual, he does not undervalue the power of baptism as ritual. Rather, my discussion will demonstrate that Paul often attributes more significance to baptism than his audience, emphasizing its performative force. Baptism does create an exclusive bond between Christ and his devotees (thus, exclusive obligations are created), moves these devotees from their pagan past to their present in Christ, rewrites the genealogy of ex-pagans so that they can share in the blessings of Israel's deity, and realizes a new social reality among the members of the Christ-cult. Furthermore, Paul's interpretation of baptism, which appears in its fullest form throughout Rom 5–8, is not merely a product of literary research. Paul's discourse of baptism was shaped by his bodily experiences as well as engaging in actual rituals practiced within his communities.

Additionally, by paying attention to the question of religious virtuosity, my discussion will emphasize the seemingly contradictory messages implied in Paul's presentation of baptism. On the one hand, Paul interprets baptism as a radicalized form of mystery initiation that democratizes religious virtuosity. That is, Paul's message says the logic of virtuosity is applied to all Christ-devotees, not only to a few virtuosos. This is most clearly seen in Paul's idea that all believers experience death/burial and rising with Christ through baptism—this particular emphasis is not found in any of the other mysteries considered. On the other hand, Paul implies that he himself is the virtuoso par excellence, who embodies the demands of initiation. Paul presents his own body as a living, ekphrastic example in which the promise of initiation and its radical demands are actualized by his apostolic suffering and dying-process, which are beneficial to his audience. He thereby re-centralizes religious virtuosity pertaining to Christ-initiation and the initiation-shaped life. In short, Paul incorporates the pattern of initiation into his own bodily existence, so that his dying body becomes an intermediary *mysterium* through which others participate in the mysteries of Christ.

2 Paul and the Mysteries: Retrospective and Prospective

2.1 The History of Scholarship

The purpose of this chapter is to provide a survey of the scholarship on the relationship between the ancient mysteries and early Christianity (or more specifically, the apostle Paul). This subject captivated the history of religions school and those who were under the influence of this school of thought in the late nineteenth and the early twentieth century.[1] Romans 6:1–14 has been the *locus classicus*, because of its distinctive understanding of baptism, namely, dying and rising with Christ. Many scholars of this era saw a close parallel between the understanding of baptism in Rom 6 and the initiation rituals of the Greco-Roman mysteries. A sampling of passages from two leading scholars, Rudolf Bultmann and Wilhelm Bousset, could exemplify this intellectual atmosphere. For example, Bultmann comments on baptism in Rom 6:

> It can be regarded as certain that from the very beginning [baptism] was practiced in the earliest Church as the rite of initiation, for Paul assumes that all Christians are baptized (Rom 6:3, I Cor. 12:13)[2] … In the worship (the Kultus) of the congregation, the Lord Jesus Christ is present. An individual gets into the congregation through baptism; and that means that in this way he enters into relation with the Lord. In all probability it was as a rite of initiation into the eschatological Congregation that baptism had been practiced in the earliest Church[3]

---

[1] This comparison is not a modern invention. See, for example, Tertullian's comparison between the initiation rituals of the mysteries and early Christian baptism (*Bapt.* 5). The origin of the modern discussions of the mysteries can be traced back to the early seventeenth century (I. Casaubon), as noted by Richard L. Gordon, "Mystery Religions, Religious Studies," *RPP* 8:652. Yet, it is the history of religions school that is well-known for this comparative task. It is a matter of debate who should be generally counted as members of the history of religions school, although its narrow definition focuses on the group of Göttingen scholars in 1880s and 1890s, such as William Wrede, Johannes Weiss, Hermann Gunkel, Albert Eichhorn, Wilhelm Heitmüller, and Wilhelm Bousset. For a broader definition of the history of religions school, see William Baird, *History of New Testament Research* (Minneapolis: Fortress, 2003), 2:222. Cf. Gerd Lüdemann, "Die 'Religionsgeschichtliche Schule' und die Neutestamentliche Wissenschaft," in *Die "Religionsgeschichtliche Schule": Facetten eines theologischen Umbruchs*, ed. Gerd Lüdemann (Frankfurt am Main; New York: Peter Lang, 1996), 9–22.

[2] Rudolf Bultmann, *Theology of the New Testament*, trans. Kendrick Grobel (Waco: Baylor University Press, 2007), 1:39. The original German was published in 1948–1952 and the first English translation appeared in 1951–1955.

[3] Bultmann, *Theology of the New Testament*, 1:133.

> ... Rom. 6:2 ff. clearly implies that Paul was not the first to give baptism this mystery interpretation, but that it was already current before him in Hellenistic congregations, as his question (v. 3), "or do you not know . . ." might indicate by itself.⁴

Bultmann basically views baptism in the earliest phase as "the rite of initiation into the eschatological Congregation," and he suggests the "mystery interpretation" of baptism already existed prior to Paul in the "Hellenistic congregations" whose "Kultus" was the locus of the presence of the Lord Jesus Christ.⁵

In this era, the motif of *dying and rising with Christ through baptism* was considered the strongest piece of evidence for the comparison between "Hellenistic piety" and Pauline thought. For many scholars of the early twentieth century the idea that all the Greco-Roman mysteries shared the notion of a dying-and-rising deity was regarded as a fact—largely due to James Frazer's influential theory.⁶ Thus, Bousset notes,

> [L]ong before the Pauline era, people had become aware of the kinship of all these divine figures to one another [e.g., Adonis, Osiris, etc.]⁷ ... Thus there grows up beyond the individual divine figures the one figure of the suffering, dying, and rising god⁸ ... One will not be able to avoid the impression that here is given the spiritual atmosphere within which the Pauline dying-with-Christ and rising-with-Christ is located⁹ ... [A]s those Hellenistic speculations devel-

---

4 Bultmann, *Theology of the New Testament*, 1:141. This understanding and research procedure were shared by many scholars in the early twentieth century. Scholars excavated the so-called "sacramentalism" of the "Hellenistic Church" through textual layers, and they located it between the kerygma of the primitive "Palestinian Church" and Pauline/Johannine theology. The results of this comparison formed the grand narratives about early Christianity up to the Apostolic Fathers or to the late-second-century Fathers. For a critique of the "Hellenistic Church aside from Paul" (entertained by Bultmann and previous German scholars), see Mack, "Rereading the Christ Myth," 65–72.
5 Bultmann could be included in the generation of scholarship that takes a more subtle approach to the relationship between the mysteries and baptism, compared to the "absolute dependence" position taken by some earlier scholars of the history of religions school. See Agersnap's discussion of Bultmann in the section called "Romans 6.1–14 as a Pauline modification of Hellenistic baptism mysticism." Søren Agersnap, *Baptism and the New Life: A Study of Romans 6.1–14*, trans. Christine Crowley and Frederick Crowley (Aarhus: Aarhus University Press, 1999), 24–33.
6 To be sure, Frazer's theory, as exemplified by his magnum opus, *The Golden Bough*, is not limited to the study of the Greco-Roman mysteries. For a helpful survey of scholarship on the dying-and-rising deity from Frazer on, see Tryggve N. D. Mettinger, "The 'Dying and Rising God': A Survey of Research from Frazer to the Present Day," *SEÅ* 63 (1998): 111–23.
7 Wilhelm Bousset, *Kyrios Christos: A History of the Belief in Christ from the Beginning of Christianity to Irenaeus*, trans. John E. Steely (Waco: Baylor University Press, 2013), 188. The original German edition was published in 1913.
8 Bousset, *Kyrios Christos*, 189.
9 Bousset, *Kyrios Christos*, 193.

oped out of the cultus of the dying and rising god, so also behind Paul's statements about dying and rising with Christ there stands quite plainly and clearly (cf. Rom. 6; Gal. 3:26–27) the sacrament.[10]

It was no surprise to Bousset and his contemporary scholars that Paul, born and raised in this universal "spiritual atmosphere" of the Hellenistic period, also developed the concept of dying and rising with Christ. These scholars were part of the intellectual "atmosphere" of their days—i.e., the late nineteenth and early twentieth century.

From that period to the present, the history of scholarship cab be organized into three stages: the Inaugurated Quest, the Moratorium on the Quest, and the Continued Quest. The term "Quest" means scholarly attempts to investigate the relationship between the mysteries and early Christianity (and/or Paul). I use terms similar to that used in Historical Jesus studies (the Old Quest, No Quest, the New Quest, etc.) because such well-known phrases help one grasp the complicated positions on this subject throughout the modern history of scholarship.[11]

- *The Inaugurated Quest* (e.g., Franz Cumont [1909], Alfred Loisy [1911; 1914], and Richard Reitzenstein [1927]) claims that Paul/early Christianity was dependent on the mysteries, or at least, that Paul/early Christianity borrowed some theological ideas and ritual practices from the mysteries.
- *The Moratorium on the Quest* (e.g., Günter Wagner [1962] and A. J. M. Wedderburn [1987]) refers to the scholarly position that considered the former quest a

---

10 Bousset, *Kyrios Christos*, 194. Yet, Bousset also emphasizes Paul's "moral-religious power" and "spiritual originality" over generalized Hellenistic piety.
11 What I see in the Continued Quest is in fact analogous to a mixture of the "New Quest" and the "Third Quest" in Historical Jesus studies. The Continued Quest seeks to locate Paul/early Christianity firmly in the social, cultural, historical milieu of the first century (similar to the Third Quest in Historical Jesus studies), but also attempts to identify distinctive characteristics of Paul and early Christianity (similar to the New Quest in Historical Jesus studies). Of course, there are indeed differences. Most significantly, the Old Quest in Historical Jesus studies was focused on the critical analysis of the NT in order to recover the historical figure of Jesus, whereas the Inaugurated Quest in the present study does not focus on the historical reconstruction of a singular figure. The two fields of studies are most similar at the No-Quest/Moratorium on the Quest stage. As the Old Quest for the Historical Jesus was ended by scholars, such as Albert Schweitzer and Rudolf Bultmann, the Inaugurated Quest for the relationship between Paul/early Christianity and the mysteries entered a moratorium due largely to the works of Günter Wagner and A. J. M. Wedderburn. Furthermore, I am aware of the criticism of taxonomy in Historical Jesus studies (e.g., Mark Allan Powell, *Jesus as a Figure in History: How Modern Historians View the Man from Galilee*. 2nd ed. [Louisville: Westminster John Knox, 2013], 22–24). Yet, I am inclined to support the partial usefulness of such taxonomies. They help one find patterns and better understand the complex attitudes and approaches of scholars. I will use this modified taxonomy for heuristic purposes.

failure because Paul/early Christianity was not actually dependent on the mysteries nor were similarities found between them. Thus, by implication, these scholars terminated the previous quest.

- *The Continued Quest* is less interested in creating or rejecting the grand narrative about dependency or genealogical relationship between Paul/early Christianity and the mysteries. It rather explores (a) the dynamic relationship between early Christian groups and other organizations at the local level, often done through archaeological, social-historical, and/or cultural-anthropological lenses (e.g., Helmut Koester [1990], Hans Dieter Betz [1995], Richard DeMaris [1995], Bert Jan Lietaert Peerbolte [2012], Terri Moore [2018]), or (b) the mysteries in their own right, without much discussion about their relationship to early Christianity (e.g., Walter Burkert [1987] and Jan Bremmer [2014]), or (c) the mysteries as philosophical and literary phenomena (e.g., María José Martín-Velasco and María José García Blanco [2016]).

The keyword for the first two "Quests" is "dependence," while the third explores a more fluid relationship. This organizational structure does not exhaust the entirety of scholarship on this subject, but it does serve as a heuristic device to locate this study in relation to previous inquiries into this topic. Although the three stages are largely chronological, there are significant overlaps and co-existence among the three. In reality, the three stages form more of a continuum than a linear progression, which makes it difficult to state definitively where one begins and ends.

2.1.1 The Inaugurated Quest: Paul/Early Christianity Was Dependent on the Mysteries

The Inaugurated Quest refers to scholarship from the late nineteenth and early/mid-twentieth century that posited a close relationship between the mysteries and early Christianity (as found in the New Testament, especially the Pauline letters). A comprehensive review of scholarship of this period is not necessary, since this has been done meticulously by other scholars (especially Günter Wagner).[12] Instead of a comprehensive review, three seminal figures whose writings exerted

---

12 Using the notion of dependency as a grid, Günter Wagner divides scholars into three larger categories ("the thesis of an absolute dependence of Paul on the mysteries"; "connection and contradiction"; "the acceptance of a mere terminological dependence of Paul on the mysteries, and the rejection of their influence on him") and eleven sub-categories.

great influence on subsequent scholarship are worth mentioning: Franz Cumont (1909), Alfred Loisy (1911; 1914), and Richard Reitzenstein (1927).[13]

2.1.1.1 Franz Cumont

Franz Cumont examined the rise and role of "Oriental religions" in transforming the landscape of Roman "paganism," and understood the appearance of Christianity against this backdrop. Although Cumont's historical project was not focused solely on comparing Christianity/Paul and the mysteries, his work had commonalities with other scholars of the Inaugurated Quest. By "Oriental religions," he means the religious traditions associated with certain deities (especially their mysteries[14]) that allegedly originated from the eastern Mediterranean world—e.g., Isis and Sarapis in Egypt, Cybele in Asia Minor, Mithras in Persia, etc. According to Cumont, the cults of these Oriental deities differed from the worship of traditional Roman deities ("civic duty") in that the Oriental cults were "the expression of personal belief."[15] They satisfied the needs of the Romans who suffered from spiritual deficiency in three ways: "to the senses and passions," "to the intelligence," and "to the conscience."[16] Cumont argued that the "invasion" of these Oriental religions significantly changed the nature of the religious climate in the Roman world, there-

---

13 Note that these three scholars (Cumont, Loisy, and Reitzenstein) are not officially members of "the history of religions school," despite sharing common perspectives with representative scholars of the school. Also, the three scholars' primary purposes differ from one another, and they had different views on the extent to which Paul was dependent on the mysteries. Yet, several commonalities allow them to be categorized together. In addition to Cumont, Loisy, and Reitzenstein, the following scholars can also be included in the Inaugurated Quest: James G. Frazer, Wilhelm Bousset, and Rudolf Bultmann. Frazer's work (*The Golden Bough* [2 vols.; London: Macmillan, 1890]; the 12-volume edition appeared in 1906–15 and its abridged version appeared in 1922) was far broader than early Christian studies, but his notion of the dying and rising mythic deity framed many subsequent scholarly investigations in the field. Both Bousset (e.g., *Kyrios Christos*) and Bultmann (e.g., *Theology of the New Testament*), as mentioned earlier, gave consideration to the mysteries when examining Pauline theology and the history of early Christianity. Their focus was often on sacramental practices (e.g., baptism) and the theology of sacraments as found in Paul's letters and in other portions of the NT.
14 Thus, the Eleusinian mysteries and the Dionysiac mysteries, which had long histories in the Greek world, are not thoroughly discussed in Cumont's book because they are not "Oriental" religions. Cumont thinks the longevity of the Eleusinian mysteries caused Greece to be less effected by the arrival of Oriental religions. Franz Cumont, *Oriental Religions in Roman Paganism*, trans. Grant Showerman (New York: Dover Publications, 1956), 221 n. 23. The French original appeared in 1906 and 1909.
15 Cumont, *Oriental Religions*, 44.
16 Cumont, *Oriental Religions*, 28.

by preparing the way for the universal "triumph" of Christianity.[17] One of the distinctive features of Cumont's work, when compared with other scholars in the Inaugurated Quest, is that he is relatively careful about expressing in detail his view of Christian origins. This is understandable because his primary area of research was not early Christianity or the New Testament, but Greco-Roman paganism.[18] Despite this, he found many similarities between the mysteries and early Christianity and presented the rise of Oriental religions in the Roman world as a prelude to the rise of Christianity.

2.1.1.2 Alfred Loisy

Early Christianity's dependence on the mysteries and the former's replacement of the latter is more explicitly articulated in Alfred Loisy's work. Loisy argues that (Pauline) Christianity was rooted in but eventually departed from its Jewish heritage and Jesus's message of the kingdom of God. As Christianity established itself as a "new religion," the Greco-Roman mysteries exerted great influence, especially with regard to its rituals. Consequently, Christianity became a new mystery religion (or, *the* Mystery) that replaced all other mystery religions. Loisy's 1911 article "The Christian Mystery" begins with a paragraph that exemplifies many assumptions (which are now contestable) shared by early-twentieth-century scholars; that is, Christianity was a new, independent religion, albeit indebted to Judaism and the "Gospel of Jesus."[19] After Jesus's expectation of the fulfillment of Israel's hope and the imminent kingdom of God "terminated in the Cross of Golgotha,"[20] the mysteries of the "East" came in and shaped the concept of salvation and salvific rituals in

---

[17] Cumont, *Oriental Religions*, 19.

[18] Yet, in other works, Cumont spoke of Paul's appropriation and Christianization of the mysteries. For a detailed discussion about the relationship between Paul and the mysteries made in Cumont's other writings and personal letters, see Annelies Lannoy, "St Paul in the Early 20th Century History of Religions. 'The Mystic of Tarsus' and the Pagan Mystery Cults after the Correspondence of Franz Cumont and Alfred Loisy," *ZRG* 64 (2012): 223, 229.

[19] His essay begins with this passage: "The Gospel of Jesus was not a religion ... However, less than thirty years after the death of Christ, a religion had issued from the Gospel; and this religion was not a split (*dédoublement*) from Judaism ... it was an independent religion." Alfred Loisy, "The Christian Mystery," *HJ* 10 (1911): 45. The first sentence of that paragraph and the subsequent treatment of early Christianity as a new religion somewhat foreshadows the famous beginning paragraph of Bultmann's *Theology of the New Testament* four decades later. Of course, for Bultmann, it was a contrast between Jesus's message and the theology of the New Testament (i.e., the former is not a part of the latter, but a presupposition of the latter). See Bultmann, *Theology of the New Testament*, 1:3

[20] Loisy, "The Christian Mystery," 47.

Christianity.²¹ According to Loisy, the characteristics of the mysteries indicate a type of "universal" religion (i.e., not restricted to people of a particular "nationality," but appealing to a diverse range of individuals). This "universal" religion was centered on the legend of mystery deities who suffered, died, and arose, and on the initiation ritual that provided the initiates with the means to participate in the prototypical experience of the mystery deities, to be united with these deities, and ultimately to attain salvation, primarily related to a happy afterlife.²² Here Loisy finds similarities with the "myth of universal salvation" in early Christianity:

> [Jesus Christ] was a savior-god, after the manner of an Osiris, an Attis, a Mithra. Like them, he belonged by his origin to the celestial world; like them, he had made his appearance on the earth; like them, he had accomplished a work of universal redemption, efficacious and typical: like Adonis, Osiris and Attis he had died a violent death, and like them he had returned to life; like them, he had prefigured in his lot that of the human beings who should take part in his worship.²³

Christianity's transition from the Gospel of Jesus to the "universal religion" took place under the influence of the mysteries. This is especially true for Christian rituals—baptism and the Eucharist—as they developed according to the pattern of pagan rituals, and ultimately "displaced" the pagan mysteries; Christianity itself became a mystery.²⁴ Loisy maintains that Paul, though himself being "imbued with the spirit of the mysteries"²⁵ and playing an important role in this crucial process toward the establishment of the "Christian Mystery," was part of the wider atmosphere of the time, rather than a lone genius: "Paul was the most important worker in this metamorphosis [of Christianity], but he was not the only one."²⁶ Also, it was not Paul's intended plan to imitate the pagan mysteries in his construction of Christianity and promulgation.²⁷ Nevertheless, Loisy views the whole process from the perspective of historical progression, saying, "[T]he analogy of the evangelic data and the primitive Christian rites with the beliefs and customs of the mysteries determined, under the rule of circumstances, the fu-

---

21 As Cumont, Loisy also connects these cults to the East/Orient, although Loisy acknowledges and begins with the Eleusinian mysteries of ancient Greece.
22 Loisy, "The Christian Mystery," 47–50.
23 Loisy, "The Christian Mystery," 51.
24 Loisy, "The Christian Mystery," 50.
25 Loisy, "The Christian Mystery," 60.
26 Loisy, "The Christian Mystery," 57. Loisy's minimization of Paul's contribution (thereby resisting "the Protestant idealization of Paul's individual religious role") might be attributed to Loisy's Catholic background. See Lannoy, "St Paul," 233.
27 Loisy, "The Christian Mystery," 61.

sion of the one with the other."²⁸ Thus, finally, "[h]aving borrowed much from the pagan mysteries, [Christianity] went on to supplant them and to eliminate them."²⁹

2.1.1.3 Richard Reitzenstein

Richard Reitzenstein emphasized that the religious and theological ideas of Christianity (especially of Paul) were greatly indebted to those of the Hellenistic mysteries (which he regarded differently than the Greek mysteries). He maintained that borrowing the ideas from the Hellenistic mysteries was a conscious act. In Reitzenstein's *Hellenistic Mystery-Religions*, he presented the "basic perspectives of Hellenistic religions" (especially, the mysteries in general) and situated Paul and early Christianity within them.³⁰ According to Reitzenstein, earliest Christianity "grew up between two thought-worlds which had begun to intermingle, the Greek and the Oriental."³¹ Focusing on the "really Oriental part of Hellenistic religions" throughout his project,³² Reitzenstein argues that Hellenistic mysteries differed from the older, Greek mysteries, in that one's participation in the mysteries was not taken for granted based on one's nationality, but was a matter of personal choice; hence Hellenistic mysteries were individualistic, voluntary, inwardly-experienced (as opposed to traditional "polis-cult/religion"), as well as "missionary."³³ The Hellenistic mysteries provided one's "voluntarily chosen death" and a "new life granted by grace."³⁴ The initiate's union with the mystery deity, especially the deity's lot as his/her dying and rising, and thereby the initiate's becoming the deity himself/herself, loom large in all Hellenistic mysteries.³⁵ Thanks to the migration of people and commodities in the period,³⁶ and the activities of wander-

---

28 Loisy, "The Christian Mystery," 61.
29 Loisy, "The Christian Mystery," 64.
30 Richard Reitzenstein, *Hellenistic Mystery-Religions: Their Basic Ideas and Significance*, trans. John E. Steely (Waco: Baylor University Press, 2018), 4, 111. The English translation first appeared in 1978 based on the third edition of the German text (1927).
31 Reitzenstein, *Hellenistic Mystery-Religions*, 17. Note that he focuses on "thought-worlds" and somehow abstracts "Greek" and "Oriental."
32 Reitzenstein, *Hellenistic Mystery-Religions*, 17.
33 Reitzenstein, *Hellenistic Mystery-Religions*, 7, 18, 20, 22, 24.
34 Reitzenstein, *Hellenistic Mystery-Religions*, 39, 20. Note his Christianized language.
35 Reitzenstein, *Hellenistic Mystery-Religions*, 13–14, 22. This characteristic is, according to Reitzenstein, indebted to the "second type of religion" from the East that includes the view that "the soul … is akin to God in essence … immortal." He finds the origin of this type from Iranian and Indian religions, and contrasts it to his first type (i.e., "the Babylonian and the early Israelite religion"). See Reitzenstein, *Hellenistic Mystery-Religions*, 8.
36 Reitzenstein, *Hellenistic Mystery-Religions*, 23

ing missionaries,[37] such a "Hellenistic form of Oriental faith" spread and reinvigorated the stagnant religiosity of the West.[38] In describing these basic patterns, he admits some local cultic diversity and relative scantiness of sources.[39] Yet, his focus is on finding commonalities among all Hellenistic mysteries. What is distinctive about Reitzenstein is that he argues for Paul's *conscious* dependence on the sacred writings of the mysteries in constructing his theology; this differs from Loisy.[40]

Specifically, Reitzenstein claimed that several exegetical problems in Rom 6 can be solved by putting the passage in the context of the mysteries and Hellenistic religious ideas. Regarding Rom 6:1–14, he pays attention to the phrase ὁ γὰρ ἀποθανὼν δεδικαίωται ἀπὸ τῆς ἁμαρτίας:

> I compare a passage like Rom. 6:1–14, which corresponds fully to Hellenistic mystery conceptions … For me, no explanation formed on the basis of the Jewish concept of δικαιοῦν (God pronounces vindication) can do justice to the words underlined above [ὁ γὰρ ἀποθανὼν δεδικαίωται ἀπὸ τῆς ἁμαρτίας] … It appears to me that the context requires first of all that the subject be seen not as a purely physical act of dying, nor a merely figurative one, but above all a *voluntary* dying and surrendering oneself to death. Everything becomes simple and clear as soon as we set the mystery conceptions in the background.[41]

Reitzenstein claims confidently that Rom 6:1–14 squares with the Hellenistic mysteries and thus, "everything becomes simple and clear" once Paul is put in this context. The Hellenistic mysteries form an indispensable context in which early Christian thought and practice (such as the notion of dying and rising with Christ through baptism) should be understood.

Currently, no NT scholar precisely follows the theses of the Inaugurated Quest (i.e., that Paul/early Christianity was largely dependent on the mysteries, deriving or borrowing their rituals or ideas from the mysteries directly).[42] Yet, as will be seen, there are some in classics and ancient history that continue to develop the

---

37 Reitzenstein, *Hellenistic Mystery-Religions*, 25.
38 Reitzenstein, *Hellenistic Mystery-Religions*, 23
39 Reitzenstein, *Hellenistic Mystery-Religions*, 27–28 (local cultic diversity); 18–19 (scantiness of sources).
40 Lannoy, "St Paul," 227–28, 232. Cumont seems close to Reitzenstein in his view of Paul's conscious adoption of pagan ideas. Lannoy, "St Paul," 229.
41 Italics original. Reitzenstein, *Hellenistic Mystery-Religions*, 327–328.
42 Dennis R. MacDonald arguing for some "literary dependency" (in terms of the source and redaction of the Fourth Gospel) is an interesting exception. *The Dionysian Gospel: The Fourth Gospel and Euripides* (Minneapolis: Fortress, 2017). Another example is John Moles, "Jesus and Dionysus in *The Acts of The Apostles* and Early Christianity," *Hermathena* 180 (2006): 65–104. Here he admits to a maximalist reading (65) and concludes that "the *Acts of the Apostles* is deeply permeated with the Dionysiac" (98).

overall framework established by these earlier scholars, especially Franz Cumont. In that regard, the Inaugurated Quest is not merely passé, but it partly resonates with present scholarship. Interestingly, if one reads this previous generation's work carefully, one would see that they already had an advanced sensibility for subtle comparisons. In his preface to *Oriental Religions*, Cumont admits that the task at hand includes "a series of very delicate problems of chronology and interrelation," which he believes require situational answers.[43] Then he goes on to say:

> We may speak of "vespers of Isis" or of a "eucharist of Mithra and his companions," but only in the same sense as when we say "the vassal princes of the empire" or "Diocletian's socialism." These are tricks of style used to give prominence to a similarity and to establish a parallel strongly and closely. A word is not a demonstration, and we must be careful not to infer an influence from an analogy.[44]

Sometimes scholars in the Inaugurated Quest did not live up to the truth of the last sentence, when they made too much out of "analogies" (i.e., early Christianity had some features analogous to the mysteries) and moved toward arguing for "influences" (i.e., early Christianity was influenced by the mysteries). The opposite also occurred with the Moratorium on the Quest when the scholars underestimated even analogies between them. Adela Yarbro Collins observes, "Bousset responded to the criticism that the Hellenistic texts cited by the historians of religion as analogues to Romans 6 ... were later than the date of Romans by stressing that it was not a question of literary dependence."[45] She continues, "Most of those who have denied that Paul was dependent on the mystery religions missed the point that the history of religions school was making."[46] The argument for Paul's (or early Christianity's) dependence on the mysteries (though not "literary") was indeed made by scholars of the history of religions school and by those who shared their perspectives. Yet, her observation is correct: the fundamental insights of the Inaugurated Quest should not be merely dismissed, and this monograph, as will be seen, is attempting to appreciate the previous scholars' insights, while modifying certain aspects.

Now, a survey of what "[m]ost of those who have denied that Paul was dependent on the mystery religions" have argued will illuminate how such criticism is fruitfully utilized to lay the foundation for furthering scholarly discussion on this subject.

---

43 Cumont, *Oriental Religions*, xviii.
44 Cumont, *Oriental Religions*, xviii.
45 Adela Yarbro Collins, *Cosmology and Eschatology in Jewish and Christian Apocalypticism* (Leiden: Brill, 1996), 236.
46 Yarbro Collins, *Cosmology and Eschatology*, 236.

2.1.2 The Moratorium on the Quest: No Dependency on the Mysteries

The next phase of scholarship (starting in the mid-twentieth century) is the Moratorium on the Quest. Roughly speaking, "No Quest" in Historical Jesus studies refers to a time when scholars became skeptical about finding direct historical facts about the figure of Jesus from the Gospels. In other words, No-Quest scholars held that there was no historical connection (or that it was impossible to find such a connection) between the portrayal of Jesus in the Gospels and the historical figure of Jesus. These scholars began to regard the Gospels as primarily representing the Christ of faith and effectively stopped the Old Quest. The Moratorium on the Quest of the mysteries can be compared to the No Quest in Historical Jesus studies in that both stopped previous scholarship. In the present study, the Moratorium on the Quest refers to a scholarly trend that denied a genuine historical connection between the pagan mysteries and Paul/early Christianity. Moratorium scholars say that perceived similarities in the Pauline letters or in other NT writings to the mysteries do not constitute real parallels or genealogical dependence.

The term "Moratorium on the Quest" does not imply that the mysteries were not seriously studied by the scholars of this category. Rather, many of the pioneers in this stage did extensive research on the mysteries and, on the basis of their work, they rejected the conclusion of the earlier scholars, thereby thwarting subsequent scholars from further pursuing the subject. In addition, the Moratorium on the Quest does not necessarily follow the Inaugurated Quest in a chronological sense; there were scholars, such as H. A. A. Kennedy and A. D. Nock, who criticized and opposed the claims of the Inaugurated Quest during the period the Inaugurated Quest flourished.[47] Likewise, the Moratorium stage does not simply end when the Continued Quest (discussed in the next section) starts, because a tone of dismissal similar to that of the Moratorium scholars is often heard in twenty-first-century scholarship. For example, one of the most recent commentaries on Romans (by Richard Longenecker) repeats this conclusion:

> Some have argued that the origin of baptism [as appearing in Rom 6] as a religious rite stemmed from the ancient Near Eastern cults of Mithra (the Persian god of light) and Isis (the Egyptian goddess of nature, who was the wife and sister of Osiris). But *that thesis is thoroughly discounted today*.[48]

---

47 H. A. A. Kennedy, *St. Paul and the Mystery-Religions* (New York; London: Hodder and Stoughton, 1913). Arthur Darby Nock, *Early Gentile Christianity and Its Hellenistic Background* (New York: Harper & Row, 1964). Though Nock's book was published in 1964, it was actually a reprint of his earlier writings published in 1928 and 1952.
48 Italics mine. Richard N. Longenecker, *The Epistle to the Romans: A Commentary on the Greek Text*, NIGTC (Grand Rapids: Eerdmans, 2016), 612. Similarly, Arland J. Hultgren, *Paul's Letter to*

Therefore, one must be aware that these heuristic stages are not clear-cut, but complicatedly overlapping.

For our purpose, the Moratorium can be subdivided in three ways in order to better understand how different approaches converged and contributed to an overall skepticism about the claims of the Inaugurated Quest.

2.1.2.1 Wagner and Wedderburn

Günter Wagner and A. J. M. Wedderburn merit attention because of the size and the decisiveness of their work, and their long-lasting, continuing influence on subsequent scholars. With some differences, both focus on Paul's notions of baptism in comparison to the mysteries and reach the conclusion that it is unlikely that Paul's theology of baptism and/or his soteriology were dependent on or influenced by the mystery cults. Therefore, their work ceased the Inaugurated Quest, and thus, any further meaningful historical comparison between Paul and the mysteries.

Günter Wagner's 1967 monograph, which comprehensively surveys the cult of Eleusis, the Osiris-Isis cult, the Tammuz and the Marduk cult, the Adonis cult, and the Attis cult,[49] is a prominent example of comparing ancient mysteries with Rom 6:1–11, producing a surprisingly negative conclusion. The tone of his assessment is definitive: "the religio-historical documents [regarding the mysteries] are of no help to us in the interpretation of Rom. VI."[50] This is mainly because the elements earlier scholars identified in the mysteries and subsequently led them to see a relationship between the mysteries and Paul were not in the mysteries, according to Wagner. Earlier in his book, he asks:

> [C]an we find a myth of a dying and rising or resuscitated god whose fortune is regarded as fundamental for the cult, and in whose worship rites actualising, repeating, or representing that fortune are celebrated—rites that give the person by whom or to whom they are done such a fellowship with the god that allows his initiates to share in his fortune?[51]

---

the Romans: A Commentary (Grand Rapids: Eerdmans, 2011), 247 ("... that view has been put to rest"). See also Siikavirta's recent monograph on baptism in Romans, which only briefly includes some negative remarks about the mysteries: "[T]he influence of the Graeco-Roman mystery cults on Paul's sacramentology [is] a position that has largely been abandoned since the 1950s." Samuli Siikavirta, *Baptism and Cognition in Romans 6–8*, WUNT II/407 (Tübingen: Mohr Siebeck, 2015), 69.
49 For recent research on Attis, see Maria Grazia Lancellotti, *Attis: Between Myth and History: King, Priest and God* (Leiden: Brill, 2002).
50 Günter Wagner, *Pauline Baptism and the Pagan Mysteries: The Problem of the Pauline Doctrine of Baptism in Romans VI.1–11, in the Light of Its Religio-Historical "Parallels,"* trans. J. P. Smith (Edinburgh; London: Oliver & Boyd, 1967), 268.
51 Wagner, *Pauline Baptism*, 61.

Wagner gives a categorical answer, *Absolutely No.* Throughout the book, he takes issue with the view that "Paul was entirely dependent on the sacramentalism and mystical practices of those cults."[52] There is "no symbolical significance" in Eleusinian baptism—unlike Pauline teaching of baptism—because the water-rite in Eleusis is "simply a preliminary purification-rite preparing for [initiation]," not the initiation proper.[53] Furthermore, "'A mystic unification of the life of man (*sic*) with the life of the godhead to whom he swears allegiance' cannot be affirmed for Eleusis."[54] Similarly, Wagner emphasizes that the water-rite in the Isis cult, described by Apuleius, has no more than "a cleansing and preparatory character."[55] Although the Osiris tradition includes the notion of drowning, says Wagner, "no thought of deification or resuscitation through the instrumentality of water" developed in the Isis-Osiris cult.[56] Furthermore, Sarapis, who replaced Osiris in the Hellenistic period, was "not a dying and rising god,"[57] which weakens its comparison with the Pauline understanding of baptism as dying and rising with Christ. As observed from this brief summary, Wagner operated on the Frazerian framework of "the dying and rising deity" in the mysteries, and attempted to refute the sacramental identification between baptism and mystery-initiations, proposed by scholars of the Inaugurated Quest.

A. J. M. Wedderburn's 1987 monograph had a slightly different agenda from Wagner's, but it also criticized the previous scholars' view that attributed the ori-

---

52 Wagner, *Pauline Baptism*, 1
53 Wagner, *Pauline Baptism*, 259. See also 71–72.
54 Wagner, *Pauline Baptism*, 259 (note: the phrase quoted by Wagner is from E. Rohde, *Psyche*; Rohde also denied its existence in Eleusis). It should also be noted that although the ancient "mysteries" and "mysticism" (or "mystic") are somehow related, they are not the same. Sometimes, general-level dictionaries link mysticism to the mysteries in the ancient world. For example, the German dictionary *Brockhaus Enzyklopädie* defines mysticism as follows: "Mysticism [the original Greek *myeomai* translates as "to be initiated," literally "to have one's eyes and mouth closed"], a structural form of religious experience and life in which the *unio mystica* – an intrinsically experienced unification (*Einung*) of the human self with the divine reality – is achieved" (*Brockhuas Enzyklopädie in Zwanzig Bänden*, vol. 13 [Wiesbanden: F.A. Brockhaus, 1971], 141. The English translation comes from Peter Schäfer, *The Origins of Jewish Mysticism* [Tübingen: Mohr Siebeck, 2009], 2). Yet, mysticism is usually applied to wider religious phenomena throughout history (e.g., medieval European mysticism, or Islamic mysticism, such as Sufism); it is not restricted to the mysteries in the Greek and Roman world. Also, the notion of *unio mystica* was not the sole emphasis of all the mysteries discussed in this study. Burkert notes, "It is … quite misleading to associate mysteries with mysticism in its true sense, that is, the transformation of consciousness through meditation" (Burkert, *Ancient Mystery Cults*, 7).
55 Wagner, *Pauline Baptism*, 260; in more detail, see 100–103.
56 Wagner, *Pauline Baptism*, 116.
57 Wagner, *Pauline Baptism*, 260.

gin of Pauline baptism to the mystery initiations.[58] According to Wedderburn, it is true that the mysteries were part of the common culture in Paul's time,[59] and generally speaking, the "life-through-death" motif in the mysteries "would provide an analogy to Paul's teaching on baptism."[60] However, Wedderburn points out that it is not possible to prove that Paul derived his view about baptism from the teaching and practice of the mysteries. For example, the notion of dying and rising (coming to life) is a "widespread idea" that is not restricted to the mysteries.[61] Also, one cannot speak of a "common theology" of the mysteries, until Neoplatonism came in later.[62] Hence, direct dependency on the mysteries by Pauline theology becomes an impossibility.[63] The conclusion of his masterful survey and careful analysis of evidence is dismissive of, rather than inviting, other perspectives (though in a polite manner):

> The interpretation of Paul is my task, and it is only just beginning. Yet it is, I hope, not an inconsiderable beginning, to have set a large warning sign at the entry to what I believe to be a 'dead-end' in Pauline studies, the interpretation of Paul's doctrine of union with Christ as derivative from the mystery-cults of his day.[64]

Throughout his book (and in his other articles on the same topic) his interest lies primarily in theological (*inter alia*, "soteriological") comparisons between Paul and the mysteries.[65] This left the unstated possibility that one could arrive at a different conclusion, if the comparison is not soteriological.

---

[58] Overall, Wedderburn's book aims to "call into question [the] dominant theory" about 1 Cor 15 and Rom 6, that is, the view that "spiritualized resurrection" attested by later documents (2 Tim 2:18; Col 2:11–13, etc.) is already presupposed in Paul's earlier writings (1 Cor 15 and Rom 6). A. J. M. Wedderburn, *Baptism and Resurrection: Studies in Pauline Theology against its Graeco-Roman Background* (Tübingen: Mohr Siebeck, 1987), 5. By extension, Wedderburn's work also tries to undermine the earlier historical reconstruction of "early Christian soteriology and baptismal theology" (this earlier reconstruction was carried out not only by using later deutero-Pauline writings, but also by studying the mysteries). Wedderburn, *Baptism and Resurrection*, 6.
[59] Wedderburn, *Baptism and Resurrection*, 393. More recently, Agersnap takes a similar position. See Agersnap, *Baptism and the New Life*, 98, 403.
[60] Wedderburn, *Baptism and Resurrection*, 379.
[61] Wedderburn, *Baptism and Resurrection*, 394.
[62] Wedderburn, *Baptism and Resurrection*, 148.
[63] Even in the twenty-first century there are several scholars who share Wagner's and Wedderburn's skepticism. As also mentioned earlier, Richard Longenecker's recent commentary on Romans (2016) exemplifies this tendency. Longenecker, *The Epistle to the Romans*, 612.
[64] Wedderburn, *Baptism and Resurrection*, 396.
[65] For his other writings: A. J. M. Wedderburn, "The Soteriology of the Mysteries and Pauline Baptismal Theology," *NovT* 29 (1987): 53–72; idem, "Paul and the Hellenistic Mystery-Cults: On Posing

In addition to the two major scholars (Wagner and Wedderburn) who directly opposed the Inaugurated Quest, there are two different approaches, which also call into question the procedures and results of the Inaugurated Quest. The first one is a scholarly trend to focus on "Jewish backgrounds" as an alternative to the Inaugurated Quest, which too often concentrated on the pagan cultic background.[66] The second is a methodological criticism, best represented by Jonathan Z. Smith, who criticized both groups—those in favor of a close relationship (the Inaugurated Quest) and others who denied that relationship (some of the Moratorium on the Quest).[67]

2.1.2.2 "Jewish Backgrounds"

Due to its diversity and broad range, it is difficult to single out a few strong voices to represent the entire scholarly trend that focuses on "Jewish backgrounds" of the New Testament. Scholars who examined terms pertaining to the mysteries and explained their origins according to Jewish backgrounds can only be mentioned here.[68] For example, in his two-part work in the 1950s, Raymond Brown attempted to demonstrate the "Semitic" background of the term μυστήριον in the NT, especially focusing on its relation to *rāz* and *sod*.[69] Prior to Brown's work, Günther Bornkamm's article in *TWNT*/*TDNT* (early 1940s) provides a general survey of

---

the Right Questions," in *La soteriologia dei culti orientali nell'Imperio Romano: Atti del Colloquio Internazionale su La soteriologia dei culti orientali nell'Impero Romano, Roma 24–28 Settembre 1979*, ed. Ugo Bianchi and Maarten J. Vermaseren (Leiden: Brill, 1982), 817–33. Note also the title of that edited volume ("*La soteriologia dei culti orientali*").

66 The term "background" may not do full justice to the material in question; hence the use of quotation marks.

67 According to Smith, both approaches are methodologically flawed because of their focus on the question of genealogical relations and dependency.

68 This movement already began when the Inaugurated Quest prevailed. For example, in the early twentieth century, H. A. A. Kennedy finds "more immediate background" in the Old Testament. See his remark in the preface: "As a matter of fact, the chief defect in the process [of the current investigations linking Paul to the mystery religions] is the failure to be sufficiently rigorous in the application of the historical method. The more immediate background of the Christian faith is apt to be strangely neglected. It will appear again and again in the course of the present investigation that the Old Testament supplies a perfectly adequate explanation of ideas and usages in the Epistles of Paul which it is the fashion to associate with Hellenistic influence." Kennedy, *St. Paul and the Mystery-Religions*, viii.

69 Raymond Brown, "The Semitic Background of the New Testament Mysterion (I)," *Bib* 39 (1958): 426–48; idem, "The Semitic Background of the New Testament Mysterion (II)," *Bib* 40 (1959): 70–87. Brown displays his impressions that the previous scholars' view on the relevancy of the mystery cults has already been sufficiently criticized and refuted. See Brown, "The Semitic Background (I)," 426 (esp. n. 2), 427, 438, 440.

the mystery cults, but affirms no relationship to the use of μυστήριον in the NT.[70] Instead, his survey suggests a more positive relationship of μυστήριον language in the NT (esp. in the Pauline letters) with Jewish apocalyptic concepts. The research trend that focuses on *terminology* is still found in recent scholarship.[71] Yet, scholars also consider several themes, passages, and patterns (i.e., not only individual terms, such as μυστήριον), previously alleged to be close to pagan mysteries, as offshoots of the revelatory tradition in the OT/HB and Jewish apocalyptic writings.[72] One example of thematic studies is Markus N. A. Bockmuehl's *Revelation and Mystery in Ancient Judaism and Pauline Christianity* (1990).[73] Overall, scholarly efforts to illuminate Jewish contexts have provided an alternative frame to make sense of the elements that were previously studied in light of the mysteries. Paul's theological ideas and some of his distinctive terms resonate with mysteries, but are not necessarily related to the pagan mysteries. Rather, this group of scholars argue that they are better understood within scriptural tradition and apocalyptic Judaism, especially regarding its spatial, revelatory, and epistemological emphasis.[74]

---

[70] G. Bornkamm, "μυστήριον, μυέω," *TDNT* 4:802–28.
[71] In Benjamin L. Gladd's survey, he only briefly mentions those who argued for the relevancy of the pagan mystery cults, then turns to other scholars who explored the Jewish milieu that "turned the tide." Benjamin L. Gladd, *Revealing the Mysterion: The Use of Mystery in Daniel and Second Temple Judaism with its Bearing on First Corinthians.* BZNW 160 (Berlin: Walter de Gruyter, 2008), 9–10. This book shows that the Moratorium is ongoing and has not been completely replaced by the Continued Quest.
[72] To be clear, I do not mean that those who focus on the apocalyptic tradition directly engage in rejecting or refuting the thesis of the Inaugurated Quest (for example, Adela Yarbro Collins, who has extensively worked on apocalyptic tradition, thinks that Paul's interpretation of baptism in Rom 6 resonates with the Greco-Roman mysteries; see Yarbro Collins, *Cosmology and Eschatology*, 237). The notion of "apocalyptic" has itself been the subject of enormous scholarly study throughout history from the time of Käsemann. See Ernst Käsemann, "The Beginnings of Christian Theology," *JTC* 6 (1969 [German original: 1960]): 162–85; Christopher Rowland, *The Open Heaven: A Study of Apocalyptic in Judaism and Early Christianity* (New York: Crossroad, 1982); Christopher Rowland and C. R. A. Morray-Jones, *The Mystery of God: Early Jewish Mysticism and the New Testament* (Leiden; Boston: Brill, 2009); see also, Benjamin E. Reynolds and Loren T. Stuckenbruck, eds., *The Jewish Apocalyptic Tradition and the Shaping of New Testament Thought* (Minneapolis: Fortress, 2017).
[73] Markus N. A. Bockmuehl, *Revelation and Mystery in Ancient Judaism and Pauline Christianity*, WUNT II/36 (Tübingen: Mohr Siebeck, 1990).
[74] Such spatial and revelatory (thus, not only eschatological) aspects are indeed apocalyptic. Note that I do not use the adjectives "apocalyptic" and "eschatological" as synonyms, although apocalyptic eschatology is an important element of many apocalyptic texts. As for the definitions of apocalypse (genre), apocalyptic eschatology (ideas/motifs), and apocalypticism (social ideology), see John J. Collins, *The Apocalyptic Imagination: An Introduction to Jewish Apocalyptic Literature*, 2nd ed. (Grand Rapids: Eerdmans, 1998), 1–14. Regarding the problem of the substantive use of the adjective "apocalyptic" in English, see Adela Yarbro Collins, "Apocalypse Now: The State of

The search for Paul's mystery-cultic background, pursued by the Inaugurated Quest, is thus regarded as misguided.

2.1.2.3 Jonathan Z. Smith

At the same time, there is another voice, not from biblical scholarship, but from the field of comparative religion, which challenged the presuppositions and procedures of the Inaugurated Quest. Jonathan Z. Smith (1987) criticizes biblical scholars or historians of early Christianity, who often do not engage the mysteries in their own right. He accuses them of flattening out the historical development of each mystery cult and each cult's particularities, thus, using them collectively as a foil for early Christianity or New Testament doctrines.[75] More importantly, Smith rebukes scholars of previous generations for being motivated by apologetic/polemical motives, that is, equating Protestantism with the pure, simple, earliest form of Christianity (before it was "contaminated" with pagan ideas) and also equating Roman Catholicism with the degenerated form of Christianity (after the influence of pagan ideas, including the mysteries). In short, in the past, the whole comparative enterprise (comparing early Christianity and the mysteries) suffered from "Protestant anti-Catholic apologetics."[76] Rather than seeking any specific genealogical relationship between early Christianity and the mysteries, Smith calls for a comparative perspective that views the individual phenomena "as analogous processes, responding to parallel kinds of religious situations."[77] For Smith, a mere comparison of words or terms (such as μυστήριον) between the NT and the mysteries (for proving or disproving any relationship) is not helpful. He notes, "the whole question of 'mystery-terminology' needs reexamination."[78] From this perspective, some scholars who turned to Jewish backgrounds of mystery terminology

---

Apocalyptic Studies Near the End of the First Century of the Twenty-First Century," *HTR* 104 (2011): 447.

75 Wedderburn also pointed out this problem. Wedderburn, "The Soteriology of the Mysteries," 53.
76 Smith, *Drudgery Divine*, 34. This type of criticism resembles G. F. Moore's (and later, E. P. Sanders') criticism that Christian theologians during the two millennia were not always free from anti-Jewish apologetics (often, combined with anti-Catholic apologetics, after the Reformation period). George Foot Moore, "Christian Writers on Judaism," *HTR* 14 (1921): 197–254. Yet, one may also point out examples in the opposite direction (i.e., some Catholic scholars explored the relationship between the mysteries and Catholic Christianity more positively because of the perceived similarity). Odo Casel, who argued that the mysteries were "the preparatory school for Christianity," is a good example of this. Regarding the summary of Casel's view, see Klauck, *The Religious Context of Early Christianity*, 151.
77 Smith, *Drudgery Divine*, 112–13.
78 Smith, *Drudgery Divine*, 79, n. 38.

(discussed in the previous section) can also be criticized for not being free from the misconceived framework.

Although Smith's point is to question (or even deconstruct) the entire scholarly endeavor of the past, his insights have played an important role for the scholars in the Continued Quest (see the next section). Similarly, the representative works of this stage—Wagner's and Wedderburn's—have provided valuable information about primary sources, as well as the history of scholarship from the earlier periods. In other words, the Moratorium on the Quest stage did not fully prevent subsequent scholars from exploring the subject matter; rather, it ironically stimulated the reconfiguration of the inquiry. In a recent volume concerning the mystery cults among Greek settlers in southern Italy (*Magna Graecia*), Giovanni Casadio begins his chapter on Dionysus with this statement alluding to Smith: "Gods rise and die— and rise again, despite the contrary opinion of an eminent Chicago professor of history of religions."[79]

2.1.3 The Continued Quest

The pendulum swings back. For a growing number of scholars, the comparative task is not to be abandoned. In his article on Rom 6 and Paul's Hellenistic context, Hans Dieter Betz expresses his dissatisfaction with the incommensurately brief conclusion of Wedderburn's massive book. By modifying a sentence from Wedderburn's conclusion (quoted before), Betz sarcastically notes, "Indeed, the interpretation of Paul's doctrines of baptism and resurrection has barely begun."[80] Betz is

---

[79] Giovanni Casadio, "Dionysus in Campania: Cumae," in *Mystic Cults in Magna Graecia*, ed. Giovanni Casadio and Patricia A. Johnston (Austin: University of Texas Press, 2009), 33. See also Marvin W. Meyer, "Mysteries Divine," *Numen* 39 (1992): 235–38. While agreeing with Smith's concerns and critiques found in *Drudgery Divine*, Meyer mentions "several examples of deities from the mystery religions who may not rise or be resurrected in a Christian sense but who still provide in their deaths and lives hints of the continuation of life or the manifestation of new life" (237). Meyer finds similarities between Christianity and the mysteries more than the Moratorium scholars did, although he also acknowledges that these similarities do not always mean dependence and that both Christianity and the mysteries are better understood in light of the wider religious context of the Greco-Roman world. See Marvin W. Meyer, *The Ancient Mysteries: A Sourcebook of Sacred Texts* (Philadelphia: University of Pennsylvania Press, 1999), 225–27, 252–54 (the initial version of this book was published by HarperCollins in 1987—note that it is the same year when Wedderburn published his *Baptism and Resurrection*).
[80] Hans Dieter Betz, "Transferring a Ritual: Paul's Interpretation of Baptism in Rom 6," in *Paul in His Hellenistic Context*, ed. Troels Engberg-Pedersen (Minneapolis: Fortress, 1995), 100, n. 66.

not alone. In her recent influential monograph on Roman faith and Christian faith, Teresa Morgan signals the possibility of comparing the worship of Christ and that of other mystery deities (while also mentioning some caveats): "In some ways ... if not all, the worship of Isis makes an interesting comparison with the worship of God and Christ."[81] Simply speaking, the quest is not dead; I am one of those who believe that it is not dead but still alive. The Pauline passages, including Rom 6, and the ritual practices of early Christians still present intriguing historical, exegetical, and theological problems. Indeed, a number of scholars are currently revisiting the quest by consciously addressing ideological biases, refining methodological issues, and paying attention to more recent research outcomes by classicists and scholars of ancient religions. I call them the Continued Quest, and this section will focus on surveying its various aspects.

Compared with the other two quests, the Continued Quest is distinct in two important ways. First, due partly to the lessons from the scholars of the Moratorium on the Quest, the notion of dependency, or the either-or question, does not take a central place in the debate. Rather, more fluid positions on the relationship between the mysteries and Paul/early Christianity begin to appear. Second, specialization in the academy has accelerated, and this enabled diverse perspectives and approaches to arise. Many scholars in the Inaugurated Quest in the late nineteenth and early twentieth centuries practiced what are now multiple disciplines (e.g., early Christianity, New Testament, ancient religions, classics, etc.). The impact of specialization can be seen in the Moratorium camp, as these scholars are largely New Testament specialists (except J. Z. Smith), not classicists/historians of ancient religion or generalists who cover various fields. Now, the scholars in the Continued Quest are drawn from several different specialized fields—for example, historians exploring material culture, classic philologists of literary sources, and NT scholars with various foci.[82]

There are three distinctive strands within the Continued Quest. Speaking of "strands" by no means implies that the members of one category think of themselves as one group (an emic view). Rather, these are heuristic categories to organize the multifaceted recent scholarship on the mysteries and situate my work with-

---

[81] Teresa Morgan, *Roman Faith and Christian Faith: Pistis and Fides in the Early Roman Empire and Early Churches* (Oxford: Oxford University Press, 2015), 498. Of course, the mystery cults are not the main subject of her book.
[82] It should also be mentioned that the scholars discussed in this section respond differently to the previous stages (the Inaugurated Quest and the Moratorium on the Quest), and how they handle the history of scholarship also differs.

in this emerging scholarly discourse that attempts to look at the old question in a new light.[83]

2.1.3.1 New Testament and Early Christianity Scholars

The first group within the Continued Quest consists of New Testament and early Christianity scholars, who continue to show their interest in the mysteries, or more broadly, Greek and Roman cults. Compared with the Inaugurated Quest, the approaches of these scholars put more emphasis on archaeological findings, particular locales, and social-cultural dynamics. Additionally, they sometimes combine other theoretical perspectives, such as cultural anthropology or ritual studies. Two seminal articles can be mentioned. Helmut Koester's 1990 article on the mystery cult of Melikertes-Palaimon in Roman Corinth surveys archaeological and literary evidence about this lesser-known mystery cult, and suggests the potential value of this particular mystery cult in comparison to Paul and his community in Corinth.[84] Hans Dieter Betz's 1995 article on Rom 6 raises the issue of cultic transfer and the role of initiation rituals in this context.[85] These scholars can be seen as successors of the history of religions school and have continued to pay attention to Paul's and early Christianity's contact with the pagan cultic environment.

This line of inquiry that focuses on reconstructing the social, cultural milieu of early Christianity (and Paul) by exploring material findings has continued to produce scholarly outcomes that focus on either (a) constructing the milieu itself, or (b) applying a particular spatial/temporal context to the interpretation of NT writings. Daniel N. Schowalter and Steven J. Friesen's edited volume, *Urban Religion in*

---

[83] The end result would be rearticulating and transforming old questions in new ways, rather than providing definitive answers. Matthew Novenson has similarly demonstrated how new research can rearticulate old questions in new ways—in his case, with regard to the topic of ancient "messianism." Matthew V. Novenson, *The Grammar of Messianism: An Ancient Jewish Political Idiom and Its Users* (Oxford: Oxford University Press: 2017). Acknowledging that he revisits an old issue, Novenson notes, "In my case, the justification is not so much new evidence ... but rather an alternative model for understanding a familiar set of primary texts. Novenson, *The Grammar of Messianism*, 4. He continues, "My project is not simply to do what the classic surveys ... have done ... but rather to ask a different set of questions altogether." Novenson, *The Grammar of Messianism*, 9–10.
[84] Helmut Koester, "Melikertes at Isthmia: A Roman Mystery Cult," in *Greeks, Romans, and Christians: Essays in Honor of Abraham J. Malherbe*, ed. David L. Balch et al. (Minneapolis: Fortress Press, 1990), 355–66.
[85] Betz, "Transferring a Ritual," 84–118.

Roman Corinth (2005), is a valuable example of the former.⁸⁶ This volume demonstrates a convergence of scholarly effort, not only from New Testament scholars but also from classical archaeologists/historians. Its purpose is to shed light on the social, cultural, religious context of Roman Corinth, which involves a discussion of the mysteries and other related cults.⁸⁷ Examples of the latter (linking the context to NT interpretation) are increasing. An earlier article by Richard DeMaris (1995) on baptism for the dead in Corinth in light of archaeology and anthropology is a good example.⁸⁸ By examining both iconographic and literary tradition, David Balch (2003) reconstructs household situations with paintings and sculptures evocative of mythic stories and explores symbolic spaces where Paul's message of Christ crucified (Gal 3:1) was possibly understood in comparison with the suffering of Isis.⁸⁹ Also, through her analysis of myth, pagan cults, and particularly, the mysteries carried out in Corinth, Laura Nasrallah (2012) attempts to construct a coherent picture of the cultural context of Roman Corinth, within which she highlights pervasive "grief," and applies this contextual understanding to passages in the Corinthian correspondence.⁹⁰ With less reliance on archaeology, but still linking the reconstruction of the mystery-cultic context and the interpretation of Pauline passages, Susan Elliott (1999) interprets Gal 4:21–5:1 in light of the mysteries of the Magna Mater in Asia Minor.⁹¹ Also, Terri Moore (2018) compares the eschatology of 1 Cor 15 with particular mysteries pertaining to Roman Corinth.⁹²

Particularly relevant to my project are Bert Jan Lietaert Peerbolte's article, "Paul, Baptism, and Religious Experience" (2012) and Stephen Richard Turley's monograph, *The Ritualized Revelation of the Messianic Age* (2015). Peerbolte draws on ritual studies (especially, that of Roy Rappaport) to explore Paul's interpretation of baptism as a rite of passage in close connection to the initiation rituals

---

86 Daniel Schowalter and Steven J. Friesen, eds., *Urban Religion in Roman Corinth: Interdisciplinary Approaches* (Cambridge: Harvard Theological Studies, 2005).
87 Particularly, Elizabeth R. Gebhard, "Rites for Melikertes-Palaimon in the Early Roman Corinthia," in *Urban Religion*, 165–203; Nancy Bookidis, "Religion in Corinth: 146 B.C.E. to 100 C.E.," in *Urban Religion*, 141–64.
88 Richard E. DeMaris, "Corinthian Religion and Baptism for the Dead (1 Corinthians 15:29)," *JBL* 114 (1995): 661–82.
89 Balch, "The Suffering of Isis/Io," 24–55.
90 Laura S. Nasrallah, "Grief in Corinth: The Roman City and Paul's Corinthian Correspondence," in *Contested Spaces: Houses and Temples in Roman Antiquity and the New Testament*, ed. David L. Balch and Annette Weissenrieder (Tübingen: Mohr Siebeck, 2012), 109–39.
91 Susan M. Elliott, "Choose Your Mother, Choose Your Master: Galatians 4:21–5:1 in the Shadow of the Anatolian Mother of the Gods," *JBL* 118 (1999): 661–683.
92 Terri Moore, *The Mysteries, Resurrection, and 1 Corinthians 15: Comparative Methodology and Contextual Exegesis* (Lanham: Lexington/Fortress, 2018).

of the mysteries, and to determine how Paul's "visionary-experiential" aspect embedded in his "apocalyptic background" worked together with the "experiential dimension" of baptismal practices.[93] His article has many things in common with my own project, for example, his use of ritual studies, his positive reevaluation of the relationship between Paul and the mysteries, his focus on how baptism functions for the Pauline group in a way analogous to initiation rites of the mysteries, and his emphasis on the experiential dimension, both in Paul and his communities. Yet, since his short essay does not engage extensively with primary sources regarding the mysteries, many assertive claims made in the essay are not actually strong enough to overcome the earlier critiques raised by the scholars of the Moratorium on the Quest, such as Wagner and Wedderburn.[94] Turley's monograph, which is a revision of his PhD dissertation, does not engage in the issue of the mystery cults (thus, technically, he is not in the Continued Quest). His project is a study of rituals in the Pauline letters through the lens of ritual theories, rather than a comparative investigation as mine, and I suspect that this has led him to emphasize the "uniqueness" of early Christian baptism.[95] Also, he discuss both baptism/washings and meal practices, i.e., a scope broader than that of the present study.[96] While differing in several exegetical points, I concur with Turley's insight about baptism as an "apocalyptic ritual" and his use of Rappaport's ritual theory. My project is both indebted to and improving on Peerbolte's and Turley's, thereby demonstrating the ways in which one can advance the discussion of this topic, surmounting the Moratorium scholars' critiques.

2.1.3.2 Classicists and Ancient Historians

The second subgroup consists of several scholars of classics or ancient history, who were only minimally influenced by the call for moratorium by biblical scholars,

---

[93] Bert Jan Lietaert Peerbolte, "Paul, Baptism, and Religious Experience," in *Experientia, Volume 2: Linking Text and Experience*, ed. Colleen Shantz and Rodney A. Werline (Atlanta: SBL, 2012), 181–204.

[94] For example, Peerbolte admits: "Bousset came to his theory on the basis of the observation that the celebration of the death and resurrection of a deity in a cultic context was a pagan Hellenistic phenomenon [but] [r]ecent study has indicated that this type of deity was hardly the central figure in mystery cults" ("Paul, Baptism," 202). Despite this admission, he makes the following remark in his conclusion without providing substantial evidence: "The parallel with the mystery cults is evident; in these cults too members were initiated into a unity with the deity" ("Paul, Baptism," 203). Such claims without sufficient evidence could still be criticized by Moratorium scholars.

[95] For example, see Turley, *Ritualized Revelation*, 55, 58.

[96] Thus, relevant to my project are Chapters 2–5 of his book discussing ritual washings in Gal 3, 1 Cor 6, and 1 Cor 12.

such as Wagner, Wedderburn, et al., and continued their research agenda and framework regarding the mystery cults, provided by earlier scholarship. Of course, it should be noted that their primary quest was not for the relationship between mysteries and early Christianity, but for studying the mysteries in their own right.

There are again some differences within this group, which need to be articulated. I divide this group into two further subgroups. (1) The first group consists of European scholars who advocate positions close to those in the Inaugurated Quest (especially, Franz Cumont).[97] As Jaime Alvar notes:

> [T]he influence of the various branches of the History of Religions school, especially the School of Rome (notably Raffaele Pettazzoni, Ugo Bianchi), and of Maarten J. Vermaseren's enormous series, Études préliminaires aux religions orientales dans l'Empire romain [EPRO; this series was published by Brill], remained dominant and continued largely to underwrite the traditional grand narrative [like Franz Cumont's].[98]

Some recent scholars are still greatly indebted to Cumont's framework of the "Oriental" cults. For example, Gasparro notes:

> Bien que la recherche actuelle ait "déconstruit" plus ou moins radicalement la catégorie cumontienne des "religions orientales" impliquées dans un mouvement de diffusion vers l'Ocident à travers le monde hellénistique, puis romain, on ne peut toutefois nier l'évidence historique d'une série de phénomènes présentant, malgré tout, quelques points communs.[99]

Here, Gasparro advocates the value of Cumont's fundamental insights. Similarly, Athanassiadi and Macris note, "[N]ous nous sommes concentrés sur les mutations du paganisme romain sous l'influence de deux catalyseurs : la philosophie grecque et les sagesses des cultes orientaux."[100] The language of "mutation" of "Roman paganism" under the influence of the "Oriental cults" sounds Cumontian.

(2) The other subgroup has turned toward other methods and perspectives in the research on ancient mysteries, rather than sticking to the traditional narratives. The primary example is Walter Burkert. In his book *Ancient Mystery Cults* (1987), Burkert suggests new ways to conceptualize the ancient mysteries by overcoming the shortcomings of the previous investigations done by scholars under the

---

97 Cf. Jean-Marie Pailler, "Les religions orientales, troisieme epoque," *Pallas* 35 (1989): 95–113.
98 Jaime Alvar, *Romanizing Oriental Gods: Myth, Salvation and Ethics in the Cults of Cybele, Isis and Mithras*, trans. and ed. Richard Gordon, RGRW 165 (Leiden; Boston: Brill, 2008), 7.
99 Giulia Sfameni Gasparro, "Identités religieuses isiaques: pour la définition de'une catégorie historico-religieuse," in *Individuals and Materials in the Greco-Roman Cults of Isis: Agents, Images, and Practices*, ed. Valentino Gasparini and Richard Veymiers (Leiden: Brill, 2018), 1:77.
100 Athanassiadi and Macris, "La philosophisation du religieux," 46.

influence of the history of religions school. To Burkert, the earlier scholars' works were based on a couple of unfounded "stereotypes" about mystery cults: (a) that they are "late" (thus, not genuinely classical Greek but on the way to deterioration to the "dark" middle ages); (b) that they are "oriental" in origin; and (c) that they are "religions of salvation" which can be "preparatory" for "the rise of Christianity."[101] Jan Bremmer has also contributed to the advancement and refinement of the discussion, updating Burkert's work. For example, in his *Initiation into the Mysteries of the Ancient World* (2014), Bremmer provides detailed descriptions of the initiation rites of the mysteries by examining literary and archaeological evidence and by engaging with recent scholars.[102] In addition, interdisciplinary approaches are increasing within this strand of scholarship, combining insights from cultural anthropology, ritual studies, comparative history, and technology. For example, Sandra Blakely's work has extensively engaged with anthropology, cross-cultural studies, and digital approaches, suggesting new possibilities of methodological innovation in the study of the mysteries (especially, the Samothracian mysteries).[103] Large projects also continue to emerge. An edited volume *Greek Mysteries: The Archaeology and Ritual of Ancient Greek Secret Cults* (2003) displays the interdisciplinary cooperation of scholars who have expertise in archaeological, ritual, and textual studies, in order to explore experiential aspects of the Greek mysteries.[104] Also, recent monographs and edited volumes published in Brill's Religions in the Graeco-Roman World series (RGRW; this is a new name for the EPRO series I mentioned earlier, and thus some partly follow the Qumontian tone of EPRO) display remarkable scholarly advancement regarding the Greek and Roman mysteries and of the methodologies used to study them.[105]

---

101 Burkert, *Ancient Mystery Cults*, 2–3. Burkert refutes these assumptions.
102 Bremmer calls his work a "thin" (rather than "thick") description because of the scantiness of the available sources, as opposed to ethnographic investigations of modern societies. Bremmer, *Initiation*, 1–2.
103 For example, Sandra Blakey, "Toward an Archaeology of Secrecy: Power, Paradox, and the Great Gods of Samothrace," *AP3 A* 21 (2012): 49–71; "Daimones in the Thracian Sea: Mysteries, Iron, and Metaphor," *ARG* 14 (2013): 155–82; "Maritime Risk and Ritual Responses: Sailing with the Gods in the Ancient Mediterranean," in *The Sea in History. The Ancient World*, ed. Philip de Souza et al. (Woodbridge, Suffolk: Boydell, 2017), 362–79.
104 Michael B. Cosmopoulos, ed., *Greek Mysteries: The Archaeology and Ritual of Ancient Greek Secret Cults* (London; New York: Routledge, 2003).
105 Several of these volumes are indispensable for this comparative project. For example, Laurent Bricault, Miguel John Versluys, and Paul G. P. Meyboom, eds., *Nile into Tiber. Egypt in the Roman World: Proceedings of the Third International Conference of Isis studies, Faculty of Archaeology, Leiden University, May 11–14 2005*, RGRW 159 (Leiden: Brill, 2007); Alvar, *Romanizing Oriental Gods*, RGRW 165 (2008); Alberto Bernabé and Ana Isabel Jiménez San Cristóbal, eds., *Instructions for the*

Since these scholars (whether they remain closer to the Inaugurated Quest's framework or they move away from it) do not primarily deal with the question of the mysteries and early Christianity (or Paul), further analysis of their work is not necessary at this point. Yet, it is obvious that the new and ongoing studies among this group provide significant resources for this project and future research on the topic.

2.1.3.3 Scholars who Focus on Philosophical/Literary Aspects of Mystery Language

The final subgroup within the Continued Quest intersects several fields of study, but their commonality (whether the discipline be classics, ancient history, Jewish studies, or early Christian studies) is their focus on literary aspects of mystery language (as opposed to actual cultic practices).[106] In other words, they explore the significance of the mysteries as *philosophical and literary phenomena*. One prominent example can be found in the recently edited volume titled *Greek Philosophy and Mystery Cults* (2016). In this book, several European scholars (mainly Spanish) explore how classical Greek philosophers' writings intersected with the mysteries. For example, Plato takes the image of the mysteries in order to describe the initiation into "divine wisdom."[107] Of course, it is possible that philosophical groups were actually adopting cultic activities,[108] so I am not posing a sharp distinction between a purely cultic activity and a purely literary-philosophical activity. This blurred line is also detected in Hellenistic Judaism. There has been a strand of Philonic research initiated by E. R. Goodenough's influential work *By Light, Light* (1935), in which he pays attention to Jewish mysteries or mysticism appearing in Philo's writings.[109] Goodenough's thesis was not only that Philo picked up the lan-

---

Netherworld: The Orphic Gold Tablets, RGRW 162 (Leiden: Brill, 2013); Laurent Bricault and Corinne Bonnet, eds., *Panthée: Religious Transformations in the Graeco-Roman Empire*, RGRW 177 (Leiden: Brill, 2013); Cornelia Isler-Kerényi, *Dionysos in Classical Athens: An Understanding through Images*, RGRW 181 (Leiden: Brill, 2015); Valentino Gasparini and Richard Veymiers, eds., *Individuals and Materials in the Greco-Roman Cults of Isis: Agents, Images, and Practices: Proceedings of the VIth International Conference of Isis Studies (Erfurt, May 6–8, 2013 – Liège, September 23–24, 2013)*, 2 vols. RGRW 187/I,II (Leiden: Brill, 2018).
106 It should be noted again that these scholars do not consider themselves one group.
107 Francesc Casadesús, "The Transformation of the Initiation Language of Mystery Religions into Philosophical Terminology," in *Greek Philosophy and Mystery Cults*, ed. María José Martín-Velasco and María José García Blanco (Cambridge: Cambridge Scholars, 2016), 4–6.
108 Richard Last, *The Pauline Church and the Corinthian Ekklēsia: Greco-Roman Associations in Comparative Context* (Cambridge: Cambridge University Press, 2016), 38–40.
109 Erwin R. Goodenough, *By Light, Light: The Mystic Gospel of Hellenistic Judaism* (New Haven: Yale University Press, 1935). He also had predecessors, such as F. C. Conybeare (*About the Contem-*

guage of the mysteries in his allegorical writings, but also that Hellenistic Judaism in the diaspora became in effect a mystery religion (like the thesis about early Christianity, held by other earlier history of religion scholars)—a thesis no longer entertained today.[110] Yet, his attempt to read Philo's writings in light of the mysteries stimulated other scholars, including his critics, to explore the ways in which Philo appropriates the language of the mysteries in his "religious philosophical" program,[111] in comparison to philosophical reflections by other philosophers.[112]

Similarly, there have been studies of early Christian writers' appropriating mystery language, which may or may not be connected to actual mystery-cultic setting. For example, in *Mysterienterminologie bei Platon, Philon und Klemens von Alexandrien* (1987), Christopher Riedweg discusses Clement of Alexandria, along with Plato and Philo, in terms of how he uses mystery language.[113] In a monograph examining the *Sentences* of Pseudo-Phocylides, Walter T. Wilson includes a discussion of how Pseudo-Phocylides (as other Jewish authors) appropriates the language of the mysteries in the context of ancient moral/philosophical discourses.[114] More recently, Ilaria Ramelli (2017) also compares the mystery language of Clement with other philosophical traditions, focusing on Clement's mode of scriptural exegesis.[115] In addition, in *Mystery and the Making of a Christian Historical Conscious-*

---

plative Life [Oxford: Clarendon, 1895]) and P. Ziegert ("Über die Ansätze zu einer Mysterienlehre aufgebaut auf den antiken Mysterien bei Philo Judäus," *Theologische Studien und Kritiken* 67 [1894]").

110 Many subsequent scholars have pointed out that his project was based on the distinction between "normative Judaism" (i.e., rabbinic Judaism) and the "deviant" form of Judaism in the diasporic settings, and on the presupposition that this "deviant" form of Judaism can provide a "missing link" between Palestinian Judaism and early Christianity. For a critical summary, see Gary Lease, "Jewish Mystery Cults since Goodenough," *ANRW* 20 (1987): 864–71. Although the form and the content of claims are different, there are still scholars who explore ancient Jewish communities as "secret societies," which can be compared to Greco-Roman mystery-cultic groups (e.g., Michael E. Stone, *Secret Groups in Ancient Judaism* [Oxford: Oxford University Press, 2018]).

111 For example, Harry A. Wolfson, *Philo: Foundations of Religious Philosophy in Judaism, Christianity and Islam*, 2 vols. (Cambridge: Harvard University Press, 1947), esp., 1:27–55.

112 Ursula Früchtel, *Die kosmologischen Vorstellungen bei Philo von Alexandrien: Ein Beitrag zur Geschichte der Genesisexegese* (Leiden: Brill, 1968). According to her, "Das Mysterium bei Philo ist daher kein Kultakt, sondern ein Geschehen, das sich am Schreibtisch und im Studierzimmer abspielt" (113). She thus uses the term "Schreibtischmysterium" for Philonic mysteries (112).

113 Christopher Riedweg, *Mysterienterminologie bei Platon, Philon und Klemens von Alexandrien* (Berlin: Walter de Gruyter, 1987).

114 Walter T. Wilson, *The Mysteries of Righteousness: The Literary Composition and Genre of the Sentences of Pseudo-Phocylides* (Tübingen: J. C. B. Mohr, 1994), 147–77.

115 Ilaria L. E. Ramelli, "The Mysteries of Scripture: Allegorical Exegesis and the Heritage of Stoicism, Philo, and Pantaenus," in *Clement's Biblical Exegesis: Proceedings of the Second Colloquium on Clement of Alexandria*, ed. Veronika Černušková et al. (Leiden; Boston: Brill, 2017), 80–110.

ness (2015), T. J. Lang examines various uses of the term μυστήριον from the Pauline letters and compares it to those of the apostolic and early church fathers, in order to understand the emergence of the distinctive historical consciousness characterized by the revelation of God's plan.[116] Another recent piece by C. Andrew Ballard (2017) also conducts a textual investigation of three different texts (*Symposium*, 4QInstruction, and 1 Corinthians) to see how mystery language is used to claim a particular form of *paideia*.[117]

Overall, scholars in this third subgroup of the Continued Quest shift their attention from actual cultic practices or the social-historical dimensions to how mystery language and concepts were appropriated by various authors for particular philosophical (or religious-philosophical) and literary purposes.

2.1.4 The Need for an Analytical Framework

My project is built upon all three subgroups of the Continued Quest (New Testament and early Christianity scholars, classicists and ancient historians, and scholars who focus on philosophical/literary aspects of mystery language) and fits within its broad parameters. I do not primarily attempt to prove (the Inaugurated Quest) or disprove (the Moratorium on the Quest) the dependence of Paul/early Christianity on the mysteries. Following other scholars in the Continued Quest, I am looking at particular dynamics at the local level, employing both literary and archaeological materials, and paying attention to how Paul theologizes the images of baptism (as an initiation ritual) in his letters.[118]

Yet, I find the lack of clear theoretical frameworks in many of the previous attempts in the Continued Quest (some exceptions exist—e.g., Bert Jan Lietaert Peerbolte) unsatisfactory. By "theoretical framework," I mean analytical tools and categories that govern the process of sorting out and examining various an-

---

[116] T. J. Lang, *Mystery and the Making of a Christian Historical Consciousness: From Paul to the Second Century*, BZNW 219 (Berlin: Walter de Gruyter, 2015), 6–9.
[117] C. Andrew Ballard, "The Mysteries of Paideia: 'Mystery' and Education in Plato's *Symposium*, 4QInstruction, and 1 Corinthians," in *Pedagogy in Ancient Judaism and Early Christianity*, ed. Karina Martin Hogan et al. (Atlanta: SBL, 2017), 243–81.
[118] By saying this, I do not mean that Paul was a systematic theologian. I rather focus on the dynamic process reflected in Paul's letters—i.e., his deep convictions, his (and others') lenses of experience, and particular situations of communities interact with each other and produce certain theological dynamics. Cf. Jouette M. Bassler, "Paul's Theology: Whence and Whither?" in *Pauline Theology Volume II: 1 & 2 Corinthians*, ed. David M. Hay (Minneapolis: Fortress, 1993), 11.

cient data in heuristic, meaningful, and controlled ways.[119] This lack of analytical framework is perhaps related to a broader issue: that is, some biblical scholars (including some historians of the ancient world) regard "theory" as unnecessary and stick to close readings of ancient data or historical "facts."[120] The latter is, of course, quintessential to any serious study of the New Testament and the ancient world, and to historical inquiry in general, but it does not invalidate the need for theories or theoretical frameworks. Also, scholars who do not explicitly state a theoretical framework still operate by utilizing some theoretical tools (at least, implicitly). As Horrell critically notes, "Any attempt … to concentrate upon 'the facts' and to avoid 'theory' is likely to be an approach which merely conceals its own presuppositions and commitments."[121] Therefore, these tools (or frameworks) should be more consciously employed and articulated for the reader. Within the Continued Quest, my particular approach will be a combination of two perspectives—cultural anthropology and the sociology of religion. In the next section, I will detail my analytical framework. This framework will be used in Chapters 3–7 to sort out all the data pertaining initiation rituals of Isis and Dionysus and baptism in the Pauline communities; raise questions that have not been asked previously; and identify some neglected aspects of those mysteries and Pauline baptism.

2.2 The Analytical Framework of this Study

To analyze ancient primary data in controlled and meaningful ways, it is crucial to clarify one's analytical framework—or more adequately, "heuristic" framework, since asking new sets of question of old data can help find (*heuriskein*) new networks of meaning that have not been clearly seen before. As mentioned in the introduction, I draw on Roy Rappaport's anthropological theory of ritual appearing in *Ritual and Religion in the Making of Humanity* (1999) and Martin Riesebrodt's sociological theory from *The Promise of Religion: A Theory of Religion* (2010).[122]

---

[119] I prefer the term "theoretical framework" (I will also use "analytical framework" interchangeably) to other related terms, such as "models" or "theories." This preference arises from David G. Horrell, *The Social Ethos of the Corinthian Correspondence: Interests and Ideology from 1 Corinthians and 1 Clement* (Edinburgh: T&T Clark, 1996), 9–18.
[120] Although it is more related to the issue of "literary theory" in biblical studies, Dinkler also discusses some biblical scholars' aversion to theory in general. Michal Beth Dinkler, *Literary Theory and the New Testament* (New Haven: Yale University Press, 2019), 1–4.
[121] Horrell, *The Social Ethos of the Corinthian Correspondence*, 28.
[122] Both books are the final scholarly treatise of these now-deceased scholars, and therefore, reflect the culmination of their scholarly research.

These scholars employ different presuppositions about religion: Rappaport relies on the Durkheimian tradition that locates religion in the origin of society and regards its function as maintaining the system of society,[123] whereas Riesebrodt follows the Weberian perspective that religion should represent interest in salvation that brings social consequences. Nevertheless, they both focus on ritual or liturgy. I will first review each scholar's theory and their relevance for the present study (and problems with application, too), and then I will articulate how I synthesize and utilize their views and why this integrated framework benefits my project.

2.2.1 Roy Rappaport

According to Roy Rappaport, religion, like language, is very old and can be traced back to the origins of human evolution; it actually played an important role in making humanity by "[ameliorating] problems of falsehood intrinsic to language to a degree to allow human sociability to have developed and to be maintained."[124] Such aspects of religion were achieved by ritual (or liturgy, terms he often uses interchangeably[125]), which he defines *formally:* the term ritual denotes "the performance of more or less invariant sequences of formal acts and utterances not entirely encoded by the performers."[126] His definition of ritual may be contestable, but it works well within his overall project.

Rappaport's distinction between "two types of messages" and the ways in which the two are interrelated in the generation and enactment of the meaning of ritual are informative for the present study.[127] After demonstrating that the ef-

---

[123] To be sure, Rappaport's perspective goes beyond the sphere of human society and looks at the larger ecosystem, as demonstrated by his research on New Guinea tribes. For a brief summary of this, see Bell, *Ritual*, 29–30.
[124] Rappaport, *Ritual and Religion*, 15. This claim, that ritual as communication overcomes the untrustworthy and falsifiable nature of language, is both the greatest contribution of his theory, and at the same time, the point where other scholars raise questions. See Joel Robbins's criticism that Rappaport's theory presupposes a particular linguistic ideology. He points out that Rappaport's thesis works better within cultures in which language is viewed skeptically, while it fits less with cultures where language is regarded as more fundamental and emptiness of ritual (which, for Rappaport, is the power of ritual that cures the falsifiability of language) is considered more problematic. Joel Robbins, "Ritual Communication and Linguistic Ideology: A Reading and Partial Reformulation of Rappaport's Theory of Ritual," *CA* 42 (2001): 591–99.
[125] Although I think ritual and liturgy are not always interchangeable, I will use them interchangeably when discussing Rappaport's theory, according to his usage.
[126] Rappaport, *Ritual and Religion*, 24.
[127] Of course, his discussion of two types of ritual messages is only a part of his entire project in his magnum opus; I pay special attention to this discussion because of its relevance.

ficacy of ritual is one of communication (i.e., ritual is not about physical efficacy, but efficacy through communication of information),[128] Rappaport claims that all rituals communicate two types of information: the self-referential and the canonical messages. Regarding the distinction of the two streams of messages, Rappaport notes,

> The self-referential represents the immediate, the particular and the vital aspects of events; the canonical, in contrast, represents the general, enduring, or even eternal aspects of universal orders ... We further see that the canonical stream is carried by the invariant aspects or components of these orders, self-referential information is conveyed by whatever variation the liturgical order allows or demands.[129]

The self-referential messages relate to variations made in ritual, while the canonical messages have to do with invariant aspects of ritual. Therefore, this is basically a *formal* distinction. Yet, these differences in form are connected to the differences in meaning and message. The self-referential messages indicate the status (or the change of status) of the individuals or groups who participate in the ritual. Since, however, any given ritual form was not entirely created by one group of participants at a specific moment in time, one's ritual participation communicates something beyond what is immediately related and applied to the participants themselves (i.e., the canonical order that sustains the self-referential messages is communicated). Again, form and message are interrelated. The canonical messages speak of what is beyond the participants because these "additional messages" are "not encoded by [the participants]," although these additional messages are "transmitted" by them.[130]

The two types of messages are interdependent, and this interrelationship between the self-referential and the canonical can be explained in several ways. The "indexical" nature of the self-referential messages necessitates the canonical messages, which are encoded in invariable aspects of liturgy mostly through "symbols."[131] By the canonical messages, "the indexically transmitted pledge" of the self-referential gains credibility and assurance of fulfillment.[132] On the other hand, without the self-referential messages (one's participation in a ritual or refus-

---

128 Rappaport, *Ritual and Religion*, 46–52.
129 Rappaport, *Ritual and Religion*, 53–54.
130 Rappaport, *Ritual and Religion*, 52. Also, the canonical messages that exceed the self-referential elements of individual ritual participants at a particular moment of space and time give some commonalities and consistency across local and chronological variations of a ritual.
131 Rappaport, *Ritual and Religion*, 58. Rappaport implicitly relies on the well-known Peircean semiotic category, i.e., icons, indices, and symbols.
132 For the use of "index" and "symbol," see Rappaport, *Ritual and Religion*, 54–58.

al to participate constitutes the self-referential messages[133]), the canonical messages are "without force" and "nonsensical."[134] Later, Rappaport expands both their distinctiveness and mutual dependence by Speech Acts theories, or theories of performatives. To guarantee the success of performatives, "[t]here must exist an accepted conventional procedure having a certain conventional effect."[135] Similarly, participating in a liturgy publicly displays the participant's acceptance (which Rappaport emphatically distinguishes from personal belief, "the inward state"[136]) of that conventional order and thereby conforms one to that order. However, the performance of a liturgy does more than merely accept the order: "liturgical performance not only recognizes the authority of the conventions it represents, it gives them their very existence."[137] In other words, "the existence of a conventional order is contingent upon its acceptance."[138] One's ritual participation communicates one's acceptance of the canonical order, but at the same time, this participation actualizes the order. This insight about reciprocity is a major contribution of Rappaport, which moves one beyond the "semiotic/somatic dualism" that some scholars found and criticized in earlier scholarship that focused on the bodily participation in ritual and the inscription of social order upon the body (e.g., Mary Douglas, Jerome Neyrey, etc.).[139]

It should be noted that Rappaport's contrast between the self-referential messages and the canonical order is not the same as a contrast between ritual and myth.[140] One could imagine that myth provides a script that has symbols, and a ritual enacts the meaning of the myth by performing the script; thus, despite the difference of medium, their contents are considered "one and the same" (Edmund Leach's view). Yet, Rappaport's theory differs from this scheme. According to Rappaport, both the self-referential and the canonical are conveyed by performing a ritual/liturgy; in other words, if there is no ritual performance, neither message is possible. Furthermore, Rappaport asserts that myth and ritual are "never one and the same." This is because myth only has "perlocutionary force" and does

---

[133] Rappaport, *Ritual and Religion*, 70.
[134] Rappaport, *Ritual and Religion*, 58.
[135] Rappaport, *Ritual and Religion*, 124. Here, he cites J. L. Austin's words.
[136] Rappaport, *Ritual and Religion*, 121.
[137] Rappaport, *Ritual and Religion*, 125. Thus, he calls the act of acceptance "the first fundamental office of ritual" and the establishment of convention the second fundamental office of ritual." See Rappaport, *Ritual and Religion*, 117–19, 126.
[138] Rappaport, *Ritual and Religion*, 137.
[139] Turley's critiques of these scholars are briefly mentioned in *Ritualized Revelation*, 14–15.
[140] For a brief summary of the history of scholarship regarding the relationship between myth and ritual, see Bell, *Ritual*, 3–22.

not demand the audience's acceptance, while ritual, by its nature, has "illocutionary force" and thus demands the acceptance of the order.[141]

For the present study, Rappaport's ritual theory, especially his theory that ritual communicates two types of messages, has both strengths and weaknesses. I will first present why his theory benefits my project. The theory is beneficial in that the distinction between the self-referential (i.e., what is indicated regarding the status, or the future status, of the current participants of a given ritual) and the canonical (i.e., the symbolic network as the larger convention that simultaneously sustains the fulfillment of the indexically transmitted pledges of the self-referential and is realized and given its existence only by actual participation in the ritual; this decision is part of the self-referential) is useful in parsing the immediate messages and the underlying logic of the initiation rituals. For example, one's participation in an initiation ritual makes the candidate an actual initiate of the mystery cult, as the ritual of dubbing makes a person a knight—the example Rappaport frequently adduces. This change of status is one of the self-referential messages of each ritual, and it also means that the person (an initiate or a knight) should accept the canonical order that sustains the efficacy of the self-referential messages but is not itself part of the self-referential messages. As the dubbing ritual presupposes the authority and legitimacy of the king or queen, or the entire kingdom under their control, the initiation rituals presuppose canonical messages about the power and legitimacy of the mystery deities and the symbolic reality populated and organized by these deities and their devotees. This distinction between the self-referential messages and the canonical messages is also useful for systematically comparing the initiation rituals of different mystery cults (i.e., regarding to what extent they communicate similar or different messages). Thus, by examining the primary sources through Rappaport's lens, one can identify the impacts (or perceived impacts) of initiation, which are "the self-referential messages," and one can also detect underlying structures that guarantee the efficacy of initiation, "the canonical messages."

Rappaport's theory can shed light on Pauline baptism as well. It provides a helpful methodology for understanding what baptism achieved for the baptized, how and why it was considered effective, and what obligations were created by baptism—all in comparison with the initiation rituals of the mysteries. Further-

---

141 Rappaport, *Ritual and Religion*, 134–35. For the meaning of terms, such as perlocutionary and illocutionary force, see Rappaport, *Ritual and Religion*, 479, n. 6: drawing on the Speech Acts theorists, he notes, "An act or utterance is said to have illocutionary force if it achieves its effect in its very utterance or enactment. An effect is intrinsic to an illocutionary act or performance ... In contrast, an act or utterance is said to have perlocutionary force if it achieves its result through its effect upon receivers. Its effect is not intrinsic to the act or utterance itself, but is realized only if the act or utterance persuades, threatens, cajoles (or whatever) some party into taking action."

more, the use of these messages is helpful in resolving some of the persistent exegetical questions in the history of interpretation of the Pauline letters. For example, scholars have often noted that in Rom 6, Paul understands believers' union with Christ (or with Christ's death) through baptism as something *real/actual* rather than *symbolic*—that is, the baptized people have really been united with Christ. Yet, interpreters have also noted that there is the possibility of committing sin and thus the ethical imperatives are repeated in Rom 6. This negative possibility (the ability to sin) exists, even though the believers' baptismal union and their transfer to the realm of Christ are real, not symbolic. These issues are usually addressed by theological explanations (e.g., Paul's eschatological reservation, Paul's indicative-imperative scheme, etc.), but they are unsatisfactory.[142] This is because, first, the context is ritual or at least interpretations of ritual, not merely abstract theological concepts, and second, the logic and premise underlying theological explanations lose much of their explanatory force outside the boundaries of Christian theology. If one Christian scholar insists that baptism in Rom 6 was not merely symbolic, but real, how much more real (and how can we know that?) was the Christian baptism, compared to other rituals conducted by other cultic groups in antiquity? Using Rappaport's theory provides a way to better understand baptism as it appears in the Pauline letters not as *sui generis*, but by fully considering how ritual works—what it can do, and what logic is used to do it—in comparison with other rituals.

One example of this new way of understanding can be described briefly. According to Rappaport, the dancing ritual of Maring people (a tribe in New Guinea) at the *kaiko* festival of another group "does not simply symbolize" their pledge for military support for that group in the future but "indicates it"; in other words, "[T]here is no ambiguity or vagueness. To dance is to pledge and that is that."[143] Yet, the indexical nature of ritual's self-referential message is different from that of general statements. In line with theories of performatives, Rappaport argues, "Statements *report* autonomously existing states of affairs," whereas "performative acts [as in the ritual] *realize* states of affairs."[144] He continues, "The state of affairs [in the case of a general statement] is the criterion by which the truth, accuracy or adequacy of a statement is assessed," but in the case of a performative act, "we judge the statement of affairs by the degree to which it conforms to the stipulations

---

142 For more on this issue, see Chapter 7, especially the discussion of Rom 6.
143 Italics original. Rappaport, *Ritual and Religion*, 57. Rappaport conducted intensive ethnographic research in Papua New Guinea, which resulted in his early major work, *Pigs for Ancestors: Ritual in the Ecology of a New Guinea People* (New Haven: Yale University Press, 1967).
144 Rappaport, *Ritual and Religion*, 132–33.

of the performative act."¹⁴⁵ In short, an inversion occurs in performatives, when compared to how general statements work. This insight illuminates how baptism and mystery initiations—these rituals are performatives—configured reality differently from the ways in which general doctrinal statements functioned. Likewise, Rappaport's discussions about how acceptance (though not precisely "belief"¹⁴⁶) of the canonical order creates obligation, how the breach of obligation is considered immoral, and how canonical order is imposed upon the private self of a performer will be helpful in understanding both Pauline baptism and the initiation rituals of the mysteries.¹⁴⁷

Despite these benefits, using Rappaport's theory for the current project on ancient rituals presents three challenges. First, as an anthropologist, Rappaport works with a theory based on his empirical field study, for example, engaging the Maring people in Papua New Guinea. This ethnographic research allowed him to make direct observations of the ritual performance as well as explore both the self-referential and the canonical messages communicated through the ritual form. In contrast, modern scholars of ancient rituals cannot conduct ethnographic research in the same way that anthropologists do with contemporary groups. Modern scholars cannot make direct observations of ancient ritual performance—including the initiation rituals of the mysteries—but they can only get information through other indirect, often fragmentary media (i.e., some mythic references, inscriptions, artifacts, iconography, etc.).¹⁴⁸ Similar concerns already appeared in Cumont's work more than a century ago. Pointing out that modern scholars do not have any true "liturgic book" of ancient mysteries, he laments: "Shut out from the sanctuary like profane outsiders, we hear only the indistinct echo of the sacred songs and not even in imagination can we attend the celebration of the mysteries."¹⁴⁹ Despite Rappaport's claim that "[m]yth as such carries no self-referential information, nor does its telling either presuppose or establish any

---

145 Rappaport, *Ritual and Religion*, 133.
146 Rappaport, *Ritual and Religion*, 132–34. Yet, Rappaport indeed speaks of "belief." See Robert Levy's observation and comment on Rappaport's use of "shifting terms, 'faith' and 'belief,'" as to what ritual generates. According to Levy, "Rappaport's argument that ritual is of primary importance in the generation of religious belief is perhaps biased or at least weighted by his focal concern with monotheism." Robert I. Levy, "The Life and Death of Ritual: Reflections on Some Ethnographic and Historical Phenomena in the Light of Roy Rappaport's Analysis of Ritual," *Ecology and the Sacred: Engaging the Anthropology of Roy A. Rappaport*, ed. Ellen Messer and Michael Lambek (Ann Arbor: The University of Michigan Press, 2001), 156.
147 For his discussions of the three aspects, see Rappaport, *Ritual and Religion*, 105–106, 132–34.
148 Similar difficulties apply to "historical sociology" (i.e., exploration of ancient societies). See D. Tidball, *An Introduction to the Sociology of the New Testament* (Exeter: Paternoster, 1983), 21.
149 Cumont, *Oriental Religions*, 11 (see 11–19).

particular relationship between the myth and he or she who recounts it,"[150] one cannot make a clear-cut contrast between myth and ritual with regard to the rituals of the ancient cults. In many cases, myth is part of important evidence used to reconstruct ancient rituals and their messages.

Second, Rappaport's definition of the ritual form and the distinction between the two streams of the messages are contingent upon the crucial condition: the ritual in question must have a long history and invariable elements (either in reality or as perceived by them) despite some variables. In short, "transmitters should be distinguished from encoders."[151] To spell this out further, the definition of ritual in Rappaport's theory presupposes two things: (1) it is possible to distinguish between the transmitters (=performers) and the encoders; and (2) the ritual in question has a long history of stable transmission (thus, rather than change and innovation).[152] Both presuppositions cause difficulties for this project. First of all, baptism in the first century was not a time-honored ritual practiced within an isolated society. The Christ-cult communities were nascent groups of people. Ritual *bricolages* were actively being created, when Paul was interacting with his communities and writing his letters. Transmitters and encoders may not be clearly distinguished. Then, a methodological question arises: how can one distinguish between self-referential messages and canonical messages in baptism in the Pauline communities that was a relatively new ritual (compared to other rituals in their society)? This problem may be less acute with initiation rituals of the mystery cults that have a longer history. The difficulty, however, partly remains: the fragmentary nature of ancient sources regarding the mysteries does not easily lend themselves to any confident claim on those invariable, canonical elements of initiation rituals. The modern ethnographic quests, such as the one that Rappaport conducted, were often carried out over a lengthy period of time within a relatively isolated group of contemporary people (often, not large in number). In contrast, the ancient sources to be explored with regard to the mysteries in the Greek and Roman world are enormously diverse geographically, temporally, and in range of ritual partici-

---

150 Rappaport, *Ritual and Religion*, 134.
151 Rappaport, *Ritual and Religion*, 118.
152 Grimes points out that Rappaport's definition of ritual cannot capture "ritual change, creativity, and innovation" well. Grimes, *The Craft of Ritual Studies*, 189. In fact, modern anthropological studies show "subtraditional variability in performance and discourse." See Eric Wolf, "Cognizing 'Cognized Models,'" *AA* 101 (1999): 22. Wolf also mentions that Rappaport's "formal-causal" model, though it is advantageous in many ways, overlooks the power dynamics among people, i.e., the political dimension interweaved with the sacred propositions of ritual (Wolf, "Cognizing 'Cognized Models,'" 21–22).

pants and groups. To articulate a single, well-shaped, long-lasting canonical order out of such vast sources runs the risk of distorting the historical reality.

These two difficulties, however, can be overcome. First, regarding the messages of mystery initiations, my goal is to construct and present potential ranges of messages, rather than arguing that each occurrence of initiation should convey all of those messages. Although I cannot observe the actual performance of ancient ritual, the ancient people often left remarks about what they expected from initiation or how they perceived their change through initiation. Also, material culture reveals what people believed about the benefits or changes involved in initiation. These are all valuable sources for reconstructing the self-referential messages. The canonical messages can be inferred by the method of elimination (i.e., by paying attention to elements other than self-referential information in the various sources regarding the mysteries). Similar approaches will also be applied to baptism in the Pauline letters. Yet, in this case, the only direct source to reconstruct how the Pauline communities in the mid-first century practiced baptism are the Pauline letters (Acts could be used indirectly). Thus, in order to discern what Christ-believers in Paul's communities did and believed and what Paul himself did and believed, traditional historical-critical tools and procedures need to be employed. This allows one to present a somewhat complicated, but dynamic, picture of what self-referential and canonical messages the Christ-believers in the Pauline communities communicated through baptism, and what self-referential and canonical messages Paul would want to communicate through his (re)presentation of baptism in the letters.

Nevertheless, there is a third drawback to using Rappaport's theory for this project, and it is the reason that the work of Martin Riesebrodt is relevant (see the following section). Many examples Rappaport presents in his discussion are rituals that emphasize a certain set of obligations or pledges on the part of the participants. The dancing of the Maring people at the festival of their neighboring group indicates their pledge to fight for that group in the future; the Tahitian youths' supercision indicates their new obligations as adult members of society; the dubbing ritual indicates the newly dubbed knight's status and knightly duty; and all of those self-referential messages are dependent on the canonical order in each case. These rituals are concerned with the pledges that the human participants make, substantially more than divine pledges the participants receive. In short, divine obligations are less emphasized in Rappaport's writing, and this creates a problem when specifically religious rituals are in view.[153]

---

[153] Note that Rappaport's approach to and definition of ritual are not limited to religious rituals—for him, ritual is a fundamental layer of human evolution and communication. Levy, "The Life and Death of Ritual," 146.

Surely, initiation rituals of the mysteries can be fruitfully explored in this way (i.e., focusing on human pledges), but there is more involved—that is, initiation into the mysteries communicates divine pledges from the deities, as well as human pledges toward the deities or other members of the community. Through the mystery initiations, the initiates not only make their vows to the deities (and the community of initiates) but also receive (or believe to receive) certain promises from their deities for various benefits in life, here and hereafter. Thus, one's participation in initiation (it is one of the self-referential messages) indicates the acceptance of the underlying structure, or the canonical order, that guarantees not only the fulfillment of the devotees' pledges but also the ratification of the deities' promise(s) toward the devotees. It is true that Rappaport's theories made a "lasting contribution to the anthropology of religion" by paying attention to the formal intersection between ritual acts and sacred meanings,[154] and that his "cognized models" of ritual (which itself focuses on the perspective of actors, not that of anthropologists) envision the hierarchy of cognition that has "ultimate sacred propositions" at its highest level.[155] Yet, what the deities are believed to promise through ritual (from the perspective of religious participants) is not fully explored by his theory.

To some extent, in Rappaport's anthropological theory of ritual, the distinction between religious ritual and other performative activities is blurred. This blurring is not surprising because his project aims to place ritual (and by extension, religion) at the beginning of human evolution, i.e., "the making of humanity." From the perspective of those who study Greco-Roman antiquity, Rappaport's position makes a lot of sense; the attempt to distinguish between religious ritual and other rituals would be arbitrary and anachronistic, influenced by the modern Western notion of religion. In the Roman world, for example, religion was first and foremost a public, civic activity—it was a "social religion."[156] The inseparable relationship between society and religion is what underlies Rappaport's theory, which resonates with Durkheim's theory of religion and society.[157] However, this

---

154 John M. Watanabe and Barbara B. Smuts, "Explaining Religion without Explaining It Away: Trust, Truth, and the Evolution of Cooperation in Roy A. Rappaport's 'The Obvious Aspects of Ritual,'" *AA* 101 (1999): 108.
155 Wolf, "Cognizing 'Cognized Models,'" 20.
156 John Scheid, *An Introduction to Roman Religion* (Bloomington: Indiana University Press, 2003), 19.
157 According to Durkheim, religion and society, or the religious order and the socio-political order, have an inseparable relationship from the beginning. Rappaport's theory is also influenced by his predecessors. See, for example, Peacock's comment, "[Rappaport's] perspective is Durkheim infused with Weber and Tillich," because "Rappaport's anthropology of religion is always stretching toward the ineffable, ultimate, and transcendent." James Peacock, "Belief Beheld—Inside and

is not the only way to conceptualize religion in antiquity, and even religion in general. In the following section, I will turn to Martin Riesebrodt's sociological theory of religion. Based on the Weberian perspective rather than the Durkheimian, Riesebrodt provides a very different approach to religion: that is, religion's interest in salvation. Yet, there is a commonality between Riesebrodt and Rappaport: ritual/liturgy (other names for concrete religious practice as opposed to sheer intellectual discourse) are central to the theoretical works of both scholars. The theoretical framework of these scholars is not contradictory or combative; therefore, I will draw on both to construct my integrated analytical framework.

2.2.2 Martin Riesebrodt

In his *The Promise of Salvation: A Theory of Religion*, the Chicago sociologist Martin Riesebrodt sets forth a theory of religion based on what religion promises. He begins his book by expressing his dissatisfaction with two contemporary phenomena. One is that "[t]he concept of religion is in crisis," because many human activities other than what is traditionally considered religious are now regarded as religious phenomena by scholars. The second point of dissatisfaction is that many scholars view religion as a legacy of colonialism (i.e., "an invention of Western modernity" that is artificially imposed upon non-Western, premodern people).[158] Thus, he sarcastically notes, "When soccer games are seen as religious phenomena and the recitation of Buddhist sutras is not, something has obviously gone wrong."[159] The first two chapters of the book are devoted to (1) refuting modern scholars' critique of religion as (Western) discourse[160] and (2) making his case for religion as a (universal) social referent.[161] He asserts, "The distinction between religious and nonreligious is lacking neither in the premodern West nor in non-Western cultures, and the religious in the sense of institutions that are associated with superhuman powers has existed in all ages and cultures."[162] Agreeing with neither formalist nor

---

Outside, Insider and Outsider in the Anthropology of Religion," in *Ecology and the Sacred: Engaging the Anthropology of Roy A. Rappaport*, ed. Ellen Messer and Michael Lambek (Ann Arbor: The University of Michigan Press, 2001), 207. Nevertheless, it is clear that the Durkheimian aspect is more obvious in Rappaport's theory.
158 Martin Riesebrodt, *The Promise of Salvation: A Theory of Religion*, trans. Steven Rendall (Chicago: University of Chicago Press, 2010), xi.
159 Riesebrodt, *The Promise of Salvation*, xi.
160 Riesebrodt, *The Promise of Salvation*, 1–20.
161 Riesebrodt, *The Promise of Salvation*, 21–45.
162 Riesebrodt, *The Promise of Salvation*, 1.

functionalist approaches, Riesebrodt rather focuses on the question of what religious practices mean for the participants, or what religious practices promise to them.[163] Whereas religious functions vary according to different social, political conditions, Riesebrodt says, "Religion's promise ... remains astonishingly constant in different historical periods and cultures. Religions promise *to ward off misfortune, to help cope with crises, and to provide salvation.*"[164] These three aspects of religion's promise appear throughout his book.

In arguing for the threefold promise of religion that consistently exists across various periods and cultures, Riesebrodt emphasizes the need to examine religious practices and their inherent meaning for the participants. Riesebrodt first differentiates between "religion" and "religious traditions." Christianity, Hinduism, Buddhism, etc. are religious traditions, whereas religion is defined as "an empirically given system of practices related to superhuman powers."[165] In this definition of religion, the word "practice" receives prominence. Riesebrodt focuses on the concrete actions of religious participants, rather than ethical/theological teachings. In short, it is in liturgies (he also uses the term "worship") that "the meaning of religions is developed" the most.[166] Thus, the promise of religion is actually *the promise of liturgies* for the participants.[167]

It should be noted that Riesebrodt emphasizes that the threefold promise of religion is not the same as the (latent) function of religion.[168] Religious functions —for example, social integration or the creation of identity predominantly—remain unconscious to the religious practitioners, and according to Riesebrodt, those functions cannot adequately differentiate religious activities from others: "All kinds of activities can be interpreted as socially integrative or identity creating—for instance, forming associations or temporary relationships, or devotion to a hobby."[169] Thus, he argues, "The promise of salvation is not a latent function of religious practices; it is the meaning inscribed within those practices."[170] In

---

163 Riesebrodt, *The Promise of Salvation*, xiii, 72.
164 Italics mine. Riesebrodt, *The Promise of Salvation*, xiii. This statement appears throughout his book.
165 Riesebrodt, *The Promise of Salvation*, 14.
166 Riesebrodt, *The Promise of Salvation*, xiii.
167 "All religious liturgies contain promises regarding what religions are capable of doing. In their liturgies, religions usually claim the ability to ward off misfortune, surmount crises, and provide blessings and salvation by communicating with superhuman powers." Riesebrodt, *The Promise of Salvation*, 72.
168 For his content-based definition of religion (*contra* a functional definition of religion), see Riesebrodt, *The Promise of Salvation*, 72–79.
169 Riesebrodt, *The Promise of Salvation*, 73.
170 Riesebrodt, *The Promise of Salvation*, 89.

other words, Riesebrodt seeks to address what's really distinctive in religion (or religion that is expressed through liturgical activities), when compared to other activities in society.

A few remarks are needed concerning Riesebrodt's use of the term "liturgies." First, he uses the term broadly; its use is not restricted to the Christian liturgy. What he means by liturgies is the "institutionalized rules and guidelines for humans' interactions with superhuman powers" or "institutionalized practices."[171] He further comments, "By 'liturgies,' I refer to any kind of institutionalized rules and scripts that guide humans' intercourse with superhuman powers, express its meanings, and are enacted in interventionist practices or in worship."[172] Thus, the word liturgy seems to be interchangeable with other related terms such as worship, cult, ritual, or any other terms for religious practices from any religious traditions, as long as they are somehow institutionalized and connected to superhuman powers.

Riesebrodt's view of religious practices is based on the sociology of religion, especially interpretative sociology that pays attention to the meanings given by the participants to their behavior.[173] Because of this perspective, Riesebrodt can place "interventionist practices" that ritual participants find meaningful at the center of his inquiry, whereas "the sociology of religion has been chiefly interested in behavior-regulating and discursive practices or, at best, in the effects of interventionist practices on everyday action, power relationships, or the social order."[174] Here, one would naturally raise questions—*What about other religious practices, or liturgies, that are not interventionist?* Is his view of religion restricted to practices that are interventionist? What meaning would participants of non-interventionist religious rituals attribute to their practices?[175] These questions will

---

171 Riesebrodt, *The Promise of Salvation*, xiii, 72.
172 Riesebrodt, *The Promise of Salvation*, 84.
173 This is reflective of Max Weber (who is well known for interpretative sociology), whose influence can be seen throughout Riesebrodt's book. Also, Riesebrodt claims that Clifford Geertz's notion of religion (especially, the "aura of factuality") is partly defined through the interventionist perspective. Riesebrodt, *The Promise of Salvation*, 86. Note that Geertz is one of the most influential figures in interpretative anthropology.
174 Riesebrodt, *The Promise of Salvation*, 86. By interventionist practices, Riesebrodt means all practices that "aim at establishing contact with superhuman powers" (Riesebrodt, *The Promise of Salvation*, 75). Within this category, he identifies four types.
175 Similar questions have also been asked of the ritual theories that put emphasis on the superhuman, interventionist aspects of rituals. For example, Grimes's criticism of Lawson and McCauley's definition of religious ritual—according to them, "Religious rituals ... are those religious actions whose structural descriptions include a logical object and appeal to a culturally postulated superhuman agent's action somewhere within their overall structural description." E. Thomas

be addressed later. For the moment, I think his framework works favorably for some religious traditions and their liturgies whose participants operate with an interventionist premise—thus, it works for both the mystery cults and the early Christ cult.

Following Martin Riesebrodt, I find it helpful to examine the "promise" of religion, as opposed to its function, for the purpose of comparing the structural meaning of different religions or religious practices. I also agree with him that the concrete communal practice of religion (for him, it is "worship" or "liturgies"), rather than theological discourses or individuals' subjective experiences, provides a better comparison for the promises of different religions. For the present study, the term "ritual" is preferred to "liturgies," because the latter sounds highly institutionalized (at least, by its popular usage), while some of ritual activities to be examined, both from the New Testament and from other ancient sources, do not necessarily include this kind of institutionalization. Yet, his focus on action or practices, rather than discourses, makes it clear that the "distinction between religious and nonreligious phenomena [is] universal,"[176] in contrast to the recent critique of the concept of religion itself.[177] The threefold promise of religious practices (or ritual, liturgies) develops helpful analytical categories through which one can sort out primary data.

Yet, Riesebrodt's theory can be challenged in several ways, so I want to clarify how I would address those issues in order to appropriate his theory for my work. First of all, as mentioned at the end of the preceding paragraph, Riesebrodt's project goes against the critics who take issue with the concept of religion itself, and his refutation surely provides incisive points. The problem is that Riesebrodt's counterargument against postcolonial and discourse criticism sometimes caricatures their positions, not doing justice to their nuanced arguments and contributions. For example, he points out that Talal Asad's critique of religion "reduces interpretations of religion to discourses and pays no attention to religious practices," and he further criticizes discourse analyses (including Asad's) as often presupposing the monolithic nature of Western modernity, while in reality there is much diversity within Western modernity, depending on which countries are considered or the particular context.[178] Yet, as Ivan Strenski notes, Riesebrodt's critique of dis-

---

Lawson and Robert N. McCauley, *Rethinking Religion: Connecting Cognition and Culture* (Cambridge: Cambridge University Press, 1990), 176; cited in Grimes, *The Craft of Ritual Studies*, 189.
176 Riesebrodt, *The Promise of Salvation*, 20.
177 Riesebrodt, *The Promise of Salvation*, 7–19.
178 Riesebrodt, *The Promise of Salvation*, 9. Casadio's paper (which criticizes scholarly views of religion as a modern, Western, Christian concept) also points out similar problems. That is, when people argue that there was no notion of religion before Western modernity, then they tend to assume

course-theory criticism and postcolonial criticism only relies on older materials and does not fully reflect recent theoretical developments in those fields.[179] Also, I find Riesebrodt's criticism of postcolonialism simply superficial. Riesebrodt chastises postcolonial critics as "[ascribing] to the cultures of colonized peoples a role that is ultimately passive" and goes on to argue that "what are involved are interactions in which both sides, both the colonizers and the colonized, took part."[180] Yet in fact, exploring the complicated interactions between the colonizers and the colonized, which cannot be dichotomized in a clear-cut way, is what postcolonial studies are about. Similarly, his description of deconstructionism is also biased and does not capture the actual significance of deconstructionism: "I oppose my theory of religion to deconstructionism, which, fashionable as it is, hinders serious research and has confused a whole generation of students. I consider the constant repetition of these debates quite banal, once one has understood what is at issue."[181] Simply "understanding what is at issue" is not what deconstructionists and other de-centering intellectual movements aim at—their emphasis is on praxis (i.e., how to embody a new mode of knowing and living).

Nevertheless, Riesebrodt is correct in arguing that some modern discourse of religion being associated with colonial history does not have to mean that one must jettison the category of religion completely. Religion is needed for "analytical concepts" for the purpose of intellectual as well as practical quests.[182] In this regard, Riesebrodt's use of the concept religion might not be *practically* far from J. Z. Smith's view (religion as a second-order, scholarly tool),[183] despite some obvious

---

the meaning of religion in the modern Western world is fixed and monolithic, which is, according to Casadio, not true. Giovanni Casadio, "*Religio* versus Religion," *Myths, Martyrs, and Modernity: Studies in the History of Religions in Honour of Jan N. Bremmer*, ed. Jitse Dijkstra et al. (Leiden: Brill, 2010), 304, n. 11.

179 Ivan Strenski, "Martin Riesebrodt, The Promise of Salvation: A Theory of Religion," *HR* 53 (2014): 315–16. See also Strenski's (politely) sarcastic remarks at the end of his review (p. 316): "The loss is especially evident in Riesebrodt's critiques of postmodern thinkers, where typically charges are made but no names named [sic]. Skimpy, imprecise, or outdated citations but, for the greater part, none at all to the work of the past decade's leading theorists or critical historians of theory of religion. Amazingly, this book is written as if Talal Asad, Michel Despland, Tim Fitzgerald, Tom Lawson, Mark Lilla, Russell McCutcheon, Tomoko Masuzawa, Robert Segal, Jonathan Z. Smith, Mark Taylor, Donald Wiebe, and I had nothing to say about theory of religion."
180 Riesebrodt, *The Promise of Salvation*, 15.
181 Riesebrodt, *The Promise of Salvation*, 6.
182 Riesebrodt, *The Promise of Salvation*, 15–19.
183 Jonathan Z. Smith, *Imagining Religion: From Babylon to Jonestown* (Chicago: The University of Chicago Press, 1982), xi.

differences.[184] It is better to ask how to reconfigure the category, rather than abandoning it.

In connection with the task (to reconfigure the category of religion), a second set of challenges emerges. Riesebrodt's theory argues that the threefold promise of religion/liturgies—namely, warding off misfortune, helping cope with crises, and providing salvation—is found in any religion of any period/culture. Here, one can ask: Did Riesebrodt actually succeed in proving "the universal *use* of a concept of religion,"[185] while avoiding presenting "a universal *concept* of religion"?[186] Does he not virtually present a universal concept of religion? Furthermore, his approach actually gets closer to presenting an *essential* definition of religion.[187] It is certain that his intention is to emphasize that a concept of religion is not universally given, but it is part of intellectual inquiry. At the end of his second chapter, Riesebrodt notes, "no unified concept of religion emerges from the examples given above. That is not to be expected, since such conceptual unification is a result of intellectual systematization."[188] This claim, which interestingly resonates with Jonathan Smith's critique of comparative religion, is fair enough. Yet, by naming three primary contents of promise and making it almost universal—"I argue that the threefold theme of averting misfortune, overcoming crises, and providing salvation appears in all types of religious practices in the most diverse religions, regardless of time, place, or specific cultural form"[189]—Riesebrodt does actually essentialize the universal concept of religion. In short, he is not free from the scholarly practice he himself criticizes.

Perhaps the biggest problem is that this universalization and essentialization, which he denies, but actually comes close to, presupposes a particular type of religious tradition, namely, "interventionistic" or "theistic" tradition.[190] As Riese-

---

184 Riesebrodt maintains that religion exists as a social referent, whereas Smith regards religion completely as part of the scholarly imagination in modern Western society.
185 Italics mine. Riesebrodt, *The Promise of Salvation*, 44.
186 Riesebrodt claims, "The goal of my discussion is not to find a universal concept of religion. There can be no such concept." Riesebrodt, *The Promise of Salvation*, 22.
187 Again, Riesebrodt asserts, "my theory does not represent an 'essential definition' of religion." Riesebrodt, *The Promise of Salvation*, xiii.
188 Riesebrodt, *The Promise of Salvation*, 44.
189 Riesebrodt, *The Promise of Salvation*, 91.
190 Ivan Strenski, "Martin Riesebrodt," 314. Note that the interventionistic and theistic are not always the same. For example, see Peacock's comparative ethnographic investigation of the narratives between fundamentalist American Christians and fundamentalist Southeast Asian Muslims. Both can be considered "theistic," yet Peacock's research reveals that there is no emotionally-filled conversion experience (e.g., inner struggle due to one's sin and strong experience of God's forgiveness) in the narratives of the Southeast Asian Muslims. Peacock, "Belief Beheld," 207–26.

brodt himself notes, "The promise to avert misfortune, to overcome crises, and to provide salvation presupposes *powers that can keep this promise*,"[191] and the "theistic" presupposition matters considerably in his overall theoretical construction, with which a Durkheimian takes issue.[192] Nevertheless, his interventionistically and theistically-constructed framework can work well as a heuristic tool for the current task of this monograph. Of course, Strenski's criticism is valid, and if one examines other "noninterventionistic" traditions, for example, Buddhist Nirvana, Riesebrodt's theistic and interventionistic approach does not work well.[193] Considerable portions of Greek and Roman religion align with noninterventionistic traditions, which would mean that using Riesebrodt's lens to examine them would be inappropriate. Yet, that might not always be the case. As Thomas Harrison aptly summarizes, one trend in recent scholarship of Greek religion brings the "gods" back to the forefront (Jim, Naiden, Versnel, etc.).[194] This is particularly true with the mysteries and the early Christ cult at the time of Paul. The theistic and interventionistic framework holds true for the primary objective of this particular study.

In short, I will use Riesebrodt's theory, "the promise of religion (of religious ritual/liturgies)," as I examine primary sources for each mystery cult and Paul, as well as when I compare them. This perspective will allow me to overcome the remaining drawback of using Rappaport's theory—i.e., Rappaport's discussions of ritual do not include the benefits the deities promise. The self-referential messages and the canonical messages in Rappaport's examples often have to do with the social, public change of ritual participants (self-referential), social conventions that guarantee the change (canonical), and the human pledges that are created by ritual participation and at the same time obligate the participants. The inclusion of Riesebrodt allows me to expand (or in some sense, narrow down) Rappaport's framework to consider how theistic/interventionistic rituals would

---

191 Italics mine. Riesebrodt, *The Promise of Salvation*, 148.
192 Strenski, "Martin Riesebrodt," 314: "[F]or him [=Riesebrodt], the 'specific meaning' of the 'social action' that is religion 'lies in its relation to personal or impersonal superhuman powers' (71). The problem is why Riesebrodt has taken the theistic route, when others, as I shall show, are also available. In a way, of course, the entire book speaks to this question."
193 Yet, using Riesebrodt's theory to explore noninterventionistic traditions is not entirely impossible. Especially, his concept of religious virtuosity (which will be discussed soon) provides a bridge. See, for example, Mihwa Choi, "Extreme Asceticism: Confucian Practice and Riesebrodt's Religious Virtuoso," *JSSR* 51 (2012): 467.
194 Thomas Harrison, "Review Article: Beyond the *Polis?* New Approaches to Greek Religion," *JHS* 135 (2015): 165–80, especially on 170: "The gods are not just ciphers or blank screens, moreover, but personalities, a 'real and potent presence.'" For Roman religion (from a theoretical perspective), see Michael Lipka's *Romans Gods: A Conceptual Approach* (Leiden; Boston: Brill, 2009).

communicate the self-referential and canonical messages. Therefore, the self-referential messages and the canonical messages can be rephrased: benefits that ritual promises the participant and the divine assurances of the promised benefits.

Finally, one more aspect of Riesebrodt's framework will benefit my investigation of the mysteries and Pauline baptism: religious virtuosity. By describing the practices of religious virtuosos, Riesebrodt explains how his theory of religion can also address a "higher level" of religious quest that voluntarily accepts adversarial conditions, which seems to contradict his theory (i.e., religion is about averting misfortune, overcoming crises, and proving salvation):

> [Virtuosos] intentionally and systematically set conditions for themselves that most mortals try to avoid by religious means. What average laypersons consider a horror, virtuosos voluntarily accept and make the basis of their way of life ... Whereas most laypersons are content to be protected from misfortune, virtuosos seek salvation, whatever the cost ... Salvation and misfortune are reinterpreted and revaluated.[195]

This concept enables Riesebrodt to explain individual anomalies and practices found in all religious traditions.[196] Drawing on Weber's concept of virtuosos, Riesebrodt clarifies who these virtuosos are: "[V]irtuosos are neither normal laypersons nor priests attached to hierocratic organizations; rather, they are bearers of personal charisma, such as shamans, hermits, monks, ecstatics, visionaries, mystics, and prophets."[197] By exploring virtuosity, Riesebrodt primarily asks three questions: "what religious practices make them virtuosos, how their religious action and its meaning differs from that of the laity, and what effects it has on their religious status and their relation to the laity."[198] This perspective concerns the question of power: how radical religious practices (e.g., voluntary suffering) and the unique authority of that practitioner intersect and reinforce each other.[199] In my investigation of primary sources regarding initiation rituals and baptism, I will examine how religious virtuosity is expressed and actualized through ritual. Put in Rappaportian terms: religious virtuosity will be considered both a type of benefit promised by ritual (because virtuosity itself is an index of

---

195 Riesebrodt, *The Promise of Salvation*, 122.
196 Furthermore, Riesebrodt mentions three ideal types of religious virtuosity: "ascetic, contemplative, and ethical disciplines." His focus is on ascetic practices. Riesebrodt, *The Promise of Salvation*, 126.
197 Riesebrodt, *The Promise of Salvation*, 125.
198 Riesebrodt, *The Promise of Salvation*, 125.
199 Riesebrodt, *The Promise of Salvation*, 127. I think a similar concern is also found in Theissen's scheme of the relationship between "Stigma" and "Charisma." Gerd Theissen, *Die Religion der ersten Christen: eine Theorie des Urchristentums* (Gütersloh: Kaiser, 2000), 27–28.

a particular connection to the supernatural power) as well as the grounds for other benefits (since virtuosity enables one to achieve power, authority, and salvation in the radical sense). A discussion of religious virtuosity broadens the ritual comparison to areas that are often regarded as less relevant to rituals—e.g., ethical dimensions, cognitive developments, or even faith/belief. The category of virtuosity will assist with comparing the initiation rituals of the mysteries and baptism in the Pauline communities.

2.2.3 My Integrated Framework

In summary, I present here my integrated framework for my comparative investigation. The heuristic framework I will employ is threefold: (1) What benefits for the participants were promised by each ritual (self-referential messages)? (2) Why and how were the benefits believed to be effective (canonical messages)? (3) How was each ritual closely related to personal and social dimensions that might extend beyond the ritual itself—including the question of how religious virtuosity is conceived and expressed (both the self-referential and the canonical). These three questions will appear in turn in each chapter of this monograph. Detailed explanations and justifications follow:

(1) In the first section of each chapter, I will investigate what benefits each initiation ritual promises their adherents.[200] The question is simple: What was the promise of initiation? What benefits attracted people to choose initiation into a particular mystery cult, over other cultic options?[201] Of course, the model of "religious choice," which sounds more like modern individualism and consumer reli-

---

200 Birgitte Bøgh's article discusses what benefits the initiation into the Dionysiac mysteries would bring to the initiates and how (differently) ancient reports from insiders and outsiders describe those benefits. Yet, her focus is more on how the benefits could illuminate the following question—to what extent and in what ways could one speak of Dionysiac "conversion"? And she does not discuss what underlying logics guarantee the efficacy of initiation, which is the second part of the analytical framework of the present study. Birgitte Bøgh, "In Life and Death: Choice and Conversion in the Cult of Dionysos," *Conversion and Initiation in Antiquity: Shifting Identities – Creating Change*, ed. Birgitte Bøgh (Frankfurt am Main: Peter Lang, 2014), 25–46.

201 In Terri Moore's recent work on the mysteries and 1 Corinthians, she also compares "benefits" given to the mystery initiates and those given to Christ-believers. Yet, her categorization of benefits needs reconsideration, and my work is to some extent seeking to demonstrate how the benefits can be better conceived and compared. For a review of her work, see Donghyun Jeong, "Review of Terri Moore, *The Mysteries, Resurrection, and 1 Corinthians 15*," *RBL* (2020): 1–4.

gion, could be problematic.²⁰² To avoid possible confusion and anachronism, I will refrain from using the term "conversion" when it comes to the mysteries, but it does not mean that I strictly follow the Nockian distinction between Christian "conversion" and pagan "adhesion."²⁰³ It might be true that prior to the end of late antiquity (600 CE), religion or one's religious identity was not yet a separate entity from other elements within the "undifferentiated matrix."²⁰⁴ Rives raises a rhetorical question: "Plutarch was a follower of Plato, a lover of Homer, a priest of Apollo at Delphi, possibly an initiate in the mysteries of Isis, undoubtedly a participant in imperial cult, and much more. Which of these determined his 'religious identity'?"²⁰⁵ Yet, as Rives also admits, the fact that Plutarch, at some point in his life, made a decision to become an initiate of the Isis mysteries may suggest that there are some reasons, or benefits, for choosing to become an Isis initiate, while this does not exclude her or his other multiple identities.²⁰⁶ Indeed, one's de-

---

202 For example, regarding Isis devotees in the Eastern Mediterranean world, Alvar argues, "[M]ost of the followers of Isis did not arise from a process of conversion, nor even from the conscious adoption of a religious position, but they assumed the cult within their families." Jaime Alvar, "Social Agentivity in the Eastern Mediterranean Cult of Isis," in *Individuals and Materials*, 1:242. Yet, the model of Lucius in Apuleius's *Metamorphoses* would be a counter example, though Lucius is basically part of Apuleius's narrative world.
203 Birgitte Bøgh, "Beyond Nock: From Adhesion to Conversion in the Mystery Cults," *HR* 54 (2015): 261. According to Bøgh, to claim that there was never such thing as conversion in paganism is unhelpful in understanding the complicated reality of the ancient world. She comments, "Often, 'conversion' is not used in a neutral sense (e.g., as 'becoming monotheistic') but as a term with a wealth of different positive connotations, such as joy, truth, spiritual growth, strong commitment, devotion, belonging, existential meaning, and a superior morality. Hence, to claim that conversion was a phenomenon invented with or limited to Christianity and to object to the possibility of conversion in the mysteries is sometimes analogous to bereaving them of the possibility of providing their participants with such valued emotions and experiences."
204 James Rives, "Religious Choice and Religious Change in Classical and Late Antiquity: Models and Questions," *ARS* 9 (2011): 268.
205 Rives, "Religious Choice and Religious Change," 269.
206 Rives notes, "It is not that the possibility of religious choice came to exist where it had not existed before; on the contrary, religious choice of a certain sort is an inherent feature of Graeco-Roman culture more or less as far back as our evidence goes." Rives, "Religious Choice and Religious Change," 270. What Rives emphasizes is that the kind of choice in the mysteries and that of early Christianity were different: "The choice to be initiated into a mystery cult or to devote oneself to philosophy thus did not necessarily involve a person in a distinct community, and even when it did those communities were not always organized in such a way as to promote a strong sense of communal identity. Early Christian communities, by contrast, generally promoted a very powerful and sharply distinct communal identity." I largely agree with this point; it is true that initiation into mysteries did not "always" bring the initiates into an organized community. Yet, there are indeed some communal aspects of initiation, which I will examine further in subsequent chapters.

cision to become an initiate, its seriousness and complexity should receive due attention, regardless of whether or not one sticks to the controversial term "conversion."[207]

Therefore, I think it is still possible and valuable to demonstrate the range of benefits that an individual may expect from that ritual—regardless of whether those benefits will be fulfilled by humans who are obliged (Rappaport) or whether such indicated benefits remain in the form of divine promise that could be fulfilled by the deity or some supernatural power (Riesebrodt). These two may look somewhat different from one another but can be discussed within the same category because both are indexically presented by ritual form and ritual participation. So, I will refer to both as "self-referential messages" in that these messages inform some changes that occur immediately or in the future within the participants. To clarify what self-referential messages are given in each ritual, I will look primarily at what each source explicitly declares regarding the benefits of that ritual and move to excavate some implicit benefits.[208]

I will not restrict the kinds of benefits to the three universally-found promises Riesebrodt asserts (i.e., "to ward off misfortune, to help cope with crises, and to provide salvation").[209] Ritual benefits cannot be reduced to those three; there are other, more "sociological" benefits that one may expect from participating in the initiation—e.g., gaining higher social status among the cultic group, or building a strong network of trust that would be beneficial to their occupational activities, etc. These cannot be excluded from one's understanding of religion. Furthermore, the distinction of the three items in Riesebrodt's theory is not entirely satisfactory. On the one hand, all three (to ward off misfortune, to help cope with crises, and to provide salvation) can be subsumed under the overall concept of "salvation," something already suggested by the title of his book. On the other hand, the term salvation is one of the three contents of promise, and it is also used to differentiate the quest of "religious virtuosos" from that of ordinary people: "Whereas most laypersons are content to be protected from misfortune, virtuosos seek salvation, whatever the cost."[210] Given the vacillating meaning of "salvation" within Riesebrodt's book, I do not think it is helpful to merely retaining the threefold "universal" promises he proposes. Keeping the three in mind but not restricting myself

---

207 See also Bøgh, "Beyond Nock," 263.
208 These sections of each chapter can be viewed as addressing the soteriological aspects of each ritual's messages. According to Riesebrodt, the word "salvation" is among the universal promises of religion beyond the Abrahamic religions. Yet I usually avoid using the term (soteriology/soteriological) frequently, for its loaded nuance specific to Christianity.
209 Riesebrodt, *The Promise of Salvation*, xiii. See also 72.
210 Riesebrodt, *The Promise of Salvation*, 122.

to them, I will try to clarify what kind of promise each initiation or baptism in Paul's communities makes. Only through this inductive process can I articulate some common messages or common patterns of messages throughout the various traditions I examine.

(2) In the second section of each chapter, I will investigate the basis for the ritual's promise, or the canonical order of rituals—the system that legitimizes the ritual and guarantees the efficacy of the ritual, and at the same time, is only actualized by one's ritual participation. According to Rappaport's conceptualization, all participants of a certain ritual are required to accept the invariable canonical messages or the canonical order by their act of ritual participation. The questions about the basis for the efficacy are not crucial for Riesebrodt, not least because he focuses on the liturgical action itself rather than the subjective understanding of the participants.[211] The question of why one was convinced of the efficacy could be hardly answered by observing the liturgical (in my case, ritual) action itself. Yet, Riesebrodt too recognizes the importance of the presupposition that supports the fulfillment of the promise: "The promise to avert misfortune, to overcome crises, and to provide salvation *presupposes powers that can keep this promise.*"[212] Actually this "theistic" presupposition matters significantly for his overall theoretical construction.[213] In the case of my project that explores mystery initiations and early Christ-baptism, the theistic and interventionistic framework holds true. I think it is necessary to explicitly state the nature of the presupposition(s) that buttresses the promise found in the initiation rituals and baptism in the Pauline letters. Relating this aspect to the present study, the main questions are: Why did those who underwent an initiation ritual of a certain mystery cult think that it was efficacious? How were they convinced that they would really receive what was promised by the initiation? Beyond what's immediately relevant to the change of their status or benefits for them, what additional messages should the participants of the mystery initiations accept? How did these canonical messages create certain obligations with divine mandate?

The canonical messages of the mystery initiations are often not explicitly stated in the fragmentary sources, so it requires an exegetical excavation of the theological, epistemological, and sociological grammar underlying the extant sources

---

[211] As Michal Pagis notes, "practice-oriented scholars might have difficulties to accept Riesebrodt's claim that the meaning of an interventionist practice is not grounded in the subjective meaning given by the practitioners ... [but in] 'ideal type' meanings given to these practices [which are] not found in practitioners' heads, but instead ... in liturgy." Michal Pagis, "Review: *The Promise of Salvation: A Theory of Religion*, by Martin Riesebrodt," *SoR* 72 (2011): 376.
[212] Italics mine. Riesebrodt, *The Promise of Salvation*, 148.
[213] Strenski, "Martin Riesebrodt," 314.

about initiation. To be specific, I will mainly eliminate the self-referential information from the primary sources and then attempt to infer what canonical messages are embedded there. Thus, while carefully examining each source, I will ask what powers are in each mystery initiation and in Pauline baptism and how divine reality is constructed through the language of each ritual and its performance, all while keeping in mind the insights from the sociology of knowledge.[214]

(3) In the third section of each chapter, I will explore the dimensions that extend beyond the initiation ritual itself. One particular question is about how religious virtuosity is envisioned vis-à-vis initiation. In addition, I will ask other questions, such as whether ancient people thought that participating in the initiation ritual was sufficient for obtaining the desired effect, or whether there were other aspects not immediately related to the ritual itself, but still important to the initiates. To put it simply, was some kind of "faith" required for the initiates? Did they also have to "repent" and look for divine forgiveness? Did initiation lead them to greater knowledge of the divine? Did initiation shape the rest of their life? These questions might seem overly Christian. Yet, my aim is rather to do justice to the mysteries. For too often and too long, the mysteries have been regarded as "magical" procedures whose external performance can deliver the desired effect. For example, in the context of discussing religious virtuosity, the sociologist Max Weber notes,

> Ritualistic salvation ... confines his [sic] participation to simple or essentially passive manipulations ... Mysteries purport to produce their effect *ex opere operato* by means of a pious occasional devotion. They provide no inner motivation for any such requirement as the believer's demonstration in his life pattern of a religious norm ... What is of primary concern to us is that in ritualism the psychological condition striven for ultimately leads directly away from rational activity. Virtually all mystery cults have this effect ... Like every form of magic, this process has a tendency to become diverted from everyday life, thereby failing to exert any influence upon it.[215]

That is, this ritual has no bearing on one's real life—it has nothing to do with one's rational and inner activities and further obligations and relationships in life. The problem is that such notions have often been used to put the mysteries in sharp contrast to Christianity, thereby creating a false impression of both. While surveying the scholars who rejected the influence of the mysteries on Christianity, Günter Wagner summarizes at one point:

---

[214] Peter L. Berger and Thomas Luckmann, *The Social Construction of Reality: A Treatise in the Sociology of Knowledge* (New York: Anchor Books, 1967), 1–18.
[215] Weber, *The Sociology of Religion*, 152–53.

> The Greek mysteries aim at a transformation of human nature, but not as giving man [sic] the capability of realising an ethical ideal to which he cannot attain on the ground of his own natural endowment. If it is held that the pagan rites were considered to be efficacious *ex opere operato* while baptism in Paul was not, then an unbridgeable gulf opens up in the centre of the two religions. While the mystery religions are primarily concerned with the individual and his salvation, in Paul the accent is on the fact that the neophyte is admitted into the Christian community.[216]

Again, this citation shows the previously held view that there was neither ethical realization nor a communal aspect in the individualistic *ex opera operato* performance of the mysteries. Even Walter Burkert, one of the most famous scholars of the mystery cults in the last century, retains some of the sharp distinctions between the mysteries and Christianity.

> [Mysteries] could not coalesce into a "church" ... These characteristics become clearer if we ask to what extent mysteries conferred a religious identity, in the sense in which a Christian knows that "I am a Christian" ... Christians adopted the term *symbolon* for their own Credo, but this only serves to emphasize the enormous difference. In Christianity there are articles of faith, to be believed and to be confessed, whereas in the mysteries there is reference to a sequence of rituals that have taken place ... [R]itual does not need explicit theology to be effective.[217]

Yes, "ritual does not need explicit theology to be effective"—that is true, and it is also true that the mysteries did not produce any Credo comparable to what later Christians produced for their developed liturgy. Yet, it is also unlikely that early Christ-devotees in the mid-first century had a Credo similar to the fourth-century Nicene one. Nor is it likely that from the outset the first-century groups of Christ-devotees coalesced into highly organized "churches" that provided a firmly set religious identity for the congregants. The validity of all the remarks introduced here by block quotations will be examined through my exploration of self-referential and canonical messages of mystery initiations and baptism, but especially in the third sections of each chapter ("Beyond Initiation").

As with any new model, it is important to address possible objections and questions. First, one might doubt how this investigation of ancient rituals is even possible. The goal of this study is to reveal the messages communicated by each of these rituals in antiquity, but if I cannot make a direct observation of these rituals or ask the ritual participants, how can I know what messages are communicated? How can I really know anything about the rituals of these ancient

---

216 Wagner, *Pauline Baptism*, 48–49.
217 Burkert, *Ancient Mystery Cults*, 46.

people at all? How can I access the "messages" that the rituals communicated? I already addressed this issue when I discussed Rappaport's theory, which provided sufficient answers. To be clear, the present project is to present my *reconstruction* —though I think is a plausible one—of ancient rituals and of the messages communicated by these rituals. This is part of the inevitable limits of researching ancient history, and what matters is whether one seeks ways to better understand the past. I will try to do justice to the ancient sources, not only well-known literary ones but also non-literary/material ones, use careful analytical tools, and present the results with clear forms, so that other scholars can engage in constructive criticism and conversation for the advancement of our understanding of the ancient world. My investigation of the ritual messages is similar to a combination of synchronic and diachronic linguistics: it aims to present ritual's semantic ranges and to excavate its underlying grammatical structures, yet, also to explore how those semantics and deeper structures changed and were modified from time to time and place to place. This principle will also be applied to Paul's passages that allude to baptismal practices in early Christ-believing communities, so that this early Christ-cult baptism can be firmly placed within the logic and pattern of ritual of his time. In doing so, one will be able to better understand how baptism worked in Paul's communities and how Paul developed his interpretation of the ritual throughout his interactions with his communities.[218]

Second, some would object to my examination because it anachronistically imposes the notions of individuals and an individual religious experience upon the ancient data. This goes in opposition to earlier scholars' assessment of the mysteries—for example, as shown by Wagner's summary, the mysteries were often regarded as only having to do with an individual's prosperity with no relation to their communal identity or obligations. Thus, this second objection is what I would expect to hear from more recent scholars who study ancient religious phenomena in the Greek and Roman world. Surely, the people in the ancient Mediterranean world were not accustomed to the same amount and type of individualism as developed in modern Western society. Collectivity and the concept of belonging are important for understanding "identity" in the ancient Mediterranean world

---

[218] In fact, whether Paul's theology underwent development and change within the period represented by his undisputed letters is a perennial question in scholarship. It is actually one of the points of disagreement between Cumont and Loisy, both of whom were representative of the Inaugurated Quest on Paul and the mysteries. Cumont argued for the existence of such a development, whereas Loisy was more doubtful. See especially Loisy's private letter to Cumont (May 1914) quoted in Lannoy, "St Paul," 233.

(note that the term "identity" is also a modern construct).[219] Yet, collectivity without any concern for individuality is a one-side emphasis, which is not helpful and does not capture the dynamics of reality. In this regard, Jörg Rüpke's words are worth mentioning. He opens his paper by introducing the wider intellectual context of his work, agreeing with his groups' "criticism of the widespread practice of dichotomically assigning individualisation and individual religious agency to modernity, whereas antiquity is supposed to have been characterised by the collective as far as religion is concerned."[220] Rüpke criticizes this dichotomy as "a specific definition of religion," whose origin can be attributed to Durkheim.[221] Investigating individuals' religious experiences and their choice of participating in certain religious activities cannot be merely dismissed as an anachronistic quest.

Lastly, one may challenge my project because s/he thinks it attempts to present what the initiates *believed* when they participated in rituals. What I want to highlight by the help of Rappaport and Riesebrodt is that one's participation in ritual is not meaningless, but it actually indicates and conveys particular messages to the participants and others. If certain messages are always communicated by ritual, then the aspect of belief is not immediately eliminated. Of course, Rappaport strongly argues that what he means by the ritual participants' acceptance of the canonical messages is not the same as the Christian concept of faith (note that he defines Christian faith in a very narrow way—beliefs in well-defined creeds, making the same mistake as Weber). Yet, I believe the notion of belief/faith—depending on how it is defined and envisioned—cannot be totally excluded from the outset as something irrelevant to the mysteries, as well as Greek and Roman religion as a whole. This can be justified in at least two ways. First, one should rethink what many have taken for granted as the definition of faith/belief (i.e., the notion that is inclined to a private, mental, intellectual, and inner state, which is aptly contrasted with outward rituals). Recent scholars in classics, early Christianity, and New Testament have noticed more relational and communal aspects of *pistis/fides* (which may be better translated as trust), as Teresa Morgan's influential book demonstrates.[222] If one follows this trend, one cannot assume any clear-cut distinction (at least in the nascent stage of early Christianity) between what *pistis* may have meant (and how it functioned) for early Christ-devotees and what the acceptance of the canonical order of rituals may have meant for other cultic participants. Furthermore, recent ritual theorists (for example, Catherine Bell) point

---

219 As for "belonging" in relation to the discussion of Greco-Roman associations, see Kloppenborg, *Christ's Associations*, 131–61.
220 Jörg Rüpke, "Theorising Religion for the Individual," *Individuals and Materials*, 1:61–62.
221 Rüpke, "Theorising Religion for the Individual," 62.
222 Morgan, *Roman Faith and Christian Faith*.

out the embodied nature of belief, resisting the reduction of belief to a mental phenomenon.[223] Thus, to speak of belief in regard to rituals outside Christianity would not be problematic from the outset.

Second, the inclusion of interest in belief/faith in this study fits within the new tendency to illuminate the neglected aspect of ancient religion regarding belief/faith. This current revival of interest in belief/faith and even in "theology" of Greek religion begins to resist the earlier generation of scholarship that focused on "the performance of cult acts," rather than "the state of mind of the actor."[224] It is true that one can hardly find a coherent doctrinal system out of the sheer diversity of ritual practices in Greek and Roman religion, and it is also evident that religion in this ancient Mediterranean world was strongly civic with its focus on proper ritual practice, both in the "polis religion" or in the emperor/ruler-centered religion. Yet, individuals' belief—their belief in the deity and in the efficacy of various rituals in which they participated—existed. As noted, some recent scholars of Greek and Roman religion have begun to reconsider the significance and role of belief. H. S. Versnel, for example, explored how the Greeks negotiated different concepts and beliefs in the god(s), and called for scholarship to extend beyond the "ritual craze" (his term) of the late twentieth century.[225] Julia Kindt criticizes the inadequacy of the framework of polis religion because there were many other religious phenomena that cannot be captured by that framework.[226] This shift is not only found in the study of Greek religion. In discussing the Roman beliefs and practices regarding the cult of the dead, Charles W. King argues that the pattern of "nondogmatic belief" existed in Roman religion.[227] One might be worried about anachronism or bringing Christian perspectives into non-Christian tra-

---

[223] Catherine Bell, "The Chinese 'Believe' in Spirits: Belief and Believing in the Study of Religion," in *Radical Interpretation in Religion*, ed. N. Frankenberry (Cambridge: Cambridge University Press, 2002), 115. Cf. Catherine Bell, "Belief: A Classificatory Lacuna and Disciplinary 'Problem,'" in *Introducing Religion: Essays in Honor of Jonathan Z. Smith*, ed. Willi Braun and Russell T. McCutcheon (London: Equinox, 2008), 85–99. See also Kevin Lewis O'Neill, "Introduction: Further Explorations in Theory and Practice," *HR* 51 (2012): 291–98.
[224] R. Osborne, "Archaeology, the Salaminioi, and the Politics of Sacred Space in Archaic Attica," in *Placing the Gods: Sanctuaries and Sacred Space in Ancient Greece*, ed. Susan E. Alcock and Robin Osborne (New York: Oxford University Press, 1994), 144: "What mattered was the performance of cult acts, not the state of mind of the actor."
[225] H. S. Versnel, *Coping with the Gods: Wayward Readings in Greek Theology* (Leiden: Brill, 2011).
[226] Julia Kindt, *Rethinking Greek Religion* (Cambridge: Cambridge University Press, 2012).
[227] Charles W. King, *The Ancient Roman Afterlife:* Di Manes, *Belief, and the Cult of the Dead* (Austin: University of Texas Press, 2020), 62–88. Thus, King asserts, "It is … untenable to suggest that attributing beliefs to the Roman is intrinsically Christianizing or intrinsically anachronistic." King, *The Ancient Roman Afterlife*, 71.

ditions. My project is rather moderate. I do not attempt to pierce into a particular individual initiate mind or create a credo or *summa theologica.*[228] I will highlight a range of beliefs from which ritual creators and performers (as *bricoleurs*) could draw meanings for their rituals.[229]

With this theoretical framework, I will investigate the initiation rituals for the mysteries—the Dionysiac mysteries (ch. 3) and the mysteries of Isis (ch. 4)—and baptism in the Pauline communities (chs. 5–7).

---

[228] Yet, if one pays attention to the philosophical appropriation of mysteries, then one might be able to use the term "theology" (*theologia* as "le troisième élément constitutif du religieux"). See Athanassiadi and Macris, "La philosophisation du religieux," 42. See also p. 47 for their discussion of theological and philosophical "koine" in the first century.

[229] Regarding bricolage and bricoleurs—see Radcliffe Edmonds's comments on "Orphism." Radcliffe G. Edmonds III, *Redefining Ancient Orphism: A Study in Greek Religion* (Cambridge: Cambridge University Press, 2013), 394. I think they are also relevant to other areas of ancient religion including ritual and ritual order.

3 Initiation into the Dionysiac Mysteries

What benefits did the initiation ritual of the Dionysiac mysteries promise the initiates? What were the canonical messages that supported the efficacy of Dionysiac initiation? How did Dionysiac initiation envision religious virtuosity? Did the initiation ritual of the Dionysiac mysteries also involve ethical behavior, proper understanding, and even "faith" on the part of the initiates?

Some preliminary remarks are in order. First, as with other mysteries, concrete details about the initiation ritual are not usually stated publicly and are, therefore, hard to find in extant sources. The theatrical dialogue between Dionysus and Pentheus (who mistakes Dionysus for a Dionysiac initiate) in Euripides's *Bacchae* 471–474 is revealing:

> Pentheus: These rites—what is their nature?
> Dionysus: They may not be told to the uninitiated (ἀβακχεύτοισιν, i.e., to those who are not Bacchic initiates).
> Pentheus: But those who perform them—what kind of benefit do they get (ἔχει δ' ὄνησιν ... τίνα)?
> Dionysus: You are not allowed to hear—though the rites are well worth knowing.

Yet, there are some clues even for modern readers—the uninitiated—to allow inferences. What follows in this chapter is a scholarly (re)construction of the Dionysiac mysteries by sorting out various types of evidence, weighing this data, and weaving it all together.

Second, exploring the Dionysiac/Bacchic/Orphic mysteries may be a complex task, as hinted at by their nomenclature; the Dionysiac mysteries have a complicated history of convergence of several traditions over a long period of time. I will mostly use the simple title "Dionysiac mysteries" or the "mysteries of Dionysus" as umbrella terms (over against "Bacchic") and I will also not explore Orphism in detail.[1] Yet, in order to refer to the devotees of Dionysus who underwent initia-

---

[1] The "Orphic" gold tablets demonstrate that the complex relationship among the deity's name Dionysus, his famous epithet Bacchus, and the Orphic influence on the cults featuring Dionysus/Bacchus existed in the Classical and early Hellenistic period. See Fritz Graf's discussion of the history of scholarship on the tablets, including how scholars have associated the tablets with Orphism. Fritz Graf and Sarah Iles Johnston, *Ritual Texts for the Afterlife: Orpheus and the Bacchic Gold Tablets*, 2nd ed. (New York: Routledge, 2013), 50–65. One example of the convergence of Orphism and the names Dionysus and Bacchus is the Amphipolis Tablet (GJ 30 = OF 496n) from Macedonia, which dates from the fourth to early third century BCE. It begins with this sentence: "Pure and sacred to Dionysos Bacchius am I (Εὐαγὴς ἱερὰ Διονύσου Βαχχίου εἰμί)" (alternatively, it can be translated: "I am pure and sacred, belonging to Dionysus Bacchius"). Yet, given that the term "Or-

tion, I will continue to use the name "Bacchants," along with the term Dionysiac initiates.²

Third, my investigation of the mysteries of Dionysus covers a wide range of time periods from classical Greece to the early Roman empire. The emergence of the Dionysiac mystery cults, not only other (more general) forms of Dionysiac worship, traces back to the Classical period; thus, it is important to remember

---

phism" covers a broader, sometimes independent, phenomenon than the Dionysiac mysteries and that the term itself has been contested by several scholars, it would not be reasonable to use the term Orphic mysteries as a primary name for the phenomena discussed in this chapter (for the history of scholarship on Orphism: Graf, "Appendix 1: Orphism in the Twenty-First Century," in *Ritual Texts for the Afterlife*, 187–94). Similarly, the combination of the two names, Dionysus and Bacchus (Βάκχος or Βάκχιος [adj. Bacchic; of the Bacchants, etc.]), began to appear early on in the history of tradition, but I will not use Bacchus as a primary name for the deity. This combination between Dionysus and Bacchus is shown by the gold tablets mentioned above, but also by literary sources, including Euripides's tragedy, *Bacchae*, and Herodotus's *The Persian Wars* (both are dated to the fifth century BCE). It is also known from the fact that in the later period among the Romans, the name Bacchus gained predominance over against Liber, which was a traditional Italic deity identified with Dionysus/Bacchus (Marco Antonio Santamaría, "The Term βάκχος and Dionysos Βάκχιος," in *Redefining Dionysos*, ed. Alberto Bernabé et al. [Berlin: Walter de Gruyter, 2013], 38, n. 2). Yet, recent scholars have pointed out that Bacchus was originally not the deity's proper name. Ana Jiménez San Cristóbal notes that βάκχος refers to "an attribute that manifests a particular condition of men or gods," rather than a theonym (Ana Jiménez San Cristóbal, "The Meaning of βάκχος and βακχεύειν in Orphism," in *Mystic Cults in Magna Graecia*, 46). As Marco Antonio Santamaría also demonstrates with his philological examination, it is likely that the term βάκχος originated from the group name of the Dionysus-followers ("the Bacchant") and was later applied to Dionysus himself as an "epithet," not the other way around (Santamaría, "The Term βάκχος and Dionysos Βάκχιος," 38–57; thus, Dionysus Βάκχιος [which is more often used than the single term βάκχος in referring to the deity] means "Dionysus of the Bacchants"). So, although it is true that the application of the term βάκχος not only to the Bacchants but also to the deity himself became common within the broadly conceived Dionysiac tradition, I think using the terms Dionysus and Dionysiac in my discussion would be helpful in simplifying the presentation of nomenclature as well as emphasizing the deity's original name.

2 On the use of the term "Bacchants" for all types of people related to the Dionysiac cult: See Bøgh, "In Life and Death." 25–26, n. 3. As Bremmer notes, it is possible that the "Bacchants" (βάκχοι) as initiates of a higher degree were sometimes distinguished from other Bacchic/Dionysiac initiates (μύσται) (see the Hipponion Tablet; GJ 1 = OF 474), similar to the distinction between ἐπόπται and μύσται in the Eleusinian mysteries. Yet I do not retain such a distinction between βάκχοι and μύσται throughout my investigation. This is because the distinctive use of βάκχοι as opposed to other μύσται faded after the fourth century BCE, and my project does not focus on sources earlier than that. Jan Bremmer, "The Construction of an Individual Eschatology: The Case of the Orphic Gold Leaves," in *Burial Rituals, Ideas of Afterlife, and the Individual in the Hellenistic World and the Roman Empire*, ed. Katharina Waldner et al. (Stuttgart: Franz Steiner Verlag, 2016), 38–39.

that the mysteries are not merely a Hellenistic and "Oriental" phenomenon.³ Yet, the Dionysiac mysteries experienced certain changes between the classical, Hellenistic, and Roman imperial periods.⁴ In this chapter, therefore, my investigation allows for chronological changes and developments.

Furthermore, the closeness/similarity between the God of Judeo-Christian tradition and Dionysus (sometimes unwittingly revealed by the contrast between them) was already theorized in antiquity.⁵ The shared divine patterns were notice-

---

3 Hence, *contra* Cumont. See Cumont, *Oriental Religions*, xvi: "In spite of the prestige that surrounded Eleusis, the word 'mysteries' calls up Hellenized Asia rather than Greece proper." The existence of the Dionysiac mysteries before the Hellenistic period has been corroborated by the discoveries of golden tablets and the Derveni Papyrus in the 1970s, and the iconographic tradition depicted on vase paintings (e. g., kylix by the "Kallix Painter"). Anne-Françoise Jaccottet, *Choisir Dionysos: les associations dionysiaques, ou, la face cachée du dionysisme* (Zürich: Akanthvs, 2003), 1:125; Cornelia Isler-Kerényi, "New Contributions of Dionysiac Iconography to the History of Religions in Greece and Italy," in *Mystic Cults in Magna Graecia*, 71.

4 When compared with the Eleusinian mysteries (the Greek mysteries *par excellence*), the most remarkable point of difference with the Dionysus mysteries is that the latter lacks a centralized location for the mysteries and the authoritative ritual related to that place (Klauck, *The Religious Context of Early Christianity*, 120). As Jaccottet highlights, the lack of a central location permits Dionysiac "associations" (e. g., *thiasoi*) to become "the natural framework" (*le cadre naturel*) for this mystery cult (Jaccottet, *Choisir Dionysos*, 1:123). Over time the word used to describe these people changed: before the Roman imperial period, θιασῖται was predominant, which was replaced by μύσται from the imperial period onward (Jaccottet, *Choisir Dionysos*, 1:129). Admittedly, it is difficult to make a definitive claim about whether the Dionysiac mysteries in the imperial period were fundamentally different from the "old orgia" in the Classical period (Nilsson), or if there was more or less continuity (or if a "rupture" happened far later, i. e., "at the edge of the second century CE" [Jaccottet, *Choisir Dionysos*, 1:131]).

5 For example, in Plutarch's *Table Talk*, the God of Jews is identified with Dionysus, and the religious customs of the Jews are regarded as connected to the Dionysiac rites (Question 6). Plutarch's etymological explanations and cultural descriptions are, of course, not historically accurate (e. g., the connection between Sabbath and *Sabi*—the latter is what the Bacchants cry out); nor is it likely that the Jews themselves identified their deity and religious customs with Dionysus and his ritual. Yet, at least, this piece of evidence suggests that some "outsiders" in antiquity saw some elements in the practices and beliefs of the Jews as comparable to those in Dionysiac traditions. The Dionysiac cult was even known in the Palestinian territories. See Jesús-M. Nieto Ibáñez, "The Sacred Grove of Scythopolis (Flavius Josephus, *Jewish War* II 466–471)," *IEJ* 49 (1999): 260–68. The famous mosaic from a house in Sepphoris (though it is dated to the third century CE) that depicts a drink competition between Hercules and Dionysus can also be mentioned. Also, *3 Maccabees*, dated approximately between the second/first century BCE and the first century CE, rhetorically presents a sharp contrast between Jewish devotion to Yahweh and the Greeks' (esp. Ptolemy Philopator's) devotion to Dionysus, but this contrast also ironically reveals many commonalities between Yahweh and Dionysus (Mercedes López Salvá, "Dionysos and Dionysism in the Third Book of Maccabees," in *Redefining Dionysos*, 452–63 [esp. 459–62]). The reception and development of Dionysiac tradition among various groups—pagans, Jews, and Christians (even making "parallels" between Christ and

able and recognized by the ancients. Of course, no simple genealogical relationship is presupposed in the current comparative investigation.

3.1 The Self-referential Messages, or the Benefits Initiation Promises

3.1.1 Transformation of One's Religious and Social Self

One of the self-referential messages that is immediately communicated through initiation ritual is the participant's rise in status to that of Dionysiac initiate. As in the case of the Erythraean ritual, as Fritz Graf observes, the initiation ritual of the Dionysiac mysteries has the power "to permanently change one's status." Just as those who participate in the rites of the Erythraean Korybantes became κεκορυβαντισμένοι, the initiates of the Dionysiac mysteries became βεβακχευμένοι.[6] Taking it a step further, Bøgh argues that Dionysiac initiation "placed the individual in a new religious community" and it even "provided him or her with a new religious – Bacchic – identity, a new perspective on life and death, new cultic behaviour, as well as a life-long loyalty and commitment."[7] This new communal reality is, according to Bøgh, highlighted by the use of συν/ ξυν and other semantically related terms throughout Euripides's *Bacchae*.

> Dionysos "joins together" with the maenads (ξυνάψει), and he "[co-]partakes" in the dances of the Bacchai (συμμετασχήσει). Teiresias and Cadmus "take hold of and join hands" (ξύναπτε καὶ ξυνωρίζου χέρα) on their way to the celebrations. The Bacchai are sisters (ἀδελφάς) and fellow revelers (συγκώμοι), they all make noise together (πᾶσα ὁμοῦ βοή) and call upon their god with a "united voice" (ἀθρόῳ στόματι). The Bacchai are Dionysos' companions (παρέδρους), his fellow travelers (ξυνεμπόρους), fellow exiles (συμφυγάδας), co-workers (συνεργούς), fellow hunters (ξυγκύναγας), and accomplices (ξυνεργάτους). The Bacchai sit together (συγκαθημένας), while the outsider, Pentheus, just sits (καθήμενος).[8]

Even if one does not fully agree with Bøgh's overall conclusion (including her claim that there was "a life-long loyalty and commitment"), it can be said that the linguis-

---

Dionysus)—have been fruitfully discussed by recent scholars as part of a wider cultural phenomenon in late antiquity. David Hernández de la Fuente, "Parallels between Dionysos and Christ in Late Antiquity: Miraculous Healings in Nonnus' *Dionysiaca*," in *Redefining Dionysos*, 464–487; Courtney J. P. Friesen, *Reading Dionysus: Euripides*' Bacchae *and the Cultural Contestations of Greeks, Jews, Romans, and Christians* (Tübingen: Mohr Siebeck, 2015).
6 Fritz Graf, "The Blessings of Madness: Dionysos, Madness, and Scholarship," *ARG* 12 (2010): 174.
7 Bøgh, "In Life and Death," 46.
8 Bøgh, "In Life and Death," 29–30.

tic features from *Bacchae* demonstrate a shared behavior and identity among the Bacchants.

In the various Dionysiac mystery associations during the Hellenistic period, this initiation-based change of status (becoming a Bacchant) and its implications were multifaceted. The initiation ritual of the Dionysiac mysteries promises a potential initiate to increase her/his status to a full member of the Dionysiac group, and also it provides further opportunities to enhance their status within the group and society as a whole. Evidence from the Hellenistic period shows that groups and individuals related to Dionysiac rituals could actually work with and within the polis system. A decree found on an inscription from Miletus (LSAM 48 = I.Miletos 8; 276/275 BCE) and an inscription from Cos (Syll.³ 3.1012; second or first century BCE) provide evidence that Dionysiac cults, though they involved ecstatic experiences, were controlled by their own bureaucratic and hierarchical orders, and these were somehow related to the polis.[9] Part of the Cos inscription reads:

> At the [time?] of monarch N[...], in the month of Batromos, 12th, at the regular meeting (ἀγορᾷ κυρίᾳ), general Nikandoros [of ...], Hagesis of Epikouros, [...], Euaratos of Eukarpos, and Phormion of Eudamos—for whom (οἷς) Euaratos of Diokleos was a secretary—they inscribed [what follows] together here: Let her pay for the priesthood of Dionysos of Thullophoros to the treasurer (τοὶ ταμίαι) in the month Batromios 16th ... She will be serving in the priesthood during her lifetime. She will make two instalments of the sum ... but the polis (πόλις) will initiate [τελέσει] the priestess (ἱέρειαν) and let the cost be paid to the treasurer. In order that the priestess may be initiated according to the customs, let one [?] be hired for the seller. Let it be allowed for the priestess to appoint a female citizen to be an assistant priestess (ὑφιέρειαν). Let it not be allowed others to do sacrifice (ἱερᾶθαι) or to preside over initiation (τελεῖν) to Dionysos Thullophoros except the [...], but if someone also transgresses something regarding the priestess, let it be allowed for the master (κυρίωι) of the priestess, but if not, let it be allowed for the other who wishes, to go into the Council (ἐς τὰν βουλάν) and announce the person who did wrong ... (translation mine)

This inscription suggests that the polis governed (or at least was deeply engaged in) the ritual activities pertaining to Dionysus—Dionysiac rituals appear to be part of civic activity, rather than some "frenzied" Bacchants. Although the priestess herself should make some financial contribution, it seems that the polis is also financially responsible for conducting the initiation of the priestess (this initiation is connected to the priesthood). The polis and its governing institution ("Council") had the authority to control and discipline Dionysiac ritual participants regarding wrong-

---

[9] For a brief discussion of this inscription, see Walter Burkert, "Bacchic *Teletai* in the Hellenistic Age," in *Masks of Dionysus*, ed. Thomas H. Carpenter and Christopher A. Faraone (Ithaca: Cornell University Press, 1993), 273–74.

3.1 The Self-referential Messages, or the Benefits Initiation Promises — 71

doings. Under such circumstances, one seeking status in Dionysiac groups is not different from her/him seeking it with the broader society.

An inscription of Miletus (LSAM 48 = I.Miletos 8) includes similar stipulations, but it should be noted that the Miletus decree adds an interesting detail: the possible tension between a Dionysiac ritual that is officially supported by the polis versus unsupported Dionysiac associations. The first lines of the inscription are lost, but the extant portion begins with this:

> whenever the priestess (ἱέρεια) accomplishes the sacred rites (ὄργια) on behalf of the city, no one is allowed to deposit (or: throw in) the raw sacrificial meat (ὠμοφάγιον) before the priestess has deposited (or: thrown in) the raw sacrificial meat on behalf of the city. No one is allowed to gather the society (τὸν θίασον) before that of the People (τοῦ δημοσίου)...[10]

Based on this description, Harland claims, "[T]here were unofficial Dionysiac 'societies' (alongside a civic-sponsored one) at Miletos by 276/275 BCE."[11] The rest of the inscription details the regulations about how one engages in Dionysiac rituals under the authority of the polis and the official priestess.[12] In this context, Dionysiac initiation likely communicated the message that those who underwent initiation not only joined a Dionysiac association as Bacchants/maenads, but they also entered into the negotiation of proper relationship between individual Dionysiac groups and the city/city-sponsored Dionysiac ritual (for some, this could provide further opportunities). Admittedly, one cannot generalize such a connection between polis and Dionysiac devotion in all periods and all places. It would be especially hard to expect the same dynamics once the traditional polis-society of the Greek world began to change.

Apart from the polis, one can still observe the existence of polis-like structures, diversified roles, and rules of order within the Dionysiac groups. Of course, this feature is not only restricted to Dionysiac groups, but also applied to many other associations in the Greco-Roman world.[13] In the Dionysiac mysteries, especially, dif-

---

10 Translation from Philip A. Harland, *Greco-Roman Associations: Texts, Translations, and Commentary. Volume II. North Coast of the Black Sea, Asia Minor* (Berlin: Walter de Gruyter, 2014), 285. This is the only portion of the inscription for which he provides translation.
11 Harland, *North Coast of the Black Sea, Asia Minor*, 285.
12 See Lefkowitz and Fant's translation: "... And whenever a woman wishes to perform an initiation for Dionysus Bacchius in the city, in the countryside, or on the islands, she must pay a piece of gold to the priestess at each biennial celebration." Mary Lefkowitz and Maureen B. Fant, *Women's Lives in Greece and Rome*, 2nd ed. (Baltimore: Johns Hopkins University Press, 1992), 274 (#384).
13 One can find many illuminating examples from sourcebooks, such as AHK. See the third-century CE membership list of an association devoted to Zeus Hypsistos from Macedonia (SEG 46, n. 800 = AHK 45). It has titles such as ἄρχων (ruler), λογιστής (auditor), γραμματεύς (secretary),

ferent offices are mentioned in the inscription found in Torre Nova (Jaccottet #188; 160–165 CE). It should also be noted that this inscription and many others demonstrate that women were able to hold offices within the Dionysiac associations (Jaccottet, ##22, 45, 147, 149, 150, 174, 181, 188). The long list of offices in the Bacchic/Dionysiac association mentioned in the Torre Nova inscription suggests that such associations somehow emulated the civic order, although many titles in the Dionysiac associations echo Dionysiac mythology.[14] Also, a late second-century CE Greek inscription from Athens (Syll.^{3} 3.1109 = IG II^2 1368 = AHK 7), which is called "the Rule of Iobacchoi," provides detailed rules about how a person enters the Dionysiac/Bacchic association, how that person behaves in that community, and what penalties would be given if those rules are not followed. Those who are responsible for this inscription (and the association related to this inscription) may have envisioned and shaped their association in a way that imitates a formal civic procedure.

The last inscription mentioned above deserves special attention. The strict Rule of the Iobacchoi (Syll.^{3} 3.1109) commands the Bacchic association to be well-ordered, structured, and disciplined, rather than being spontaneous, ecstatic, criminal, licentious—many of these are stereotypical portrayals of Bacchic groups, as prominently exemplified by Livy's report on the Roman persecution of the Bacchanalia in 186 BCE (*History of Rome* 39.8–9).[15] According to the Rule of Iobacchoi, an individual member of this group who "insulted" (ὑβρίσας) or "abused" (λοιδορήσας) other members must pay the association (τῷ κοινῷ) a penalty of "twenty-five light drachmai"; otherwise, that person will be punished with a temporary ban (lines 79–83). More interestingly, this inscription explicitly prioritizes communal order over and against ecstatic religious expressions by individual members:

> No one may either sing (ᾆσαι) or create a disturbance (θορυβῆσαι) or applaud (κροτῆσαι) at the gathering, but each shall say and act (λέγειν καὶ ποιεῖν) his allotted part (τοὺς μερισμούς) with all good order and quietness (μετὰ ... πάσης εὐκοσμίας καὶ ἡσυχίας) under the direction

---

etc., which are reminiscent of Athenian officials. See, also, a second-century CE inscription containing detailed regulations of a club from Liopesi (Attica) (SEG 31, no. 122 = AHK 9).

14 See another second-century inscription that records donations made by dead initiates for the Dionysiac association (SEG 17, no. 496 = Jaccottet #147 = AHK 203). This inscription mentions titles like "nurse" and "papas." Also, see the first-century inscription from Pergamon that lists "cowherds" (βουκόλοι) and "Silenoi" (Σειληνοί) as titles (Syll.^{3} 3.1115 = Jaccottet #94 = AHK 115).

15 To be sure, such stereotypical, negative portrayals and the refutations existed at an earlier stage of the tradition. Euripides's *Bacchae* 313–318 attempts to exonerate Dionysus of "compel[ling] women to act foolishly where sex is concerned." Rather, "even in ecstatic worship a chaste woman will not be corrupted (ἥ γε σώφρων οὐ διαφθαρήσεται)."

of the priest or the arch-bacchos (lit. "as the priest or the arch-bacchos commands [προστάσ-σοντος]) (lines 63–67; translation mine).

Note that some interesting resonance with the Pauline injunctions regarding the gathering of his *ekklesia* (e.g., 1 Cor 12–14) appears; also, the phrase μετὰ ... πάσης εὐκοσμίας καὶ ἡσυχίας further resonates with some particular speaking habits of the Pastorals (e.g., 1 Tim 2). Returning to the Rule of Iobacchoi, the priest is expected to deliver a "sermon" (τιθέτω ... θεολογίαν; perhaps, "mythic teaching" would be a better translation),[16] in addition to performing "customary services" and the drink-offering for the returning of the deity (τὴν τῶν καταγωγίων σπονδήν) (lines 111–117). As Isler-Kerényi notes, Dionysus's boundary-crossing (this is what Dionysus is well known for) "was only possible because he at first represented these very boundaries," as is suggested by pottery from the Archaic period.[17] This aspect of Dionysus and his cults in the Classical period (which Isler-Kerényi demonstrates) still held true hundreds of years later, in the second century CE (as shown by the Rule of Iobacchoi). Yet, the scope shifted—from Dionysus who imposes order on the polis to Dionysus who imposes order on a particular cultic group.

3.1.2 Blessed Civic Life

One's blessed life on earth is one of the primary benefits promised by the Dionysiac initiation; this particular promise is more clearly found in sources dating to the Classical period. Although some argue that the ecstatic ritual of the Dionysiac mysteries can be understood as a "counterpolis" ritual,[18] evidence shows that the Dionysiac ritual and the tradition pertaining to Dionysus were interwoven with the polis life of Athenians. Through her comprehensive iconographic investigation, Isler-Kerényi's *Dionysos in Classical Athens* (2015) demonstrates how ubiquitous

---

16 AHK 7 translates it as "... give the discourse about the god."
17 Cornelia Isler-Kerényi, *Dionysos in Classical Athens: An Understanding through Images* (Leiden: Brill, 2015), 2. In her other book on Dionysus images in archaic Greece, she notes, "Whether it is on the occasion of the wedding of Thetis and Peleus, the Return of Hephaistos to Olympus, or of the Gigantomachy, Dionysos always tends to strengthen the cosmic order personified by Zeus." Cornelia Isler-Kerényi, *Dionysos in Archaic Greece: An Understanding through Images* (Leiden: Brill, 2007), 216.
18 See, for example, Cassidy's article that locates "the maenadic rituals of Dionysos in the Greek religious and social worlds as a complex that counters the dominant cultural ethos." William Cassidy, "Dionysos, Ecstasy, and The Forbidden," *Historical Reflections / Reflexions Historiques* 17 (1991): 40.

the image of Dionysus is in the public life of Athens—thus, this deity is not merely a god of eccentricity and social anomaly. In Euripides's *Bacchae* 72–87, the Chorus sings, declaring that the Bacchic initiate is a happy one: "O blessed the man who (ὢ μάκαρ, ὅστις), / happy in knowing the gods' rites (εὐδαίμων τελετὰς θεῶν εἰδώς), / makes his life pure / and joins his soul to the worshipful band, / performing Bacchic rites upon the mountains, with cleansings the gods approve . . ." Why the initiate is happy or what kind of blessing is given is not clearly stated (except for the fact that the person has joined the Bacchic group). Perhaps, *Bacchae* 135–144 provides some clues in its symbolic language: "Welcome is the god when on the mountains / he leaves the coursing coves and falls to the ground[19] ... The ground runs with milk, runs with wine, runs with the nectar of bees." The imagery—milk, wine, honey (all often related to Dionysus)—obviously evokes a sense of prosperity and affluence, which would lead to a happy, earthly life. In this drama, Dionysus exemplifies the truly peaceful life in contrast to the destructive king Pentheus.[20] What is depicted here amounts to an "entire second universe created wherever Dionysos is worshipped"[21] and one might say that it is only realized by the initiates within their Dionysiac symbolic world. Yet, the fact that the image of Dionysus was prevalent in the iconographic tradition (which probably represents popular perception) and in other literary works in classical Athens (e.g., *Frogs*) increases the likelihood that the notion of a blessed, affluent life on earth brought by Dionysus was also a widespread belief throughout Athens.[22] If that is the case, one could say that Dionysiac initiation communicated this message both to the initiated and the uninitiated (thus, it was not a secret!), constantly attracting the latter.

Dionysus's gracious power of granting the blessed civic life and freedom to his devotees was malleable and useful enough for rulers to appropriate this image for their political ideology. This may have communicated a new self-referential message to the initiates in this altered political climate. During the Hellenistic period, a connection between the Dionysiac rituals and the ruler cult began to emerge and receive prominence. This phenomenon almost "supplemented" and "ousted" the older forms of "charismatic" Dionysiac rituals. As Burkert summarizes,

---

[19] Kovacs notes that this phrase would mean that Dionysus is "falling on the goat, his prey." David Kovacs, *Bacchae* (LCL 495), 23.
[20] Herbert Musurillo, "Euripides and Dionysiac Piety (*Bacchae* 370–433)," *TPAPA* 97 (1966): 301–2.
[21] Bøgh, "In Life and Death," 29.
[22] Aristophanes's *Frogs* portrays the figure of Dionysus in a way even more integral to the communal life of Athenians than Euripides's *Bacchae*. As Segal notes, "The asocial, orgiastic Dionysus of the Bacchae is rejected, along with the entire Euripidean outlook, as being hostile to this spirit of communal regeneration." Charles Paul Segal, "The Character and Cults of Dionysus and the Unity of the Frogs," *HSCP* 65 (1961): 230.

The experience of "epiphany" came to concentrate on the person of the ruler who had acted as a "savior" and inaugurated an age of bliss and abundance—a process that easily assumed a Dionysiac coloring. Royal display in the great parade took the form of a Dionysiac *pompē*. At the same time the theater had made Dionysiac enthusiasm readily available in mimetic play, at least since Euripides' *Bacchae*. The monarch was the victor, the savior, the god, "present" (*epiphanēs*) to a degree gods had hardly ever been. Not only the actors followed in his wake, but "all sorts of *thiasoi*," including those of *mustai* and *bakkhoi*.[23]

Perhaps, the most remarkable example of this kind is Demetrius Poliorcetes, who freed Athens from another "tyrant" and entered the city during a Dionysiac festival (295 BCE). He stylized himself as Dionysus, a fact attested to by an ithyphallic hymn dedicated to him and by Herodian (*Ab excessu divi Marci* 1.3.3).[24] This phenomenon (the ruler attempting assimilation with Dionysus) also occurred at the time when the Roman Republic morphed into the Roman Principate, as shown by Mark Antony, the first-century BCE Roman politician. His self-proclamation that he was a "new Dionysus" and his assumption of other Dionysiac epithets are well attested by ancient sources (e.g., Plutarch, *Life of Antony* 24.3, 60.3; Dio Cassius 50.5.3, 50.25.2–4; IG II^2 1043).[25] For the Hellenistic cities where the divine traits of Dionysus and his benefits were appropriated by the deified rulers and the ruler cult, it is likely that the Dionysiac mysteries also functioned to propagate ruling ideology and to maintain the social order.[26] Of course, this phenomenon is not restricted to the Dionysiac mysteries and Dionysiac tradition—for example, Emperor Hadri-

---

23 Burkert, "Bacchic *Teletai*," 268. See, also, Burkert, "Bacchic," 269, regarding the papyrus fragment (e.g., P.Ant. 18).
24 Litwa, *We Are Being Transformed*, 71–74. See, also, Angelos Chaniotis, "The Ithyphallic Hymn for Demetrios Poliorcetes and Hellenistic Religious Mentality," in *More than Men, Less than Gods. Studies in Royal Cult and Imperial Worship. Proceedings of the International Colloquium Organized by the Belgian School at Athens (1–2 November 2007)*, ed. P. P. Iossif, A. S. Chankowski, and C. C. Lorber (Leuven: Peeters, 2011), 157–95.
25 Litwa, *We Are Being Transformed*, 81–84. See Friesen, *Reading Dionysus*, 86–117 (ch. 6 on Philo; ch. 7 on Horace), which discusses how authors in the early Roman imperial period appropriated the image of Dionysus politically (especially in relation to *Bacchae*).
26 The relationship between Dionysiac groups and ruling ideology continued until much later. For example, a Dionysiac group who called themselves "Dancing cowherds" honored the proconsul of Asia, Gaius Antius Aulus Julius Quadratus (Jaccottet #98 = AHK 116; early second century CE from Pergamon). In the inscription, the proconsul is called a "priest of the noble ancestry of Dionysos Kathegemon (Dionysus the Leader)." See also an honorary inscription for the emperor Lucius Septimius Severus (found in Perinthos, Thrace) made by a Baccheion of Asians in the late second century (Jaccottet #37 = AHK 64). In the latter example, the emperor is not identified with Dionysus.

an and his Sabina appropriated the Eleusinian mysteries in the similar way.[27] In sum, under these socio-political circumstances where the image of Dionysus was appropriated by rulers, the Dionysiac mysteries were probably messaging that an initiate would be provided with an affluent and peaceful life under the auspices of the ruler whose identity was symbolically integrated into the Dionysiac one (or vice versa).

3.1.3 Ecstasy and Deliverance in the Present

In this section and the section that follows, I will examine two types or modes of "deliverance" (λύσις), which the initiation ritual of the Dionysiac mysteries promises.[28] The two types are temporal: deliverance in the present and future. One of the earliest witnesses of present deliverance is Plato:

> [W]hen diseases and the greatest troubles have been visited upon certain families through some ancient guilt, madness (μανία) has entered in and by oracular power has found a way of release for those in need, taking refuge in prayers and the service of the gods, and so, by purifications and sacred rites (τελετῶν; i.e., mysteries), he who has this madness is made safe for the present and the after time, and for him who is rightly possessed of madness a release from present ills (λύσιν ... τῶν παρόντων κακῶν) is found (Plato, *Phaedrus* 244E).

Here, the first type of deliverance is epitomized by the experience of ecstasy or madness through "purifications and mysteries,"[29] which can free the initiates from "present ills." As also seen in Euripides's *Bacchae*, ecstasy is thought to be the representative effect and characteristic of the Dionysiac mysteries (*Bacchae* 67–68, 157, etc.), which is why the Dionysiac mysteries were often looked upon with suspicion (*Bacchae* 215–262). Livy's account (*History of Rome* 39.8–9) about the Roman suppression of the Bacchanalian groups in 186 BCE accuses them of being morally depraved and dangerous.[30] Gruen summarizes the effects of Plau-

---

27 Theodora Suk Fong Jim, *Sharing with the Gods:* Aparchai *and* Dekatai *in Ancient Greece* (Oxford: Oxford University Press, 2014), 215. Hadrian was depicted as Ploutos, while his wife Sabina was named New Demeter (Νέα Δημήτηρ).
28 Regarding the two modes of deliverance, see Friesen, *Reading Dionysus*, 10–12.
29 It should also be noted that "the boundaries between madness and rationality were more fluid" in antiquity, when compared to modern conceptions. Friesen, *Reading Dionysus*, 9.
30 Livy depicts the Bacchanalia as a recent phenomenon. Yet, according to Gruen, this is not true historically. He notes, "The Bacchants were well known—and tolerated [from long before]." Erich S. Gruen, *Studies in Greek Culture and Roman Policy* (Leiden; New York: Brill, 1990), 51. Gruen rejects Livy's story (featuring "a romanticized and embellished tale, designed more for literary effect than for historical exactitude," Gruen, 62). He suggests rather that there were probably political

tus's negative portrayal of the Bacchic cults: "How far these descriptions approximate reality is irrelevant. Stereotypes count."[31] Yet, such stereotypes are actually illuminating as to what the popular perception in antiquity was about the Dionysiac cults.

Ecstatic madness is indeed an ambivalent phenomenon. It can be said that *curing one's madness* was part of the tradition associated with the Dionysiac mysteries; and, in this case, madness is a psychosomatic state that should be overcome. According to Apollodorus (*Library* 3.5.1), Dionysus himself is depicted as one who suffers from divine-caused madness and is healed from it through his initiation (Apollodorus narrates that Rhea purified him and taught him how to perform initiation)—in short, "purification as healing of madness and initiation go closely together."[32] Yet, madness is not purely an anomalous mental state that should be healed by ritual, but the *madness itself can also be curative* in that it releases one from some unfavorable situations in life. *Mania*, which the Dionysiac participants experienced during the initiation ritual, may have provided a type of "psychosomatic cures" for the devotees.[33] As Plato notes in passing elsewhere (*Laws* 790D–E; cf. 815), frenzied dance and singing were viewed as a cure.

The literary representation of Bacchic madness in Euripides's *Bacchae* aptly demonstrates that possession and the extraordinary behaviors involved in Dionysiac initiation are a double-edged sword: Bacchic madness can be a curative blessing, but also a destructive curse.[34] The Bacchic possession is both god's gift and god's punishment. The bacchant women possessed by Dionysus display enormous physical power, such as tearing apart live cattle with their hands, winning when fighting men (*Bacchae* 760–764), and even killing Pentheus by ripping his limbs apart (*Bacchae* 1114–1152). These actions were carried out in the ecstatic state and Agave and the other women did not even remember what they did (cf. *Bacchae* 1286). When the report about the king's death arrives, the Chorus that consists of Bacchic women from Asia joyfully cries out, "It is Dionysus, Zeus's son, not Thebes, who is my ruler!" (*Bacchae* 1037–1038). Yet, at the end of the drama, Agave, who took her son's life by her own hand in madness, eventually leaves her land in

---

reasons for the phenomenon: "The issues can be approached in two separate but ultimately converging paths: a shift in emphasis in Roman foreign policy, and an assertion of collective authority by the Roman senate. The Bacchants became victims in the implementation of those developments." Gruen, *Studies in Greek Culture and Roman Policy*, 65.
31 Gruen, *Studies in Greek Culture and Roman Policy*, 50.
32 Graf, "The Blessings of Madness," 170.
33 Burkert, "Bacchic *Teletai*," 260, 268.
34 Admittedly, one should be cautious about how much this literary destructive side reflects reality.

grief. In a sense, therefore, Bacchic madness is a destructive curse. The dark side of madness also appears in a memorable episode from Herodotus's historical writing (although there are no curative elements in his report).³⁵

Perhaps, the harsh, negative descriptions about Bacchic madness in Euripides and Herodotus can be attributed to their respective literary purpose. These literary witnesses give a different perspective than the epigraphic evidence about the Dionysiac mysteries, which is mostly honorary, celebratory, and commemorative. The tragic portrayal of the double-edged madness in Euripides's *Bacchae* is probably explained by its literary genre (i.e., tragedy). Also, Herodotus's report of Scyles's fall due to his initiation (see n. 35 below) should be understood in light of Herodotus's overall reason for introducing that episode. Though Scyles was king of the Scythians, he tended to follow Greek customs (in this case, Dionysiac initiation), and the cost of such a "treacherous" choice was expensive—his death. The conclusion of this episode exemplifies this: "So closely do the Scythians guard their usages, and such penalties do they lay on those who add foreign customs to their own" (*The Persian Wars* 4:80). Then, in the life of ordinary initiates, the consequence of Bacchic madness was perhaps not always drastically harmful. For example, a medical description of μανία in Aretaeus of Cappadocia (contemporary of Galen) is interesting in this regard: "those to whom madness is joy: they laugh, play, dance day and night, even publicly on the agora, and they walk around with wreaths as if [they] were victors coming from a contest; and their relatives receive no damage from this form of madness" (*The Symptoms and Reasons for Chronic Illness* 1.6.4).³⁶

---

35 Here, Bacchic madness is related to the tragic death of Scyles, king of the Scythians (*The Persian Wars* 4:78–80). When Scyles was eager to be initiated into the Dionysiac mysteries in the city of the Borysthenites, Zeus destroyed the house to deter his initiation (was the supreme god himself not in favor of the Dionysiac mysteries?)—despite this, Scyles completed his initiation. To the Scythians, who hated Dionysiac initiation, the Borysthenites' report that the king of the Scythians became a Bacchant was an affront. The passage reads: "Now the Scythians make this Bacchic revelling a reproach against the Greeks, saying that it is not reasonable to set up a god who leads men on to madness (ὅστις μαίνεσθαι ἐνάγει ἀνθρώπους). So when Scyles had been initiated into the Bacchic rite, some one of the Borysthenites scoffed at the Scythians: 'Why,' said he, 'you Scythians mock us for revelling and being possessed by the god; but now this deity has taken possession of your own king, so that he is revelling and is maddened by the god (βακχεύει τε καὶ ὑπὸ τοῦ θεοῦ μαίνεται). If you will not believe me, follow me now and I will show him to you.' The chief men among the Scythians followed him, and the Borysthenite brought them up secretly and set them on a tower; whence presently, when Scyles passed by with his company of worshippers, they saw him among the revellers; whereat being greatly moved, they left the city and told the whole army what they had seen" (*The Persian Wars* 4.79). Because of this, Scyles had to flee to Thrace, and he was eventually handed over to the Scythians and executed by them.

36 Translation by Graf, "The Blessings of Madness," 175.

Participation in the Dionysiac ritual also promises freedom from life's concerns. The Chorus sings from *Bacchae* 378 onwards, "These are his powers, to blend us, by dance, with the worshipful band, to laugh to the sound of piping, and to vanquish care [ἀποπαῦσαί τε μερίμνας], when to the sacred meal comes the gleam of the grape …" In the following lines, Dionysus's granting of the "painless joy of wine" is promised "equally both to the rich and to the lowly" (*Bacchae* 421–423). The marvelous scene in which the Bacchic women are automatically (αὐτόματα) released from chains and freely rushed toward "the mountain glades, calling on the god Bromios [=Dionysus]" (*Bacchae* 444–450) may also be symbolic of the freedom that people usually associated with this god. Similarly, a line from Demosthenes's oration 18 (*On the Crown* 259) contains part of an interesting Bacchic hymn: "Here I leave my sins behind, Here the better way I find (ἔφυγον κακόν, εὗρον ἄμεινον; or, literally: I have fled from what's bad, I have found what's better)." Perhaps, this joyful hymn indicates the initiates' released state from what is κακόν both in the present and future (i.e., the afterlife).[37] According to Pausanias's report (1.20.3), the image of Dionysus in Athens is named "Liberator" (Ἐλευθερεύς).

The religious experience of ecstasy and liberation related to Dionysus is not just collective. Of course, ecstasy and participation in the Dionysiac mysteries could have provided a collective occasion to cope with social norms unfavorable to certain groups of people.[38] Bremmer notes that the Dionysiac "cures" (particularly, related to maenadism) might be better considered "a collective trance," rather than "an individual treatment."[39] Yet, it is possible to find individual aspects of healing and the ecstatic experience of liberation. Graf points out that ancient evidence does not associate the ecstatic healing of Bacchic rituals to "an institutionalized setting."[40] Rather, according to Graf, private rituals performed by "itinerant specialists" provided curative experiences.[41] If so, certain individuals could have experienced Bacchic ecstasy and the curative effects of Dionysiac madness with or without "a collective trance" in a Dionysiac group. Indeed, literary evidence suggests that individual devotees' *enthusiastic* (i.e., inspired and possessed by the indwelling deity; cf. ἐνθουσιάζειν) experience was one of the prominent benefits promised by Dionysiac initiation. A good example of this is found in Teiresias's words in *Bacchae* 298–301:

---

37 Bøgh, "In Life and Death," 37.
38 Ross S. Kraemer, "Ecstasy and Possession: The Attraction of Women to the Cult of Dionysus," *HTR* 72 (1979): 55–80.
39 Jan N. Bremmer, "Greek Maenadism Reconsidered," *ZPE* 55 (1984): 284.
40 Graf, "The Blessings of Madness," 177.
41 Graf, "The Blessings of Madness," 178.

> The god [Dionysus] is also a prophet (μάντις): for the ecstatic (τὸ βακχεύσιμον; or, "the Bacchic state") and the manic (τὸ μανιῶδες) have mantic powers in large measure. When the god enters someone in force (ὅταν γὰρ ὁ θεὸς ἐς τὸ σῶμ' ἔλθῃ πολύς), he causes him in madness to predict the future (λέγειν τὸ μέλλον τοὺς μεμηνότας ποιεῖ).

According to this description, which is part of Teiresias's response to Pentheus's devaluation of Dionysus, Dionysus is portrayed as a god who enters (the verb ἔρχομαι) into someone's body (ἐς τὸ σῶμα), bringing with him a state of madness, thereby causing them to speak of what is to come (λέγειν τὸ μέλλον). It is a manic and mantic spirit that possesses and empowers the person. Similarly, Sophocles's *Antigone* (963–964) uses ἔνθεος when describing the women of the Dionysiac cult: παύεσκε μὲν γὰρ ἐνθέους γυναῖκας εὐιόν τε πῦρ ("for he tried to check the inspired women [=lit. 'god-dwelling women'] and the Bacchic fire").[42] These are poetic, dramatic representations, and this "mythological maenadism" might not reflect actual rituals.[43] Yet, as Versnel correctly points out, "[M]yth and ritual are nowhere as intricately interwoven as in Dionysiac religion."[44] In short, it is possible to say that one's participation in the Dionysiac initiation connects the deity and the devotee physically (the deity "entering" into the initiate), which means a union is created. Dionysus becomes a type of indwelling god/spirit, and this intimate god impacts not only Dionysiac groups, but also individual Bacchants.

3.1.4 Deliverance in the Future

The second type of λύσις that Dionysus brings is related to the afterlife, and this aspect is well substantiated by material witnesses from a wide geographic and temporal range; eschatological hope is one of the benefits consistently attested.[45]

---

[42] Yet, note Santamaría's comment that "ἔνθεος and ἐνθουσιάζειν do not appear in the *Bacchae*." Santamaría, "The Term βάκχος and Dionysos Βάκχιος," 49, n. 71. However, passages in *Bacchae*, such as one cited above, include expressions (e.g., ἔρχομαι and ἐς τὸ σῶμα) that are close enough to the notion of ἔνθεος and ἐνθουσιάζειν, etc.
[43] This is A. Rapp's view (1872), according to H. S. Versnel, *Ter Unus: Isis, Dionysos, Hermes: Three Studies in Henotheism* (Leiden: Brill, 1990), 135.
[44] Versnel, *Ter Unus*, 137.
[45] One might oppose my use of eschatology/eschatological in relation to the individual afterlife without reference to an "end time scenario." I admit that I use the term eschatology/eschatological in a broad sense. Ancient historians who discuss the issue of afterlife also employ the term eschatology. For example, Theodora Suk Fong Jim, "'Salvation' (*Soteria*) and Ancient Mystery Cults," *ARG* 18–19 (2017): 255–82. See also the use of the term in Graf and Johnston, *Ritual Texts for the Afterlife*.

Iconographic evidence, such as the Apulian vases from Southern Italy, also supports the overall impression that one of the primary benefits Dionysus promises his initiates is a blessed afterlife.⁴⁶ The hope for a blessed afterlife as a result of one's initiation also appears in inscriptions (for example, CIL 3.686 = CLE 1233, from Philippi, third century CE).

> While we are tormented by our grief, you live, restored to life in Elysium ... Whether, according to Fate, in the flowery meadow, among the assembly of the Satyrs, the initiates marked [i.e., tattooed] for Bacchus demand you for themselves, or the basket-bearing nymphs equally demand you to lead their festal ranks with torches preceding, be now anything your age has brought you.⁴⁷

The band of Bacchic initiates and the flowery meadow in this third-century inscription resonate with the Underworld scene in the Classical Athenian drama, Aristophanes's *Frogs*.⁴⁸ This inscription clearly presents hope for the deceased boy, who was presumably an initiate, while acknowledging the grief of those left behind.⁴⁹

Yet, the most significant evidence that Dionysiac initiation communicates hope for a blessed afterlife can be found in the "Orphic" gold tablets, which were possibly used as a "ritual script" in the setting for oral performance.⁵⁰ These tablets indicate Dionysiac initiation would effectively lead the initiates into a blessed afterlife, although it is impossible to construct "a single, complete, and coherent eschatological system" out of these fragmentary sources.⁵¹ The "mnemonic tablets" contain instructions (including a passcode) for how the deceased (who have already been initiated presumably; e.g., μύσται καὶ βάχχοι in GJ 1; ὁ μύστης in GJ 27) should act and what they should say to the "stern guardians or Persephone" in the Underworld.⁵² The deceased are supposed to say, for example, "I am a child of Earth and starry Sky, but my race is heavenly ... I am parched with thirst and am dying; but

---

46 Paloma Cabrera, "The Gifts of Dionysos," in *Redefining Dionysos*, 488–503.
47 Graf and Johnston, *Ritual Texts for the Afterlife*, 164.
48 E. Courtney, *Musa Lapidaria: A Selection of Latin Verse Inscriptions* (Atlanta: Scholars Press, 1995), 385–86.
49 Graf and Johnston, *Ritual Texts for the Afterlife*, 164.
50 For example, Graf regards short passages that deviate from hexameter (e.g., line 5 in GJ 3) as "ritual acclamations inserted into a hexametrical frame" (all the gold tablets are written in hexameter). Graf and Johnston, *Ritual Texts for the Afterlife*, 137. Translations of the gold tablets in the present work are from Graf and Johnston.
51 Graf and Johnston, *Ritual Texts for the Afterlife*, 96. These are mainly "mnemonic devices" comparable to "a grocery list," which does not give a full narrative. Moreover, the expensive cost of the tablet material (gold) only allows for short texts. Graf and Johnston, *Ritual Texts for the Afterlife*, 95.
52 Graf and Johnston, *Ritual Texts for the Afterlife*, 157.

quickly grant me cold water flowing from the Lake of Memory" (GJ 2; and see variations in GJ 1, 8, 10, 11, 12, 13, 14, 16, 18, 25, 29), or "the Bacchic One himself released (ἔλυσε) [me]" (GJ 26a, b). As for the former ("I am a child of Earth and starry Sky ..."), it can be understood as evoking the origin of the gods themselves (Hesiod, *Theogony* 106: "[the gods] who were born from Earth and starry Sky") as well as evoking human origin (Hesiod, *Works and Days* 108); thus, the initiates can establish "the familial relationship" between themselves and gods/heroes.[53] The latter ("Tell Persephone that the Bacchic One himself released you"), however, highlights the motif of λύσις more. Also interesting are the "proxy tablets," which contain relatively short descriptions about the deceased person.[54] In this case, the deceased are not supposed to say the words of the tablets but rather "Persephone or her deputy was to read these labels and consult a list of initiates to see whether the name appeared there."[55] There is even a table from a Hellenistic cist-grave in Aigion (GJ 20 = OF 496e) on which only one word is inscribed: Μύστης. Johnston notes, "[This Aigion Tablet] must have functioned like a theater ticket."[56] Inscriptions on both types of tablets (mnemonic or proxy) clearly show a blessed afterlife was among the messages communicated by Dionysiac initiation.

This Dionysiac afterlife is also communal. The tablets envision that the initiates will form Dionysiac cultic groups (θίασοι) in the hereafter, as they did on earth. In the Pherae Tablet 2 (GJ 28 = OF 493a; late fourth to early third century BCE), line 1, reads: "Send me to the *thiasoi* of the initiates (πέμπε με πρὸς μυστῶ<ν> θιάσους); I possess the tokens (ἔχω ὄργια)."[57] Also, the Pelinna Tablet a (GJ 26a = OF 485; late fourth century BCE) reads: "And below the earth there are ready for you the same offices/rites (τέλεα) as for the other blessed ones" (cf. Pherae Tablet 2, line 2: τε<τέ>λη). Those who carefully and successfully follow this afterlife instruction will join the procession of Bacchic initiates in the Underworld, probably in a similar way to when they were alive. The Hipponion Tablet (GJ 1 = OF 474) finishes with these lines: "And you, too, having drunk, will go along the sacred road on which other glorious initiates and *bacchoi* (μύσται καὶ βάχχοι) travel,"[58] which resonates with the afterlife picture of the Eleusinian initiates por-

---

53 Graf and Johnston, *Ritual Texts for the Afterlife*, 114.
54 Graf and Johnston, *Ritual Texts for the Afterlife*, 134–36.
55 Graf and Johnston, *Ritual Texts for the Afterlife*, 135.
56 Graf and Johnston, *Ritual Texts for the Afterlife*, 135.
57 The last part of this line is missing, and it is difficult to reconstruct. See Graf and Johnston, *Ritual Texts for the Afterlife*, 205–207.
58 Are μύσται and βάχχοι different groups? It seems there are no major differences for the deceased, who follow the instruction and are promised glorious procession. Perhaps, in this instance, these terms are a hendiadys.

trayed in Aristophanes' *Frogs*, who are marching and crying out, "Iacchus" (a deity that can be equated with Bacchus).

Epigraphic evidence suggests that the deceased initiates will be participating in similar ritual activities to those living on earth, and this tradition appears to continue into the Roman Principate. A second-century CE funerary epigram from Rome (Jaccottet #180), dedicated (probably by her father) to a young girl named Julia, reads: "Dionysus Bacchus led me [i.e., Julia] into his *thiasoi* [pl.] to dance, like a commander of his *speira*" (Διόνυσος ὁ Βάκχιος ἐν θιά<σ>οισιν [ἤγ] ἤτειραν ἐμὲ σπείρης ἐ[ν]έβησσε [χ]ορεύειν). As Jaccottet comments, this conception of the afterlife was "quite common" (très courante) and it does not necessarily refer to any "particular mystical teaching" (un enseignement mystique particulier).[59] Yet, it is still important to note that Dionysus and the technical term for his groups (θίασοι) appear here to be associated with this type of afterlife vision, and the deceased participate in the same ritual as she would do on earth—i.e., dancing with fellow initiates. The role and significance of Dionysus for the individual's afterlife will be revisited in detail in the next section discussing the canonical messages of Dionysiac initiation. For now, suffice it to say that Dionysiac initiation communicates and indicates benefits for the afterlife, despite the fact that this aspect is not expressed by the language of *salvation* (σωτηρία, σώζειν, *salus*, etc.).[60]

So far I have explored the self-referential messages that Dionysiac initiation would communicate. Canonical messages are also communicated by the ritual, and, at the same time, sustain the efficacy of the self-referential messages. These will be examined next.

---

59 Jaccottet, *Choisir Dionysos*, 2:293.
60 Theodora Jim correctly points out that the afterlife benefits in the Dionysiac mysteries are not linguistically connected to the terms that are often translated as salvation (see her "'Salvation' (*Soteria*) and Ancient Mystery Cults," 261–66). However, a biblical scholar (e.g., James Barr, *The Semantics of Biblical Language* [London: Oxford University Press, 1961]) would say that words and concepts are not the same. The notion of salvation may not be limited to a few etymologically related words (σωτηρία, σώζειν, *salus*), but it can be constructed and conveyed by combinations of many other words and phrases.

3.2 The Canonical Messages, or the Grounds for the Efficacy of the Initiation's Promises

3.2.1 Dionysus Established the Initiation Ritual

The message that the deity himself established and commanded initiation is a canonical message supporting the efficacy of the self-referential benefits. This etiological aspect is clearly found with the Eleusinian mysteries: the goddess Demeter "went to the kings ... and revealed the conduct of her rites and taught her Mysteries to all of them, holy rites that are not to be transgressed, nor pried into, nor divulged" (Homeric Hymn to Demeter 473–79).[61] "The Great Commission" that includes Jesus's command to baptize (Matt 28:16–20) can be similarly understood as communicating the canonical message that the initiation ritual was instituted by the deity, although there is no emphasis on secrecy in this Matthean passage. Then, what about the mysteries of Dionysus?

Like other deities in antiquity, Dionysus was also thought to be a god of epiphany (e.g., Homeric Hymn to Dionysus 53–57).[62] Sometimes this epiphany is accompanied by the notion that Dionysus himself established his mysteries. In Euripides's *Bacchae*, Dionysus is portrayed as a god who reveals himself to people in various forms, including a human disguise (*Bacchae* 1–5, 53–54). He jealously claims the rights of a god. In *Bacchae* 43–50 (cf. Homer, *Il.* 6.138–40), complaining that Pentheus, Cadmus's son, "[excluded Dionysus] from libations and [made] no mention of [him] in prayer," Dionysus declares, "I will demonstrate (ἐνδείξομαι) to him and to all the Thebans that I am a god. And when I have set all here to rights, I shall journey to another land and show myself (δεικνὺς ἐμαυτόν) there." Within this opening speech, Dionysus recounts that he has returned to Greece, after "having set everything in Asia a-dancing and having established my rites [or, "mysteries"] (καταστήσας ἐμὰς τελετάς) so that my divinity (δαίμων) may be made manifest to mortals" (*Bacchae* 20–23). In stating that he was spreading his mysteries in Asia (indicated by τἀκεῖ[63]), he provides his native people, the Thebans, the reason for his late arrival.[64] One interesting variation of the etiolog-

---

[61] This translation is from Helene P. Foley, ed., *The Homeric Hymn to Demeter: Translation, Commentary, and Interpretative Essays* (Princeton: Princeton University Press), 26.
[62] See also Jáuregui, "Trust the God," 30–31.
[63] The word "Asia" does not appear in that sentence. Thus, τἀκεῖ (21) could perhaps include other regions mentioned in lines 13–19, too.
[64] E. R. Dodds, *Euripides. Bacchae* (Oxford: Clarendon Press, 1960), 65. Dodds refutes another possible translation: "I came to this city first in Greece." He argues that the adverb "first" (πρῶτον)

ical story of Dionysiac initiation is the mid-second-century CE inscription from Magnesia on the Maeander (west coast of Asia Minor) (SEG 17, no. 495 = Jaccottet #146 = AHK 202). This inscription relates an event from the remote past (i.e., the fourth or third century BCE) about how the Dionysiac associations and rituals were first established in Magnesia by following a Delphic oracle.[65] Yet, this version of the cult founding is, strictly speaking, not about Dionysus himself commanding or establishing the initiation rituals. Rather, it is the Delphic oracle that commands the foundation of the cult, when "an image of Dionysos was discovered in a plane tree" in Magnesia.

Thus, apart from the few literary sources mentioned above (Homeric Hymn to Dionysus and *Bacchae*), I would conclude, there are not many resources that emphasize Dionysus's establishment of initiation as the grounds for its efficacy. This could prompt one to ask, what alternative canonical messages could there be?

3.2.2 Dionysus Suffers and Overcomes

Another possible canonical message is that Dionysus's suffering and overcoming are somehow "meritorious" for his initiates. There are both literary and iconographic traditions about Dionysus's own madness and cure through purification/initiation. This archetypal portrayal provided assurance for those who participated in the mysteries of Dionysus and expected deliverance as the benefit of their initiation. This particular connection does not necessarily mean some "identification" between Dionysus and his initiates (although this will be discussed). The emphasis is more on the value of the story of Dionysus as an exemplar with regard to the efficacy of initiation and the power of Dionysus.

Some earlier mythic tradition may have contained Dionysus's death and resuscitation (e.g., the myth of Dionysus Zagreus). The essence of the story is that Dionysus was murdered by Titans and his limbs were torn apart and eaten, but he was "resurrected."[66] The so-called Eudemian Theogony is not extant but the narrative about Dionysus's dismemberment is reconstructed through various fragmen-

---

should be rendered together with the participles in line 20: thus, "I came to this city of Greeks *first when* (i.e., only when) I had set Asia dancing . . ."

[65] The story in the inscription is comparable to other stories of the cult foundation and/or transfer—for example, the foundation of the cult of Sarapis in Alexandria in the early third century BCE (Tacitus, *Histories* 4.83). See also Betz, "Transferring a Ritual," 90–91.

[66] M. L. West, *The Orphic Poems* (Oxford: Oxford University Press, 1983), 140–75.

tary sources.[67] It seems unlikely that every individual who participated in the Dionysiac ritual at various times and places consciously learned or even confessed a single, coherent Zagreus myth.[68] Likewise, it is hard to retain any longer the old assumption that behind this Zagreus myth there was "a unified 'Orphic' church, an almost Christian religion with dogma based on a central myth—specifically, salvation from original sin through the death and resurrection of the suffering god," a notion that Edmonds convincingly challenges.[69] Yet, mythic elements regarding Zagreus could contribute to various traditions (including rituals) associated with Dionysus from as early as the fifth century BCE (Euripides, *Cretans*, fr. 472).[70] Also, if one slightly expands the motif of Dionysus's death, one can see that Dionysus as one who courageously faces the political authority's threat of punishment and death was vividly portrayed in Euripides's *Bacchae*. This expanded motif influences much later appropriations of *Bacchae* and/or Dionysus, as shown by the Roman author Horace's *Epistles* 1.16 and Origen's *Contra Celsum* 2.33–35.[71] In the second

---

[67] See the helpful table in Anthi Chrysanthou, *Defining Orphism: The Beliefs, the Teletae and the Writings* (Berlin: Walter de Gruyter, 2020), 85–88. The table includes each portion of the narrative, the ancient primary sources that includes each narrative, and the date of these sources.

[68] I agree with Radcliffe Edmonds's critique of the long-lasting scholarly view that assumed a single, coherent Zagreus myth. Edmonds, *Redefining Ancient Orphism*, 297. He argues against the scholarly convention that "weave[d] together four strands [="the dismemberment of Dionysos Zagreus by the Titans, the punishment of the Titans by Zeus, the generation of human beings from the ashes of the lightning-blasted Titans, and the burden of guilt that human beings inherited from their Titanic ancestors because of this original sin"] into this central mythic narrative [="the Zagreus myth"]."

[69] Radcliffe Edmonds, "Tearing Apart the Zagreus Myth: A Few Disparaging Remarks on Orphism and Original Sin," *Classical Antiquity* 18 (1999): 36. Edmonds calls the Zagreus Myth a "modern fabrication."

[70] This fragment does not relate the Zagreus myth in detail. Yet, it has significance as the earliest source that identifies Zagreus with Dionysus and its relation to the ritual context. On this fragment, Chrysanthou comments,

> This passage has a clear ritual context and the fact that Zagreus is mentioned alongside deities of mystery cults implies that he was also associated with mysteries ... By becoming an initiate of Idaean Zeus, Zagreus and the Mountain Mother, the person has become a βάκχος. The importance of this passage, then, is that it allows for an identification of Zagreus with Dionysos and his association with Dionysiac rites from the 5th century B.C. (Chrysanthou, *Defining Orphism*, 89–90).

The myth of Dionysus's dismemberment by the Titans is attested later. For example, see Origen's use of that myth to refute Celsus (*Cels.* 3.23). Friesen, *Reading Dionysus*, 168.

[71] As for Horace, see Friesen, *Reading Dionysus*, 96–117. Friesen explores how Horace presents Dionysus as a Stoic sage in the context of competitive political propaganda in which the image of Dionysus was evoked and appropriated by various people. As for Origen's *Cels.* 2.33–35, see

century CE, Pausanias speaks of the Titans as "the authors of the god [Dionysus]'s sufferings (εἶναι τοὺς Τιτᾶνας τῷ Διονύσῳ τῶν παθημάτων ... αὐτουργούς)" (Pausanias 8.37.5), and the tradition is taken up by several Neoplatonic philosophers in late antiquity. In other words, the notion of Dionysus's own struggling (including his death or his death threats) is part of the well-known tradition of later generations, and not just for those who were directly familiar with the myth of Dionysus Zagreus. With the Dionysiac initiation rituals, one does not have to rely on the Orphic "original sin" interpretation. Nevertheless, Dionysus's suffering and overcoming permeate Dionysiac tradition,[72] and it is possible that the initiates were reminded of the story of Dionysus as part of their initiation.

A variety of evidence from the Classical period to the Roman imperial age depicts Dionysus suffering, specifically from madness, and recovering through an initiation ritual (in these cases, Dionysus was not the one who established initiation, but the first beneficiary of initiation—cf. Jesus in the canonical Gospels who was baptized [Mark 1:9–11 and parallel passages]). Thus, Bacchic madness and the cure that his initiates experience are part of Dionysus's own archetypal story. For example, in Apollodorus 3.5.1, Dionysus, who was driven mad by Hera (cf. Plato, *Laws* 672B), was "purified (καθαρθείς) by Rhea and learned the rites of initiation (τὰς τελετὰς ἐκμαθών)." A relief from Cos (circa. 150 BCE) matches this literary tradition; Burkert interprets this iconography as Dionysus being "purified by Meter in the Cybela mountains and [receiving] his mysteries."[73] Thus, Burkert, drawing on the dual nature of Dionysus Βάκχειος (one who maddens people) and Dionysus Λύσιος (one who cures) (cf. Pausanias 2.2.6 and 2.7.6), suggests,

> The god experienced the suffering and salvation that his adherents are going to experience themselves in the course of their "cures." *Mania* is affliction and a means of healing, is revenge or blessing or both; the outcome is purification, "feeling better now," through the acceptance of a rite of initiation (*teletē*).[74]

Reading Dionysus, 161–64. In that section, Origen selectively reports Celsus's argument, featuring *Bacchae*. Celsus (Origen's interlocutor) tends to interpret allegorically the deity's suffering in Greek mythology.
72 Here, one could add the iconographic tradition of Dionysus as the victor, which is most evident in the Roman imperial period. Dionysus's career as the conqueror of India (this tradition itself goes back to the fourth century BCE) became a very popular theme in the Roman empire, and is often portrayed with him riding on a chariot. Katherine Dunbabin, "The Triumph of Dionysus on Mosaics in North Africa," *Papers of the British School at Rome* 39 (1971): 52–65.
73 Burkert, "Bacchic *Teletai*," 272.
74 Burkert, "Bacchic *Teletai*," 273.

That Dionysus experienced the same hardship as his initiates builds a strong, intimate, and personal connection between the deity and the devotees. This aspect leads to the next section: Dionysus is a deity who constantly returns and revisits his devotees.

3.2.3 Dionysus Returns

In addition to Dionysus's suffering and overcoming, there is another ancient tradition, which is traceable to classical Athens, about the ritual expectation of Dionysus's "return" or "arrival." This is not to say that one could build a linear story that begins from his suffering, leads to his death, and culminates in his returning to life (like Christ's passion, death, and resurrection). The point here is that Dionysus's presence and promise to return may also underlie the initiation ritual and support its efficacy. Walter Otto titled the fifth chapter of his 1948 book *Dionysos. Mythos und Kultus* (ET: 1965) "The God Who Comes."[75] He notes, "These [cult] forms present him as the god who comes, the god of epiphany ... He had disappeared, and now he will suddenly be here again."[76] Indeed, *Bacchae* begins with the memorable line about this deity's arrival in Thebes after his long journey outside Greece: the Greek verb Ἥκω ("I have come") comes first (Ἥκω Διὸς παῖς τήνδε Θηβαίαν χθόνα Διόνυσος, "To this land of Thebes I have come, I Dionysus, son of Zeus"). The entire story of *Bacchae* depicts a group of people who welcome and accept this god's return versus another group of people who reject his arrival. Though a dramatic representation, it testifies to this particular aspect of Dionysus.

Material evidence suggests that in the Classical period, the returning/arrival of Dionysus primarily had to do with the wider polis, but it also had individual implications (i.e., his personal intimacy to the devotees and benefits for them).[77] Isler-Kerényi examines three types of images depicting Dionysus with chairs that were found on cups, kraters, choes, and other items from classical Athens, especially in the fifth century BCE. One type of iconography contains a figure of a satyr

---

75 Walter F. Otto, *Dionysus: Myth and Cult*, trans. Robert B. Palmer (Bloomington: Indiana University Press, 1965). The German original, *Dionysos. Mythos und Kultus*, appeared in1948. See also Santamaría, "The Term βάκχος and Dionysos Βάκχιος," 48.
76 Otto, *Dionysus*, 79
77 Note that Anthesteria, a major Athenian civic festival in honor of Dionysus, involved rituals for dead individuals' better afterlife. Sarah Iles Johnston, *Restless Dead: Encounters Between the Living and the Dead in Ancient Greece* (Berkeley: University of California Press, 1999), 63–71. The images discussed in this section (Figures 1–3) are associated with Anthesteria.

carrying a chair (or stool), going before or after Dionysus (Figure 1).⁷⁸ Another type is an image of an unoccupied chair, usually large in size and adorned (Figure 2).⁷⁹ The third type of chair-images has Dionysus sitting on a chair, being greeted by women (Figure 3).⁸⁰

Figure 1: Pelike, art trade, side A (Sotheby's, London 1995, 36 Nr. 72); Isler-Kerényi, *Dionysos in Classical Athens*, 136. Reproduced by permission of Cornelia Isler-Kerényi.

According to Isler-Kerényi, these images were "used to evoke the arrival of the god [Dionysus] at the Anthesteria." She further suggests that the chair was not only "an element of the imagery," but also possibly "part of the actual ritual."⁸¹ The unoccupied chair (Figure 2) will soon be occupied by the coming deity. It should also be noted that these chair images appear only in domestic (rather than polis) rituals for Dionysus. Thus, Isler-Kerényi concludes:

---

78 Isler-Kerényi, *Dionysos in Classical Athens*, 136–42.
79 Isler-Kerényi, *Dionysos in Classical Athens*, 142–46.
80 Isler-Kerényi, *Dionysos in Classical Athens*, 146–52.
81 Isler-Kerényi, *Dionysos in Classical Athens*, 152.

Figure 2: Chous, Meidias Painter, New York, Metropolitan Museum of Art 75.2.11 (Richter 1936, pl. 158 a); Isler-Kerényi, *Dionysos in Classical Athens*, 144. Reproduced by permission of Cornelia Isler-Kerényi.

Figure 3: Calyx krater, Polygnotos group, Copenhagen, The National Museum of Denmark ABC 1021, side A (CVA Copenhagen 4, pl. 146 a-b); Isler-Kerényi, *Dionysos in Classical Athens*, 147. Reproduced by permission of Cornelia Isler-Kerényi.

We have to keep in mind that, of all the gods who are represented in vase painting as seated on an elegant klismos, only Dionysus has it carried before him; and only Dionysos has a chair prepared for him with cloths and gifts: no other god's arrival is expected. Only Dionysos' arrival is ritualized in this way: he is the only god who always returns to visit people's home.[82]

Her emphatic use of "only" shows the distinctive place Dionysus held in Athenians' symbolic and ritualized world, as a god who not only returns to the festival but also visits individual homes.

This tradition of Dionysus who returns seems long lasting; there is some evidence of its existence hundreds of years later. For example, a second-century CE Athenian inscription (Syll.³ 3.1109) stipulates that the priest should "set before the meeting the drink-offering for the return of Bacchos (τὴν τῶν καταγωγίων σπονδήν)." It is that association's ritual that envisions Dionysus as the returning one. The verbal form (κατάγειν) is also attested in *Bacchae* 84–85 (Βρόμιον παῖδα θεὸν θεοῦ Διόνυσον κατάγουσαι, "Bring [back] the roaring son of a god, Dionysus"). The precise title "Dionysus Katagogios" appears in a contract of sale for the priesthood of Dionysus Phleos at Priene in the second century BCE.[83] Admittedly, the term καταγώγιος, as an epithet of Dionysus, is not frequently attested. The name, however, is obviously related to the more widely known festival, Katagogia, celebrating the return of Dionysus.[84]

Based on—but beyond—what has been discussed so far, there are now two more fundamental canonical messages regarding Dionysus, which sustain and guarantee the benefits of Dionysiac initiation promises. The first is that Dionysus is identified with his devotees and the other is, especially in the afterlife, Dionysus takes on the role of intercessor for his devotees.

3.2.4 Dionysus Is Identified with His Devotees

Previously, I have shown that Dionysus experienced suffering (madness and sometimes death), but overcame it through initiation, and that he was also thought to draw close to his devotees. Taking these in combination means he could be identified with his initiates (i.e., Dionysus is the *arche-initiate*, or conversely, the Bac-

---

82 Isler-Kerényi, *Dionysos in Classical Athens*, 152.
83 CGRN 176, l. x-x (http://cgrn.philo.ulg.ac.be/file/176/); J.-M. Carbon, S. Peels and V. Pirenne-Delforge, Collection of Greek Ritual Norms (CGRN), Liège 2015- (http://cgrn.ulg.ac.be, consulted in 2019).
84 According to the CGRN commentators, "the god (i.e. his image, in the form of a mask or a statue) was brought (back), possibly on a ship set up on a chariot, during a procession through the city. The ceremony is to be led by the priest of Dionysus Phleos, at the head of 'those bringing him back' (it is unclear whether these were members of a specific association or, more simply, the participants in the processional ceremony)." CGRN 176, l. x-x (http://cgrn.philo.ulg.ac.be/file/176/)

chants become like Bacchus). In short, a logic of metonymy is at work in the substructure of this ritual, and the efficacy of the benefits promised by Dionysiac initiation was partially supported by the underlying identification between the deity and the initiates. In some sense, therefore, this ritual transformation could be both the promise of initiation (self-referential messages; i.e., "the initiates become like Dionysus") as well as the grounds that guarantee other benefits given through initiation (canonical messages; i.e., "Dionysus as the arche-initiate will fulfill the promises given to his initiates"). Yet, the reason why it is discussed with the canonical messages is that emphasis is put on the deity's coming and becoming like one of his devotees, rather than on the initiates' becoming like Dionysus. As Santamaría demonstrates, the fact that "both the god and his worshippers are given the same name" (Βάκχος and βάκχοι) is because βάκχοι was originally the group name for the initiates and later extended to Dionysus himself as an epithet.[85] Thus, Βάκχος or Dionysus Βάκχιος, which became almost another proper name for Dionysus in the development of Dionysiac tradition, communicates the message that this deity is "(god) of the Bacchants, showing the god's proximity to and interest in his followers."[86] Although there is some imbalance (e.g., initiates were given the name Bacchus but never the name Dionysus),[87] one finds sufficient evidence, including iconographic one, which suggests that the initiates' identification with the deity was among the messages conveyed by Dionysiac initiation.

Children's initiation into the Dionysiac mysteries, an interesting phenomenon in itself, can further illuminate this point. These initiations potentially were modelled after Dionysus himself the archetypal initiate. Literary evidence for this is found in the later period. Himerius's orations from the fourth century CE include descriptions about babies initiated into the Dionysiac mysteries.[88] Epigraphic and iconographic evidence dates to earlier periods. For example, a second-century CE funerary epigram from Rome shows that young children could be initiated, probably according to their parents' will, into the Dionysiac mysteries in the hope of providing a better afterlife (Jaccottet #180). Other intriguing witnesses come from iconographic representations, such as a relief in Bologna (probably from the third century CE) that depicts a seated boy with a thyrsus,[89] and two Arretine cups (Augustan period) in which a baby is carried by the Silenus.[90] According to G.

---

85 Santamaría, "The Term βάκχος and Dionysos Βάκχιος," 38.
86 Santamaría, "The Term βάκχος and Dionysos Βάκχιος," 45.
87 San Cristóbal, "The Meaning of βάκχος and βακχεύειν in Orphism," 46.
88 Martin P. Nilsson, *The Dionysiac Mysteries of the Hellenistic and Roman Age* (New York: Arno Press, 1975), 106.
89 Nilsson, *The Dionysiac Mysteries*, 107.
90 Nilsson, *The Dionysiac Mysteries*, 93–95.

E. Rizzo, the baby (the initiate) represented in the cups is Dionysus himself, and for Rizzo, it explains one of his epithets, *Dionysus Mystes:* Dionysus the Initiate.[91] This emphasizes that Dionysus himself was an initiate—he had to become like his brothers and sisters in every respect.[92] In contrast, Nilsson interprets the baby in the cups as a human baby who was initiated, rather than Dionysus himself.[93] Yet, Nilsson also admits that "The child Dionysos may have been considered as a prototype of the human child initiate" in the complicated tradition history, in which later writers (e.g., Nonnus of Panopolis,[94] Himerius, etc.), who were already familiar with children's initiation, somehow conversely "embellished their description of Dionysos' childhood with new features."[95] If one moves outside the area of the initiation ritual per se, one could also find various iconographic representations of the child Dionysus, who was handed over to nymphs or Silenus by his father, Zeus. Examining fifth-century BCE images from cups, kraters, stamnoi, etc., Isler-Kerényi proposes an interpretation based on the social situation in Athens, especially regarding fathers who have children out of wedlock: "every Athenian father who acknowledged his son through a legitimization ritual could identify with Zeus,"[96] and she further notes, "There was no other god [than Dionysus] with whom young children could be identified."[97] Detailed interpretations based on iconography are contestable and remain suggestive, yet, it is clear that Dionysus occupied distinctive iconography featuring children's initiation both in the classical Greek period and in the Roman imperial period.

What about initiates who are not children? The "Orphic" gold tablets are worth considering in two ways. First, these tablets focus on the initiates' becoming like the deity, rather than the other way around. Second, this identification is thought to be fully realized and revealed in the afterlife. In the afterlife envisioned

---

91 Rizzo's view is mentioned in Nilsson, *The Dionysiac Mysteries*, 95, 110.
92 Here I deliberately echo the language of Heb 2:17. See also the Gospel accounts of Jesus's baptism (Mark 1:9–11 and parallel passages) in which the deity of the Christ cult is himself displayed as an initiate.
93 Nilsson, *The Dionysiac Mysteries*, 95.
94 According to Nonnus, the nurse Mystis taught Dionysus the Bacchic initiation (Graf, "The Blessings of Madness," 170) Yet, according to Apollodorus (also in the A scholia on *Iliad* VI; this tradition goes back to Eumelos), it was Rhea-Kybele who taught the initiation ritual to Dionysus (see Graf, "The Blessings of Madness," 172). Either way, this tradition could imply that the history of the Bacchic initiation is more ancient than the deity himself. In the Nonnus version, the baby Dionysus was initiated—if such tradition was also known to others earlier, this could make a good model for other babies/children initiated into the Dionysiac mysteries.
95 Nilsson, *The Dionysiac Mysteries*, 110.
96 Isler-Kerényi, *Dionysos in Classical Athens*, 111.
97 Isler-Kerényi, *Dionysos in Classical Athens*, 113.

on the tablets, the deceased would be asked questions, such as, "What [are you] seeking in the darkness of murky Hades?" (e.g., Hipponion, GJ 1 = OF 474), or "Who are you? Where are you from?" (τίς δ' εἶ ἤ πῶ δ' εἶ) (Rethymnon 2, GJ 18 = OF 484a; similarly, Eleutherna 1–5, GJ 10–14 = OF 478, 479, 480, 482, 483; Mylopotamos, GJ 16 = OF 481; Thessaly, GJ 29 = OF 484). The exemplary answers from the deceased person contain self-declarations, such as, "I am a child of Earth and starry Sky" (Γῆς παῖς εἰμι καὶ Οὐρανοῦ), and "my race is heavenly" (γένος οὐράνιον) (Petelia Tablet, GJ 2 = OF 476; similarly, Hipponion; Rethymonon 2; Eleuterna 1–5; Mylopotamos; Thessaly; also, Entella, GJ 8 = OF 475). This declaration implies that the deceased person is already a member of the "heavenly race," being "a child of Earth and starry Sky," before s/he died, presumably as a result of their initiation. The Petelia Tablet further notes that the person will "rule among the other heroes" (ἄ[λλοισι μεθ'] ἡρώεσσιν ἀνάξει[ς]; cf. Matt 19:28).

This, of course, does not state that the person is immediately equated with the deity through their participation in an initiation ritual—the context of the tablets is the afterlife. To be clear, the initiate who was buried was already a *bacchos*, i.e., one who "has lived like a *bacchos*." For example, a fifth-century BCE funerary inscription found in Kyme (southern Italy) includes this sentence: "Οὐ θέμις ἐντοῦθα κεῖσθαι ἰ (= εἰ) μὲ (= μὴ) τὸν βεβαχχευμένον ("Lying buried in this place is illicit unless one has become *bakchos* [i.e., has lived like a *bakchos*]")."[98] In the fourth century BCE Thurii Tablet 1 (GJ 3 = OF 487), the deceased person is supposed to hear a welcoming voice in the Underworld (it is unclear who says this): "Greetings, you who have suffered the painful thing; you have never endured this before. You have become a god instead of a mortal (θεὸς ἐγένου ἐξ ἀνθρώπου). A kid you fell into milk" (lines 3–4). Similarly, the Thurii Tablet 3 (GJ 5 = OF 488), a voice speaks to the deceased, "Happy and blessed, you will be a god instead of a mortal" (θεὸς δ' ἔσηι ἀντὶ βροτοῖο), followed by the deceased's own word, "A kid I fell into milk." The final line of the Rome Tablet (GJ 9 = OF 491) from the second or third century CE (which is later than the other tablets) suggests a similar deification of Caecilia, who is presumably the deceased: "Caecilia Secundina, come, by law grown to be divine" (νόμωι ἴθι δῖα γεγῶσα). These tablets suggest that the deceased's transformation, or deification, may have already begun on earth (by virtue of initiation), but it is nevertheless completed through death.

In addition to the gold tablets, iconographic witnesses, as exemplified by Apulian vases, also display the hope for a blessed afterlife where one becomes like Dionysus. That is, after their death, the Dionysiac initiates will be received by Dionysus, join the group of the blessed θίασος as an undifferentiated member (they will

---

[98] Text and translation are from Casadio, "Dionysus in Campania," 35–36.

all look the same), and ultimately "become a new Dionysus."[99] The afterlife scene appearing on an Apulian krater (fourth century BCE; Figure 4, Madrid) shows half-naked male figures (they look similar to each other) with Dionysian motifs, such as the thyrsus, and a dancing woman with a large tambourine.

Figure 4: Apulian bell-krater by the Truro Painter. © Archivo del Museo Aqueológico Nacional. Inv. 1999/99/124

Cabrera's interpretation is that in this scene, men "do not differentiate one from another [and] [t]he woman become[s] a new maenad or a divine bride."[100] With *theological* overtones, Cabrera concludes his survey of several vases, including the one above (Figure 4), saying,

> [The initiates'] destiny will be to enter in the divine entourage as βάκχοι, fully participating in the ecstatic commotion of the θίασος, in an eternal banquet in the Netherworld, achieve a blessed existence, a new joyful and full life, enter into Dionysian paradise, space for the final possession by the god, of self-dissolution to enter a radically new sphere of [existence] and fulfil [a] total and definitive union with the god.[101]

The blurring of identities between Dionysus and his initiates is more clearly detected on another interesting Apulian krater (Pulsano), which puts a twist on the typical Dionysiac "paradisal garden" scene. This Pulsano krater included in Trendall and Cambitoglou's book (Plate 213.5 [20/57a])[102] attracts our attention when compared to the more typical scene on a similar, more typical krater (Vienna, Plate 227.2 [20/299]).[103] The Vienna krater depicts the "Dionysian Eros," holding a situla, provides a larger flower to a seated woman as "a welcoming present and a gift" for the woman "who is going to celebrate her nuptials with the god."[104] Yet, the Pulsa-

---

99 Cabrera, "The Gifts of Dionysos," 493.
100 Cabrera, "The Gifts of Dionysos," 493.
101 Cabrera, "The Gifts of Dionysos," 501.
102 A. D. Trendall and A. Cambitoglou, *The Red-Figured Vases of Apulia, Volume II* (Oxford: Clarendon Press, 1982), Plate 213.5 (20/57a).
103 Trendall and Cambitoglou, *The Red-Figured Vases of Apulia, Volume II*, Plate 227.2 (20/299).
104 Cabrera, "The Gifts of Dionysos," 501.

no krater depicts the one who holds a situla and offers the flower in the form of Dionysiac μύστης—or, as Cabrera suggests, the man is perhaps Dionysus himself, and thus, a clear distinction between Dionysus and his μύστης (not only between his initiates) is not possible in these afterlife scenes.[105]

Both on the Madrid krater (Figure 4) and on the Pulsano krater, it is male initiates who may be identified with the deity (compare the case of Isis and the female devotees of Isis in the following chapter). Theoretically, it is still possible that in terms of symbolic, metonymical identification through ritual, the gender of the deity and that of the devotees would not have to be the same. In fact, Dionysus is the most flexible and fluid deity, having both male and female characteristics (cf. *Bacchae* 233–238; see, also, a second-century CE androgynous statue of Bacchus in the Louvre).[106] Yet, this gender fluidity is not reflected in the aforementioned Apulian kraters regarding the afterlife.

The ritual element of ecstasy may have offered a symbolic assimilation between the deity and female devotees, and this is experienced in the present, not the afterlife. An image of a maenad engraved on a red jasper (Figure 5; the third century BCE; Munich, SMM 2587) and another maenad image on a red-orange cornelian (Figure 6; the second century CE; Munich, SMM 537) portray the maenad's head thrown back with her eyes looking upward, probably in ecstasy (the first woman on a jasper is standing, while the woman on the cornelian appears to dance).[107] The same pose is found on another orange cornelian from the first century CE with the figure of Dionysus (Figure 7; Munich, SMM 2190). On this stone, the deity stoops slightly with his head thrown back and with his eyes looking upward, perhaps in ecstasy. A wine cup seems to slip from his left hand about to drop. Bernhard and Mechtild Overbeck note that this is "a pose that is normally typical of his followers rather than himself, as it is a sign of total abandonment and surrender to the cult."[108] In this distinctive artwork, Dionysus is envisioned as if he himself were an initiate of his cult, and it is female devotees who assume this posture in this ritualized ecstatic moment that the gems celebrate. In all these images on the stones, there is no particular sign that indicates it is the afterlife—they capture a characteristic moment of Dionysiac ritual and monumentalize it.

---

105 Cabrera, "The Gifts of Dionysos," 501.
106 The photo is found here: https://commons.wikimedia.org/wiki/File:Bacchus_in_Louvre.jpg. I also want to note that the androgynous iconography of some deities may be a cross-cultural phenomenon. Cf. the image of Guanyin Bodhisattva in Buddhism. This Bodhisattva has been depicted as either male or female, or sometimes in an ambiguous, gender-fluid form.
107 Bernhard Overbeck and Mechtild Overbeck, *Dionysus and His World: The Fascination of Precious Gems* (Athens: Hatzimichalis Estate, 2005), 76–77.
108 Overbeck and Overbeck, *Dionysus and His World*, 66.

Figure 5: SMM 2587. Reproduced with permission of Staatliche Münzsammlung München.

Figure 6: SMM 537. Reproduced with permission of Staatliche Münzsammlung München.

Figure 7: SMM 2190. Reproduced with permission of Staatliche Münzsammlung München.

In light of this evidence, I now return to the famous scene in *Bacchae*—the scene where the disguised Dionysus has a conversation with Pentheus.[109] This representation is evidence of certain beliefs among his devotees, that Dionysus has become an arche-initiate, like one of his siblings (cf. Heb 2:17), and he identifies himself with his initiates either in the earthly ritual or in the afterlife. In *Bacchae*, when Dionysus is dragged before the king, the king Pentheus (who does not know that he is Dionysus) asks Dionysus where he is from and where he learned the mystery rites of Dionysus ("What is the source of these rites [τελεταί] you bring to Greece?" *Bacchae* 465). Then, Dionysus answers, "Dionysus himself initiated me, Zeus's son (Διόνυσος αὐτός μ' εἰσέβησ', ὁ τοῦ Διός)" (466). When threatened with prison, Dionysus also declares, "Dionysus himself will free me when I so desire (ὅταν ἐγὼ θέλω)" (498)—note that he emphasizes that Dionysus will do so "when I so desire." Pentheus sarcastically retorts, and Dionysus continues, "Yes, even now he is near (πλησίον παρών) and sees what I am undergoing (lit. what I am experiencing/suffering [ἃ πάσχω])" (500). As Pentheus raises his voice, "Where is he?" then Dionysus claims, "He's with me (παρ' ἐμοί): since you are a godless man you do not see him" (502). Finally, the dialogue ends with Dionysus being led away to prison while saying: "You wrong me (lit. us; ἡμᾶς ... ἀδικῶν), but it's him [i.e., Dionysus] you're leading off to prison (κεῖνον ἐς δεσμοὺς ἄγεις)" (518).[110] Although this dialogue is a theatrical one, the contents might reflect a popular understanding of Dionysus and what kind of relationship exists between him and his initiates.[111] If Euripides's *Bacchae* played an important role in the subsequent history of tradition regarding Dionysus, as Friesen argues throughout his book *Reading Dionysus*, then it is possible for one to imagine that an individual in-

---

109 The dialogue scene interestingly resonates with some of the Johannine passages, as Dennis MacDonald argues in his *The Dionysian Gospel*, though I do not follow his source-critical and redaction-critical proposals.
110 Dodds comments on this verse by invoking a Jesus saying in Matthew: "Irony again: the words are literally true, but for the people on the stage they express the same religious truth as 'Inasmuch as ye have done it unto one of the least of these my brethren, ye have done it unto me.'" Dodds, *Euripides*, 142.
111 There is no mention that the initiates participate in the dying/suffering and resurrection of Dionysus; one must not look for the precise Christ story in the Dionysiac (or other mystery) tradition. Still, some interesting comparisons can be made, for example, between this story about Dionysus and Matt 25:31–46. Yet, these can also be understood in the topoi of the disguised deity and lack of recognition that are found broadly in ancient mythology, literature, and biblical traditions. As for some famous examples from Homer, Genesis, Tobit, and Ovid, etc., see Gregory E. Sterling, "Deities in Disguise: The Care of Strangers as a Criterion for Discipleship," in *Scripture and Social Justice: Catholic and Ecumenical Essays*, ed. Anathea E. Portier-Young and Gregory E. Sterling (Lanham: Lexington Books/Fortress Academic, 2018), 159–75 (esp. 164–69).

itiate would feel the presence/nearness of Dionysus in the midst of her/his suffering. This is because Dionysus is the archetypal initiate, has already experienced unfavorable events (e.g., the king being disrespectful to Dionysus and his rites), and has overcome them. The deity who is near me and like me guarantees the efficacy of initiation done by his name.

3.2.5 Dionysus Is the Intercessor in the Afterlife

Finally, the image of Dionysus as intercessor can be discussed in relation to his power that provides benefits for dead initiates.[112] Johnston and McNiven argue that an Apulian volute krater (dating to 330 BCE; now in the Toledo Museum) has Dionysus helping his dead devotees (Figure 8a and Figure 8b).[113] They call this krater "the first artistic illustration of soteriological doctrines alluded to in ancient Orphic sources." As they note, this depiction of Dionysus is rare on other Apulian funerary kraters.[114] For them, the most compelling evidence is that on one side of the krater (Figure 8a), Dionysus (standing on the left side of the *naiskos*) is portrayed as shaking hands with Hades (who is seated in the *naiskos*). While diverse interpretations are possible—most notably it could be a greeting marking Dionysus's arrival in or departure from the Underworld—Johnston and McNiven regard this handclasp as an agreement between two equally powerful deities.[115]

One may not agree with Johnston and McNiven's assessment that this Apulian krater reflects beliefs about Dionysus as intercessor in the Underworld. Two criticisms, in particular, can be mentioned as follows, but Johnston and McNiven's interpretation still looks more convincing than these criticisms. First, in a recent article, Karolina Sekita disagrees with Johnston and McNiven, arguing that the handshake represents the greeting between the two figures when Dionysus visited the realm of Hades for his mother Semele.[116] However, that Semele does not ap-

---

[112] Another example of an intercessory deity is the Mesopotamian goddess Lama who raises both hands at the height of her chest with the palms forward. https://www.metmuseum.org/art/collection/search/325092.
[113] Sarah Iles Johnston and Timothy J. McNiven, "Dionysos and the Underworld in Toledo," *MH* 53 (1996): 25–36; cf. Bremmer, *Initiation*, 76.
[114] Johnston and McNiven, "Dionysos and the Underworld," 25–26.
[115] Johnston and McNiven, "Dionysos and the Underworld," 29–30, 33–34.
[116] Karolina Sekita, "*Orphica non grata?* Underworld Palace Scenes on Apulian Red-Figure Pottery Revisited," in *Greek Art in Motion: Studies in Honor of Sir John Boardman on the Occasion of his 90th Birthday*, ed. Rui Morais et al. (Oxford: Archaeopress, 2019), 467.

Figure 8a and Figure 8b (both sides): Toledo Museum of Art. Object number: 1994.19. Reproduced with permission of the Toledo Museum of Art.

pear in the scene weakens Sekita's point.[117] Additionally, the other side of this Apulian krater (Figure 8b) has Dionysus himself (rather than Hades or Persephone) standing at the center of the funerary *naiskos*, surrounded by other Dionysiac devotees outside the *naiskos*. This suggests a particular afterlife expectation of the Dionysiac initiates (rather than representing Dionysus visiting Hades for Semele). Note that here Dionysus and his (male) devotees are almost indistinguishable, as in the afterlife scene in the aforementioned Apulian krater (Figure 4). Second, William Slater criticizes Johnston and McNiven, saying that "[Johnston and McNiven's claim] is an over-interpretation, and that the vase represents in an entirely Greek tradition another aspect of the theatrical 'Dionysiasm' that Richard Green has delineated for this period."[118] One should be cautious about "over-interpretation," as Slater warns, but I suspect that his view underestimates the evocative power of Dionysiac elements by limiting it to "the good life" in the here and now. Accordingly,

---

[117] One may vaguely infer her myth from the figure of Actaeon (who appears in the scene). Yet, this may cause a similar problem to what she criticizes regarding the "Orphic interpretation"—that is, imposing a particular myth onto the scene.

[118] William J. Slater, "Life as a Party: A Pindaric Look at Dionysus in the Underworld," *MA* 17 (2004): 223–29 (here, 224).

this Apulian volute krater can be seen as revealing a canonical message of Dionysiac initiation about the intercessory role of Dionysus in the Underworld.

This image of Dionysus in the krater as interpreted by Johnston and McNiven corresponds to the image of Dionysus in the Underworld that appears in the gold tablets.[119] It does not matter whether one should call both (the iconography on the Apulian krater and the texts in the gold tablets) "Orphic" or not; what seems important is that both imagine a similar scene in the underworld in which Dionysus does something before the chthonic deities on behalf of his initiates.[120] For example, the Pelinna Tablets (GJ 26 a, b = OF 485, 486), two ivy-shaped tablets from a woman's grave dated to the fourth century BCE, begin with these lines: "Now you have died and now you have come into being, O thrice happy one, on this same day. Tell Persephone that the Bacchic One himself released you (Β<ακ>χιος αὐτὸς ἔλυσε)." The deceased woman can have confidence even in front of Persephone because of what Dionysus has done for her. The ritual context related to this tablet could have been either a funeral or an initiation, as Graf notes.[121] Although Graf slightly prefers the funerary context, he points out that "the reference to 'this same day'" (the addressee experiences death and coming into being simultaneously) might be a reason to consider it an initiation, since a funeral takes place three days after death.[122] Yet, whether the ritual context of this tablet is strictly related to an initiation or to a funeral does not make much difference, because both rituals have the same mythic foundation, and it is likely that one who received a Dionysiac funeral had already undergone the Dionysiac initiation.

Perhaps the notion of forgiveness is implied by this triad—between Persephone, Dionysus, and the deceased person. The narrator of the Pelinna Tablets urges the deceased woman to tell Persephone, Queen of the Underworld, that she (the deceased) is a Bacchic initiate and that Dionysus has already "released" (ἔλυσε) her. Here, one can hear an echo of Euripides's *Bacchae*. Bacchic women who were incarcerated by Pentheus are miraculously released (*Bacchae* 443–450). Also, when Dionysus himself was threatened with prison by Pentheus (who does not recognize Dionysus), Dionysus said, "Dionysus himself will release

---

119 Bremmer, *Initiation*, 74–75.
120 As Johnston and McNiven note, "It might be objected that Dionysos clasps Hades' hand, not Persephone's, in the krater, as we would perhaps expect from the references to the goddess throughout the Orphic texts." Yet, they explain this difference "by the formality of the gesture" (i.e., the formality is needed between Hades and Dionysus, whereas it is not needed between Dionysus and Persephone, who is thought to be Dionysus's mother). Johnston and McNiven, "Dionysos and the Underworld," 33–34.
121 Fritz Graf, "Dionysian and Orphic Eschatology," in *Masks of Dionysus*, 247–50.
122 Graf, "Dionysian and Orphic Eschatology," 248.

(λύσει) me when I so desire" (*Bacchae* 498; my translation). In this story, it is obvious that their release is from imprisonment. Yet, what do the Pelinna Tablets mean? What has the person been released from? Based on other similar tablets from various regions, perhaps, it is from punishment (for unjust deeds while on earth) that the person has been released. For example, the Thurri Tablets 4 (GJ 6 = OF 492) and 5 (GJ 7 = OF 489) include this line: "I have paid (ἀνταπέτεισ') the penalty for unrighteous deeds (ἔργων ... δικαίων)." Also, the Pherae Tablet 1 (GJ 27 = OF 493), after introducing the σύμβολα for the deceased to know ("Man-and-child-thyrsus . . ." etc.), declares, "Enter the holy meadow, for the initiate is redeemed (ἄποινος γὰρ ὁ μύστης)." The last phrase (ἄποινος γὰρ ὁ μύστης) can also be translated thus: "for the initiate has entered a state without penalty." Some type of "forgiveness" of sins is envisioned, due to Dionysus's act of releasing. Thus, "proxy" tablets (i.e., the texts are expected to be read by Persephone or other chthonic authorities, not by the deceased person her/himself) often emphasize the pious status of the deceased person—perhaps by her/his devotion to the merciful Dionysus (GJ 30 = OF 496n; GJ 31 = OF 496b). Through initiation, a canonical message of assurance is communicated: Dionysus will help the deceased initiate get through Persephone's scrutiny in the Underworld.

Although the tablets thus far discussed are mostly from Classical or early Hellenistic periods, some other gold tablets suggest a continuation of this canonical message in much later periods. For example, a second or third-century CE tablet from Rome (GJ 9 = OF 491), following a general description, shows an illuminating dialogue between two anonymous figures. It is possible to interpret this tablet as a conversation between Dionysus and Persephone, in light of the traditions suggested above. The entire text of the Rome Tablet reads (trans. Graf and Johnston):

> Ἔρχεται ἐκ καθαρῶν καθαρά, | χθονίων βασίλεια
> Εὔκλεες Εὐβου|λεῦ τε, Διὸς τέκος, ἀλλὰ δέχε<σ>θε
> Μνημο|σύνης τόδε δῶρον ἀοίδιμον ἀνθρώποισιν.
> Καικιλία Σεκουνδεῖνα, νόμωι | ἴθι δῖα γεγῶσα.
>
> She comes pure from the pure, Queen of the Chthonian Ones.
> Eucles and Eubouleus, child of Zeus. "But accept
> this gift of Memory, sung of among mortals."
> "Caecilia Secundina, come, by law grown to be divine."

The first two lines consist of phrases that can be found in other earlier tablets. Yet, beginning from the end of the second line to the end of the fourth line, Graf and Johnston put two separate sets of quotation marks (which are not part of the original text), indicating that this is a conversation between two figures. This interpretative decision is reasonable. One could read the former ("But accept . . .") as an intercessory request on behalf of the deceased (or the mortal ones), and the latter

("Caecilia Secundina, come . . .") as a declaration by an authoritative figure. The former could be Dionysus (in the text, "child of Zeus" refers to Dionysus).[123]

3.3 Beyond Initiation

After this examination of the Dionysiac initiation ritual, two questions remain. The first one is whether one's participation in Dionysiac initiation is sufficient for obtaining the benefits promised by the ritual. This question might seem strange after the discussion about canonical messages being the underlying grounds for the efficacy of benefits that initiation promises. Yet, these underlying, canonical messages are mainly related to who this deity is, what he does (has done), and how this deity encounters his initiates. The current question focuses on human agency and responsibility, and I seek to address this issue because in previous studies, scholars have assumed that the mystery cults remained "magical sacramentalism," often labelled with phrases like *ex opere operato*, whereas they have claimed that Paul's notion of baptism emphasized the participants' faith. The first question of this section ("Is initiation alone sufficient?") is, therefore, an attempt to investigate whether this contrasting depiction is accurate. The second question is, how does Dionysiac initiation envision religious virtuosity? As mentioned in Chapter 2, religious virtuosity can be understood both at the level of the self-referential and the canonical messages. The two questions in this section will further help one compare the Dionysiac mysteries, the mysteries of Isis, and Pauline baptism, articulating each ritual's distinctive characteristics as well as commonalities.

3.3.1 Is Initiation Alone Sufficient?

Despite some restraints that are characteristic of his time, Alfred Loisy's remarks on the mysteries cited below (the term *gallus* suggests that he is referring to the mysteries of the Great Mother) are still instructive. The passage shows the possibil-

---

[123] Perhaps, the notion of Dionysus as a meditator or intercessor is also associated with the view that Dionysus is a deity that overcomes binary oppositions, as Aelius Aristides's hymns show. For these hymns, see Robert Parker, "Religion in the Prose Hymns," in *In Praise of Asclepius: Aelius Aristides, Selected Prose Hymns*, ed. Donald A. Russell et al. (Tübingen: Mohr Siebeck, 2016), 81. This god is so versatile and multifaceted that, when asked by Pentheus, "The god—what did he look like?" Dionysus answers, "He looked as he wished to look" (*Bacchae* 477–478). Even Dionysus was once pejoratively called the "effeminate stranger" (τὸν θηλύμορφον ξένον, lit. "stranger having a women-like form") who deceives women (*Bacchae* 353).

ity that one can speak of the relationship between initiates' participation in ritual and the cognitive aspects of this participation (i.e., their convictions and/or understanding of the ritual).

> The absolute distinction [Paul] draws between faith and the Law, which is works and rites, mainly had a polemical value ... Faith and works or rites are not mutually exclusive, because it's faith which makes up the merit of works and the power of rites. The mutilation of the gallus doesn't save him independently of the faith which has provoked this mutilation. And the mosaic rites are only incompatible with the Christian faith because they express another faith. (Loisy's letter to Cumont, December 26, 1915)[124]

To be clear, one cannot prove the singular, linear process: i.e., a would-be initiate of any mysteries had "faith" in the deity before her or his initiation, then it "provoked" her or him to be initiated, and the initiation ritual itself cannot "save" the initiate without that faith—unless one imports the whole array of Christian theological presuppositions. However, as Rappaport's theory suggests, ritual participation publicizes the fact that the participant accepts the canonical order underlying the ritual. Although this public acceptance is not the same as faith (in the sense of creedal faith in later Christian theology), participants of initiation ritual come to the ritual with some expectations about the benefits it promises.

It matters whether the initiate or would-be initiate properly understands the promises of the ritual, or the "true" nature of the ritual. Some evidence pertaining to Dionysiac initiation reveals that concern. Admittedly, this question is deeply rhetorical, and therefore, includes power dynamics and boundary-markings. As a fragmentary saying goes, "For there are many that carry the thyrsus, but few are the Bacchi" (πολλοὶ μὲν ναρθηκοφόροι, παῦροι δέ τε βάκχοι, OF 576).[125] One may hear echoes of the Gospels (e.g., Matt 22:14; cf. Luke 14:7), or the other way around. Some among the Orphic groups in the Classical period seem to have regarded true understanding as necessary for obtaining what is promised.

In the Derveni Papyrus, which is associated with the Dionysiac mysteries, one finds a polemic against some fraudulent ritual practitioners from whom initiates cannot learn proper knowledge. That, however, presupposes that experiences of the initiation ritual are supposed to lead to learning, if initiation is properly ad-

---

124 The translation is from Lannoy, "St Paul," 236.
125 This translation is from Fritz Graf, "Derveni and Ritual," in *Poetry as Initiation: The Center for Hellenic Studies Symposium on the Derveni Papyrus*, ed. Ioanna Papadopoulou and Leonard Muellner (Washington, DC: Center for Hellenic Studies, 2014), 76. Plato's *Phaed.* 69D has the saying in a slightly different order, but it has the same sense: ναρθηκοφόροι μὲν πολλοί, βάκχοι δέ τε παῦροι.

ministered.[126] In the Derveni Papyrus, Col. 5 reads, "Why do they disbelieve (ἀπιστοῦσι) in the horrors of Hades? Without knowing (οὐ γινώσκοντες) (the meaning of) dreams or any of the other things, by what kind of evidence would they believe ... Disbelief (ἀπιστίη) and ignorance (ἀμαθίη) [are the same thing]." According to Tsantsanoglou's interpretation, the Derveni author "views that participation in sacred rites is only one of the conditions that must be met if salvation in Hades is to be ensured ... the initiates must also obtain through teaching special knowledge about eschatology, divination [etc.]."[127] The Derveni author's similar criticism about ignorance and disbelief is also found in Col. 20: "Although they believe before they perform the rites that they will learn, they go away after performing them before having learned (πρὶν εἰδέναι), without even asking further questions, as if they knew something of what they saw or heard or were taught (ἔμαθον) ... they also go away devoid even of their belief (γνώμης, or, "thought")." Thus, criticizing such ignorance, "[p]art of the Derveni author's program is ... to offer knowledge of the true significance of bizarre and scandalous stories about gods."[128] The Derveni author was trying to give a proper interpretation of ritual activity; in his view, his version of interpretation has to be recognized and accepted in order to achieve the promised effects of the ritual. The date of this papyrus is not certain (the end of the fourth century or the beginning of the third century BCE would be a terminus ante quem[129]), and one cannot know how widespread and common this view was. It does, however, demonstrate that from the earliest period, not everyone related to the Orphic/Bacchic ritual took for granted the efficacy by virtue of participating in the ritual itself, but some people sought further knowledge and even *pistis* to corroborate its efficacy of the promise (in this case, the blessed status in the afterlife).

---

126 The rhetorical contrast between suffering/experience and learning based on the παθεῖν-μαθεῖν word-play was not unusual in antiquity. It is in some sense almost proverbial in Greek literature, as one can see from Aeschylus's *Agamemnon* (177–178): "wisdom (μάθος) comes alone through suffering (πάθος)." Yet, there are some examples that this relates to the context of initiation. One of Aristotle's fragments (*frag.* 15; Synesius, *Dio* 10) runs: "Aristotle thinks that the initiates (τοὺς τελουμένους) should not learn (μαθεῖν) something but experience (παθεῖν) (something) and change (διατεθῆναι), that is, becoming suitable for a certain purpose (ἐπιτηδείους)." Aristotle portrays mystery initiation negatively—that is, initiation lacks real knowledge (this differs from the position of the Derveni author). This fragment can be found in Valentinus Rose, *Aristotelis qui ferebantur librorum fragmenta* (Lepzig: Teubner, 1886), 31.
127 Theokritos Kouremenos et al. eds., *The Derveni Papyrus* (Firenze: Leo S. Olschki Editore, 2006), 46.
128 Kouremenos, *The Derveni Papyrus*, 50.
129 Yannis Z. Tzifopoulos, "The Derveni Papyrus and the Bacchic-Orphic *Epistomia*," in *Poetry as Initiation*, 135–64.

3.3.2 Religious Virtuosity as Both What is Promised and What Enables Other Benefits

Mystery initiation is by definition a way of achieving virtuosity because it is not a general practice performed by everyone. Bacchic madness is a strong indicator of virtuosity (as defined by Riesebrodt, following Weber). It redraws and rearranges one's physical and social bodies, as well as brings spiritual transformation, i.e., becoming like a Bacchic one. As shown by the sources, Dionysus, an archetype of initiates, experiences suffering/madness and overcomes it through initiation. He himself is a religious virtuoso. The madness in the Dionysiac initiation is a way to participate in the virtuosity of Dionysus. At the same time, this virtuosity makes other benefits possible.

What is characteristic in the virtuosity of the Dionysiac mysteries is that it is not a higher, separate stage differentiated from general practices—notwithstanding differentiated roles and offices that are often found within Dionysiac associations, as discussed earlier in this chapter. The Dionysiac mysteries' lack of differentiated stages of initiation stands out when compared with the most famous mysteries in the Greek world, i.e., the mysteries of Eleusis. The Eleusinian mysteries contain differentiated stages that require additional practices, for example, further fasting or purificatory activities, over an extended period of time.[130] In contrast, the madness in the Dionysiac mysteries seems to be given to the initiates without requiring additional practices to set an initiate apart from others. In this sense, religious virtuosity in the Dionysiac mysteries is accessible to all initiates; or one could say that it is "democratized." Interestingly, the lack of differentiated stages (coupled with few remarks about the afterlife) in the Bacchic initiation that Scyles, the king of the Scythians, underwent (reported in Herodotus) and in "the maenadic cult" appearing in Euripides' *Bacchae* led Kevin Clinton to claim that they are "not necessarily a mystery cult, according to classical usage of the term *mysteria*."[131] This might be correct if one sticks to the classical use. Yet, Clinton's observations could be reversed: those sources can provide the distinctive

---

[130] For a good classical reconstruction and discussion of the Eleusinian mysteries see George E. Mylonas, *Eleusis and the Eleusinian Mysteries* (Princeton: Princeton University Press, 1961), 224–85. For a more recent treatment of the Eleusinian mysteries: Kevin Clinton, "Stages of Initiation in the Eleusinian and Samothracian Mysteries," in *Greek Mysteries*, 50–77.
[131] Clinton, "Stages of Initiation," 55.

characteristics of the Dionysiac mysteries, as differentiated from the Eleusinian mysteries.[132]

3.4 Summary

In terms of the self-referential messages communicated by ritual participation, Dionysiac initiation plays with seemingly contradictory ideas. On the one hand, the initiation ritual of the Dionysiac mysteries points to the new self- and social identity as a Bacchant and it integrates (or further integrates) the initiated person into the regulated order of a polis (Classical and Hellenistic period) or of Dionysiac associations (late Hellenistic and Roman imperial period), often with rules of order and various roles. Initiation ritual turns one into a Bacchant, imposing a group identity of the same name and opening access to various other benefits within the symbolic world where Dionysus as an arch-initiate flourishes and helps his devotees flourish, too. On the other hand, the Dionysiac mysteries provide particular benefits that are not necessarily related to one's position in the traditional civic or social space, highlighting the eccentric nature of Dionysus. An initiate receives the promise of deliverance from various life-concerns through ecstatic madness, which is itself somehow "curative," but comes under suspicion by outsiders. Also, Dionysiac initiation offers the initiates the divine pledge of a blessed afterlife, envisioned as continuous worship of the deity along with a group of fellow-initiates, and clearly differentiates the fate of initiates from that of non-initiates.

Various witnesses help us reconstruct the canonical messages of Dionysiac initiation, and these messages can be summarized as *the nearness of Dionysus to his initiates*, both in life and the afterlife. From the Classical period onward, Dionysus was portrayed as a deity who frequently returns and even enters *into* his initiates, and who archetypally experiences and overcomes human suffering—including madness and death. This image of Dionysus supports the efficacy of Dionysiac initiation. The initiates can be assured that they will also experience the same benefits as Dionysus. The identification between Dionysus and his initiates is also a canonical message, attested both in literary and material evidence. This identification is often envisioned in the context of the afterlife (i.e., an initiate's assimilation to Dionysus will be realized in the hereafter), but some evidence suggests that initiates may have experienced this identification through their ecstatic ritual in

---

[132] Also, as discussed through various pieces of evidence, the promise of a blessed afterlife is among the benefits communicated by Dionysiac initiation, although it is not clearly found in *Bacchae*, as Clinton notes.

life. A related idea is the role of Dionysus as intercessor for his initiates in the Underworld. To summarize, (1) Dionysus's archetypal experiences and his returning through ritual guarantee the benefits of λύσις that his initiates enjoy on earth, whereas (2) both the identification of the initiates with Dionysus and Dionysus's intercession with other deities in the Underworld (these conceptions are not contradictory) guarantee the benefits related to the fate of the initiates in the afterlife.

Two points can be mentioned in terms of matters beyond Dionysiac initiation itself. First, according to some evidence, notably inferred from the Derveni Papyrus, Dionysiac initiation requires more than one's participation in the initiation ritual. It requires a true understanding of what initiation means to an initiate. Yet, it is not certain how consistently, persistently, and widely one can find such a view throughout the diverse Dionysiac tradition. Second, the religious virtuosity of Dionysiac initiation is "democratized," owing to ecstatic madness. Although differentiated offices and roles are found among Dionysiac associations (sometimes emulating civic structures), there were no clear low and high (or lesser and greater) stages of initiation in Dionysiac initiation, unlike in the Eleusinian mysteries. Through the initiation ritual, the initiates of the Dionysiac mysteries proleptically participate in the virtuosity of Dionysus himself, which will lead them to the promised, blessed afterlife along with other Bacchants.

4 Initiation into the Mysteries of Isis

In order to examine the messages that the initiation rituals of the mysteries of Isis communicated, some methodological issues need to be addressed first. Chronology is the first issue that must be discussed, as the evidence related to the Isis mysteries vis-à-vis the early Christ cult is slightly different from the difficulty involved in discussing the Dionysiac mysteries (for the latter, some evidence goes back to classical Greece). It is evident that the Isis mysteries were quite popular in the Roman imperial world at least by the second century CE. Yet, it is debatable whether and to what extent the *mysteries* of Isis (thus, not other forms of Isis worship) already existed in the Hellenistic period and the early Roman imperial period at the turn of the era.[1] The heyday of the mysteries of Isis might postdate Paul's life and ministry in the mid-first century.[2] I begin my investigation with the presupposition that the mysteries of Isis were already to some degree known and practiced in the world of the first-century Christ-devotees; that is, I follow the theories of some scholars who offer a positive assessment of the early existence of the Isis mysteries.[3] Furthermore, even if this early dating is contested, it will not be a serious problem. My comparative project is not affected by whether Paul or his com-

---

[1] While major scholars in the field have taken different positions, Jan Bremmer is doubtful about the early existence of the mysteries of Isis: "It is striking that the earliest, still Hellenistic, aretalogies, those of Maroneia and Andros, do not contain the claim, 'I revealed Mysteries unto men' ... Mysteries were a relatively late arrival among the achievements of Isis as perceived by her propagandists." Bremmer, *Initiation*, 113.

[2] The most valuable literary sources for the Isis mysteries, Plutarch's *Isis and Osiris* and Apuleius's *Metamorphoses* (Book 11) were written decades after Paul. Material evidence also suffers from this issue. For example, coins from Corinth depicting Isis began flourishing during and after Hadrian's time, i.e., the early second century CE. For the numismatic evidence, see Laurent Bricault and Richard Veymiers, "Isis in Corinth: The Numismatic Evidence. City, Image and Religion," in *Nile into Tiber*, 392–413. This is one of the reasons why Wagner doubts any concrete connection between the Osiris/Isis cult and Pauline baptism. See his *Pauline Baptism*, 91–92.

[3] It is possible that Paul and his contemporaries were acquainted with some form of Isis initiation. Bricault claims the Maroneia inscription (RICIS 114/0202; from the end of the second century BCE) alludes to the existence of the Isis mysteries in the Hellenistic world before the common era. Such a view is supported by his observation that the inscription modifies a more traditional formula featuring Egypt by adding Hellenistic elements (e.g., "in Greece you honored Athens above all") and it includes a reference to Eleusis. Laurent Bricault, *Les cultes isiaques dans le monde gréco-romain* (Paris: Les belles lettres, 2013), 430. Regarding the exact period when the traditional Egyptian cult of Isis morphed into the mysteries (comparable to that of Eleusis), Bricault maintains that it was probably at the early stage of the Ptolemaic dynasty, following Plutarch's report. Isis devotion in general was already known in Roman Palestine. See, for example, Nicole Belayche, "Les dévotions à Isis et Sérapis dans la Judée-Palestine Romaine," in *Nile into Tiber*, 448–69.

munity members knew the mysteries of Isis in their second-century form, because the question of Paul's (or early Christianity's) dependence on the mysteries is not my investigative question.

Second, one might also point out some caveats in using Plutarch (*Isis and Osiris*) and Apuleius (*Metamorphoses*) for any historical reconstruction of the mysteries of Isis. Literary sources have their own literary devices, purposes, and agenda, and therefore, they are not transparent windows through which historians can directly access the past (in the earlier chapter, Euripides's *Bacchae* had similar issues).[4] Yet, acknowledging the literary devices, purposes, and agenda does not necessarily mean that one cannot use the information gleaned from the literary sources as illuminating the ancient religious practices mentioned in the texts. If there was no correspondence to reality, the texts would not have successfully achieved their literary goals with their contemporary audiences. Perhaps analogously, one could think about the usefulness of Acts of the Apostles in the study of early Christian history, despite the document's literary embellishment and theological agenda.[5] Furthermore, there are historians of antiquity who affirm the validity of using Plutarch and Apuleius in their historical investigations of Isis initiation.[6]

---

[4] The description of the Isis myth in Plutarch's *Isis and Osiris* should be read with caution because that work functions as a vehicle to convey Plutarch's middle-Platonism. Similarly, as for the eleventh book of Apuleius's *Metamorphoses*, some recent scholars pay attention to this work's "literary aspect" and Apuleius's "literary ambition" as an author. For example, Stefan Tilg, "Aspects of a Literary Rationale of *Metamorphoses* 11," in *Aspects of Apuleius' Golden Ass: The Isis-Book: A Collection of Original Papers*, ed. W. H. Keulen (Leiden: Brill, 2011), 132–55. Also, Apuleius's descriptions of Lucius's initiation into the Isis mysteries can be interpreted as a "satirical parody," i.e., insinuating that "the now-human Lucius is simply another example of a duped religious believer." Brigitte B. Libby, "Moons, Smoke, and Mirrors in Apuleius' Portrayal of Isis," *AJP* 132 (2011), 317. For a more detailed discussion of *Metamorphoses* Book 11 as a "sophistic satire," see Stephen J. Harrison, *Apuleius: A Latin Sophist* (Oxford: Oxford University Press, 2000), especially Chapter 6. He discusses *Metamorphoses* in the context of the entire Apuleian corpus and in light of the Second Sophistic.
[5] One cannot argue that the writing chronicles events regarding early Christians exactly as they happened. However, Acts includes significant information about early Christian beliefs and practices in various regions of the Mediterranean world. Some historians have suggested that one can even use apparently fictional documents from antiquity to explore social history. For example, see Keith Hopkins, "Novel Evidence for Roman Slavery," *PP* 138 (1993): 3–27.
[6] Richter notes that several Egyptologists and Roman historians have regarded Plutarch's *Isis and Osiris* as a relatively reliable source. Daniel S. Richter, "Plutarch on Isis and Osiris: Text, Cult, and Cultural Appropriation," *TAPA* 131 (2001): 192 (see, also, Cumont, *Oriental Religions*, 14). As for the validity of using Apuleius's *Metamorphoses* for the exploration of possible "contents" of Isis initiation, see Bricault's assessment: "Le text d'Apulée contient probablement d'authenique formules cultuelles, à peine stylisées." Bricault, *Les cultes isiaque*, 436–37. It is striking to see how much Bricault's view of *Metamorphoses* ("... à peine stylisées") differs from the scholars mentioned above, who focus on the literary agenda of that work. Reinhold Merkelbach is more optimistic about the

Thus, by attending to literary and ideological features of Plutarch's and Apuleius's texts, I will use them carefully to reconstruct the social reality of the Isis mysteries in the earliest centuries of the common era.

Finally, some recent scholars of Isis studies caution against approaching the cults of Isis with a narrowly defined "religious" focus and with an acontextual synthesis, contrary to earlier scholarship. Versluys summarizes the *status quaestionis* in two ways:

> First of all the aprioristic religious interpretation has been *challenged*. Things Egyptian have been made part of different frameworks of interpretation like Augustan imperial ideology, Roman exoticism and colonial discourse or the Roman construction of 'Gegenwelten'. Secondly the cults of Isis themselves have been *contextualised*. They have been brought out of the domain of the history of religions alone and made part of frameworks of interpretation like elite self fashioning [sic], Hellenisation or Romanisation.[7]

This recent trend is indeed significant; the mysteries of Isis should be examined in their multi-layered contexts. Although my interest primarily lies in the religious aspect (especially, religious ritual), I will try not to isolate the religious aspect of the Isis mysteries from all other aspects in their contexts, which was the same approach used for the Dionysiac mysteries.

4.1 The Self-referential Messages, or the Benefits Initiation Promises

4.1.1 Transformation of One's Religious and Social Self

After John Scheid's succinct and accurate statement that "Mystery cults changed an individual's relationship with the deity in the present world by means of rituals of initiation and purification," he adds, "But ... those initiations did not rep-

---

value of Apuleius's account for understanding Isis initiation, calling *Metamorphoses* "das wichtigste ... Zeugnis über die Isismysterien," and even, "eine Missionsschrift." Reinhold Merkelbach, *Isis regina, Zeus Sarapis: die griechisch-ägyptische Religion nach den Quellen dargestellt* (Stuttgart: B. G. Teubner, 1995), 266, 291. Of course, Merkelbach's view that *Metamorphoses* was a "Missionsschrift" might go too far. I am doubtful about Merkelbach's view that the Greek novels featuring mysteries are "mystically encrypted text[s] written by initiates for initiates." See Miguel Herrero de Jáuregui, "'Trust the God': *Tharsein* in Ancient Greek Religion," *HSCP* 108 (2015): 18. Nevertheless, with all caveats, a judicious use of the literary sources, both Plutarch and Apuleius, is required in any historical investigation of the mysteries of Isis.

7 Italics in original. Miguel John Versluys, "Aegyptiaca Romana: The Widening Debate," in *Nile into Tiber*, 3.

resent a visible or definitive change of state for an individual."⁸ This may be true, because, using modern analogies, Isis initiation neither confers a knighthood on the person nor physically reformulates her/his body with medical surgery.⁹ Yet, evidence shows that there were indeed some visible changes (that occurred once or continuously) for individuals who participated in the mysteries of Isis. In this section, I will demonstrate that one's participation in the Isis initiation observably transforms the person's religious and social self. This relationship was also found in the previous chapter's survey of Dionysiac initiation (note that a phrase like βεβακχευμένοι is not found with Isis initiation).

The transformation of one's social and religious self through initiation is indicated by one's outward appearance. This becomes more conspicuous in the cultic setting where initiates and the uninitiated occupy the same space. According to the narrative of *Metam.* 11, the initiates and the uninitiated participate together in the public rituals of the Isis cult. In the public procession, the initiates' clothing matters, because it explicitly represents the indexical nature of this ritual. The public procession, including masquerade,¹⁰ culminates in the procession of the "savior goddess," including the procession of the initiates, "men and women of every rank and age" (*viri feminaeque omnis dignitatis et omnis aetatis*) (*Metam.* 11.10). The initiates are distinguished in the public procession by their linen clothes and distinctive hairstyle—women with a transparent hair covering and men with the shaven heads.¹¹ Apuleius's account compares the light reflected on their shaven head to "earthly stars of the great religion" (*magnae religionis terrena sidera*). This metaphor is naturally regarded as literary elaboration, but it perhaps relates to the popular notion of the initiates' status—although they live on earth, their shaven heads and light from them could symbolize their "heavenly" status, achieved by their initiation into the Isis mysteries. Also, *Metamorphoses* presents

---

8 Scheid, *An Introduction to Roman Religion*, 187.
9 Of course, there were members in other mysteries who attain visible change by physically mutilating their bodily parts; for example, the *galli* in the mysteries of Cybele.
10 Note Takács's warning: "Procession and initiation were two different matters." Sarolta A. Takács, *Isis and Sarapis in the Roman World* (Leiden: Brill, 1995), 87. Nevertheless, that Isis initiates participate in this procession and segregate themselves with special clothing indeed conveys some of the ritual messages of initiation—ones available even to the uninitiated.
11 Note that Lucius, after his human transformation, was given "a piece of linen cloth" to cover his naked body; he actually received "an outer tunic" from "a member of a religious cohort" (*e cohorte religionis unus*) (*Metam.* 11.14). The Latin term *cohors*, which has military connotations, would be understood in light of the portrayal of Isis cult in the next section (11.15) as "a spiritual struggle with quasi-military significance," as Griffiths suggests (cf. *da nomen sanctae huic militia*, 11.15). J. Gwyn Griffiths, *Apuleius, The Isis-Book* (Leiden: Brill, 1975), 240.

Lucius's deification at the end of initiation through his outward appearance.[12] Standing on "a wooden platform set up in the very centre of the holy shrine in front of the goddess's statue," Lucius is "decorated in the likeness of the Sun and set up in the guise of a statue" (*ad instar Solis exornato me et in vicem simulacri constituto*; *Metam.* 11.24).[13] That Lucius takes the role of the Sun-god, or even, Sarapis, through initiation is indicated by this visual representation.

Various rules and purity rituals that were required as part of the initiation, as well as the ways in which the initiated appears in public, are a visual index of the change of status that comes through initiation. After the public scene at the beginning of *Metam.* 11, the life of an initiate is highlighted. One can be a "companion" of priests of Isis, fully devoting oneself to Isis (e.g., 11.19) even before initiation, but it is only a beginning—actual initiation is difficult to achieve. Lucius is hesitant due to the many obligations involved in initiation: "I had learned from thorough investigation that the obligations of her cult were difficult, that the abstinence required by the rules of chastity was quite strenuous, and how necessary it was to guard with caution and circumspection a life subject to countless vicissitudes" (11.19). One's decision to be initiated and acceptance of all ritual requirements virtually demarcate the person's past/present status and that of the future in a "digitalized" way (that is, either yes or no). That is, the initiation ritual replaces a "more-or-less continuum" with a "yes/no question."[14] As Rappaport notes, "Whereas vagueness is reduced by the digitalization of aspects of ritual's contents, ambiguity concerning the current state of the performers may be reduced, or even eliminated by ritual's occurrence."[15] Following certain rules and requirements specifically for initiates is an index of their transformed status.

One may object that these visual signs are restricted to one's change of symbolic status in the religious imagination.[16] There is, however, evidence that one's participation in the mysteries of Isis also brought some concrete changes of social and economic status and, by extension, led to social and economic benefits. First of all, while women did not make up of the majority of Isis devotees in all periods and

---

12 Thus, *pace* Wagner, *Pauline Baptism*, 113–14.
13 A later report by Rufinus of Aquileia about the Sarapis temple in Alexandria is a useful comparison (*Church History* 11.23). Philip R. Amidon, *The Church History of Rufinus of Aquileia, Book 10 and 11* (New York: Oxford University Press, 1997), 467.
14 Rappaport, *Ritual and Religion*, 76, 90–91.
15 Rappaport, *Ritual and Religion*, 89.
16 Even so, this symbolic status represented by visual signs does not disappear immediately once the initiation rituals (or public processions where the initiates and uninitiated are distinguished) end. A good example is the initiates of the Eleusinian mysteries (especially, in the lesser mysteries); they "continued to wear the garments of their initiation until they were worn out." Mylonas, *Eleusis and the Eleusinian Mysteries*, 280, n. 214.

places,[17] Heyob demonstrates with massive epigraphic evidence that women did indeed participate in the higher priesthood and "perform[ed] the same priestly duties as men."[18] The Isis litany in P.Oxy. 1380 contains this intriguing sentence (lines 214–216), "... Thou didst make the power of women equal to that of men (σὺ γυναιξὶν ἴσην δύναμιν τῶν ἀνδρῶν ἐποίησας)."[19] Wall paintings from Pompeii depict "the reception of Io by Isis," in which female and male priestly figures serve Isis equally.[20] Sometimes this priestly role of women is for their entire lifetime (ἱέρειαν διὰ βίου τῆς <Τ>αποσειριάδος Εἴσιδος; RICIS 105/0895 = SIRIS 62; third century CE). Taking religious leadership roles were not forbidden to women in many other cultic groups in the Greco-Roman world—including Jewish and early Christian groups.[21] Therefore, female leadership in the Isis groups was conventional rather than controversial behavior. Yet, there are some distinctive characteristics in the Isis initiation about the transformation of female devotees on earth or in the afterlife.

Secondly, there is an economic side, one's participation in initiation indicates one's participation in the communal economy of the group of initiates. According to a first-century CE inscription (RICIS 113/0537, Thessalonica), certain initiates (μύσται) donated a portion of their vineyards to the deity, and they were given the right to partake in the produce of these vineyards as long as they live and

---

[17] Sharon Kelly Heyob, *The Cult of Isis among Women in the Graeco-Roman World* (Leiden: Brill, 1975), 81–110.

[18] Heyob, *The Cult of Isis among Women*, 110; cf. 95. She also notes that priestesses who played the primary role (thus, not "secondary priestesses") appeared only after the first century CE (see Heyob, *The Cult of Isis among Women*, 90).

[19] This translation is found in Bernard P. Grenfell and Arthur S. Hunt, *The Oxyrhynchus Papyri. Part XI* (London, 1915).

[20] Heyob, *The Cult of Isis among Women*, 99.

[21] There has been a persistent tendency in scholarship to downplay the existence of women's leadership in the religious activities of the Greek and Roman world, including among early Christian groups. Yet, various examples of women's religious activities, including their participation in leadership, are listed in Ross Shepard Kraemer, *Women's Religions in the Greco-Roman World: A Sourcebook* (Oxford: Oxford University Press, 2004). For a recent discussion on women in the New Testament period: Susan E. Hylen, *Women in the New Testament World* (New York: Oxford University Press, 2019). For an earlier discussion of women leaders in Jewish groups, see Bernadette J. Brooten, *Women Leaders in the Ancient Synagogue: Inscriptional Evidence and Background Issues* (Atlanta: Scholars Press, 1982). Particularly regarding early Christian groups, Carolyn Osiek and Margaret Y. MacDonald, with Janet H. Tulloch, *A Woman's Place: House Churches in Earliest Christianity* (Minneapolis: Augsburg Fortress, 2006). Sometimes, the spatial notion of "public" and "private" has been brought in to explain the women's religious activities and leadership roles, but this dichotomy is questionable. For a recent critique of this dichotomy, see Susan E. Hylen, "Public and Private Space and Action in the Early Roman Period," *NTS* 66 (2020): 534–53.

keep certain regulations, as stipulated in the inscription—e. g., some of the produce should be used for "the festival of the bread for the *threpsantes*" (ἡ ἐπὶ τῶν θρεψάντων ἄρτου ἑστίασις; *threpsantes* = lit. "those who have supported/nourished"). What this inscription envisions is community property, that the members invest together and from which they receive interest. In addition, although not directly related to the initiation ritual, RICIS 101/502 (Rhamnous, third century BCE) is also illuminating. This inscription reports a certain Apollodoros's donation of the land for the Isis/Sarapis shrine and, accordingly, the appreciation of his benefaction by the local Sarapis-devotees or the Sarapis-cultic association (Σαραπιασταί / τὸ κοινὸν τῶν Σαραπιαστῶν). In addition to the fact that this person was praised and honored by the local Sarapis community, they also granted him a golden crown (στεφανῶσαι χρυσῶι στεφάνωι) for his piety towards the gods (i.e., Isis and Sarapis) (εὐσεβείας ἕνεκα τῆς πρὸς τοὺς θεούς), which displays the economic resourcefulness of this community of Isis/Sarapis initiates.[22] Perhaps, for those who live in or near this town, the initiation into this cohort of initiates indicated benefiting from that economic resource. Needless to say, cultic communities and associations in antiquity were deeply intertwined with social and economic reality, and it seems reasonable to think about one's own initiation or one's relationship with a group of initiates on social and economic terms.

Furthermore, joining an Isis group could indicate a change in one's social identity outside the local Isis groups. A sense of "universal" community, which expanded beyond particular geographic locations, is part of the mysteries of Isis—although one should not overstate this. A first-century graffito from Pompeii written for political purposes provides a good example (RICIS 504/0208 = SIRIS 487). It reads: "The entire/universal Isis-followers request Gnaeus Helvius Sabinus to be elected for aedileship" (*Cn. Helvium Sabinum aed[ilem] Isiaci universi rog[ant]*). The Latin term *Isiaci universi*, according to Burkert, functions to "make the group seem as large as possible," though he cautiously points out that this has to do with "a political construct rather than an actual religious 'movement.'"[23] Yet, it is possible that this "political construct" reflects certain aspects of the "actual religious movement." Conversely, such an intersection between the political and the religious, which is not unusual in antiquity, may have influenced Isis initiates and their practices.

---

[22] As Alvar notes, "[Apollodoros] expressed his *pietas* by giving the land to those who already had the resources to make the purchase." Alvar, "Social Agentivity," 224.
[23] Burkert, *Ancient Mystery Cults*, 48.

4.1.2 *Sōtēria:* Protection/Deliverance

Above all, Isis is a σώτειρα (fem. of σωτήρ), and therefore σωτηρία/*salus* is one of the prominent benefits the goddess Isis promises her devotees.[24] Here, one sees a more explicit link between the canonical message (Isis is the goddess of salvation) and the self-referential message (those who join the worship of Isis receives salvation). For Lucius, the day of his transformation is described as "the day of salvation" (*dies salutaris*; *Metam.* 11.5; cf. "hope of salvation" [*spem salutis*] in 11.1; cf. ἡμέρα σωτηρίας in 2 Cor 6:2). Technically, this is before initiation proper, and it mainly indicates the transformation of Lucius from bestial form back into a human being. Also, one should not impose a Christian connotation on the Latin term *salus* (Greek σωτηρία), especially with eschatological connotations.[25] Yet, it is still noteworthy that this mystery deity is portrayed primarily promising the initiates *salus*. This phenomenon is more distinctive when compared with the mysteries of Dionysus, where his benefits are not usually referred to as σωτηρία/*salus* nor is he himself called σωτήρ.[26]

In addition to the literary sources, Isis as a goddess of salvation and healing is also well attested in inscriptions from the Hellenistic period. For example, a marble stele found in Maroneia (RICIS 114/0202 = Totti #19; the end of the second century BCE), in which a Greek man praises and gives thanks to Isis for the "greatness of the beneficial action" that healed his blindness.[27] Giving ἐγκώμιον to Isis, the man rhetorically asks, "If you came for my requested salvation, how could you not come for your own honor?" (εἰ γὰρ ὑπὲρ τῆς ἐμῆς καλουμένη σωτηρίας

---

[24] Note Versnel's definitive tone: "In short, [Isis] was the *soteira par excellence* even to the degree of becoming the device of salvation." Versnel, *Ter Unus*, 45. Of course, the epithet σώτειρα applied to goddesses (or σωτήρ to gods) may not be unique to Isis, as Vanderlip points out. Vera F. Vanderlip, *The Four Greek Hymns of Isidorus and the Cult of Isis* (Toronto: A. M. Hakkert, 1972), 31–32. See the references on p. 32 of that book. On the epithet σωτήρ or its feminine form frequently used in relation to various Greek gods, who are not necessarily mystery deities, see Fritz Graf, "Theoi Soteres," *Archiv für Religionsgeschichte* 18–19 (2017): 239–53. On the concept of savior in popular philosophy, see Johan C. Thom, "God the Saviour in Greco-Roman Popular Philosophy," in *Sōtēria: Salvation in Early Christianity and Antiquity: Festschrift in Honour of Cilliers Breytenbach on the Occasion of his 65th Birthday*, ed. David S. du Toit et al. (Leiden: Brill, 2019), 86–100.
[25] For the language of *soteria* in Isis, see, Jim, "'Salvation' (*Soteria*) and Ancient Mystery Cults," 269–72.
[26] Perhaps, a famous line from the later Christian author, Firmicus Maternus, would contain a grain of truth (though it would have more to do with Osiris, than Isis): "Have courage, initiates, now that the god has been rescued. For we shall receive salvation from pains (ἐκ πόνων σωτηρία)."
[27] Giulia Sfameni Gasparro, "The Hellenistic Face of Isis: Cosmic and Saviour Goddess," in *Nile into Tiber*, 40.

ἦλθες, πῶς ὑπὲρ τῆς ἰδίας τιμῆς οὐκ ἂν ἔλθοις; lines 10–11).²⁸ As Gasparro notes, "The intervention of the goddess, configured as an epiphany, is perceived by the worshipper as a real action of σωτηρία."²⁹ The salvation given by Isis is mainly related to one's prosperity in life, overcoming tribulations and adversities. One's participation in Isis initiation primarily indicates the divine promise that the initiate will begin a life under the goddess's salvation, in which further reciprocity between the goddess and the initiate is also expected.

The goddess's *salus*/σωτηρία, of course, covers much more than an individual's life and that person's relationship with the deity—the goddess's *salus* extends to the wellbeing and order of society as a whole. *Metamorphoses* 11.16 describes the purification of a ship and its dedication to the goddess—the ship's sail includes an inscription "whose text renewed the prayer for prosperous navigation during the new sailing season." This is actually the climax of the public procession (ending with the priest's ritual declaration of the "navigation season" [τὰ πλοιαφέσια] and with the crowd's joyous celebration; 11.17). The efficacy of the mystery deities for safety in the sea is widely believed, especially in the case of the Samothracian mysteries.³⁰ This was also true of the Isis devotion; the ritual involving the ship has some particular significance in the history of Isis tradition in the Greco-Roman world.³¹ Furthermore, the prayer for the members of the Roman empire—the emperor, other privileged groups, "and the entire Roman people" (*totoque Romano populo*), as well as "the sailors and ships under the rule of our world-wide empire" (*nauticis, navibusque, quae sub imperio mundi nostratis reguntur*)"—is made when the procession arrives at the Isis temple, according to *Metam.* 11.17 (also, see 11.25: "you protect men [sic] on sea and land"). Such large-scale prayers for the entire Roman world in *Metam.* 11.17 resonate with the earlier Eleusinian mysteries, which were part of the polis-religion and presumably functioned to maintain the social wellbeing and order of the polis. Therefore, in the Roman context, Isis initiation can indicate and reaffirm one's place within the larger symbolic order of the empire, rather than leading initiates out of it.

Nevertheless, individual aspects—one could even call her a "personal" deity³² —were more prominent with the *salus*/σωτηρία that Isis promises. Particularly,

---

28 The translation is mine. The Greek text is from Yves Grandjean, *Une nouvelle arétalogie d'Isis à Maronée* (Leiden: Brill, 1975).
29 Gasparro, "The Hellenistic Face of Isis," 40, n. 2.
30 Blakely, "Maritime Risk and Ritual Responses," 362–79. She notes that performing maritime rituals creates "symbolic connections between the maritime and the divine worlds" (363).
31 R. E. Witt, *Isis in the Ancient World* (Baltimore: Johns Hopkins University Press, 1997), 165 ff.
32 See the discussion of Isidorus's *Hymn to Isis* in Vernon K. Robbins, *The Invention of Christian Discourse* (Blandford Forum: Deo Publishing, 2009), 45–50.

Isis initiation promises transcending one's place, a place conditioned by external forces, often personified as Fate/Fortune. In the Isis aretalogy from Kyme (RICIS 302/0204 = I.Kyme 41; perhaps the first century CE[33]), Isis solemnly declares, "I overcome Fate; Fate obeys me" (Ἐγὼ τὸ ἱμαρμένον[34] νικῶ. Ἐμοῦ τὸ εἱμαρμένον ἀκούει).[35] Similar ideas are found in the earlier parts of Apuleius's *Metam.* 11.[36] Especially in 11.6, Isis appears to Lucius and says, "But if by assiduous obedience, worshipful service, and determined celibacy you win the favour of my godhead, you will know that I—and I alone—can even prolong your life beyond the limits determined by your fate (*ultra statuta fato*)."[37] The entire narrative of *Metamorphoses* is full of remarks about how Fate/Fortune has driven Lucius (and other characters) into calamities (e. g., 1.6 – 7; 3.14 [savage Fortune]; 7.2 [blind Fortune]; 7.20; 8.24]). Finally, Book 11 shows how Lucius overcomes this savage and blind Fortune through Isis's protection; when Lucius the donkey sees the Isis priest holding a sistrum in the procession "exactly according to the prescription of the divine promise," he says to himself, "I would overcome Fortune, who was so savagely battering me …" (11.12). In the following passages, after Lucius's transformation, the Isis priest explains at length about the victory over Fortune enabled by the goddess Isis. What is interesting is that contrary to the "blind" Fortune (*Fortunae caecitas*;

---

[33] Bricault dates it to the first century CE, but signals his uncertainty with a question mark. Bremmer thinks it could be dated to the first or second century CE (Bremmer, *Initiation*, 111).
[34] Probably a variation of εἱμαρμένον.
[35] Jan Bergman suggests that the unusual neuter εἱμαρμένον instead of the feminine εἱμαρμένη indicates an Egyptian concept, and thus he takes it as evidence against previous scholars' view that these concluding lines in the aretalogy are not part of the original aretalogy but a later addition. Jan Bergman, "'I Overcome Fate, Fate Harkens to Me,'" in *Fatalistic Beliefs in Religion, Folklore, and Literature: Papers read at the Symposium on Fatalistic Beliefs held at Åbo on the 7th–9th of September, 1964*, ed. Helmer Ringgren (Stockholm: Almqvist & Wiksell, 1967), 41. In the history of scholarship, Bergman (especially, his *Ich bin Isis* [1968]) takes a position that strongly argues for the Egyptian influence on the putative original form of all Isis aretalogies, differing from the view of other scholars, such as A. D. Nock and A. J. Festugière. For further discussion, see Versnel, *Ter Unus*, 41.
[36] According to Gasparini, Apuleius's *Metamorphoses* depends on aretalogical literature. Valentino Gasparini, "Isis and Osiris: Demonology vs. Henotheism?" *Numen* 58 (2011): 710.
[37] Bergman notes that this idea is traced back to a hieroglyphic text in the *Leiden Hymn to Amun* (III, 7) (the thirteenth century BCE). It reads, "He lengthens the time of life, he shortens it, he grants an addition to fate to the one he loves." Bergman, "I Overcome Fate," 37. One reason Isis appears as a goddess who overcomes fate can be explained by her long-established close connection with Sothis/Sirius (Sothis/Sirius was used for measuring time; it indicates when the Nile arises), which is attested in the old tradition (like the Pyramid texts) and in the later Hellenistic period (the litany in P.Oxy. 1380; cf. the Isis aretalogy in Kyme, etc.). See also Bergman, "I Overcome Fate," 38–39.

"the blindness of Fortune," 11.15),[38] another Fortune who is not blind but able to see (... *Fortunae, sed videntis*; "of a Fortune who can see," 11.15) is also depicted. This *videns* Fortune is, according to Griffiths, Isis herself. In other words, it is implied that Isis can help her devotees overcome blind Fortune because she herself is a kind of Fortune, the true fortune (therefore, this becomes a canonical message, not only a self-referential message). Again, as Griffiths points out, the connection between Isis and Fortune (Isis-Fortuna or Isis-Τύχη; even the combined form Ἰσι-τύχη) is attested in other ancient sources, including iconographic and epigraphic witnesses.[39] In light of such conventions, I also suggest that it is possible to take the phrase τύχην, ἀγαθήν in the Isis litany in P.Oxy. 1380 (line 51) as one amalgamated title (thus, *contra* the P.Oxy. editors), and thus as another example of the fusion between Isis and Fortune.[40] In short, Isis becomes the true Fate/Fortune, who has already overcome fate and thus is able to help her devotees overcome fate. One's participation in Isis initiation communicates the self-referential message that the initiate's new life journey is no longer bound by her/his fate, thanks to the salvation of Isis.[41]

Lastly, for female initiates, one of the "soteriological" aspects indicated by ritual participation is Isis's divine favor toward and protection of women. For example, a second-century CE inscription from Spain states that Isis, who is called *Isis puellaris*,[42] favorably protects prepubescent girls (RICIS 603/0101 = SIRIS 761 = CIL II 3386). Also, identified with various mother-goddesses in antiquity,[43] Isis is also expected to help women during pregnancy and childbirth (e.g., Ovid, *Metam.* 9.685–

---

38 Bergman notes that "blind fate [is] a common topos" in antiquity. Bergman, "I Overcome Fate," 44, n. 3.
39 Bergman, "I Overcome Fate," 48; Griffiths, *Apuleius*, 241–42. For example, Isidorus's Hymns to Isis found in the Isis temple in Alexandria (dating from the first century BCE) include such connections: Χαῖρε, Τύχη Ἀγαθή, μεγαλώνυμε Ἴσι μεγίστη (SEG 8, n. 549 = Hymn II in Vanderlip's edition; the same phrase is also found in Hymn I; yet, Hymn III has a more distinctive form: Ἀγαθή τε τύχη—how does this single τε function here?). Also, see CED 120: Τύχηι Πρωτογενείαι Ἴσιδι.
40 The editors of the Oxyrhynchus Papyri suggest that ἀγαθήν in line 51 is "probably separate from τύχην." Grenfell and Hunt, *The Oxyrhynchus Papyri. Part XI*, 211.
41 Consider how fate was regarded as an inevitable force, both deities and human beings, in antiquity. For example, in Homer's *Il.* 16.419–507, Zeus pities his son Sarpedon for his death is "destined" (the Greek word μοῖρα [fate/lot/portion] is used). Though Zeus already anticipates this impending death of Sarpedon (15.67), this supreme deity does not seem to go against fate.
42 The first line begins with *Isidi puel[lari]*. The bracket indicates a reconstruction. Bricault translates this line as "À Isis patronne des jeunes filles."
43 Heyob, *The Cult of Isis among Women*, 70–71; Gail Paterson Corrington, "The Milk of Salvation: Redemption by the Mother in Late Antiquity and Early Christianity," *HTR* 82 (1989): 398.

701; *Amores* 2.13⁴⁴; RICIS 113/0301; RICIS 302/0204). These ideas are often expressed by the goddess's self-revelatory discourse. In the Isis aretalogy from Kyme (RICIS 302/0204), Isis herself declares, "I appointed to women to bring their infants to birth in the tenth month" (Ἐγὼ γυναικὶ δεκαμηνιαῖον βρέφος εἰς φῶς ἐξενεγκεῖν ἔταξα).⁴⁵ Also, in Ovid, *Metam.* 9.696 onwards, Isis appears to Telethusa and promises to save her newborn girl from her husband's death threat:

> O Telethusa, one of my own worshippers, put away your grievous cares, and think not to obey your husband's orders. And do not hesitate, when Lucina has delivered you, to save your child, whatever it shall be. I am the goddess who bring help and succour to those who call upon me; nor shall you have cause to complain that you have worshipped a thankless deity.

As Heyob notes, "[W]omen in the Graeco-Roman world viewed Isis as among other things the goddess whose protection they might seek in the whole span of events connected with the reproduction process."⁴⁶ This is, of course, not only limited to Isis; several goddesses in antiquity, such as Hera, Artemis, and Demeter, seem to share similar roles.⁴⁷ It should be noted that this does not mean that women only participated in religious rituals for the specific purposes of childbearing or fertility; women participated in rituals for diverse reasons and expectations.⁴⁸

4.1.3 Isis's Guardianship: Permanent Relationship with the Goddess

Initiation enables one to enter into a permanent relationship with the goddess. This means that the σωτηρία that Isis offers is not a onetime only deliverance, but the equivalent of a lifelong warrantee. In Apuleius, *Metam.* 11.6, Isis says, "You will clearly remember [*plane memineris*] and keep forever sealed deep in your heart the fact that the rest of your life's course is pledged to me [*mihi reliqua vitae tuae curricula ... vadata*] until the very limit of your last breath ... you will

---

44 In *Amores* 2.13 the prayer is said by a man (not by the pregnant woman herself) to ask Isis's mercy on and healing of his lover.
45 This translation is from Kraemer, *Women's Religion*, 457.
46 Heyob, *The Cult of Isis among Women*, 73.
47 Susan Guettel Cole, *Landscapes, Gender, and Ritual Space: The Ancient Greek Experience* (Berkeley: University of California Press, 2004), 211–12.
48 There are also methodological problems surrounding ancient sources produced by male authors. To what extent do they reflect women's ritual reality? In what ways do they construct it for their rhetorical/ideological purposes? These must be carefully examined. See the essays in Maryline Parca and Angeliki Tzanetou, eds., *Finding Persephone: Women's Rituals in the Ancient Mediterranean* (Bloomington; Indianapolis: Indiana University Press, 2007).

live in happiness, you will live in glory, under my guardianship [*in mea tutela*]." This relationship will be permanent even in the afterlife: "While you dwell in the Elysian fields I will favour you and you will constantly worship me" (*Metam.* 11.6).[49] Such a relationship is expressed through several images. In Apuleius, *Metam.* 11.15, the priest envisions this relation between devotee and deity, established by initiation, as the slave-and-master relationship (in addition to the image of joining "this holy army" [*sanctae huic militiae*]). This religious slavery is thought to be "voluntary," rather than compulsory, liberative, rather than suppressive: "Dedicate yourself today to obedience to our cult and take on the voluntary yoke of her service (*ministerii iugum subi voluntarium*); for as soon as you become the goddess's slave you will experience more fully the fruit of your freedom (*magis senties fructum tuae libertatis*)" (*Metam.* 11.15; cf. Matt 11:28–30). What is interesting here is that the image of sacred warfare, cultic/religious slavery, and the notion of freedom and choice are clustered together, as in Rom 6 (see, for example, footnote 82 of Chapter 7 in this book). For now, suffice it to say that one's initiation actually creates her/his relationship with Isis; its beneficial effects and the obligations it creates extend to the rest of one's life.

This relationship is constantly negotiated before and after one's initiation, which is demonstrated, at least in part, by the oath to/before Isis. As a ritual strategy for one's negotiation with the deity, oath taking was indeed a large part of the newly constituted relationship between Isis and the initiate (as was probably the case in other mysteries, too). Recall the Maroneia inscription discussed in the previous section (RICIS 114/0202). Additionally, a Latin inscription from Rome (RICIS 501/0127 = SIRIS 390; the first to the second century CE), written by an Isis initiate (possibly a former slave), recounts the oath that person made: "I made a vow: if I go out well, they ask the sixth part of a congius of wine (be given) inside (*Votum feci, / se recte exiero, / qu(a)erunt / intro vini / sextarios*). Then, this person, in the inscription, exhorts other initiates: "The initiate of god (*Mystes Dei* [*deus* is masculine]). Trust/believe in her/him (*Crede ei* [*ei* can be either masculine or feminine]), and do not doubt (*noli deficere*). If only you are not conscious (of one's guilt?), then you are of good courage (*animo bono sis*)." Who is this *deus* [m.]? Would it be Osiris? This is not certain because the first line of the inscription is damaged. A few lines later, however, the inscription reads: *Te, Isi, te salus ad tuos*. The meaning and syntax of this line is also not clear, because there is no verb. Yet, given the mention of a sick person two lines later ("The sickness of Theon"), the line in question can be understood as a petition to Isis. Hence, the line can be rendered: "[I ask] You,

---

49 A very similar notion is found in Aristophanes, *Frogs* 449–59, with respect to the Initiates of the Eleusinian mysteries.

Isis, you. [May] your salvation [be given] to your people." The inscription ends with the declaration, "Amphion, the initiate, be happy!" and a Greek term, μνήμη (in memory of [him?]).[50] Contrary to common assumptions, the mysteries do not guarantee whatever desirable outcomes one wants, and the oath is part of the process of negotiation (to achieve the outcomes).[51] At the end of this chapter, this aspect will be revisited.

4.1.4 Blessed Afterlife

Both literary and material evidence demonstrates that initiation into the mysteries of Isis promised a blessed afterlife to her initiates. In Apuleius's *Metamorphoses*, the blessed afterlife is clearly stated as part of the benefits that Isis promises to her initiates, although this does not mean that benefits one receives on earth are less important. In *Metam.* 11.6, Isis says,

> You will clearly remember and keep forever sealed deep in your heart the fact that the rest of your life's course is pledged to me until the very limit of your last breath. Nor is it unjust that you should owe all the time you have to live to her by whose benefit you return to the world of men. Moreover you will live in happiness, you will live in glory, under my guardianship. And when you have completed your life's span and travel down to the dead, there too, even in the hemisphere under the earth, you will find me, whom you see now, shining among the shades of Acheron and holding court in the deep recesses of the Styx, and while you dwell in the Elysian fields I will favour you and you will constantly worship me.

In this passage, Isis's protection extends beyond one's earthly life. Yet, the following sentences in 11.6 suggest that a prolonged life *on earth* remains an important benefit of Isis initiation. As Burkert puts it, "The main emphasis [of the mysteries of Isis] … is on the power of Isis ruling in this cosmos, changing the fates here and now for her protégé."[52] Nevertheless, it is fair to say that Apuleius's text envisions

---

50 This person could be the person who was responsible for this inscription and the oath mentioned in it.
51 The oath to Isis (or before Isis) is also one of the stock images used in romance novels. In Apuleius, *Metam.* 11.6, Lucius's commitment to Isis is noteworthy, but oaths sworn between human beings before this deity also have a strong binding force. In *Leucippe and Clitophon* 5.26, Melite bitterly tells Clitophon, with whom she cannot consummate her love: "Remember Isis [ἀναμνήσθητι τῆς Ἴσιδος], respect the oaths you swore before her altar [αἰδέσθητι τοὺς ὅρκους τοὺς ἐκεῖ]; if you had been willing to be my lover, as there you swore, I would have recked nought of ten thousand Thersanders. If, now you have found Leucippe, marriage with another woman is no longer possible for you, I willingly grant you even this."
52 Burkert, *Ancient Mystery Cults*, 27.

Isis's protection as covering not only an initiate's life in the "here and now," but also her/his life after death.

Additionally, a funerary inscription from Bithynia (RICIS 308/1201; second century BCE) provides further insight into the promise of a blessed afterlife for Isis initiates:

> I did not tread (οὐ ... ἔβαν) the dark funerary road to Acheron, but I, Meniketes, hastened to the harbors of the Blessed (μακάρων ... λιμένας). For I furnished the linen-covered beds of the goddess, forbidden to the laymen (ἄρρητα βεβήλοις), for the opulent dwellings of Egypt. And, honored after my death by mortals, oh stranger, I gained the remarkable reputation of the Isiacs (τὰν ἐπίσαμον φάμαν Ἰσιακῶν), in pledge (of my action). I honored my father Menestheus, leaving behind three children. May you, too, walk this way free from harm![53]

This inscription shows that the first person speaking, Meniketes, was an Isis initiate (as opposed to the "laymen" [βέβηλοι]) and he believed that, after his death (i.e., at the time when passers-by happened to read this inscription) he would have already attained a blessed afterlife ("I did not tread the dark funerary road ..."). The meaning of the Greek word (μάρτυρ') that Vermiers translates as "in pledge (of my action)" is unclear. The entire Greek sentence reads: τὰν ἐπίσαμον φάμαν Ἰσιακῶν μάρτυρ' ἐπεσπασάμαν (lit. "I gained the remarkable reputation of the Isiacs as witness [to what?]"). On what basis does Meniketes have a "remarkable reputation" postmortem? Because of the deeds that he performed while living, or the benefits Isis promised, or the oaths that he or Isis initiates made? All are possible; what is clear is the close connection between Meniketes's Isis initiation while living and his now-blessed afterlife. Moreover, it should be noted that his deeds of Isis devotion that can only be performed by the initiates ("furnishing the linen-covered beds of the goddess") are considered his "merits in life." This gives one insight into the historical development of "personal strategies" for obtaining a better afterlife.[54]

The link between Isis initiation and the afterlife is rather suggestive in other material witnesses, but still illuminating. For example, a second-century CE votive altar dedicated to Isis (Figure 9a, Figure 9b, Figure 9c, Rome) provides evidence (both in its iconographic and text) that Isis initiation may have communicated the message that initiates would enjoy a continuing, blessed relationship with the goddess in the afterlife.

---

53 The translation is from Richard Veymiers, "Introduction: Agents, Images, Practices," in *Individuals and Materials*, 1:1. Also note this inscription's use of the word ἄρρητος (cf. 2 Cor 12:4).
54 Valentino Gasparini, "I will not be thirsty. My lips will not be dry," in *Burial Rituals*, 135.

Figure 9a, Figure 9b, Figure 9c: Inv. no. MA 1544, Musée du Louvre (photo: Maurice et Pierre Chuzeville). © RMN-Grand Palais / Art Resource, NY.

The inscription on one side of the altar (Figure 9c) reads: *Isidi / sacrum / Astragalus / aeditimus / D. M.* Several interpretations of the abbreviation (*D. M.*) have been suggested: for example, in the early nineteenth century, Ossan read *D. M.* as *dedicavit monumentum*, which makes sense within the sentence.[55] Rüpke mentions other possibilities such as *dat meritae*, or *divino mandato*, but as he notes, such usage is not found elsewhere.[56] Instead, Rüpke argues that *dis manibus* is most likely, and if that is the case, this dative construction at the end corresponds to the first part of the inscription.[57] Together with other indicators such as *sacrum* and *aeditimus*, the abbreviation *D. M.* in this inscription shows that Astragalus's "permanent ritual activity" and "[t]he relationship of both [Astragalus and Isis] [that] reaches beyond death."[58] Furthermore, one side of the altar (Figure 9a) de-

---

55 F. G. Osann, *Sylloge inscriptionum antiquarum graecarum et latinarum* (Leipzig: Leske, 1834), 375.
56 Rüpke, "Theorising Religion for the Individual," 71.
57 Admittedly, this use of *dis manibus* (here, the dative *Isidi* and the dative *dis manibus* are in apposition) would be unusual because *di manes* are "the deified spirits of dead Romans," rather than other preexisting deities. For a definition of *manes*, see King, *The Ancient Roman Afterlife*, 2. Interestingly, a table on p. 11 in King's book shows two groups of Roman deities according to whether the gods in question were formerly human. The "No" column includes most public deities and (perhaps, some) *lares*, whereas the "Yes" column includes *manes, divi Augusti*, a few public cult deities, and (some) *lares*. Then, would this votive alter, which identifies Isis as *manes*, imply that Isis also had a past life as a human? King rules out the discussion of the mysteries in relation to the topic of *di manes*, which he clarifies from the outset (*The Ancient Roman Afterlife*, xxix).
58 Rüpke, "Theorising Religion for the Individual," 71.

picts a man bringing a dove offering and the other side (Figure 9b) shows a woman dressed like Isis, holding a sistrum. Rüpke interprets the woman to be Isis, rather than a priestess of Isis. These two figures seem to be approaching each other[59]—perhaps from different realms (one from the human and the other from the divine), as represented by their placement on different sides of the altar. These images evoke a emotional bond between the male devotee of Isis and his goddess that extend into the afterlife.

Female devotees of Isis experience a more explicit form of assimilation in the afterlife: these devotees become like Isis herself. There are many Attic grave reliefs dated to the Roman period that feature women with characteristics usually associated with Isis (such as her dress, hairstyle, garlands, sistrum etc.). A good example is the Isis stele, dating to the Tiberian era (Figure 10). It has been suggested that the women clothed in Isis-like dresses represent Isis priestesses or even Isis herself. Yet, based on a careful survey, Walters argues that the women on the Isis reliefs are likely Isis initiates—these women were probably from "the prosperous middle class" families and were initiated into Isis at an early age.[60] Some of the reliefs, such as one from third century CE Athens (Figure 11), exhibit a "competitive" and "ostentatious" nature. The deceased woman, Parthenope, is "not only honored on one of the few stelai signed by the sculptor, her proud husband, but also the only relief figure to have held sistrum and situla of bronze" (i.e., this figure held actual objects—they are now missing, but the holes on her hands testify to their existence).[61] What these images mean is open to various interpretations. Yet, it is possible to infer, as Frederick Brenk does, that these images reflect "women's desire to be frozen forever in marble assimilation to the goddess."[62] These images that suggest the deceased woman's "Isification" are comparable to inscriptions that identify the deceased person with Osiris (i.e., "Osirification"). The latter appears, for example, in a funerary inscription (probably the first century CE) found in the church of Santa Maria in Monticelli in Rome (RICIS 501/0196 = SIRIS 463 = IG XIV 2098).[63] The monumentality of the reliefs and inscriptions works well with these messages of initiates' Isification and Osirification.

---

59 Rüpke, "Theorising Religion for the Individual," 71.
60 Elizabeth J. Walters, *Attic Grave Reliefs that Represent Women in the Dress of Isis* (Hesperia Supplement XXII; Princeton: American School of Classical Studies at Athens, 1988), 56.
61 Walters, *Attic Grave Reliefs*, 57, 24.
62 Frederick E. Brenk, "A Gleaming Ray: Blessed Afterlife in the Mysteries," *ICS* 18 (1993): 157.
63 Gasparini, "I will not be thirsty," 125–127. The translation of the inscription reads: "Flavia Servanda, also called Agrippina, very virtuous, be of good cheer in the company of Osiris (ΜΕΤΑ ΤΟΥ ΟΣΕΙΡΙΔΟΣ; or, "with Osiris")." Gasparini notes that this last phrase could be interpreted as indicating a kind of "hierogamy" (i.e., the deceased woman, Servanda, replaces Isis and becomes Osir-

Figure 10: National Archaeological Museum, Athens, Theseion 140 (photographer: Eleftherios Galanpoulos). Reproduced by the permission of the National Archaeological Museum in Athens. © Hellenic Ministry of Culture and Sports/Hellenic Organization of Cultural Resources Development (H.O.C.RE.D).

is's consort). Yet, he argues that it should be understood as this woman being "osirified." Even if

4.1 The Self-referential Messages, or the Benefits Initiation Promises — 127

Figure 11: National Archaeological Museum, Athens, NAM inv. no. 1244 (photographer: Athanasios Meliarakis). © Hellenic Ministry of Culture and Sports/Hellenic Organization of Cultural Resources Development (H.O.C.RE.D).

---

one disagrees with Gasparini's interpretation and takes the view of hierogamy, it still holds true that the deceased woman is somewhat deified—in this case, as Isis, like other women appearing in Attic grave reliefs mentioned above. Also, note that the deceased person's assimilation with Osiris reveals long-standing Egyptian influence.

In the literary witnesses to the Isis mysteries in the second century (i.e., Plutarch's *Isis and Osiris* and Apuleius's *Metamorphoses*), the picture of a blessed afterlife takes a more Platonic tone. Brenk notes, "In Apuleius' *Metamorphoses* ... the trials of Lucius and his ultimate release through Isis probably is a Platonic allegory of the soul's entrapment in the world we love, its release through appreciation of the intelligible realities, and its expectation, in the next life, of the blessed vision of the Form."[64] How much these literary representations reflect the actual messages communicated through ordinary people's participation in the initiation ritual is a matter of debate. But some elements in Isis rituals might have been conducive to further philosophical interpretations. Once such interpretations of ritual developed in texts, the particular message represented in the textualized ritual, conversely, began to influence and shape people's experience of ritual participation, which is also the case with textualized ritual in the Hebrew Bible and the New Testament.

4.1.5 Development of One's Cognitive Capability

A certain tradition related to the mysteries of Isis shows that Isis initiation may have communicated a message about the enrichment of an individual initiate's inner life—including cognitive development. The concept of individual cognitive development sounds very modern, but the "discovery of the individual" is not necessarily a modern invention.[65] Apuleius and Plutarch interpret the Isis mysteries as the medium for developing the individual initiate's cognitive capability. This line of ritual interpretation or the emphasis on the self (esp. inwardness) did not begin in the second century CE.[66] The tradition that appropriates and interprets mystery in-

---

64 Brenk, "A Gleaming Ray," 149.
65 Regarding the emergence of an individual self in history, David Lambert makes an interesting observation on the history of scholarship: "Not surprisingly, scholars working within a wide range of historical periods have discovered that it is in the period of their specialization that the self, more or less as we know it today, first emerged." Lambert then lists several examples of scholars who argue for the invention/emergence of the individual self in the period that they examine: such as B. Snell (ancient Greece); P. Cary (Augustine); C. Morris (the eleventh to twelfth century); C. Walker Bynum (the twelfth century); S. Greenblatt (Renaissance); S. Bercovitch (the Puritans); and J. Lyons (the eighteenth century). David Lambert, "'Desire' Enacted in the Wilderness: Problems in the History of the Self and Bible Translation," in *Self, Self-Fashioning, and Individuality in Late Antiquity: New Perspectives*, ed. Maren R. Niehoff and Joshua Levinson (Tübingen: Mohr Siebeck, 2019), 25.
66 Historians of the ancient world (or early Christianity) often think that late antiquity (or at the earliest, at the turn of the era) was the period in which one can detect the notion of individuality

itiations for philosophical enterprises already emerged in the Platonic corpus.[67] Burkert points out that the literary appearance of the "self-conscious ego" traces back to classical Greece in the seventh/sixth centuries BCE.[68] The seeking of individuality with respect to religious activity did not merely result from the "invasion" of the "Oriental" cults that modified the classical polis religion; it was already rooted in Greek religious tradition. Burkert continues:

> Alongside participation in the polis festivals as fixed by the calendar there emerges the interest in something special, chosen by oneself, and hence in additional initiations and mysteries. At the same time individual death, which is built into the system of communal life as an unquestionable fact, becomes a *personal problem* more than before.[69]

Apuleius's and Plutarch's literary texts depict a noticeable development within the mysteries of Isis. This development places emphasis on how initiation affects one's inward aspect, including enhanced cognition.

Another interesting point is that in both texts, Isis, though powerful, becomes an intermediary deity who leads initiates to the higher deity, Osiris. This staged upward movement corresponds to one's cognitive growth. In this philosophically constructed interpretation of Isis initiation, one's participation in the Isis initiation is a step towards Osiris initiation. This is quite distinctive when compared to the Dionysiac mysteries and interpretative traditions. As has been noted, sometimes Dionysus also functions as an intermediary (or intercessory) in the afterlife, as depicted in the gold tablets or on the Apulian volute krater (Figure 8), but Dionysus was not presented as the means to access a higher deity (yet, the myth of Dionysus's

---

or some type of human inwardness. This is the position argued in most of the essays found in Niehoff and Levinson, eds., *Self, Self-Fashioning*.
67 For example, see the essays in Martín-Velasco and Blanco, eds., *Greek Philosophy and Mystery Cults*. For more on this book, see ch. 2.
68 Burkert, *Greek Religion*, 278.
69 Italics mine. Burkert, *Greek Religion*, 278. Burkert's description better captures the dynamic reality of antiquity than Scheid's statement about Roman religion in his introductory book. Scheid notes, "[Roman religion] was a religion that involved no initiation and no teaching. Religious duties were imposed on individuals by their birth, adoption, affranchisement or grant of Roman citizenship. In short, these duties were linked to the social status of an individual and not to any personal decision of a spiritual kind (such as baptism or conversion, for example)." Scheid, *An Introduction to Roman Religion*, 19. It is doubtful whether this generalized statement can adequately embrace the diversity and plurality of religious phenomena in the Greco-Roman world, which included the mysteries rooted in Greek tradition as part of its overall cultural system. One wonders where one could locate the mysteries—that actually flourished in the Roman world—within Scheid's picture of Roman religion, if there was "no initiation and no teaching" in Roman religion and no room for "any personal decision of a spiritual kind."

dismemberment by the Titans was somehow allegorized; for example, see Plutarch, *On the Eating of the Flesh* 1.7).[70] In Apuleius's *Metam.* 11, the initiate's cognitive growth is clearly one of the benefits Isis provides (one which would eventually lead Lucius to the ineffable deity, Osiris).[71]

Admittedly, this would relate more to those who combine philosophical interests with Isis devotion, or those who appropriate the mysteries of Isis for her/his philosophy, rather than every ordinary initiate. The narrative of *Metam.* 11 reveals how a particular relationship between the mystery deity and a newly converted devotee is developing and maturing. This individual, Lucius, participates in the public procession for the goddess, but he also separates himself from others, or more precisely, he develops separately his inner religiosity. A vivid contrast appears at the end of the procession; the celebrant crowd has at last left for their homes, while Lucius remains there in the contemplation of his deity. The text reads, "For my part, my heart would not let me go a nail's breadth away from that spot, but I continued to concentrate on the goddess's image as I pondered my former misfortunes." In a later scene, Lucius bears witness to his former misfortunes and present joy (enabled by the goddess), and then "return[ed] again to the contemplation of the goddess [*ad deae ... conspectum*; or, "the presence of the goddess"], which was [his] greatest delight" (11.19). The inner life, in *Metamorphoses*, includes deeper cognitive activity, which one could call spiritual discernment. When a dream vision comes to Lucius, featuring abundant gifts, the chief priest, and a slave named Candidus, he ponders in his mind/thought (*cogitationes*) the meaning of the vision for a long time (11.20). The remarks about the individual's inward devotion and contemplation, which are quite distinguished from the public procession of the cult, are unmistakable.[72]

Plutarch's *Isis and Osiris* clearly relates Isis and her mysteries to the acquisition of true knowledge, especially the knowledge of the true God in the Platonic sense. Thus, Brenk notes, "*On Isis and Osiris* reveals how all these mysterious, and at first sight barbarous, myths, rites, and symbols conform to the principal ten-

---

[70] Such an allegorical approach to Dionysiac tradition is also found in later Christian writers. See, for example, Fulgentius, *Myths* 2.12.
[71] Jeffrey Thomas Winkle, "Daemons, Demiurges, and Dualism: Apuleius' *Metamorphoses* and the Mysticism of Late Antiquity" (PhD diss. Northwestern University, 2002), 18.
[72] My interpretation of *Metam.* 11 maintains that the author Apuleius presents the story of Lucius's initiation and religious experiences as serious and genuine. Yet, there are recent critical views about the religious awakening of Lucius. Nathan Watson notes, "[T]he joy Lucius finds is misplaced—he has not achieved an enlightened state." "Dreams and Superstition: A Reinterpretation of Satire in Apuleius, *Metamorphoses* 11," *AN* 11 (2014): 155. However, I do not think that *Metam.* 11 presents Isis and Osiris as "no less flawed than the other characters of the novel."

ets of Plutarch's Middle Platonism."[73] The close relationship between Isis devotion and true knowledge seems, at least partly, based on Plutarch's (inaccurate) etymology about Ἴσις and οἶδα.[74] According to Plutarch, Isis is "a goddess exceptionally wise and a lover of wisdom (φιλόσοφον), to whom, as her name at least seems to indicate, knowledge (τὸ εἰδέναι) and understanding (τὴν ἐπιστήμην) are in the highest degree appropriate" (351E-F). Right after this introduction, Plutarch continues to speak of the divine benefits she provides to her initiates in two ways: first, she "collects and puts together" the "sacred writing," which was torn by her enemy, and "hands it over" (παραδίδωσι) to her initiates (τοῖς τελουμένοις) who are ascetic and morally excellent; second, as the "end/aim" (τέλος) of their devotion to her is the knowledge (γνῶσις) of the ultimate deity, "the First, the Lord of All, the Ideal [νοητός] One," whom she "urges [them] to seek (παρακαλεῖ ζητεῖν)" (351F–352A).[75] This supreme deity is probably Osiris,[76] because in 355E, Plutarch also reports the Egyptian description of the birth of Osiris, accompanied by a voice, "The Lord of All advances to the light" (ὁ πάντων κύριος εἰς φῶς πρόεισιν). In Plutarch's view, similarly to that of Apuleius, Isis functions as an intermediary deity that advances her devotees toward the knowledge of the highest deity, by virtue of her wisdom and giving of wisdom.

4.2 The Canonical Messages, or the Grounds for the Efficacy of the Initiation's Promises

4.2.1 Isis Established the Initiation Ritual

Earlier (ch. 3) it was noted that the understanding that Dionysus established initiation and commanded his devotees to practice it was a canonical message that sustains the efficacy of initiation. The message of the deity's establishment of initiation is more strongly detected in the Isis tradition than the Dionysiac tradition.

---

73 Brenk, "A Gleaming Ray," 148.
74 Frank C. Babbitt, *Plutarch, Moralia V* (LCL 306), 8, note b. Plutarch regards Isis's name as Greek (Ἑλληνικὸν γὰρ ἡ Ἴσίς ἐστι, *Is. Os.* 351F; cf. 352A, which interprets her sanctuary, Ἰσεῖον, in a similar way.
75 Note that the verbs are in the present tense, although it is possible that they are historical present.
76 Hans Dieter Betz and Edgar W. Smith, Jr., "De Iside et Osiride (Moralia 351C – 384C)," in *Plutarch's Theological Writings and Early Christian Literature*, ed. Hans Dieter Betz (Leiden: Brill, 1975), 40.

In addition to the fact that Isis is a goddess who reveals herself,[77] she frequently appears as the deity who establishes her initiation and thereby guarantees the legitimacy and efficacy of Isis initiation. This idea that Isis herself established initiation appears both in literary and non-literary sources.

Among the many identities (ἐγώ εἰμι form) and deeds of Isis (ἐγώ + other verbs) in the Isis aretalogy in Kyme (RICIS 302/0204), Isis reveals herself as the founder of her mysteries: Ἐγὼ μυήσεις ἀνθρώποις ἐπέδε[ι]ξα ("I myself displayed [my] mysteries to people"). Another inscription from the Serapeum in Thessalonica (RICIS 113/0545 = IG X,2 1.254; the first to the second century CE), which has a self-aretalogy of Isis similar to the one from Kyme, appears to contain the same line Ἐγὼ μυήσεις ἀνθρώποις ἐπέδειξα, although it is uncertain due to the inscription's fragmentary condition (The extant line reads ... ΟΙΣΕΠΕΔΕΙΞΑ ...).[78] If the aretalogies were used in ritual contexts, as Paraskevi Martzavou suggests, then this canonical message was probably communicated clearly through ritual, and the initiates naturally accepted the authority and efficacy of the initiation.[79]

This idea that Isis establishes her mysteries and instructs people in them is also implied in literary sources (but less directly than in evidence drawn from material culture). Here, it is emphasized that she takes the initiative with individual devotees. In Apuleius' *Metamorphoses*, any performance related to the initiation into her mysteries (including the public procession) depends on the oracular signal of this deity and her "good will" toward those who wish to be her devotees. Isis says to Lucius: "At my command [*meo monitu*; "at my admonition by oracles/ omens"],[80] my priest, as part of his equipment for the procession, will carry in his right hand a garland of roses attached to the sistrum. So do not hesitate, but eagerly push through the crowd and join the procession, relying on my good

---

77 E.g., *Metamorphoses* 11 begins with a scene in which Lucius sees "the full circle of the moon glistening with extraordinary brilliance." He recognizes the mysterious light of the moon in the night as the sign that "the supreme goddess now exercised the fullness of her power" (*summatem deam praecipua maiestate pollere*; 11.1). This is divine revelation.
78 Indeed, many other sentences in the printed form of this inscription (in RICIS) are bracketed, which indicates reconstruction. The sentences in question read: [... Ἐγὼ μετὰ τοῦ ἀδελφοῦ] Ὀσίριδος τὰς ἀν[θρωποφαγίας ἔπαυσα. Ἐγὼ μυήσεις ἀνθρώπ]οις ἐπέδειξα. The Ἐγὼ μυήσεις ἀνθρώπ- part is in brackets. The reconstruction is not without reason; there are several comparable, complete Isis aretalogies from which to draw. The Kyme inscription (see above) is such an example. Yet, another inscription found in Ios (RICIS 202/1101 = IG XII,5 14; the third century CE) has ἀνέδειξα instead of ἐπέδειξα.
79 Paraskevi Martzavou, "Isis Aretalogies, Initiations, and Emotions: The Isis Aretalogies as a Source for the Study of Emotions," in *Unveiling Emotions: Sources and Methods for the Study of Emotions in the Greek World*, ed. Angelos Chaniotis (Stuttgart: Franz Steiner Verlag, 2012), 267–68.
80 Also, later in this section, a similar phrase, *meo iussu* ("at my command"), appears.

will [*mea volentia fretus*]" (*Metam.* 11.6). Her ability to be present in different places simultaneously also increases the reliability of her power and favor. Isis encourages Lucius not to be overwhelmed by the apparent difficulty of the task she commands: "Do not shrink from any of my instructions because it seems difficult; for at this very moment when I come to you I am present there too [*simul et ibi praesens*] and am instructing my priest in his sleep about what he must do next" (*Metam.* 11.6). This contemporaneous revelation of Isis to Lucius and the priest is confirmed in 11.13, in which the priest recognizes the ass, Lucius. After Lucius's human transformation and his new life as an Isis devotee in the temple, Isis appears in a vision and again takes the initiative urging him to be initiated, for which he has "long been destined" [*iam dudum destinatum*] (11.19). In short, *Metam.* 11 shows that Isis orchestrates Lucius's initiation with the greatest care. To use a Christian analogy, Isis's grace/favor toward her would-be initiate always precedes the human response through her divine providence.

4.2.2 Isis is the All-powerful, Universal Deity

In addition to Isis's establishing initiation and taking the initiative with her initiates, the efficacy of benefits promised by Isis initiation is also predicated upon the far-reaching power of Isis—Isis is an all-powerful, almost "universal" goddess. In a striking way, the deity reveals herself as an omnipotent creator god in the epigraphic witnesses. An Isis aretalogy from Kyme (RICIS 302/0204) states, "I divided earth from heaven" (Ἐγὼ ἐχώρισα γῆν ἀπ' οὐρανοῦ), which is, Versnel notes, "an act of creation no Greek god could boast."[81] The many names of Isis are also related to her power and universality. Although it is common that deities in antiquity had different names, or that deities of different names were identified with one another, this phenomenon receives particular prominence in the case of Isis. In *Metam.* 11.2, Lucius, who does not know precisely the identity of the goddess he feels, calls upon the names of several famous goddesses, such as Ceres (i.e., Demeter), Venus, Phoebus's sister (Diana?), and Proserpina (i.e., Persephone). As Lucius says, "by whatever name, with whatever rite, in whatever image it is meet to invoke you" (*quoquo nomine, quoquo ritu, quaqua facie te fas est invocare*), the goddess appears and reveals herself as a universal deity, who is "worshipped by all the world (*totus veneratur orbis*) under different forms, with various rites, and by manifold names." He then adds several other names (e.g., Cybele, Minerva, etc.) by which people in various areas call her (11.5). This flexibility and universal ap-

---

[81] Versnel, *Ter Unus*, 43.

plicability may have been appealing to many. The Isis litany (P.Oxy. 1380; the second century CE) also emphasizes Isis's many-names (she is πολυώνυμος), providing a long list of her names in Egyptian towns as well as in other regions throughout the Mediterranean world.[82]

The power of Isis is implicitly contrasted with that of other deities and other mysteries. The hope that the Isis devotees overcome fate, as discussed earlier in relation to the Isis aretalogy, also relies on Isis being strong enough to overcome her own fate as well as that of her devotees.[83] The narrative of *Metamorphoses* occasionally reveals that Isis is the most (or even the sole) powerful deity. For example, before Lucius's transformation into a donkey, he had already undergone many other mystery initiations (*sacris pluribus initiatus*) (3.15); yet, these did not deliver Lucius from his calamities. The story of Cupid and Psyche, embedded within *Metamorphoses*, also portrays Ceres (Demeter; the Eleusinian mysteries) as unable to help Psyche (6.2–3). The priests of the Syrian goddess (in Book 8) are sarcastically depicted as charlatans. In contrast, Isis appears at the end of the story as the genuinely powerful and merciful deity who can help Lucius, making him wholly devoted to her.

4.2.3 Isis Sympathizes with Her Devotees

The efficacy of Isis initiation was not only based on her all-powerful and universal nature; it is also her sympathy for human beings that may have been an important part of the canonical messages that sustain the effectiveness of her initiation (this somehow resonates with the discussion of her initiative and providence). As Witt

---

[82] *Metamorphoses* also suggests that only the Egyptians had true knowledge of the real name of the goddess (*regina Isis*) and also knew the right way of her *ritus* (11.5). Similarly, the Isis ἐγκώμιον in Maroneia (RICIS 114/0202; the end of the second century BCE) mentions Egypt as her dwelling place (κατοίκησις), which she particularly loves (σοὶ πρὸς κατοίκησιν Αἴγυπτος ἐστέρχθη; lines 34–35). Yet, as Gasparro points out, it is noticeable that the encomium does not describe Egypt as her place of origin, but only her favorite κατοίησις, and the next line ("in Greece you honored Athens above all") also "specifies the clear Hellenic orientation of her sphere of action." Gasparro, "The Hellenistic Face of Isis," 42.

[83] Commenting on the mystery cults in the Roman world, Scheid notes with a definitive tone: "There is no similarity between these [mystery] cults and Christianity. They conveyed no message of triumph over death nor did they offer any fundamentally new revelations." (*An Introduction to Roman Religion*, 188). Yet, the mysteries of Isis do indeed provide messages of a "triumph over death" by highlighting Isis as a universal and all-powerful deity who overcomes fate. Also, despite Scheid's negative view, Isis aretalogy (such as that of Kyme) functions to reveal herself to human beings in its declarative literary form of ἐγώ εἰμί.

noted a half century ago, "[I]n one respect at least she is unique among pagan deities, for she overflows with affection and compassion."[84] Particularly, Isis pays attention to human affliction and shows sympathy to human beings, because she herself experienced suffering.[85] There are a few pieces of evidence for this, for example, PGM 36, 134 ff, but it appears most memorably and extensively in Plutarch's report of her myth and his interpretation of it.[86] In *Is. Os.* 361D–E, when he talks about virtues and vices of "demigods" (δαίμονες),[87] he describes what happened after Isis achieved her revenge:

> But the avenger, the sister and wife of Osiris, after she had quenched and suppressed the madness and fury of Typhon, was not indifferent (οὐ περιεῖδε) to the contests and struggles (τοὺς ἄθλους καὶ τοὺς ἀγῶνας) which she had endured, nor to her own wanderings (πλάνας αὐτῆς) nor to her manifold deeds of wisdom and many feats of bravery, nor would she accept oblivion and silence for them, but she intermingled (ἀναμείξασα) in the most holy rites (ταῖς ἁγιωτάταις … τελεταῖς) portrayals and suggestions and representations (εἰκόνας καὶ ὑπονοίας καὶ μιμήματα) of her experiences at that time (τῶν τότε παθημάτων; or, "of her *sufferings* at that time"), and sanctified them, both as a lesson in godliness (εὐσεβείας … δίδαγμα) and an encouragement (παραμύθιον) for men and women who find themselves in the clutch of like calamities (ὑπὸ συμφορῶν ἐχομένοις ὁμοίων) (*Is. Os.* 361D–E).

Four notable things are found in this quotation. First, Isis appears as a deity who experienced human-like sufferings, depicted with the help of athletic imagery, such as "contests" and "struggles." She wandered in searching for her murdered husband Osiris, and that is an important part of her παθήματα. Second, Isis did not overlook (οὐ περιεῖδε) her παθήματα; rather, she was self-conscious about them, even immortalizing her experiences by establishing the cult. Third, in doing so, she mixed the "portrayals and suggestions and representations of her former ex-

---

84 Witt, *Isis in the Ancient World*, 18.
85 This aspect is also found in Dionysiac traditions. Yet, the portrayal of Dionysus as one who experiences grief for other humans who also experience grief for grieving humans is much later: e.g., the *Dionysiaca* of Nonnus ("Bacchus, the Lord, cried to liberate mortal from weeping" [12.171: Βάκχος ἄναξ δάκρυσε, βροτῶν ἵνα δάκρυα λύσῃ], de la Fuente, "Parallels between Dionysos and Christ," 482). In contrast, this portrayal of Isis is found much earlier, i.e., in Plutarch's writing (the late first century to the early second century CE).
86 Although Plutarch was mostly influenced by Middle Platonism, "the notion of a universal *sympatheia*" as seen in this passage regarding Isis is "more Stoic than Platonic." Gasparini, "Isis and Osiris," 717.
87 Plutarch regards Osiris, Isis, and Typhon as "demigods" ("daimons") from 360D onward; in 361E, Plutarch adds that Isis and Osiris were transformed from demigods to gods due to their virtues.

perience (or sufferings)" into the ritual of her mysteries.[88] Therefore, fourth, the initiates, who suffer "from similar kind of calamities," can find both "a lesson in piety" and "encouragement" from Isis by participating in her mysteries (cf. Heb 2:18). According to this passage, the efficacy of the benefits of initiation (in this case, the benefit is to obtain a lesson and encouragement in the midst of calamities) is predicated upon the goddess's suffering, her sympathy for people, and the ritual elements instituted by her, which reflect her own experiences.

The compassionate nature of Isis is also reflected in Apuleius's literary presentation. In *Metam.* 11.5, Isis says to Lucius, "I have come in pity at your misfortunes; I have come in sympathy and good will" (*Adsum tuos miserata casus, adsum favens et propitia*). She is the "savior goddess" (*Metam.* 11.9). Implicitly, the narrative of *Metamorphoses* demonstrates that the transformation of Lucius was not achieved by his own "faithfulness" or favor toward the goddess, but by the favor (and initiative) of the goddess who sympathizes with Lucius's calamities. Right after Lucius's public transformation (his "rebirth," according to the crowd) from an ass to a human, everyone in the crowd begins to talk about him:

> He is the one who was transformed back into a human being today by the majestic force of the all-powerful goddess. How fortunate he is, by Hercules, and thrice blessed! It is doubtless because of the innocence and faithfulness of his past life [*vitae ... praecedentis innocentia fideque*] that he has earned [*meruerit:* "merited"] such remarkable patronage from heaven that he was in a manner reborn [*renatus*] and immediately engaged to the service of her cult [*sacrorum obsequio desponderetur*] (*Metam.* 11.16).

A reader of this narrative, who knows the former life of Lucius, and who has just heard the priest's words in 11.15 ("... on the slippery path of headstrong youth you plunged into slavish pleasures and reaped the perverse reward of your ill-starred curiosity"), will recognize that the crowd's response is not accurate; Lucius was neither innocent nor faithful in his past life.[89] Perhaps, this irony and inaccuracy

---

[88] See also Betz and Smith's comments on this phrase (εἰκόνας καὶ ὑπονοίας ...) in 361E: "This statement, with many of its terms being religious technical terms, describes the purpose of the mystery ritual as initiating the worshipper into the imitation of the god ... Comparable is Paul's interpretation of baptism as an initiation into the faith-experience of the imitation of dying and rising with Christ (Ro vi)." Betz and Smith, "De Iside et Osiride," 55–56. This general comparison is valid, even though the Isis mysteries do not have precisely the same notion of "dying and rising" with the deity. On this topic (Isis initiates share the fate of Isis), more will be discussed in the following section.

[89] His transformation into a donkey occurred due to his excessive curiosity (3.14, 22), but he blames Photis for his misfortune (9.15) (throughout *Metamorphoses*, curiosity is a repeated problem: it causes people to stumble and make serious mistakes that bring catastrophic results. This is not only for Lucius, but also for other characters [e.g., Psyche in 5.22–24; 6.20]). Bestiality

can be resolved by viewing the audience's remark about Lucius's meritorious life as referring back to his life *before* all his "adventures," as Griffiths mentions.[90] Yet, it is more likely that the narrator intends the crowd's words to be read proleptically: after Lucius experienced his remarkable transformation, he becomes a devout Isis-devotee (11.19 onwards), for whom the word *innocentia* makes sense. To put it simply, not only "priority" (see my earlier discussion in 4.2.1) but also "incongruity" and "efficacy" are essential to Isis's grace.[91]

4.2.4 The Initiates Share the Fate and Suffering of Isis

The most significant canonical message is that the initiates share the fate of the deity through their participation in her mysteries, and this guarantees the efficacy of the other promised benefits, such as deliverance from tribulations and/or a blessed afterlife. As discussed in an earlier section, iconographic tradition suggests that female initiates of Isis were identified with Isis in the afterlife, which indicates a shared identity between Isis and her devotees. In addition to that, one particular aretalogy of Isis (Andros; RICIS 202/1801 = IG XII,5 739) provides intriguing evidence that Isis initiation communicated this identification through the ritual process. Martzavou, who claims that Isis aretalogies indeed played important roles in the initiation rituals of Isis mysteries,[92] observes a distinctive shift from the "You-are-Isis" type to the "I-am-Isis" type, which is made midway in the Isis aretalogy from Andros. Martzavou notes,

> The significant detail is present only in the text of Andros: it is the shift to the first person in the enumeration of Isis deeds, attributes, and powers. This self-asserting formula, enhanced by the personhood-altering initiatic experience and by the blurred perception of the divine that we analysed in the previous section, would allow the initiate to experience a very powerful identification with the divine, and allow him to 'become' god for the few moments that the recitation of this text lasted.[93]

---

also appears when a lady enticed and forced Lucius (as the donkey) to have sex with her (10.20–22). Ultimately, this leads to greater humiliation of Lucius in public that is supposed to culminate in Lucius's theatrical marriage to a female criminal (though Lucius manages to escape) (10.23, 29–35).
90 Griffiths, *Apuleius*, 257 (this interpretation was suggested by Berreth).
91 These terms are from John M. G. Barclay, *Paul and the Gift* (Grand Rapids: Eerdmans, 2015). Barclay presents six ways to "perfect" the gift/grace in the Judeo-Christian tradition: they are superabundance, singularity, priority, incongruity, efficacy, and non-circularity.
92 Martzavou, "Isis Aretalogies," 267–68.
93 Martzavou, "Isis Aretalogies," 285–86.

That is, one who recites this aretalogy in a ritual setting possibly impersonates the deity (or unwittingly obtains such emotional experiences) with the "I-am-Isis" statements. Similar to Dionysiac initiation, the shared identity between the deity and the devotee is both a self-referential message (the initiate partakes in the deity's identity) and a canonical message (this identity guarantees the efficacy of the other benefits indicated by initiation).

Admittedly, none of this means that the initiates were precisely experiencing "dying and rising" with the "dying and rising deity." Furthermore, in the aretalogy above, Isis does not appear as a dying and rising goddess. Reitzenstein claims that the initiates of Osiris share his dying and rising by "putting on [Osiris's] clothing or by employing the means by which the god was awakened from the dead."[94] But this claim about Osiris initiation needs to be more nuanced, and it is doubtful whether *Isis* initiation can be understood in the same way. There are stories about Isis's suffering and hardship, but one must look beyond the dying-and-rising deity model to better understand Isis's experiences. Therefore, I do not focus on this dying-and-rising aspect.

Indeed, that the initiates share the fate and suffering of Isis is both the self-referential and canonical messages of Isis initiation. Various types of evidence confirm that a deeper relationship between the deity and her initiates is one of the self-referential messages communicated by the initiation ritual. At the same time, this relationship also provides the canonical dimension that guarantees the other promised benefits.[95] To substantiate this claim, three issues are to be discussed in detail: first, the suffering of Isis and/or Osiris is part of the message conveyed in Isis initiation; second, taking Osiris into account is justified to some extent; and third, devotees could experience some type of identification with the deities through initiation.

First, it is reasonable to infer that the actual Isis initiation rituals accompanied the representations of sacred stories concerning Isis/Osiris's suffering. Isis is a suffering deity, though not a dying and rising deity.[96] Admittedly, Apuleius's account

---

94 Reitzenstein, *Hellenistic Mystery-Religions*, 13.
95 Reitzenstein, *Hellenistic Mystery-Religions*, 11.
96 As already mentioned, many scholars from the Moratorium on the Quest stage onward have pointed out that the old model of a dying-and-rising god may not fit the mysteries of Isis, because in no tradition is Isis a deity who dies and rises. According to Wedderburn, many mystery deities are mourning deities, and this is also the case with Isis. Osiris can probably be regarded as a deity who dies and rises (e.g., Firmicus Maternus, *de errore* 22.1). Yet, in the mysteries of Isis, Osiris does not always play a significant role. Thus, scholars have concluded that it is not likely that the initiates of the mysteries of Isis participated in the fate of Isis as a dying and rising deity. This criticism is valid in itself, but it needs qualification. Above all, although Isis does not form a precise parallel to the dying-and-rising deity model, it is still remarkable that Isis experiences some

does not clearly state that there was a "sacred drama" performed during initiation.[97] Yet, one cannot entirely exclude such a practice. Bremmer admits that Lucius's appearance with his new clothes before the public after the night of initiation signals his new status "publicly dramatised and advertised."[98] If there were no dramatic representation leading to this culmination, the final appearance would arise out of thin air. According to Merkelbach, the communal meal following Lucius's appearance is also part of the initiation drama ("Einweihungs-Schauspiel").[99] The whole initiation process may include other elements of "sacred drama." Apart from Apuleius's text, some indirect witnesses corroborate this theory. The first-century CE poet Statius's *Silvae* 5.3.242–245 could be referring to women's ritual mourning over the death of Osiris,[100] although his tone is quite sarcastic. Elements of the deity's suffering were probably part of Isis/Osiris cults in the pre-Hellenistic period, as Herodotus's report suggests (the fifth century BCE). Herodotus makes this intriguing remark about the nocturnal dramatic representation at Sais (according to him, the Egyptians called it the mysteries): "On this lake they enact by night the story of the god's sufferings (τὰ δείκηλα τῶν παθέων αὐτοῦ), a rite which the Egyptians call the Mysteries (τὰ καλέουσι μυστήρια Αἰγύπτιοι). I could speak more exactly of these matters, for I know the truth, but I will hold my peace" (*The Persian Wars* 2.171). In this passage, "his (masculine αὐτοῦ; probably, Osiris, not Isis) sufferings" seem to have been dramatically represented during the mysteries. Caution is required when interpreting Herodotus's report, and one cannot find concrete evidence in this report that ritual participants shared the deity's suffering through ritual.[101] At the least, the passage could be evidence

---

type of suffering, through her loss, separation, and mourning (even though it is not her "death"). Because of this suffering, she obtained sympathy for human beings who also are struggling with various types of suffering. The initiation into her mysteries reminds people of her suffering and provides the opportunity to establish a special and intimate relationship with her by reflecting on their own past and present. This sharp contrast between the deity's mythical past and present is replicated in Lucius's testimony to others; it embodies the contrast between his "former suffering" and his "present joys" (*meis ... pristinis aerumnis et praesentibus gaudiis*) (*Metam.* 11.19).
97 Bremmer, *Initiation*, 124, is skeptical about its existence.
98 Bremmer, *Initiation*, 124.
99 Merkelbach, *Isis regina*, 295.
100 Heyob, *The Cult of Isis among Women*, 56–57.
101 This passage does not say whether the initiates thought that they were participating in the deity's suffering. Also, one does not know to what extent the same practice existed in later periods and other areas. Furthermore, it is possible that this ritual was not part of the mysteries at all. Bremmer strongly argues that "the Egyptians did not call these performances Mysteries, which is clearly Herodotus' interpretation, as they did not have a general term or exact equivalent for what the Greeks called Mysteries." Bremmer, *Initiation*, 110–11. Bricault also notes that the Egyptian ritual mentioned by Herodotus is not a mystery initiation, as in the Greek world (which Bri-

that Herodotus found some elements in these Egyptian cults analogous to the prominent mysteries of his culture (i.e., the Eleusinian mysteries), probably dramatic representations of the deity's suffering before the eyes of the ritual participants.

Second, it is possible to bring Osiris tradition into the discussion of the mysteries of Isis when one pays careful attention to detail. This will strengthen the hypothesis that the mysteries of Isis communicated the message about shared experience (esp. suffering) between the deity (or deities) and the initiates. The objection to using Osiris tradition when discussing Isis initiation primarily comes from the unclear connection between Isis and Osiris in *Metamorphoses*.[102] Despite the existence of a separate mystery cult for Osiris mentioned at the end (*Metam.* 11.30), there is no mythic story for Osiris included in the Isis initiation as described in *Metam.* 11.[103] Given other ancient evidence, however, Osiris (and the seeking/finding of him) is not entirely absent from the mysteries of Isis in the Roman period (cf. Ovid, *Metam.* 9.693: *numquamque satis quaesitus Osiris*). Even in Apuleius's *Metam.* 11.9, the Isis procession entails "pipers dedicated to mighty Sarapis," that is, Osiris.[104] In the procession of the gods (11.11), Apuleius's account suggests that both Isis and Osiris are visually present for the ritual, the former by a cow that is "the fertile symbol of the divine mother of all" (cf. Plutarch) and the latter by an *urnula*, which contains "the venerable image of the supreme deity."[105] As Winkle argues, if Osiris is envisioned as a highest, "ineffable" deity in the Platonic sense, and Isis takes the role of the "intermediary" deity who leads Lucius to that deity,[106] it is possible to see Isis and Osiris as separate figures with distinct

---

cault thinks includes the establishment of some direct, personal relationship between the deity and the individuals), but it was rather "une allusion à des drames sacrés représentant la passion d'Osiris." Bricault, *Les cultes isiaques*, 430. Regardless of whether the Egyptians actually called them mysteries, Herodotus's report should receive serious attention, because he found it reasonable to label the ritual enactment of god's sufferings "mysteries" back in the fifth century BCE. Yet, the passage demonstrates that Herodotus found the Egyptian ritual at Sais similar to the Eleusinian mysteries.

102 Also, regarding the passage from Herodotus, Herodotus mainly speaks of Osiris's suffering, not that of Isis's.
103 Wagner, *Pauline Baptism*, 106.
104 Yet, Bricault distinguishes the remark about Sarapis from that of Osiris in *Metamorphoses*. According to him, the conception of mysteries is applied only to Osiris, and Sarapis never appears to be a god of mysteries in Apuleius's work. Bricault, *Les cultes isiaques*, 431. (Wagner briefly mentioned the difference between Osiris and Sarapis, especially focusing on the fact that the Hellenistic deity Sarapis was never "a dying and rising god." Wagner, *Pauline Baptism*, 92–93.)
105 For linking the *urnula* to Osiris Hydreios, see Griffiths, *Apuleius*, 215, 227–32.
106 Winkle, "Daemons," 18.

roles, and yet still present with each other in the Isis mysteries envisioned in *Metam.* 11.

Other pieces of material and literary evidence also point toward the interwoven net of meanings in Isis/Osiris initiation. The popularity of Osiris, along with Isis, is also seen in the archaeological evidence from Corinth.[107] Scholarly views vary. Whereas Wagner rejects the possibility that the seeking/finding of Osiris in the Isis initiation rituals was prevalent in that region,[108] Merkelbach thinks the story of Isis's seeking and finding Osiris was a constant element of the Isis procession. He notes, "Die Umzüge im Dienst der Isis haben bei den Zeitgenossen Eindruck gemacht. Sie fanden in wechselnden Formen statt; der Inhalt war aber immer der gleiche: Isis hat den toten Osiris gesucht und ihn im Wasser wiedergefunden."[109] To be sure, Merkelbach's claim appears to be an overstatement, but there is indeed evidence that shows the seeking/finding of Osiris might have been part of the mysteries in the imperial period.[110] For example, a second-century inscription from Acerra (southern Italy) (RICIS 504/0701 = SIRIS 501 = CIL X 3759) begins with the Latinized Greek word, *Heuresi* (i.e., εὕρεσις = "finding" or "discovery"), which appears to be a part of the name of the patron to whom the inscription is dedicated. The word *Heuresi*/εὕρεσις may allude to the festival *Inventio Osiridis* (late October to early November).[111] Plutarch's report of the Isis mysteries points to this ritualized seeking and finding of Osiris (*Is. Os.* 366E–F). Although Plutarch philosophically equates Osiris with the highest, ideal deity, whom Isis urges her devotees to seek and whose knowledge is the goal/aim of her mysteries (*Is.*

---

107 The location of the sanctuaries of Isis and Osiris, which Pausanias mentions (2.4.6–7), may be plausibly identified with the north slope of Acrocorinth (the modern name of this place is Hadji Mustafa). Nancy Bookidis and Ronald S. Stroud, *Corinth XVIII/3* (Princeton: American School of Classical Studies at Athens, 1997), 5–7; also, Nancy Bookidis, "The Sanctuaries of Corinth," in *Corinth XX: The Centenary*, ed. Charles K. Williams and Nancy Bookidis (Princeton: The American School of Classical Studies at Athens, 2003), 257–58.
108 Wagner notes, "The chief festival of the cult, the seeking and finding of Osiris at harvest-time, is not recorded for Greece." Wagner, *Pauline Baptism*, 93. Yet, consider SIRIS 501.
109 Merkelbach, *Isis Regina*, 153.
110 Cf. Witt, *Isis in the Ancient World*, 161–62. The contrast between the Isaeum Campense in Rome (where Osiris/Serapis is the ultimate deity) and the Isaeum in Pompeii (where Isis predominates) shows how people in different regions negotiate and conceptualize the relationship between the two deities. Frederick Brenk, "'Great Royal Spouse Who Protects Her Brother Osiris': Isis in the Isaeum at Pompeii," in *Mystic Cults in Magna Graecia*, 217–34.
111 Witt, *Isis in the Ancient World*, 162; RICIS 2:614.

Os. 351F–352 A), it is likely that his philosophical interpretation reflects a ritual reality.[112]

Third, the first-person narrative about Lucius's near-death experience in the famous passage from *Metam.* 11—the narrative resembling the genre of *synthēma*—can be viewed as reflecting a genuine experience of Isis initiates.[113] The fact that *Metamorphoses* is fiction does not mean that the ritual experiences described in it are purely fictive.[114] If this description from the novel somehow reflects the initiates' actual experience, a parallel fate between that of the deity and that of the initiates is enhanced. It is intriguing that there was a near-death experience on the part of initiates during their initiation into the mysteries of Isis, which recalls the suffering of these mystery deities. Lucius recounts the night of initiation, saying,

> I came to the boundary of death and, having trodden the threshold of Proserpina, I travelled through all the elements and returned. In the middle of the night I saw the sun flashing with bright light. I came face to face with the gods below and the gods above and paid reverence to them from close at hand. Behold, I have told you things which perforce you may not know, although you have heard them. Therefore I shall relate only what can be expounded to the minds of the uninitiated without atonement.
>
> *Accessi confinium mortis et, calcato Proserpinae limine, per omnia vectus elementa remeavi; nocte media vidi solem candido coruscantem lumine; deos inferos et deos superos accessi coram et adoravi de proximo. Ecce tibi rettuli quae, quamvis audita, ignores tamen necesse est. Ergo quod solum potest sine piaculo ad profanorum intelligentias enuntiari referam* (*Metam.* 11.23).

Yet, the evidence only allows for a tantalizing and ambiguous picture. Even in this passage, it is not clearly stated that Lucius experiences the death that Osiris (or Isis, indirectly) experienced in his myth. One could interpret this as a report on Isis's universal power and protection extending into the underworld.[115] Thus,

---

112 Note the following statement: "The end and aim of [the sacred services to Isis] is the knowledge of Him who is the First, the Lord of All, the Ideal One. Him does the goddess urge us to seek, since He is near her and with her and in close communion (ὧν τέλος ἐστὶν ἡ τοῦ πρώτου καὶ κυρίου καὶ νοητοῦ γνῶσις, ὃν ἡ θεὸς παρακαλεῖ ζητεῖν παρ' αὐτῇ καὶ μετ' αὐτῆς ὄντα καὶ συνόντα)." The verb ζητεῖν is primarily associated with some kind of religious-philosophical search for ultimate truth, but it acquires a special sense if one remembers the myth of Isis's seeking (ζητεῖν) and finding of Osiris.
113 Klauck, *The Religious Context of Early Christianity*, 137.
114 On the promising use of fictions for reconstructing social history in antiquity, see Hopkins, "Novel Evidence for Roman Slavery," 3–27. Hopkins focuses on Roman slavery.
115 After closely examining the passage above, Wagner concludes, "[Lucius's] initiation is not to be comprehended from the standpoint of the Osiris myth; it bears rather all the marks of the Hellen-

the passage offers insufficient ground for supporting the idea that the initiates participated in the deity's *death*. Nevertheless, if one uses a more flexible conceptual model, one can infer that some type of extreme physical and emotional extreme experience was involved in the process of Isis initiation (as presumably in the case of the Eleusinian mysteries; e. g., blinded in the dark; flickering torchlight; perhaps including psychological effects, such as disorientation and confusion).[116] Lucius's testimony suggests that he embodies the deity's suffering and recovery through his "former suffering" and his "present joys" (*meis ... pristinis aerumnis et praesentibus gaudiis*) (*Metam.* 11.19). The extraordinary experiences of initiates, including their physical pains/hardship, endurance, and recovery, would be conducive to recalling the stories about the deity, even though the precise experiences are not described.[117]

Finally, some material evidence also corroborates such a reconstruction about a shared identity between the deities (Osiris/Isis) and devotees. As already discussed, Attic grave reliefs (Isis initiates resembling Isis herself), or a funerary inscription in the church of Santa Maria in Monticelli at Rome (RICIS 501/0196 = SIRIS 463 = IG XIV 2098) featuring "Osirification" demonstrate that initiates envisioned their identity merging with the deity. In addition, the underground crypt found in the sanctuary of Sarapis and Isis in Thessalonica offers an interesting piece of evidence concerning this issue.[118] A relief depicting people who sacrifice contains the following inscription: Ὀσείριδι μύστει Ἀλέξανδρον Δημητριοῦ καὶ Νίκαιαν / Χαριξένου Δημήτριος τοὺς αὑτοῦ γονεῖς. The first phrases, Ὀσείριδι μύστει ("to Osiris the initiate/mystic"), could imply, as Robert Wild suggests, "Osiris is the prime analogate of all μύσται, the first of all initiates, the one whom all other initiates follow (imitate?)."[119] As noticed by the question mark in the author's parenthesis, Wild is cautious about over-extending his analysis. There is another possible

---

istic Isis cult. Isis is Queen of the universe, sovereign mistress of heaven, the elements and the Nether World." Wagner, *Pauline Baptism*, 110.
116 Hugh Bowden, *Mystery Cults of the Ancient World* (Princeton: Princeton University Press, 2010), 15, 40–42; Clinton, "Stages of Initiation," 50–77.
117 See Klauck, *The Religious Context of Early Christianity*, 137–38 for some examples of scholarly suggestions about what was actually done to Isis initiates to trigger such experiences.
118 IG X,2.1.83 (dated from the early first century BCE) shows that the sanctuary's water facility was dedicated by "a priest of Sarapis and Isis" (ἱε]ρεὺς Σαράπιδος καὶ [Ἴσι]δος) to "Isis and all the other male and female deities dwelling in the precinct" (Ἴσιδι καὶ τοῖς ἄλλοις θεοῖς τοῖς ἐντεμενίοις πᾶσι καὶ πάσαις). The fact that Isis's name is given prominence among the deities to whom this facility was dedicated can, according to Wild, be interpreted as "devotional enthusiasm ... directed primarily toward Isis." Robert A. Wild, *Water in the Cultic Worship of Isis and Sarapis* (Leiden: Brill, 1981), 186.
119 Wild, *Water in the Cultic Worship*, 191.

interpretation of this appellation. If the crypt in this Isis-Sarapis sanctuary at Thessalonica represents "a local adaptation" of the Isis-Sarapis cult into "an old mystery cult honoring Zeus Dionysus Gongylos,"[120] it is reasonable to regard the term μύστης as drawing on one of the epithets of Dionysus (e.g., the epithet Διόνυσος μύστης appears in Pausanias, 8.54.5). The identification of Osiris with Dionysus has a long history—not only in Plutarch's second-century *Is and Osiris* (356B, 362B, 364E, etc.),[121] but also in the Classical period, for example, in Herodotus's *Persian Wars* (2.42, 47–48, etc.). Either way, Ὀσείριδι μύστει in the relief suggests that, as in the case of the Dionysiac mysteries, the initiation ritual in the Isis/Osiris tradition can be thought to have mediated between the deities and initiates to the extent that they share the same label and experiences—μύστης.[122]

> Excursus 1: Water in Isis-Osiris Worship
> Apuleius's *Metam.* 11.11 and Plutarch's *Is. Os.* 365B give examples of a ritual vessel containing water that was used in Isis-Osiris worship.[123] According to Wild, this "cultic pitcher" is related to two other material finds—i.e., images of Osiris Hydreios and the so-called "cool water" inscriptions ("May Osiris give you cool water" or similar formulas).[124] First of all, one should look at Apuleius's description of the vessel in the context of the *Navigium Isidis* in Roman Corinth and Plutarch's report and philosophical interpretation of the Egyptian rites.
>
> > Immediately thereafter came the gods, deigning to walk with human feet ... Another carried in his happy arms the venerable image of the supreme deity. This did not resemble any domestic animal, or bird, or wild beast, or even the human form itself, but by an ingenious discovery inspired reverence by its very strangeness, an ineffable symbol of a somehow deeper sanctity which must be cloaked in great silence. But it was formed of flashing gold in exactly this manner: it was a small urn (*urnula*), skillfully hollowed out, perfectly round at the bottom, its outer surface engraved with strange Egyptian images. Its mouth was raised only a little and stretched out into a beak, projecting in a long

---

[120] This is Wild's suggestion; "Zeus Dionysus Gongylos" appears in another inscription found in the same sanctuary (RICIS 113/0537 = IG X,2 1.259; the first century CE; cf. Christopher Steimle, *Religion im römischen Thessaloniki: Sakraltopographie, Kult und Gesellschaft 168 v.Chr. –324 n.Chr.* [Tübingen: Mohr Siebeck, 2008], 183 ff).

[121] See also RICIS 501/0174, which can be dated to a similar period as Plutarch's writing. In this inscription, one can find a "double identité cultuelle" like Clea, whom Plutarch relates to both the Isis/Osiris tradition and the Dionysiac tradition. Gasparro, "Identités religieuse isiaques," 79.

[122] Of course, the link is more clearly shown in the Dionysiac mysteries: the deity is *Bacchos* and the devotees are *Bacchoi*.

[123] This may not be a universal component of Isis-Osiris ritual in antiquity. While early scholarship took the description of the cultic vessel in Apuleius (*Metam.* 11.11) as almost universal of Isis-Osiris cultic activity, Wild examines archaeological evidence and claims, "the use of such a vessel can be verified only within a restricted geographical area and only from about the first century BC onward." Wild, *Water in the Cultic Worship*, 101–2.

[124] Wild, *Water in the Cultic Worship*, 103.

spout. To the opposite side was attached a handle extending far back in a wide curve; on top of the handle sat an asp in a coiled knot, rearing high the striped swelling of its scaly neck (Apuleius, *Metam.* 11.11).

Not only the Nile, but every form of moisture they call simply the effusion of Osiris; and in their holy rites the water jar (τὸ ὑδρεῖον) in honour of the god heads the procession (Plutarch, *Is. Os.* 365B).

Wild sees the latter as a clarification that the content of the cultic *urnula* (in the latter passage, the term is τὸ ὑδρεῖον) used in Isis-Osiris ritual was primarily Nile water.[125] He also points out abundant iconographic evidence for this—for example, from frescoes in the so-called *Aula Isiaca* (Rome), the Isis sanctuary at Pompeii, two Isis sanctuaries in Rome, and the sanctuary of Isis and Sarapis at Philippi—all of which provide images of the cultic pitcher in the proximity of the Nile. Its function in actual cultic processions is one of a sacred object for adoration (as widely accepted), but based on the Isis procession scene on the Vatican relief featuring the pitcher, Wild adds an additional function, namely, libation of Nile water, "a practice which perhaps recalled the fruitful union of Isis and Osiris."[126]

Combining this tradition about the cultic pitcher with material findings of the Osiris Hydreios statue (high-shouldered, decorated jar) and the so-called "cool water" inscription related to funerary contexts, Wild presents an interpretation that "the symbolism involved in all three must have had reference to life after death ... the Nile water associated with this assemblage of materials was the source not only of a bountiful earthy life but also of a joyous life beyond the grave."[127] The geographic convergence of the examples (e.g., especially, the Osiris Hydreios images and the "cool water" inscriptions are found in north Egypt and Italy) provide the strong possibility of their mutual relationship and corroborate his claim. It is admittedly hard to directly apply this interpretation to the mysteries of Isis, a particular form of Isis devotion. Apuleius's description of the procession is a part of public activity. Also, the cool water inscriptions are very terse and do not give any further insights into its use, e.g., about whether the deceased was an initiate of Osiris (or even Isis). Nevertheless, the set of examples assembled by Wild suggests the possibility that at least from the Roman imperial period, the use of water symbolism in the ritual activities featuring Isis and Osiris provided both self-referential messages and canonical messages beyond "purification" (purification is a more intuitive function of any water-rite).[128] A blessed afterlife is promised, or at least, envisioned by the participants, and the canonical messages (the basis for the benefit) were probably the myth of Isis's finding of Osiris and her reunion with him, as well as the continuity between the sacred Nile water (embodying Osiris) and water used in the ritual.

---

125 Wild, *Water in the Cultic Worship*, 104; also, 237, n.14.
126 Wild, *Water in the Cultic Worship*, 111, 113.
127 Wild, *Water in the Cultic Worship*, 103.
128 For example, many of the extant "cool water" inscriptions are dated to the late imperial period, and only one is dated to the end of the first century CE. For detailed information about the inscriptions: see Wild, *Water in the Cultic Worship*, 248–249.

4.3 Beyond Initiation

As in the earlier chapter regarding the Dionysiac mysteries, here I turn to two issues that go beyond initiation itself. First, I will examine the question of human agency, i.e., whether one's participation in the initiation is sufficient for obtaining the desired benefits or whether more human responsibilities are required. Second, I will explore how the Isis mysteries distinctively envision religious virtuosity and how this becomes part of the self-referential and canonical messages.

4.3.1 Is Initiation Alone Sufficient?

First, according to our literary sources, belief/trust appears to have been required of Isis initiates; participation in the ritual itself is not enough. To be sure, from the Rappaportian perspective, one's participation in any ritual amounts to the person's acceptance of the canonical order (Rappaport emphasizes that this public acceptance is not identical to faith or belief as an "inner" quality), and it is, therefore, no surprise that the same is true of the mysteries of Isis. Yet, there is some clear evidence that one's inner state of trust (which is not necessarily contrasted to one's public participation in the ritual) is a prerequisite. In *Metam.* 11, Lucius's metamorphosis from an animal to a human, which is the most remarkable event in the narrative, is not the result of the initiation ritual that occurs later in Book 11. Nor is this transformation achieved by Lucius's action, i.e., devouring the wreath of roses in the midst of the procession. In fact, one of the biggest ironies in *Metamorphoses* is that from the moment he became a donkey, Lucius already knew how to reverse the process (i.e., by eating roses; 3.25), but every time he tried to find and eat roses, his attempts were thwarted (e.g., 3.29–4.2; 7.15). Only when Isis reveals herself to Lucius and instructs him to eat roses (11.6) does Lucius actually have the opportunity to eat them (11.13). Lucius follows the divine instruction and he somehow "believes" in the efficacy of what is promised by the gracious deity (of course, in the text, the term belief/faith does not appear; it is only stated that Lucius, "eager for the promised results, most eagerly devoured" [*cupidus promissi cupidissime devoravi*[129]]). Isis's command, "join the procession, *relying on my good will* [*mea volentia*

---

[129] There is a text-critical issue regarding this phrase. Three variants are found in the manuscript tradition: 1) *cupidus promissi devoravi* (F B3 D O); 2) *cupidissime devoravi* (Φ B2); 3) *cupidus cupidissime devoravi* (A B1 U E S R). The present text (*cupidus promissi cupidissime devoravi*; both in LCL and Griffiths) is a conflation of the traditions, which is, according to Griffiths, justifiable in light of Apuleius's pleonasm. See Griffiths, *Apuleius*, 235. Yet, even if one takes one of the other readings, my argument would not be much affected. For example, if one takes out *promissi*

fretus]" (Metam. 11.6), according to Griffiths, comes closer to "Christian doctrine of πίστις."[130] In short, in the world of this narrative, any ritual (or non-ritual) action taken by human beings for the goddess is not a manipulation of the goddess's favor; nor is the ritual action itself expected to be automatically effective.

Plutarch, drawing on a well-known moral lesson in antiquity ("having a beard and wearing a coarse cloak does not make philosophers"; cf. Epictetus, *Diatr.* 2.19.19, 3.7.17), emphasizes that the external features of initiation, linen clothing and shaven head, do not make one a true Isis devotee (*Is. Os.* 352C). Nor is it sufficient to see the δρώμενα in the initiation. Rather, "the true votary of Isis is (ἀλλ' Ἰσιακός ἐστιν ὡς ἀληθῶς ...) he who, when he has legitimately received what is set forth in the ceremonies (τὰ δεικνύμενα καὶ δρώμενα; lit. "things shown and things done") connected with these gods, uses reason (λόγῳ) in investigating and in studying (ζητῶν καὶ φιλοσοφῶν) the truth contained therein" (352C; cf. 351E). Of course, this is Plutarch's philosophical interpretation of Isis initiation, but it resonates with other traditions, suggesting the possibility that it is not merely Plutarch's idiosyncratic thought. For example, it provides an interesting point of comparison with the saying about the true Bacchant (see the previous chapter; OF 576) and with Paul's view about the true Jew (Rom 2).

Additionally, one can find references to the confession of sins and forgiveness among Isis's devotees. It is too sweeping and problematic to characterize it as part of the "Oriental penitential ideas."[131] Yet, there is some evidence from Roman authors that provide insights into this aspect of Isis devotion that the authors' contemporaries may have perceived as penitence. Penitence/confession is expected not only before one's initiation (esp. in order to prove the candidate's "innocence" [132]), but as an ongoing part of their relationship with the deity. Here, indirect witnesses are potentially helpful. A passage from Ovid's letters written while he was in exile in Pontus is relevant:

> Because I have earned or felt the Prince's wrath, do not suppose that I would not worship the Prince himself. I have seen one who confessed to have outraged the deity of linen-wearing Isis sitting before Isis's shrine [*vidi ego linigerae numen violasse fatentem Isidis Isiacos ante sedere focos*]. Another bereft of sight for a like cause was crying out in the midst of the street that he had deserved it. The gods rejoice in such heraldings that witnesses may attest their power. Often do they mitigate penalties and restore the sight they have taken away when they behold

---

from this phrase, the next sentence (*Nec me fefellit caeleste promissum*) still emphasizes the fulfillment of the divine promise and suggests that Lucius acts upon his assurance of that promise.
130 Griffiths, *Apuleius*, 257.
131 Reitzenstein, *Hellenistic Mystery-Religions*, 170.
132 R. Merkelbach, "Fragment eines satirischen Romans: Aufforderung zur Beichte," *ZPE* 11 (1973): 82. Also, Versnel, *Ter Unus*, 66.

sincere repentance for sin [*cum bene peccati paenituisse vident*]. I too repent! O, if any wretched man is believed in anything, I too repent! I feel the torture of my own deed! (*Ex Ponto* 1.49–60)

In his letter to Brutus, Ovid compares his painful situation of exile in Pontus and his "repentance" to a certain Isis devotee, who confesses (*fatentem*) his wrongdoing that violated (*violasse*) the deity or another person. This penitent Isis devotee lost his sight, but regains it by sincerely repenting of his sin (*bene peccati paenituisse*) before the gods (*caelestes*; lit. "heavenly ones"). Just as these people are worshippers and devotees of Isis even though they made mistakes and thus were required to repent, Ovid asserts that he also remains devoted to the emperor, although he is exiled and now repenting. If one does a mirror-reading, the passage suggests that penitence is an ongoing practice for Isis initiates who have entered into a close relationship with this mystery goddess. Perhaps, confession of sins and request for forgiveness are not unique to Isis devotion, but are part of a wider religious phenomenon in antiquity. Nevertheless, it is noteworthy that Ovid singles out Isis devotees as an example, which may attest to the fact that such characteristics were stereotypically related to Isis devotion in the mind of Ovid and his contemporaries.[133]

4.3.2 Religious Virtuosity as Both What is Promised and What Enables Other Benefits

The story of Lucius in *Metam.* 11 exemplifies a story of religious virtuosity, since his path to initiation into Isis includes almost ascetic devotion and it overlaps with the priesthood (although this does not mean that all initiates of Isis are priests). After

---

[133] One can also consider Juvenal's infamously misogynic work, the sixth book of his *Satires:* "If white Io tells her to, she'll go to the ends of Egypt and bring back water fetched from sweltering Meroë to sprinkle in Isis' temple, towering next to the ancient sheepfold. You see, she thinks her instructions come from the voice of the Lady herself! There you have the kind of mind and soul that the gods converse with at night! Consequently, the highest, most exceptional honour is awarded to Anubis, who runs along, mocking the wailing populace, surrounded by his creatures in linen garments and with shaved heads. He's the one that asks for a pardon whenever your wife does not refrain from sex on the days which should be kept sacred and a large fine is due for violation of the quilt. When the silver snake has been seen to move its head, it's his tears and his practised mumblings which ensure that Osiris will not refuse to pardon her fault [*veniam culpae*]—provided, of course, he's bribed by a fat goose and a slice of sacrificial cake" (*Satire* 6.526–541). The whole Isis cult is mentioned here, including other related deities such as Osiris and Anubis. As Ovid's passage does, this also reflects the popular perception that the cult requires its devotees to confess their wrongdoing and ask for the deit(ies)' forgiveness.

his extreme calamities in the form of a donkey, Lucius experiences a revelation of Isis and a subsequent physical transformation from animal to human. In order to become an initiate, he goes through several steps, including a long period of purification. The enigmatic report of near-death that he experiences himself in the precinct is not available to other general practitioners of Isis worship. By completing several stages and his own physical, social hardship, Lucius finally appears like a living Osiris before the crowd. The virtuosity of Lucius is what his initiation promises, and at the same time, what ensures the other benefits (such as Isis's permanent guardianship and a blessed afterlife). Between the promise of initiation and the basis for the initiation's efficacy, virtuosity is actually an obligation indicated by ritual. In this sense, one can speak of wholehearted devotion and ethical lifestyle being expected of the initiates for the rest of their lives. It is interesting to see that Wagner, whose work so vehemently refutes any similarities between initiation in the mysteries and Pauline baptism, describes Lucius's initiation into the Isis mysteries in terms that sound like Paul's theology of baptism:

> Lucius dies to his old life, to his former lusts and frivolities, to the prying and magic that had exposed him to the tricks of malevolent Fortune (II. 1 ff.; XI. 6, 15, 19, 21). Entering the service of the goddess, he submits to her discipline (XI. 19, 23, 28, 30). The initiation of Lucius has rightly been regarded as comparable to the ordination of a monk; here the novice sets out on a new course of life, and hence he is wrapped in a shroud to symbolise that he is dead to the world.[134]

One hears echoes of Rom 6, when Wagner depicts Lucius's initiation and his "d[ying] to the world" and "his old life," and "entering the service of the deity," thereby starting "a new course of life." According to this interpretation, Lucius's "voluntary death" (*voluntaria mors*) described in *Metam.* 11 amounts to his being "dead to the world," thereby living a life of full dedication to Isis. When compared to the Dionysiac mysteries, the concept of virtuosity in the mysteries of Isis reflected in *Metamorphoses* seems less "democratized," and it seems to support some differentiated stages of initiation, as in the case of the Eleusinian mysteries. Also, in the sources pertaining to the mysteries of Isis, one does not (usually) find something like ecstatic madness in the Dionysiac cult that reconfigures (all) initiates' minds and bodies into the Dionysiac virtuosity (in reality, however, such ecstatic experiences as part of general religious experiences could happen in Isis initiation—not only in the Dionysiac mysteries).

Yet, the differentiated virtuosity in the mysteries of Isis should be understood in light of the tendency of "sacerdotisation" (Martzavou's term) of Isis devotees in

---

134 Wagner, *Pauline Baptism*, 112–13.

the late Hellenistic and Roman contexts. According to Martzavou, sacerdotisation means "the diffusion of some sort of freelance priestly status, through ceremonies of initiatory character, to a significant portion of the Isis devotees, who may be represented in their funerary reliefs as performing rituals in the service of the deity."[135] The symbolic configuration of sacerdotisation suggests that the notion of religious virtuosity in the mysteries of Isis may be no less democratized than in the Dionysiac mysteries. This does not mean that initiates all officially functioned as priests and their job descriptions were diversified and formulated in hierarchical ways (although there is some papyrological evidence from Oxyrhynchus [Papyrus Washington University inv. 138] that suggests some overlap between joining the priesthood and initiation into the mysteries of Isis[136]). For example, Bricault's epigraphic study that focused on the Latin west of the similar period demonstrates no noticeable trace of sacerdotal hierarchy that was developed and sophisticated.[137] In conclusion, it is possible to say that a new symbolic network

---

[135] Paraskevi Martzavou, "Priests and Priestly Roles in the Isiac Cults: Women as Agents in Religious Change in Late Hellenistic and Roman Athens," in *Ritual Dynamics in the Ancient Mediterranean: Agency, Emotion, Gender, Representation*, ed. Angelos Chaniotis (HABES 49; Stuttgart: Franz Steiner Verlag, 2011), 81.

[136] Thus, there is evidence of such phenomena apart from literary (e.g., Apuleius's *Metamorphoses*) or iconographic (e.g., Attic grave reliefs) representations. The Papyrus Washington University inv. 138, a second-century fragment papyrus that was excavated from Oxyrhynchus, contains oaths that should be taken for the priesthood. The verso, which is probably a different work from the recto, is a fragment of μοσχοσφραγιστικά (instructions for animal slaughter) (see R. Merkelbach, "Ein ägyptischer Priestereid," *ZPE* 2 [1968]: 13). Although there is no explicit mention of the name Isis, the papyrus's provenance and several allusions in the papyrus to specific customs pertaining to the Isis cult (e.g., prohibition of sheep sacrifice, col. ii, lines 11–13) suggest an Isis connection. Furthermore, the recto of the papyrus includes the specific term μυστηριασθῆναι (col. i, line 12) (according to Schuman, this is the earliest occurrence of the word in extant literature. Verne B. Schuman, "A Second-Century Treatise on Egyptian Priests and Temples," *HTR* 53 [1960]: 166) and the remark about taking oaths (col. I, line 16 ff). Taken together, they suggest a close connection between those who *should* be initiated (the papyrus has the verb δεῖ) and the list of priestly oaths. The contents of the oaths are not fully known, due to the fragmentary status of column i, but a more substantial list appears in column ii (col. ii, lines 6–16): "'I will not eat and I will not drink the things that are not lawful nor all those things which have been written in the books nor will I attach my fingers to them; I will not measure a measure on a threshing floor; I will not lift a balance in my hand; I will not measure land; I will not go into an unclean place; I will not touch sheep's hair; I will not hold the *machaira* until the day of my death.' All these things are written down together [in a book]. Taking it up he reads it aloud as testimony..." (trans. Schuman, "A Second-Century Treatise," 170).

[137] Laurent Bricault, "Les prêtres isiaques du monde romain," *Individuals and Materials*, 1:197.

emerged, in which Isis initiates gained a sacerdotal identity available not only to a small number of priestly figures, but to the broader group of initiates.[138]

4.4 Summary

Similar to Dionysiac initiation, one's participation in Isis initiation communicates the benefits or self-referential messages about the change of self- and social identity and the protection/deliverance from life concerns. What is more distinctive about Isis initiation, when compared to the Dionysiac, is the repeated emphasis on the "permanence" of its effects. Through initiation, a message is communicated that the initiate enters into a permanent relationship with the universally powerful goddess, who provides σωτηρία/*salus* (this "salvation" language is not explicitly found in Dionysiac tradition). Isis becomes the guardian of the initiate, and the initiate is bound to obligations to the goddess that extend for the initiate's entire life. Accordingly, this salvific and protective benefit transcends life on earth; thus, initiation is indexical of one's blessed afterlife under the guardianship of Isis. Finally, improved cognitive capability might be viewed as a benefit communicated by initiation, at least according to the literary evidence of the Roman imperial period (Apuleius, Plutarch).

While the canonical message about the nearness of Dionysus is given prominence in the Dionysiac mysteries, one observes that Isis initiation highlights the universally powerful and yet compassionate image of the deity, tending to the suffering of her devotees.[139] She always takes the initiative with her devotees, not only establishing the mysteries, but also choosing, inviting, and inaugurating individual devotees into her initiation. The identification of initiates with the deity (with Isis, but also Osiris) may also be part of the canonical messages, especially in the iconographic tradition, but this is less emphasized and thus more ambiguous, when

---

138 Admittedly, "priests" and the priesthood are complicated and pluriform phenomena in Greek and Roman antiquity, and scholars have pointed out the risk of reading Christian notions of priesthood into ancient pagan materials. See, for example, caveats about speaking of priests in the Greek world discussed in Albert Henrichs, "Introduction: What is a Greek Priest?" in *Practitioners of the Divine: Greek Priests and Religious Officials from Homer to Heliodorus*, ed. Beate Dignas and Kai Trampedach (Cambridge: Center for Hellenic Studies, 2008), 1–14. The term "practitioners of the divine," as suggested by the title of the volume, could be an overall term that covers diverse priestly phenomena. See also Martzavou's comment that "Isiac priests do not seem to constitute a coherent category." Paraskevi Martzavou, "What is an Isiac Priest in the Greek World?" in *Individuals and Materials*, 1:128, 152.
139 According to Gasparini, these two aspects, which were viewed by some scholars (e.g., N. Méthy, R. Turcan) as problematic, are compatible. Gasparini, "Isis and Osiris," 698, 717.

compared to the Dionysiac mysteries. The canonical messages of the mysteries of Isis are further complicated by the fact that Isis and Isiac devotion are often located in the cultural network of other deities, including her spouse Osiris/Sarapis and several other deities originally from Egypt.

The evidence also illuminates two intriguing aspects of the mysteries of Isis. First, one's trust/faith in the goddess is highlighted, especially in the literary sources related to the Isis mysteries, and the language of repentance and forgiveness (not only a pre-condition of initiation but as a continuous practice) appears in relation to Isis devotees. In terms of religious virtuosity (part of both self-referential and canonical messages), virtuosity in the Isis mysteries was perhaps not widely and equally available to all devotees when compared to the radical means found in the Dionysiac mysteries, namely, ecstatic madness. Yet, a closer look at the material evidence suggests that Isis initiates in the late Hellenistic and Roman periods came to understand themselves in priestly terms; that is, symbolic "sacerdotisation" may have emerged, which was available not only to a small number of priestly figures, but to a broader group of initiates.

5 Initiation into the Pauline Communities (I): Baptism in 1 Corinthians

Paul's letters will now be examined with a focus on the benefits baptism promises (self-referential messages), the underlying logic that sustains the efficacy of these promises (canonical messages), and aspects that extend beyond the baptismal ritual itself. Although the heuristic framework used in the previous chapters will be largely retained, some changes are needed, because the primary sources in this chapter—the undisputed Pauline letters—are relatively long literary works written by one person. This is in contrast to the diverse (even fragmentary) literary and material sources examined in the previous chapters that come from various places, periods, and people. Thus, a modified strategy is required. Key Pauline passages that are most relevant to our subject will be discussed, passage by passage, chronologically. In doing so, an attempt will be made to articulate how Paul and his communities understood baptism (sometimes Paul and his communities understood baptism differently from each other). A synthetic discussion focusing on ritual messages will follow each exegetical discussion.

With regard to baptism, what Pauline passages should be examined? The following section is devoted to establishing the scope of sources.

5.1 Preliminary Considerations

In order to establish focal passages that are relevant to the topic of this chapter (i.e., baptism in Paul's letters), one can begin with using a concordance. In what passages does Paul use vocabulary or expressions associated with baptism? Yet, Paul's use of certain baptismal words does not necessarily mean that Paul focuses on baptism as ritual. It is possible that he mentions the baptism-related words figuratively. Conversely, it is also entirely possible that even if specific word groups usually associated with baptism do not appear in a given text, Paul is actually indirectly referring to baptism. Therefore, caution should be used with this type of word-search, but an attempt to look for words and expressions commonly used to refer to baptism is necessary for a controlled investigation.

After surveying words and expressions related to baptism from the undisputed Pauline letters, I have sorted them into four categories: the A group has explicit reference to baptism, and this explicit relevancy decreases gradually in the B, C, and D groups. In other words, Group A is lexically most tight, whereas Groups B, C, and D further broaden the semantic range. One can find detailed results in the Appendix.

Verbs and nouns that are most explicitly related to baptismal practice are categorize as Group A. They share the same root with the English word baptism, namely, the Greek verb βαπτίζω and the nouns βάπτισμα and βαπτισμός. The verb βαπτίζω is used disproportionately: it appears once in Gal 3:27, twice in Rom 6:3, and ten times in 1 Corinthians (it is absent from 1 Thessalonians, 2 Corinthians, Philippians, and Philemon). Furthermore, of the ten times it appears in 1 Corinthians, six of them are clustered in the first chapter (1:13, 14, 15, 16 [twice], 17; the other four: 10:2; 12:13; 15:29 [twice]). The noun βάπτισμα occurs only in Rom 6:4 among the undisputed Pauline letters.[1] The noun βαπτισμός is never used in the undisputed Pauline letters, but it appears in Col 2:12 (cf. Heb 6:2, 9:10). This simple survey suggests that 1 Corinthians will play a primary role in any discussion of baptism in Paul. It also reveals that Paul prefers to speak about baptism actively (using verbs) rather than abstractly (using nouns).

Baptism is, by definition, a water ritual. Therefore, the next place to look is in passages that include ritual actions related to water. Words included in Group B are mostly associated with ritual washing and purification, and by extension, sanctification.[2] The verbs ἀπολούομαι, καθαρίζω, ἁγιάζω, the nouns λουτρόν, ἁγιασμός, ἁγιωσύνη, and the adjectives καθαρός and ἅγιος fit this category. The verb ἀπολούομαι (cf. the connection with baptism found in Acts 22:16) appears only in 1 Cor 6:11 among the Pauline corpus (in fact, this is a rare word in the NT). Καθαρίζω appears in 2 Cor 7:1.[3] The verb ἁγιάζω appears in Rom 15:16, 1 Cor 1:2, 6:11, 7:14 (twice).[4] The noun λουτρόν appears in Eph 5:26 and Tit 3:5, but it does not occur in the undisputed Pauline letters. The noun ἁγιασμός appears more frequently; it is used in Rom 6:19, 6:22, 1 Cor 1:30, 1 Thess 4:3, 4:4, and 4:7.[5] The noun ἁγιωσύνη is less frequent; it is found in Rom 1:4, 2 Cor 7:1, and 1 Thess 3:13. The adjective καθαρός occurs only in Rom 14:20 in the undisputed Pauline letters,[6] whereas ἅγιος is far more frequent. The latter occurs 20 times in Romans (1:2, 7; 5:5; 7:12 [twice]; 8:27; 9:1; 11:16 [twice]; 12:1, 13; 14:17; 15:13, 16, 25, 26, 31; 16:2, 15, 16), 12 times in 1 Corinthians (1:2; 3:17; 6:1, 2, 19; 7:14, 34; 12:3; 14:33; 16:1, 15, 20), eight times in 2 Corinthians (1:1; 6:6; 8:4; 9:1, 12; 13:12 [twice]; 13:13), three times in Philippians (1:1; 4:21, 22),

---

1 Among the disputed Pauline letters, Eph 4:5 contains the word (cf. 1 Pet 3:21). The word frequently appears in the Synoptic Gospels and Acts.
2 See, for example, Käsemann's discussion of the term ἁγιασμός (and by extension, ἅγιος as in 1 Thess 4:7) as part of baptismal vocabulary. Ernst Käsemann, *Commentary on Romans*, trans. Geoffrey W. Bromiley (Grand Rapids: Eerdmans, 1980), 183.
3 It is also found in the disputed Pauline letters: Eph 5:26 and Tit 2:14.
4 In the disputed Pauline letters, it occurs in Eph 5:26, 1 Tim 4:5, 2 Tim 2:21.
5 In the disputed Pauline letters, it is used in 2 Thess 2:13 and 1 Tim 2:15.
6 Cf. 1 Tim 1:5, 1 Tim 3:9, 2 Tim 1:3, 2 Tim 2:22.

five times in 1 Thessalonians (1:5, 6; 3:13; 4:8; 5:26), and twice in Philemon (5, 7).[7] The question is to what extent each occurrence of those verbs, nouns, and adjectives is relevant to baptism. This should be examined case by case.

Group C emerges based on the interpretative presupposition that baptism is primarily an entry ritual in the Christ cultic communities (see the introduction). Thus, Group C contains words/expressions that can be regarded as the social and communal result of baptism especially in the Pauline letters. This requires justification. What I mean is the famous construction, ἐν Χριστῷ and ἐν κυρίῳ (these two expressions are not identical, but interrelated), with other slightly different variants.[8] Through baptism, according to Paul's phraseology, Christ-believers are collectively located ἐν Χριστῷ (Käsemann).[9] In Gal 3:27–28, Paul claims that those who are baptized into Christ (εἰς Χριστόν, 3:27) are considered to be in Christ (ἐν Χριστῷ, 3:28).

My basic presupposition about Paul's ἐν Χριστῷ/ἐν κυρίῳ is indebted to several scholars' views. One is Schnelle's eschatological and ecclesiological interpretation of ἐν Χριστῷ language,[10] which can be traced back to A. Schweitzer, W. D. Davies, and E. Käsemann (each of whom had different reasons for that view).[11] Paying attention to the local sense of ἐν+dative, Schnelle argues:

> The primary meaning of ἐν Χριστῷ is understood in a local sense, indicating a sphere of being: by baptism the believer is incorporated into the sphere of the pneumatic Christ,

---

[7] In the disputed Pauline letters, it appears 15 times in Ephesians, six times in Colossians, once in 2 Thessalonians, once in 1 Timothy, twice in 2 Timothy, and once in Titus.
[8] Recently, J. Thomas Hewitt argues that ἐν Χριστῷ and ἐν κυρίῳ should be distinguished—for example, only the former (that he translates "in messiah") expresses the solidarity with Christ's death, resurrection, and glory. Hewitt claims, "'In the Lord' and 'in Christ' are two quite distinct expression." J. Thomas Hewitt, *Messiah and Scripture: Paul's "In Christ" Idiom in Its Ancient Jewish Context*, WUNT II/522 (Tübingen: Mohr Siebeck, 2020), 240 n. 114. See also N. T. Wright's comment on ἐν κυρίῳ in Philemon. N. T. Wright, *The Climax of the Covenant: Christ and the Law in Pauline Theology* (Minneapolis: Fortress, 1992), 45. Also, I want to mention that it is disputed whether the combination of the preposition εἰς and the proper name (or title) Χριστός envisions a physical movement into that figure or the construction is merely a shorthand of εἰς τὸ ὄνομα Χριστοῦ/κυρίου (cf. Acts 8:16; 19:5; 1 Cor 1:13), which can be interpreted in various ways, including one that is based on Semitism. Yet, since the phrase ἐν Χριστῷ is quite distinctive in Paul's letters and there is some evidence that ἐν Χριστῷ appears in proximity to baptism εἰς Χριστόν, it is possible to look at the phrase in other places of Paul's letters for further evidence.
[9] Ernst Käsemann, *Leib und Leib Christi* (Tübingen: Mohr, 1933), 159–62, 183–86.
[10] Udo Schnelle, *Apostle Paul: His Life and Theology*, trans. M. Eugene Boring (Grand Rapids: Baker Academic, 2005), 481–82.
[11] Albert Schweitzer, *The Mysticism of Paul the Apostle*, trans. W. Montgomery (Baltimore: Johns Hopkins University Press, 1998), 101; W. D. Davies, *Paul and Rabbinic Judaism: Some Rabbinic Elements in Pauline Theology* (London: S.P.C.K., 1948), 102. For Käsemann, see n. 9 of this chapter.

and the life is constituted by the conferral of the Spirit as the down payment on salvation, which begins in the present and is fulfilled in the eschatological future redemption.[12]

There are a few caveats. Schnelle's claim results from his theological synthesis; thus, it is not intended to be read full-fledged into every use of ἐν Χριστῷ in Paul's letters. Various "syntactical uses" of the phrase should also be taken into consideration,[13] and it should be noted that I do not intend to read the alleged mystical meaning into every occurrence of ἐν Χριστῷ.[14] Nevertheless, Schnelle's claim points to the possibility that the phrase ἐν Χριστῷ can be meaningfully examined in relation to baptism. In this regard, Isaac Morales also recently argues that "Being 'in Christ' is closely connected to baptism"[15]—the insight observed by Eduard Lohse in the mid-twentieth century:

> If one considers the exceedingly frequent use of the formula 'in Christ' in Paul, with which the apostle shows that the transfer to the Lord effected in baptism and the claim of the baptized by his Lord associated with it actually extends to all areas of life and puts the human being under the control of the Lord in his entire thinking, working, and action, then one can rightly characterize the whole of Paul's theology as an exposition of baptism.[16]

Despite the risk of overstatement (see Lohse's last sentence), such scholarly views show sufficient cause for serious attention to be given to the Pauline passages fea-

---

12 Schnelle, *Apostle Paul*, 481.
13 Novenson, *Christ among the Messiahs*, 119–20. For example, adverbial (Gal 2:17), adjectival (Rom 16:3), substantive (Rom 8:1), verbal-complementary (1 Cor 15:19), etc. Yet, interestingly, Novenson himself places more emphasis on the adverbial sense of the phrase, making it central to Paul. Novenson, *Christ among the Messiahs*, 126.
14 Since Deissmann, many scholars have advanced the mystical-participatory interpretation of Paul's phrase, ἐν Χριστῷ. Yet, in her recent book, Teresa Morgan challenges this line of interpretation and instead argues that ἐν Χριστῷ is best understood "encheiristically" (while acknowledging some occurrences that can be understood instrumentally). That is, ἐν Χριστῷ in Paul's letters primarily means "in Christ's hands" (encheiristic), and in some cases, the phrase could mean "through Christ['s death]" (instrumental), but it does not refer to union with/participation in Christ. Morgan also argues that her proposal is not only philologically sound, but it also helps one better unpack Paul's thought. Teresa Morgan, *Being 'in Christ' in the Letters of Paul: Saved through Christ and in his Hands* (Tübingen: Mohr Siebeck, 2020).
15 Isaac A. Morales, "Baptism and Union with Christ," in *"In Christ" in Paul*, ed. M. J. Thate et al. (Tübigen: Mohr Siebeck, 2014), 159.
16 Eduard Lohse, "Taufe und Rechtfertigung bei Paulus," *KD* 11 (1965): 318. The English translation of the passage is taken from Morales, "Baptism and Union with Christ," 159. On the same page, Morales comments, "Lohse's characterization no doubt goes too far – certainly Paul's understanding of God, of the mission of Christ, and of the role of the Spirit, to name but a few examples, are not derived from baptism. Nevertheless, Lohse's emphasis on the importance of baptism is refreshing."

turing "in Christ" language and its baptismal implication. Detailed analysis will follow.[17]

Lastly, Group D consists of words that are related to the mysteries and initiation rituals in the mysteries: the verbs τελέω, τελειόω and μυέω, the nouns τελετή, μύησις, μυστήριον, τέλος, and the adjective τέλειος. Paul does not usually use these words in a baptismal context, and for this reason, these words have been relegated to Group D. The verb τελέω occurs in Rom 2:27; 13:6; 2 Cor 12:9; and Gal 5:16. Philippians 3:12 is the only place where τελειόω occurs within the Pauline corpus. As for μυέω, Phil 4:12 is also the sole Pauline passage that includes this word. Nouns related to the mysteries do not appear much in the New Testament. The noun τελετή is never used in the New Testament,[18] and there is no occurrence of μύησις in either the LXX or the New Testament. The noun μυστήριον frequently appears in the Pauline letters, as well as other parts of the New Testament and the LXX. It appears in the singular form in Rom 11:25, 16:25, 1 Cor 2:1, 7, and 15:51; and it is used in the plural form in 1 Cor 4:1, 13:2, and 14:2.[19] The noun τέλος appears in Rom 6:21, 22; 10:4; 13:7 (twice); 1 Cor 1:8; 10:11; 15:24; 2 Cor 1:13; 3:13; 11:15; Phil 3:19; and 1 Thess 2:16. The adjective τέλειος is found in Rom 12:2; 1 Cor 2:6; 13:10; 14:20; and Phil 3:15 (cf. Col 1:28; 4:12). Not all those occurrences of this mystery language have actual connections to mystery initiation or baptism. Frequently, the words are used in a general sense. As I mentioned in Chapter 1, a comparison between mystery initiations and Pauline baptism merely focused on mystery vocabulary may not be fruitful.

The detailed results of this concordance analysis are presented in the Appendix (see the tables). From this survey, "shaded" passages emerge, which I will focus on this chapter. Passages that contain noticeable clusters of the most relevant word groups are shaded. The criteria for shading are 1) whether the passage has Group A words (explicit reference to baptism), 2) whether words belonging to other groups (B, C, D) also cluster in the passage that already has Group A words, and 3) whether other interesting convergences are detected even if there is no word belonging to Group A (still Group B words and Group C words carry more weight than Group D

---

17 Here is the list of ἐν Χριστῷ occurrence in the Pauline corpus: Rom 3:24; 6:11, 23; 8:1, 2, 39; 9:1; 12:5; 15:17; 16:3, 7, 9, 10; 1 Cor 1:2, 4, 30; 3:1; 4:10, 15, 17; 15:18, 19, 31; 16:24; 2 Cor 2:27; 3:14; 5:17, 19; 12:2, 19; Gal 1:22; 2:4, 17; 3:14, 26, 28; Phil 1:1, 13, 26; 2:1, 5; 3:3, 14; 4:7, 19, 21; 1 Thess 2:14; 4:16; 5:18; Phm 8, 20, 23. Also, ἐν κυρίῳ appears in Rom 14:14; 16:2, 8, 11, 12 (twice), 13, 22; 1 Cor 1:31; 4:17; 7:22, 39; 9:1, 2; 11:11; 15:58; 16:19; 2 Cor 2:12; 10:17; Gal 5:10; Phil 1:14; 2:19, 24, 29; 3:1; 4:1, 2, 4, 10; 1 Thess 3:8; 4:1; 5:12; Phm 16, 20. The ἐν κυρίῳ may not exclusively refer to Jesus Christ, especially when it appears in the LXX quotations (e.g., 1 Cor 1:31; 2 Cor 10:17, etc.).
18 In the LXX, it is used in 1 Kgs 15:12, 3 Macc 2:30, Wis 12:4; 14:15, 23; Amo 7:9.
19 Cf. In the disputed Pauline letters, six times in Ephesians, four times in Colossians, once in 2 Thessalonians, and twice in 1 Timothy.

words). In addition, 4) if certain words seem to have meanings that are obviously irrelevant to the semantic range of this investigation (e.g., ἐν Χριστῷ can occur in the letter-closings, where any baptismal reference is hard to detect), they are excluded from shading, and 5) even in the same group, some words may receive more weight than others: for example, contrary to ἁγιασμός, the use of ἅγιος is sometimes too general, and it can be used merely to modify the Holy Spirit, rather than community members that are called holy. Evaluating the Pauline passages with these criteria, I will make distinctions among primary passages (darker shades), secondary passages (lighter shades), and other passages that are not relevant.

In summary, the passages discussed in Chapters 5–7 are 1 Cor 1:10–17; 1:26–31; 6:9–11; 10:1–5; 12:12–13; 15:18–19, 29; Gal 3:25–29; and Rom 6:1–14.[20] They will be presented in chronological order as this can be relevant to the discussion (e.g., the relationship between 1 Cor 15 and Rom 6).[21] In general, however, the chronological

---

20 First Corinthians 1 is the passage where the verb βαπτίζω is concentrated most intensively in all the Pauline letters, and also where words from other groups appear. First Corinthians 15 also has a reference to baptism, as well as other group words. First Corinthians 10:2 and 12:13 will also be counted as primary passages because they contain the verb βαπτίζω. First Corinthians 6:9–11 could be a secondary passage (rather than a primary), but this passage is actually one of the passages scholars have discussed in relation to baptism, despite lacking specific words for baptism. Thus, I will give close attention to 1 Cor 6:9–11. Galatians 3:10–29 will be examined as a primary passage, since it has a clear reference to baptism. Romans 6:1–23 is shaded because it contains all four groups, and thus, is a primary passage. Romans 8 is a secondary passage because of its distinctive use of ἐν Χριστῷ as an *inclusio*, although there is no explicit reference to baptism. Thus, the discussion of Rom 8 will be more suggestive rather than definitive. Romans 12 is also partly considered when necessary (although no reference to baptism [Group A] is found, the chapter has words from all the other three groups, and furthermore, the first few verses have strong resonance with Rom 6). The word τέλος in 10:4 and μυστήριον in 11:25 are interesting, yet their immediate contexts lack the other word groups, so they will not be discussed. The appearance of τελέω and τέλος in Rom 13 (e.g., τέλος in Rom 13:7 refers to a form of tax) and the cluster of ἅγιος language in Rom 15 are not relevant to our discussion. It is interesting that ἐν Χριστῷ/ἐν κυρίῳ is repeated several times in Rom 16 in the exceptionally long greetings (far longer than greetings in other Pauline letters), but there is no meaningful baptismal reference.
21 Among the seven undisputed letters of Paul, the chronological order of the four letters (1 Thessalonians—1 Corinthians—2 Corinthians—Romans) is widely accepted. The other letters are fitted around these references, but conclusions vary. Thus, a brief remark on my view of the relative chronology of Paul's letters is presented here. As widely accepted, 1 Thessalonians is likely the earliest. It is not certain whether 1 Corinthians or Galatians is earlier than the other, although it is highly likely that both precede Romans. Following Schnelle's hypothesis (based on textual evidence), I think 1 Corinthians was likely earlier than Galatians (Schnelle, *Apostle Paul*, 269–71). As for Philippians, the issue of dating is far more difficult; some scholars argue that it was written in the Roman prison (making it the last of Paul's undisputed letters), while others think it was writ-

order does not demonstrate a development in Paul's thought. In general, 1 Thessalonians, 2 Corinthians, Philippians, and Philemon will not be included in the discussion, but may be mentioned when necessary.[22]

5.2 Discussions of Key Passages

5.2.1 1 Corinthians 1:10–17

5.2.1.1 Exegetical Discussion

Chronologically speaking, the first Pauline reference to baptism is found in 1 Corinthians. First Thessalonians, the first extant Pauline letter, lacks a verbal reference to baptism (i.e., Group A words).[23] This does not necessarily mean that

---

ten before Romans (probably from his [presumed] imprisonment in Ephesus). Considering Paul's frequent contacts with the Philippians during his imprisonment (Raymond Brown, *An Introduction to the New Testament* [New York: Doubleday, 1997]), and Paul's expressed hope of seeing them again (In Romans, Paul does not plan to go back to the eastern areas of the Mediterranean world, but to move westward), I think Philippians was written prior to Romans. Still, uncertainty remains about the chronological order among Galatians, 2 Corinthians, and Philippians. I will not go in detail on this issue, and the precise order of these books does not really affect this investigation (I follow Calvin Roetzel's theory, i.e., Galatians—2 Corinthians—Philippians, Calvin J. Roetzel, *The Letters of Paul: Conversations in Context*, 6th ed. [Louisville: WJK, 2015], 100). In this monograph, I focus on 1 Corinthians, Galatians, and Romans.

22 In 1 Thessalonians, Paul does not make explicit reference to baptism, although 1 Thess 4 shows an intensive concentration of ἁγιασμός language. It is interesting to note that ἐν Χριστῷ language is less frequent in 1 Thessalonians, compared to other letters. Second Corinthians lacks Group A words, and there is also no cluster relevant to our investigation. Yet, some passages in 2 Corinthians (esp. ch. 4) will be brought into discussion later to see how passages that are not related to baptism can also contribute to one's understanding of Paul's baptismal theology. Philippians does not have a direct reference to baptism, but there is an interesting cluster of τελ- words, coupled with the ἐν Χριστῷ expression, in ch. 3; yet, there are no Group A and B words included. Thus, I do not include Philippians in my primary discussion of the messages of baptism. It will, however, be used later for illuminating the issue indirectly.

23 Although there is no explicit baptism in 1 Thessalonians, one can find faint allusions to baptism, if one takes into account Group B and Group C words (especially in 1 Thess 4:1–8). The Thessalonians receive Paul's exhortation regarding how to live as Christ-devotees. The will of God is summarized in the catchword, ἁγιασμός, which appears in vv. 3, 4, and 7. The life of ἁγιασμός seems to consist primarily of two aspects: first, to guard against sexual immorality (in v. 4, "how to acquire one's own vessel [σκεῦος] in consecration and honor," has been a *crux interpretum*: namely, whether it speaks of taking one's wife or controlling one's body; see Raymond F. Collins, "'This is the Will of God: Your Sanctification.' (1 Thess 4:3)," in *Studies on the First Letter to the Thessalonians* [Leuven: University Press, 1984], 311–17), and second, not to harm other members of the same Christ-be-

Christ-devotees in Thessalonica (probably artisans) were never baptized.[24] Rather, the lack of reference to baptism in 1 Thessalonians may indicate baptism was taken for granted, and that there was no special issue concerning baptism at Thessalonica to attract Paul's attention. In contrast, one encounters many direct and indirect references to baptism in 1 Corinthians. This may reflect the situation in Corinth that was controversial enough that Paul felt the necessity to address it.[25]

The first passage that deserves exploration is 1 Cor 1:10–17, where several direct remarks on baptism (Group A) are found. The verb βαπτίζω occurs six times in 1 Cor 1:13, 14, 15, 16 (2x), and 17, and in terms of frequency, there are no other passages in the Pauline letters like this. The reference to baptism in 1 Cor 1 emerges out of the context where Paul rhetorically rebukes the discord and conflicts among the Corinthians and urges unity.[26] First Corinthians 1:10–17 reads:

---

lieving community in domestic affairs (it is possible that the two are more interrelated than they appear, if both relate to instructions about wives. Collins, "This is the Will of God," 316). Also, v. 7 suggests that the term ἁγιασμός stands in contrast to impurity (ἀκαθαρσία) that may refer to *ritual* impurity. In his book that maps out different approaches within ancient Judaism to moral and ritual impurity, Klawans argues that Paul is only concerned about moral defilement (Jonathan Klawans, *Impurity and Sin in Ancient Judaism* (Oxford: Oxford University Press, 2000), 150–56; his focus is on examining how different Jewish authors/communities participated in the debates over purity [thus, intra-Jewish debates]). Yet, it is not impossible to say that Paul's use of ἁγιασμός evokes the image of ritual purity from his gentile audience, for whom ἁγιασμός/ἀκαθαρσία relates to one's devotion to certain deities or cults and his/her embodiment of that devotion by following ritual procedures. In other words, put into their pagan context, Paul's words in 1 Thess 4:1–8 may have been understood to mean that the audience has acquired "ritual purity" through their initiation into a new cultic group, which is interpreted as "turning from idols they served in their gentile past to the living God (=the Jewish God)" (1 Thess 1:9; cf. Philo, *Virt.* 102–103). Paul encourages his new converts to live in purity by conforming to particular moral behaviors, both in their sexual relationships and in other types of relationships in their association. In a sense, Paul applies religious virtuosity to all the members of the community.

24 As for the view that the Thessalonian community was an artisan association, see Richard S. Ascough, *Paul's Macedonian Associations: The Social Context of Philippians and 1 Thessalonians*, WUNT II/161 (Tübingen: Mohr Siebeck, 2003), 162–90.

25 Even in 1 Cor 1, baptism itself (and issues surrounding baptism) might not be "a major concern," as suggested by Margaret M. Mitchell, *Paul and the Rhetoric of Reconciliation: An Exegetical Investigation of the Language and Composition of 1 Corinthians* (Tübingen: J. C. B. Mohr Paul Siebeck, 1991), 201. But it is worth asking whether Mitchell fails to see the crucial role that baptism plays throughout the letter, both explicitly and implicitly.

26 The problem of discord and factionalism is not only found in this chapter, but it permeates the entire letter. Mitchell, *Paul and the Rhetoric of Reconciliation*, 67. Yung Suk Kim challenges it by arguing that Paul's solution is to promoting diversity, not unity. Yung Suk Kim, *Christ's Body in Corinth: The Politics of a Metaphor* (Minneapolis: Fortress, 2008), 71. To be specific, the majority of interpreters regard discord as the problem in Corinth and unity as Paul's solution. Kim rather notes, "The problem in the community is not a lack of 'unity' but an overpowering, hegemonic ideology of

10 Now, I urge you, brothers and sisters, by the name of our Lord Jesus Christ, that all of you say the same thing, that there be no schisms among you, that you have been restored in the same mind and in the same purpose. 11 For it has been made clear to me concerning you, my brothers and sisters, by Chloe's people that there are discords among you. 12 What I am saying is this: that each of you says, "I belong to Paul," or "I belong to Apollos," or "I belong to Cephas," or "I belong to Christ." 13 Has Christ been divided? Paul was not crucified on behalf of you, was he? Or, were you baptized into the name of Paul? 14 I give thanks to God that I baptized none of you except Crispus and Gaius, 15 so that no one may say that you were baptized into my name. 16 And I baptized also Stephanas's household, but for the rest, I do not know whether I baptized anyone else. 17 For Christ did not send me to baptize but to proclaim the gospel, not with wisdom of speech, lest the cross of Christ should be made in vain.

Paul purposefully detaches himself from the role of performing baptism (vv. 14–17). Verse 17 is quite interesting, since cult founders in antiquity often transferred rituals, including acting out, not only verbal transmission of myths.[27] Betz

---

'power' over the weak and against the voice of women's freedom and equality." Kim, *Christ's Body in Corinth*, 56. While I fully agree with his point that Paul does not present hierarchically-conceived unity and that Paul urges "Christic embodiment," I think that his reading and the "dominant" reading he criticizes are not sharply contradictory; they can be compatible and complementary. What matters is not the scheme itself (discord and unity) but how to (re)define discord and unity. The "overpowering, hegemonic ideology" indeed engendered *discord* in the community, harming the marginalized; Paul urges the Corinthians to be *"united* in the gospel of the cross of Christ," which will eventually build a mutually-loving community where diversity of gifts and ministries flourishes.

27 Detailed discussions about Paul in light of founder figures, see James C. Hanges, *Paul, Founder of Churches: A Study in Light of the Evidence for the Role of "Founder-Figures" in the Hellenistic-Roman Period*, WUNT 292 (Tübingen: Mohr Siebeck, 2012). Cult-founding activities are not only done at the communal level. There were some religious freelancers who were travelling and implementing one's own cult. Lucian of Samosata, the second-century CE rhetorician and satirist, provides one interesting example. He wrote a satirical account about Alexander the false prophet, known for visiting several places and deceiving gullible people into his cult using a snake, called Glykon (so, the ritual is not water ritual like baptism but a theatrical representation of theogony). Alexander claimed that the God Asklepius appears in the form of Glykon. The mysteries Alexander performed are similar to what is known about the Eleusinian mysteries: "Also aimed at the Italian trade was the following scheme. He worked up a mystery ceremony of his own, complete with torchbearers and presiding priests. It lasted three whole days in a row. On the first there was, as at Athens, an initial proclamation. Here it took the form. 'If any atheist, Christian, or Epicurean [τις ἄθεος ἢ Χριστιανὸς ἢ Ἐπικούρειος] has come here to spy, let him be gone. And may the true believers of the god conduct their rites with heaven's blessing.' Immediately thereafter the ceremony led off with an expulsion ritual. Alexander opened it with the words, 'Christians, begone! [Ἔξω Χριστιανούς]' and the crowd responded with one voice, 'Epicureans, begone! [Ἔξω Ἐπικουρείους]' Then came the acting out of Leto in labor, of the birth of Apollo, his mating with Coronis, and the birth of Asklepios [Ἀσκληπιὸς ἐτίκτετο]. On the second day there was the birth [γέννησις τοῦ θεοῦ, i.e., Glykon] and presentation [manifestation] of the god Glykon [Γλύκωνος ἐπιφάνεια]..." (Lucian,

notes, "In Hellenistic religions, one of the methods for founding new cults was by the transferal of rituals, myths, statues, and cult personnel from one place to another (*Kultübertragung*)."[28] Was Paul not the actual founder of the Corinthian community (1 Cor 3:6, 4:15)? Why then does Paul seems to downplay his role in transplanting the ritual? Sociologically, this feature might be explained by considering the characteristics of the "wandering charismatics." Paul may have thought that baptism is a task for local communities, not traveling missionaries like himself.[29] Yet, other explanations are also possible within the context of 1 Corinthians. Paul's intentional detachment from the role of baptizer is probably because baptism was understood by the Corinthians as establishing an exclusive relationship between the baptized and the baptizer (including the former's personal allegiance to the latter), and Paul disagreed with this. Paul may not have wanted to give added prestige to those he personally baptized.[30] Additionally, that Paul did not baptize much suggests that Paul was not alone in his cult planting activity. Let us examine the passage more closely.

First, vv. 12–13 confirm that the Corinthians were baptized into Christ's name. Reading vv. 12–13, especially v. 13c, as though the Corinthians were actually baptized in the name of the person who baptized them (e.g., some were baptized in Paul's name, others in Apollos's name) is untenable. Rather, their baptism was carried out in the name of Christ, which was probably part of a baptismal tradition. Paul's twisted phrase in v. 13c and his expectation that it would work rhetorically for the Corinthians imply the existence of a pre-existing baptismal tradition. Mi-

---

Alexander the False Prophet 38; translation is from Lionel Casson, *Selected Satires of Lucian* [New York: Norton, 1968]).

28 Betz, "Transferring a Ritual," 90; also 87.

29 Gerd Theissen, *Sociology of Early Palestinian Christianity*, trans. John Bowden (Philadelphia: Fortress, 1978), 21. In discussing the early Palestinian communities, Theissen notes that "membership ... had to be determined by the local community itself," and not by the wandering charismatics. The administration of baptism was not a job assigned to the latter.

30 As Brigidda Bell hypothetically proposes, if baptism as a ritual was a "paid service" (distinctive from the proclamation of the gospel as a "free service"), baptism by Paul was perhaps "a prestigious good, a rarefied offering, whose limited availability heightened status differences between members." Then Paul's reluctant attitude toward baptism would make more sense. See Brigidda Bell, "The Cost of Baptism? The Case for Paul's Ritual Compensation," *JSNT* 42 (2020): 444. Bell notes, "If baptism is an additional, paid service offered after the reception of the (free) gospel, not everyone will be able or willing to partake in it, making baptism a limited good." This is an intriguing inference from examining *comparanda* about paid rituals (actually, one should remember that mystery initiation also required fees!), but baptism was not necessarily a "limited good" in Pauline communities. Several passages presuppose baptism as a common experience applied to all of his audience (e.g., 1 Cor 12:13; Gal 3:26–29). Yet, baptism by important leaders (including Paul) could be considered "prestigious" by some members.

chael Wolter notes, "Paul did not initiate baptism for newly converted Christians. Rather, he discovered baptism already as an institution in Christian communities."³¹ The rhetorical question in v. 13b, "Paul was not crucified on behalf of you, was he? (μὴ Παῦλος ἐσταυρώθη ὑπὲρ ὑμῶν),"³² does not mean that some Corinthians actually claimed that Paul died for them, because μή expects a negative answer. The same principle could be true for the next question (i.e., the initial μή in the previous question may govern this one, too): "Or, you were not baptized into the name of Paul, were you? ([μή] ... ἢ εἰς τὸ ὄνομα Παύλου ἐβαπτίσθητε)." They were not baptized into Paul's name. The rhetorical question indirectly bears witness to the fact that they were baptized εἰς τὸ ὄνομα τοῦ Χριστοῦ³³—otherwise, Paul's twist (εἰς τὸ ὄνομα Παύλου) loses its force. The phrase "to baptize εἰς τὸ ὄνομα of Christ/Jesus/Lord" could have begun to convey some mystical relationship among early Christ-cult communities. Yet, linguistically,³⁴ the phrase εἰς τὸ ὄνομα may not have expressed mystical ideas.³⁵ It primarily conveys a relationship of possession (to whom does one belong, etc.).³⁶ Whether or not "baptism εἰς τὸ ὄνομα τοῦ Χριστοῦ" can be equated with "baptism εἰς Χριστόν" will be discussed later.

Second, vv. 14–17 provide further insight into Pauline practice. Despite being the "founder" of the *ekklesia* in Corinth, Paul did not baptize all of the individual members himself. Presumably, all the members were baptized (cf. 1 Cor 12:13), but by whom? Two things are clear. First, Paul was not solely responsible for founding the Christ cult in Corinth, but he was just one of many, some of whom may have worked together. This is also revealed in other passages. Even though Paul portrays

---

31 Michael Wolter, *Paul: An Outline of His Theology*, trans. Robert L. Brawley (Waco: Baylor University Press, 2015), 126. The term "institution" may sound too institutionalized in the context of the mid-first century.
32 In some manuscripts (P⁴⁶ᵛⁱᵈ 326. 2464* syᵖ sa), μή is also added before μεμέρισται ὁ Χριστός. This inclusion of μή makes the question μεμέρισται ὁ Χριστός clearly lead to a negative answer ("No, Christ has not"). Additionally, in P⁴⁶ and (syᵖ), μή before Παῦλος ἐσταυρώθη ὑπὲρ ὑμῶν is replaced by ἤ (this makes the phrase similar to the following question ἢ εἰς τὸ ὄνομα Παύλου ἐβαπτίσθητε).
33 Rudolf Schnackenburg, *Baptism in the Thought of St. Paul*, trans. G. R. Beasley-Murray (Oxford: Blackwell, 1964), 18.
34 Regarding papyrological evidence ("to the account of" in the economic sense; cf. Heitmüller) and Rabbinic literature (*le-shem*, indicating "to what purpose an ablution took place"; cf. Bietenhard, Hartman), see Schnackenburg, *Baptism*, 19–20 and Joseph A. Fitzmyer, *First Corinthians: A New Translation with Introduction and Commentary.* AB 32 (New Haven: Yale University Press, 2008), 146.
35 Wolter, *Paul*, 130.
36 Schnackenburg, *Baptism*, 19–20. Fitzmyer points out some difficulties in these readings, *First Corinthians*, 146. Yet, see also Wolter's positive treatment of this view (especially, summarizing Hartman's). Wolter, *Paul*, 129–30.

himself as a "planter" and Apollos as a "waterer" in 1 Cor 3:6 (ἐγὼ ἐφύτευσα, Ἀπολλῶς ἐπότισεν), it does not mean that he was the only planter. Rather, if one understands the aorist verb ἐπιστεύσατε in 3:5 (both Paul and Apollos are διάκονοι δι' ὧν ἐπιστεύσατε) as expressing the "inception of the event,"[37] it implies that both of them were regarded as founders for this community. There is every reason to expand the scope of the Pauline "team," although one cannot be sure of precisely who else was involved.[38] The second point is that baptism in this period was conducted in a less systematic way and thus with various ritual messages that were not yet doctrinally controlled (cf. 1 Cor 15:29). When he was initially with the Corinthians, Paul probably did not spend much time explaining the meaning of baptism or constructing the ritual procedure in detail. Baptism might have occurred more spontaneously by several leaders in Corinth (in addition to apostles/missionaries such as Paul, Apollos, Cephas[39]), rather than strictly controlled by a few apostles. Perhaps, for some of the Corinthians, the self-referential message of baptism may have been the creation of a personal bond with, and political allegiance to, the human baptizer.[40]

Initially at Corinth, Paul may have had a relatively laissez-faire attitude toward baptism; only after the issue of factionalism (which also features baptism) emerged from the Corinthian community did Paul begin to address it.[41] Even so, this passage

---

37 Anthony C. Thiselton, *The First Epistle to the Corinthians: A Commentary on the Greek Text*, NIGTC (Grand Rapids: Eerdmans, 2000), 300.
38 For example, in 1 Thessalonians in which Paul, Silvanus, and Timothy are listed as co-senders, Paul speaks of his and his team's εἴσοδος into the region (1 Thess 1:9). The same is probably true of Corinth (i.e., Paul had coworkers), although it is not certain whether Sosthenes, the co-sender of 1 Corinthians, is also included among them.
39 One cannot be sure whether Paul actually means that there were indeed groups for these four factions (including "Christ") among the Corinthians, or whether Paul merely uses them as figurative examples (cf. 1 Cor 4:6) indicating the phenomenon of factionalism among the Corinthians.
40 Perhaps, baptism was not unrepeatable. See a recent work that refutes the scholarly assumption of the unrepeatability of baptism in the New Testament: Lynn Mills and Nicholas J. Moore, "One Baptism Once: The Origins of the Unrepeatability of Christian Baptism," *EC* 11 (2020): 206–26. The authors date the clear appearance of baptism's unrepeatability ("once-only") to the early third century CE, the time of Tertullian.
41 This does not mean that the Corinthians actually came up with the political "slogans"—i.e., "I belong to Paul," or "I belong to Apollos," or "I belong to Cephas," or "I belong to Christ" (1:12). As for the effective refutation of the previous view that 1:12 represents the Corinthians' actual "slogans," see Mitchell, *Paul and the Rhetoric of Reconciliation*, 83–86. The precise reconstruction of the Corinthian situation is hard because what one finds here in 1 Cor 1 is Paul's caricature of the Corinthians' behavior and Paul's rebuke. Yet, several speculations can be mentioned. Perhaps, the Corinthian community consisted of several small groups from the outset (as in Rome—cf. Peter Lampe, *From Paul to Valentinus: Christians at Rome in the First Two Centuries*, trans. Michael Stein-

does not mean that Paul rejects baptism as such entirely.[42] As Wolter puts it, "[Paul] relativizes not the meaning of *baptism*, but merely his own significance as a *baptizer*."[43] By implication, Paul relativizes any person who puts emphasis on her/himself as a baptizer. This distinction between Paul's basic affirmation of baptism per se and his criticism about some understanding of baptism is important, which will be clarified as my discussion progresses. In 1 Cor 1, Paul does not reject the power of baptism that creates a personal bond (the self-referential message of baptism), but he attempts to redirect it. Baptism should foster the unity of the whole community (cf. 1:10)—Christ is not divided (cf. 1:13). More fundamentally, the bond resulting from baptism should be formed primarily between the deity and the devotee, which is implied in 1:13 (μὴ Παῦλος ἐσταυρώθη ὑπὲρ ὑμῶν, ἢ εἰς τὸ ὄνομα Παύλου ἐβαπτίσθητε;). In emphasizing this divine-human bond, Paul's understanding of the ritual message of baptism resonates more with the initiation rituals of the mysteries, than how his Corinthian community members understood baptism, even though Paul does not use any mystery vocabulary.

Finally, it should be noted that there is not anything "magical" in the Corinthians' understanding of baptism reconstructed from this passage, despite some scholars' claims. For example, Witherington comments:

> This section of 1 Corinthians cautions against too exalted a view of baptism. For Paul what was central to his ministry and to the whole process of making converts was preaching, *not* baptizing. This counts against all magical views of baptism, whether of infants or of adults.[44]

---

hauser, ed. Marshall D. Johnson [Minneapolis: Fortress, 2003]). Individuals joining a certain small group of Christ-believers by receiving baptism from the leader of that group (household group?) might have naturally felt allegiance to that person (as opposed to other leaders of other groups). See Richard B. Hays, *First Corinthians* (Louisville: WJK, 1997), 24 (but Hays adds that the passage could also be understood as Paul's rhetorical strategy of *reduction ad absurdum*—rather than precisely reflecting the situation). Or, it is also possible that the Corinthian community did not start as several small groups. If there were several distinctive groups in Corinth at the outset, Paul would have been less surprised when he heard the report of schism among the Corinthians. Also, that Paul sets the recipient of the letter as τῇ ἐκκλησίᾳ θεοῦ τῇ οὔσῃ ἐν Κορίνθῳ (1:2) suggests that Paul understood this community as one unit, rather than several different communities (cf. Gal 1:2, ταῖς ἐκκλησίαις τῆς Γαλατίας), even though he has heard the news of conflict and discord (see also 1 Cor 11:17 that assumes the Corinthians came together as a collective). First Corinthians 1 suggests that at least some people in Corinth viewed baptism as creating a personal bond.
42 Fitzmyer, *First Corinthians*, 147.
43 Italics in original. Wolter, *Paul*, 125.
44 Italics in original. Ben Witherington, *Conflict and Community in Corinth: A Socio-Rhetorical Commentary on 1 and 2 Corinthians* (Grand Rapids: Eerdmans, 1995), 104.

In 1 Cor 1, there is hardly any polemic against the significance of baptism. Questions such as whether conversion comes from preaching or from (magically) baptizing are not the focus of the passage. Ironically, it is Paul who may show more "magical" characteristics, if one utilizes an ancient understanding of "magic." Note, for example, Graf's explanation about magic in antiquity:

> What constitutes a magician, again, is his unusual closeness to the divine sphere. This definition reflects current Greco-Roman thinking: magic has its foundation in the possibility of contact between humans and superhuman beings, and *its main vehicle is speech, the powerful word (and not ritual, the powerful act).*[45]

Paul emphasizes not only his role as a κῆρυξ, but also the effective performativity of his κήρυγμα, which is enabled not by human eloquence, but by the demonstration of the divine spirit: καὶ ὁ λόγος μου καὶ τὸ κήρυγμά μου οὐκ ἐν πειθοῖ[ς] σοφίας [λόγοις] ἀλλ' ἐν ἀποδείξει πνεύματος καὶ δυνάμεως (1 Cor 2:4). Of course, it is unlikely that Paul viewed himself as a "magus."[46] This was to point out that the notion of magic is not helpful for understanding the issue of baptism behind 1 Cor 1:10–17. It could be Paul, not some Corinthians, who attach significant value (thus, "exalted view") to baptism in the name of Christ—which will be made clear in 1 Cor 10.

---

[45] Italics mine. Fritz Graf, "Theories of Magic in Antiquity," in *Magic and Ritual in the Ancient World*, ed. Paul Mirecki and Marvin Meyer (Leiden: Brill, 2001), 94. Admittedly, ritual and magic should not be distinguished too sharply; in fact, magic can be seen as a certain type of ritual. As for magic as "a discourse pertaining to non-normative ritualized activity," see Radcliffe G. Edmonds, *Drawing the Moon: Magic in the Ancient Greco-Roman World* (Princeton: Princeton University Press, 2019), 5. See also a similar definition of magic as deviant religious behavior in David E. Aune, "Magic in Early Christianity," *ANRW* 2.23.2 (1980): 1507–57. Aune demonstrates that magic is a fruitful area of study in relation to early Christianity and its context if one is cautious to avoid the pejorative use of the term that existed even among scholars (especially, Aune critically notes the history of research that created a sharp distinction between magic and religion). Yet, Klauck expresses his reservations about completely abandoning "a consideration of the goals intended by those who engage in magical or religious practices." He rather presents a comparison table that treats magic and religion "as antithetical poles within a continuum," that is, "as the two end points joined by a common line." Klauck, *The Religious Context of Early Christianity*, 217.

[46] See also Seon Yong Kim, *Curse Motifs in Galatians: An Investigation into Paul's Rhetorical Strategies*, WUNT II/531 (Tübingen: Mohr Siebeck, 2020), 92–94 (esp. 94), on how Paul rhetorically employs the theme of magic in Gal 1 "to wards off any slight possible suspicion of his being an unreliable rhetor or evil magician (or a combination of the two)."

5.2.1.2 The self-referential messages, the canonical messages, and things beyond baptism

First Corinthians 1:10–17 suggests that baptism among the Corinthians was practiced in a less systemic and organized way, and that Paul himself did not engage much in the enactment of baptism. Based on the passage, one can infer that the primary self-referential message of the baptismal ritual as perceived by the Corinthians was that baptism is the entry point into this cultic group and it creates a personal bond, or even a political allegiance, between the human leader/baptizer and the baptized. Paul does not relativize or denigrate the power of baptism that creates the intra-human relationship. Instead, Paul subtly shifts the focus of baptism in two ways: (1) The intra-human relationship created and communicated by the ritual should be formed with the whole community, and (2), more fundamentally, the bond should be located between the deity and the devotee—1 Cor 1:13 implies that baptism is primarily related to and predicated upon the name of Christ, rather any human cultic founder or leader. These two are not separate matters, but they are fundamentally interconnected. Schrage comments, "Wo die im gekreuzigten Christus vorgegebene Einheit der Kirche und die durch die Taufe begründete ausschließliche Zugehörigkeit zu Christus ernst genommen wird, werden σχίσματα unmöglich."[47] Only when the Corinthians' "exclusive belonging to [the crucified] Christ based on baptism" is secured can the dysfunctional σχίσματα of the community be eradicated.

This passage does not explicitly state what the canonical messages of baptism are—either as perceived by the Corinthians or interpreted by Paul. Yet, Paul's rhetorical detachment from baptismal activities (vv. 14–17) and his long discourse on the epistemological, soteriological, and sociopolitical force of Christ crucified (starting from v. 18, i.e., the immediately following verse) imply that Paul is signaling to the Corinthians that the proclamation of the gospel (with which Paul is preoccupied, 1:17) is indispensable to the full realization of the meaning of baptism. Paul assumes the role of a proclaimer who interprets the message of ritual, rather than a cult founder who transfers the ritual itself. In 1 Cor 1, Paul suggests that his gospel, namely, the message of the cross (1:18), is the canonical message that guarantees the efficacy of baptism. By ritual logic, the baptized person is obliged to accept this canonical order and to conform her/his behavior to that underlying reality.

---

[47] Wolfgang Schrage, *Der Erste Brief an die Korinther (1Kor 1,1–6,11)*, EKK VII/1 (Zürich: Benziger Verlag; Neukirchener Verlag, 1991), 162. Schrage considers baptism to be important for the unity of the community: " Nicht theologische Schultraditionen und der Konsens der *doctrina* verbürgen die Einheit der Gemeinde. Das tun allein Kreuz und Taufe." Note how he juxtaposes the "cross" and "baptism."

5.2.2 1 Corinthians 1:26–31

5.2.2.1 Exegetical Discussion

Although terms related to baptism (Group A) do not occur explicitly in 1 Cor 1:26–31, the close connection between the deity and the devotees characterized by the expressions ἐν Χριστῷ (Group C) and ἁγιασμός (Group B), along with the fact that Paul's reference to baptism has already appeared in the same chapter (1:10–17), increases the possibility that an echo of Paul's baptismal discourse also continues here in vv. 26–31.[48] Before employing the second person plural in v. 26 (the plural imperative), Paul in vv. 18–25 uses the inclusive first person plural pronoun ("we") to refer to himself and his audience and describes who they are: (1) we are "those who are being saved" (v. 18); (2) we are contrasted with both Jews and Greeks in that "we are proclaiming Christ crucified," whereas they seek signs (Jews) and wisdom (Greeks), respectively (vv. 22–23); and (3) we are "the called" (v. 24, dat., τοῖς κλητοῖς). In v. 26, Paul takes up the language of calling and begins to address the audience in a more direct way (second plural).

> 26 For consider your calling, brothers and sisters, that not many are wise according to the flesh, not many are powerful, not many are of noble birth. 27 But God chose the foolish things of the cosmos, so that he may shame the wise, and God chose the weak things of the cosmos, so that he may shame the things that are strong, 28 [and God chose] the base things of the cosmos, the things that are despised, things that are not, so that he may nullify things that are, 29 so that no flesh should boast before God. 30 But, out of him, you are in Christ Jesus, who has become wisdom for us from God, and righteousness, consecration, and redemption, 31 that, just as it is written, "Let the one who boasts boast in the Lord."

The changed status of the baptized Christ-believers in Corinth is summarized in this short expression in v. 30: "you are in Christ Jesus" (ὑμεῖς ἐστε ἐν Χριστῷ Ἰησοῦ). In the same verse, the phrase ἐξ αὐτοῦ suggests that Paul is rewriting the genealogy of his audience (cf. Gal 3). Despite their unremarkable origin "according to the flesh," they are called by God and now considered originating ἐξ αὐτοῦ (i.e., ἐκ τοῦ θεοῦ) and being ἐν Χριστῷ Ἰησοῦ.

In terms of ritual messages, this passage is comparable to 1 Thess 4:1–8. According to 1 Cor 1:26–31, the self-referential message of baptism is that the baptized receives a new, semi-ethnic (perhaps trans-local) identity, as implied in 1 Thess 4:1–8.[49] Paul further spells out this idea in Gal 3. Also, one can notice that

---

[48] Schnelle, *Apostle Paul*, 481, gives a positive assessment of a "pre-Pauline baptismal tradition" in 1 Cor 1:30.
[49] The characteristically Pauline expressions, ἐν Χριστῷ and ἐν κυρίῳ, already occur in 1 Thessalonians (ἐν Χριστῷ: 2:14; 4:16; 5:18; ἐν κυρίῳ: 3:8; 4:1; 5:12), and several of them would suggest a link

as in 1 Thess 4:1–8, the ἁγιασμός language appears in 1 Cor 1:26–31: the term resonates with the dedication to the cultic deity and ritual-moral purity. Fitzmyer notes: "'Sanctification' is ... an abstract way of expressing the dedication of Christians to God and his cultic service that is derived from the crucified Christ."[50] Yet, the role of the Holy Spirit with regard to Christ-believers' ἁγιασμός is not explicitly found within 1 Cor 1:26–31, in contrast to 1 Thess 4:1–8.

> Excursus 2: Conversion and Baptism in 1 Thessalonians 4:1–8
> No precise reference to baptism is found in 1 Thess 4:1–8, but the passage points out the results of the Thessalonians' conversion (of which the baptismal ritual was likely a part). In 1 Thess 4:1–8, Paul notes that the conversion of the Thessalonians (cf. 1 Thess 1:9–10) brought about ritual purity, and he attributes this transformation to divine agency, divine knowledge, and the Holy Spirit.
>
> First, divine agency underlies the purity of the Thessalonians. The life of ἁγιασμός is described as divine mandate (4:3), in which God called the Thessalonians (who were gentiles). Yet, the life of ἁγιασμός is not a demand that is disconnected from the demander: rather, as Collins notes, "'holiness' [ἁγιασμός] retains the basic connotation of *divine action*—in this case that of a divine activity which is manifest in concrete activity on the part of the faithful."[51]
>
> Second, the Thessalonians' knowledge of God (and of God's will), i.e., their cognitive dimension, may be presupposed as the source of the Thessalonians' pure status. Admittedly, Paul does not explicitly say that the gentiles/nations (τὰ ἔθνη, 4:5) are ritually unclean, and in the biblical tradition, ritual purity/impurity may be only temporary, without necessarily moral implications.[52] Yet, ritual purity and moral purity are conceptually blended in Paul, and this leads to some connection between the gentiles (esp. in relation to their idolatry)

---

between baptism, new local/trans-local community of the ἅγιοι, and their being-in-Christ in the here and hereafter. First, in 1 Thess 2:14, Paul applies ἐν Χριστῷ to the *ekklesiai* in Judaea (Paul urges the Thessalonians to be imitators τῶν ἐκκλησιῶν τοῦ θεοῦ τῶν οὐσῶν ἐν τῇ Ἰουδαίᾳ ἐν Χριστῷ Ἰησοῦ). It could be inferred that even before Paul, the ἐν Χριστῷ language was accepted and used as a form of reference to the Christ-believing groups in various regions, including Judaea. Yet, it is more plausible that Paul purposefully uses this phrase to emphasize the shared identity between the Christ-believers in Thessalonica and those in Judaea. For the invention of shared identity and tradition, see Sarah E. Rollens, "Inventing Tradition in Thessalonica: The Appropriation of the Past in 1 Thessalonians 2:14–16," *BTB* 46 (2016): 127–30.

50 Fitzmyer, *First Corinthians*, 164.
51 Italics mine. Collins, "This is the Will of God," 309. Yet, his distinction (or contrast) between "the ethical" and "the religious register" seems unnecessary.
52 Fredriksen, *Paul*, 51. Yet, depicting gentiles as intrinsically "impure" is a rhetorical trope attested in some Jewish writings (such as the *Animal Apocalypse*). It also occurs in early Christian writings. See Matthew Thiessen, "Gentiles as Impure Animals in the Writings of Early Christ Followers," in *Perceiving the Other in Ancient Judaism and Early Christianity*, ed. Michal Bar-Asher Siegal et al. (Tübingen: Mohr Siebeck, 2017), 19–32.

and their impurity.⁵³ In 4:5, the stock image of "people who do not know God" characterizes gentile identity (cf. Jer 10:25, Ps 79:6), echoing other passages in Paul that link the stereotypical portrayal of gentiles to their unclean status (e.g., Rom 1:24 [ἀκαθαρσία]; 1 Cor 6:11 says that the unjust ones have now been "washed," implying that they were unclean before). Contrary to the rest of the ignorant nations, these newly converted Thessalonians have been called to embody ritual-moral purity in their lives as they live in the knowledge of God (e.g., the Lord as the "avenger," which Paul says he already taught them before; v. 6). In short, the epistemological aspect is part of the divine transformation toward the new life of ἁγιασμός.

Third, 4:8 suggests that God's Holy Spirit (τὸ πνεῦμα αὐτοῦ τὸ ἅγιον) sent into (εἰς) the Thessalonians (at the time of conversion?) may be the source of their ἁγιασμός; the Holy Spirit is a concrete manifestation of the divine action. The preposition εἰς in v. 8 could be rendered as "toward," which would suggest that the Spirit remains as a power or guidance that is external to the believer. Yet, what Paul envisions here may be the indwelling divine Spirit. Refusing to follow Paul's instructions about the life of ἁγιασμός amounts to refusing God who works in that person through the indwelling Spirit. Later in the letter, Paul warns them not to "quench" the Spirit, which is the will of God (5:18–19), harking back to 4:1–8.⁵⁴

The three points above (divine agency, knowledge, and the Holy Spirit as the indwelling divine source of transformation), which have transformed (purified) the Thessalonians before God, resonate with Rom 6–8, which will be discussed later. To what extent all three are related to baptism is, of course, a matter of debate (both in 1 Thessalonians and in Romans). Yet, if baptism marked their conversion in the visual and embodied way, then it is possible that baptism could function as a synecdoche. That is, baptism as an entry ritual into the Christ asso-

---

53 Cf. Fredriksen, *Paul*, 53. "Perhaps ... because of pagan traditions of idol-worship, Jews (or at least some Jews, like Paul) considered pagans as somehow intrinsically 'impure.'" Yet, Fredriksen's basic position is that the binary of pure/impure and that of holy/profane are two different categories, and neither of them is directly related to moral issues. But in Paul, the two distinct categories are blended to some degree. For example, 1 Thess 4:7 contrasts ἀκαθαρσία (belonging to the pure/impure binary) and ἁγιασμός (the holy/profane binary), suggesting that the two domains overlap into a new space in Paul's discourse.

54 First Thessalonians 4:1–8 and 5:18–22 are closely related. First Thessalonians 5:18 contains the expression τοῦτο γὰρ θέλημα θεοῦ once again (cf. 4:3), and this time it is coupled with ἐν Χριστῷ Ἰησοῦ. What the pronoun τοῦτο refers to (i.e., whether it points backward or forward) is not entirely clear, but in light of 1 Thess 4:3 (cf. John 6:39–40), it is more likely that τοῦτο points forward. That is, the will of God (5:18) is what follows from 5:19 onward (Abraham J. Malherbe, *The Letters to the Thessalonians: A New Translation with Introduction and Commentary*, AB 32B [New York: Doubleday, 2000], 330). This includes instructions "on the proper attitude towards the Spirit in prophecy," but also admonition to "abstain from every form of evil" (5:22). This last element, with its verb ἀπέχεσθε in 5:22, forms an *inclusio* with ἀπέχεσθαι in 4:3. Seen together with 4:3–8, τοῦτο γὰρ θέλημα θεοῦ ἐν Χριστῷ Ἰησοῦ εἰς ὑμᾶς in 5:18 suggests that ἐν Χριστῷ refers to the communal boundary for following those instructions characterized by the extension of ritual purity language (ἁγιασμός as opposed to ἀκαθαρσία) to everyday life, but at the same time, it refers to the source of such divine knowledge. The Holy Spirit is closely connected to this pure/consecrated life in both passages.

ciation can indicate the whole array of transformation that follows one's conversion to the Jewish God (and to Christ).

In 1 Cor 1:26–31, the role of the indwelling Holy Spirit is not explicitly found; rather, Christology receives more prominence. Christ-believers' current status is closely connected to the identity of their new cultic deity, Christ. The Corinthians are "in Christ," according to the rewritten genealogy (enabled by their joining the Christ-cult group—presumably through baptism). They are now enjoying righteousness (δικαιοσύνη), consecration (ἁγιασμός), and redemption (ἀπολύτρωσις), mainly because Christ himself is the δικαιοσύνη, ἁγιασμός, and ἀπολύτρωσις from God for Paul and his Corinthian audience (1:30). Paul's claim that Christ Jesus "has become (ἐγενήθη) wisdom for us from God, righteousness, consecration, and redemption" goes back to v. 24.[55] There, Paul says that "for us, the called," Christ is "the power of God" and "the wisdom of God." It is the figure of Christ that guarantees these "effects" to be fulfilled in the baptized Christ-believers. This language recalls Gal 3:13: "Christ redeemed (ἐξηγόρασεν) us from the curse of the law by himself becoming a curse for us (γενόμενος ὑπὲρ ἡμῶν κατάρα)." There is of course a difference: in Gal 3:13, what Christ has become (=curse) is the *reverse* of what Christ-believing gentiles are supposed to become (=the blessing [of Abraham]). Yet, there is an underlying similarity: in Gal 3:13, the infusion of the blessing "into the gentiles/nations" (εἰς τὰ ἔθνη) is only made possible ἐν Χριστῷ Ἰησοῦ, as in 1 Cor 1:30–31. Thus, generally speaking, the metonymical logic is similar. As is the cultic deity, so also are his devotees, since those who are ἐν Χριστῷ have become part of this deity—i.e., Christ's body. Then, this underlying pattern—"as is the cultic deity, so also are his devotees" (cf. 1 Cor 15:48)—should be considered a canonical message of baptism according to Paul. He did not necessarily borrow it from the mysteries (the pattern is already there in Jewish Scripture [e.g., Lev 11:44–45, 19:2; cf. in the NT, 1 Pet 1:15–16]). Still, Paul's logic of association echoes the messages of mystery initiations as discussed in the earlier chapters, for example, the identification between Dionysus and his devotees (3.2.4) or Isis devotees' sharing of Isis's fate and suffering (4.2.4).

---

[55] Within the Pauline corpus, the link between wisdom and the other "three effects of the Christ-event" (δικαιοσύνη, ἁγιασμός, and ἀπολύτρωσις) is peculiar to 1 Corinthians. Fitzmyer, *First Corinthians*, 164.

5.2.2.2 The self-referential messages, the canonical messages, and things beyond baptism

Little new information can be obtained from 1 Cor 1:26–31 about what ritual messages the Corinthians believed. Rather, this passage further illuminates Paul's understanding and interpretation of baptism. Two self-referential messages are noticeable. First, Paul presupposes that baptism communicates the ἁγιασμός of the baptized person (cf. 1 Thess 4). Second, by telling the Corinthians, "out of him [God], you are in Christ Jesus," Paul implies that baptism rewrites one's genealogy (cf. Gal 3).

The baptized person's close connection with the new cultic deity, Christ, continues to receive emphasis (as in 1 Cor 1:10–17). This serves both as a self-referential message and a canonical message of baptism that sustains the other self-referential messages at a deeper level. Christ himself has become wisdom, righteousness, consecration, and redemption for the Corinthians. The Christ-initiate shares the traits of Christ through metonymic logic ("as is the cultic deity, so also are his devotees," cf. Gal 3:13; 1 Cor 15:48), which then creates obligations to which these initiates are bound (Rappaport). This close relationship between the deity and the devotees in terms of their identity could have been drawn from the HB/LXX tradition (e.g., Lev 11:44–45, 19:2) in light of Paul's Jewish heritage. Our survey of the initiation rituals of the mysteries allows us to see how this shared identity (based on association) fits the cognitive pattern of mystery initiation attested among the gentiles in Pauline cities. For Paul, this ritual metonymy is a good strategy for conveying his exhortation, emotionally appealing to the Corinthians and intellectually making sense to them. If the baptized Corinthians are related to Christ and to his foolish and weak crucifixion, then their own boasting (self-pride) is strongly discouraged. Furthermore, Paul exhorts the Corinthians to realize that baptism demands religious virtuosity in an embodied way by participating in the crucified identity of this cultic deity.

5.2.3 1 Corinthians 6:9–11

5.2.3.1 Exegetical Discussion

Although no word in this pericope uses the βαπτιδ-root (Group A), most agree that 1 Cor 6:9–11, especially the image of washing/cleansing in v. 11 (ἀπελούσασθε), refers to baptism. Cleansing one's body or objects with water is perhaps the most universal mechanism of purification in antiquity, including the Jewish world.[56] Wash-

---

[56] For a classic discussion about washing in a Greek context, see Robert Parker, *Miasma: Pollution*

ing with water for the purpose of ritual is intuitive: as one's external body is cleansed with water, one's ritual purity is also restored. This image of washing is also frequently connected to early Christian baptism throughout the NT, although it takes a moral tone. It is usually a way of authenticating one's repentance and of cleansing one's sins (e.g., Acts 2:38; cf. Mark 1:5 and parr.). Schnackenburg begins his famous book on Pauline baptism with 1 Cor 6, noting, "Of all expressions which Paul uses in connection with baptism ἀπολούεσθαι [1 Cor 6:11] indicates the closest link with the material of baptism, the water."[57] Although it is hard to determine whether the verse actually contains a "baptismal formula" recited by the baptizer or the baptized, Paul assumes his readers' common experience of baptism as ritual washing and makes use of the ritual for his particular rhetorical purposes.

The structure of the Greek text needs to be examined.

⁹Ἢ οὐκ οἴδατε
    ὅτι ἄδικοι θεοῦ βασιλείαν οὐ κληρονομήσουσιν;
      μὴ πλανᾶσθε· οὔτε πόρνοι
        οὔτε εἰδωλολάτραι
        οὔτε μοιχοὶ
        οὔτε μαλακοὶ
        οὔτε ἀρσενοκοῖται
        ¹⁰οὔτε κλέπται
        οὔτε πλεονέκται,
        οὐ μέθυσοι,
        οὐ λοίδοροι,
        οὐχ ἅρπαγες
    βασιλείαν θεοῦ κληρονομήσουσιν.

¹¹καὶ ταῦτά τινες ἦτε·

    ἀλλ' ἀπελούσασθε, ἀλλ' ἡγιάσθητε, ἀλλ' ἐδικαιώθητε

---

and Purification in Early Greek Religion (Oxford: Clarendon Press, 1983). For a survey of Jewish washing from the Hebrew Bible through Second Temple literature, see Lawrence, *Washing in Water*. His threefold categorization ("ritual washing," "metaphorical washing," and "initiatory washing") is understandable—what he means by "ritual" basically has to do with cultic purity —but is not entirely satisfactory. From the perspective of rituals in the broader Mediterranean world, initiation is also a ritual.

57 According to Schnackenburg, at least two arguments can be made against the claim that 1 Cor 6:11 refers to baptism: first, in light of the LXX usage of the verb λούεσθαι, the verb ἀπολούεσθαι in 1 Cor 6:11 could be "simply a picture [of] cleansing from sins"; and second, the middle voice of ἀπολούεσθαι is strange, given that in Paul's letters baptism is mostly expressed in the passive voice. Schnackenburg responds by making three points: first, "a comparison with Acts xxii. 16 shows that this picture does relate to baptism"; second, "[a]s to the middle voice, it can scarcely be maintained ... that it expresses the action of man [sic] in contrast to the action of God"; third, [t]he aorists support a once for all, foundational act in the past." Schnackenburg, *Baptism*, 3.

ἐν τῷ ὀνόματι τοῦ κυρίου Ἰησοῦ Χριστοῦ
καὶ ἐν τῷ πνεύματι τοῦ θεοῦ ἡμῶν.

In this passage, Paul contrasts the Corinthians' gentile past (cf. 1 Cor 12:2) and their present status in Christ. Paul begins to enumerate a vice list in 6:9–10, rhetorically asking the audience whether they do not know that such ἄδικοι will not inherit the kingdom of God (the phrase "to inherit the kingdom of God" is an *inclusio*; it appears at the beginning of v. 9 and at the end of v. 10). Does the short imperative remark, μὴ πλανᾶσθε ("Don't be deceived/misled"), imply that some Corinthians were actually deceived by others about eschatological teachings or moral norms? Or, would that also be part of Paul's rhetoric (cf. 1 Cor 15:33; Gal 6:7)? At any rate, Paul then declares that in the past, some of Paul's Corinthian audience were (τινες ἦτε; "some of you were") also engaging in the vices of the gentiles, but they have undergone a dramatic change that is in sharp contrast (using ἀλλά) with their past. This change is explained by three aorist middle/passive verbs, ἀπελούσασθε (mid),[58] ἡγιάσθητε, and ἐδικαιώθητε, whose rhythmical arrangement has led some scholars to suspect a vestige of a baptismal formula. The three aorist verbs can be translated in the perfect: "you have washed (yourselves), you have been sanctified, and you have been justified." The first verb ἀπελούσασθε (inf. ἀπολούεσθαι) especially evokes the visual and tactile image of ritual washing (cf. Acts 22:16, which juxtaposes βάπτισαι and ἀπόλουσαι). As Rappaport demonstrates, regardless of continuing personal ambivalence, rituals signal one's social status digitally (e.g., yes/no, before/after, etc.), marking the definitive change.[59] Paul reminds his audience of the bodily experience of baptism as ritual washing in order to emphasize that baptism marked the moment that separated their present life in Christ from their gentile/pagan past.

One gets a glimpse of how early Christ-believers practiced and understood baptism and how Paul modified it. Within the Pauline corpus, it is only in this passage that the verb ἀπολούεσθαι appears. Furthermore, nowhere else does Paul portray baptism primarily as a washing event, although this intuitive connection is frequently found in other parts of the NT. This might increase the possibility that Paul draws on baptismal tradition (though not necessarily a "formula") known to his audience and perhaps to the broader early Christ-believing commun-

---

58 Scholars often argue that the middle voice should be understood as passive (cf. the list of scholars in Turley, *Ritualized Revelation*, 61). Yet, such an assumption is based on a particular interpretation of the verb. If one takes into account that the verb is actually referring to washing activities in a ritual setting, where participants often washed themselves for purification (i.e., not all washings were conducted by other special agents), one can retain the middle force in this verse.
59 Rappaport, *Ritual and Religion*, 89–106.

ities of the first century.⁶⁰ The basic self-referential message of baptism as understood by the Corinthians would be this: similar to other washing activities in antiquity, baptism promised the would-be baptized people ritual purity before the deity that they serve now. Paul does not reject this understanding of baptism (held by the Corinthians). Rather, he leverages this image for his rhetorical purposes by blending it into his moral discourse. The first two ritually-related words, ἀπελούσασθε and ἡγιάσθητε, are blended with ἐδικαιώθητε—a verb that is probably less directly related to cleansing rituals, but fits better with Paul's theological vocabulary. In that sense, the last verb, ἐδικαιώθητε, could be Paul's own contribution, something he adds to existing baptismal tradition. Similar to 1 Thess 4, baptism in 1 Cor 6:9–11 is a ritual that communicates the participant's purity—a hybrid of ritual and moral purity.

How the last part of 6:11 (ἐν τῷ ὀνόματι τοῦ κυρίου Ἰησοῦ Χριστοῦ καὶ ἐν τῷ πνεύματι τοῦ θεοῦ ἡμῶν) is related to the three verbs that precede is not entirely clear.⁶¹ Probably, this is part of the baptismal tradition.⁶² Beyond that general state-

---

60 Schnackenburg, *Baptism*, 9. The other two verbs (ἁγιάζειν and δικαιοῦν, especially the latter) are more frequently found in Paul's letters, yet their appearance in the aorist indicative is rare (of the six occurrences in the undisputed Pauline letters, ἁγιάζειν only appears here in this form; in the aorist indicative, δικαιοῦν appears only here and in Rom 4:2 and 8:30 [twice] of the 23 occurrences of the verb). The rarity of a certain verbal form or phrase does not necessarily prove that Paul draws on tradition.
61 Grammatically, this double ἐν τῷ phrase in 1 Cor 6:11 could be applied to all three verbs (ἀπελούσασθε, ἡγιάσθητε, and ἐδικαιώθητε), or it might modify only the third one (ἐδικαιώθητε). The former is more likely. Fitzmyer, *First Corinthians*, 258.
62 Turley, *Ritualized Revelation*, 62, 73. The phrase may not be the baptismal *formula* actually used in baptism. First of all, as one can see from 1 Cor 5:4 (ἐν τῷ ὀνόματι τοῦ κυρίου [ἡμῶν] Ἰησοῦ), Paul uses similar phrases in contexts with no connection to baptism. Second, the historicity of the baptism depicted in Acts can be questioned. It is only in Acts that one finds a liturgical formulaic use of ἐν τῷ ὀνόματι τοῦ [κυρίου] Ἰησοῦ Χριστοῦ (e.g., Acts 10:48; cf. Acts 2:38 [ἐπὶ τῷ ὀνόματι], 8:16 [εἰς τὸ ὄνομα]; cf. Matt 28:19). That being said, the baptismal reference of this phrase still holds true. The difference between εἰς (which is more Pauline) and ἐν caused Gupta to be skeptical about relating 1 Cor 6:9–11 to baptism at all. Nijay. K. Gupta, *Worship That Makes Sense to Paul: A New Approach to the Theology and Ethics of Paul's Cultic Metaphors*. BZNW 175 (Berlin: Walter de Gruyter, 2010), 71. Nevertheless, his argument based on the difference between εἰς and ἐν is not definitive, considering the overlapping use of them in the New Testament (e.g., Luke 9:62, 11:7; John 1:18, 3:15; see Daniel B. Wallace, *Greek Grammar beyond the Basics: An Exegetical Syntax of the New Testament* [Grand Rapids: Zondervan, 1996], 363, 369, and 372; cf. Turner's remarks on Matthew's careful distinction between the two prepositions: Nigel Turner, *A Grammar of New Testament Greek* by James Hope Moulton, vol. 4 [Edinburgh: T.&T. Clark, 1976], 42 [Paul is not mentioned there]). Also, one cannot exclude the possibility that Paul included the traditional phrasing (in this case, using ἐν in the baptismal context) as he heard it. I think the ἐν τῷ ὀνόματι τοῦ κυρίου Ἰησοῦ Χριστοῦ phrase can

ment, several exegetical questions remain, which cannot be addressed at this point.[63] Two things are clear: First, this prepositional phrase functions as a boundary marker that demarcates this initiation ritual from other analogous rituals. This is a Christ initiation, hence the focus on the name of the deity, *Christos*. Second, this phrase suggests that the Holy Spirit is the agent of baptismal transformation.[64] Whether the Holy Spirit is bestowed at the moment of baptism is not clear in this passage alone (yet, cf. 1 Cor 12:13).[65]

5.2.3.2 The self-referential messages, the canonical messages, and things beyond baptism

Regarding self-referential messages of baptism, Paul in this passage emphasizes two benefits of baptism. Also, his warning against some form of ritual failure provides insight into the canonical messages, although the canonical messages of baptism are not explicitly mentioned in 1 Cor 6:9–11.

First, Paul reminds them that baptism as ritual is "the digital representation of analogic processes" (Rappaport's phrase); baptism changes one's identity from the morally "depraved/unjust" gentile (past) to the washed, sanctified, justified being-in-Christ (present), reducing any ambiguity or ambivalence.[66] As shown above, it is

---

be seen as a baptismal reference (cf. 1 Cor 1:13; although εἰς is used there), especially in conjunction with other words in this verse (including ἀπελούσασθε and ἡγιάσθητε).

63 Only a few of those questions can be mentioned briefly. First, elsewhere in the undisputed Pauline letters, baptism is not combined with the phrase ἐν τῷ ὀνόματι of Jesus, Christ, the Lord, or any other person (cf. εἰς τὸ ὄνομα, e.g., in 1 Cor 1:13, 15), which Gupta also points out. Then, the question about the nature and extent of pre-Pauline tradition arises. Second, in 1 Cor 6:11, "the name of Lord Jesus Christ" and "the Spirit of our God" are paralleled, but how these two are related to each other is not clear in this passage. Are they a form of hendiadys? Or, do they have different meanings and functions? Third, it is also uncertain whether the ἐν τῷ phrase is instrumental ("by the name of … and by the Spirit of …") in the sense that Jesus's name and God's Spirit enabled the change indicated by the three verbs, or whether it is locative ("in the name of … and in the Spirit of …") in the sense that the name and the Spirit are construed as a realm within which this change occurs. Finally, the question of the precise role of the divine Spirit for believers also arises. Does the verse imply that the baptized receive the πνεῦμα through their participation in baptism? Or, does the ἐν τῷ phrase suggest that the πνεῦμα was a true medium (not water?) by which they were washed? Or, is the πνεῦμα (in conjunction with the "name of the Lord Jesus Christ"?) the true agent of this transformation?

64 Turley, *Ritualized Revelation*, 70. He criticizes previous commentators who "have largely overlooked the significance of the Spirit for Paul's argument in 1 Corinthians 6.9–11." Turley reads too much extra-textual information into the text of 1 Cor 6:9–11 in his intertextual investigation.

65 Cf. Schrage, *Der Erste Brief an die Korinther (1Kor 1,1–6,11)*, 434.

66 Rappaport's ethnographic examples and explanations are helpful (Rappaport, *Ritual and Religion*, 102–103): "Continuous more-less processes … may trigger the performance of a ritual, but it is

possible that the Corinthians (or other Christ-believers, too) already understood baptism as a cleansing event, as well as an entry ritual that marks the boundary of the group—Paul agrees. In addition, he spells out the ethical potential of that understanding of baptism by blending it into his hortatory discourse. The verb ἁγιάζειν in 6:11 echoes how Paul portrays his audience in 1:2—the Corinthians are already ἡγιασμένοι (note the nuance of the perfect participle) and κλητοὶ ἅγιοι. One might ask whether "to justify" should be placed before "to sanctify" from the doctrinal perspective,[67] but one can hardly expect a full-fledged expression of *ordo salutis* from the first-century author.[68] By reminding them of their past baptism and the significance attached to it (i.e., they are now ἅγιοι and no longer ἄδικοι; see also the vice list in 6:9–10),[69] Paul indirectly chastises them for their unjust actions toward their fellow-members, found in 6:8 (ὑμεῖς ἀδικεῖτε … ἀδελφούς). This is quite natural, considering how ritual works. By the ritual's illocutionary force, one's change of socio-religious identity also creates obligations that must be accepted by the participants.[70] Thus, Turley rightly notes, "Paul is calling the Corinthians to realize in their behavior the sanctified and righteous obligations that their washings in the name of Christ unambiguously established."[71] In short, it is not that Paul merely uses the image of baptism as a secondary device to his discourse; rather, he fully exploits how ritual—baptism—works

---

in the binary nature of such occurrence to signal the transition from one to the other of two possible discrete states. Such a reduction of ambiguity … enhances the clarity of messages so transmitted. I would now add that it 'purifies' them, so to speak, as well. That is, although it may not eliminate all of the ambivalence that may attend their transmission, it does tend to neutralize the possibly polluting social effects of that psychic condition … The planting of the *rumbim* signals to those planting it, as well as to others; the slash of the supercisor's knife signals to the boys having themselves cut even more than to others, that *regardless* of their continuing ambivalence they have taken *definitive* action, action, that is, redefining their social status. [A]nd that, in social terms, is that … The new social status is not nullified or even modified by ambivalence with respect to its assumption, or even by emotions and attitudes incompatible with it."

67 Schnackenburg mentions in passing that the place of ἐδικαιώθητε after ἡγιάσθητε is "remarkable," yet he also notes that ἐδικαιώθητε in v. 11 is placed there as the "opposite pole to ἄδικοι" in v. 9. Schnackenburg, *Baptism*, 4.

68 Moreover, the order of the three (wash—sanctify—justify) does not likely suggest a sequence, but it could illuminate the significance of the same event in various ways.

69 It is true that there is some cognitive aspect in this chapter (e.g., οὐκ οἴδατε in v. 9). But Siikavirta's claim, *Baptism and Cognition*, 91, that "the cognitive force of Paul's ethical appeal in 1 Cor. 6 is very strong" is dubious. This explanation makes sense in Rom 6–8, but the cognitive-ethical aspect is not yet fully developed in 1 Cor 6.

70 Rappaport, *Ritual and Religion*, 134–35.

71 Turley, *Ritualized Revelation*, 74.

and its full implications. Perhaps, a canonical message similar to what appears in 1 Cor 1:26–31 is also implied here.

Secondly, but related to the first, baptism indicates an eschatological benefit. Paul's discourse implies that baptism promises the participants that they will inherit the kingdom of God. This too turns into an explicit warning in 6:9 and 11 (οὐχ … βασιλείαν θεοῦ κληρονομήσουσιν), which closely parallels Gal 5:21. The language of inheritance is deeply rooted in biblical tradition, in which the promise of the land (though not "the kingdom of God") is found alongside the injunction to obey and the warning against disobedience (e.g., the long discourse in Deut 5–9; for the particular verb κληρονομεῖν: e.g., Gen 15:7–8; Exod 23:30; Deut 1:38–39). These promises, obligations, and warnings were probably (re)created by ritual moments (see, for example, Gen 15:10–11; Gen 17 [circumcision]; Exod 13 [Passover]), in which the covenant God made with ancestors (or individuals like Abraham) in the past were constantly fused with the present. While retaining the frame of covenantal ritual, Paul appropriates the language of inheritance and reformulates it for baptism and conversion. Baptism indexically communicates that the baptized has changed from ἄδικοι (detailed by the vice list) to ἅγιοι, indicating their inheritance in the kingdom of God, simultaneously demanding the acceptance of the obligations created by the ritual.[72] The implied canonical message is that baptism is a ritual amounting to, or even fulfilling, the covenantal rituals and ritualized moments found in the HB/LXX. God's covenant sustains the efficacy of this new ritual of the Christ cult.

5.2.4 1 Corinthians 10:1–5 and 1 Corinthians 12:12–13

5.2.4.1 Exegetical Discussion

There are two short references to baptism in 1 Cor 10 and 12 (Group A). Though they are brief, they illuminate how baptism was understood by the Corinthians and how Paul used the baptismal messages for a specific purpose. First Corinthians 10 is the final chapter of the three sustained chapters (chs. 8, 9, 10) in which Paul wades through the issue of food offered to idols (περὶ τῶν εἰδωλοθύτων, 8:1).

One must begin by examining 10:1–5, focusing on the remark about baptism.

> 1 For I do not want you to be unaware, brothers and sisters, that our fathers were all under the cloud and all passed through the sea, 2 and all were baptized (ἐβαπτίσθησαν) into Moses

---

[72] As Morales correctly observes, 1 Cor 6:9–11, along with certain passages in Galatians (e.g., Gal 3:26–29 and 5:19–21), puts together "baptism, a vice list, and becoming heirs of the kingdom." Morales, "Baptism and Union with Christ," 166.

in the cloud and in the sea, 3 and all ate the same spiritual food, 4 and all drank the same spiritual drink, for they were drinking from a spiritual rock that followed—and the rock was Christ. 5 But God was not pleased with most of them, for they were struck down in the desert.

As such, this passage offers little information about the actual baptismal ritual among the Corinthians, since Paul uses baptism with an expanded and unusual meaning. The Israelites were not baptized, but were escaping and fleeing from the Egyptian army, and there is no extant evidence in the HB/LXX, or in other Jewish writings, or even in the NT (but, cf. 1 Pet 3:20–21),[73] that the exodus event was interpreted as baptism. Perhaps for the first time, Paul interprets the story of the Israelites' wandering in the wilderness in terms of baptism. Thus, this passage does not seem to inform us much about actual baptismal practices among early Christ-believers. Rather, it shows an early Christian interpretation of the exodus: Paul sees a typological relationship between the exodus and Christian baptism.

In light of other Pauline passages, one might presume that rewriting the gentile believers' genealogy may be included in the self-referential message of baptism in 1 Cor 10:1–5, but that is not the case. Rhetorically employing the disclosure form (here, οὐ θέλω γὰρ ὑμᾶς ἀγνοεῖν), Paul sets forth a new interpretation of the exodus story, in which he brings together "two horizons"—i.e., Israel's ancestors (past) and the Corinthian gentiles (present).[74] By calling the Israelites "our fathers" (οἱ πατέρες ἡμῶν, 10:1),[75] Paul indeed rewrites the audience's (especially the gentile members') genealogy. In this regard, this passage is similar to 1 Cor 1:30–31,[76] and even more so to Gal 3 (which will be discussed below). Galatians 3, especially, contains remarks about baptism in which Paul discusses the connection between present Christ-believers and the figure(s) from Israel's past. There is a slight differ-

---

[73] First Peter 3:20–21, where an event from the HB/LXX is compared to baptism, postdates Paul's letters, thus it is possible that 1 Peter was influenced by Paul's application of baptism to the exodus story. Baptism and water in 1 Pet 3:20–21 are not understood in the same way they are in 1 Cor 10. First Peter 3:20–21 says that the household of Noah was saved through water and Christians are saved through Christ's resurrection. John H. Elliott, *1 Peter: A New Translation with Introduction and Commentary*, 37B (New York: Doubleday, 2000), 667, 673. Other than that, it is hard to find comparable sources from which Paul may have drawn this analogy.
[74] This hermeneutic is already hinted in 1 Cor 9 (e.g., 9:10, "Or, doesn't he speak entirely for our sake?"). The conscious appropriation of older tradition for the present had a long history—even traced back to Moses himself speaking to the second generation in the wilderness (e.g., Deut 5:3; unlike 1 Cor 10, it is about God's "covenant" and has nothing to do with ethnic reasoning).
[75] The inclusive first person plural presumably includes not only Paul (or Jewish Christ-believers) but also the gentile audience. Fitzmyer, *First Corinthians*, 380; Wolfgang Schrage, *Der erste Brief an die Korinther (1Kor 6,12–11,16)*, EKK VII/2 (Zürich: Benziger Verlag; Neukirchener Verlag, 1995), 388.
[76] In 1 Cor 1:30, Paul writes their genealogy in a way that is connected to God himself.

ence in that in 1 Cor 10, the Christ-believers are linked to *Israelites from the exodus period* (i.e., the Corinthians are the descendants of those rebellious Israelites who perished), whereas in Gal 3, the Christ-believers are connected to *Abraham* (i.e., the Galatians are "the seed of Abraham" [τοῦ Ἀβραὰμ σπέρμα], to whom the promise is given, 3:29). Furthermore, what is distinctive in 1 Cor 10 is that the connection between the Corinthians and the Israelites is taken for granted; Paul does not need to explain that presupposition. This situation is quite different from that of Gal 3, in which Paul labors to prove that the Galatians have become the seed of Abraham (3:29) through Christ who is the ultimate seed of Abraham (3:16). This difference implies that appropriating Israel's history for the Christ-believing gentiles in Corinth was already part of common knowledge among the Corinthians, either taught by Paul, or others (Apollos?), or both. Paul is not disclosing a new fact (despite the disclosure form in 10:1) that the Israelites in the wilderness are the Corinthians' ancestors; nor is he saying that baptism establishes this relationship (cf. Gal 3: baptism is indeed involved in the establishment of the gentiles' genealogical connection to Abraham via Christ). Rather, Paul wants to draw the audience's attention to his new interpretation of the exodus as a baptism: "our fathers" were also "baptized," just like the Corinthians are.

Furthermore, it seems that the physical process of baptism has little to do with Paul's interpretation of the exodus story in 1 Cor 10. Grammatically, Paul says that the Israelites were baptized *into* (εἰς) Moses, not *by* (ὑπό) Moses. Furthermore, it was into *Moses* (εἰς τὸν Μωϋσῆν), not into the *sea* (εἰς τὴν θάλασσαν—this is my coinage). The latter ("into the sea") might be more accurate if Paul really wanted to highlight a physical event shared by both (i.e., the Israelites' entered the Reed Sea, just like the Corinthian Christ-believers entered baptismal water [either the sea or other water]). In 1 Cor 10:2, the sea that the Israelites entered is mentioned with the preposition ἐν (as in ἐν τῇ θαλάσσῃ), also accompanied by the phrase ἐν τῇ νεφέλῃ ("in the cloud"). It can be inferred that the crucial imagery that attracts Paul's attention for his analogy between the exodus event and baptism was not physically entering the sea (which could be compared to the baptized entering the water).[77]

This passage shows how Paul's distinctive "ecclesiocentric hermeneutics" is at work in his retelling of the story of Israel in the wilderness; he is not telling how baptism works as a ritual or what messages it communicates.[78] Since Paul and his contemporary Christ-believers were expecting an eschatological consummation

---

77 Thus, *contra* Schnackenburg, *Baptism*, 92.
78 Richard B. Hays, *Echoes of Scripture in the Letters of Paul* (New Haven: Yale University Press, 1989), 101–2.

(εἰς οὓς τὰ τέλη τῶν αἰώνων κατήντηκεν, 10:11), he uses his experience of a contemporary ritual (baptism) as a framework for interpreting Jewish tradition in a new way.

However, this is not all. A closer look at 1 Cor 10:1–5 illuminates (1) the logic of baptism for early Christ-believers, and (2) how much Paul emphasizes the significance of baptism. First, the prepositional phrase in 10:2—the Israelites were baptized "into Moses" (εἰς τὸν Μωϋσῆν)—demonstrates the underlying message of baptism, specifically what it means to be baptized into Christ. If one reads 10:2 in light of the previous passages about baptism in 1 Corinthians, the phrase εἰς τὸν Μωϋσῆν can be understood as a shortened form of εἰς τὸ ὄνομα Μωϋσέως, as in 1:13 (εἰς τὸ ὄνομα Παύλου).[79] Paul's rhetorical question in 1:13 expects a negative answer (with μή), and ironically implies this unfulfilled possibility:

> μὴ Παῦλος ἐσταυρώθη ὑπὲρ ὑμῶν, ἢ εἰς τὸ ὄνομα Παύλου ἐβαπτίσθητε;
> Paul was not crucified on behalf of you, was he? ("No, he wasn't.") Or, you were not baptized into Paul's name, were you? ("No, we weren't.")

If the Corinthians had been baptized into Paul's name (εἰς τὸ ὄνομα Παύλου), they would have become Paul's people (cf. ἐγώ εἰμι Παύλου, 1:12). But they are not Paul's people. Why? It is presumably because they were baptized in/into Christ's name (cf. 6:11). Hence, the implicit logic of the baptismal ritual is: *if X is baptized into Y (or Y's name), then X belongs to Y.* The ownership and the direction of allegiance are highlighted.[80] Since this logic is not the main focus of Paul's passage, but presupposed in it (i.e., Paul does not labor to prove this), one can infer that this structure is part of the baptism tradition shared by Paul and his fellow Christ-believers. In 1 Cor 10, Paul states that the fathers were "baptized into Moses" (or Moses's name). The unfulfilled ritual pattern implied in 1:13 (if X is baptized into Y, then X belongs to Y) is applied to the relationship between Israelites and Moses. By being baptized into Moses, they became Moses's people, and this is what the formula "to be baptized εἰς τὸν Μωϋσῆν" indicates. Similarly, the Corinthians who were baptized into Christ are Christ's people.[81]

Second, this passage reveals how seriously Paul takes the power and implications of baptism. It is not that the Corinthians put too much emphasis on the "sac-

---

79 Schrage, *Der erste Brief an die Korinther (1Kor 6,12–11,16)*, 390.
80 Schrage, *Der erste Brief an die Korinther (1Kor 6,12–11,16)*, 391. The close relationship between baptism and Christ's name is intriguing and deserves further investigation, especially in connection with initiation rituals (e.g., Isis was often described as "many-named" [πολυώνυμος]).
81 Moses and Christ appear to have a typological relationship; Christ is seen as a "new Moses," *pace* Hays, *Echoes of Scripture*, 101.

raments." Paul made the interpretative connection between the exodus and baptism in 1 Cor 10 because of issues in the Corinthian *ekklesia*. Yet, in spite of what many interpreters claim, Paul does not try to refute the Corinthians' "magical" view that baptism automatically brings them salvation.[82] For example, Schnackenburg notes:

> The Apostle does not see in this "means of deliverance" a magical happening with infallible effects. His chief thesis in I Cor. x. 1 ff is that the recipients can go astray despite their deliverance. He obviously contends *against* a false sacramental concept current among the Corinthians, according to which such miracles and signs guarantee eternal salvation. If this danger has always been present in the popular view, it was particularly great at that time through the Mystery religions. Similar sacramental views, divorced from ethics, are characteristic of Gnosticism right up to Manichaeism. For Paul the gift of God must not be separated from the moral responsibility of man.[83]

In a similar vein, Witherington comments:

> Possibly the Corinthians had a magical view of the Christian sacraments and thought that since they had partaken of the Christian initiation rite (baptism) and the Christian communion rite (the Lord's Supper) they were immune to spiritual danger at pagan feasts ... Paul is trying to dissuade them from this false sense of security.[84]

Even, Schrage considers this passage a warning against the sense of security held by the "pneumatics, who think themselves safe from all danger through sacraments":

> In 10,1–13 führt Paulus den Korinthern midraschartig das warnende Beispiel der Wüstengeneration vor Augen, um die Perfektionisten und Sakramentalisten Korinths zur Ordnung und die exklusive Bindung an den Kyrios in Erinnerung zu rufen. Auch dieser Abschnitt ist mit seiner Warnung vor der *securitas* von Pneumatikern, die sich durch die Sakramente vor aller Gefährdung gefeit wähnen, als exemplum mit paränetischer Funktion zu charakterisieren, soll also nicht über "Sakramente", Schriftverständnis u. ä. belehren.[85]

---

82 Several scholars still hold such a view (see my block quotations). But, not all scholars claim this line of interpretation. Michael Wolter gives a more balanced view: "In 10:1–11, it is self-evident that Paul does not intend to claim that baptism alone is insufficient and that still other actions must be added so that it can be effective. Rather, the claim applies precisely the other way around: baptism is completely sufficient for the assured participation in God's salvation—if certain ethical boundaries are not transgressed." Wolter, *Paul*, 136.
83 Italics in original. Schnackenburg, *Baptism*, 94.
84 Witherington, *Conflict and Community*, 220.
85 Schrage, *Der erste Brief an die Korinther (1Kor 6,12–11,16)*, 381.

At first, this view seems quite reasonable. There is a noticeable contrast between the long description about "all of them" (see the repeated πάντες) participating in various blessed experiences and privileges in 10:1–4 and the tragic conclusion that happened to "most of them" (ἐν τοῖς πλείοσιν αὐτῶν) in v. 5.[86] In the wilderness, the Israelites were in danger of falling back into idolatry despite their having escaped from Egypt. Sometimes such danger had tragic consequences. The lesson Paul draws from this typology (vv. 6, 11) is that, although all of them were "baptized into Moses" and received "spiritual nourishment," these experiences did not save them from the consequences of their idolatry. Neither does the Corinthians' baptism automatically guarantee their salvation. According to this reading, the Corinthians overestimate the efficacy of baptism at the expense of their moral behavior.

But this line of interpretation is unconvincing, although the importance of moral behavior in Paul's discourse is clear. It is not that the Corinthians overestimate the efficacy of baptism; rather, they *underestimate* it (see the discussion of 1 Cor 1:10–17). This is closely connected to the different *theology* (or theological ontology) between Paul and the Corinthians. There is no textual evidence to support the assumption that the issue concerning the food offered to idols (1 Cor 8–10) arose from (or was partly related to) some Corinthians' "sacramentalism" about baptism's "magical" power and its full effectiveness. For Paul, the problem was not false "sacramentalism," but knowledge (γνῶσις)—some Corinthians know that "no idol in the world really exists" (8:4; in principle, Paul agrees with it ["we know that"]). Their "free" attitude toward τὰ εἰδωλόθυτα (arising from their conviction about the nonexistence of idols) caused the weak to stumble (8:9–13). Baptism, knowledge of the one true God, and purity are intertwined (see the discussion on 1 Thess 4:1–8 [pp. 169–71]). The declaration of one God and the relativization of idols (8:4–6) resonates with the Jewish confession, the Shema. In the wider Mediterranean context, however, the belief in one God is neither monolithic nor unique to Jews; it can be found in a broad spectrum of pagan mono/henotheism.[87] Then, the

---

86 In addition, τινες αὐτῶν in the following verses are also aligned with "most of them," contrasting with πάντες. Hays, *First Corinthians*, 163.
87 On pagan monotheism, see Polymnia Athanassiadi and Michael Frede, eds., *Pagan Monotheism in Late Antiquity* (Oxford: Clarendon Press, 1999); Stephen Mitchell, ed., *One God: Pagan Monotheism in the Roman Empire* (Cambridge: Cambridge University Press, 2010). The wider definition and use of the term monotheism has also been frequently criticized by several camps. In classics and ancient history, scholars, such as Jens-André P. Herbener, argue for the expanded use of other terms that have been traditionally distinguished from monotheism, such as henotheism ("the temporary elevation of one deity as the only god [or at least superior] within a polytheistic religion") or monolatry ("characterized by the permanent worship of only one god, but without denying the existence of other gods"). They suggest that the term monotheism should be used in a restricted way.

real point of difference between Paul and the (ex-pagan) Corinthians is not Paul's ethically grounded baptismal understanding versus their magical sacramentalism. Rather, the Corinthians and Paul differ in what knowledge about this one God and other suprahuman powers is communicated and negotiated by baptism, and equally, by other ritual activities outside the community.

Paul buys into the power of ritual (not only Christ-rituals, but also rituals engaging other deities) more than some Corinthians are willing to do, while he is firmly rooted in Jewish monotheistic tradition.[88] This seems somehow inconsistent. In some sense, the Corinthians Paul criticizes show more consistency in their thought. Paul and some Corinthians agree on two points (see οἴδαμεν ὅτι ...): 1) that there is only one God, and 2) that an idol is nothing/there is no idol in the world (1 Cor 8:4). Many people in the ancient Mediterranean world (not only Jews and Christ-believers) could have agreed on the second statement (οὐδὲν εἴδωλον ἐν κόσμῳ), despite all the polemics against pagans in Jewish and Christian literature.[89] Ancient pagans were not ignorant of the distinction between

---

Jens-André P. Herbener, "On the Term 'Monotheism,'" *Numen* 60 (2013): 616–48; especially 620. For henotheism, see Versnel, *Ter Unus*, especially 35–38). On the other hand, theologians such as Mark Edwards criticize the extended application of the term monotheism to religions other than Christianity and Judaism in antiquity (he sarcastically asks, "Is there an air of triumph among the classicists?"). Mark J. Edwards, "Review of Pagan Monotheism in Late Antiquity Edited by Polymnia Athanassiadi and Michael Frede," *JTS* 51 (2000): 339–42. It is better to envision a spectrum of belief rather than separate, sharply distinguished categories. It is also possible that the same principle within the same tradition could have been understood and interpreted differently by individuals and groups. Even though 1 Cor 8:4–6 contains common tradition upon which Paul and the Corinthians agree, it is entirely possible that they understood it in different ways.

88 It can also be noted that even in the history of ancient Israel and in the Hebrew Bible, "monotheism" was not always strong and dominant. See, for example, Juha Pakkala's proposal that the well-known monotheistic views are only found in a "thin and late layer" of the Hebrew Bible. For him, Israelites held an "intolerant monolatry" (i.e., the presence of other deities is not denied, but worship of them is prohibited) over a long time before the "nomist editors" appeared later in the sixth century BCE. Juha Pakkala, *Intolerant Monolatry in the Deuteronomistic History* (Helsinki, Göttingen: Vandenhoeck & Ruprecht, 1999); idem. "The Monotheism of the Deuteronomistic History," *SJOT* 21 (2007): 159–78.

89 Christoph Auffarth, "The Materiality of God's Image: The Olympian Zeus and Ancient Christology," in *The Gods of Ancient Greece: Identities and Transformations*, ed. Jan N. Bremmer and Andrew Erskine (Edinburgh: Edinburgh University Press, 2010), 465: "In the ancient world people imagined a god or a goddess by referring to a double 'image' of the divine being: one is the invisible and immaterial god in opposition to the visible and material world of humankind; the other represents it as a material image, in shape and size almost that of a human being ... most people were aware of the difference between these two images. Christians, however, accused their pagan adversaries of confusing the two – by taking the material representation as the invisible living god, they worshipped a dead stone, a tree or a beast. Yet the Christians themselves blurred the border be-

actual deities and their earthly representations made of stone, bronze, or ivory (τεχνιτῶν … ἀγαθῶν δημιουργήμασιν λίθου καὶ χαλκοῦ ἢ ἐλέφαντος πεποιημένοις), as one passage from Lucian reveals (*Essays in Portraiture Defended* 23). Paul differs from the Corinthians in that he believes in the performative, illocutionary force of ritual (this is a Rappaportian view; of course, Paul did not use these modern terms). Paul differentiates an *idol* that is only a visual representation from *demons* (δαιμόνια) who have ontological status by virtue of ritual activity and are actually interacting with those who sacrifice (10:19–22). Paul agrees that an idol (εἴδωλον) is only wood or metal; yet he holds that when people participate in pagan sacrifice, this ritual act creates a particular reality. They sacrifice to demons (δαιμόνια), not to God (cf. Deut 32:17), and these people become the κοινωνοί of demons (1 Cor 10:20). Similarly, baptism matters not because of the medium, but because of its power—it is not only a purificatory rite (see 1 Cor 6) or a personal avenue to group formation (see 1 Cor 1), but it also creates a relationship between the baptized and Christ/God. This creates and actualizes a particular canonical order that the baptized people must accept. In Paul's understanding, the obligation to exclusive cultic life is demanded by baptism. Considering the cultic situations in antiquity, including the mysteries, an individual's participation in a particular initiation does not necessarily hinder that person's participation in the cultic activities of other deities. Presumably some early Christ-believers understood baptism in a similar way—i.e., participating in baptism does not prohibit one from participating in other cultic activities. Yet, Paul insists that *this* ritual is different—this ritual activates a different, incompatible canonical order, and this ritual requires exclusive devotion to the Christ cult. The Israelites in the wilderness underestimated the significance of their archetypal baptism and did not fully understand the power and demand of the ritual; the same problem, Paul insists, is found among the Corinthians.[90]

Communal implications of baptism found in 1 Cor 10:1–5 can be further expounded, and this exploration is possible when one reads 1 Cor 10:1–5 in light

---

tween the divine and humankind, since they identified the invisible god with the material and visible man Jesus."

[90] Interestingly, Num 25:3 LXX expresses Israel's idolatry by using mystery language (καὶ ἐτελέσθη Ισραηλ τῷ Βεελφεγωρ· καὶ ὠργίσθη θυμῷ κύριος τῷ Ισραηλ), suggesting that the LXX translators may have understood this story in the Hebrew Bible in light of cults and rituals found in their contemporary world. Would Paul also understand the Numbers story (it echoes 1 Cor 10) the same way? This would make Paul's discourse more interesting. The problem in 1 Cor 10 would be confusion about initiation: even though the Israelites were "initiated" through Moses-baptism, they went on to be "initiated" into Baal of Peor. I thank my colleague Steve Marquardt for drawing my attention to Num 25:3 LXX.

of 1 Cor 12:12–13. But there is one issue that needs to be addressed first: some have found allusions to the Lord's Supper (not baptism) in both passages by reading 1 Cor 12:12–13 in light of 10:1–5, which is the opposite of what I suggest here. Above all, what does Paul mean by spiritual food and drink in 1 Cor 10? In 1 Cor 10:3–4, the food and drink consumed by the Israelites are modified by the adjective πνευματικός. All of them ate "the same pneumatic food" and all of them drank "the same pneumatic drink" (vv. 3–4). Several commentators see an analogy to (and a prefiguration of) the Eucharist. According to Fitzmyer, the food and drink are "spiritual" because they are God-given (manna as "the bread of angels" [Ps 78:24–25] and "God's gift of his good spirit" [Neh 9:20]), and it is possible that "Paul sees it prefiguring the eucharistic bread."[91] Conzelmann also speaks of "the presentation of the second sacrament" in terms of "a prefiguration."[92]

Now that 1 Cor 10 can be interpreted in terms of the Lord's Supper, some regard even 12:13 as a reference to it (rather than to baptism), and this was already a theory by the time of Augustine.[93] Turley notes that the eucharistic understanding of 12:13 is due to the parallel between 10:2–4 and 12:12–13.[94] His reasoning is that since 10:2–4 includes the allusion to the Eucharist (i.e., eating and drinking), ἐποτίσθημεν in 12:13 should also be understood as referring to the Eucharist. If so, the temporal order of this newly interpreted, Israel's story in 1 Cor 10 would fit that of the Corinthians' ritual experiences. The Corinthians first join the Christ cult by receiving Christ-baptism and then they participate in communal meals (including the Lord's Supper, cf. 1 Cor 11), as their Israelite ancestors also received Moses-baptism first and then they participated in some type of spiritual meal. In 1 Cor 10:4, Paul adds ἡ πέτρα δὲ ἦν ὁ Χριστός: Christ existed at the foundation of Israel's archetypal Eucharist.

Yet, eating and drinking spiritual nourishment in 1 Cor 10 can be linked not only to the Lord's Supper but also to baptism itself. In 12:12–13, Paul may have understood baptism (not only the Eucharist) as the experience of Spirit-drinking. As Fitzmyer notes, the last part of 12:13 (including ἐποτίσθημεν) is "a literary parallel

---

91 Fitzmyer, *First Corinthians*, 382.
92 Hans Conzelmann, *1 Corinthians: A Commentary on the First Epistle to the Corinthians*, trans. James W. Leitch, Hermeneia (Philadelphia: Fortress, 1975), 166. See also, Schnackenburg, *Baptism*, 91.
93 Fitzmyer, *First Corinthians*, 479. For the interpretation of the verb ἐποτίσθημεν as reference to the Lord's Supper, see further Raymond F. Collins, *First Corinthians*, SP (Collegeville: Liturgical Press, 1999), 463; Käsemann, *Leib und Leib Christi*, 176. Conzelmann suggests the reference to the Lord's Supper as a possibility. Conzelmann, *1 Corinthians*, 212, n. 17.
94 Turley, *Ritualized Revelation*, 83–84.

to the first [ἐβαπτίσθημεν], that affirms the same thing about water baptism."⁹⁵ Then, my suggestion is the reverse of Turley's—one can move from ch. 12 to ch. 10 (reading 10:2–4 in light of 12:12–13). Since Paul uses the language of drinking/giving water in 12:13 to allude to baptism, it is possible that the drinking activity in 10:4 is also an extension of the baptismal framework, not only the prefiguration of the Lord's Supper.⁹⁶ Since 1 Cor 12:12–13 is embedded in Paul's broad discourse, one might argue that it does not directly reflect the Corinthians' ritual practice. Yet, because 1 Cor 12:12–13 talks about baptism among the present community (not the typological baptism in the wilderness as in 10:1–5), it clearly reveals how Paul understands baptism as an actual ritual. The benefit of comparing the two passages (10:1–5 and 12:12–13) is that the latter can illuminate the meaning of the unclear prepositions (ἐν and εἰς) in 10:1–5.

One must look at the remarkable verbal overlap between 10:1–5 (esp. 2–4) and 12:12–13. First Corinthians 12:12–13 states:

> 12 For just as the body is one and it has many members and all the members of the body, though being many, are one body, so also Christ. 13 For even in one spirit we were all baptized into one body, whether Jews or Greeks, whether slaves or free, and we were all made to drink one Spirit.

These verses are located in Paul's call for unity and harmony in the community in which he appeals to the metaphor of body in a way similar to what appears in *homonoia* speeches in the Greek and Roman world.⁹⁷ While their contexts are different, 1 Cor 10:1–5 (esp. vv. 2, 4) and 12:12–13 have the following verbal overlaps.

Table 1. 1 Corinthians 10:2, 4 and 12:12–13

10:2, 4	12:12–13
καὶ **πάντες εἰς** τὸν Μωϋσῆν **ἐβαπτίσθησαν ἐν** τῇ νεφέλῃ καὶ **ἐν** τῇ θαλάσσῃ	καὶ γὰρ **ἐν** ἑνὶ πνεύματι ἡμεῖς **πάντες εἰς** ἓν σῶμα **ἐβαπτίσθημεν**
καὶ **πάντες** τὸ αὐτὸ πνευματικὸν ἔπιον πόμα	καὶ **πάντες ἓν πνεῦμα**⁹⁸ ἐποτίσθημεν.

---

95 Fitzmyer, *First Corinthians*, 479. Richard Hays also holds this view. Hays, *First Corinthians*, 214.
96 One interpretation of 10:4 (drinking the spiritual nourishment as a prefiguration of the Eucharist) should not be totally excluded in favor of another (drinking the spiritual nourishment as a prefiguration of baptism); both are possible. The point is that the reference to baptism is not restricted to 10:2, but can also be extended to 10:4.
97 Michelle V. Lee, *Paul, the Stoics, and the Body of Christ* (Cambridge: Cambridge University Press, 2006).
98 Some witnesses (630. 1505. 1881 sy^h; Cl) read πόμα instead of πνεῦμα, thereby making 12:13 closer to 10:4. Considering the weight of external evidence, this variant reading is weak.

Both passages use the passive voice of βαπτίζω (the third person plural in 10:2 and the first person plural in 12:12). Regarding prepositions, both passages employ both εἰς and ἐν with regard to baptism. The two passages use slightly different verbs to refer to drinking (and accordingly, different voice), but there is little difference in meaning. The reference to the Spirit is also similar, although not exactly the same. In 10:4, what the Israelite ancestors drank is "the same spiritual drink" (τὸ αὐτὸ πνευματικὸν ... πόμα), while in 12:13, the Corinthians were made to drink "one Spirit" (ἓν πνεῦμα). Functionally, ἕν is almost the same as the use of αὐτό as an identical adjective. Also, in both passages, the repeated πάντες language accentuates that these (the Israelite ancestors' exodus and the present-day Corinthians' ritual) are communal experiences shared equally by all the members. What is distinctive in 12:13 is that the middle part of the verse (not appearing in the table above) further spells out a social implication of baptism within the community: εἰς ἓν σῶμα ἐβαπτίσθημεν ... εἴτε Ἰουδαῖοι εἴτε Ἕλληνες εἴτε δοῦλοι εἴτε ἐλεύθεροι. This issue is taken up again in Gal 3:28, which will be discussed later.

This comparison helps explore the function of prepositions in the statements about baptism and identify additional layers of meaning. First, the preposition εἰς needs to be examined. As already noted, the construction of "to be baptized εἰς Moses" in 1 Cor 10:2 could be shorthand for "into/in the name" as in 1 Cor 1:13: hence, "to be baptized into the name of Moses." Yet, the comparison of 1 Cor 10:2–4 with 12:12–13 provides another possible layer of meaning. The phrase ἡμεῖς πάντες εἰς ἓν σῶμα ἐβαπτίσθημεν in 12:12 can hardly be rendered as "we were all baptized into the *name* of one body"—it is just "into one body." Then, is it possible that Moses (10:2), a human figure, is also considered a kind of communal body as in the case of ἓν σῶμα in 12:12? This is not impossible, considering Paul's use of baptismal language with respect to another figure, Christ (cf. εἰς Χριστόν in Gal 3:27, which will be discussed later).[99] Reading the baptismal experiences of his contemporary community into the story of the Israelites in the wilderness, Paul could have envisioned Moses as a figure that played a somewhat comparable role to Christ.[100] If baptism εἰς Χριστόν means forming one communal body, baptism εἰς τὸν Μωϋσῆν could be understood as expressing a similar notion.

---

[99] Yet, the expression (εἰς τὸν Μωϋσῆν ἐβαπτίσθησαν) is peculiar, because a precise antecedent to this notion of baptism ("into [εἰς] a person") is rare (Rom 6, which is often adduced by Fitzmyer or others, is later than 1 Corinthians, which leaves only Gal 3:27).

[100] Fitzmyer, *First Corinthians*, 382. Fitzmyer notes, "It is Paul who formulates the baptism 'into Moses,' in imitation of the expression he will use about Christian baptism in Rom 6:3. He means only that the Israelites had in Moses someone analogous to Christ, into whom Christians are baptized."

Second, the co-appearance of two different prepositions, ἐν and εἰς, in both passages (1 Cor 10 and 12) deserves further discussion. Below is a brief comparison of the two passages, focusing on the prepositions.

Baptism of all the exodus ancestors (10:1–5): ἐν τῇ νεφέλῃ καὶ ἐν τῇ θαλάσσῃ / εἰς τὸν Μωϋσῆν
Baptism of all the Corinthians (12:12–13): ἐν ἑνὶ πνεύματι / εἰς ἓν σῶμα

One should read ἐν in the local sense (rather than instrumental) and εἰς as resulting a condition (rather than indicating physical movement, like the image of going into water). In both verses, the ἐν construction could have either the instrumental sense (i.e., "by"), or the local/spatial sense (i.e., "in"). At first glance, ἐν τῇ νεφέλῃ καὶ ἐν τῇ θαλάσσῃ in 10:2 may fit well with the local sense (they were baptized into Moses *in* the cloud and *in* the sea), while ἐν ἑνὶ πνεύματι in 12:13 with the instrumental sense (=they were baptized into one body *by* one Spirit). Paul could have used the same grammatical structure with these different senses, and pure grammar cannot resolve this issue.[101] My suggestion is that ἐν in 12:13 likely has the local sense (though metaphorical[102]). Hays notes, "The Spirit is not the agent who does

---

[101] Whether ἐν in 12:12 is local or instrumental is not entirely clear at a grammatical level (cf. BDF §195). One might take ἐν (12:12) as instrumental, especially in light of ἐν τῷ αὐτῷ/ἑνὶ πνεύματι (12:9).

[102] Turley is right when he criticizes previous scholars' dichotomy of interpretation (Dunn, Fee, etc.) for 1 Cor 12:13, "baptism as a metaphor versus a rite." Turley, *Ritualized Revelation*, 79. The way that Turley distinguishes his solution (as a metonymic transition and as a metaphoric predication) does not necessarily invalidate the metaphorical nature of Paul's use of the phrase "baptism in the Spirit." Yet, there is one possible exception: if one follows more "realistic" and materialistic understanding of the pneuma, baptism ἐν ἑνὶ πνεύματι could be understood as entirely literal. This materialistic understanding of the pneuma is proposed by a number of recent scholars such as Troels Engberg-Pedersen (*Cosmology and Self in the Apostle Paul* [Oxford: Oxford University Press, 2010], 69), G. Strecker (*Theology of the New Testament* [Berlin: Walter de Gruyter, 2000], 162), T. Martin ("Paul's Pneumatological Statements and Ancient Medical Texts," in *The New Testament and Early Christian Literature in Greco-Roman Context: Studies in Honor of David E. Aune*, ed. John Fotopoulos [Leiden: Brill, 2006], 105–26), and Stanley K. Stowers ("What is 'Pauline Participation in Christ?" in *Redefining First-Century Jewish and Christian Identities: Essays in Honor of Ed Parish Sanders*, ed. Fabian E. Udoh et al. [Notre Dame: University of Notre Dame Press], 355–56 [although he does not talk about 1 Cor 10]), to name a few. From their perspectives, baptism in the Spirit could be more literal than metaphorical, given that it envisions substantial unity. Yet, Turley rejects this understanding of the pneuma. I also find difficulty in equating Paul's understanding of pneuma and pneumatic participation with the materialistic-realistic understanding of pneuma appearing in philosophical and medical writings in antiquity. For a critique of the scholarly views that read Stoic/Stoicized philosophical views of the material pneuma into Paul's use of pneuma in particular discourses, see Volker Rabens, *Holy Spirit and Ethics in Paul: Transformation and Empow-*

the baptizing, but the figurative element into which the new converts were immersed, being plunged into a new world of Spirit-experience."[103] As for the other preposition εἰς, it indicates *the result* rather than another locality that is connected to the physical act of baptism (such as "plunging into").[104] Similarly, Schnackenburg points to the possibility of interpreting εἰς here in the "final" sense.[105] This understanding of εἰς has some significant implications for the reading of a similar expression in Rom 6. Based on this understanding of the prepositions ἐν and εἰς, the two verses, 10:2 and 12:13, can be paraphrased this way:

> 10:2 καὶ πάντες εἰς τὸν Μωϋσῆν ἐβαπτίσθησαν ἐν τῇ νεφέλῃ καὶ ἐν τῇ θαλάσσῃ.
> And they were all baptized *in* (ἐν) the cloud and in the sea, *which results in their belonging to* (εἰς) Moses (τὸν Μωϋσῆν)—[possibly forming one body?].
>
> 12:13 καὶ γὰρ ἐν ἑνὶ πνεύματι ἡμεῖς πάντες εἰς ἓν σῶμα ἐβαπτίσθημεν, εἴτε Ἰουδαῖοι εἴτε Ἕλληνες εἴτε δοῦλοι εἴτε ἐλεύθεροι, καὶ πάντες ἓν πνεῦμα ἐποτίσθημεν.
> For we were all baptized *in* (ἐν) one Spirit, *which results in our belonging to* (εἰς) one body (ἓν σῶμα)—regardless of Jews or Greeks, slaves or freepersons, and we were all made to drink one Spirit.

Taken this way, two social/communal implications of baptism come to the fore more clearly, and they constitute the self-referential messages of baptism in 1 Cor 12:12–13. First, this initiation ritual into a cultic community relativizes and reconfigures the effect of social power and status based on difference: εἴτε Ἰουδαῖοι εἴτε Ἕλληνες εἴτε δοῦλοι εἴτε ἐλεύθεροι (which is similar to Gal 3:28 to be discussed later).[106] Second, this ritual indicates the unity of community because all, regardless of their ethnic identity and status, participate in the same ritual activity, "being given to drink the same spirit." The first message (relativizing previous power relations attached to one's social, cultural, political, and ethnic identities) may not have originated with Paul. Instead, it probably reflects one benefit that early Christ-believers experienced with baptism. But in this passage, that is not

---

ering for Religious-Ethical Life (Minneapolis: Fortress, 2013). For my own critique, see Donghyun Jeong, "1 Corinthians 15:35–58: An Assessment of Stoic Interpretation." *KJCS* 109 (2018): 45–70.
103 Hays, *First Corinthians*, 214. Contrary to Hays, this metaphorical locality conveyed by the expression baptism "in the Spirit" should not be treated as a separate event from water baptism. Hays notes, "Immersion in water provides the literal reference point for Paul's metaphorical description," but he does not think that baptism in the Holy Spirit is "identified with" water baptism.
104 BDAG, s.v. "εἰς," has this meaning (4-e), but it does not list any of these passages as an example.
105 Schnackenburg, *Baptism*, 27.
106 Yet, the phrase εἴτε Ἰουδαῖοι εἴτε Ἕλληνες εἴτε δοῦλοι εἴτε ἐλεύθεροι in 12:13 differs from Gal 3:28 in that the former is stated in the form of conditions (using εἴτε), and it also lacks the remark about male and female. See Jill E. Marshall, "Uncovering Traditions in 1 Corinthians 11:2–16," *NovT* 61 (2019): 82.

what most interests Paul. Given Paul's repeated use of words such as ἓν σῶμα and the goal of the entire chapter (ch. 12), Paul's particular point of emphasis lies in baptism's indexical feature pointing to *unity* (the second message).[107] Paul's rhetorical movement in 12:12–13 is similar to that of 6:9–11. By mentioning the benefits of ritual, Paul calls for obligation fulfillment that was simultaneously created by one's participation in the ritual—in this case, the obligation to maintain and foster unity within this body. In this passage, Paul does three things: he refers to the existing ritual practice (i.e., actual ritual is used as a frame of reference); he articulates the messages of ritual, and finally, he uses them as leverage for his paraenetical discourse.[108]

5.2.4.2 The self-referential messages, the canonical messages, and things beyond baptism

The analysis of 1 Cor 10:1–5 shows that this passage contains the same self-referential message as 1 Cor 1:10–17, i.e., baptism creates a bond between Person A who is baptized and Person B (human or deity) into whose name A is baptized. Contrary to popular interpretation, it is the Corinthians who underestimated the effectiveness of that bond and it is Paul who gives it more prominence. For Paul, this bond created by the ritual is so strong and real that the baptized must be exclusively devoted to this deity alone; one's participation in the cultic practice related to other deities (even if they appear as "idols" merely made of wood and metal), including meals, would create an alternate reality and change their ontological status (i.e., idols become demons and they interact with the ritual participants). Thus, read in light of Paul's practical discourse through 1 Cor 8–10, 1 Cor 10:1–5 unexpectedly reveals an important canonical message of baptism as conceived by Paul. Ritual activities, which are not limited to Christ-rituals, create divine-human reality by virtue of their performative, illocutionary force. Paul's strong warning against idolatry in ch. 10 does not mean that he regards baptism as less

---

107 Morales, "Baptism and Union with Christ," 170.
108 If water baptism is a point of reference in his expression "baptized in one Spirit" (that is, there was baptism in water among the Corinthians, and Paul now interprets it as baptism in the Spirit), then one could even say that the next phrase, "we were all made to drink one Spirit," could have also been literal in the Corinthians community. It might have included drinking some type of wine or other liquid not only in the Eucharist but also as part of the baptismal ritual. One cannot prove it, but if at this stage there was no fixed ritual procedure for this newly found Christ cult, it is entirely possible that they brought in such elements as drinking wine or other liquid (like *kykeon*) from other initiation rituals (like the familiar mysteries) to construct their version of this ritual. Instead of repudiating the practice, Paul would have clarified the meaning—such an attitude is also found in 1 Cor 15:29.

important than the Corinthians' moral behavior. Rather, Paul's moral exhortation makes sense when baptism's power of creating reality and obligating the participant to accept it are taken seriously. Paul is warning against ritual failure because of a breach of obligations.

In addition, the comparison between 1 Cor 10:1–5 and 12:12–13 reveals another aspect of Paul's use of baptism for his exhortation, especially in the latter context. The common grammatical features between the two passages imply that baptism transforms each ritual participant into one cultic body that drinks from "the same Spirit" (remarks about the Spirit and other terms, such as "spiritual," have communal implications). The idea that initiation rituals indicate one's entry into the cult is widespread. This is one of the most noticeable self-referential messages of baptism understood by the Corinthians. Paul blends this ritual logic with political language about the body and its unity. By identifying the communal body of this Christ cult with Christ's body (or Christ as body), Paul's discourse provides a new canonical message. Members of the Christ-group can effectively constitute one real body through baptism (a self-referential message), which requires them to maintain unity within this body (an obligation) because of the symbolic identification between this communal body and Christ's body (a canonical message).

5.2.5 1 Corinthians 15:18–19

5.2.5.1 Exegetical Discussion

Although there are no Group A words, such as baptism or to baptize (yet, cf. 15:29!), in 1 Cor 15:18–19, the ἐν Χριστῷ language (Group C) could be understood as indicating the communal status of those who have joined the Christ cult through baptism (cf. the discussion of 1 Cor 1:30 in the context of 1 Cor 1). These verses suggest what benefits baptism has when it comes to the afterlife.

Verses 18–19 fall within Paul's rhetorical argument against dissenting Corinthians who allegedly claim that there is no resurrection (ἀνάστασις νεκρῶν οὐκ ἔστιν, 15:12). To do justice to Paul's discourse, the entire chapter should be discussed, but for the sake of brevity, the following structure analysis includes only vv. 12–22.

> **Paul's articulation of the problem**
> [12] If Christ is proclaimed as raised from the dead, how are some of you saying that there is no resurrection of the dead?
>
> **Paul's argument *ad absurdum*, or his hypothetical scenario**
>   **A. An immediate consequence: Christ's resurrection is impossible**
>   [13] If there is no resurrection of the dead, not even Christ has been raised.

B. Further consequences
¹⁴ And if Christ has not been raised,
Our proclamation is in vain,
And your faith is also in vain.
¹⁵ And we are also found to be false witnesses of God, because against God we bore witness that he raised Christ, whom he did not raise if indeed the dead are not raised.

A'. A restatement of A
¹⁶ For if the dead are not raised, not even Christ has been raised.

B'. A restatement of B
¹⁷ And if Christ has not been raised,
Your faith is meaningless,
And you are still living in your sins.
¹⁸ And those who have fallen asleep in Christ have also perished.
¹⁹ If we only hope in this life in Christ, we are the most miserable among all people.

Paul's counterargument
A. The reversal of the hypothetical scenario (vv. 13–19) and its consequences
²⁰ Now, however, Christ has been raised from the dead as the first fruits of those who have fallen asleep.

B. A proof based on the Adam-Christ myth
²¹ For since death came through one man, the resurrection of the dead also came through one man.[109]
²² For just as in Adam all die, so also in Christ all will be made alive.

First of all, the aim of Paul's argument is quite apparent and clear, regardless of how one understands the precise meaning and background of the claim, "there is no resurrection of the dead" (15:12). Paul is arguing that resurrection is indeed a necessary concept by demonstrating what would logically happen if one holds the view that there is no resurrection (i.e., an argument *ad absurdum*). Paul initially states that if there had been no resurrection of the dead, then Christ would not have been raised. On this premise/condition (if Christ has not been raised …), Paul shows that his (and his team's) proclamation of the gospel would lose its meaning, and the Corinthians' πίστις would also be rendered meaningless; furthermore, the problem of the Corinthians' sins would not have been fully resolved. From v. 20 onward, however, Paul reverses the hypothetical scenario. He declares that Christ has indeed been raised, and by extension, this reverses all the negative, imaginary corollaries (*ad absurdum*) listed in vv. 14–19. Finally, Paul uses an interesting mythic proof in vv. 21–22 (as in Rom 5 and in the later part of 1 Cor 15, Christ and Adam come to the fore), which is connected to v. 20 with the conjunction γάρ. It is not

---

109 Note that in the Greek text, there is no verb in 15:21. A more literal rendering is: "For since through one man, death; also through one man, the resurrection of the dead."

likely that vv. 21–22 proves the claim that Christ has been raised. This claim was already "proved" by Paul's report of many witnesses to the resurrected Christ, including Paul himself (vv. 3–8).[110] Rather the reasoning in vv. 21–22 is connected to the last part of v. 20 (i.e., Christ's resurrection as the first fruits ushered in the resurrection of those who have fallen asleep). Just as one ἄνθρωπος was able to cause the death of all people, another ἄνθρωπος's resurrection will cause all people's resurrection. How Christ's resurrection can usher in the resurrection of all who are in Christ is never explicitly explained by Paul. What is just presupposes is a metonymic logic based on close association (something like, "as is the cultic deity [Christ's resurrection—first fruits], so also are his devotees [their resurrection that will follow]"; cf. a similar, but slightly different use of the ἀπαρχή metonymy/synecdoche in Rom 11:16). The pattern of thought in 15:20–21 will appear again later in 1 Cor 15:48 (cf. 1 Cor 1:30–31).

Now, let us closely look at what would happen if there was no resurrection. Verses 13–19 are divided into two parts (vv. 13–15 and vv. 16–19): the latter is a restatement of the former. Verses 13 and 16 present an immediate consequence when the resurrection of the dead is denied. Verses 14–15 and 17–19 detail further consequences, after repeatedly stating the premise εἰ δὲ Χριστὸς οὐκ ἐγήγερται (v. 14 and v. 17). In the first half, Paul predicts that "our (Paul and his team's) proclamation" and "witness" would be rendered meaningless and even false, and "your (the Corinthians') faith would be in vain." The second half contains similar contents, yet it focuses more on what would happen to "you," the Corinthians. In addition to the result that their faith would become futile, Paul notes that the Corinthians would remain in their sins. This strongly echoes 1 Cor 1:30 and 6:11. As already discussed, Paul contrasts the Corinthians' past as pagans and their present as Christ-believers in 1 Cor 6:11 (cf. 1 Cor 12:2). Their past is characterized by the vice list in 6:9–10, but Paul declares to them directly, "However, you have been ritually washed (ἀπελούσασθε), you have been consecrated (ἡγιάσθητε), you have been made righteous (ἐδικαιώθητε) in the name of the Lord Jesus Christ and in the Spirit of our God." Also, this type of ritual purification allows the individual to enter the group consisting of ritually purified members (this is also seen in 1 Thess 4, 1 Cor 1, etc., as discussed). Although ritual purity/impurity may not always

---

110 Bultmann criticizes this point: "I can understand the text [15:3–8] only as an attempt to make the resurrection of Christ credible as an objective historical fact. And I see only that Paul is betrayed by his apologetic into contradicting himself. For what Paul says in vv. 20–22 of the death and resurrection of Christ cannot be said of an objective historical fact." Rudolf Bultmann, "Karl Barth, *The Resurrection of the Dead*," in *Faith and Understanding I*, trans. Louise P. Smith (London: SCM, 1969), 83–84. The original German work appeared in 1926.

correspond to "sins,"[111] the two realms overlap to some extent in 1 Cor 6.[112] Given this picture, Paul's *ad absurdum* argument in 1 Cor 15:17 provides another canonical message of baptism, which could have been known to his audience.[113] The efficacy of baptism's benefit of resolving sins is predicated upon the resurrection of Christ; therefore, if one denies the resurrection of the dead, baptism is not efficacious in resolving sins. Paul's thought can be reconstructed as follows:

> Corinthians, we all agree that when you were baptized, your past sins were washed and you have now transferred to a new realm, ἐν Χριστῷ (1 Cor 1:30, 6:11).
>
> Yet, if your sins are truly washed, you should also accept that there is resurrection.
>
> This is because if there is no resurrection, then Christ has not been raised, and if Christ has not been raised, then your sins are not actually washed away (15:17), despite the fact that you have been baptized—this conclusion is absurd and not what you want!

5.2.5.2 The self-referential messages, the canonical messages, and things beyond baptism

Based on the discussion above, three points can be made: 1) it is implied (probably already known by the audience) that baptized people have been washed of their sins (the self-referential message); 2) Paul's rhetorical flow in this passage highlights that baptism is linked to Christ's death and resurrection through the acceptance of Paul's proclamation about Christ's death and resurrection (this was likely part of his εὐαγγέλιον[114]), and 3) Paul communicates the canonical message that it is Christ's death and resurrection (not water as material medium that washes one's external body) that guarantees the removal of sins. Christ's death and resurrection are the canonical order that sustains the efficacy of Christ-initiation. Therefore, one's denial of resurrection amounts to ritual failure.

---

111 See Mary Douglas, *Purity and Danger: An Analysis of Concepts of Pollution and Taboo* (London: Routledge Classics, 1966). According to her, ritual purity is a way of securing the boundaries of classification and avoiding any ambiguities and anomalies.
112 Klawans, *Impurity and Sin*, 151.
113 If one remembers that 1 Cor 15:17 is within Paul's extreme rhetoric, which forces his opponent to agree, perhaps it is possible that Paul's position in 15:17 (i.e., Christ's resurrection is crucial to Christ-believers' removal of the past sins) is also part of what the Corinthians accepted when they first heard the Christ-message and decided to be baptized. In addition, if one believes Rom 4:25 (ὃς παρεδόθη διὰ τὰ παραπτώματα ἡμῶν καὶ ἠγέρθη διὰ τὴν δικαίωσιν ἡμῶν) as part of pre-Pauline tradition, then it would also strengthen the inference that Paul did not create the view reflected in 1 Cor 15:17, but rather picked up tradition known to him and his audience.
114 For full reconstruction of the shape and content of the εὐαγγέλιον τοῦ Χριστοῦ in Paul, see Schnelle, *Theology of the New Testament*, 215.

In addition, vv. 17–19 reveal that the divine-human and intra-human relationship created by baptism transcends one's life on earth (self-referential message) and Christ's resurrection guarantees that benefit (canonical message). These messages are comparable to the messages of other mysteries discussed in earlier chapters. As in 1 Thess 4, Paul in 1 Cor 15:18 presupposes that one's relationship with Christ survives one's physical death. Thus, they become οἱ κοιμηθέντες ἐν Χριστῷ. That Paul does not attempt to prove this point suggests that it was probably already known to, and accepted by, the Corinthians. From this common ground, Paul rhetorically drives his point home: if Christ has not been raised (the premise in v. 14 and v. 17), then those who are already dead but still ἐν Χριστῷ (an extension of their status of ἐν Χριστῷ while living) have also perished, i.e., the effect of ἐν Χριστῷ (the effect of baptism) is nullified—this is, for Paul, an impossible possibility. Again, it is clear that one's blessed status ἐν Χριστῷ even after death is one of the benefits baptism promises, and the underlying logic or canonical message is that it is Christ's resurrection that sustains one's remaining ἐν Χριστῷ beyond their physical death.[115]

Whether this underlying connection among all those elements—one's baptism, Christ's death, the baptized people's physical death, and their after-death status—was apparent in the baptismal practices among the Christ groups at this early stage (including Pauline communities) is by no means clear. Such a connection was probably not fully articulated and by and large remained implicit in all baptismal practices. In other words, people were performing baptism with different understandings and for different reasons, and *even Paul* did not attempt to give the Corinthians a single, authoritative set of instructions about baptism. This leads to the discussion of 1 Cor 15:29 in the following chapter.

---

115 Similarly, Moore, *The Mysteries*, 109–110.

6 "Baptism for the Dead" (1 Cor 15:29): Ritual Blending and Innovation

6.1 Introductory Remarks

The present chapter of this study is an "interlude" between the discussion of baptism in 1 Corinthians (Chapter 5) and that in Galatians/Romans (Chapter 7). While Chapters 5 and 7 maintain the same structure (exegesis of key passages, followed by synthetic discussion of ritual messages), a slightly different approach is taken in Chapter 6. Here, I consider a particular ritual practice, namely, baptism for the dead (1 Cor 15:29), by exploring the ritual context of Roman Corinth and by employing the theory of conceptual blending. The result of this investigation develops one's understanding of the Corinthians' ritual practice reflected in 1 Cor 15:29, and it also illuminates Paul's discourse on baptism in Rom 6, which will be discussed in Chapter 7.

In 1 Cor 15:29, Paul tantalizingly alludes to an actual baptismal practice among the Corinthians (this verse belongs to Group A). This verse has puzzled many interpreters in the history of interpretation.[1] Paul's words reveal that some members among the Corinthian audience were baptized for the dead. The immediate question arises: How can one be baptized on behalf of a dead person? The verse and its literal translation are as follows:

> Ἐπεὶ τί ποιήσουσιν οἱ βαπτιζόμενοι ὑπὲρ τῶν νεκρῶν; εἰ ὅλως νεκροὶ οὐκ ἐγείρονται, τί καὶ βαπτίζονται ὑπὲρ αὐτῶν;
>
> Otherwise, what will those do who are baptized for the dead? If the dead are not raised at all, why are they even baptized for them?[2]

To illuminate this verse and the ritual practice reflected there, I will first examine two possible contexts in Roman Corinth that have been occasionally suggested by scholars to explain the emergence of baptism for the dead: namely, the mysteries of Melikertes-Palaimon and funerary rituals. I will demonstrate that neither of these contexts can fully explain how this baptismal practice came into being within the Corinthian Christ-group. Second, I will suggest that the notion of conceptual

---

[1] This single verse deserves a book-length discussion. For example, Hull's monograph is solely devoted to this single verse. He surveys the history of interpretation and offers his reading in light of its historical and rhetorical context. Michael F. Hull, *Baptism on Account of the Dead (1 Cor 15:29): An Act of Faith in the Resurrection* (Atlanta: SBL, 2005).
[2] It is also possible to render τί καί as "why at all." BDF 442 (14), but I prefer "why ... even."

blending can help one make sense of how the two partially helpful contexts actually illuminate the emergence of this innovative ritual practice. Baptism for the dead in 1 Cor 15:29 is best understood as ritual innovation. This understanding is not surprising because the beginning of early Christian baptism was itself ritual innovation. Risto Uro argues that John's baptism was ritual innovation that differed from other Jewish ritual bathing by highlighting the special agent, and once again, earliest Christ-believers turned John's baptism into an initiation ritual.[3] Despite Rappaport's theory that views ritual as more stable and less changeable, ritual does change and evolve.[4] First Corinthians 15:29 is located in the dynamic ritual matrix of the mid-first century CE, where the forms and messages of water rituals within Jewish and early Christ-cult groups fluctuated and underwent changes.

Not all scholars understand the verse as referring to some type of proxy or vicarious baptism. To be sure, the majority hold that the verse evidences such a baptismal practice among the Corinthians.[5] Yet, two problems have been identified. The first is a historical issue. Previous attempts to identify an exact parallel or precedent to this vicarious baptismal practice from ancient Judaism, Greek and Roman religion, earliest Christianity, or other Pauline letters, have been largely unsatisfactory.[6] The second is a theological issue. The notion of proxy baptism created a theological conundrum for some Christians, especially among Protestants.[7] These difficulties have led NT scholars to adopt one of two options. One approach is to accept the traditional exegetical understanding of the verse (i.e., vicarious baptism), but then to criticize this Corinthian practice of vicarious baptism as anomalous, aberrant, and magical (thus, Paul's mention of it is merely *ad hoc* rather than a full endorsement). Another approach is to argue that Paul does

---

[3] Risto Uro, *Ritual and Christian Beginnings: A Socio-Cognitive Analysis* (Oxford: Oxford University Press, 2016), 71–98.
[4] Bell, *Ritual*, 210–52
[5] See the standard commentaries: Conzelmann, *1 Corinthians*, 275–77; Fitzmyer, *First Corinthians*, 580; Hays, *First Corinthians*, 266–68; Gordon D. Fee, *The First Epistle to the Corinthians*, NICNT (Grand Rapids: Eerdmans, 1987), 760–67. Joel R. White calls it the *communis opinio*. "Recent Challenges to the *communis opinio* on 1 Corinthians 15.29," *CBR* 10 (2012): 379–80.
[6] See Schnackenburg's simple rejection of such parallels in the mysteries, as claimed by Reitzenstein, Bousset, J. Weiss, Lietzmann, etc.: "These texts (e.g., Plato, Dionysiac mysteries) may well have in view a religious care for the dead, but they do not offer a convincing parallel." Schnackenburg, *Baptism*, 100–101.
[7] Yet, this baptism is not abnormal to some contemporary Christians. It is currently practiced by Mormons, or The Church of Jesus Christ of Latter-day Saints. The present study does not engage what this baptism exactly means and how it functions in this denomination, or how it operates within the overall theological/ministerial system. Cf. Daniel B. Sharp, "Vicarious Baptism for the Dead: 1 Corinthians 15:29," *SBA* 6 (2014): 36–66.

not mean vicarious baptism in this verse at all, but something else.[8] Schnackenburg's strong remark is a combination of both approaches, resonating deeply with the history of Pauline studies and that of western Christianity: "A magical custom, according to which living people get baptized for dead, would contradict not only the Apostle's opposition to a magical interpretation of the sacrament ... but also everything else that we know about baptism in the primitive Church."[9] Then he starts to search for another exegetical solution.

I want to make sure that I start from the presupposition that 1 Cor 15:29 can mean what many people see here, but do not welcome due to its enigmatic, problematic nature: namely, some Corinthians engaged in vicarious baptism for dead people. It is historically unsound to chastise the "superstitious" and "magical" Corinthians for misunderstanding a "true" Pauline teaching on baptism. Also, as previously discussed, textual evidence for the Corinthians' alleged magical view of baptism is weak. Furthermore, it is exegetically unsatisfactory to divert the meaning of the verse from the straightforward interpretation of vicarious baptism.[10]

---

8 An exhaustive survey of the reception history of 1 Cor 15:29 is not necessary for this study. As Conzelmann notes in passing, almost two hundred different interpretations have been suggested so far (Conzelmann, 1 Corinthians, 276, n. 120; he refers to K. C. Thompson's overview). Recently, Joel White offers a concise summary of various interpretative options. See White, "Recent Challenges," 380–81. Though I do not agree with White's conclusion, his summary is helpful in understanding the exegetical options for each segment of the phrase, οἱ βαπτιζόμενοι ὑπὲρ τῶν νεκρῶν (15:29a).
According to White's article, exegetical options for Corinthians 15:29 are:
1. for *hoi baptizomenoi*
   a. those who undergo literal baptism with water
   b. those who undergo baptism, metaphorically speaking (i.e. endure suffering or martyrdom)
   c. those who undergo a ritual washing
2. for *hyper* + genitive
   a. substitutionary: 'instead of'
   b. final: 'for the benefit of'
   c. causal: 'because of or 'on account of'
   d. locative: 'over' (indicating the place where an event occurs; cf. lat. super)
3. for *tōn nekrōn*
   a. dead people (the adjective *nekrōn* functions as a substantive)
   b. dead bodies (the adjective *nekrōn* assumes an implied substantive *sōmatōn* = 'bodies')
   c. people who are portrayed as being dead (metaphorical use).

9 Schnackenburg, *Baptism*, 95.

10 I mention three examples that I think are not exegetically satisfactory. The first alternative reading is to supplement "bodies" to the adjective "dead" (a combination of 1-a, 2-b, 3-b). The verse is thus thought to mean that the Christ-believers are baptized for their own dead bodies (more precisely, dying bodies). This interpretation has a long history traceable to Tertullian and Erasmus and is also supported by some modern scholars (see Garland, A. R. Krauss, R. P. Martin,

What seems more fruitful and productive is to explore the social, cultural, and religious contexts of Roman Corinth to see how this type of practice (vicarious/proxy baptism) was able to emerge and might make sense for the people living in that context. As in the earlier discussions of the mysteries, various types of materials from mythology, historical writings, philosophical treatises, archaeological finds (tombs, temples, coins, ancient art, etc.) will be explored in a synthetic way to piece together the cognitive framework of the Corinthians, as shaped by the sociocultural world of mid-first century Corinth.[11]

Two ritual contexts in Roman Corinth could have influenced the beliefs and practices of the Corinthians, as related to 1 Cor 15:29: first, mystery initiation, especially that of the mysteries of Melikertes-Palaimon, and second, funerary rituals and mythic beliefs related to them. The significance of the mysteries of Melikertes in understanding the context of Paul's Corinthians was proposed initially by Oscar Broneer and Helmut Koester. Richard DeMaris explores it particularly with regard to 1 Cor 15:29.[12] DeMaris also examines funerary rituals and proposes them as a better parallel to baptism for the dead in Corinth. More recently, Laura Nasrallah attempts to reconstruct the general ambience of Roman Corinth.[13] In this work she

---

etc. See a summary in Fitzmyer, *First Corinthians*, 579). Second, Murphy-O'Connor bases his argument on the general, non-sacramental denotation of βαπτίζειν ("to destroy," "to perish") and on the metaphorical understanding of the dead (spiritually dead) (a combination of 1-b, 2-c, 3-c). He thus regards 1 Cor 15:29 as referring to apostolic suffering and the Corinthians' ignorance of it. According to this view, the verse can be rendered: "Supposing that there is no resurrection from the dead, will they continue to work, those who are being destroyed on account of an inferior class of believers who are dead to true Wisdom?" Jerome Murphy-O'Connor, "'Baptized for the Dead' (I Cor XV, 29) A Corinthian Slogan?" *RB* 88 (1981): 542. Third, White's own view is also unsatisfactory (1-a, 2-c, 3-c). White's argument is based on the metaphorical/metonymical understanding of "the dead" as referring to Paul and other suffering apostles, and he also buttresses his case by taking into account the sociological dimension, namely, the personal affinity and factionalism in Corinth. Then the verse refers to the practice that some Corinthians are baptized because of influential apostles and their personal affinity with these apostles. Joel R. White, "'Baptized on Account of the Dead': The Meaning of 1 Corinthians 15:29 in its Context," *JBL* 116 (1997): 487–99. This does not fully account for why 1 Cor 15:29 appears in the midst of Paul's discourse that criticizes those who deny resurrection.

11 The discussion of this section is methodologically indebted to Teresa Morgan's investigation of "*l'histoire des mentalités*" on the topic of *pistis/fides*. Her book is focused on a particular concept (*pistis/fides*) in its sociocultural context, while this study is on rituals and the cognitive framework related to the rituals. Morgan, *Roman Faith and Christian Faith*.

12 DeMaris, "Corinthian Religion and Baptism," 661–82. See also his discussion in *The New Testament in Its Ritual World*.

13 Nasrallah, "Grief in Corinth," 109–39.

links baptism for the dead particularly to pervasive "griefs [sic] over dead children and memorializations of mythic grief" in Corinth.[14]

6.2 Investigation of the Context in Roman Corinth

6.2.1 Rituals for Initiation: focusing on the Mysteries of Melikertes-Palaimon

In the earlier chapters, the Dionysiac mysteries and the mysteries of Isis were extensively discussed. In this section, the scope is narrower focusing on a "minor" mystery cult that is particularly related to Roman Corinth: i.e., the mysteries of Melikertes-Palaimon. Technically speaking, it could have been discussed in the earlier chapters with the other mysteries. Yet, it was not since it is more specifically related to Corinth, and there is insufficient information to complete a full reconstruction of this cult and its rituals. Despite the paucity of sources, the mysteries of Melikertes-Palaimon offer an interesting avenue to understand baptism for the dead in Corinth for two reasons. First, the Melikertes-Palaimon cult is a mystery cult that is, by definition, characterized by initiation rituals. Second, the myth of Melikertes-Palaimon and his mother Ino-Leukothea is characterized by the tragic death of family members and yet their transformation and commemoration. Baptism for the dead can also be understood as related to one's dead family members and their transformation/commemoration, and as a baptism, it is a type of initiation ritual. One can expect that the mysteries of Melikertes-Palaimon might explain how baptism for the dead arose in the Corinthian context.

The mythical story about the infant/boy Melikertes-Palaimon and his mother Ino-Leukothea needs to be examined.[15] Ino, a daughter of Cadmus[16] and a wife of the Boeotian king Athamas,[17] either driven by her madness[18] or in order to escape her mad husband,[19] leapt into the sea with her little son Melikertes on her

---

14 Nasrallah, "Grief in Corinth," 138.
15 There are many variations. Earlier sources tend to be fragmentary; full narratives are found in later sources, such as Ovid, Apollodorus, Pausanias, etc. For a detailed and careful review of each literary source, see Corine Ondine Pache, *Baby and Child Heroes in Ancient Greece* (Urbana; Chicago: University of Illinois Press, 2004), 135–80.
16 Apollodorus, *Library* 3.4.2.
17 Apollodorus, *Library* 1.9.1.
18 Euripides, *Medea* 1282–1291; Ovid recounts that both Ino and her husband Athamas were driven mad by Juno (*Metam.* 4.416–542).
19 Apollodoros, *Library* 1.9.2.

arm.[20] Ino herself was received by the Nereids and transformed into the sea-goddess Leukothea, while the dead body of Melikertes was carried by a dolphin to the shore of Isthmia,[21] where Sisyphos[22] found Melikertes's corpse, buried it, and established a funeral game in honor of Palaimon (Melikertes's new name). This myth was well known not only in Corinth but also in various regions in the Mediterranean world from the classical era (the first record is found in Homer, *Odyssey* 5:333–335) to the Roman imperial period. Ino-Leukothea and Melikertes-Palaimon are already, to some extent, an intriguing example of mythic blending/hybridity. The features of maritime, chthonic (e.g., underground *adyton* in Palaimonion), vegetation (roasted seed in the story), and *kourotrophos* deities are contained and blended in their myth and cult.[23] Ovid portrays mother and son reaching Italy (not Isthmia) and receiving new names there; thus, Ino-Leukothea and Melikertes-Palaimon became Roman gods (Ovid, *Fasti* 6.501–502).[24] The far-reaching influence of the myth of Ino-Leukothea and Melikertes-Palaimon in Italy is well attested in iconographic tradition. For example, a stucco in the underground basilica near Porta Maggiore in Rome (ca. first century BCE) depicts this mythic leaping of Ino into the sea. Ino-Leukothea was worshipped even far north, in Samothrace, along with the Samothracian gods.[25]

One does not have to agree with the bold claim by Oscar Broneer, who led the excavation at Isthmia in the mid-twentieth century, that Paul chose Corinth as "the chief base of his missionary work in Greece" partly *because of the Isthmian games*

---

20 According to Apollodorus's *Library* 3.4.3, Melikertes was already dead when Ino leapt into the sea with him: "Ino threw Melicertes into a boiling cauldron, then carrying it with the dead child she sprang into the deep".
21 Pausanias, 1.44.8; also see schol. Pindar, *Isthmians* (Drachmann 3.194).
22 One of Pindar's fragments (*Isthmian fr.* 5, the fifth century BCE) describes Melikertes as if he was Sisyphus's own son with the ambiguous ᾧ: "They ordered Sisyphus, son of Aeolus, / to raise up a far-shining honor / for his dead son, Melicertes (ᾧ παιδὶ ... φθιμένῳ Μελικέρτᾳ)".
23 Ingrid Krauskopf, "Leukothea nach den antiken Quellen," in *Akten des Kolloquiums zum Thema die Göttin von Pyrgi: archäologische, linguistische und religionsgeschichtliche Aspekte (Tübingen, 16–17 Januar 1979)* (Florence: Olschki, 1981), 141–42. A good example of such blending is found in the imperial-era inscription in the Dionysian theater in Athens, in which Ino-Leukothea is depicted as a savior and goddess of the harbor (Krauskopf, "Leukothea," 142). Yet, Krauskopf is cautious not to link the leaping into sea to the notion of dying and rising of vegetation deities. "Ein Sprung ins Meer impliziert also nicht notwendig Sterben und Wiederauferstehen. Das Meer nimmt die Verzweifelten auf, wäscht die irdischen Verwirrungen hinweg und erfüllt sie mit neuem, ewigen Leben. Es handelt sich dabei um einen einmaligen Vorgang, nicht um das zyklische Sterben und Wiederauferstehen der Vegetationsgottheiten" ("Leukothea," 144–45).
24 Pache, *Baby and Child Heroes*, 144.
25 Sandra Blakely, "Leukothea's Sash, Lucretius' Magnets, and Samothracian Rings/Maritime Amulets" (unpublished article), 1, and 10, n. 1.

and that Paul would have watched the games and the nocturnal ritual.²⁶ Yet, it is at least plausible to assume that the ex-pagan Christ-devotees in Corinth were familiar with the Isthmian games and the myth of Melikertes, given the pervasive Melikertes tradition around Roman Corinth. The mystery cult of Melikertes-Palaimon had a particular significance in Isthmia (part of the Corinthia, the larger area surrounding Corinth), and by extension, in Corinth. The Panhellenic games, combined with the mystery cult of Melkertes-Palaimon, were celebrated in Isthmia. This increases the possibility that this cult contributed substantially to the outlook of the Corinthians with whom Paul is interacting.

Three literary witnesses are relevant to this study. First, Plutarch (late first/early second century CE) reports on the cult in *Theseus* 25:

> For the games already instituted there in honour of Melicertes were celebrated in the night, and had the form of a religious rite (τελετῆς; or, "of initiation") rather than of a spectacle and public assembly (μᾶλλον ἢ θέας καὶ πανηγυρισμοῦ τάξιν).

According to Plutarch, these nocturnal games celebrated in honor of Melikertes resemble (secret?) initiation than public events. This description of the nocturnal ritual for Melikertes may be corroborated by the discovery of several lamps near Palaimonion.²⁷ Second, Pausanias (second century CE) gives a tantalizing portrayal of the Melikertes mysteries (Pausanias 2.2.1):

> Within the enclosure is on the left a temple of Palaemon, with images in it of Poseidon, Leucothea and Palaemon himself. There is also what is called his Holy of Holies, and an underground descent to it (ἔστι δὲ καὶ ἄλλο Ἄδυτον καλούμενον, κάθοδος δὲ ἐς αὐτὸ ὑπόγεως), where they say that Palaemon is concealed (τὸν Παλαίμονα κεκρύφθαι). Whosoever, whether Corinthian or stranger, swears falsely here, can by no means escape from his oath.

---

26 Oscar Broneer, "Paul and the Pagan Cults at Isthmia," *HTR* 64 (1971): 169–70. It is worth quoting his words at length because his statement is provocative and somehow illuminating, regardless of whether one agrees or disagrees with it: "Since Paul remained in Corinth for eighteen months on his first visit, he would have been there in the spring of 51, when the games were held at Isthmia. If, as I believe, the biennial Isthmian festival played a contributing, if not decisive, role in his choice of Corinth as the chief base of his missionary work in Greece, he would have come to the Isthmus for the occasion, and this gave him the opportunity to become familiar at first hand with the pagan rites that formed an integral part of the festival. In particular he would have witnessed the nightly celebrations in the Sanctuary of Palaimon, which probably constituted the most impressive religious act in the celebration. The things he saw made a profound effect on Paul; this is evident from his letters to the Christian church at Corinth."
27 DeMaris, "Corinthian Religion and Baptism," 666.

Pausanias reports the existence of an underground shrine (Ἄδυτον which is accessed through a κάθοδος) in which "Palaemon is concealed (τὸν Παλαίμονα κεκρύφθαι)"[28] and people had to take solemn oaths. How far this description can match the archaeological sites will be discussed later. Finally, there is another literary witness to the mysteries of Melikertes from the early third century CE, Philostratus's *Heroikos* 53.4:

> That's the right attitude! Since you are willing, listen: what the Corinthians do to commemorate Melicertes (for these are the ones I meant by Sisyphus' descendants), and what they also do for the children of Medea, whom they killed to avenge Glauke, are similar to a dirge (θρήνῳ) that is mystical (τελεστικῷ)[29] and ecstatic (ἐνθέῳ): Medea's children they attempt to appease, Melicertes they praise.

Interestingly, the ritual for Melikertes and that for the children of Medea are juxtaposed here.[30] One also gets the impression that the ritual is a mixture of several elements. It looks like a funerary lament (θρήνῳ) and a mystery cult (τελεστικῷ) that is divinely inspired (ἐνθέῳ—recalling Dionysiac tradition). As Pache notes, both "consist of a blend of initiation rituals and heroic offerings."[31] Regarding the blended nature of the Melikertes/Palaimon ritual, a witness from a second-century inscription (IG IV 203) is also comparable: "The same [Iuventianus] also made ... the Palaimonion with its decorations and the place for the offerings for the dead ..." (ὁ αὐτὸς καὶ <τ>ὸ Παλαιμόνιον σὺν τοῖς προσκοσμήμασιν καὶ τὸ ἐναγιστήριον ...).[32]

If one wants to use the mysteries of Melikertes-Palaimon to illuminate baptism for the dead (1 Cor 15:29) in first-century Corinth, three issues should be carefully addressed:[33] first, the dating of this mystery cult; second, the function of ritual me-

---

28 What it means is not clear (a statue? an urn?). Given φασίν, perhaps Pausanias did not have first-hand experience of this underground *adyton*.

29 The word "mystical" may not be the best translation of τελεστικός. It is retained because this study mainly uses the LCL translation of the ancient sources.

30 See also Pache's remark: "The death of the children of Medea, whether killed by the citizens of Corinth or by their own mother, serves as an aetiological myth for a ritual that includes both mourning and initiatory rites." Pache, *Baby and Child Heroes*, 46.

31 Corinne Ondine Pache, "Singing Heroes: The Poetics of Hero Cult in the Heroikos," in *Philostratus's* Heroikos: *Religion and Cultural Identity in the Third Century C.E.*, ed. E. B. Aitken and K. B. Maclean (Atlanta: SBL, 2004), 11.

32 Translation is from Koester, "Melikertes at Isthmia," 361.

33 This is related to whether one finds more continuity between the Roman practice of the Melikertes cult and the earlier (pre-146 BCE) Greek tradition (Gebhard) or more discontinuity between them (Koester). For example, there is the third-century BCE poetry of Euphorion (frag. 84), which speaks of the Melikertes cult, but it is basically a hero cult, and there is no explicit mention of the mysteries. How much continuity can one speak of between this third-century BCE cult and the second/third-century CE cult described by Pausanias, Plutarch, and Philostratus?

dium; and third, whether any vicarious action existed in the initiation ritual of this mystery cult.

First, can the similar form of the Melikertes-Palaimon mysteries as reported by authors in the second/third century CE be applied to the mid-first-century Corinthians? This challenge might be intensified by the comparison of these literary sources (which are later than Paul) with archaeological findings. Archaeologists have found several layers of strata around the Temple of Poseidon in Isthmia and the nearby Palaimonion. At least five phases are distinguished (see Figure 12a and Figure 12b): (a) Classical/Hellenistic, pre-Roman; (b) Palaimonion I, ca. 50 CE; (c) Palaimonion II, ca. 80/90 CE; (d) Palaimonian III, ca. 130/150 CE; (e) Palaimonion V, ca. 161/169 CE.[34] Elizabeth Gebhard thinks that Pausanias describes the first temple of Melikertes (Palaimonion II: the Hadrianic period) to the east of the Temple of Poseidon (thus, the *adyton* is a separate place [ἄλλο Ἄδυτον]),[35] whereas Helmut Koester views it as the second temple of Melikertes (Palaimonion V: the Antonine period) to the south of the Poseidon temple (thus, the *adyton* included in the temple).[36] Either way, they agree that these Melikertes temples were built after Paul. In other words, when Paul arrived in the Corinthia in the mid-first century, there was probably no separate "temple" dedicated for Melikertes in Isthmia. The third-century witness of Philostratus (see above) is also connected to the last phase of Palaimonion, which may have looked very different from what Paul and his community experienced.

Yet, the chronological issue of the temple of Melikertes-Palaimon does not necessarily mean that there was no cultic activity for this deity, including the mysteries, before the establishment of the temple. There was already Pit A in the mid-first century (Palaimonian I) and some sacrificial activities were enacted around the pit during the time of Paul (charred bones, carbonized remains of wheat, phialai, cups, etc. were found).[37] (Also, one can remember that the first-century Christ cult in the diasporic environment also did not have a temple, but it does not mean that there was no ritual for Christ.)

Iconographic witnesses provide insight about the persistence of Melikertes-Palaimon tradition over a long period of time. A fair number of coins—depicting Melikertes, or Ino, or both of them—were found in the early Imperial period, and

---

34 Gebhard, "Rites for Melikertes-Palaimon," 190–91.
35 Gebhard, "Rites for Melikertes-Palaimon," 197.
36 Koester, "Melikertes at Isthmia," 360.
37 Regarding the use of pits in the pre-temple period, see Broneer, "Paul and the Pagan Cults at Isthmia," 176. Broneer emphasizes that "[t]he Palaimonion was a purely Roman creation." This is true to the extent that there is no cultic site in the pre-Roman period. Yet, not everything about the cult of Palaimon is a Roman invention.

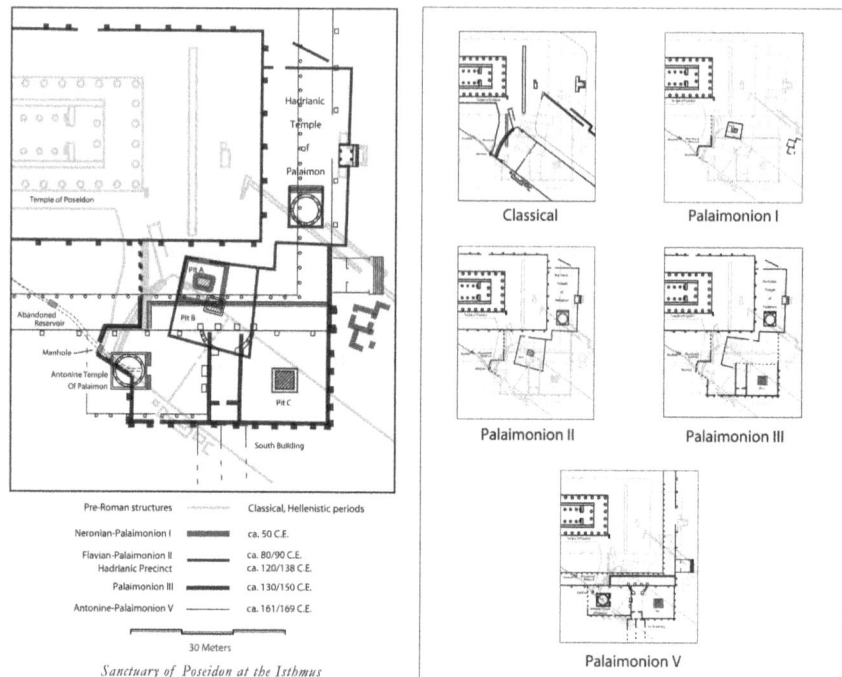

Figure 12a and Figure 12b: The two plans are reproduced by the permission of the University of Chicago "Excavations at Isthmia." Image credit: Peggy Sanders, American School of Classical Studies, University of Chicago "Isthmia Excavations."

they often include pine trees and the altar, both of which have ritual connotations.[38] Many of them are dated to the second century (thus, postdate Paul), but two things are worth mentioning. First, a certain iconographic continuity between earlier Greek tradition and Roman tradition regarding Melikertes-Palaimon (esp. Melikertes as a rider of a dolphin/sea monster[39]) can be strengthened by the existence of earlier visual representations of Melikertes, such as a fragmentary terracotta votive plaque from the late sixth century BCE (a boy riding a dolphin; Figure

---

38 Pache, *Baby and Child Heroes*, 166–67.
39 Note its resonance with Dionysiac tradition: the figure of the dolphin rider sometimes with the thyrsus in hand recalls Dionysus. Also note Philostratus's description of the Melikertes cult as ἔνθεος.

13).⁴⁰ Iconographic continuity may indicate some long-lasting continuity of the Melikertes-Palaimon tradition. This also suggests that the cultic activities that were somehow similar to what the later literary sources report could be conducted even before the construction of the temples (Palaimonion II onwards) dedicated to this particular deity, i.e., when people performed ritual activities around the pit.⁴¹

Figure 13: Pache, *Baby and Child Heroes*, 161. The line drawing is reproduced here by the permission of Corinne Pache and Zoie Lafis.

Figure 14: LA 105, 700. © Numismatik Lanz. Reproduced by the permission of Hubert Lanz.

Figure 15: LA 105, 752. © Numismatik Lanz. Reproduced by the permission of Hubert Lanz.

More importantly, iconographic witnesses often transmit the transformative characteristic of Melikertes-Palaimon more than the literary sources. In most literary sources, Melikertes appears as a baby/infant who died because of his mother's

---

40 Pache also mentions another sixth-century BCE terracotta votive plaque (a sea monster, not a dolphin, appears) found from the same region (Penteskouphia, near ancient Corinth). *Baby and Child Heroes*, 160.

41 Whether the ritual in the *adyton*, as described by Pausanias, already existed around Pit A (or in other places) in Paul's time is not entirely clear. Regarding the rite of oath, one has Aristides's report (*Isthmikos* 46.40), but it is also a second-century witness.

leaping into the sea; it is Melikertes's *corpse* that a dolphin carried to Isthmia. However, Roman bronze coins found in Corinth, depicting deified Melikertes, portray him not only lying on the dolphin's back (Figure 14; 161–180 CE), but also standing or riding the dolphin (Figure 15; 161–169 CE), as if he is not dead but *alive*. This deified Melikertes is not a baby/infant who was passively killed, but quite a big boy, who can control the dolphin by himself (see also the old terracotta votive, Figure 13).[42] The transformation of Melikertes-Palaimon through the sea water/death into an immortal being, which also involves growth and maturity (from a baby to a boy), is suggestive of characteristics of the mysteries of Melikertes-Palaimon as a rite of passage. Note that the coins with the image of Melikertes (with CLI COR, i.e., *Colonia Laus Iulia Corinthiensis*) also have the figure of the emperors on the other sides of the coins: Marcus Aurelius on the coin of Figure 14, Lucius Verus for Figure 15. The mythic story of Melikertes and his transformation through death in the sea is no parochial or peripheral concern; it was taken up and incorporated into the Roman imperial iconography and propaganda.

Although these considerations do not resolve the problem of locating the same exact picture in Paul's time, cumulative evidence enables one to see how deeply the tradition of Melikertes may have been entrenched in the mind of ordinary Corinthians. The myth of Melikertes, which includes death and revival/deification through water and the transformative aspects of this water-death, is a valuable point of comparison with baptism. The issue of dating poses little challenge when one brings the mysteries of Melikertes into the discussion of baptism for the dead reflected in 1 Cor 15:29.

The second issue relates to the ritual medium: whether, to what extent, and what kind of, water was used in the actual ritual for the mysteries of Melikertes-Palaimon. Did people leap into the sea and emulate the mythic leaping of Ino and Melikertes?[43] Or, did they perform some water ritual in recalling the trans-

---

[42] This "tendency" that "[represents] the mortal child (i.e., before death) as a baby (typically with his mother), and the hero (usually with the dolphin) as boy" corresponds well to other mythic tradition, such as that of Opheltes-Arkhemoros. Pache, *Baby and Child Heroes*, 169. Pache also sees these two stages appearing in Aristides's report of Melikertes (*Isthmikos* 46.40); she notes, "before the jump, when Melikertes is with his mother, he is consistently described as an infant; yet after the jump, when he is depicted alone, the boy is older. As he is heroized as Palaimon, his metamorphosis from baby to youth takes place, and the body brought to the Isthmus by the dolphin is that of a boy."

[43] The sea water was generally regarded as good for purification. Parker, *Miasma*, 226. This might also explain the connection between the sea and initiation rituals for other mysteries. For example, the public ceremonies of the Eleusinian mysteries included all participants' cleansing in the sea, marked by the shout ἅλαδε μύσται. Mylonas, *Eleusis and the Eleusinian Mysteries*, 249; Bowden, *Mystery Cults of the Ancient World*, 33.

formative power of water that changed Melikertes into the god Palaimon? Regarding the constituent elements of the Melikertes mysteries, the literary sources only provide brief descriptions, and there is no mention about a water ritual as a whole or part of the initiation into Melikertes. According to the Euphorion fragment (before the Roman period), lament and an athletic game were conducted in/around the cult. As discussed, the Melikertes cult in the Roman period later described by Philostratus (*Heroikos* 53.4) includes singing laments and hymns to Melikertes, which make this cult look like both τελεστικός and ἔνθεος. In addition, Statius (first century CE) leaves the tantalizing words (*Thebaid* 6.11): "After that came a black cult (*nigra superstitio*) observed at Palaemon's gloomy altars as often as brave Leucothea renews her lamentations and returns to the friendly shore at festival time." The precise picture of the Melikertes mysteries emerging from this set of literary sources remains vague. There is no explicit mention of any water ritual. This is odd because at the heart of the myth about Ino-Leukothea and Melikertes-Palaimon lies death and transformation/apotheosis through water (the sea in particular) and their saving power from the danger of the sea. In the mythic tradition of Ino and Melikertes, the sea could be seen as the "pathway to immortality," since Leukothea who was transformed through the sea also rescues Odysseus from "drowning."[44] No definitive answer can be given from the literary evidence.

Comparisons with other mysteries, as well as archaeology, could further illuminate this second issue. For example, as discussed in the earlier chapters, Apuleius (*Metam.* 11) depicts Lucius's sevenfold self-immersion into the sea near Corinth as purification (this is not part of his initiation per se), which later leads to the theophany of Isis (transformation and initiation follow, which also include water purification). The Eleusinian mysteries, famous for being the model that other mysteries emulated, included a purification in the sea before the initiation proper.[45] In addition, the fact that the underground *adyton* in Palaimon intersects with the ancient subterranean reservoir, which was uncovered in archaeological excavations, may suggest that some type of water ritual could have been performed in the *adyton*. Admittedly, it is not clear whether it is for purification, or for initiation, or the means of intensifying the solemnness of the oath taken there, or something else. Did the participants in the mysteries of Melikertes plunge into the sea water before they came to the Palaimonion? Or, did they purify themselves with the underground water found in the *adyton?* Beyond purification, did the ritual participants also dramatize the death and transformation of Melikertes-Palaimon by using

---

[44] Blakely, "Maritime Risk and Ritual Responses," 370.
[45] See the ancient sources cited in Bremmer, *Initiation*, 5, n. 27. Also, Parker, *Miasma*, 283.

water? What, if anything, did they experience with these water-rites? There are more questions than answers. Any conclusion remains suggestive and tentative.

The third issue is more critical. The investigation in this section demonstrates that the mysteries of Melikertes-Palaimon only provide a broad, circumstantial point of comparison, thus not fully explaining baptism for the dead. What is distinctive in baptism for the dead in 1 Cor 15:29 is that some Corinthians receive baptism, an initiation ritual, not for themselves but for those who have died. The mysteries of Melikertes-Palaimon have initiation rituals, and the mythic story of Melikertes and his mother Ino is characterized by their tragic death, grief, and transformation through death (thus, suggestive of a rite of passage). However, in the Melikertes-Palaimon mysteries, one cannot find evidence that devotees were initiated on behalf of their dead family members or friends. How baptism for the dead emerged and why some Corinthians performed it are not yet answered. This leads to our second contextual investigation: funerary rituals and other rituals engaging dead people.

6.2.2 Funerary Rituals and Beyond

Funerary rituals, along with other types of interactions between the living and the dead, possibly illuminate the baptismal practice in 1 Cor 15:29. Funerary rituals and other rituals engaging the dead might be promising because baptism for the dead is—however its precise details are understood—apparently a ritual for the dead performed by the living. While DeMaris also discusses the mysteries of Melikertes-Palaimon, he primarily considers baptism for the dead in 1 Cor 15:29 in light of funerary rituals in Roman Corinth. In Greco-Roman antiquity in general, the recently deceased person was regarded as lying in a liminal state. According to DeMaris, "[l]iving society must, therefore, exert itself to help the deceased pass through the transition, so that the uncertain status that dying imposes on the deceased can be resolved."[46] He also presumes that "conflicting burial practices" (he refers to the coexistence of cremation and inhumation) likely "heightened concern about the disposition of the dead" in Roman Corinth, and that the Corinthians Christians were also "preoccupied" with it.[47] Against such backgrounds, DeMaris argues, "vicarious baptism was one among several funerary rituals the Corinthian Christians used to help the deceased community member through the

---

46 DeMaris, "Corinthian Religion and Baptism," 675.
47 DeMaris, "Corinthian Religion and Baptism," 671.

difficult transition between life and death."⁴⁸ This ritual was also practical for the living: "Baptism for the dead would have alleviated any apprehension the Corinthian Christians might have had about the destiny of the newly deceased, because the ritual allowed them to enact, and thus to be assured of, the departed one's transition to the next world."⁴⁹ DeMaris also emphasizes that this reconstruction gains more plausibility, considering the Corinthian women's active role in their assembly, which Paul attempted to restrict. Baptism for the dead, DeMaris claims, was a funerary practice carried out by the Corinthian *women*.⁵⁰ In this section, DeMaris's proposal will be examined in detail to see how far the context of funerary rituals and other rituals associated with the dead can illuminate baptism for the dead in Corinth.

First, one might ask whether Roman Corinth in the first century would have been more influenced by Roman funeral customs, rather than by the customs of classical Greece where women in the family played important roles throughout the funeral from prothesis through the subsequent stages.⁵¹ Such Greek customs are reflected in iconographic tradition (Figure 16: seventh century BCE, Athens).⁵² In contrast, according to Roman customs, funerals were conducted by professional undertakers (*libitinarii, vespillones, dissignatores*, etc.).⁵³ Here is a sample of how Roman authors describe funerary customs in Rome:⁵⁴

> You show patience when I'm ill; so show patience when I fear becoming ill, when the heat that ripens the first figs brings the undertaker [*dissignator*] out with his black-dressed attendants, when fathers and fond mothers are pale with fear for their children (Horace, *Epistles* 1.7, 3–7).

> Diaulus was a doctor until recently; now he's an undertaker's assistant [*vispillo*]. What the undertaker does the doctor used to do (Martial, *Epigrams* 1.47).

---

48 DeMaris, "Corinthian Religion and Baptism," 676.
49 DeMaris, "Corinthian Religion and Baptism," 677.
50 DeMaris, "Corinthian Religion and Baptism," 680.
51 Donna C. Kurtz and John Boardman, *Greek Burial Customs* (Ithaca: Cornell University Press, 1971), 142–61.
52 As for the discussion of this cart, see John H. Oakley, "Women in Athenian Ritual and Funerary Art," in *Worshiping Women: Ritual and Reality in Classical Athens*, ed. Nikolaos Kaltsas and Alan Shapiro (New York: Alexander S. Onassis Public Benefit Foundation in collaboration with the National Archaeological Museum, Athens, 2008), 335–41.
53 J. M. C. Toynbee, *Death and Burial in the Roman World* (Ithaca: Cornell University Press, 1971), 45; also, Kathleen Warner Slane, *Corinth Vol. XXI: Tombs, Burials, and Commemoration in Corinth's Northern Cemetery* (Princeton: The American School of Classical Studies at Athens, 2017), 225.
54 The reference and translation are from Valerie M. Hope, *Death in Ancient Rome: A Sourcebook* (New York: Routledge, 2007).

212 —— 6 "Baptism for the Dead" (1 Cor 15:29): Ritual Blending and Innovation

Figure 16: National Archaeological Museum, inv. no. 26747 (photographer: Irini Miari). Reproduced by the permission of the National Archaeological Museum in Athens. © Hellenic Ministry of Culture and Sports/Hellenic Organization of Cultural Resources Development (H.O.C.RE.D).

The role of undertakers in the Roman funeral is not only recorded in the literary sources but also found in inscriptions (e.g., AE 1971, n.88. Column 2, 1–23). Hence the inference: if Roman Corinth was more Roman than Greek, their funerals and burials were likely performed according to Roman customs.[55]

This evidence cannot guarantee that all people in Roman Corinth followed Roman customs. Thus, DeMaris's reconstruction that funerary practices in Corinth, including baptism for the dead, were probably performed by ordinary women is not impossible. First of all, the literary sources and the inscriptions regarding the distinctive Roman practice of professional undertakers are focused in Italy. One cannot be sure the same custom was followed in Greece, where Roman Corinth is located. It is well known that Corinth was destroyed by Mummius in 146 BCE, and was rebuilt as a Roman colony by the order of Caesar in 44 BCE. The new colonists from Rome (freedpeople, urban plebeians, veterans, etc.) migrated to the new Roman Corinth.[56] Contrary to the view of some scholars, the city itself was not completely destroyed in 146 BCE; nor was it abandoned in the sense that no one continued to live there. As Donald Engels explains, "most [buildings] still stood during this period," and "[some] of the old Corinthians still lingered like ghosts among its ruins."[57] Engels's phrase "lingering like ghosts" may be slightly depreciatory. Nancy Bookidis more positively assesses the occupation in the interim period between 146 and 44 BCE. She notes that "the portable remains [excavated from Corinth] indicate that the reoccupation began after only forty or fifty years of abandonment following the Roman sack."[58] More significantly, important religious structures, including the Sanctuary of Demeter and Kore, were intact despite the Roman raid.[59] Undoubtedly, the Roman invasion of Corinth in 146 BCE and its

---

55 Even though the use of undertakers in the funeral cost more than family members, funerary clubs (*collegia tenuiorum, collegia funeraticia*) meant that even the poor were not entirely excluded from burials/funerals performed by people outside one's immediate family. Valerie M. Hope, *Roman Death: The Dying and the Death in Ancient Rome* (London; New York: Continuum, 2009), 68–69. For the burial clubs, see Toynbee, *Death and Burial in the Roman World*, 54–55. The existence of clubs that are solely devoted to funerals has been questioned recently. John S. Kloppenborg, "Collegia and *Thiasoi:* Issues in Function, Taxonomy and Membership," in *Voluntary Associations in the Graeco-Roman World*, ed. John S. Kloppenborg and Stephen G. Wilson (London; New York: Routledge, 1996), 20–23; also, Philip A. Harland, *Associations, Synagogues, and Congregations: Claiming a Place in Ancient Mediterranean Society* (Minneapolis: Fortress, 2003), 28–29. But as Kloppenborg notes, "Indeed, burial and funerary activities are among the most common activities of [all] associations." Kloppenborg, *Christ's Associations*, 267.
56 Donald Engels, *Roman Corinth: An Alternative Model for the Classical City* (Chicago: University of Chicago Press, 1990), 14–16
57 Engels, *Roman Corinth*, 16.
58 Nancy Bookidis, "Religion in Corinth: 146 B.C.E. to 100 C.E.," in *Urban Religion*, 149.
59 Bookidis, "Religion in Corinth," 151.

refounding in 44 BCE radically changed this Greek city into a Roman colony (Roman Corinth was considered "mini-Rome"[60]), but one cannot ignore the possibility that Greek customs were still alive even in Roman Corinth—there were some descendants of the old Corinthians, along with Greek migrants from adjacent cities in the Corinthia that were not subject to the same degree of destruction as Corinth was.[61] As Concannon demonstrates, Roman Corinth was a locus of hybridity, cultural blending, and ethnic negotiation.[62] It is entirely possible that people in some quarters of Roman Corinth continued to conduct funerals for their loved ones as old Greeks did. Perhaps DeMaris's suggestion that women in Paul's Corinthian *ekklesia* actively conducted funerary rituals is not entirely unfounded.[63]

Yet, DeMaris's claim can be questioned in two aspects. First, DeMaris's view depends on his presupposition that there was a local "preoccupation with the dead" and the underworld."[64] According to him, the coexistence of inhumation and cremation indicates conflicting practices that reveal the Corinthians' particular concern about—and preoccupation with—the problem of death. This claim is unconvincing and not strongly supported by archaeological evidence. It is true that the Corinthians in Paul's time practiced both ways of disposing of a corpse. Yet, this is not exceptional, and the implication of the concurrence should not be exaggerated. In general, the Greek world saw fluctuation between the two methods of burial without noticeable reasons underlying the change. Although in archaic Greece cremation burials were found more frequently than inhumations (both were coexistent, though),[65] both inhumation and cremation were practiced to a similar degree in classical Greece.[66] Kurtz and Boardman attribute the method choice to "a matter of personal or family preference."[67] The fluctuation/coexistence between inhumation and cremation also appears throughout Roman his-

---

[60] James Walters, "Civic Identity in Roman Corinth and its Impact on Early Christians," in *Urban Religion*, 401.

[61] The adjacent areas were not without damage; for example, the Isthmus played no role in the festival between 146 BCE and the mid-first century BCE (i.e., until the games resumed; perhaps, 43 BCE). Gebhard, "Rites for Melikertes-Palaimon in the Early Roman Corinthia," 185.

[62] Cavan W. Concannon, *When You Were Gentiles: Specters of Ethnicity in Roman Corinth and Paul's Corinthian Correspondence* (New Haven; London: Yale University Press, 2014), 23–90.

[63] This does not rule out the possibility that some Corinthians may have received help from professional undertakers and were thus familiar with that custom.

[64] DeMaris, "Corinthian Religion and Baptism," 665, 671, 672, 674. A similar tendency is also detected in Nasrallah, "Grief in Corinth."

[65] Kurtz and Boardman, *Greek Burial Customs*, 71–74.

[66] Kurtz and Boardman, *Greek Burial Customs*, 96–99. Compared to the Archaic period, cremation in the Classical period became simplified. *Greek Burial Customs*, 98.

[67] Kurtz and Boardman, *Greek Burial Customs*, 96.

tory. The Twelve Tables (fifth century BCE) show that the two methods were practiced side by side in the earlier period.[68] Although cremation became dominant from the Republic through the Imperial period, inhumation gained more popularity from the second century CE onward.[69] Scholars in the twentieth century (including A. D. Nock) have refrained from interpreting this phenomenon as the result of developing theology about the afterlife or to the influence of the mysteries or Christianity.[70]

DeMaris seems to overstate the significance of archaeological data regarding burial methods. It is true that locally focused information in Corinth (i.e., the North Cemetery [1964]; see the map in Figure 17[71]) allows one to see the ongoing influence of Greek burial custom during the time of Paul. Yet, these cemeteries do not clearly reveal any conflict relating to funerary methods. In the North Cemetery, the burial method in the pre-Classical and Classical period was predominantly one of inhumation, with "exceedingly few exceptions."[72] The same trend continued in the Roman period. Among twenty-eight graves of the Roman period, only four show evidence of cremation (see some examples in Figure 18: Grave 516 has the urn at the center, which is evidence of cremation, while Grave 512 is an inhumation burial in the Roman period).[73] Another recent publication on the Northern Cemetery (2017) also shows that cremation and inhumation appeared together in the same tomb.[74] This set of data may indicate that, contrary to the general view of Roman Corinth as a fairly "Romanized" city ("mini-Rome"), the Corinthians retained some old burial customs, perhaps while negotiating both the old and new customs. But the differences between inhumation and cremation should not be exaggerated. Actual customs vary place to place,[75] and this may account for some of the differences. There is no clear evidence of conflict, at least among the Corinthi-

---

68 Toynbee, *Death and Burial in the Roman World*, 39.
69 Toynbee, *Death and Burial in the Roman World*, 40.
70 Arthur Darby Nock, "Cremation and Burial in the Roman Empire," *HTR* 25 (1932): 321–59.
71 The North Cemetery (publication: 1964) and the Northern Cemetery (2017) are different cemeteries. The North Cemetery is located outside the classical wall, to the northwest. The Northern Cemetery refers to several groups of graves and tombs scattered near the aqueduct at the north edge of ancient Corinth.
72 Carl W. Blegen, Hazel Palmer, Rodney S. Young, *Corinth Vol. XIII: The North Cemetery* (Princeton: The American School of Classical Studies at Athens, 1964), 69.
73 Blegen et al., *Corinth Vol. XIII*, 70, note, "The cremations may represent the foreign colonists."
74 Slane, *Corinth Vol. XXI*, 6. All of the cremations in such cases are dated to the Roman period, which indicates that the Corinthians embraced the Roman practice. Even so, inhumation and cremation existed side by side.
75 Mary E. Hoskins Walbank, "Unquiet Graves: Burial Practices of the Roman Corinthians," in *Urban Religion*, 270.

an believers, over the relative merits of these two methods of burial. Nor can the archaeological finds support the claim that the Corinthians were particularly preoccupied with the realm of the dead.

A second criticism relates to whether funerary rituals constitute a precise parallel to, or antecedent of, baptism for the dead. The use of water in funerary rituals and in baptism should be compared critically before positing close parallels. Did people in Corinth (or in the Roman world) use water for funerals and burials in a manner resembling baptism? And if so, did members of Paul's Corinthian *ekklesia* incorporate baptism for the dead into their funerary practices? In the Greek context, water was important for funerals as a means of purification. Women in the family used to bathe the corpse with water as the first step in the funeral process.[76] Since contact with the dead could render one impure, the person who washes the corpse also needs to undergo a purification ritual after the funeral. This is true in both Greek and Roman customs, and the family of the dead has agency in terms of purification.[77] Yet, purification involving water is a universal practice and is not specific to funerals and burials. It is not certain whether the meaning of water rituals in funerary rites can be directly linked to baptism for the dead in Corinth.

Even so, funerary rituals might be related to the Corinthians' practice of baptism for the dead. How people in the ancient world thought about the relationship between the dead and the living can shed valuable light on the issue of baptism for the dead in 1 Cor 15. This depends on how one understands parallels—whether one can expand the conceptual scope of the investigation by including occasions in which the living and the dead encounter and interact with each other (not only funerals but also commemorations, cults of the dead, magical practices involving the dead or implying the power of the dead, *goēteia*,[78] apotropaic rites).[79]

First of all, practices performed by the living for the dead aim to benefit the dead, as was probably the case with baptism for the dead. This was widespread and not limited to Corinth. For example, in Homeric epics (e.g., *Il.*, Book 23; *Od.*,

---

76 Kurtz and Boardman, *Greek Burial Customs*, 149.
77 Kurtz and Boardman, *Greek Burial Customs*, 150; Toynbee, *Death and Burial in the Roman World*, 50. Toynbee notes, "There were ... a number of other acts to be performed by the family. On returning from the funeral the relatives had to undergo the *suffitio*, a rite of purification by fire and water. On the same day there began a period of cleansing ceremonies (*feriae denicales*) held at the deceased's house . . ."
78 A simple definition of *goēteia* is found in *Suda* (http://www.stoa.org/sol/): γοητεία δὲ ἐπὶ τῷ ἀνάγειν νεκρὸν δι' ἐπικλήσεως. Regarding the origin and roles of *goēs* in the Greek world, see Johnston, *Restless Dead*, 82–123.
79 Cf. Johnston, *Restless Dead*, x.

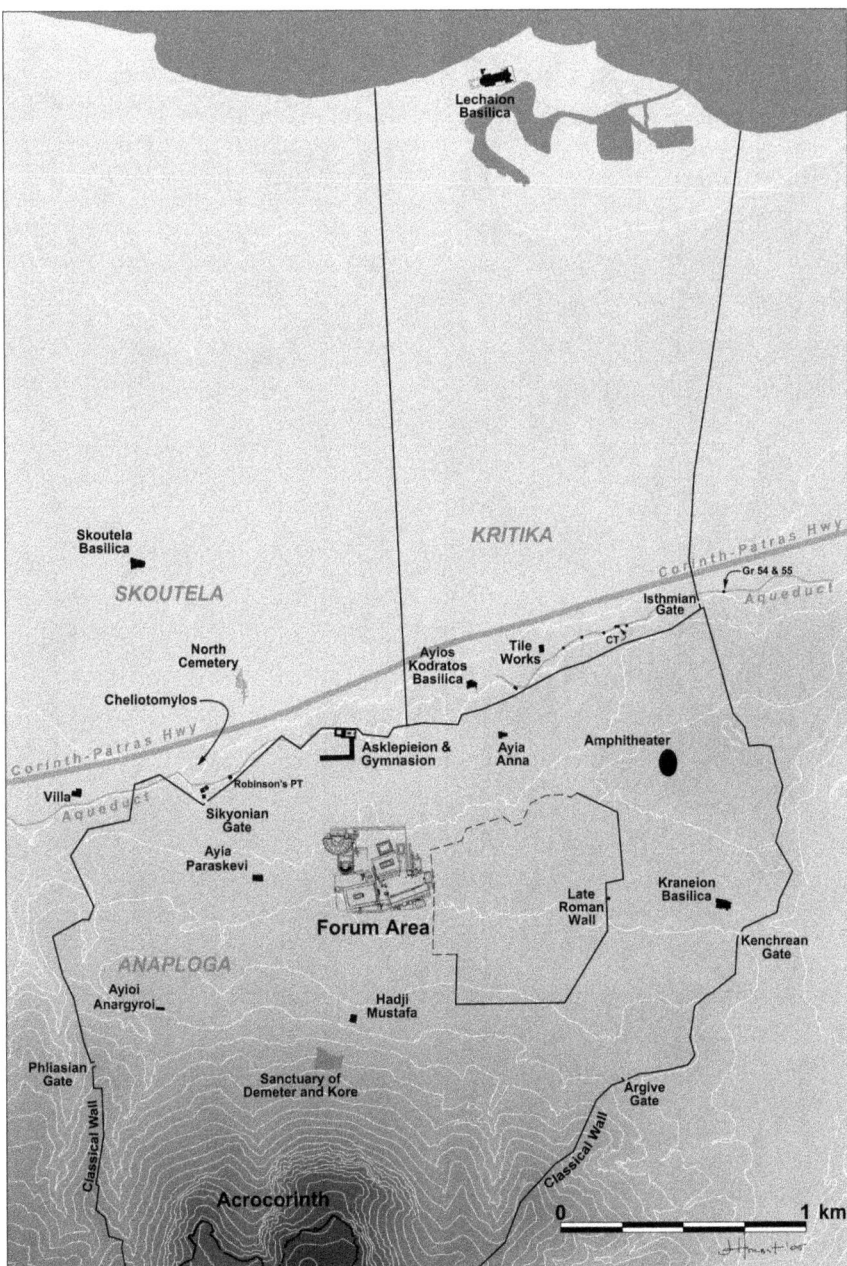

Figure 17: Slane, *Corinth Vol. XXI*, xxx. Reproduced by permission. Courtesy of American School of Classical Studies at Athens, Corinth Excavations.

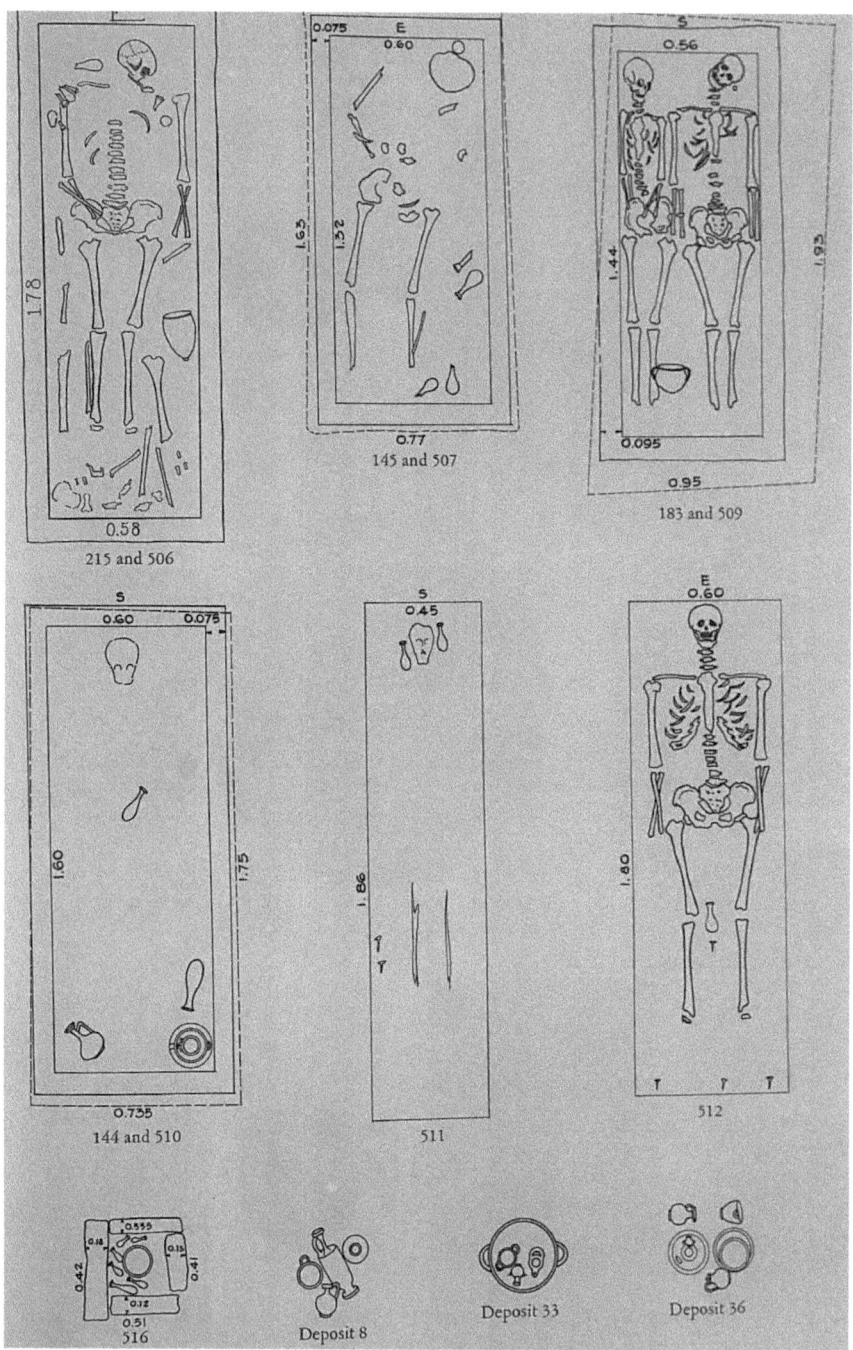

Figure 18: Blegen et al., *Corinth Vol. XIII*, Plate 123. Reproduced by permission. Courtesy of American School of Classical Studies at Athens, Corinth Excavations.

Book 11), if a corpse is not properly buried, the dead person suffers from shame and cannot successfully transition from the world of the living to the world of the dead.[80] Archaeological finds, including grave goods and holes for libation, also substantiate this ancient belief that the dead need things like the living—a belief found in numerous myths, poems, and narratives in antiquity.[81] This first point, in connection with Roman Corinth, was thoroughly investigated by DeMaris.[82] There are two other examples to consider: one is 2 Macc 12:43–45, which appears in the outer margin of 1 Cor 15:29 in NA28 (most commentaries also mention this reference):

> [Judas] also took up a collection, man by man, to the amount of two thousand drachmas of silver, and sent it to Jerusalem to provide for a sin offering. In doing this he acted very well and honorably, taking account of the resurrection. For if he were not expecting that those who had fallen would rise again, it would have been superfluous and foolish to pray for the dead. But if he was looking to the splendid reward that is laid up for those who fall asleep in godliness, it was a holy and pious thought. Therefore he made atonement for the dead, so that they might be delivered from their sin (NRSV).

Here is clear evidence showing that the living, through a ritual performance, can bring about posthumous salvation. To some extent, Paul's argument in 1 Cor 15:29 ("If the dead are not raised at all, why are they even baptized for them") is a variation of 2 Macc 12:44 ("If he were not expecting that those who had fallen would rise again, it would have been superfluous and foolish to pray for the dead"). Another example is from Plato, *Republic* 2.362E–367E (dealing with "Orphic religiosity") and its comparison with the fourth century BCE Orphic/Bacchic texts written on tablets from graves (discussed in Chapter 3). Although there is some unclarity and controversial points of interpretation, Trumbower argues that *Republic* 2.365A, 2.366A, and the Orphic tablets speak of the "posthumous succor for the dead."[83] If so, this is not just a local issue in Corinth—it relates to a widespread concern in the ancient Mediterranean world.

---

80 For a succinct summary of this aspect from Greek, Roman, and Jewish literary sources, see Jeffrey A. Trumbower, *Rescue for the Dead: The Posthumous Salvation of Non-Christians in Early Christianity* (Oxford: Oxford University Press, 2001), 19–23.
81 For example, Herodotus relates a story about the Corinthian tyrant Periander who stripped the Corinthian women and burned their clothes to appease and get information from his dead wife, Melissa, whose ghost had told him that she was cold and naked, thus needed "properly burned" clothes (Herodotus, 5.92). See Johnston, *Restless Dead*, vii.
82 DeMaris, "Corinthian Religion and Baptism," 675–76.
83 Trumbower, *Rescue for the Dead*, 23–26.

Second, there are some practices in the Greek and Roman world in which the living engage the dead, and the act is meant to benefit the living. In this case, the underlying belief is that the dead can influence the living either positively or negatively. Even worse, the dead can return to the world of the living. In this regard, properly conducted funerary rituals are not only devised *for* the dead, but also *against* the dead, that is, against the harms the dead can bring.[84] The permeability between the living and the dead, and the dead's potential (negative) influence on the living, led to two very different customs. On the one hand, there are many stories about actively conjuring up a dead person—often, the soul of the person is summoned, but the dead body itself is sometimes raised up (e.g., a story of the Thessalian Erictho reanimating a dead solider [Lucan, *Pharsalia* 6.588–830; first century CE], or the story of an old woman of Bessa in Egypt reanimating the corpse of her son [Heliodorus 6.12–5; fourth century CE]).[85] Conjuring up the dead usually occurred through divination, and the dead whose rest was broken by this *goēteia* tend to get angry (cf. 1 Sam 28:15). The use of curse tablets, though somehow different, can also be understood as efforts by the living to derive benefit from the power of the dead or chthonic gods. An example is found in the Demeter Sanctuary in Roman Corinth.[86] On the other hand, there are other practices that put the dead back in their place and attempt to prevent the dead from doing harm or even returning. A *lex sacra* on a lead tablet from Selinus is an example: on each side of the tablet are instructions for apotropaic rituals with respect to the dead ancestors. Johnston notes,

---

[84] Johnston, *Restless Dead*, 38. See also Jonathan Z. Smith's comments: "In such locative traditions, what is soteriological is for the dead to remain dead. If beings from the realm of the dead walk among the living, they are the objects of rituals of relocation, not celebration." *Drudgery Divine*, 124.

[85] Daniel Ogden, *Magic, Witchcraft, and Ghosts in the Greek and Roman Worlds* (Oxford; New York: Oxford University Press, 2002), 193–201.

[86] Bookidis and Stroud note that "a vivid link with the underworld and a reminder of the predominance of women in the life of the Sanctuary is provided by a number of lead tablets which were found rolled up and pierced by iron nails." Plate 32 from the Sanctuary of Demeter and Kore reads: "I consign and entrust Karpime Babbia, the weaver of garlands, to the Fates who exact justice so that they may expose her acts of insolence, and to Hermes of the Underworld, to Earth, to the children of Earth, so that they may overcome and completely destroy her [_ _ _] and her heart and her mind and the wits of Karpime Babbia, the weaver of garlands. I adjure and I implore you and I beg of you, Hermes of the Underworld, [to grant] heavy curses." The translation is from N. Bookidis and R. S. Stroud, *Demeter and Persephone in Ancient Corinth* (Princeton: American School of Classical Studies at Athens, 1987), 30. The tablet is also mentioned in John G. Gager, *Curse Tablets and Binding Spells from the Ancient World* (New York: Oxford University Press, 1999), 37, n. 92.

[A]lthough the evidence is too scant for us to be certain, the ritual described on Side A of our *lex sacra* from Selinus may be interpreted as a sort of "mass for the dead," in which the living endeavored to improve the postmortem lot of certain dead progenitors, not only out of sympathy but because the condition of these ancestors affected things of vital interest to the living themselves, such as fecundity.[87]

As already discussed with 2 Macc 12:43–45 and the *Republic* 2.362E–367E, the unwashed sins of the dead are thought to be atoned for by proxy (rituals performed by the living). If those literary sources are viewed alongside the Selinunitan tablet (improving the life of the living by improving the lot of the dead), it is possible that baptism for the dead also reflects such a motive. The living can purify the sins of the dead by practicing proxy baptism, in order to derive benefits for themselves, as well as for the dead.

Yet, some questions remain: Are practices associated with death, and preoccupation with the realm of death, confined to Corinth? Are they not fundamental concerns within the ancient Mediterranean world? As Zeller comments, "Es wird allerdings schwerfallen, derartige Gebräuche als spezifisch für Korinth zu erweisen."[88] Nasrallah's view faces the same problem. She highlights pervasive "grief" in Corinth and connects it with the practice of baptism for the dead. Nasrallah notes, "This context of grief likely formed the traditions that the Corinthian *ekklesia* in Christ engaged, traditions that predated Paul: baptism on behalf of the dead. This baptism emerged out of a context encysted with the griefs over dead children and memorializations of mythic grief."[89] This may be true, but one can still ask: Was the context of grief specific to Corinth, or could that be connected to any other city that experienced wars, destruction, famine, slavery, loss of family members, and some tragic, mythic stories endemic in the region?[90] If so, why is baptism for the dead found only in 1 Cor 15:29?

---

87 Johnston, *Restless Dead*, 58.
88 Dieter Zeller, "Gibt es religionsgeschichtliche Parallelen zur Taufe für die Toten (1Kor 15,29)?" *ZNW* 98 (2007): 75.
89 Nasrallah, "Grief in Corinth," 138.
90 Emphasis on the Corinthians' "preoccupation with death" or pervasive "grief" seems to go beyond what the archaeological data can reasonably allow. There might be a specter of the centuries-old Christian perspective on the pagan world—i.e., the pagans suffered from fear and anxiety about the afterlife, so they sought the mystery cults and other remedies, but they were nevertheless in need of a genuine solution (Christianity). For a recent critique of such an understanding, see Antigone Samellas, *Death in the Eastern Mediterranean (50–600 A.D.)* (Tübingen: Mohr Siebeck, 2002). On the other hand, I do not deny the existence of such fear and anxiety at all; indeed, to deny them is to make another mistake found in earlier scholarship—that is, to idealize the Greeks and the Romans as being without any "superstitious" fear or "irrational" anxiety. This is noted by

Perhaps, the question of *how* it emerged is easier to answer than the *why* question. My suggestion is that the emergence of baptism for the dead in Corinth can be better understood by considering the possibility of conceptual blending between the mystery initiation (especially, of Melikertes), funerary rituals, and Paul's message of baptism. Nasrallah's theory is already beginning to blend. When she speaks about grief over dead children and their memorialization, the tradition of Melikertes (his death, transformation, and memorialization) is presupposed in her argument. This should be more clearly articulated. Each context, i.e., initiation, funeral, and early Christ-cult baptism, does not fully explain the particular phenomenon in 1 Cor 15:29, but the convergence and blending of the three can offer an answer as to how baptism for the dead appeared in Corinth.

6.3 Ritual Blending and Innovation

As previously discussed, neither rituals for initiation (the mysteries of Melikertes) nor funerary rituals (and other rituals for/against the dead) exactly correspond to baptism for the dead in 1 Cor 15:29, but there are many possible correlations. In addition, Roman Corinth was a place where several mythic and ritual traditions existed, becoming fused and transformed. A theoretical framework is needed to coordinate different possible explanations and to account for the emergence of baptism for the dead. To be specific, insights from cognitive science—especially the notion of conceptual blending or conceptual integration advanced by Fauconnier and Turner[91]—help to understand how this new ritual (baptism for the dead) could emerge from the social, cultural, and religious contexts of first-century Roman Corinth.

Conceptual blending refers to a process of the human brain that selectively combines information from multiple domains and creates a new mental image. According to Fauconnier and Turner, conceptual blending "always involves at least four spaces: two input spaces, a generic space, and a blended space."[92] These are all "mental spaces,"[93] and the aim of the authors (Fauconnier/Turner) is to articulate what is going on in the *mind*. By drawing on the notion of conceptual

---

Johnston, *Restless Dead*, vii–xiii. My discussion complements the overall perspective and research of DeMaris and Nasrallah and hopefully produces a more nuanced understanding of the practice in Roman Corinth.

91 Gilles Fauconnier and Mark Turner, *The Way We Think: Conceptual Blending and the Mind's Hidden Complexities* (New York: Basic Books, 2002).
92 Fauconnier and Turner, *The Way We Think*, 279.
93 Fauconnier and Turner, *The Way We Think*, 47.

blending for the discussion of 1 Cor 15:29, I am applying this idea to the blended rituals that were created in the *mind* of Corinthians when they encountered and received Pauline/early Christian teaching, and when they practiced baptism in their own ritually filled social, cultural, and religious context.

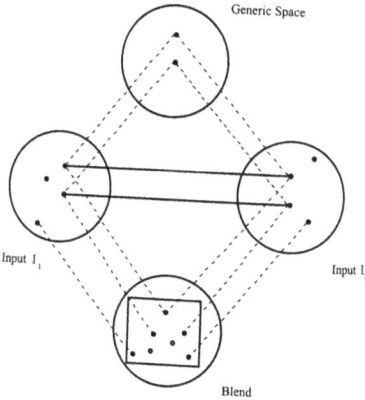

Figure 19: This diagram is from *The Way We Think: Conceptual Blending and the Mind's Hidden Complexities* by Gilles Fauconnier and Mark Turner, copyright © 2002. Reprinted by permission of Basic Books, an imprint of Hachette Book Group, Inc.

A simplistic description of the four spaces (see Figure 19) is as follows. When two different input spaces are juxtaposed and a partial cross-space mapping emerges (indicated by the dotted lines), some elements in both input spaces are abstracted and merge in the generic space. Then, a new space, a blended space emerges; as Fauconnier and Turner note, "Blends contain generic structure captured in the generic space but also contain more specific structure."[94] This new structure is related to, but not identical with either input space.[95] What is important in this blending process is selectivity: "not all elements and relations from the inputs are projected to the blend."[96] As discussed, the myth and cult of Melikertes and Ino already contain many interesting examples of blending (e.g., the features of maritime deities and those of chthonic deities are mixed; various regions in the Mediterranean world appropriated the myth and cult of Melikertes and Ino as their own, etc.). Also, funeral rituals in Roman Corinth may have hybridity, as discussed, because of social, historical, and geo-political reasons. Additionally, other rituals engaging the dead may have interacted with the funerary concepts, shaping people's mind vis-à-vis their relationship with the dead. In all these examples, selectivity occurred. This is also the case with baptism for the dead. Some elements

---

94 Fauconnier and Turner, *The Way We Think*, 47.
95 Fauconnier and Turner, *The Way We Think*, 42.
96 Fauconnier and Turner, *The Way We Think*, 47.

from each input space are abstracted and projected to the generic space, and then they morph into a new, blended space that retains a general structure of the generic space, as well as some specific details from input spaces.

Although the basic diagram (Figure 19) is helpful in understanding the notion of conceptual blending, an actual blending can take various forms.[97] For example, blending can be "single-scope networks," in which "the organizing frame of the blend is an extension of the organizing frame of one of the inputs but not the other."[98] It also can form "double-scope networks" organizing frames from each input and each partly contributes to the organizing frame of the blended space.[99] Furthermore, the basic four-space picture can be extended by adding more spaces (thus, "multiple blends," see Figure 21),[100] which is the case with bap-

---

[97] Yet, the basic diagram itself also works. For example, Paul's view of baptism in Rom 6 can be regarded as an example of conceptual blending. The basic diagram (Figure 19) is employed to produce a diagram below (Figure 20). It may be a mistake to assume that Paul taught the Corinthians the view of baptism expressed in Rom 6. The latter was possibly shaped by his earlier encounter with the Corinthians' blended ritual practice (1 Cor 15:29). The simple figure below, which I drew, is provided purely as an example of the cognitive blending process.

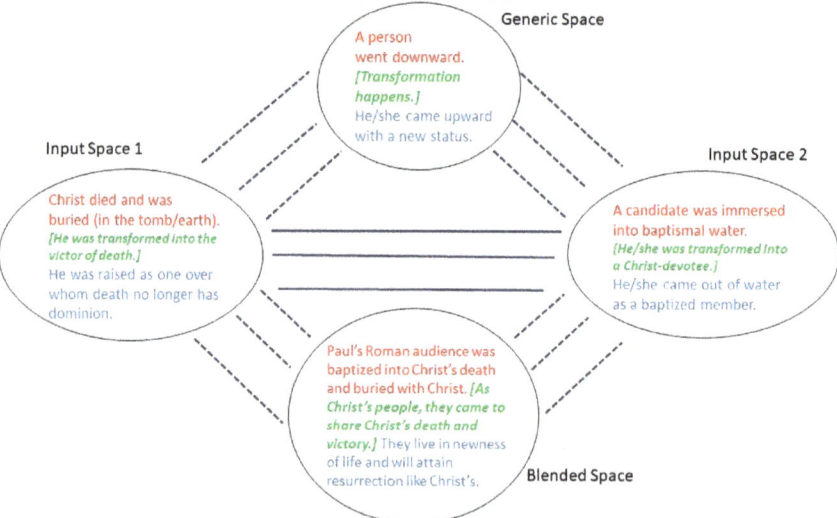

Figure 20

A more elaborate diagram that explains the process of conceptual blending in Romans 6 can be found in Frederick S. Tappenden, *Resurrection in Paul: Cognition, Metaphor, and Transformation* (Atlanta: SBL, 2016), 138. See also Kai-Hsuan Chang, *The Impact of Bodily Experience on Paul's Resurrection Theology*, LNTS 655 (London: T&T Clark, 2022), 125 (in connection with 111 and 119).
[98] Fauconnier and Turner, *The Way We Think*, 126.
[99] Fauconnier and Turner, *The Way We Think*, 131.
[100] Fauconnier and Turner, *The Way We Think*, 279–98.

tism for the dead in Roman Corinth. Then, using the concept of multiple blends, the complete map of conceptual blending is seen in Figure 22.

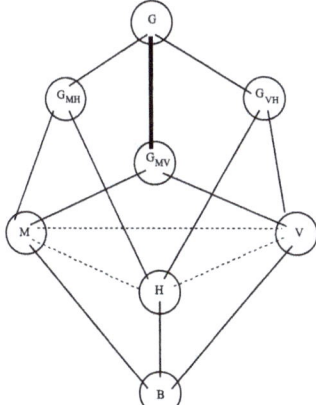

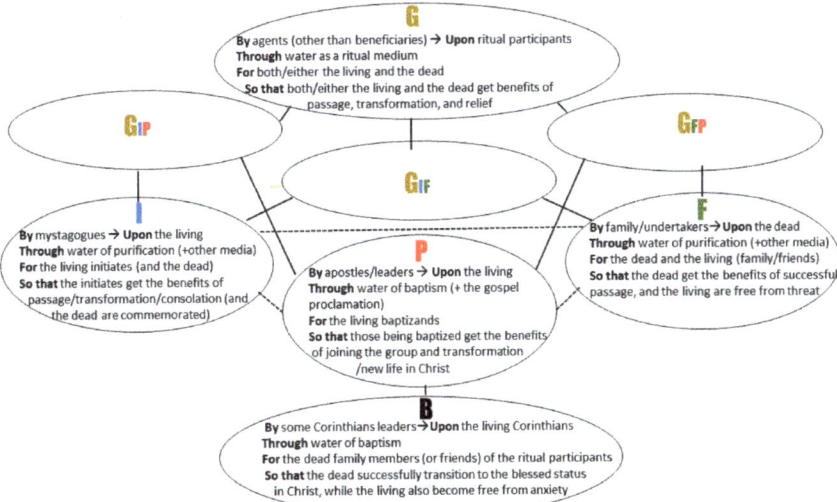

Figure 21: From *The Way We Think: Conceptual Blending and the Mind's Hidden Complexities* by Gilles Fauconnier and Mark Turner, copyright © 2002. Reprinted by permission of Basic Books, an imprint of Hachette Book Group, Inc.

Figure 22: Space descriptions:
G: Generic Space
I: Initiation into the mysteries (esp. the mysteries of Melikertes-Palaimon in Corinth) (Input Space 1)
P: Paul's initial teaching of baptism in Corinth (Input Space 2)
F: Funerary rituals, including other rituals engaging the dead (Input Space 3)
B: Blended Space: Baptism for the dead (1 Cor 15:29)
Solid lines: matching and cross-space mapping
Dotted lines: connections between inputs

Figure 22: by conceptually describing each ritual in each input space, one can obtain some common structures that can create some partial cross-space mapping (dotted lines). All input spaces (I, P, F) include elements, such as who performs the ritual, upon whom it is performed, what the medium is, who benefits from the ritual, and what the benefits are.[101] Specific contents of each input space are partly generalized and incorporated into a generic space (G), but since this is a case of multiple blends, intermediaries such as G_{IP}, G_{IP}, G_{FP} emerge first—these will not be described in detail. The generic space (G) can combine mystagogues in the mysteries of Melikertes (I), apostles/leaders in baptism (P), and family members (in the Greek context) and/or professional undertakers in funerals (especially in the Roman context), along with other agents who can engage with the dead (F), into the generic category, "agents" (other than those who benefit from the ritual). Diverse people upon whom initiation (I), baptism (P), and the funerary rituals (F) are performed can be seen as a comprehensive group of "ritual participants" (e.g., in some sense, the dead are also regarded as participating in the funerary ritual) in the generic space (G). The beneficiary of the ritual, and the specific content of the benefit can also be made generic in the same way. The generic space (G) is again projected to the blended space (B), which contains new specific content. For the final blended space, one is left with speculation because the description of 1 Cor 15:29 is brief. Since it is still called "baptism" by Paul, and Paul also mentions upon whom and for whom it is performed, some elements are relatively certain. The agents of this ritual are difficult to identify, but one can safely exclude Paul as a candidate. The most likely agents are some unnamed Corinthian leaders with authority. The benefits the dead and the living receive would be a blending of benefits that one would expect from baptism, initiation, and funerary rituals—though not all of them. Primarily, the images of passage and transformation from one state to another, as well as consolation/relief for the living, in both the mysteries of Melikertes-Palaimon and funerary rituals are combined with certain structural counterparts in baptism. These images symbolize a specific benefit from the deities—Christ and God—associated with this baptism ritual.

Even when one speaks of conceptual blending, this does not mean that the blending is created only in theory or in the abstract. Some in the Corinthian community perhaps participated in mystery initiation in the past or likely observed other people participating in initiation with visual, auditory, or other sensory stimulation. Many, or most, people in this Christ group experienced the death of their

---

[101] It should be noted that each input space is already a blended space from previous inputs spaces (all three, I, P, F, have blended properties). For example, the input space F (funerary rituals) can be a blended ritual space, where ordinary funerary practices and other types of practices that engage the dead are integrated.

close friends or family members and participated in their funerals and burials. All (or at least, most) people in the Corinthian congregation underwent baptism when they joined the Christ cult. The blending may not have been a conscious process. Individuals' embodied practices of several rituals converged in an unexpected way when they formed a new cult group and encountered a new message and ritual.

The provisional conclusion of this "interlude" chapter is that 1) when the gentiles in Corinth first encountered or learned about the baptismal practices that Paul or other early Christian missionaries brought in, they understood the ritual within their cognitive framework that included other existing rituals—especially initiation rituals and funerary rituals; 2) thus, "baptism for the dead" in 1 Cor 15:29 is a showcase in which one can see how a relatively new ritual could evolve and develop with the help of conceptual blending; 3) the meaning and significance of early Christian baptism were not officially fixed at this period, and even Paul was tolerant about their practices and how they made meaning out of these processes; 4) finally, it is possible that Paul's more explicit remarks about baptism, which appear later in Rom 6, are the result of his thought development through his interactions with the Corinthians and their practices of baptism.[102] This last point will be discussed further in the section on Rom 6. Before approaching Romans, another important passage from Galatians needs to be examined. Thus, in the following chapter, we will discuss Gal 3 and Rom 6, focusing on ritual messages in the same way that we did in previous chapters.

---

102 According to Risto Uro, ritual innovations often function as catalysts for new religious movements. Uro, *Ritual and Christian Beginnings*, 76–78. Admittedly, the innovative baptism in 1 Cor 15:29 did not lead to a new movement per se. Yet it impacted the understanding and practice of baptism in Christian history.

7 Initiation into the Pauline Communities (II): Baptism in Galatians and Romans

7.1 Discussions of Key Passages

7.1.1 Galatians 3:25–29

7.1.1.1 Exegetical Discussion

Galatians 3:25–29 is located at the end of Paul's discourse κατὰ ἄνθρωπον (beginning from 3:15), in which he restates what he has said so far. The passage includes Group A words which appear in vv. 27–28. This passage, whether it is formulaic or not,[1] "references the performance of the baptism ritual," given the performative and social indicators.[2] Setting aside the first part of 3:28 ("there is neither Jew nor Greek/Hellene"), the rest of 3:28 ("there is neither slave nor free, there is not male and female") seems like residual tradition,[3] because it is not directly connected to Paul's discourse in Gal 3 (i.e., the male/female relations are not the focus of this passage). This suggests that Paul draws on a pre-existing baptismal tradition rather than creating an ad hoc phrase himself.[4]

---

[1] It was often assumed by scholars (Betz, Martyn, Meeks, etc.) that one can find a "baptismal formula" in this passage through a form-critical analysis. See, for example, Betz's words: "[W]e have before us a form of a saying, made up of a number of components, which must have had its place and function in early Christian baptismal liturgy." Hans Dieter Betz, *Galatians: A Commentary on Paul's Letters to the Churches in Galatia* (Philadelphia: Fortress, 1979), 181 (also, 184). Yet, even if one employs form criticism, one cannot *prove* that this passage contains an actual baptismal formula—one that was recited during baptism at this early stage. McGowan's critical approach to scholarly assumptions about NT eucharistic passages would be relevant to this issue. Andrew Brian McGowan, "'Is There A Liturgical Text in This Gospel?': The Institution Narratives and Their Early Interpretative Communities," *JBL* 118 (1999): 73–87. This does not mean that baptism is used figuratively, or even peripherally, or that Paul invented all these images *ex nihilo*.
[2] Turley, *Ritualized Revelation*, 36.
[3] A similar point is made by Betz, *Galatians*, 182; also, Wayne Meeks, "The Image of the Androgyne: Some Uses of a Symbol in Earliest Christianity," *HR* 13 (1974): 181. Paul's removal of the boundaries between slave and free is not necessarily connected to baptismal tradition (e.g., 1 Cor 7:22; cf. circumcision/non-circumcision, 1 Cor 7:18–19). Yet, I regard these remarks in 1 Cor 7 as examples in which the implications of baptism morph into practical exhortations within the community.
[4] Turley, *Ritualized Revelation*, 31. Turley persuasively demonstrates that Paul refers to an actual ritual and, at the same time, interprets it theologically. Turley's analysis, however, cannot (and does not aim to) reveal how the Galatians were practicing this ritual, what it meant for them, and what benefits it promised them.

Galatians 3 is divided into three subsections. The first section, ranging from v. 1 to v. 14, is Paul's interpretation of scripture in light of his Christ-experience. In vv. 1–5, Paul rebukes the Galatians with a rhetorical question. The implied answer is that the Galatians' reception of the Spirit was not ἐξ ἔργων νόμου, but ἐξ ἀκοῆς πίστεως. Then, in vv. 6–9, Paul recounts God's promises to Abraham (Gen 12:1–3; 15:1–6; cf. 18:18) and its relevance to the Galatians. Abraham trusted (ἐπίστευσεν) in God, which was considered δικαιοσύνη, and thus, those who are ἐκ πίστεως are the children of Abraham. That all the nations will be blessed in Abraham (ἐν σοί, "in you") was "pre-preached" (προευηγγελίσατο) in Scripture.[5] By drawing on Deuteronomy (27:26; cf. 28:58, 30:10) and Habakkuk (2:4), Paul then employs a striking contrast between the law and πίστις in Gal 3:10–12. Those who are ἐξ ἔργων νόμου are under the curse, and the law is not ἐκ πίστεως. Paul aptly summarizes the meaning and effect of Christ's death in relation to the Abrahamic promise and current Christ-believers. Christ redeemed "us" by becoming "the curse for us" (ὑπὲρ ἡμῶν κατάρα), so that "unto the nations/gentiles" Abraham's blessing may be realized ἐν Χριστῷ Ἰησοῦ, with the result that "we" may receive "the promise (sg.) of the Spirit" through πίστις (vv. 13–14).[6]

Paul begins the second subsection (3:15–22) by rephrasing what he has said in vv. 1–14; he calls his mode of speech κατὰ ἄνθρωπον ("according to/in the human manner," or "according to the common estimation"[7]). In this section, Paul relies heavily on legal images and reasoning, especially the law of succession/inheritance (e.g., διαθήκη, v. 15; σπέρμα, v. 16; κληρονομία, v. 18),[8] even though he continues to engage Jewish Scripture. First of all, Paul contrasts Abraham's promises (pl. in v. 16; yet, the difference between promises and promise does not seem as significant as

---

5 This is the only occurrence of this verb in the NT; it should be understood in light of Paul's use of other verbs with the prefix προ (e.g., Rom 1:2, 15:4). See, for example, Hays, *Echoes of Scripture*, 107.
6 The first-person plural "we" includes both Jewish (thus, Paul) and gentile believers. J. Louis Martyn, *Galatians: A New Translation with Introduction and Commentary*, AB 33 A (New York: Doubleday, 1997), 323, 334–36; Martinus C. de Boer, *Galatians*, NTL (Louisville: WJK, 2011), 214–16.
7 The latter rendering is from Jerome Murphy-O'Connor, "The Irrevocable Will (Gal 3:15)," *RB* 106 (1999): 234.
8 Scholars have pointed out that the law of inheritance in the ancient world (whether Jewish or non-Jewish) does not precisely correspond to what Paul describes, especially, Paul's point that the testament/will (διαθήκη) cannot be changed once it is ratified (v. 15). Yet, if Murphy-O'Connor's theory, based on his survey of Paul's use of κατὰ ἄνθρωπον, is correct, then Paul's remark about the custom in v. 15 is not rigid. Rather, "Paul knew perfectly well that what he was going to say did not accurately reflect the letter of the law regarding adoption. He explicitly based his argument on the common estimate, the popular perception, of what were the rights of an adopted son." Murphy-O'Connor, "The Irrevocable Will," 235.

the contrast between seed and seeds[9]) with the Mosaic law chronologically; the promises were given earlier, and the law came in later. These promises, which take chronological precedence, cover Abraham and his seed (sg.). Paul plays on the grammatical singularity of the word; the promises were not made to many seeds (οὐ ... ὡς ἐπὶ πολλῶν), but to one seed (ὡς ἐφ' ἑνός). In other words, Paul's discourse implies the question, who is the legitimate heir of these promises? (cf. Philo, *Her.*).[10] Beginning in v. 17, Paul clarifies: the law came in and encompassed all people under its authority until the arrival of πίστις, but the appearance of the law does not invalidate the original promise given as a διαθήκη. After a complicated discussion about the law's origins (vv. 19–21), Paul ends the section on a positive note: Scripture's (γραφή) temporary incarceration of all under sin was ultimately meant to bring about the promise for those who believe (τοῖς πιστεύουσιν) through "Jesus-Christ-faith" (ἐκ πίστεως Ἰησοῦ Χριστοῦ, 3:22)—or, simply, "Christ-faith."[11]

---

9 In this chapter, Paul uses the singular promise (vv. 14, 17, 18, 22, 29) and the plural promises (vv. 16, 21). Scholarly views vary. For example, on v. 16, Martyn notes, "It is curious that Paul should use the plural in a passage in which he is intent on emphasizing the covenantal promise as a punctiliar event (Abraham) that refers to a singular and punctiliar seed (Christ). The plural may reflect the fact that God repeated his promise to Abraham several times." Martyn, *Galatians*, 339. According to de Boer, the plural promises may indicate several instances of the same promise (similar to Martyn's view) or specifically, "the promise of land . . ., that of a son and heir . . ., and that of many descendants" (de Boer thinks that the promise of the Spirit fulfills the latter two). De Boer, *Galatians*, 223–24. Betz's position is more speculative. From the plural promises and the singular promise, Betz finds Paul's "polemic against the opponents." Betz, *Galatians*, 156, n. 31 (see also 329, n. 7).
10 In this treatise that begins with the statement, "Now our task is to inquire *who is the heir of divine things* (τίς ὁ τῶν θείων πραγμάτων κληρονόμος ἐστίν, *Her.* 1)," Philo gives a detailed allegorical interpretation of Gen 15:2–18. In the end, the land promised to Abraham's seed is understood in relation to the promise of God's wisdom (*Her.* 313–15). Genesis 15:6, which Paul cites, appears in *Her.* 90–95 (cf. other passages where Philo mentions Gen 15:6: *Leg.* 3.228; *Deus* 4; *Migr.* 44; *Mut.* 186; *Abr.* 262; *Virt.* 216; *Praem.* 28; I thank an anonymous reviewer of my manuscript for drawing my attention to these passages, which actually merits further study).
11 The question as to whether the genitive phrase *pistis Christou* (here and elsewhere in the Pauline corpus) should be understood as an objective genitive (i.e., [our] faith in Christ) or a subjective genitive (i.e., Christ's own faith[fulness]) has been debated among many NT scholars since the second half of the twentieth century. For a useful summary of this debate, see Matthew C. Easter, "The *Pistis Christou* Debate: Main Arguments and Responses in Summary," *CBR* 9 (2010): 33–47. As Easter and many others have pointed out, this issue cannot be settled purely by grammar, and interpreters often incorporate their own theology and understanding of Pauline theology. Given the possibility of this phrase's inherent ambiguity (and its resultant evocative power), I render the phrase ambiguously. The current trend in scholarship is to regard the phrase as referring to the entire chain of trust among God-Christ-humans (Teresa Morgan) or the chain of imitation among these agents (Sierksma-Agteres) (thus, rather than making an either-or choice). Morgan, *Roman Faith*

The third subsection starts in v. 23, when Paul continues his legal metaphor about the law of inheritance. Paul now merges the reference to the practice of inheritance with household circumstances familiar to the wider Greco-Roman world, for example, παιδαγωγός (vv. 24, 25) and δοῦλος (4:1)—this blended visual rhetoric extends to 4:11.[12] With that in mind, see Gal 3:25–29:

> 25 But after the πίστις has come, we are no longer under a *paidagogos* (ὑπὸ παιδαγωγόν). 26 For you are all the children of God through Christ-Jesus-faith (πίστις ἐν Χριστῷ Ἰησοῦ). 27 For as many of you as were baptized into Christ (ὅσοι γὰρ εἰς Χριστὸν ἐβαπτίσθητε) have clothed yourselves with Christ (Χριστὸν ἐνεδύσασθε). 28 There is neither Jew nor Greek, slave nor free, male and female, since you are all one in Christ Jesus (ἐν Χριστῷ Ἰησοῦ). 29 If you are of Christ, then you are the seed of Abraham, heirs according to the promise.

Thus, as in 1 Cor 1 and 15, Paul's remark about baptism is embedded in a discussion focused on another topic.[13] Yet, this indirect discourse can offer insight into how the Galatians and Paul understood baptism and its promise.

Many scholars and non-specialists alike have paid attention to Gal 3:27–29, for these verses provide a potentially "egalitarian" vision for early Christianity. This vision was probably part of the *Galatians'* understanding of baptism (see my discussion at the beginning of this section regarding baptismal tradition).[14] This radical removal of differences is possible because of their new collective identity and status (i.e., their being-in-Christ) created through baptism. This process is articulated in vv. 27–29: they have been baptized into Christ (εἰς Χριστόν) and clothed with Christ (v. 27), so that they are all ἐν Χριστῷ Ἰησοῦ (v. 28) and belong to Christ (ὑμεῖς Χριστοῦ, "you are of Christ," v. 29). In this passage, one finds an explicit link among these three aspects (baptism into Christ, being in Christ, and belonging to Christ)

---

and Christian Faith, 288–92; Suzan J. M. Sierksma-Agteres, "Imitation in Faith: Enacting Paul's Ambiguous *Pistis Christou* formulations on a Greco-Roman Stage," *IJPT* 77 (2016): 119–53. See also Morna D. Hooker, "Another Look at πίστις Χριστοῦ," *SJT* 69 (2016): 46–62. While acknowledging that πίστις Χριστοῦ can mean both our faith in Christ and the faithfulness of Christ, Hooker is inclined to say that the latter is the primary meaning.

12 While some interpreters (e.g., James Scott) have suggested the exodus as the background for Gal 4:1–2, John Goodrich's recent article argues that guardianship and inheritance practices in the Greco-Roman world are the primary context for this passage. His argument is based on his exploration of verbal parallels between Gal 4:1–2 and P.Ryl 2.153 (a second-century Roman will). John K. Goodrich, "'As long as the heir is a child': The Rhetoric of Inheritance in Galatians 4:1–2 and P.Ryl 2.153," *NovT* 55 (2013): 61–76.
13 Longenecker even claims that the omission of vv. 27–28 makes better sense. Richard N. Longenecker, *Galatians*, WBC 41 (Dallas: Word Books, 1990), 154.
14 Betz also notes, "The baptismal theology which is reflected in Paul's remark appears to antedate Paul's own theology." Betz, *Galatians*, 186.

that was only hinted at in 1 Corinthians. In other words, this passage suggests that baptism promises that an individual can only enter the Christ cult through the ritual participation in this deity, Christ (which is also seen in 1 Corinthians), and as a result, other social/cultural markers are now relativized within the Christ community (as is sometimes seen in the mysteries;[15] but again, new markers and hierarchies sometimes arise!).

The use of εἰς in the phrase, "to be baptized εἰς Χριστόν" (3:27), may help conceptualize baptism as a devotee's entering εἰς the divine figure, and as such, this is linguistically peculiar, because the other way (i.e., the divine figure [comes] εἰς a devotee [see also my discussion of Dionysus in Chapter 3]) would make more sense in the ritual context of the ancient Mediterranean world.[16] Yet, as I already discussed (see my discussion of 1 Cor 10 and 12), baptism into Christ does not primarily mean that the individual *mystically* enters into this deity, but rather signals that the person is joining this cultic group and becomes a single cultic body, belonging to Christ. Nevertheless, Gal 3:27b, Χριστὸν ἐνεδύσασθε, which is perhaps Paul's interpretation of baptism, takes a step further: it suggests that the baptized are identified with Christ. The baptized person's identification with Christ reminds one of the ritual identification found in the Dionysiac mysteries and the mysteries of Isis (see 3.2.4 and 4.2.4).[17]

---

15 The temporary overcoming of sociocultural and economic differences by all participating in the same ritual was not unprecedented (cf. the Eleusinian mysteries). Bremmer notes that the Eleusinian mysteries were "open to men and women, free and slaves, young and old, Greeks and non-Greeks." Yet, one needed to pay to participate, and therefore, "not everyone could afford the Mysteries." Bremmer, *Initiation*, 2–3.

16 The infusion of the divine Spirit into the devotees (cf. 1 Thess 4:8, "God gave his Holy Spirit into you" [τὸν θεὸν τὸν διδόντα τὸ πνεῦμα αὐτοῦ τὸ ἅγιον εἰς ὑμᾶς]) is more easily explained in light of other comparable expressions appearing in cultic contexts, including that of the Dionysiac mysteries (for example, expressions like ἔνθεος, ἐνθουσιασμός, ἐνθουσιάζειν, etc.). It is interesting to note that the group of prophets in 1 Sam 19:20–24 and Saul who suddenly happened to join them are portrayed almost like corybants or bacchantes; Josephus even uses the phrase ἔνθεος γενόμενος for Saul (*A.J.* 6.56, 76). For 1 Samuel and Josephus, see John Ashton, *The Religion of Paul the Apostle* (New Haven: Yale University Press, 2000), 183. Admittedly, initiation rituals into the mystery deities may be conceptually similar to baptism into Christ/Moses, but this concept is not articulated in pagan sources in precisely the same way as in Paul. In this regard, the criticism of the Moratorium scholars is valid.

17 As Agersnap observes, Gal 3:29 continues to depict Christ-believers as belonging to Christ (thus, distinguished from Christ). This demonstrates that this passage envisions "no literal fusion." Agersnap, *Baptism and the New Life*, 107. Perhaps, this "literal fusion" may be excluded from other conceptions of deification/divine participation found in the ancient Mediterranean world. See Litwa, *We Are Being Transformed*, 32. Yet, this puts too much emphasis on the point; the idea that deification (including Paul's notion of deification) is not the same as "literal fusion" is somewhat anach-

When compared to 1 Corinthians, Paul's discourse in Galatians gives prominence to different aspects of baptism. This is because in Galatians, Paul adopts baptismal tradition and uses it for rhetorical purposes differing from those of 1 Corinthians. Thus, baptism's promise of afterlife, or baptism's implications for church unity (both of which are prominent in 1 Corinthians) are not highlighted in Galatians. Here, Paul employs baptism in his discourse that dissuades the gentile believers in Galatia from circumcision by proving that they have become Abraham's children without circumcision. Galatians 3:29 reveals the goal of the chapter: the Galatian audience is Abraham's seed (sg.) and the legitimate heir of the Abrahamic promise(s). This is somewhat unexpected because Paul already said that Christ is the singular seed (v. 16).[18] Yet, that is where one can see what baptism can do for the Galatians, according to Paul.

The clothing metaphor in Gal 3:27b shows how Paul creates connections between Christ-baptism and this new genealogy for the ex-pagan believers in Galatia. In order to better understand the clothing metaphor, one needs to examine Paul's argument in Gal 3. It can be presented in detail:

1) God gave promises to Abraham and his seed (sg.), i.e., Christ, and these promise(s) take precedence over the Mosaic law.
2) The Christ-believing gentiles (the Galatians) can participate in the promise(s) without following Mosaic law, because they are also the seed (sg.) of Abraham.
3) The transformation of the gentiles into Abraham's seed can be explained in two ways. First, it is because πίστις has come. The Galatians received the Holy Spirit (or, the promise of the Spirit) by hearing of πίστις, not by the works of the law, and the Galatians' πίστις corresponds to Abraham who trusted/believed (ἐπίστευσεν). As is Abraham, so is the seed of Abraham.
4) A second explanation is needed because Paul does not directly connect Abraham and the Galatians: the Galatians are the seed (sg.) in so far as they are in Christ (ἐν Χριστῷ) and identified with Christ by being clothed in him in baptism. This is prefigured in Scripture: all the nations/gentiles will be blessed in Abraham (ἐν σοί), who trusted/believed (ἐπίστευσεν) God and was himself faithful (πιστός).
5) This εὐλογία is finally realized at the present age (Paul's time) in Christ Jesus through baptism.

---

ronistic. In many cases, the ambiguity inherent in the language of deification actually contributed to its rhetorical power in antiquity.

18 The Hebrew *zera* (seed/offspring) is a collective noun (e.g., Gen 3:15; 1 Sam 2:20). Although Paul exploits the difference between the singular σπέρμα and the plural σπέρματα in 3:16, which implies that Paul does not treat the singular σπέρμα collectively, 3:29 suggests that Paul eventually uses σπέρμα almost as a collective noun.

It is tempting to regard the clothing metaphor of "putting on Christ" (cf. Col 3:10; Eph 4:24) as referring to changing one's clothes during baptism (consider Lucius's change of clothes after his initiation into the mysteries of Isis); indeed, the *Apostolic Tradition* 21 indicates that early Christian baptism included a rite of changing clothes. Yet, it is hard to prove that the same procedure already existed in the Pauline communities. This phrase (3:27b, Χριστὸν ἐνεδύσασθε) should be read as Paul's interpretation of baptism, which he adds to baptismal tradition in 3:27a and 3:28 (εἰς Χριστὸν ἐβαπτίσθητε ... [therefore] ... οὐκ ἔνι Ἰουδαῖος οὐδὲ Ἕλλην, οὐκ ἔνι δοῦλος οὐδὲ ἐλεύθερος, οὐκ ἔνι ἄρσεν καὶ θῆλυ· πάντες γὰρ ὑμεῖς εἷς ἐστε ἐν Χριστῷ Ἰησοῦ).[19]

Considering the household imagery pertaining to the wider Greco-Roman world in the third subsection (Gal 3:23–29; perhaps, to 4:11), Harrill proposes that one should read Paul's rhetorical use of "putting on Christ" in baptism in light of the *toga virilis* ceremony in the Roman household.[20] This proposal fits into the literary context of the passage. Since the *toga virilis* ceremony is a "rite of passage," this explanation demonstrates how baptism can change one's status and at the same time require new moral responsibilities of the baptized. Yet, his proposal does not (nor does it aim to) fully address how and to what extent this *toga virilis* interpretation fits with (1) pre-Pauline baptismal tradition, i.e., that baptism relativizes various identity markers for those in Christ (Gal 3:28), and (2) Paul's message here, i.e., baptism's power (in contrast to circumcision) to rewrite the gentiles' genealogy in order to reconfigure them as the seed of Abraham in Christ (a new kinship as the people of God).[21]

---

[19] Other examples of the clothing metaphor (Col 3:10; Eph 4:24), as well as actual rites of changing clothes during baptism (*Apostolic Tradition* 21), were possibly influenced by the seminal Pauline passage in Galatians. This does not mean that Paul's use of the clothing imagery is unique. Rather, the connection between change of clothing and rites of passage is a widespread phenomenon found in several religious and cultural traditions. See Meeks, "The Image of the Androgyne," 183–84.

[20] J. Albert Harrill, "Coming of Age and Putting on Christ: The *toga virilis* Ceremony, Its Paraenesis, and Paul's Interpretation of Baptism in Galatians," *NovT* 44 (2002): 252–77. From the outset, Harrill states that his project does not explore the origins of "putting on Christ" language but examines how Paul interprets the tradition and uses it for his rhetorical purpose. Harrill, "Coming of Age," 253.

[21] Paul's thought might be based on "the ideology of patrilineal decent," as Caroline Johnson Hodge points out (*If Sons, Then Heirs: A Study of Kinship and Ethnicity in the Letters of Paul* [Oxford: Oxford University Press, 2007], 93). Yet, it is entirely possible that the gentile Galatians understood their new identity in Christ through Christ-baptism in another way. Note that the identification between Dionysus and the Dionysiac devotees are not relevant to patrilineal decent.

To understand the multiple connections Paul creates here, one should take into consideration the connection between one's dress and her/his ethnicity in iconographic and literary evidence. Applying the term ethnicity (and even, "race") to the ancient world is contested. What factors precisely constitute an *ethnos* in antiquity is a complicated question; one should be careful about reading modern understandings of ethnicity and race into ancient materials. Nevertheless, in antiquity, there were diverse ways of distinguishing peoples, or more precisely, constructing such distinctive identities among peoples. These strategies include "shared ancestry, toponyms, or rituals or ... cultural markers such as dress and hairstyle, prestige goods (often imported), symbols, and cuisine."[22] In Greek iconography, skin color—one of the primary markers for modern constructions of race/ethnicity—was "never used to distinguish 'Hellene' from 'barbarian,'" while *garments do function that way.*[23] The latter is not only true for iconography, but is also found in the literary sources. One noticeable example is from Herodotus 4.78, a story of the Scythian king Skyles who changed his clothes to Greek. As Dahl and Hellholm observe, "The change of garments [in this story] can mark a change of customs and nationality."[24] In addition to the *toga virilis* custom suggested by Harrill, therefore, this trans-ethnic/national context sheds further light on Paul's expression "putting on Christ" in relation to baptism (3:27) and his subsequent statement that "there is neither Jew nor Greek" (3:28). Having clothed oneself with Christ (like putting on a new garment) in baptism amounts to superimposing a new ethnic identity (which is linked to the deity's name) upon the preexisting one (rather than completely replacing it).

Admittedly, Paul does not explicitly speak of "the third race" (*tertium genus*; τρίτον γένος), as one finds in later writers, such as Tertullian (*Ad nationes* 1.8) and pseudo-Cyprian (*De pascha computus* 17). Furthermore, Paul's discourse in Gal 3 seeks to support the claim that the gentile Galatians' incorporation into Abraham's genealogy, and thus, their participation in Abraham's blessing is not through the works of the law. What receives prominence is the gentiles' inclusion into God's (preexisting) people, rather than a creation of a brand-new people. Nevertheless, Paul—especially his arrangement of 3:27–28—unwittingly creates an inchoate,

---

[22] S. Rebecca Martin, "Ethnicity and Greek Art History in Theory and Practice," in *Theoretical Approaches to the Archaeology of Ancient Greece: Manipulating Material Culture*, ed. Lisa Nevett (Ann Arbor: University of Michigan Press, 2017), 144.
[23] Martin, "Ethnicity and Greek Art History," 150.
[24] Nils Alstrup Dahl and David Hellholm, "Garment-Metaphors: The Old and the New Human Being," in *Antiquity and Humanity: Essays on Ancient Religion and Philosophy Presented to Hans Dieter Betz on his 70th Birthday*, ed. Adela Yarbro Collins and Margaret M. Mitchell (Tübingen: Mohr Siebeck, 2001), 139.

pseudo-ethnic image of this group of Christ-believers (something like Christ's *ethnos*).²⁵ For Paul, the radical egalitarianism alluded to in Gal 3:28 is partially subordinate to his use of that vision to emphasize their identity pertaining to Christ, specifically, their identity *as Christ*.²⁶ This identification of initiates with the deity recalls some examples from the mysteries (such as the Attic grave reliefs in which women are dressed like Isis and identified with her [Figures 10 and 11]; or the Apulian kraters, where male initiates are dressed like Dionysus, thus are identified with him [Figure 4]). But when compared to these examples, Paul's ethnic reasoning is much stronger: the baptized become Abraham's seed through their identification with Christ, the very seed of Abraham.

The place of the πνεῦμα within this whole picture remains relatively ambiguous, although, given other passages (e.g., 1 Cor 12:13), Paul may have taken for granted that the reception of the πνεῦμα was accompanied by baptism. *Contra* Matthew Thiessen, the πνεῦμα does not appear as the material agent that makes such transformation possible,²⁷ although it appears to be the content of the promise (cf. Gal 3:2, 13), which they receive ἐξ ἀκοῆς πίστεως and ἐν Χριστῷ.

Excursus 3: The Promise of the "Material" *Pneuma?*
Thiessen's thesis in *Paul and the Gentile Problem* is that (1) the promise given to Abraham in Gen 15 (Abraham's seed will be like stars) already includes the promise of the "material" *pneuma* (to the eyes of Jewish interpreters in Paul's days) and (2) Paul asserts that the infusion of material *pneuma* into the gentile believers by πίστις is the way to turn the gentiles into Abraham's seed. This is an ingenious reading; however, his reasoning requires multiple steps of identification (Abraham's seed will be like "stars" = being like stars has a qualitative, not just quantitative sense = these stars are angelic beings = the stars' pneumatic composition =

---

25 Regarding the tension between Paul's creation of new identity in Christ and his lack of the precise designation (like "Christians"), see Wolter, *Paul*, 6–7, 434–35. Similarly, regarding the Corinthians: see Jonathan Z. Smith, "Re: Corinthians," in *Redescribing Paul and the Corinthians*, ed. Ron Cameron and Merrill P. Miller (Atlanta: SBL, 2011), 33.
26 The reference to baptism here in Galatians does not emphasize (or even imply) "hierarchization" between Paul as the "ritual agent" and the Galatians (thus, *contra* Yuh). Jason N. Yuh, "Analyzing Paul's Reference to Baptism in Galatians 3.27 through Studies of Memory, Embodiment and Ritual," *JSNT* 41 (2019): 489–90. Throughout Galatians Paul highlights his authority over the Galatians, and Yuh's use of cognitive science and memory theories indeed help illuminate the rhetorical force of Paul's brief remark of baptism. But there is no evidence that Paul actually baptized all the Galatians, so that Paul's reference to baptism also functions to remind them of Paul's authority (cf. 1 Cor 1:13–17, which makes it unlikely that Paul baptized all congregants in his communities).
27 Thiessen does not pay attention to the relationship between baptism and the πνεῦμα, but only that between πίστις and πνεῦμα. Matthew Thiessen, *Paul and the Gentile Problem* (New York: Oxford University Press, 2016).

Christ's pneuma in the gentiles is also pneumatic in this sense).[28] Furthermore, Thiessen's understanding of the πνεῦμα and the pneumatic transformation in Paul (which depends on previous scholars, such as Stanley Stowers, Dale Martin, Troels Engberg-Pedersen) unnecessarily forces Paul's pneumatology and his notion of reality into a physical and material understanding.[29] Above all, it was not common in the ancient world to think about one's genealogy as purely determined by one's material constitution; nor should one restrict the ancient people's (including Paul's) epistemological options to binary options, either "metaphorical" or "material."[30] As Sanders observes, modern people lack the "concept of reality" that characterized Paul's realism.[31] Yet, Thiessen notes,

> Through the reception of Christ's material *pneuma*, gentiles receive the very substance—to use a modern conception (and admittedly rough analogy), the very DNA—of Abraham's seed … In receiving the *pneuma*, then, gentiles undergo a material transformation—again, to use a modern analogy, they undergo gene therapy—which addresses their genealogical deficiencies as gentiles.[32]

Thiessen's analogies reveal that this materialistic interpretation of Pauline pneumatology would fall into another type of anachronism (e.g., employing a modern biological model), despite his intention to overcome other scholars' anachronistic, overly Christianized reading of the first-century figure Paul.

"The promise of the *pneuma*" in Gal 3:14 should be understood as manifestations of the spiritual experiences among the Christ-believers, rather than intrinsically related to the Abraham account (later NT writers link the promise of the *pneuma* to Christ's promise [e.g., Acts 1:8; John 14:16–17, 15:26]).[33]

---

[28] Each of these elements can be partly demonstrated by his survey of relevant material. For example, Philo's passages (*Her.* 86–87; *QG* 4.181) are evidence that some Jewish authors did interpret the Abrahamic promise that his seed will be like stars in Gen 15 with a qualitative (not just quantitative) meaning. Likewise, several passages from the HB (e.g., Ps 148:1–3) and extracanonical Jewish writings (1QH^a 9.11b–14a) show the stars as angelic beings. Also, there is evidence in Jewish writing, including the HB/LXX (Ps 103 LXX), that angels are regarded as pneumatic beings. Thiessen, *Paul and the Gentile Problem*, 135–147. Despite all these impressive primary sources, what is missing is a strong link throughout the multiple steps of identification. For example, although it is true that the angels are portrayed as *pneumata* in Ps 103 LXX, does it necessarily mean that these pneumatic angels are made up of material *pneuma* in the Stoic sense?
[29] As for my own critique of Dale Martin and Troels Engberg-Pedersen, see Jeong, "1 Corinthians 15:35–58," 45–70. More recently, see John Granger Cook, "1Cor 15,40–41: Paul and the Heavenly Bodies," *ZNW* 113 (2022): 159–79. He correctly notes, "It is time for scholars to stop assuming without evidence that the Stoics believed the stars comprised πνεῦμα" (Cook, "1Cor 15,40–41," 173, n. 55).
[30] Such a binary view is found in Stowers, "What is 'Pauline Participation in Christ?" 356.
[31] E. P. Sanders, *Paul and Palestinian Judaism: A Comparison of Patterns of Religion* (Philadelphia: Fortress, 1977), 520.
[32] Thiessen, *Paul and the Gentile Problem*, 117.
[33] Syntactically, "the blessing of Abraham" and "the promise of the *pneuma*" in Gal 3:14 could be understood as apposition (Thiessen, *Paul and the Gentile Problem*, 107 and Francis Watson, *Paul*

7.1.1.2 The self-referential messages, the canonical messages, and things beyond baptism

To summarize, the self-referential messages of baptism as the Galatians perceived them are two: baptism is an entry ritual that enables the baptized to obtain membership in the cult, and it also relativizes parts of one's identity and status that matter outside of the community. In addition to these, Paul's interpretation of baptism in Gal 3 shows that another important self-referential message of baptism is its power to rewrite the genealogy of the gentiles ἐν Χριστῷ, so that they participate in the blessing of Abraham. It is not clear what canonical messages the Galatians previously expected, but one can see how Paul creates and conveys the canonical messages that support the efficacy of the self-referential messages. The gentiles can become Abraham's seed through baptism (self-referential message) because baptism depicted as a clothing ritual has the power to clothe the gentiles with Christ, causing them to be identified with Christ, Abraham's seed (canonical message). This canonical message actually produces another self-referential message that was not emphasized in this passage. Since Christ, with whom believers are identified, is the crucified one who "became a curse (γενόμενος ... κατάρα) for us" (3:13) and publicly exhibited (προεγράφη) before the eyes of the Galatians (3:1),[34] then baptism communicates the self-referential message that the baptized now share Christ's cruciform identity and suffering.[35] In this regard, one could agree with Siikavirta who regards even Gal 2:19–21 as part of Paul's baptismal reference.[36] Yet, the connection between baptism and Gal 2:19–21 is not explicitly made in the text. In Rom 5–8, however, Paul makes this connection between baptism and one's participation in Christ's cruciform identity clear.

---

and the Hermeneutics of Faith [London: T&T Clark, 2004], 192). This identification arises because Paul begins from his contemporary experience and then reinterprets the content of Abraham's blessing. Betz notes, "[Paul] arrives at this conclusion for these reasons: the Gentile Christians did receive the Spirit (3:2, 5), and they did so 'through [the] faith' (διὰ τῆς πίστεως). If this is the fulfillment of the promise God made to Abraham (3:8), the blessing which is the content of the promise must be the gift of the Spirit." Betz, *Galatians*, 153.

34 If one accepts (or at least is sympathetic toward) Balch's suggestion that Paul's remark in Gal 3:1 (i.e., the crucified Christ was publicly exhibited before the Galatians) can be read in light of household wall-paintings exhibiting deities' suffering (including Isis), then the emotional force of Paul's canonical message about baptism would increase. Balch, "The Suffering of Isis/Io," 24–55.
35 Morales, "Baptism and Union with Christ," 173.
36 Siikavirta, *Baptism and Cognition*, 87, 89.

7.1.2 Romans 6:1–14 within Romans 5–8

7.1.2.1 Exegetical Discussion

Romans 6 has been the *locus classicus* on the issue of Pauline baptism, especially vis-à-vis the mysteries (Moratorium scholars pronounced a negative verdict on this comparative case). Yet, against previous scholars' preoccupation with baptism when interpreting Rom 6 (both in the Inaugurated and Moratorium stages), some scholars argue that baptism is neither Paul's primary interest nor the center of his argument in Rom 6. Tannehill observes that "Paul is not primarily concerned to set forth an interpretation of baptism."[37] Nevertheless, the ritual reality of baptism provides a basis for Paul's theological reflections in this overall discourse. In other words, one could distinguish the topic at hand and the deeper structure that underlies it: while Rom 6 is not primarily about baptism, baptism shapes the discourse. The mysteries still constitute interpretative *comparanda*, as discussed in Chapters 3 and 4. In this final section, I will demonstrate how the pattern of baptism and the perceived ritual reality inform the whole discourse in Rom 6 (and 5–8), and conversely, how Paul's theological convictions enable him to appropriate the image of baptism as an effective vehicle for his exhortation.

Romans 6:1–14 is arranged in a (incomplete) chiasm. This passage does not have to be understood strictly as a chiasm.[38] This arrangement is given only for heuristic purposes to help clarify the connections between the sentences and to identify some distinctive features in the passage. A brief description about the structure of Rom 6:1–14 follows:[39]

---

[37] Robert C. Tannehill, *Dying and Rising with Christ: A Study in Pauline Theology* (Berlin: Verlag Alfred Töpelmann, 1966), 7. The view that baptism in Rom 6 is *merely* figurative language and not central to this passage (e.g., Ashton) does not do justice to the dynamics between ritual and ritual interpretation. Ashton comments: "For although the passage is generally assumed to be *about* baptism, it is far from certain that baptism figures in this passage as anything more than a simile. I shall argue that *this does not matter*, since the central message is none other than the appropriation by individual Christians of the victory over sin accomplished by Christ through his own death and resurrection" (italics original). Ashton, *The Religion of Paul*, 131; see also, 133.
[38] Hendrikus Boers suggests another formulation of the chiastic structure of this passage, which begins with 6:4cd and ends with 6:11. Hendrikus Boers, "The Structure and Meaning of Romans 6:1–14," *CBQ* 63 (2001): 676.
[39] In parentheses, I indicate whether each description envisions what was done in the past, what lies in the present, or what is reserved for the future. The temporal relationship between statements in this passage is complex and needs more detailed exegesis. As for what is expressed in the perfect tense (e.g., γεγόναμεν in 6:5), I treat it as an event in the past. The subjunctive mood (e.g., 6:4, 6:6) is ambiguous with respect to temporality, but I place them in the present rather than the future.

Table 2: The structure of Romans 6:1-14

A: 6:1–2a				It is absurd to claim that we remain in Sin to make grace abound.
	B: 6:2b			We who died to Sin (past) will not live in it (fut.).
		C: 6:3		We were baptized into Christ, i.e., into his death (past).
			C-1: 6:4	We, co-buried with Christ (past), walk by the newness of life (now)
			C-2: 6:5	We, co-planted with Christ's death (past), will be with his resurrection (fut.)
			C-3: 6:6–7	We, co-crucified with Christ (past), have been freed from Sin (now)
	B': 6:8			We who died with Christ (past) will live with him (fut.).
		C': 6:9–11		Just as Christ died to Sin (past) but lives to God (now), you consider yourselves to be dead to Sin, living to God (now).
A': 6:12–14				Do not let Sin reign over you; present yourselves to God, not to Sin.

A few preliminary observations on the baptismal images and messages in Rom 6:1–14: (a) in Rom 6:1–14, there is no explicit mention of purification and repentance, although these are the characteristics most frequently attached to baptism outside the Pauline corpus (1 Cor 6 has a vestige of the concept);[40] (b) unlike the

---

[40] A brief review of NT passages outside the Pauline letters regarding baptism provides the broader context:

First, Mark 1:4–8 is the baptism of John the Baptist. It is primarily a "baptism of repentance for the forgiveness of sins." Only Jews in Judaea are included (rather than including gentiles), and this baptism has nothing to do with conversion into the Christ-believing movement or even the mystical union with Christ. It is possible that the picture in Mark 1:4–8 reflects baptismal practice among certain Jews in the early first-century Judaea.

Second, John 3:22–26 and 4:1–2 enable one to infer that not only the baptism by John the Baptist but also the baptism by Jesus and his disciples was something several early Christian writers struggled to fit in their overall theological understanding. Still, baptism in John 3–4 is understood as a means to forgiveness and purification, but there is no connection between baptism and Jesus's name.

Third, in Acts, baptism begins to involve Jesus's name. His name is linked to three different prepositions, ἐπί (2:38), εἰς (8:16), ἐν (10:48), but they are used interchangeably. Unlike baptism in the Gospels, baptism in Acts initiates converts into a new community that is "devoted ... to the apostles' teaching and fellowship, to the breaking of bread and the prayers" (2:42). Yet, this baptism still resonates with John the Baptist's baptism found in the Gospels due to its emphasis on repent-

previous Pauline baptismal passages, Rom 6:1–14 lacks the emphasis on the social messages of baptism, such as joining the community (it is implied by εἰς Χριστὸν Ἰησοῦν, 6:3); as relativizing other sociocultural identity markers; or as promoting unity within the community; (c) within the undisputed Pauline letters, the notion that believers die and are buried with Christ through baptism appears only here (though, cf. Col 2:12),[41] which has naturally led many scholars to explore its origins (i.e., "where did this unique idea come from?");[42] and (d) as shown in the structural analysis of Rom 6:1–14 (see above), the particular image of baptism is combined with, or embedded in, a series of other images (see C-1, C-2, C-3 above),[43] which rais-

---

ance. Also, 2:38 connects the receiving of the Holy Spirit to baptism in the name of Jesus Christ. The baptism of the Spirit is mentioned in the Gospels in a prophetic way, but Acts now actualizes the baptism of the Spirit by the apostles' baptismal practice (8:14–17, 10:44–48). The connection between water baptism and the bestowal of the Spirit does not always appear as successive steps that happen automatically. Finally, baptism in Acts includes gentiles and their conversion (esp. Acts 10), contrary to that of the Gospels (except Matt 28:19, which portrays the baptism of all the nations/gentiles not only εἰς τὸ ὄνομα τοῦ υἱοῦ but also τοῦ πατρός and τοῦ ἁγίου πνεύματος).
41 This refers to the explicit combination of baptism and believers' death with Christ. The dying-and-rising-with-Christ pattern is more widespread and significant throughout the Pauline corpus, as Tannehill demonstrates. Tannehill, *Dying and Rising with Christ*, 1. For example, the notion of believers' unity with the one who died and was raised for them and their reception of soteriological benefits from that unity already appears in Paul's earliest document, i.e., 1 Thessalonians (e.g., 5:9–10). Daniel G. Powers, *Salvation through Participation: An Examination of the Notion of the Believers' Corporate Unity with Christ in Early Christian Soteriology* (Leuven: Peeters, 2001), 35–46 (esp. see 46). Yet, there is no explicit remark about baptism; nor is clearly explained "how" this unity is achieved. Colossians 2:12–13 is largely based on Rom 6, but it differs from the latter: (1) Col 2:12–13 states more clearly that the believers have already been raised and (2) it emphasizes the forgiveness of sins (which does not appear in the baptismal context of Rom 6). Walter T. Wilson, *The Hope of Glory: Education and Exhortation in the Epistle to the Colossians* (Leiden: Brill, 1997), 19.
42 One might think that Paul's connection between baptism and death has its precedent in Jesus's words (Mark 10:38–40). James D. G. Dunn, "'Baptized' as Metaphor," in *Baptism, the New Testament and the Church: Historical and Contemporary Studies in Honor of R. E. O. White*, ed. Stanley Porter and Anthony R. Cross (Sheffield: Sheffield Academic, 1999), 306–7. Since the Gospel of Mark postdates Paul, it is possible that the link between baptism and death found in Rom 6 influenced the words of the Markan Jesus. As Schnackenburg notes, "There is no evidence to show that the interpretation of baptism in terms of dying (and rising) with Christ, as expounded [in Rom 6], was already current in the Church." Yet, he also mentions 1 Cor 15:3–4 as a possible link: "The possibility remains, then, that the baptismal instruction in the primitive Church set the first sacrament in relation to the death of Jesus in a general way only (cf. 1 Cor. xv. 3), while Paul … gave his own interpretation of it in v. 4." Schnackenburg, *Baptism*, 33–34.
43 Dunn has suggested a similar view, that is, Rom 6:3–6 consists of three metaphors intertwined: baptismal, agricultural, and burial. James D. G. Dunn, *Baptism in the Holy Spirit: A Re-examination of the New Testament Teaching on the Gift of the Spirit in Relation to Pentecostalism Today* (London:

es questions about whether (or to what extent) baptism is central to this passage.⁴⁴ Not all questions can be sufficiently addressed here.

Why and how does Paul express a virtually unique notion of baptism as dying/burial with Christ in this passage? Although there have been numerous proposals,⁴⁵ I think that the combination between (believers') baptism and (Christ's)

S.C.M., 1970), 140–42. It is preferable to see the images of burial, planting, and crucifixion as three metaphors, all of which are incorporated into the image of baptism.

44 As mentioned earlier, Tannehill argues that the cross or co-crucifixion with Christ, rather than baptism, is the center of this passage. Tannehill, *Dying and Rising with Christ*, 42–43. In other words, Paul brings a particular understanding of baptism only to support his overall argument and to persuade the audience, rather than focusing on baptism itself. On the contrary, Schnelle maintains that ch. 6 should be read "from the perspective of the baptismal event." Schnelle, *Apostle Paul*, 332, n. 113. Wolter represents a mediating position: "In this passage Paul develops a theology of baptism in order to make clear that the 'once' of life before conversion and the 'now' of Christian existence are separated from each other … On this level, baptism is first of all not the *subject matter* of interpretation but the *medium* of interpretation. However, because only a particular understanding of baptism can take on this function, Paul must then make it the subject matter of interpretation" (italics original). Wolter, *Paul*, 137.

45 As a matter of fact, Jesus of Nazareth did not die through water, i.e., by drowning, and conversely, the baptized do not undergo literal crucifixion, death, and burial the way Jesus did. Thus, as James Dunn points out, "the symbolism of immersion provided no self-evident link" (James D. G. Dunn, *Romans 1–8*, WBC 38 A [Dallas: Word, 1988], 312). See also Bultmann, *Theology of the New Testament*, 1:140. Then, how did this combination come into being? If this connection was not an accident, was there any intrinsic reason to connect the two? Where can one find the religious-historical "background"? Among the prominent examples in the history of interpretation, the top five are noted here: (1) **The Greco-Roman mysteries:** Reitzenstein maintains that this passage, particularly its view on "a voluntary dying and surrendering oneself to death" through baptism, "corresponds fully to Hellenistic mystery conceptions." Reitzenstein, *Hellenistic Mystery-Religions*, 327–28. According to Reitzenstein, the concept of baptism in Rom 6 was obviously part of the world in which Paul and other early Christians lived. This idea, largely shared by the Inaugurated Quest, has been criticized for decades (see Ch. 2); (2) **Christ-mysticism:** Schweitzer claims that this notion of baptism derived from Paul's mysticism based on eschatology rather than the sacramentalism of the mysteries. Schweitzer, *The Mysticism of Paul the Apostle*, 19–20, 227–29. Bousset also used the term "Christ mysticism" with regard to Paul, although Bousset's understanding of the nature of Christ mysticism was different from Schweitzer's in that Bousset understands Paul primarily within the "Hellenistic" religious-historical context. Bousset, *Kyrios Christos*, 153–210. For a recent view similar to Schweitzer's, see Ashton, *The Religion of Paul*, 130–35; (3) **Paul's apocalyptic thought:** see Teresa Kuo-Yu Tsui, "'Baptized into His Death' (Rom 6,3) and 'Clothed with Christ' (Gal 3,27): The Soteriological Meaning of Baptism in Light of Pauline Apocalyptic," *ETL* 88 (2012): 395–417. Similar ideas are found in J. C. Beker's work, although he does not fully explain how Pauline apocalyptic enables the combination of two seemingly discrete images, Christ's death and believers' baptism. J. C. Beker, *Paul the Apostle: The Triumph of God in Life and Thought* (Philadelphia: Fortress, 1984), 83–89, 160–70, 204–208, 287–91; (4) **The Jewish notion of corporate personality/solidarity** found in the OT and rabbinic literature: notably, Wedderburn, "The Soteriology of the Mysteries,"

death in Rom 6:3–4 is indebted to the distinctive baptismal activity implied in 1 Cor 15:29, namely, baptism for the dead among the Corinthians (see the earlier section). The combination between baptism and death, or baptism and burial/funeral, does not easily arise from the way Jesus died nor from contemporary Jewish practice (see Theissen's remarks in footnote 45 of this chapter.). I suggest that 1 Cor 15:29 and the baptismal practice reflected in it can provide a link.[46] Put in the context of Roman Corinth, baptism for the dead in 1 Cor 15:29 can be understood as the conceptual blending between baptismal ritual, mystery initiation, and funerary ritual. It is unlikely that Paul himself invented baptism for the dead or taught it to the Corinthians; but Paul did not criticize or strongly prohibit this practice. Furthermore, the echo of the Corinthian practice in Rom 6:3–4 does not necessarily imply that the Romans also practiced the same type of blended baptism.[47] Yet, the particular combination between baptism and death/burial in Rom 6:3–4 indicates the possibility that Paul may have received insight from observing the practice in Corinth, developed its christological potential, and recontextualized it in his discourse in Rom 6. In short, the distinctive notion of baptism as dying/burying

---

71–72. With different emphasis, see also Peter Stuhlmacher, *Paul's Letter to the Romans: A Commentary*, trans. Scott J. Hafemann (Louisville: Westminster John Knox, 1994), 91, 99. Stuhlmacher regards the Danielic notion of "the Son of Man" who "represents the people of God made up of the 'saints of the Most High'" as a whole" as underlying Paul's view of baptism in Rom 6. Yet, such suggestions do not satisfactorily answer the question why Paul connects the rite of baptism to the notion of corporate-participation into the messianic figure. In fact, Paul's language, especially the ways in which he connects baptism with "burial," may have been offensive to Jewish sensibility, as Theissen points out; it is less likely that such a connection naturally arose from the notion of the OT and other Jewish tradition because the symbolic language of baptism transgresses "jüdische Tabuvorstellungen" in that "[d]ie Identifikation der Taufe mit einem Begräbnis verband sie mit einem Ort der Unreinheit." Theissen, *Die Religion der ersten Christen*, 94; (5) **Rejection of all those options:** Wagner thinks that no such extra effort for religious-historical investigation is needed because the "disciples'" participation in Christ's fate is quite natural. Wagner, *Pauline Baptism*, 293–94. Similarly (but with different reasons), Luke Johnson believes this religious sensibility of "participation" is universal and common to virtually all ages. Luke Timothy Johnson, *Reading Romans: A Literary and Theological Commentary* (New York: Crossroad, 1997), 96. If it is natural for the Jesus followers, or for all people, how does one explain this particular combination between baptism and participation in Christ's death and resurrection found only here in the NT (possibly, Col 2:12)?

46 Similarly, DeMaris, "Corinthian Religion and Baptism," 682.

47 One might suggest that similar ritual blends occurred in Rome (which is possible in principle). One needs to know more about the social and cultural contexts of Rome to make such an assessment (that the Christ devotees in Rome were also blending baptism, mystery initiation, and funeral as some believers in Corinth did). What seems more likely from the extant evidence is that (1) such ritual innovation is found in Corinth and (2) Paul was writing this letter to the Romans from Corinth, knowing and probably reflecting on the ritual practice there.

with Christ in this chapter reflects the embodied experience of Paul's audience, especially ritual experience.

A recent monograph by Kai-Hsuan Chang emphasizes the significance of bodily experience for understanding Paul's resurrection discourse, including 1 Cor 15 and Rom 6. He persuasively demonstrates how the repeated experience of death rites and bodily decomposition are conceptually blended with the sowing metaphor Paul uses in 1 Cor 15, resulting in the bodily transformation that overcomes the problem of cosmic polarity.[48] Yet, this insight does not fully extend to his discussion of the conceptual blending in Rom 6. When Chang talks about the role of bodily experience in Paul's theological construction of believers' participation in Christ's death and burial, it is focused on baptism, not death rites.[49] This happens despite the fact that the death language is pervasive in this chapter of Romans and Chang himself makes connections between 2 Cor 4 and Rom 6 in terms of Paul's sharing in Christ's suffering/dying and life.[50] Extending Chang's argument, I suggest that Paul's blend of believers' baptismal experience and Christ's death-burial-resurrection can be understood better when one also considers the bodily experience of death rites. The Corinthians' ritual blending reflected in 1 Cor 15:29 may have facilitated Paul's development of the particular blend in Rom 6:3–4.

In addition to Paul's development of the blend arising from his Corinthian experience, one can also detect a pre-Pauline layer of baptismal tradition (already known to his Roman audience) in Rom 6 and infer what Paul was doing with that tradition.[51] The grammatical clue within Rom 6:3 suggests the existence of a tradition that Paul uses and modifies.[52] The rhetorical question in the first part of Rom 6:3, with the disclosure formula (ἢ ἀγνοεῖτε ὅτι, ὅσοι ἐβαπτίσθημεν εἰς Χριστὸν Ἰησοῦν), probably indicates common knowledge (thus, pre-Pauline tradition) shared by Paul and his Roman audience,[53] although one cannot be entirely certain

---

48 Chang, *Impact of Bodily Experience*, 41–70.
49 For example, see Figure 5.3 in Chang, *Impact of Bodily Experience*, 125.
50 Chang, *Impact of Bodily Experience*, 107–36.
51 As with Gal 3, it is hard to prove that the possible baptismal tradition in Rom 6, known to Paul's audience, was a baptismal "formula" that was recited during the ritual.
52 Similarly, Wolter, *Paul*, 139.
53 Many scholars hold this view (see the introduction). Also, Tannehill, *Dying and Rising with Christ*, 12–14. For a more nuanced view, Wedderburn, *Baptism and Resurrection*, 37–69; idem, "Hellenistic Christian Tradition in Romans 6?" *NTS* 29 (1983): 337–55. Jewett is more cautious. As he suggests, using examples from classical literature, this phrase could be just a rhetorical question to alert his audience, not necessarily indicating a common tradition. Robert Jewett, *Romans: A Commentary*, Hermeneia (Minneapolis: Fortress, 2007), 396.

of the precise extent of the tradition.[54] At the very least, Rom 6:3 reveals both the existence of tradition and Paul's modification of it; especially the latter part (εἰς τὸν θάνατον αὐτοῦ ἐβαπτίσθημεν) is likely Paul's contribution.[55] Therefore, the phrase ἢ ἀγνοεῖτε ὅτι has a dual function. It indicates common knowledge between Paul and his audience, but it also rhetorically appeals to the audience who may be surprised by Paul's introduction of a new idea (this view follows Jewett's suggestion; see footnote 53 of this chapter.). The content of the tradition actually resonates with the picture of baptismal practices previously reconstructed in the other Pauline passages. As discussed earlier in relation to 1 Corinthians, the phrase "baptism into (εἰς) Christ" was not likely coined by Paul, and it does not necessarily mean a mystic union; rather, it primarily refers to a joining of devotees in a community considered to be "in Christ" (see the discussion of 1 Cor 12 and Gal 3).[56] Yet, in this chapter, Paul redefines baptism *into Christ* as baptism *into Christ's death*.[57] In this way, Paul individualizes as well as adds a mystical interpretation to baptismal tradition. This is an important point for understanding the self-referential

---

[54] Earlier scholarship, as mentioned by Beasley-Murray, finds a "primitive kerygma" and early Christian "liturgy" or "hymn" in Rom 6:3–4, based on the co-occurrence of "died," "(was) buried," and "(was) raised," as in the case of 1 Cor 15:3b–4. Beasley-Murray himself is skeptical: "The difficulty of adopting this view without qualification lies in the absence from the other New Testament writers of this interpretation of baptism as a dying and rising with Christ and the fact that later writers who do mention it depend on Paul." George Raymond Beasley-Murray, *Baptism in the New Testament* (New York: St Martin's Press, 1962), 127. He is correct in pointing out that the explicit connection between this pattern (Christ's death—burial—resurrection) and believers' baptism is unique to Paul, especially Rom 6. Also, the co-occurrence of the three verbs with regard to Christ does not necessarily imply an early Christian "hymn." Yet, I think that this pattern commonly found in Rom 6:3–4 and 1 Cor 15:3b–4 was probably part of the earliest *euangelion*, which Paul also received/learned and then proclaimed to the Corinthians (see Paul's introductory remarks in 1 Cor 15:1–3a). Again, the extent of tradition in and around both passages (Rom 6:3–4 and 1 Cor 15:3b–4) is not easily confirmed (e.g., Are all the appearance accounts in 1 Cor 15:5–8 also part of the same tradition as 15:3b–4? Is 15:8 [leading to 15:9–11] a Pauline addition to the tradition Paul received?).
[55] Dunn, *Romans 1–8*, 312. Thus, *contra* C. E. B. Cranfield: according to Cranfield, it is "highly probable" that both the notion of baptism into Christ and baptism into Christ's death "have belonged to the common primitive Christian teaching (as opposed to being a Pauline contribution)." C. E. B. Cranfield, *A Critical and Exegetical Commentary on the Epistle to the Romans*, vol. 1, ICC (Edinburgh: T&T Clark, 1975), 300. However, the rhetorical force of Paul's words can be fully appreciated when one presupposes a distinction between what the Roman audience knew and what Paul was contributing.
[56] Also, see C. K. Barrett, *The Epistle to the Romans*, rev. ed. (Grand Rapids: Baker Academic, 2011), 114.
[57] Wolter, *Paul*, 139 (also, 129).

messages (benefits for participants) and the canonical messages (grounds for the indicated benefits) of baptism in Rom 6.

In Paul's theological appropriation of baptism, what benefits does baptism provide? Interestingly, this passage does not say that the primary benefit is joining the cult as one body or being cleansed of former sins, both of which were found in Paul's other passages and/or other New Testament passages. Rather, "unity with Christ" is the benefit (or "effect") of baptism in Rom 6.[58] This union between Christ and the Christ-devotee as the explicit benefit or result of baptism found in 6:4–5 can be further delineated in three ways, using Paul's own words: (1) "we were buried with Christ" (συνετάφημεν αὐτῷ)/"we have been united with the likeness of Christ's death" (σύμφυτοι γεγόναμεν τῷ ὁμοιώματι τοῦ θανάτου); (2) "(so that) we may walk/live in the newness of life" (ἐν καινότητι ζωῆς περιπατήσωμεν); and (3) "we will be united with the likeness of Christ's resurrection" ([probably σύμφυτοι τῷ ὁμοιώματι is omitted] τῆς ἀναστάσεως ἐσόμεθα). The first is quite remarkable; baptism in Rom 6 promises one's death, or more precisely, one's co-death/burial with Christ. Even though Paul already expressed the notion of being baptized into Christ/the body of Christ (1 Cor 12; Gal 3), which can be explained by sociology and the body politics in antiquity, being baptized into *Christ's death* is quite startling and new. Death, which most people want to "avert" (Riesebrodt) by practicing various religious rituals, both in Paul's context and elsewhere in human history (even the mysteries never clearly state that initiation offers one's death with the deity), is cast in a positive light in Rom 6. This baptismal death is not the same as one's physical death, but this language creates the symbolic reality in which this particular death is viewed as a positive experience, shaping one's disposition and behavior. Baptism in Rom 6 is presented primarily as a practice of "religious virtuosos."[59] Paul attributes this practice of virtuosity not to a small number of virtuosos, but to all baptized Christ-believers: "as many of us as (ὅσοι) were baptized into Christ" were indeed "baptized into Christ's death." Baptism, which all Christ-believers receive equally, becomes an index of religious virtuosity.

Why is one's participation in Christ's death beneficial? How does this ritual practice, which includes an element that non-virtuosos would avoid (i.e., death), bring about something desirable for the practitioners? The reason for this is found in relation to Paul's mythography in Rom 5, which will be discussed

---

[58] Schnackenburg, *Baptism*, 30.
[59] In reviewing religious virtuosos in various cultures, Riesebrodt notes, "[Virtuosos] intentionally and systematically set conditions for themselves that most mortals try to avoid by religious means. What average laypersons consider a horror, virtuosos voluntarily accept and make the basis of their way of life." Riesebrodt, *The Promise of Salvation*, 122.

below. For now, Paul's discourse suggests that death is crucially related to solving the problem of Sin (note my use of the capitalized Sin).⁶⁰ According to Rom 6, death is necessary to "nullify the body of Sin" (ἵνα καταργηθῇ τὸ σῶμα τῆς ἁμαρτίας, v. 6), and this is based on Paul's underlying presupposition that "one who is dead has been released/justified from Sin" (ὁ γὰρ ἀποθανὼν δεδικαίωται ἀπὸ τῆς ἁμαρτίας, v. 7). The fundamental benefit of baptism for participants (the self-referential message of baptism) can be summarized as gaining release from Sin through one's death—this Sin-breaking death is made possible by one's baptism into Christ's death. The effect of the baptismal death is irreversible and non-repetitive, as Christ has been raised and does not die again (this is one of the canonical messages Paul highlights).⁶¹

The second and third benefits/promises of baptism appear in the same verses (6:4–5). The participants are promised new life. Here, the dilemma or eschatological tension between the present and the future has vexed many interpreters.⁶²

---

60 I treat Sin as a mythic/dramatic persona in Romans. Gaventa notes, "In Romans in particular, sin is Sin—not a lower-case transgression, not even a human disposition or flaw in human nature, but an upper-case Power that enslaves humankind and stands over against God. Here, Sin is among those anti-God powers whose final defeat the resurrection of Jesus Christ inaugurates and guarantees." Beverly Roberts Gaventa, "The Cosmic Power of Sin in Paul's Letter to Romans," *Interpretation* 58 (2004): 231.

61 Anders Klostergaard Petersen, "Shedding New Light on Paul's Understanding of Baptism: A Ritual-Theoretical Approach to Romans 6," *ST* 52 (1998): 19.

62 Regarding this tension, scholars have asked various questions: What was achieved through (or before/after) baptism (coupled with other factors, such as πίστις)? What is still reserved for the future? and What is required as ethical imperatives in the present. Some scholars think that Paul was fighting with "enthusiasts" who operated with an over-realized eschatology. Paul makes his exhortation ("you should present yourselves to God, not Sin") **dependent on the reserved portion of resurrection** (e.g., the exhortation is based on the fact that, although you have already been dead and given new life with Christ, you have not yet attained full resurrection as long as you live in your body). This position is supported by Käsemann, *Romans*, 161; Gerhard Barth, *Die Taufe in frühchristlicher Zeit*, 2nd ed. (Neukirchen-Vluyn: Neukirchener, 2002), 89. J. C. Beker does not use the term "enthusiasts" but notes, "Sacramental realism does not mean an ontological usurpation of premature blessedness ... Paul integrates them [a juridical hermeneutic and a participation hermeneutic] to protect ontology from disintegrating into a realized eschatology and so preserves the apocalyptic perspective of the lordship of Christ." Beker, *Paul the Apostle*, 275. In contrast, other scholars think that Paul bases his exhortation **on the already-happened aspect** (e.g., the exhortation is based on the fact that, although you live in the mortal body, you have already been released from the sphere of Sin and transferred to the Christ-sphere). This view has also been supported by many. For example, Günter Bornkamm, "Baptism and New Life in Paul (Romans 6)," in *Early Christian Experience*, trans. Paul L. Hammer (New York: Harper & Row, 1969), 71–86; Beasley-Murray, *Baptism*, 126–46 (esp. 142–44). See also Wolter, *Paul*, 140, n. 42. Wolter is critical of views that presuppose the existence of "enthusiasts" as Paul's opponents: "[T]

Does one's baptism mean this new life both in the present and the future, or should it be understood that baptism only means the beginning of the renewed life in the present, and therefore, the future resurrection is not directly related to baptism?[63] More questions arise if one takes into account (1) Paul's claim that all believers have died through their baptism into Christ's death and (2) Paul's moral exhortation throughout this chapter. If believers are already dead to Sin through baptism (Rom 6:2, 7, 11) and their transfer to the new sphere and master has already occurred (6:22; note νυνὶ δέ), why are there still existential possibilities of their coming back to and serving Sin? Conversely, if there are such possibilities for whatever reason (e. g., they are still living in an earthly body; the parousia has not come yet, etc.) so that Paul feels it necessary to address this moral exhortation (6:12–14), how can he boldly argue for the already-fulfilled death of believers through baptism and their transfer from Sin to the new sphere/master? How can the death and transfer actually be efficacious? Is the baptismal union with Christ's death and their transference to the new Christ-sphere "real," or merely "metaphorical"?[64] These are the theological (and philosophical) questions that fre-

---

he rhetorical slant of Paul's argument [in Rom 6] makes it perceptible that the point for him is not criticism, but assurance: in v. 5 and v. 8 Paul does not wish to say '*not until* then,' but 'then *also*!" See also Schweitzer's remark (although Schweitzer's overall view is different from Wolter's): "Paul's logic [in Rom 6] is the converse of [the mysteries' thought], and takes the objective form: Christ's death and resurrection is effectively present in us; therefore we are no longer natural men and cannot sin any more." Schweitzer, *Paul and his Interpreters*, 226. Bousset diverges from Schweitzer on many points but holds a position. *Kyrios Christos*, 181.

63 Grammatically, v. 4 takes the subjunctive in the subordinate clause (ἵνα … ἡμεῖς ἐν καινότητι ζωῆς περιπατήσωμεν) and v. 5 takes the future indicative (τῆς ἀναστάσεως ἐσόμεθα). The aorist subjunctive περιπατήσωμεν is usually understood as ingressive, meaning that it marks the (already-started) beginning of an action. Fitzmyer, *Romans*, 434; Cranfield, *Romans*, 305.

64 Interpreters have long been caught in the dichotomy of "reality" and "metaphor/symbol." For example, Wolter highlights the "categorical distinction" between Christ's death and the believer's death through baptism into Christ's death—the former is "real" and the latter is "metaphorical." Wolter, *Paul*, 141–42. By calling it a metaphor, Wolter does not mean that the believer's death with Christ has no real impact on the moral/ethical life of believers; he just highlights the fact that this death is not physical like that of Jesus. He also notes, "[F]or Christians the separation from sin is not still outstanding, but already a reality—and that on the basis of their baptism. Anyone who is baptized no longer has anything to do with sin." Wolter, *Paul*, 138. Some other scholars take Paul's language of baptism into Christ's death as reality. For example, Udo Schnelle comments, "That the εἰς (into) should be understood in terms of an objectively real space is indicated by the parallel formulations εἰς τὸν θάνατον … in 6:3b and 4a and the expression in 6:2, πῶς ἔτι ζήσομεν ἐν αὐτῇ … which presuppose a force field or sphere of influence … effecting the death of the Christian to sin as something that happens in reality (not merely 'in symbol')" (parentheses original). Schnelle, *Apostle Paul*, 329. See also Siikavirta, *Baptism and Cognition*, 108: "[E]xpressions such as ἀπεθάνομεν σὺν Χριστῷ and συζήσομεν αὐτῷ (6:8) are not to be taken as merely ethical or met-

quently appear when interpreting this chapter of Romans,[65] and they are also important for understanding baptism's benefits.

---

aphorical expressions, but as referring to the real death to sin (6:10) that the Christians have experienced by participating in the real death and resurrection of Christ." Yet, what do they mean by "real/realistic"? Luke Johnson notes, "Whatever its roots, Paul's understanding of baptism is *startlingly realistic*; he does not think of ritual in terms of an arbitrary set of signs but rather a symbol that participates in that which it signifies" (italics mine). Johnson, Reading Romans, 96. What Johnson thinks is in fact not a contrast between realistic and unrealistic; rather, he seems to envision a contrast between a *less arbitrary symbol* (immersion into water is somehow seen similarly to being buried because both have downward and upward movements) and a *more arbitrary symbol* (as is the case of any linguistic sign, according to the well-known Saussurian notion of the signifier and the signified). Johnson's remark raises the question: Is the connection between baptism and Jesus's death less arbitrary than other pairs of signifier-signified? (cf. Theissen's argument that there does not necessarily exist a pictorial relationship [anschauliche/ikonische Beziehung] between Jesus's death on the cross/his burial and believers' baptism. Theissen, *Die Religion der ersten Christen*, 184–86). What difference do interpreters make by pitting what's actual/real against what's not (be it figurative, metaphorical, or symbolic, etc.—these terms are not identical, but they often stand together in contrast to what's real/realistic in this matter in the scholarly discussion)? To what extent can this type of claim for realism, as opposed to symbolism and metaphor, be intelligible outside the realm of theological studies? In principle, metaphor is the basic mode of human cognition, rather than a secondary adornment. See George Lakoff and Mark Johnson, *Metaphors We Live By* (Chicago: University of Chicago Press, 1980). Also, Susan E. Hylen, "Metaphor Matters: Violence and Ethics," *CBQ* 73 (2011): 781–84. Someone's identity (or identities) in reality is always intertwined with, shaped by, and articulated through series of metaphors and symbolic structures. If one follows a radical version of constructivism, reality itself can be regarded as invented and constructed by symbols. Paul Watzlawick, *The Invented Reality: How Do We Know What We Believe We Know? Contributions to Constructivism* (New York: Norton, 1984).

65 Recent discussions about the "death of the soul" in Platonic philosophical traditions, especially focusing on Philo, may illuminate this issue in Paul. For example, see Dieter Zeller, "The Life and Death of the Soul in Philo of Alexandria: The Use and Origin of a Metaphor," *SPhiloA* 7 (1995): 19–55 and John T. Conroy, Jr., "Philo's 'Death of the Soul': Is this Only a Metaphor?" *SPhiloA* 23 (2011): 23–40 (but, note that Conroy's article has a similar issue to what I discussed in the previous footnote, i.e., sharply contrasting the metaphorical with the real/ontological). In addition to the Platonic notion, the *topos* of the "living dead" (e.g., due to lack of knowledge or of virtue) seems to have existed more widely (Zeller, "The Life and Death of the Soul," 50–54). Thus, Rom 6 could also be understood in this broader literary-philosophical context, especially in a Platonic context. Reading Romans in this light, Wasserman points out that modern scholars are confused by Paul's language in Rom 6–8 because of their "modern ideas of the self as a more or less unified center of consciousness, experience, and reflection." Emma Wasserman, *The Death of the Soul in Romans 7*, WUNT II/256 (Tübingen: Mohr Siebeck, 2008), 146. Rather, she suggests, "Paul's already statements explain a new form of self-mastery, whereas his not yet statements warn that the lower faculties still threaten" (Wasserman, *Death of the Soul*, 134). Her discussion from the perspective of ancient philosophy explains the apparent tensions in Rom 6 (or Rom 6–8) better than previous theological solutions did, but her appeal to the death-of-the-soul traditions does not fully account for Paul's

Yet, this could be framed better,[66] if one considers how ritual works and what messages ritual conveys. The indexical nature of ritual, which Rappaport theorizes (see ch. 2), is particularly helpful. According to him, for example, the Maring people's dancing at the *kaiko* festival of another group "does not simply symbolize the Maring man's pledge [to fight for that group]. It indicates it."[67] He notes,

> There is surely no intrinsic or causal relationship between dancing and fighting, particularly dancing now and fighting later, but the dance is nevertheless indexical. What it indicates is not fighting in the future, but, rather, a pledge undertaken in the present to fight in the future ... [T]here is no ambiguity or vagueness. To dance is to pledge and that is that.[68]

In Paul's version of baptism in Rom 6, one's participation in baptism in the present *indicates* that person's new life in the present and in the future alike without ambiguity. By combining the Rappaportian ritual theory and the theistic focus of Riesebrodt on the promises of ritual, the theological tension between realized eschatology and reserved eschatology can be resolved, or at least, mitigated: the ritual of baptism in the present indicates both the participants' pledge and the divine pledge, linking the present and future.[69] Alternatively, employing Arnold van Gennep's tripartite phase of initiation (preliminal – liminal – postliminal), Petersen notes, "The Christian is not in baptism resurrected with Christ, but he is following from his incorporation by baptism into a sphere defined by Christ with an inevitable certainty oriented towards the future resurrection with Christ."[70] With either theory, the two different timeframes—the present and the future—merge together in the enactment of baptismal ritual. The past (which is mythically constructed in Rom 5) also merges into this ritual enactment in Rom 6. Paul refers to an actual ritual, although he interprets and appropriates the ritual. How rituals work can illuminate the theological conundrums.

---

distinctive connection between believers' baptism into Christ's death (Rom 6:3) and their death to sin (6:2, 11).

66 Petersen points out that many dead-end dichotomies in the interpretation of baptism in Rom 6 emerged from the Reformation tradition (Petersen, "Shedding New Light," 7), and he suggests that "contemporary scholarship on rituals and their meaning" can overcome such "perceptual filters" ("Shedding New Light," 3).
67 Rappaport, *Ritual and Religion*, 57.
68 Rappaport, *Ritual and Religion*, 57.
69 As discussed in Chapter 2 of this study, the promises/pledges communicated by rituals in Rappaport's theory are promises/pledges made by human beings, while Riesebrodt examines how religious rituals (or "liturgies" in his words) promise divine benefits.
70 Petersen, "Shedding New Light," 16–17.

The indexicality of ritual does not mean that the indicated pledge is always brought successfully into fulfillment. This is also the case in Rom 6. In Rappaport's terms, the indexically transmitted pledge of the ritual can be "violated" (though it cannot be "falsified").[71] The violation, leading to ritual failure, undermines the canonical order that underlies the ritual.[72] According to Rappaport, general descriptions or statements "report autonomously existing states of affairs," while "[p]erformative acts *realize* states of affairs."[73] He continues:

> *The state of affairs is the criterion by which the truth, accuracy or adequacy of a statement is assessed.* In the case of performatives there is an inversion ... *We judge the state of affairs by the degree to which it conforms to the stipulations of the performative act.*[74]

Ritual performance not only actualizes the pre-existing convention that underlies the ritual, but it also creates obligations. Conformity to them or violation of them is crucial to the canonical order. In Paul's representation of baptism in Rom 6, the violation of pledge on the part of Christ or God is not in view (God is faithful and truthful [Rom 3:3–4]); Paul's warning is for possible human violations. This ritual perspective enables one to overcome the dichotomized interpretation, whether one's transfer from the realm of Sin/law into the realm of Christ/grace has been completed through baptism (cf. 6:14, 22) or the person is in "limbo" despite baptism, so that they still need to be cautious not to fall back (cf. 6:12–13). As Paul envisions in this discourse, one's transfer from Sin and obtaining of the newness of life ("state of affairs") appears *as a pledge* indicated by participating in baptism that creates obligations. The transfer of the baptized person is clearly indicated by this performative act (i.e., the transfer is reality), while this "state of affairs" (the baptized person's transfer from Sin to life/grace/God) is judged "by the degree to which [the baptized person] conforms to the stipulations of the performative act."[75] The baptized must present her or his bodily members to God (6:13) for sanctification (ἁγιασμός, 6:19). Through this ritual lens, the alleged

---

[71] Rappaport, *Ritual and Religion*, 108.
[72] A similar point was made by Peter-Ben Smit, "Ritual Failure in Romans 6," *HTS Teologiese Studies/Theological Studies* 72 (2016): 11. "The failure of the ritual to produce its results, for whichever reason, in fact, would also indicate the failure of the narrative into which it initiates people; in other words: if the ritual fails to produce people that are indeed dead to sin and living in newness of life, then the lordship of Christ and ultimately YHWH is denied, or, worse (from Paul's perspective), to be a claim only, without any basis in reality."
[73] Rappaport, *Ritual and Religion*, 132–33.
[74] Italics original. Rappaport, *Ritual and Religion*, 133.
[75] Modifying Rappaport's phrase: Rappaport, *Ritual and Religion*, 133.

tensions between the present and future, or between the "indicative" and "imperative," can be understood in a more organically integrated way.

Paul's use of ἁγιασμός (6:19, 22; cf. 1 Thess 4:3–7) to describe both the benefit of the baptismal ritual and the obligation that it naturally creates suggests that in Romans he envisions the baptized believers with priestly language.[76] Morales correctly points out "the close relationship in Paul's thought between holiness and eternal life."[77] He goes on to argue that "baptism makes possible a life of holiness in the present that leads to eternal life."[78] This "close relationship" needs further clarification. While helpful, Siikavirta's view, which considers ἁγιασμός a category of identity ("God-given status") and cognition in his cognitive-theological terms,[79] should also be explored in ritual terms. Sanctification/holiness (ἁγιασμός) is the benefit (for both the present and the future, leading to "eternal life") indicated by one's ritual participation, and at the same time, this participation is an index for one's acceptance of the canonical order conveyed by this ritual—the order that is imposed upon the private self of a ritual performer.[80] A breach of obligation is considered immoral in all rituals,[81] even more so with baptism in this passage.[82] Paul presents ἁγιασμός as both a promise of baptism (as in 1 Thess 4; cf. 1 Cor 6) and the obligation to which one must conform. If one understands the notion of ἁγιασμός primarily as pertaining to the people/things/spaces/times that are "set aside," as opposed to "profane" (i.e., of common use),[83] the implication of ἁγιασμός

---

[76] This does not mean that Paul strictly regards all Christ-believers in his communities as priests. It is rather likely that Paul, applying a priestly role to himself (e.g., Rom 15:16), considers his gentile converts (collectively) primarily to be sacred offerings to God. Yet, as living human bodies (thus, as consecrated human beings), these converts themselves should live out the life of ἁγιασμός.
[77] Morales, "Baptism and Union with Christ," 164.
[78] Morales, "Baptism and Union with Christ," 161.
[79] Siikavirta, *Baptism and Cognition*, 133–49.
[80] Rappaport, *Ritual and Religion*, 105–106.
[81] Rappaport, *Ritual and Religion*, 132.
[82] The baptized believers' obligation for the life of holiness receives much seriousness and urgency by Paul's juxtaposition of slavery image and cosmic warfare, resonating with what the Greek historian Peter Hunt calls "bidding war model." As for interpretation of Rom 6 focusing on the juxtaposition of slavery metaphor and ancient warfare (including Hunt's theory), see Donghyun Jeong, "God's Hoplites: Slaves and Warfare in Romans 6:12–23," *KJCS* 105 (2017): 47–72. Cf. Peter Hunt, *Slaves, Warfare, and Ideology in the Greek Historians* (New York: Cambridge University Press, 1998), 118. One may also recall how Apuleius uses the language of slavery and of soldiers together in *Metam.* 11 with regard to Isis initiation.
[83] Regarding the difference between the binary of pure/impure and that of holy/profane for ancient Jews, see Matthew Thiessen, *Jesus and the Forces of Death: The Gospels' Portrayal of Ritual Impurity within First-Century Judaism* (Grand Rapids: Baker Academic, 2020), 9–12; also, Fredrik-

in relation to baptism becomes more noticeable.[84] Baptism in Rom 6 grants a kind of consecrated identity to all baptized Christ believers, not only a few priests or virtuosos.[85] This metaphorical expansion of virtuosity would somehow be comparable to the democratized virtuosity of Dionysiac initiates (ritually experienced *mania*), or the "sacerdotisation" of Isis initiates sometimes detected in the Hellenistic and Roman periods.[86]

In summary, the self-referential messages of baptism textualized in Rom 6 are (1) the baptized person's co-death with Christ; (2) her/his gaining new life in the present; (3) her/his conformity to Christ's resurrection in the future; and in addition, (4) ἁγιασμός that is presently realized in/through the bodies of individual initiates—of which the fourth one is also an obligation (i.e., ἁγιασμός *should* be realized) toward the canonical order that sustains the efficacy of the self-referential messages. Now, canonical messages of baptism in Rom 6 need to be further explored.

One common expression of the canonical message of ritual (as seen in the mysteries) is a foundational story for that ritual. If there was tradition about the deity's establishment or direction of the initiation ritual, then one has assurance about the ritual's legitimacy and efficacy. It is true that in other parts of the New Testament, Jesus appears to establish or to order baptism (e.g., Matt 28:19–20) or Jesus himself receives baptism (Mark 1:9–11 and parr.), so that he becomes an archetype of all the baptized (cf. in some tradition, Dionysus undergoes

---

sen, *Paul*, 51. Yet, also see footnote 53 of Chapter 5 on the partial overlap of the two categories (pure/impure and holy/profane) in Paul's letters (e.g., 1 Thess 4).

84 See Käsemann's remark that the term ἁγιασμός is "part of the baptismal vocabulary," linking it to 1 Cor 6:11. Käsemann, *Romans*, 183. On the same page, he also notes that "an originally cultic term has already been taken up by Judaism [and primitive Christianity] into both the ethical and the eschatological sphere of language." For Käsemann, what can be regarded as a distinctive development found in Rom 6 is that "sanctification is described as the daily task of the living out of justification."

85 "Priests" (or "hierocratic elites") and "virtuosos" are not always the same in the sociology of religion. According to the Weberian view, for example, the distinction is prominent in Buddhist tradition. See Stephen Sharot, *A Comparative Sociology of World Religions: Virtuosi, Priests, and Popular Religion* (New York: New York University Press, 2001), 39. Sharot notes, "[t]he virtuosos ... were often concerned with their individual salvation rather than that of the collective. The hierocratic elite, in comparison, sought to organize the religious behavior, soteriological and otherwise, of the masses." In my discussion of the Pauline communities, this distinction is less important. Also, see my earlier discussion about the difficulty of defining priest/priesthood in antiquity, and especially, in relation to the mystery cults.

86 See the summary sections in Chapters 3 and 4.

initiation and becomes an archetype of initiates).[87] Paul never states that Christ or God commanded or established the ritual of baptism (not in Rom 6 or anywhere else in the Pauline corpus), despite presenting this type of foundational story for the Lord's Supper, another significant ritual (1 Cor 11:23–26). In contrast, Paul does not labor to legitimize the ritual of baptism nor explicitly communicate a tradition that he received. Rather, in 1 Cor 1, Paul tries to detach himself from the role of baptizer. He was commissioned to proclaim the gospel, not to baptize. Recourse to the deity's command to practice the ritual cannot be the underlying structure that sustains baptism's efficacy in Rom 6.

Another possible reason for the efficacy of baptism (again drawn from comparative rituals) is that the actual procedure of baptism could have been *intuitively* (within their own cultural contexts) associated with the effect it promises. For example, the link between washing one's external body and obtaining ritual purity (or even cleansing of moral wrongdoings) is one prominent example found both in the Jewish and wider Mediterranean context. Yet, there is insufficient evidence that baptism in the Pauline communities is intuitively linked to the baptizand's participation in Christ's death. There is no indication that baptism provides dramatic/theatrical representation of Christ's death,[88] or at least narration of a formula (e.g., "you are now baptized into Christ's death") during the baptism ritual. One can find a hint that in post-Pauline Christianity (i.e., after Paul's letters, including Romans, obtained their authoritative status), the recitation of the expressions in Rom 6 (with accompanying movement) may have been part of baptismal ritual or at least catechesis before baptism (e.g., Cyril of Jerusalem, *Catechetical Lectures* 3; *Lectures on the Mysteries* 2.4–8).[89] In the ambiguous remark in *Didache* 7.1 ("Having said all these things, baptize ... [ταῦτα πάντα προειπόντες, βαπτίσατε ...])," what does ταῦτα πάντα refer to? Coote argues that the Gospel of Mark, which he identifies as an extended account of Jesus's baptism as well as a baptismal instruction, was narrated during baptism.[90] The claim that Mark was read as part of the actual

---

[87] Regarding Jesus's baptism in Mark, see Theissen's remarks: "Die Taufe Jesu wird zum Urbild der chirstlichen Taufe." *Die Religion der ersten Christen*, 240. According to Theissen, the Gospel of Mark is constructed by the framework of the founding stories about the two new sacraments for Christians: namely, baptism (at the beginning of Mark) and the Eucharist (at the end of Mark). *Die Religion der ersten Christen*, 239.

[88] S. G. F. Brandon, "The Historical Element in Primitive Christianity," *Numen* 2 (1955): 166. See also the summary of J. Leipoldt's and H. Lietzmann's views in Wagner, *Pauline Baptism*, 27–32.

[89] As for the figure of Paul as the mystagogue in the writings of Cyril of Jerusalem, see Benjamin A. Edsall, *The Reception of Paul and Early Christian Initiation: History and Hermeneutics* (Cambridge: Cambridge University Press, 2019), 193–96.

[90] According to Coote's interpretation, the Markan notion of baptism connects death and baptism/rebirth, similar to Rom 6. Robert B. Coote, "The Gospel of Mark: Baptism and Passover Initiation,"

baptismal ritual is far from certain. Also, Cyril of Jerusalem and *Didache* are chronologically later. Whether such practices were already present in Paul's time cannot be shown. Cognitively, there are two possibilities. One is that the "non-sacramental" and "metaphorical" use of baptism already contained connotations of death (meaning "to destroy" or "to perish").[91] The other is the conceptual blending between funerary, initiation, and baptism that occurred in Corinth; such a blending could offer an intuitive ground that baptism can be associated with the desired effect (death and life). The first suggestion (the philological solution) is not convincing, while the second is a good possibility. But even that cannot explain why baptism links the baptized person to *Christ's* death.

Rather than relying on preexisting canonical messages, Paul creates a canonical message of baptism by means of his mythographic activity throughout Romans (esp. in Rom 5–8).[92] One of the central pieces of the myth is the representativeness of Adam and that of Christ vis-à-vis humanity.[93] Petersen correctly asserts, "The

---

in *Worship, Women and War: Essays in Honor of Susan Niditch*, ed. John J. Collins, T. M. Lemos, and Saul M. Olyan (Providence, RI: Brown University, 2015), 63–64, 73.

91 Murphy-O'Connor, "Baptized for the Dead," 534.

92 I use the problematic term "myth" rather than "narrative" or "story" (Richard Hays prefers narrative/story), because I want to highlight its intersection with ritual. In his Emory dissertation four decades ago, Hays pointed out at least five problems arising from using the term myth or mythic structure in the study of the Pauline letters (Richard B. Hays, *The Faith of Jesus Christ: The Narrative Substructure of Galatians 3:1–4:11* [Grand Rapids: Eerdmans, 2002], 15–18). He prefers to speak of the single foundational "story." The term myth is multivalent and perhaps of little use for an analytical tool, because of its polemical connotations in the history of Christianity. Nevertheless, by using the term, we can see more clearly what Paul does in terms of ritual practices among early Christ-believing communities, and in terms of social-communal dynamics. Paul did not live solely as a theological exegete who created early Christian midrash out of Jewish Scripture in the light of the foundational story of Jesus Christ's faithfulness. Rather, he lived as a community builder, a cult founder (with others), and mythographer/interpreter of rituals, who negotiated the boundaries and meanings of practices that were used and developing in various regions.

93 The definition of myth is complicated and elusive. Some NT interpreters avoid the term because of its negative (especially, pejorative) connotation. But speaking of the NT as mythical or as containing myth does not necessarily mean that it is false. Rather, "[The New Testament's] language and stories [are] true in the sense that they create meaning for their adherents." Steven J. Kraftchick, "Recast, Reclaim, Reject: Myth and Validity," in *Myth and Scripture: Contemporary Perspectives on Religion, Language, and Imagination*, ed. Dexter E. Callender (Atlanta: SBL, 2014), 181. Kraftchick correctly notes, "[T]he New Testament does employ myths and is itself mythical," and he clarifies the claim in two ways (Kraftchick, "Recast, Reclaim, Reject," 180–81): "First, the New Testament writers (like the Hebrew Bible writers before them) used elements of cultural and religious myths drawn from their social and intellectual environment in order to define their own nascent community's beliefs and to distinguish those beliefs from those of competing religious/philosophical groups. Second, the New Testament invokes and assumes a larger enveloping story of the origin

contrast of Adam and Christ (distinctly expressed in the typologies of Rom 5:12–21 and 1 Cor 15) can be apprehended as the fundamental narrative structure structuring all other components of the Pauline theology."[94] The analogy (and contrast[95]) between Adam and Christ cannot directly explain how baptism achieves the promised benefit. Yet, intense verbal links between Rom 5 and Rom 6 increase the possibility that the mythic narrative of Adam and Christ is part of the canonical messages that are actualized and conveyed by participation in baptism, according to what Paul envisions in the text of Romans.[96] As Petersen argues, "In baptism a linkage is established between the individual believer and the founding story."[97]

Paul's use of ὁμοίωμα (6:5) deserves particular attention since it is key to understanding the connection between Rom 5 and 6 and how it relates to baptism.[98] In the LXX, ὁμοίωμα sometimes has sacramental connotations when it relates to divine-human contact and communication. This dimension of meaning is often implied by Paul's use of the term ὁμοίωμα.[99] Three different meanings of ὁμοίωμα in

---

of the world, its current conditions, the place of humans in that world, and the relationship of those humans and that world to unseen otherwordly powers and beings."

94 Petersen, "Shedding New Light," 10. Petersen's claim, though exaggerated, is basically true.

95 Note Cranfield's emphasis on how Rom 5:12–21 highlights "the vast dissimilarity" (thus, not the similarity) between Adam and Christ. He pays attention to the fact that Paul suddenly breaks the sentence about the Adam-Christ parallel in v. 12 (its apodosis only appears in v. 18) and rather goes into detail about how Adam and Christ differ. Cranfield, *Romans*, 270. See also Otfried Hofius, "The Adam-Christ Antithesis and the Law: Reflections on Romans 5:12–21," in *Paul and the Mosaic Law*, ed. James D. G. Dunn (Grand Rapids: Eerdmans, 2001), 165–205.

96 Comparing Rom 5:12–21 and Rom 6:1–14 (or including the rest of Rom 5 and 6), there are several points of verbal correspondence, such as words related to reigning/ruling (βασιλεύειν in 5:14, 17 [2x], 21 [2x], 6:12; κυριεύειν in 6:9, 14) and obeying (ὑπακούειν in 6:12 [cf. 6:16, 17], ὑπακοή in 5:19 [cf. 6:16–2x] / cf. disobeying in 5:19), particular abstract nouns that may or may not be personified (ἁμαρτία in 5:12 [2x], 13 [2x], 20, 21, 6:1, 2, 6 [2x], 7, 10, 11, 12, 13, 14 [cf. 6:16, 17, 18, 20, 22, 23] θάνατος in 5:12 [2x], 14, 17, 21, 6:3, 4, 5, 9 [cf. 5:10; 6:16, 21, 23]) and their cognates (ἀποθνῄσκειν in 5:15, 6:2, 7, 8, 9, 10 [2x] [cf. 5:6, 7–2x, 8]; ἁμαρτάνειν in 5:12, 14, 16 [cf. 6:15, 18]). Also found in both passages are other abstract nouns that are contrasted with them (ζωή, ζῆν, δικαι-word group, χαριτ-word group) and the causal link between one and all/many (εἷς ἄνθρωπος brings far-reaching results toward πάντας ἀνθρώπους or πολλούς; whoever/as many of us ... and Christ [=one person], etc).

97 Petersen, "Shedding New Light," 22.

98 For a history of interpretation of the term ὁμοίωμα in Rom 6:5 (e.g., a corresponding reality, a form, or a representation of Christ's death), see the survey in Sorin Sabou, "A Note on Romans 6:5: The Representation (ΟΜΟΙΩΜΑ) of His Death," *TynBul* 55 (2004): 219–29. Sabou argues that ὁμοίωμα means "representation"—i.e., "a 'representation' of Christ's death and resurrection" by "the proclamation of the gospel." Sabou, "A Note on Romans 6:5," 229. One does not have to limit the meaning of ὁμοίωμα in Rom 6:5 to the gospel proclamation.

99 Paul's awareness of the Septuagintal use of ὁμοίωμα can be clearly seen in Rom 1:23, where Paul alludes to Ps 105:20 LXX (=106:20 MT), so this search for a tradition-historical background

the LXX can be distinguished: one negative, one positive, one more neutral and mundane.[100] I focus on the first two, both of which are related to the divine/human relationship (one is a false relationship and the other is true). The negative use of ὁμοίωμα is related to idolatry especially, and the positive use of ὁμοίωμα is found in the context of theophany or mystic-visionary experience, mostly in Ezekiel.

The negative use of ὁμοίωμα refers to passages in which the true God has no visible representation (ὁμοίωμα) and, thus, any ὁμοίωμα amounts to an idol (εἴδωλον) and a false attempt to encounter the divine. This negative use is found in Exod 20:4, Deut 4:12, 15, 16 (2x), 17 (2x), 18 (2x), 23, 25; 5:8; 1 Sam 6:5; 1 Macc 3:48; Ps 105:20 LXX (106:20 MT); Sir 34:3 (a bit different here); and Isa 40:18, 19. In the LXX, Exod 20:4 reads (ὁμοίωμα is in apposition to an idol): "You shall not make for yourself an idol or a likeness (ὁμοίωμα) of anything." Also, Deut 4:12 reads (God has no ὁμοίωμα): "And the LORD spoke to you from the midst of fire and you heard the sound of the words but did not see his likeness/representation (ὁμοίωμα)—but only a sound."

In contrast, the word ὁμοίωμα is often used positively to describe a theophany or other visionary experiences in a way that avoids a direct description of the divine beings, including God. Despite the claim that the true God cannot be compared to any ὁμοίωμα (e.g., Isa 40:18), other authors can actually speak of a certain ὁμοίωμα of God with reverence. This use is characteristically found in Ezekiel—1:5 (2x), 16, 22, 26 (3x), 28; 8:2, 3; 10:1, 8, 10, 21, but it also appears in Dan 3:92 LXX. In some sense, ὁμοίωμα represents a space of constant mimicking and negotiation between sameness and difference[101]—*almost the same but not quite* (to borrow Homi Bhabha's expression).[102]

Ὁμοίωμα in the context of baptism in Rom 6:5 (along with Rom 8:3 and Phil 2:7) is best understood in light of the positive, theophanic usage in the LXX. One should interpret this ὁμοίωμα as part of Paul's theological grammar for the divine-human encounter in baptism rather than trying to find a one-word referent of ὁμοίωμα,

---

is not far-fetched. Yet, in addition to (or rather than) Ps 105:20 LXX, Gen 1:20–26 (and perhaps 3:1–7) lies behind Rom 1:22–23 (this was suggested by Hyldahl and Jervell in the mid-twentieth century). See John R. Levison, "Adam and Eve in Romans 1.18–25 and the Greek *Life of Adam and Eve*," *NTS* 50 (2004): 523–25. Possibly, both LXX passages are in view.

100 In this final case, ὁμοίωμα means something like a "copy" (Josh 22:28; Judg 8:18; 2 Kgs 16:10; 2 Chr 4:3; Ps 143:12 LXX; Song 1:11; Sir 38:28; Ezek 23:15).

101 Wolter emphasizes that difference/distinction is always there in the language of ὁμοίωμα, especially in Paul's usage of that word. Wolter, *Paul*, 142.

102 Homi K. Bhabha, *The Location of Culture* (London; New York: Routledge, 2004), 128.

such as death, baptism, the body of Christ.[103] This does not mean that Paul is operating only at the level of theological abstraction; rather, his usage of the term is rooted in the ritual reality of early Christ groups. As Betz points out, ὁμοίωμα is an apt reference for the baptismal ritual that differs from other pagan rituals in that "no cult image (εἰκών) is used and no dramatic episodes (μιμήματα) are performed."[104] Paul appropriates the malleable word ὁμοίωμα and recasts or reformulates its theophanic nuance in the ritual context of Rom 6:5 according to his Christology.

The New Testament has six occurrences of ὁμοίωμα, and five of them are in Paul's letters (Rom 1:23, 5:14, 6:5, 8:3; Phil 2:7; cf. Rev 9:7). Among the five occurrences, only Rom 1:23 clearly reflects the negative use related to idolatry, especially alluding to Ps 105 LXX. Its use in Rom 8:3 and Phil 2:7 could be the theophanic usage in the LXX (here, a kind of Christophany), although there is a twist. The use of ὁμοίωμα in relation to Christ's revealing himself to humanity does not function to avoid a direct description of the unapproachable divinity. See the passages below:

> Ezek 1:28 ὡς ὅρασις τόξου, ὅταν ᾖ ἐν τῇ νεφέλῃ ἐν ἡμέρᾳ ὑετοῦ, οὕτως ἡ στάσις τοῦ φέγγους κυκλόθεν. αὕτη ἡ ὅρασις **ὁμοιώματος δόξης κυρίου**· καὶ εἶδον καὶ πίπτω ἐπὶ πρόσωπόν μου καὶ ἤκουσα φωνὴν λαλοῦντος.
>
> Ezek 8:2 καὶ εἶδον καὶ ἰδοὺ **ὁμοίωμα ἀνδρός**, ἀπὸ τῆς ὀσφύος αὐτοῦ καὶ ἕως κάτω πῦρ, καὶ ἀπὸ τῆς ὀσφύος αὐτοῦ ὑπεράνω ὡς ὅρασις ἠλέκτρου.
>
> Rom 8:3 ... ὁ θεὸς τὸν ἑαυτοῦ υἱὸν πέμψας ἐν **ὁμοιώματι σαρκὸς ἁμαρτίας** καὶ περὶ ἁμαρτίας κατέκρινεν τὴν ἁμαρτίαν ἐν τῇ σαρκί
>
> Phil 2:7 ἀλλ' ἑαυτὸν ἐκένωσεν μορφὴν δούλου λαβών, ἐν **ὁμοιώματι ἀνθρώπων** γενόμενος· καὶ σχήματι εὑρεθεὶς ὡς ἄνθρωπος

Ezekiel 1:28 is typical of this ὁμοίωμα usage in Ezekiel. To avoid speaking of "the glory of the Lord" directly, the visionary qualifies his experience: what he saw was "a likeness of the glory of the Lord." In Ezek 8:2, in which he saw "a likeness of (or, someone like) a man," the divine figure's body is extraordinary in that it appears like "fire" and "electron" (ἤλεκτρον; perhaps, pale gold). None of the six NT occurrences of ὁμοίωμα precisely corresponds to this Ezekiel usage. If the concept is flexibly considered and Christophany is included, then Rom 8:3 and Phil 2:7 count as examples. The word ὁμοίωμα occurs in these verses in the context of Christ's becoming like a human being in reference to his *sarkic* nature and

---

[103] For various proposals, see Dunn, *Romans 1–8*, 316–18.
[104] Betz, "Transferring a Ritual," 115.

death of crucifixion.¹⁰⁵ In terms of its overall pattern, the use of ὁμοίωμα in Rom 8:3 and Phil 2:7 can be taken as a variation of the positive usage of the word in the LXX, which depicts the moment of theophany, or an extraordinary tangent of divine-human encounter.¹⁰⁶ It can retain the gap between the divine and the human, while at the same time expressing the possibility that it is overcome by the revelatory moment. All this helps one understand the meaning of ὁμοίωμα in Rom 6:5.

By applying his theological grammar (ὁμοίωμα) to the discussion of baptism in Rom 6:5, Paul suggests that the ritual of baptism provides a divine-human encounter—this is the canonical message Paul freshly attaches to baptism. Rather than other means, such as a cultic image or dramatic episodes that correspond to the divine reality, the word ὁμοίωμα effectively represents the nature of this aniconic ritual that still "makes mythic realities present in symbolic fashion."¹⁰⁷ What is distinctive about this divine-human encounter in baptism is that this ritual as ὁμοίωμα does not lead the candidate to a glorious theophany (unlike Ezekiel), but into Christ's death (τῷ ὁμοιώματι τοῦ θανάτου αὐτοῦ),¹⁰⁸ and thus, Christ's faithful

---

[105] Paul's words (Christ was sent ἐν ὁμοιώματι σαρκὸς ἁμαρτίας) do not mean that he had a docetic view. Fitzmyer, *Romans*, 485. It could mean either (1) Paul's distinction between Christ and other human beings in terms of Sin/sins, or (2) the idea that Jesus was more than merely a sarkic man ("He never ceased to be the eternal Son of God") even though he assumed the sarkic nature of human beings (cf. Gal 4:4). For the former, see Stuhlmacher, *Romans*, 119; for the latter, see Cranfield, *Romans*, 381–82. As widely recognized, docetism as a historical phenomenon is hard to define (there may not have been a unified docetism), and its pejorative use in the history of Christianity has contributed to the difficulty of its fair use in scholarly discourses. A recent study emphasizes that the "core of docetism" is found in the "rejection of Jesus's passion of the cross." Goldstein and Stroumsa note, "In all probability, the original core of Docetism did not lie in its Platonic elements, which became apparent only at later stages, but in the rejection of Jesus's passion on the cross, 'stumbling block (σκάνδαλον) to Jews and foolishness to gentiles', to use Paul's terms (1 Cor 1,24)." Ronnie Goldstein and Guy G. Stroumsa, "The Greek and Jewish Origins of Docetism: A New Proposal," *ZAC* 10 (2006): 425. Even if Paul's use of ὁμοίωμα might continue to cause some difficulties, it is relatively obvious that Paul himself emphasizes the message of Christ's cross and its scandalous nature, rather than rejecting such ideas.
[106] Given Paul's Jewishness, this LXX connotation is probably what he primarily had in mind when he adopted this expression. It is possible that various people in the Mediterranean world found further resonance with other "metamorphic myths," especially the use of γίνομαι along with ὁμοίωμα. See Paul A. Holloway, *Philippians: A Commentary.* Hermeneia (Minneapolis: Fortress, 2017), 121–24.
[107] Betz, "Transferring a Ritual," 115.
[108] As for resurrection (6:5b), τῷ ὁμοιώματι is omitted probably to avoid repetition, rather than the phrase only applying to death (6:5a). Dunn, *Romans 1–8*, 318; Jewett, *Romans*, 401; Fitzmyer, *Romans*, 435; Hultgren, *Romans*, 248.

obedience demonstrated through his death (cf. Rom 5:19; Phil 2:8).[109] In part, this use of ὁμοίωμα in a divine/human mimetic context also resonates with the philosophical tradition of "becoming like (a) god/likeness to (a) god" (*homoiōsis theōi*, ὁμοίωσις θεῷ).[110] In Plato, *homoiōsis theōi* is for human beings "to become righteous and holy and wise" (δίκαιον καὶ ὅσιον μετὰ φρονήσεως γενέσθαι, *Theaet.* 176A–B), which means their escape (φυγή) from the earthly dwelling. The same might be true with Paul, but for him, this ὁμοίωσις/ὁμοίωμα is understood primarily as a divine initiative. Christ was sent in the likeness of flesh of Sin (Rom 8:3; cf. Phil 2:7), and then believers are united with Christ in the ὁμοίωμα of his death and will be in the ὁμοίωμα of his resurrection (Rom 6:5). Even when Paul says in an earlier verse that believers were baptized into Christ's death (6:3), the difference or the gap between Christ's death in the past and believers' baptismal death still remains.[111] At the same time, it is overcome by the enactment of this ritual that communicates the canonical message of ὁμοίωμα that is rooted in the divine-human encounter tradition.

In summary, drawing primarily on the revelatory tradition of Scripture and echoing some philosophical reflections,[112] Paul in Rom 6 reconfigures baptism as a revelatory space in which the divine-human encounter is actualized. The two different horizons of spatiality (divine/human) and three different horizons of temporality (past-present-future) are fused. Upon this canonical foundation (which Paul creates), the self-referential benefits of baptism are eventually guaranteed. This en-

---

109 Note that Paul's remarks about Christ's own obedience (ὑπακοή) only appear in the two passages (Rom 5–6 and Phil 2), in which ὁμοίωμα occurs.
110 Regarding Paul's use of *pistis Christou* in light of the tradition of *homoiōsis theōi*, see Sierksma-Agteres, "Imitation in Faith," 119–53. She understands *pistis Christou* as "a mimetic movement of faith(fulness) via Christ towards God." It can also be noted that the notion of *homoiōsis theōi* later became the *telos* of Middle Platonism. See a helpful summary in John Dillon, *The Middle Platonists, 80 B.C. to A.D. 220*, 2nd ed. (Ithaca: Cornell University Press, 1996), 43–44 (more discussions: 122–23 [Eudorus], 145–46 [Philo], 299–300 [Albinus]).
111 Wolter, *Paul*, 141–42.
112 Elsewhere, Plato discusses ὁμοίωμα in relation to mystery initiation (*Phaedr.* 250). One must not assume that Paul knew Plato's work or that Paul was a professional Platonic philosopher. Some familiarity with Plato could have been part of the common/intellectual matrix in which Paul lived, especially in Jewish exegetical traditions. This influence of Platonizing Jewish exegetical traditions regarding the "likeness to God" (or the imitation of God") can also be found in the deutero-Pauline letters. See, for example, Gregory E. Sterling, "*Imitatio Dei* (Eph 5:1–2): The Soteriological Basis for Ethics," *Sōtēria: Salvation in Early Christianity and Antiquity*, 345–60 (Sterling does not argue that Ephesians is directly dependent on Philo).

counter is the foundation that enables the baptized person to participate in (or "become like") Christ—i.e., dying and rising with Christ through baptism.[113]

One more theological question should be addressed: Why is the believer's ὁμοίωμα with Christ's *death* through baptism necessary? Why do believers not participate directly in the ὁμοίωμα of Christ's glory, similar to the Ezekiel accounts, or in the ὁμοίωσις of divinity escaping earthly constraints as in Platonic tradition? To answer these questions, one needs to consider another occurrence of ὁμοίωμα in Paul's mythographic activity in Rom 5. In this chapter, Paul views everyone after Moses (yet, death ruled even before Moses) under the power of death *due to their participation in the ὁμοίωμα of Adam's transgression*. This remark metaleptically evokes the figure of Adam in Genesis who was created according to the divine ὁμοίωσις (Gen 1:26 LXX [Hebrew cog. דמות]).[114] A new conformity, a new ὁμοίωσις θεῷ through ὁμοίωμα with Christ's death is needed for them to overcome the universal problem resulting from Adam's transgression and to be freed from death—baptism in Rom 6 appears on the basis of that necessity. Although its fullest form appears in Rom 5, the contrast between (a) Adam and Adam-like humanity and (b) Christ and Christ-like humanity was foreshadowed in Rom 1, and it also resonates with 1 Cor 15.[115] Paul's ὁμοίωμα in Rom 5–6 does double-duty: (1) it represents the revelatory function of the baptismal ritual that enables the divine-human encounter, and (2) it also highlights what baptism can mean in relation to the universal human problem (i.e., death, which Paul traces back to Adam, his transgression, and Adamic humanity).[116]

---

113 Regardless of Paul's intention or the existence of direct cultural influence on him, the way in which he presents baptism in Rom 6 shows a certain commonality with that of mystery initiation, especially in terms of this type of ritual's power to create a divine/human bond to the extent that the deity and the devotee co-mingle. Paul speaks of ὁμοίωμα despite the difference between the way Jesus died and believers' ritual death in baptism. This is not a problem because ὁμοίωμα in Paul is a malleable theological concept that can resolve qualitative differences.
114 As for the notion of metalepsis in literary theory and its use in discussing scriptural intertextuality in the NT, see Hays, *Echoes of Scripture*, 20–21, 23.
115 Levison notes, "On the basis of these analogies between the men of dust and of heaven [in 1 Cor 15:47–49], Paul extrapolates the same contrast between immortal and mortal that characterizes Rom 1.23 ... This developed contrast in 1 Cor 15 provides an interpretive key to the more compact contrast in Rom 1.23, where the glory of the immortal God is exchanged for the likeness of the image of (the) mortal human. In 1 Cor 15 and Rom 1 alike, then, Paul has reached much the same goal: he has deftly related Adam to his progeny, the mortal human to those who bear his image, who share his likeness." Levison, "Adam and Eve in Romans 1.18–25," 525.
116 The Greek *Life of Adam and Eve* (LAE; also called "Apocalypse of Moses") and its retelling of the Genesis story are helpful for understanding Rom 1, as discussed in detail in Levison, "Adam and Eve in Romans 1.18–25," 519–34. Such a close relationship could be contested, especially because of different views about the date of composition, and whether it was a Jewish or Christian

The complex theological reasoning behind the Adam-Christ typological myth (Rom 5) and its relation to the ritual of the present community (Rom 6) is not explicitly stated in Paul's text and requires unraveling. In Rom 5:14, Paul uses the word ὁμοίωμα in the context of universal death. Romans 5:14 describes the universal power of death ruling over even those who did not sin in the likeness (ὁμοίωμα) of Adam's transgression between the time of Adam and Moses (cf. LAE [Gk.] 14.2–3).[117] Implied is the idea that after Moses and the law, death ruled over those who actually sinned in the likeness of Adam's transgression, which includes everyone (5:12). Paul's theological reasoning in 5:12–21, including unstated assumptions, can be displayed as follows:

A. From Adam to Moses:
 - There was indeed ἁμαρτία (it had already entered the world through Adam), but people's ἁμαρτία did not count because there was no νόμος (v. 13). (Therefore, no παράβασις [transgression] existed yet except for Adam's transgression.)
 - Yet, through ἁμαρτία, θάνατος also entered[118] and ruled universally—even over those who did not sin in the ὁμοίωμα of Adam's transgression (vv. 12, 14).

B. From Moses onward:
 - Due to the coming of the νόμος, people's ἁμαρτία began to count (vv. 13, 20). Implied is that the word παράβασις gains actual meaning (because the νόμος can be transgressed).
 - θάνατος still ruled universally. Whenever people transgressed (and it is the case with all people), it was regarded as the ὁμοίωμα of Adam's transgression (this is implied in vv. 14 and 20).

C. From Christ onward:
 - The universally negative effect of one man's action is reversed by the universally salvific effect of another man's action (vv. 18–19), whose benefits surpass the effect of the former (vv. 15–17).
 - In order to overcome the universal reign of θάνατος, the ὁμοίωμα of Adam's transgression must be replaced.
 - Participation in baptism means the enactment of one's new ὁμοίωμα of Christ's θάνατος in the present (6:3–4); over this Christ, θάνατος no longer reigns (6:9). Those who were baptized into Christ's θάνατος are not under

---

work (Levison also does not argue that Paul drew on the precise form of the extant LAE). The following discussion of Rom 5–6 does not engage (much) or rely on the Adam tradition in LAE.
117 Levison, "Adam and Eve in Romans 1.18–25," 527 n. 23; 534.
118 Paul differs from Wis 2:24, which says, φθόνῳ δὲ διαβόλου θάνατος εἰσῆλθεν εἰς τὸν κόσμον ("through the devil's envy death entered the world," NRSV).

νόμος (6:14), and they are freed from ἁμαρτία (6:2, 7, 11) and (by extension) from θάνατος (6:23).

The period of Christ does not correspond symmetrically to that of Adam prior to Moses, but it presupposes (and reflects) the change made from Moses onward. Before Moses, all died regardless of their ὁμοίωμα of Adam's transgression, but after the arrival of the νόμος, ἁμαρτία began to count as "transgression." This change implies that people began to transgress the νόμος as Adam transgressed God's command (thus, they sin in the ὁμοίωμα of Adam's transgression). The solution to the problem of the ἁμαρτία/θάνατος cluster should also address this ὁμοίωμα, which is what Paul suggests in Rom 6. The promise of renewed life and future resurrection given to believers is only made possible by their being planted/united with the ὁμοίωμα of Christ's death through baptism (6:5).[119] Christ died on the cross, was raised, and dies no more; therefore, θάνατος no longer rules over him (6:9), which is the canonical message Paul presents. In the ritually enacted death, the same pattern is also appropriated by the baptized people as the self-referential message (6:8–11). Even though they do not die in the same manner as Jesus did (crucifixion), the old self (ὁ παλαιὸς ... ἄνθρωπος) has been in effect crucified in the ὁμοίωμα of Christ's death through baptism (6:6).[120] Consequently, the universal effect of the ἁμαρτία/θάνατος forces on them is over: they are dead to ἁμαρτία and alive to God (6:11), and they will live with Christ as they died with Christ (6:8).[121]

---

[119] See Theissen's remarks about this "limited" universality of Christ (as opposed to Adam's universality): "Aber diese Universalität ist de facto eingeschränkt." Theissen, *Die Religion der ersten Christen*, 309. According to Theissen, this "limited" universality of the new redemption in Christ led Paul to struggle with the question of Israel's future (Rom 9–11).

[120] The term "our old man" (ὁ παλαιὸς ἡμῶν ἄνθρωπος), as well as "the body of Sin" (τὸ σῶμα τῆς ἁμαρτίας) could be understood collectively. According to Tannehill, these terms mean "the old dominion as a corporate entity." Thus, "the destruction of the 'old man' in the cross of Christ meant the death of the believers as men [sic] of the old aeon." Tannehill, *Dying and Rising with Christ*, 30. I tend to agree with this, but considering the context of baptism, Paul's words still give prominence to the realization of this apocalyptic destruction of the "old aeon" at the individual level (thus, *pace* Tannehill: "Paul is not speaking of the death of individual believers one by one," 30).

[121] Romans 6:7 is connected to 6:6 with the conjunction γάρ (ὁ γὰρ ἀποθανὼν δεδικαίωται ἀπὸ τῆς ἁμαρτίας), seemingly providing the rationale of 6:6. The precise meaning and function of 6:7 is not easy to explain, partly because the phrase (δεδικαίωται ἀπὸ τῆς ἁμαρτίας) is not characteristic of Paul (Dunn, *Romans 1–8*, 320) and because of its generic tone that may not fully correspond to the particular meaning of death (i.e., Christ's death and the believers' death with Christ). Perhaps it is a "gnomic saying" adopted by Paul for the present discourse. Jewett, *Romans*, 404–5. One peculiar interpretation of 6:7 is to take ὁ ἀποθανών as referring to Christ. This is Conleth Kearn's interpretation in his short study, which is mentioned in a footnote in Jewett's commentary, but immediately

Romans 6 recasts the cosmic myth of Rom 5, including Paul's reading of Genesis, in ritual terms. The universal problem of Sin and death resulting from Adam's transgression extending to all who transgress in the ὁμοίωμα of Adam's transgression (since Moses) has now been resolved in Christ (5:12–21; the fulfillment is in the future tense [5:19] or subjunctive mood [5:21]) and in the lives of those who participate in the ὁμοίωμα of Christ's death through baptism (Rom 6). To put it differently, Paul's canonical message is that baptism replaces one type of ὁμοίωμα (Adamic) with another type of ὁμοίωμα (Christ-like), so that the ritual participants can be assured of the self-referential messages' success. The effectiveness of this mythic unity or identification—between Adam or Christ and the baptism candidate—relies on the performative force of the ritual.[122]

---

rejected (Jewett, *Romans*, 404, n. 147). Conleth Kearns, "The Interpretation of Romans 6,7," in *Studiorum Paulinorum Congressus Internationalis Catholicus 1961: simul Secundus Congressus Internationalis Catholicus de Re Biblica. Completo undevicesimo saeculo post S. Pauli in urbem adventum*, vol. 1 (Romae: E Pontificio Instituto Biblico, 1963), 303–307. At first, Kearns's suggestion would make little sense (e. g., why does Christ have to be "released/justified from sin"?), but his observation is worth considering—that is, this article + aorist participle phrase (ὁ ἀποθανών; in various grammatical cases) appears four times in the NT, including Rom 6:7, and the other three clearly refer to Christ (Rom 8:34; 2 Cor 5:15; 1 Thess 5:9–10; Kearns, "The Interpretation of Romans 6,7," 304). His view that Rom 6:7 is "an echo of a baptismal creed" ("The Interpretation of Romans 6,7," 305) is hard to prove, despite other alleged NT parallels he adduces concerning baptismal liturgy. Yet, it is possible that Paul applies Rom 6:7 to both Christ and Christ-devotees ("The Interpretation of Romans 6,7," 307). Tannehill's view on ὁ παλαιὸς ἡμῶν ἄνθρωπος (6:6) as the corporate entity of the old aeon is one option for revising Kearns's insight. Tannehill notes, "In 5 $_{12-21}$ Adam and Christ are contrasted. In 6 $_6$ the 'old man' is crucified with Christ, which implies that Christ is related to this 'old man.' Indeed, the fact that the 'old man' and the 'body of sin' are destroyed in Christ's crucifixion seems to imply that Christ is the bearer of this inclusive reality of the old aeon." Tannehill, *Dying and Rising with Christ*, 27. Possibly, ὁ ἀποθανών in 6:7 refers back to ὁ παλαιὸς ἄνθρωπος, i. e., Christ as "the bearer of this inclusive reality of the old aeon." Tannehill himself does not proceed to argue that way. Yet, his corporate and apocalyptic reading of ὁ παλαιὸς ἄνθρωπος somehow resonates with Kearn's reading of ὁ ἀποθανών (6:7) as Christ.

122 Sellin explains that myth itself enables "deep identity" (Tiefenidentität) between discrete people and events. Myth also promotes corporate/typological thinking and connects different spaces and times in the here-and-now. Gerhard Sellin, "Mythologeme und mythische Züge in der paulinischen Theologie," *Mythos und Rationalität*, ed. Hans Heinrich Schmid (Gütersloh: Gütersloher Verlagshaus G. Mohn, 1988), 209–23 (esp. 210–15). Sellin's idea about the power of myth is partly related to an understanding of myth as a kind of "speech act." He notes, "Man kann sagen: Der Mythos ist ein Sprechakt, in dem sich der semantische Gehalt selber pragmatisch verwirklicht" (Sellin, "Mythologeme und mythische Züge," 214). If so, his explanation of myth presupposes the activation of myth by the performance of narration, which is, in some sense, a ritual. Geertz observes: "In a ritual, the world as lived and the world as imagined, fused under the agency of a single set of symbolic forms, turn out to be the same world." Clifford Geertz, "Religion as a Cultural System," in *The Interpretation of Cultures*, 3rd ed. (New York: Basic Books, 2017 [1973]), 121.

This whole scheme does not necessarily require a precise precedent from the mystery cults (Wagner and Wedderburn were correct in this regard); Jewish writings may better explain where Paul draws particular ideas and words/phrases (e.g., the previous discussion of the LXX). Yet, Paul writes about ritual, and thus, one should pay attention to the process of how ritual combines with and conveys such religious ideas. A comparison with the initiation ritual in the mysteries is helpful (see the synthetic discussion at the end of this chapter). It is true that many of the mythic ideas in Rom 5–6 strongly resonate with the world of Jewish apocalyptic literature.[123] Apocalyptic tradition illuminates the cosmic myth in Rom 5. Free from the reign of θάνατος, the people who receive abundant divine favor (they are the "elect") will reign through one person, Jesus the Messiah (5:17). Paul draws on Jewish traditions about Adam that interpret the Genesis story a particular way, which includes Adam bringing death into the world and his becoming a paradigm for everyone who sins (2 Bar 54:19; 4 Ezra 7:118–119).[124] Or, if one follows Kuo-Yu Tsui's proposal (i.e., "baptized into Christ's death" in Rom 6 and "clothed with Christ" in Gal 3 are closely related), then the motif of "the garment of glory" would also be added to this list of Jewish traditions (e.g., LAE Gk. 20–21; cf. Genesis Rabbah 20.12).[125]

The recognition of the tradition-historical background does not fully explain why Paul combines these interpretations with a particular ritual. Wedderburn's theory does include some ritual aspects; the concept of "corporate personality" (he actually prefers the term "solidarity"), as in the Mishnah (Pesaḥ 10.5), Passover Haggadah, or in the Hebrew Bible (Amos 3:1), may sufficiently explain the background of "the idea of a ritual in which participants find themselves ... in some sense involved in past events."[126] There he sees a "clear expression of the solidarity and unity from generation to generation."[127] Wedderburn does not pay the same amount of attention to the difference between corporate "solidarity" (at the national level) in the Jewish literature he adduces and what Paul describes in Rom 5–6, as he does to the difference between the soteriology of the mysteries and Paul's baptismal theology.[128] For Paul's audience, solidarity with Christ was not

---

123 Kuo-Yu Tsui, "Baptized into His Death," 395–417.
124 James D. G. Dunn, *The Theology of Paul the Apostle* (Grand Rapids: Eerdmans, 1997).
125 Kuo-Yu Tsui, "Baptized into His Death," 407–13.
126 Wedderburn, "The Soteriology of the Mysteries," 71–72.
127 Wedderburn, "The Soteriology of the Mysteries," 72.
128 Participation in the ritual of Passover does not create "the solidarity and unity of the nation from generation to generation." Such a "national" solidarity was already given, and the repetitive ritual functions as a reminder that they are already in the covenant (the Lord's Supper probably functions similarly for Christ believers).

given before their participation in the ritual of baptism. Rather, baptism is the ritual of *transfer* (i.e., from one place/status to another),[129] and as many scholars of the history of religion school rightly observed, this feature of baptism as a ritual of transfer can render baptism comparable to other initiation rituals, i.e., the mysteries (although this does not mean any dependence). Paul's distinctive transfer (and transformative) ritual effectively imposes the cosmic myth (apocalyptically envisioned dualism between Adam and Christ, reign of death and that of life/grace) on the body of ritual participants,[130] and their physical participation "gives ... their very existence"[131] to the canonical messages that are based on the apocalyptic significance of Christ's death.[132] Tannehill, a scholar who generally minimizes the function of baptism qua ritual *in the present* in favor of the theological meaning of Christ's unrepeatable (cf. ἐφάπαξ, 6:10) death *in the past* that already established "the new aeon," still admits the importance of baptism for individual believers:

> The believer is baptized into Christ's death and released from the old dominion not because baptism repeats Christ's death or enables it to be present in some unique way, but because in baptism the destruction of the old world and founding of the new which the cross brings about reaches its goal in the life of the individual.[133]

Why not say more clearly that baptism as ritual is crucial to embodying this fundamental change from the old dominion to the new in individuals? What is at stake is not just how Paul constructs the myth of universal death and its universal solution, but also how he presents this myth in relation to a particular ritual that marks the moment of initiation into the Christ cult. This observation justifies the examination of the messages of baptism as ritual in comparison with the messages of other initiation rituals in the Greco-Roman world.

---

[129] Sanders's view of righteousness in Paul would provide a similar distinction. For Paul, the language of righteousness is transfer terminology (i.e., the change of status), while in Judaism it represents the maintenance of status. Sanders, *Paul and Palestinian Judaism*, 544 and 463–72. Sanders does not fully appreciate the role of baptism in his view of Pauline participation theology, and this influenced many other scholars who followed him so that they also undervalue the role of baptism. Morales, "Baptism and Union with Christ," 157–58.
[130] Turley, *Ritualized Revelation*, especially chs. 2–5.
[131] Rappaport, *Ritual and Religion*, 125.
[132] The difference between the mythic and the apocalyptic is not as sharp as Sellin states. Discussing myth and apocalyptic in general, Sellin observes, "Die Apokalyptik zerreißt zeitlich die mythische Identität zwischen dem Materiellen und dem Ideellen." Sellin, "Mythologeme und mythische Zuge," 216. If one specifically looks at Rom 5–6, it appears that the apocalyptically envisioned figures and events support the "mythische Identität."
[133] Tannehill, *Dying and Rising with Christ*, 42.

7.1 Discussions of Key Passages — 267

Finally, as in earlier sections, the role of the Spirit in baptism and baptismal messages in Rom 5–6 needs to be examined. The reception of the Spirit is one of the important benefits that baptism promises elsewhere in the New Testament (esp. baptismal references in Acts; also, in the Gospels, John the Baptist proclaims that one who comes after him will baptize in/with the Spirit and fire, Matt 3:11/ Luke 3:16). In other Pauline passages, the reception of the Spirit as the benefit that baptism promises is not always clearly articulated, but it is obvious that the Spirit plays an important role in cleansing those who are baptized (1 Cor 6:11) and dwelling in and leading the baptized believers to the continuous life of ἁγιασμός (1 Thess 4:8, cf. 5:19). Galatians 3 uses a particular phrase, "the promise of the Spirit" (τὴν ἐπαγγελίαν τοῦ πνεύματος, 3:14), for the gentiles' participation in Abraham's blessing in Christ. All these baptismal passages include some remark about the Spirit. In contrast, except for Rom 5:5 and 7:6, Paul does not discuss πνεῦμα in his most well-known passage of baptism (Rom 6).

The role of the Spirit becomes clear only when one reads Rom 5–8 as a continuous discourse. A detailed discussion about the Spirit will be provided in the next section, which reads Rom 5–8 as a whole from the perspective of baptism. The coherence of Rom 5–8 and these chapters' distinctive nature from the preceding and the following chapters should be discussed. Some frequently occurring theological terms provide a particular coherence throughout Rom 5–8, as opposed to other parts of Romans. This is interesting especially when one compares them with other equally significant theological terms that are distributed throughout all chapters or with those that sometimes occur less frequently in Rom 5–8. This does not necessarily mean that Rom 5–8 is inconsistent with and separate from Rom 1–4 to the degree that one should regard them as two different sources or two different understandings of the gospel.[134] Linguistically, many verbal overlaps are found between Rom 1–4 and 5–8. For example, the word νόμος, which is not included in the table below (Table 3), appears frequently both in Rom 1–4 and 5–8.[135] Nevertheless, the table below shows some simple, but helpful, statistics about some noticeable quantitative features of Rom 5–8, compared with other

---

[134] Cf. Scroggs's view that two homilies are combined in the process of composing Romans. Robin Scroggs, "Paul and Rhetorician: Two Homilies in Romans 1–11," in *Jews, Greeks, and Christians: Religious Cultures in Late Antiquity: Essays in Honor of William David Davies*, ed. Robert Hamerton-Kelly and Robin Scroggs (Leiden: Brill, 1976), 271–98. See also Campbell's proposal of rereading Rom 1–4 not as Paul's gospel but as Paul's critique of the "Teacher's" (Paul's rival) gospel. Douglas A. Campbell, *The Deliverance of God: An Apocalyptic Reading of Justification in Paul* (Grand Rapids: Eerdmans, 2009) (e.g., see pp. 590–600).
[135] Rom 2 (19), Rom 3 (11), Rom 4 (5), Rom 5 (3), Rom 6 (2), Rom 7 (23), Rom 8 (5), Rom 9 (1), Rom 10 (2), Rom 13 (2). Note the high volume of occurrence in chs. 2–3 and 7.

chapters in Romans. The numbers represent how many times each word occurs in each chapter of Romans; other numbers in parenthesis represents how many times a cognate verb appears in addition to the noun form. For example, ἁμαρτία occurs two times in Rom 3, and its verbal form ἁμαρτάνω occurs once in the same chapter. So the table shows 2 (+1). As for θάνατος, there are two parentheses: the first one indicates ἀποθνῄσκω and the second one refers to θανατόω.

Table 3. Quantitative features of Romans 5–8

	θάνατος	ἁμαρτία	ζωή	σῶμα	σάρξ	ἄνθρωπος	χάρις	δικαιοσύνη	πίστις	πνεῦμα
Rom 1	1		(+1)	1	1	2	2	1	6 (+1)	2
Rom 2		(+1)	1		1	5		(+1)		1
Rom 3		2 (+1)			1	3	1	5 (+6)	9 (+2)	
Rom 4		2		1	1	1	2	8 (+2)	10 (+6)	
Rom 5	6 (+5)	4 (+3)	4			6	6	2 (+2)	2	1
Rom 6	7 (+6)	16 (+2)	3 (+5)	2	1	1	4	5 (+1)	(+1)	
Rom 7	5 (+4)(+1)	15	1 (+4)	2	3	3	1			1
Rom 8	3 (+2)(+1)	5	4 (+3)	4	13			1 (+3)		21
Rom 9		(+1)			3	1		4	2 (+1)	1
Rom 10		(+1)				1		7	3 (+7)	
Rom 11		1	1		1		4		1	1
Rom 12		(+1)	3			2	2		2	1
Rom 13					1				(+1)	
Rom 14	(+6)	1	(+7)			2		1	4 (+1)	1
Rom 15							1		(+1)	4
Rom 16						1	1		1	

These numbers should be used with caution, because one also needs to pay attention to how each word is used in each context (sometimes its meaning differs from context to context), not only to how many times it is used. Also, words and concepts should not be equated (cf. James Barr[136])—i.e., the lack of certain words would not necessarily indicate the lack of certain concepts. Four points of observation are worth mentioning. *First of all*, some words, such as θάνατος, ἁμαρτία, and ζωή, are particularly concentrated in Rom 5–8. Among them, the most noticeable example is θάνατος. Even if its cognate verbs are included, the cluster of those words in Rom 5–8 is retained, except for Rom 14.[137] The other two words, ἁμαρτία and ζωή,

---

136 Barr, *The Semantics of Biblical Language*.
137 Despite the interesting results in Rom 14, this remains something for further study as it is beyond the scope of the current project.

gather in Rom 5–8 to a lesser degree compared to that of θάνατος, but their frequency is still impressive. For example, the number of occurrences of ἁμαρτία and ἁμαρτάνω in Rom 5–8 is 45 times, whereas the sum of their occurrences in the rest of Romans is only 8. *Secondly*, σῶμα and σάρξ appear to cluster in Rom 6–8, while the concentration is much less (but note the occurrence of σάρξ in ch. 8; cf. πνεῦμα in ch. 8). More importantly, σῶμα and σάρξ, both of which are perhaps Paul's most famous anthropological terms, are lacking in Rom 5 (rather, ἄνθρωπος comes to the fore in ch. 5). This example shows some difference between Rom 5 and 6–8. *Thirdly*, there are some words that seem to play important roles throughout Romans, but they appear less frequently in Rom 5–8 or are missing entirely. The most interesting example is πίστις/πιστεύω, considering how much importance the history of Pauline interpretation (and history of Christianity) has given to it. The noun πίστις and the verb πιστεύω never occur in Rom 7–8. *Lastly*, as briefly mentioned, the word πνεῦμα does not appear much in Rom 5–7, but its occurrence dramatically rises in (and only in) Rom 8.[138] This frequent use of πνεῦμα in Rom 8 corresponds to that of σάρξ in the same chapter, which is understandable, considering the explicit contrast between πνεῦμα and σάρξ in the first part of Rom 8. This example further distinguishes Rom 8 from 5–7 (as the lack of σῶμα and σάρξ differentiates Rom 5 from 6–8).

Considering the entirety of Rom 5–8, not only Rom 5–6, is helpful in understanding Paul's reconfiguration of baptism and baptism's implications.[139] Similarly, Samuli Siikavirta argues, "[B]aptism is in fact a central topic in Rom. 6–8, and ... it must not be reduced to a mere tangential illustration or a symbol for something more real."[140] As Snyder rightly criticizes, caution should be used to avoid "false equivalence" between baptism and other terms in Rom 6–8 without concrete evidence.[141] Yet, verbal and thematic continuities between Rom 5/6–8, some of which are demonstrated by Siikavirta's tables,[142] encourage one to rethink Rom 7–8 as a detailed exposition of the implications of baptism. Romans 5–8 amounts to Paul's extended discourse on baptism—i.e., what baptism promises to Christ-devotees (self-referential messages), how it guarantees the promised benefits (canonical messages), and what obligations are created by baptism participation. Read that way, the role of the Spirit in Paul's understanding of baptism in Romans, which

---

138 Cranfield notes that πνεῦμα is the "key-word" of Rom 8. Cranfield, *Romans*, 371.
139 Note the previous quotation from Lohse that Paul's theology amounts to his exposition of baptism. Lohse, "Taufe und Rechtfertigung bei Paulus," 318.
140 Siikavirta, *Baptism and Cognition*, 103. His book focuses on Rom 6–8.
141 Benjamin J. Snyder, "Samuli Siikavirta, *Baptism and Cognition in Romans 6–8: Paul's Ethics beyond 'Indicative' and 'Imperative,'" TJ* 38 (2017): 103–5.
142 E.g., Siikavirta, *Baptism and Cognition*, 126, 131–32.

is not explicitly included in Rom 5–7, can be inferred. The Spirit is the new (or renewed) life-principle (8:2) and the enhanced cognitive capability (8:5–6), according to which baptized believers can now walk (6:4, 8:4). The development of one's cognition through the initiation process may be comparable to the literary treatment of Isis initiation found in Apuleius and Plutarch (and back to Plato's use of the Orphic initiation topoi). This would suggest that Paul somehow participates in the ancient philosophical discourse of how initiation could (or could not; cf. Aristotle, *Fr.* 15 [Synesius, *Dio* 10]) contribute to the development of the epistemological dimension. The indwelling Spirit (8:9–11, 26) could be understood as an effect of baptism (cf. 1 Thess 4), and the link among baptism, the promise of the Spirit, and the rewriting of genealogy (cf. Gal 3–4) would also be hinted at (8:14). The connection between baptism and the πνεῦμα in Romans is not explicit; it is inferred. More discussions about the Spirit will be provided in the following section.

7.1.2.2 The self-referential messages, the canonical messages, and things beyond baptism

Based on the exegetical discussion so far, coupled with the statistical observations in Table 3, I present a new reading of Rom 5–8 focused on Paul's baptismal theology.[143] Paul's reference to baptism in Rom 6 is not merely an example brought in to make other arguments, but it is the center of Rom 5–8, the long discourse that is analogous to philosophical mythography. My reading consists of six subpoints, some of which are not new. The contribution of my discussion is to gather them together in a way that supports a sustained reading of Rom 5–8 with an eye on the promise/self-referential benefits, the grounds/canonical order, and the obligation(s) of baptism, as Paul presents them.

1. The universal human problem Paul struggles with throughout Rom 5–8 is one of θάνατος and ἁμαρτία, which stand in opposition to ζωή. These nouns sometimes function as personified beings;[144] they are, nevertheless, more than narrowly defined personification as a literary device, as Matthew Croasmun challenges.[145]

---

[143] In this regard, Barclay's observation that "the event of baptism … stands at its [Rom 5–8] core" is correct. Barclay, *Paul and the Gift*, 494.
[144] Cf. Gaventa, "The Cosmic Power of Sin," 229–40. Of course, this personification is not unique to Paul. For an example of this with the Book of Wisdom, see Joseph R. Dodson, *The 'Powers' of Personification: Rhetorical Purpose in the 'Book of Wisdom' and the Letter to the Romans*. BZNW 161 (Berlin: Walter de Gruyter, 2008). For virtue worship in Greece, see Emma Stafford, *Worshipping Virtues: Personification and the Divine in Ancient Greece* (London: The Classical Press of Wales, 2000).
[145] Focusing on ἁμαρτία in Romans that appears to have agency and personhood, Croasmun points out that exegetes have often been caught in the dichotomy between interpreting ἁμαρτία

The words, θάνατος and ἁμαρτία, represent suprahuman powers that actually govern and orient the ways in which individuals behave toward concrete manifestations of ἁμαρτία and subsequent θάνατος.

2. The solution for defeating these hostile powers, θάνατος and ἁμαρτία, and for bringing in ζωή (and δικαιοσύνη),[146] in which the elect will be rulers (5:17), is not articulated by means of πίστις/πιστεύω (see Table 3). In Rom 5–8, δικαιοσύνη/δικαιόω is basically not connected to πίστις/πιστεύω, which shows a stark contrast with the situation in Rom 1–4. The whole process—overcoming condemnation,[147] achieving δικαιοσύνη, defeating ἁμαρτία/θάνατος, and bringing in ζωή—appears to be separated from πίστις/πιστεύω at least at the linguistic level.

3. Paul's solution in Rom 5–8 is twofold—cosmic and anthropological, especially when one looks at Rom 5 and 8. In Rom 5, the solution depends entirely on "one man" Christ (the antitype of Adam)[148] and Christ's obedience (5:19, i.e., his death as obedience, 5:8; cf. Phil 2:8), and the problem is primarily dealt with at the cosmic level. In the first part of Rom 8, the solution depends on the liberating work of the πνεῦμα, and one's σῶμα and σάρξ appear to be where contests take place. As Rom 8 unfolds, the scope of discourse is again expanded, and cosmological perspectives come into view. The final verses of Rom 8 correspond to 5:1–11 in terms of its emphasis of God's ἀγάπη.

4. Baptism provides the link to connect the cosmological solution and the anthropological one. As Käsemann famously puts it, "Anthropology must then *eo ipso* be cosmology just as certainly as, conversely, the cosmos is primarily viewed by Paul under an anthropological aspect ... Anthropology is cosmology *in concreto*."[149] Baptism as a bodily ritual is key; baptism is a way for an individual to be freed from the cosmic power of ἁμαρτία/θάνατος by being "co-planted" (σύμφυτοι) τῷ ὁμοιώματι τοῦ θανάτου of Christ (6:5) who was sent ἐν ὁμοιώματι σαρκὸς ἁμαρτίας

---

as real (i.e., it is a real person) and figurative (i.e., personification as a literary device), depending on one's understanding of reality and personhood. He introduces emergence theory as an ontological framework that enables one to hold together the individual, social, and mythological levels of ἁμαρτία. Matthew Croasmun, *The Emergence of Sin: The Cosmic Tyrant in Romans* (Oxford: Oxford University Press, 2017).

146 The word δικαιοσύνη and its verbal form (regardless of whether they mean righteousness/to rectify or justice/to justify) appears sometimes in the context of speaking ζωή as a final goal (5:17–18; 6:19–22).

147 The problem of condemnation (the opposite of δικαιοσύνη) still appears in Rom 5–8 (5:16, 18; 8:1, etc.).

148 For a recent challenge to this common view: see Ryan S. Schellenberg, "Does Paul Call Adam a 'Type' of Christ?" *ZNW* 105 (2014): 54–63.

149 Italics original. Ernst Käsemann, "On Paul's Anthropology," in *Perspectives on Paul*, trans. Margaret Kohl (Philadelphia: Fortress Press, 1971), 23, 27.

(8:3). Baptism brings Christ's death into the body of the baptized, so that the baptized can be "rightwised" on the basis of their participation in Christ's death (cf. 6:7), rather than on the basis of πίστις/πιστεύω. In the context of Rom 5–8, the πίστις is rather conceived as a prepositional πίστις (πιστεύομεν ὅτι ...), believing in the rightwising effect of baptismal union with Christ's death and the following union with Christ's life (6:8). Unlike other passages in the Pauline letters, mystical ideas come to the fore in Rom 6. Even in Rom 11, Paul speaks of the gentile believers' being "grafted in" (using the verb ἐγκεντρίζω) to share the rich root along with Israel—which has mainly social-communal implications. Here in Rom 6, Christ-devotees are σύμφυτοι τῷ ὁμοιώματι τοῦ θανάτου—they are all grafted into Christ's death, thereby sharing the nature of Christ's death.

5. The Spirit, πνεῦμα, which suddenly appears in Rom 8 with high frequency, comes close to ζωή. The principle of πνεῦμα that liberates "you" from the principle of ἁμαρτία and θάνατος is called ὁ νόμος τοῦ πνεύματος τῆς ζωῆς ἐν Χριστῷ Ἰησοῦ (8:2). Further, in v. 10, Paul says, "If Christ is in you, the σῶμα is dead because of ἁμαρτία, but the πνεῦμα is ζωή because of δικαιοσύνη." This collocational relationship between πνεῦμα and ζωή enables one to read the baptismal reference in Rom 6 anew. Paul says, "Therefore, we have been buried with him through the baptism into his death, so that just as Christ was raised from the dead by the glory of the Father, so we also may walk in the newness of ζωή." In this declaration, "walking in the newness of ζωή" resulting from baptism means that the baptized person is now empowered to live a life animated by the πνεῦμα.

6. It is possible to use Rom 8 to further describe what benefits baptism promises, what underlying messages support and guarantee the efficacy of the promise, and what obligations are given to the baptized. Above all, baptism promises one's freedom from the grip of ἁμαρτία and θάνατος and from condemnation by one's participation in ζωή (8:2) that is concretized through their union with Christ's death in baptism (6:3). What guarantees the efficacy of this promise is the *likeness* achieved by ritual participation, which is anchored in the theological axiom that ὁ γὰρ ἀποθανὼν δεδικαίωται ἀπὸ τῆς ἁμαρτίας (6:7). Baptism indicates the dwelling of the Spirit within the baptized (8:9; which indicates that they are of Christ), the bodily resurrection (8:11), the Spirit's and Christ's intercession for the elect (8:26, 34), God's perpetual guardianship (8:31–39), and the cosmic glory about to be revealed (8:18).

This is not to say that all the Romans (or other Christ-believers) who were baptized understood this entire series of messages at the time of their baptism. Ritual theorists and ethnographers point out that rituals are not always clear to all participants,[150] and the same was probably true of Christ-believers who participated in baptism. In this passage, Paul interprets baptism in a distinctive way and adds this message layer to the Romans' understanding of the existing ritual. Yet, not only adding a layer, but Paul—who, as the apostle set apart for the gospel of God (Rom 1:1), has been speaking to the Romans and expressing his hope to proclaim the gospel to the Romans as well (1:15)[151]—is also promoting *this* understanding of baptism as the normative one, i.e., part of his gospel.

7.2 Synthesis: Baptism in the Pauline Communities and Paul's Interpretation of Baptism

A survey of the Pauline letters has thus far demonstrated how Christ-believers in Paul's Christ-cult groups understood baptism and the messages of baptism. As a ritual part of the requirements for entry into this new cult (1 Cor 12:12–13; Gal

---

150 Ethnographic studies provide empirical evidence of multiplicity and ambiguity of meanings of ritual(s), or the gap between what is claimed and what is understood. The anthropologist James Fernandez published an article (1965) on the African reformative cult, Bwiti, practiced by "the Fang peoples of northern Gabon and the Spanish African territory, Rio Muni" (James W. Fernandez, "Symbolic Consensus in a Fang Reformative Cult," *AA* 67 [1965]: 902–29). The goal of this ritual is to achieve "a state of *nlem-mvore* (one-heartedness), uniting all members of the cult" (Fernandez, "Symbolic Consensus," 904), and the ritual includes some Christian elements (Fernandez, "Symbolic Consensus," 905). Although the participants understand the central theme of the ritual, the one-heartedness, they had different answers and different emphasis or priorities with regard to the function of the ritual activities (Fernandez, "Symbolic Consensus," 906).
151 To some extent, my proposal that Paul offers the Romans his gospel, including a foundational myth to their community-creating ritual, has some affinity to Günter Klein's 1969 theory about Paul's purpose of writing Romans. The tension between Rom 1:15 (Paul's desire to preach the gospel to those in Rome) and 15:20 (Paul's avoidance of preaching the gospel in a place where others have already laid the foundation) has vexed interpreters for a long time. Klein's view, though not accepted unanimously, is that Paul did not think that the proper "apostolic foundation" was laid in Rome, so he felt some necessity to preach the gospel there. Günter Klein, "Paul's Purpose in Writing the Epistle to the Romans," in *The Romans Debate*, ed. Karl P. Donfried, rev. and exp. ed. (Peabody: Hendrickson, 1991), 39. (Klein's original article was published in 1969.) It is unclear whether Paul really thought the Roman Christ-followers did not have a proper apostolic foundation. Yet, it is still possible to imagine that Paul may have thought that the Roman communities needed a refoundation, or one might say, an alternative version of founding myth for segmentalized, or in Peter Lampe's term, fractionated Roman communities. As Lampe notes, in Romans, "the entirety of Roman Christianity is never designated in any passage of Romans as ἐκκλησία, not even in Rom 1:7 where, according to the standard of other Pauline letters, it would be expected" (Lampe, *From Paul to Valentinus*, 359). Lampe claims that there were "five different Christian islands" in the city of Rome at the time of Paul. Lampe, *From Paul to Valentinus*, 359.

3:25–29), baptism functions to grant membership, to purify the participants (1 Cor 6:9–11; cf. 1 Cor 15:18–19), and to create a divine-human relationship (Gal 3:27; 1 Cor 10:1–5 [when mirror-read]) and intra-human bonds among ritual practitioners and participants (1 Cor 1:10–17). Yet, as shown in 1 Cor 1:10–17 and 1 Cor 15:29, baptism among the Pauline communities in the mid-first century was not yet fully regulated or organized in a systemic way.

Eschatological benefit is apparently part of the messages of baptism as understood by Paul's communities. Baptism promises a better afterlife for the living, but can also be attained for the dead (1 Cor 15:29). Both the living and the dead are identified as those ἐν Χριστῷ, which means that the bond (to each other as well as with the deity) created by baptism transcends physical death and the earthly realm (1 Cor 15:17–19; cf. 1 Thess 4). Paul's exhortation in 1 Cor 6:9–11 implies that the Corinthians were already familiar with the message of baptism that it promises their inheritance of the kingdom of God by cleansing them and transforming them in the present (a message to which they failed to conform).

Much more has been ascertained about Paul's own interpretation of baptism and its significance throughout his letters. Paul appears as a mythographer, who negotiates the boundaries and meanings of pre-existing practices developing in various ways. Paul's interpretation and representation of baptism in his letters creates new messages of baptism. Although he detaches himself from the role of baptizer (1 Cor 1), Paul views his version of myth and his interpretation of ritual as normative.

In 1 Cor 1:10–17 and 1:26–31, Paul emphasizes baptism's power to create a bond between the deity and the devotee more than its power to create intra-human bonds (but, the latter is not denied; see 1 Cor 12:12–13 and Gal 3). Those who are baptized into Christ/Christ's name primarily belong to Christ (i.e., the self-referential message). The baptized people's participation in idolatry is strongly forbidden (1 Cor 10) not because the Corinthians overestimated the efficacy of baptism in a magical way (i.e., they are free to do anything they want because their salvation is secured by baptism), but they underestimated the illocutionary power of baptism to create an exclusive bond between the deity (Christ) and his devotees.

As seen in 1 Cor 10, Paul's discourses on baptism often form ethical exhortations. This is no surprise because messages of ritual usually create obligations one must fulfill. Ἁγιασμός is one of the self-referential messages communicated by baptism (1 Thess 4:1–8; 1 Cor 1:26–31; Rom 6:19) and the Holy Spirit that begins to indwell is the source of ἁγιασμός (1 Thess 4:1–8; cf. Rom 8:9–11) and a new life in the body, involving renewed mind/cognition (Rom 6:4; 8:2, 6; 12:2). Baptized people have already been ἡγιασμένοι and they are κλητοὶ ἅγιοι, and they are promised the kingdom of God (implied in 1 Cor 6:9–11). Yet, based on the way ritual works, Paul warns that one's negligence to conform to this identity, created by the ritual, would amount to ritual failure (e.g., the Corinthians' unjust action toward their fellow members, 1 Cor 6:9–11). Addressing the problem of division and conflict in the Corinthian community (1 Cor 1:10–17 and 1:26–31), Paul also states that the message of the cross is what makes Christ-baptism effective (i.e., canonical message), and accordingly, the baptized Corinthians are obligated to conform their behavior in the community to this new epistemological norm (the call for assuming the cruciform identity also appears in Gal 3). By building upon the Corinthians' preexisting understanding of baptism as an entry ritual into the cultic body, Paul communicates another canonical message. This message states that the effectiveness of baptism in creating a real communal body and the ensuing obligations are predicated upon the symbolic identification between the church body and Christ's body (1 Cor 12:12–13; also the same Holy Spirit from which they "drank" in baptism also supports and initiates this). One who disrupts the former body (the community of Christ-believers) is tantamount to committing sins against the latter body (Christ's body), again, resulting in ritual failure (cf. 1 Cor 11:27–34).

Paul also connects baptism to what one might call doctrines, and Paul's mythographic activity becomes more prominent here. Baptism can rewrite one's genealogy and this is part of the self-referential message for those who participate in this ritual. In Gal 3:25–29, Paul presents baptism as rewriting the genealogy of the gentiles ἐν Χριστῷ, thus, enabling them to participate in the blessing of Abraham. In 1 Cor 1:26–31, it is also presupposed that baptism reconfigures the baptized's origin —therefore, it can be said that the Corinthians come "out of God." In both passages, the canonical message that supports the self-referential benefit lies in the ἐν Χριστῷ part. Baptism can transform the pagans into Abraham's seed (self-referential) because through baptism, they are clothed/identified with Christ (self-referential), who is the very seed of Abraham (Gal 3:16, 25–29). Baptized people are regarded as coming "from God (ἐξ αὐτοῦ)" because they are ἐν Χριστῷ, who is "from God (ἀπὸ θεοῦ)" (1 Cor 1:30).

Paul's myth-writing highlights baptism as a key to communicating the message of the cross and realizing the cruciform identity within the community and within the body of individual Christ-believer. First Corinthians 1:10–17 and 1:26–31 cements baptism to the proclamation of the cross—the baptized person belongs to this crucified Christ and is required to conform to him. In 1 Cor 15:18–19, Christ's death and resurrection (these are the content of εὐαγγέλιον) come to the fore as what guarantees the efficacy of baptism. It is Christ's resurrection that sustains one's remaining ἐν Χριστῷ beyond their physical death, and those who are baptized must also accept this canonical message. In Romans, Paul more clearly articulates the significance of baptism as a performative moment where the cosmological solution to the problem of Sin/death turns into its anthropological realization (chs. 6–8). To support this idea of baptism, Paul foregrounds an Adam-Christ myth in Rom 5, and he weaves this myth into his interpretation of baptism in Rom 6 using ὁμοίωμα. Baptism indicates the baptized person's death and burial with Christ and one's being united in the ὁμοίωμα of Christ's death, which replaces her/his ὁμοίωμα of Adam in the previous/present age and promises her/his ὁμοίωμα of resurrection in the coming age. Yet, it should be emphasized that the multiple instances of identification—between Adam and humanity and between Christ and humanity—and/or the chain of faithful imitation are realized by the performative force of ritual, rather than the myth itself and, by implication, a simple understanding of faith as an intellectual consent to the myth.

Paul's use of ὁμοίωμα and of faithful imitation now leads to the final discussion of how religious virtuosity is expressed in terms of Paul's understanding of baptism. As shown by Paul's emphasis on the message of the cross and cruciform identity communicated by baptism, "Christoformity" (to borrow Scot McKnight's words) is for Paul the key to religious virtuosity, and Rom 5–8 democratizes this virtuosity. Baptized believers equally participate in Christ's death and are obligated to accept the canonical order communicated by baptism. Furthermore, the elaborate moral discourse in Rom 5–8 reveals that the radical implication of baptism is extended to their everyday lives in the pneumatic orientation of their cognition and their habitus.

Yet, it should also be noted that Christoformity as the believers' union with Christ's death is actualized by their *imitatio Pauli*, or, Pauloformity (imitation and participation often overlap). Paul recentralizes the democratized virtuosity of baptismal life under his own apostolic, bodily life—he is the "possessed" one *par excellence*,[152] and he demands all believers to be completely possessed by the Spirit of Christ for the entirety of their lives. Elsewhere (passages less directly connected to baptism), Paul often presents himself as suffering and even dying. In this visualized process of physical dying, Paul regards himself as imitating, participating in, and ultimately becoming united with Christ crucified. In Gal 2:19, Paul says, "I have been crucified with Christ (Χριστῷ συνεσταύρωμαι)"—or, "I have been *Christified*."[153] In Phil 3:10, Paul speaks of his epistemological (τοῦ γνῶναι ... [τὴν] κοινωνίαν [τῶν] παθημάτων αὐτοῦ) as well as physical (συμμορφιζόμενος τῷ θανάτῳ αὐτοῦ) participation in Christ's suffering and death. Note here Paul's use of the present participle (συμμορφιζόμενος), which highlights a continuous progression, rather than a single instance, of his being physically reformed into

---

152 Cf. Ashton, *The Religion of Paul*, 214–37.
153 In a personal communication about the idea of Isification and Osirification (cf. 4.1.4 of the present monograph), Carl Holladay suggested the possibility of translating Gal 2:19 this way.

Christ's dying body. In 2 Cor 4:7–12, Paul depicts his (and his coworkers?) suffering, apostolic life as one that "always carries around Jesus's corpse in his own body" (πάντοτε τὴν νέκρωσιν τοῦ Ἰησοῦ ἐν τῷ σώματι περιφέροντες, 4:10) and that is "always handed over to death" (ἀεὶ ... εἰς θάνατον παραδιδόμεθα, 4:11). Even though Paul says that suffering/dying is their (Paul and coworkers') lot, while life is his audience's lot ("death in us, life in you," 4:12), elsewhere Paul exhorts his audience to become "imitators" of him (e.g., Phil 3:17; 1 Cor 11:1), thereby enacting a life lived for others, not for themselves (e.g., 1 Cor 8–10). As Castelli points out, "Paul's act of imitation [i.e., his imitation of Christ] is an act of mediation ... he is setting himself in a structurally similar position to that of Christ."[154] She continues by explaining how power relations are constructed: "the imitation of Paul's example is itself a privileged mode of access to salvation."[155]

Paul does not explicitly present himself as a model of religious virtuosity in his lengthy discourse about baptism in Rom 5–8. Nevertheless, the description of his own apostolic, physical existence (2 Cor 4:7–12) strongly resonates with his portrayal of baptismal life as it relates to his audience's bodies (Rom 5–8)—this point was already observed by Origen (*Commentary* 5.8).[156] Second Corinthians 4:7–12 is part of Paul's *peristasis* catalogues that he employs as "the occasion for the exhibition of power," as other Hellenistic moralists did (e.g., Epictetus, *Diatr.* 2.1.39; Seneca, *Ep.* 71.26). Paul presents himself as the "suffering sage."[157] The enumeration of suffering is "the litmus test of character," demonstrating the virtuosity of the person as the true philosopher (cf. suffering and character in Rom 5:3–4).[158] While this comparison demonstrates that Paul was indeed familiar with the philosophical topoi and somehow participated in this moralist discourse, Paul's self-portrayal in 2 Cor 4:7–12 goes beyond what the moralists did because of the passage's strong evocation of Jesus's death and his appropriation of it into his mode of existence. In

---

154 Elizabeth Castelli, *Imitating Paul: A Discourse of Power* (Louisville: Westminster John Knox, 1991), 112. See also Hans Dieter Betz, *Nachfolge und Nachahmung Jesu Christi im Neuen Testament* (Tübingen: Mohr, 1967), 153–69.
155 Castelli, *Imitating Paul*, 115.
156 J. Patout Burns Jr. *Romans: Interpreted by Early Christian Commentators* (Grand Rapids: Eerdmans, 2012), 134–35.
157 John T. Fitzgerald, *Cracks in an Earthen Vessel: An Examination of the Catalogues of Hardships in the Corinthian Correspondence* (Atlanta: Scholars Press, 1988), 166. Similarly, see Aune's discussion of the Hellenistic philosophical tradition of "practice of death." Aune quotes Plato's passage: "true philosophers practice dying" (*Phaed.* 67E), which Cicero also alluded to (*Tusc.* 1.30.74). David E. Aune, "Human Nature and Ethics in Hellenistic Philosophical Traditions and Paul: Some Issues and Problems," in *Paul in His Hellenistic Context*, ed. Troels Engberg-Pedersen (Minneapolis: Fortress, 1995), 306.
158 Fitzgerald, *Cracks in an Earthen Vessel*, 203.

2 Cor 4:10, Paul says that "carrying around Jesus's corpse in his own body" means that "the life of Jesus is manifested in our body (ἡ ζωὴ τοῦ Ἰησοῦ ἐν τῷ σώματι ἡμῶν φανερωθῇ)," and the same pattern appears in Rom 5–8 (e.g., 5:3–4; 6:4, 8:10–11). Barclay notes, "the body is the place where the resurrection life of Jesus (the new self) becomes visible and active in human lives."[159] This description is true of both 2 Cor 4:7–12 and Rom 5–8.

Paul's body is an ekphratic model for all believers who need to be conformed and transformed into Christ's death through baptism—a pattern that is extended to their current bodily life (cf. Rom 8:10–11). This coincidence is no surprise. Schweitzer is correct when he points out how Paul's own suffering experience influenced the development of the "mystical doctrine" of dying with Christ.[160] Indeed, when Paul says "we [he and his coworkers] are always being handed over [παραδιδόμεθα] to death" (2 Cor 4:10–11), he actively imitates what Jesus Christ did for him (Gal 2:20, τοῦ υἱοῦ τοῦ θεου … παραδόντος ἑαυτὸν ὑπὲρ ἐμοῦ)— thus, "[Paul's] giving himself up to death is … part of his *imitatio Christi.*"[161] Paul's theology of baptism that programmatically seeks to extend the implications of baptism to all believers is tantamount to his invitation to the chain of imitation. In Rom 5–8, Paul's audience is asked to remember/be noetically renewed (cf. Rom 12:1–2; μεταμορφοῦσθε τῇ ἀνακαινώσει τοῦ νοός),[162] abide in, and live out the canonical messages indicated by baptism (their baptism into Christ's death), and they are exhorted to fulfill baptism's radical obligation bodily in priestly terms (Rom 12:1: παραστῆσαι τὰ σώματα ὑμῶν θυσίαν ζῶσαν ἁγίαν εὐάρεστον τῷ θεῷ, τὴν λογικὴν λατρείαν ὑμῶν; again, echoing the language of 6:12–13; also, note that Paul applies priestly language to himself in Rom 15:16 and Phil 2:17). In doing so, Paul implicitly demands their Christoformity through Pauloformity.[163]

---

159 Barclay, *Paul and the Gift*, 505.
160 Schweitzer, *The Mysticism of Paul the Apostle*, 147. Thus, any attempt to attribute all of (or most of) Paul's mysticism to Paul's conversion experience is not persuasive (e.g., Ashton, *The Religion of Paul*, 113–142, esp. 126).
161 Fitzgerald, *Cracks in an Earthen Vessel*, 180.
162 Note the verbal connection between Rom 12:1–2 and Rom 6. For example, see Paul's injunction παραστῆσαι τὰ σώματα ὑμῶν in Rom 12:1, which strongly recalls Rom 6:12–13.
163 To some extent, Paul's pattern of self-presentation may correspond to that of the "wandering charismatics." For the latter, Theissen notes, "The ambivalence of the sayings about exaltation and those about humiliation in the Son of man christology is a structural homologue of an inevitable conflict of roles for the early Christian wandering charismatics … The wandering charismatics identified themselves with the destiny of the Son of man." Theissen, *Sociology of Early Palestinian Christianity*, 27. This shared fate between the Son of man and the wandering charismatics is focused on the lifestyle of wandering preaching, rejection, and vindication. Theissen understands that radical ethical norms are only applicable to the wandering charismatics, and not the sympa-

All three important aspects in Paul—(a) Christ's death and resurrection, (b) Paul's apostolic life that is characterized by his body suffering and dying for others (in this body, Christ's life is manifested), and (c) believers' altered life patterns shaped by baptism—are intertwined in the metaphorical chain. This is not a one-way, top-down flow of information. Christ's death and resurrection indeed function as a "generative metaphor" that structures Paul's apostolic self-understanding and the latter in turn shapes his teaching for the audience's life in the body—individual and communal.[164] At the same time, ritual experiences and the intrinsic pattern of baptism *qua* ritual among communities create a meaningful framework for Paul's theological reflections and eventually provide the embodied ways in which Christ-devotees can mystically participate in Christ's death and resurrection.

---

thizers in the communities. Paul's theology of baptism requires all the members of the Christ cult to accept and realize the radical vision of Christoformity.
164 Steven J. Kraftchick, "Death in Us, Life in You," *Pauline Theology. Volume II: 1 & 2 Corinthians*, ed. David M. Hay (Minneapolis: Fortress, 1993), 156–81.

8 Conclusion

In this book, I have demonstrated that baptism in the Pauline communities is a ritual analogous to mystery initiation. Both the initiation rituals of the mysteries and baptismal ritual practiced in the Pauline groups are informed by similar socio-cultural understandings of how initiation constructs divine-human and intra-human/social relationships. Secondly, I have argued that Paul is an innovative interpreter of ritual who recalibrates the messages of preexisting rituals for his theological and ethical program, seeking to radically extend the implications of initiation to the social reality within his Christ-cult groups and the embodied life of every Christ-believer. Thirdly, I have argued that Paul recentralizes religious virtuosity by incorporating the pattern of baptismal initiation into his own apostolic existence.

Baptism in Paul's mid-first century communities shares a certain type of ritual messages with the initiation rituals of the Dionysiac mysteries and the mysteries of Isis. In terms of self-referential messages (or the benefits promised by initiation), baptism was primarily an entry ritual into Paul's Christ groups (largely consisting of Christ-devotees from pagan backgrounds) in a way similar to the initiation rituals of the mysteries. These rituals of initiation transform individual and communal identity (intra-human relationships are formed), and accordingly create boundaries and norms for the group by which they can identify themselves. Significantly, both Christ-baptism and mystery initiation communicate the self-referential message that ritual participation creates a personalized, trustworthy bond between the deity and devotee(s). As an extension of this bond, the divine pledge of a blessed afterlife (though what this entails might differ) for the devotees is often communicated as part of the promise of initiation, as baptism communicated eschatological promise. These general similarities hold true despite a few noticeable benefits of mystery initiation (e. g., prosperous civic-political life and other earthly-λύσις in the Dionysiac mysteries, or the healing and protection of women in the Isis mysteries) that are absent from the Pauline baptism passages.

Admittedly, some of these benefits of initiation perhaps were not restricted to the mysteries, but extended to other forms of cultic activities in the ancient Mediterranean world. Thus, more noticeable characteristics of the mysteries emerge when one also considers how the self-referential messages are supported by, and simultaneously activate, the canonical messages of initiation, thereby leading to a particular form of religious virtuosity embodied by their participants. This enables one to see how early Christ baptism participated in the pattern of mystery initiation. Canonical messages about the suffering of the deity (Dionysus, Isis, Christ), the deity's nearness to the devotees (Dionysus, Christ) as well as sympathy/mercy (Isis, Christ), and the identification (or some type of unity) between the deity and the devotees based on the logic of metonymy (Dionysus, Isis, Christ) are found, *mutatis mutandis*, in both the mysteries and the description of baptism in the Pauline letters. The emphasis on the devotees' faith/trust in the deity (in addition to the ritual activity itself), their right understanding of the meaning of ritual, and as mentioned above, their ethical behavior to maintain order within the cultic community appear in all three groups. This is not surprising given the reciprocal process: one's participation in and acceptance of ritual (this is part of the self-referential message) gives the canonical order its very existence, which guarantees the efficacy of the benefits promised by the ritual and generates the participant's obligations. Finally, cultic initiation by definition signifies some form of religious virtuosity, but when compared to the Eleusinian mysteries (where differentiated stages of initiation are found), the two mystery cults examined here have more in common with Pauline baptism. With its emphasis on the figure of Dionysus as an archetypal initiate who powerfully enables his devotees to become like this deity, Dionysiac initiation provided a more "democratized" version of virtuosity, accessible to all initiates, although rules of order and diverse roles are still found within Dionysiac groups. While some differentiation among initiates is detected in Isis initiation (e.g., as seen in Apuleius's *Metamorphoses*), a consideration of material culture suggests that the mysteries of Isis also developed a symbolic order where a larger group of initiates shared sacerdotal identity.

Since this overall contour of ritual messages was not unique to Christ-baptism and Paul's baptism discourse, pagans in the first-century Mediterranean world who were familiar with how the Dionysiac mysteries or the mysteries of Isis worked would easily understand what ritual messages baptism communicated. Baptism fits the cognitive pattern of mystery initiation attested among pagans in Pauline cities. To be clear, this analogical relationship of ritual messages does not mean that Christ-baptism directly originated from the initiation rituals of the mysteries, or that Paul's theology of baptism was dependent on the (abstracted) theology of the mystery cults.

Throughout key passages in his letters, Paul as an interpreter and mythographer of the earliest phase of the Christ cult engages and expands the images and messages of baptism. On one hand, as seen above, baptism in Paul's communities can be understood in light of the analogical framework of the mysteries. On the other hand, Paul developed distinctive messages of baptism that look different from initiation in the Dionysiac and Isis mysteries, although the differences are primarily of degree, rather than kind. Writing to his (mostly ex-pagan) audience for whom baptism was already a shared experience, Paul extends the pattern of this Christ-initiation (especially participants' conformity to Christ-like identity) to the social reality of his communities and the bodily life of individual Christ-believers in a more radical way.

Several examples of Paul's distinctive ritual messages are worth noting. First, while the initiation rituals of the mysteries create certain obligations, they do not usually prevent the initiates from participating in and fulfilling cultic requirements, other than those for the mystery deity. Paul puts more emphasis on obligations to maintain ritual/ethical exclusivism that arises from the ontological change (i.e., their "being in Christ") caused by ritual participation. This is exemplified by Paul's baptism discourse in 1 Corinthians that warns those who do not commit exclusively to Israel's God and Christ—violation of this canonical message amounts to ritual failure. Second, my survey has demonstrated that the metonymic logic ("as is the cultic deity, so also are his devotees") was communicated by participation in mystery initiation, and this relationship underlies Paul's baptism passages in 1 Corinthians and Galatians. Yet, Paul strategically employs this logic to urge his audience to embody the crucified identity of Christ in order to unify the community and reorient it towards Paul's teaching. Third, mystery initiation rituals often relate mythic stories about the deities and their personal (including ethnic) characteristics and achievements to guarantee the efficacy of the promised benefits, but these rituals do not include the reformulation of initiates' ethnic identity. Galatians 3, which recalls stories about Israel's God and Christ, shows that baptism has the ability to rewrite the genealogy of pagans (though they are still distinguished from Jews) who have been transferred into the Christ-sphere, clothed and thus identified with Christ, i.e., Abraham's seed.

Fourth, the notion of "dying and rising with Christ through baptism" (in Rom 6)—a perennial theme in previous scholarship—can be briefly revisited. In Rom 5–8, one can see how Paul's view of baptism evolved through his interactions with several types of pre-existing traditions (e.g., pre-Pauline baptismal tradition, LXX tradition, apocalyptic tradition) and with ritual innovations emerging from his Christ groups. Paul's extended discourse on baptism in these chapters theologizes baptism as a revelatory space where the conquest of the cosmic problem of death through Christ's death is enacted on individual believers' body with renewed life animated by the Spirit of the risen Christ. It is true that Isis and Dionysus experienced suffering, and a part of their ritual messages includes a shared identity between the deity and the initiates. However, the precise connection between the cosmic nature of death, the death of the deity to address that issue, and initiates' participation in this deity's death/burial through ritual is a peculiar blend that does not appear in the mysteries of Dionysus and the Isis mysteries. Thus, as scholars of the Moratorium stage correctly argued, Paul's presentation of baptism as dying and rising with Christ is not a reason to claim that Pauline baptism is dependent on the pagan mysteries. To the ex-pagans in Paul's groups, Paul's message of baptism as dying and rising with Christ would be a point that makes this ritual more distinctive from the other mystery initiations.

Another peculiar element in Paul's baptism discourse (and its broader implications for his self-understanding) is that he presents his own apostolic existence as a model that the members of his communities should imitate in the process of Christoformity. That is, Paul's dying body becomes an intermediary *mysterium* through which his communities are expected to participate in the mysteries of Christ. In this way, the figure of Paul in his letters is presented as another (perhaps, secondary) mystery deity whose archetypal suffering (and even death/dying process) is shared between himself and his followers and whose sympathy and intercessory capability toward his followers guarantees the efficacy of the ritual promises. In a sense, one could argue that the cult of Paul (and by extension, the cults of other martyrs)[1] was already latent in inchoate form at the intersection of Paul's baptismal theology and his apostolic existence in the context of the initiation rituals of the Greco-Roman mysteries. Not long after Paul, Ignatius of Antioch calls his Ephesian audience Παύλου συμμύσται ("the fellow initiates of Paul," *Eph.* 12.2 [or, I would translate "the fellow initiates belonging to Paul"]).[2]

Finally, what are the broader implications of this study? My discussion of Pauline baptism in the context of the Greco-Roman mystery cults encourages scholars to pay more attention to how ritual works in relation to key concepts in Pauline theology and ethics. Traditionally, Pauline scholars have downplayed the significance of ritual in Paul's letters and emphasized the theological or ethical aspects of Paul's writing. Teresa Morgan's recent book, *Being 'in Christ' in the Letters of Paul*, is a telling example. In her excellent philological and historical study, Morgan gives surprisingly little attention to the role of ritual in the Pauline letters, even though she is aware of how ritual has contributed to the construction of divine-human relationships in later Christianity and other religious traditions.[3]

> [Paul] has ... little to say about physical or ritual aspects of Christ-confession itself. He mentions baptism in half a dozen passages: sometimes figuratively (e.g. Rom. 6.3–4) and sometimes to make a point about what baptism should achieve (e.g. 1 Cor. 12.13). He discusses

---

[1] For the cult of Paul, see David L. Eastman, *Paul the Martyr: The Cult of the Apostle in the Latin West* (Atlanta: SBL, 2011). For the cults of the saints/martyrs, see Candida R. Moss, *The Other Christs: Imitating Jesus in Ancient Christian Ideologies of Martyrdom* (New York: Oxford University, 2010).
[2] For a detailed discussion of Ignatius's use of images and expressions related to associations and mysteries in shaping the Christian identity of his audience, see Philip A. Harland, "Christ-Bearers and Fellow-Initiates: Local Cultural Life and Christian Identity in Ignatius' Letters," *JECS* 11 (2003): 481–99.
[3] Morgan, *Being 'in Christ,'* 216.

the eucharist (1 Cor. 10.16–17, 11.23–6) only, it seems, because the Corinthians have been abusing it.[4]

At first glance, her assessment makes sense; Paul often mentions baptism or other ritual activities "to make a point about what [they] should achieve." Furthermore, it is also true that Paul and his contemporaries do not represent developed Christian liturgy.

> The fact that the institutions and rituals of Christ-confession are still inchoate in the 50s and 60s is not, of course, due to Paul. It must be possible that one of the reasons why he focuses strongly on the role of therapeutic attitudes in Christ-confession is that relatively few shared institutions and rituals yet exist. It is, however, notable how little he has to say even about those that do.[5]

Yet, in the last sentence quoted above, Morgan goes a step further and asserts that even the rituals that existed in the mid-first century did not feature much in Paul's discourse: "*It is ... notable how little he has to say even about those that [existed].*" Rather, she thinks that Paul was more concerned about certain important "therapeutic attitudes" that describe a new mode of life and relationship in Christ (by "therapeutic attitudes" she means: *charis, pistis, dikaiosynē, agapē, hagiotēs, eleutheria, eirēnē,* and *elpis*). Morgan regards ritual aspects as peripheral to Paul's construction of the new divine-human and intra-human relationships characterized by ἐν Χριστῷ ("in Christ's hands"). Her view on ritual is not idiosyncratic—despite her innovative approaches to Paul and early Christianity in this book and her previous monograph (*Roman Faith and Christian Faith*), she seems to follow the well-trodden path taken by generations of scholars regarding the issue of ritual.[6]

---

4 Morgan, *Being 'in Christ,'* 216.
5 Morgan, *Being 'in Christ,'* 217.
6 Morgan attempts to dispel any misunderstandings of her position and makes sure that she does not fall into an old bias against ritual:

> In case, to some readers, this observation raises the alarming ghost of long-defunct comparisons between the supposed ritualism or legalism of Greeks, Romans or Jews compared with the supposed preoccupation of Christians with belief and orthodoxy, it is worth emphasizing that no such comparison is at stake here ... I am not suggesting that Paul is against ritual, or rituals, nor that he is preoccupied with belief or orthodoxy (which is an anachronistic concept in first-century Christianity). Rather, the letters suggest that Paul is concerned first and foremost with the nature of the relationship between God, Christ, and the faithful, and how that relationship is acknowledged and enacted in every situation by the faithful, above all by means of key therapeutic attitudes (Morgan, *Being 'in Christ,'* 217–18).

My comparative study of ritual has demonstrated that ritual does *not* remain peripheral to Paul. Admittedly, Paul was not an "eisegete" (εἰσηγητής) of rituals in the emerging early Christ cult groups, transferring new cultic rituals to various places. Yet, he was certainly an active and creative "exegete" (ἐξηγητής) of rituals (most significantly, baptism), who reinterpreted pre-existing rituals and expanded their theological, social, and ethical implications. A closer look at Paul's references to baptism shows that Morgan's "therapeutic attitudes" are actually among the very messages communicated through one's participation in baptism. A few examples will demonstrate this point. First, Christ-baptism establishes the trusting relationship—hence, *pistis*—between God, Christ, and Christ-believers. Second, one of the clear benefits (or self-referential messages) of baptism is Christ-believers' *elpis* in resurrection. Third, baptism's effects are inseparable from the story of Christ, his crucifixion, and the power of his death in destroying the power of Death. It has been demonstrated that baptism enacts God's cosmological intervention for *dikaiosynē* in communal and individual bodies. Fourth, one's participation in baptism indexically refers to the person's obligations to abide in the canonical order that sustains the efficacy of baptism—and thus, leads to a life of *hagiotēs*. In a sense, every "therapeutic attitude" that Morgan highlights is embodied in, and conversely, gives meaning to, baptism. Rather than contrasting ritual and theology/ethics, one will find more fruitful avenues for Pauline scholarship by closely examining how Paul's and the Pauline communities' ritual experiences shaped Paul's theology and ethics, and at the same time, how Paul's theological-ethical convictions informed his distinctive interpretation of ritual.

Nevertheless, Morgan still does not explore whether and how Paul's ritual experiences can work with Paul's "first and foremost" concerns (i.e., "the nature of the relationship between God, Christ, and the faithful" [i.e., theology] and "how that relationship is acknowledged and enacted in every situation" [i.e., ethics]).

Appendix: References to Baptism in the Undisputed Pauline Letters

Table 1. Romans

Romans	Group A	Group B	Group C	Group D
1:2		ἅγιος		
1:4		ἁγιωσύνη		
1:7		ἅγιος		
2:27				τελέω
3:24			ἐν Χριστῷ	
5:5		ἅγιος		
6:3	βαπτίζω (2x)			
6:4	βάπτισμα			
6:11			ἐν Χριστῷ	
6:19		ἁγιασμός		
6:21				τέλος
6:22		ἁγιασμός		
6:22				τέλος
6:23			ἐν Χριστῷ	
7:12		ἅγιος (2x)		
8:1			ἐν Χριστῷ	
8:2			ἐν Χριστῷ	
8:27		ἅγιος		
8:39			ἐν Χριστῷ	
9:1		ἅγιος		
9:1			ἐν Χριστῷ	
10:4				τέλος
11:16		ἅγιος (2x)		
11:25				μυστήριον (sg.)
12:1		ἅγιος		
12:2				τέλειος
12:5			ἐν Χριστῷ	
12:13		ἅγιος		
13:6				τελέω
13:7				τέλος (2x)
14:14			ἐν κυρίῳ	
14:17		ἅγιος		
14:20		καθαρός		
15:13		ἅγιος		
15:16		ἁγιάζω		

https://doi.org/10.1515/9783110791389-011

Table 1. Romans *(Continued)*

Romans	Group A	Group B	Group C	Group D
15:16		ἅγιος		
15:17			ἐν Χριστῷ	
15:25		ἅγιος		
15:26		ἅγιος		
15:31		ἅγιος		
16:2		ἅγιος		
16:2			ἐν κυρίῳ	
16:3			ἐν Χριστῷ	
16:7			ἐν Χριστῷ	
16:8			ἐν κυρίῳ	
16:9			ἐν Χριστῷ	
16:10			ἐν Χριστῷ	
16:11			ἐν κυρίῳ	
16:12			ἐν κυρίῳ (2x)	
16:13			ἐν κυρίῳ	
16:15		ἅγιος		
16:16		ἅγιος		
16:22			ἐν κυρίῳ	
16:25				μυστήριον (sg.)

Table 2. 1 Corinthians

1 Cor	Group A	Group B	Group C	Group D
1:2		ἁγιάζω		
1:2		ἅγιος		
1:2			ἐν Χριστῷ	
1:4			ἐν Χριστῷ	
1:8				τέλος
1:13	βαπτίζω			
1:14	βαπτίζω			
1:15	βαπτίζω			
1:16	βαπτίζω (2x)			
1:17	βαπτίζω			
1:30		ἁγιασμός		
1:30			ἐν Χριστῷ	
1:31			ἐν κυρίῳ	
2:1				μυστήριον (sg.)
2:6				τέλειος
2:7				μυστήριον (sg.)

Table 2. 1 Corinthians *(Continued)*

1 Cor	Group A	Group B	Group C	Group D
3:1			ἐν Χριστῷ	
3:17		ἅγιος		
4:1				μυστήρια (pl.)
4:10			ἐν Χριστῷ	
4:15			ἐν Χριστῷ	
4:17			ἐν Χριστῷ	
4:17			ἐν κυρίῳ	
6:1		ἅγιος		
6:2		ἅγιος		
6:11		ἀπολούομαι		
6:11		ἁγιάζω		
6:19		ἅγιος		
7:14		ἁγιάζω (2x)		
7:14		ἅγιος		
7:22			ἐν κυρίῳ	
7:34		ἅγιος		
7:39			ἐν κυρίῳ	
9:1			ἐν κυρίῳ	
9:2			ἐν κυρίῳ	
10:2	βαπτίζω			
10:11				τέλος
11:11			ἐν κυρίῳ	
12:3		ἅγιος		
12:13	βαπτίζω			
13:2				μυστήρια (pl.)
13:10				τέλειος
14:2				μυστήρια (pl.)
14:20				τέλειος
14:33		ἅγιος		
15:18			ἐν Χριστῷ	
15:19			ἐν Χριστῷ	
15:24				τέλος
15:29	βαπτίζω (2x)			
15:31			ἐν Χριστῷ	
15:51				μυστήριον (sg.)
15:58			ἐν κυρίῳ	
16:1		ἅγιος		
16:15		ἅγιος		
16:19			ἐν κυρίῳ	

Table 2. 1 Corinthians *(Continued)*

1 Cor	Group A	Group B	Group C	Group D
16:20		ἅγιος		
16:24			ἐν Χριστῷ	

Table 3. 2 Corinthians

2 Cor	Group A	Group B	Group C	Group D
1:1		ἅγιος		
1:13				τέλος
2:12			ἐν κυρίῳ	
2:27			ἐν Χριστῷ	
3:13				τέλος
3:14			ἐν Χριστῷ	
5:17			ἐν Χριστῷ	
5:19			ἐν Χριστῷ	
6:6		ἅγιος		
7:1		καθαρίζω		
7:1		ἁγιωσύνη		
8:4		ἅγιος		
9:1		ἅγιος		
9:12		ἅγιος		
10:17			ἐν κυρίῳ	
11:15				τέλος
12:2			ἐν Χριστῷ	
12:9				τελέω
12:19			ἐν Χριστῷ	
13:12		ἅγιος (2x)		
13:13		ἅγιος		

Table 4. Galatians

Gal	Group A	Group B	Group C	Group D
1:22			ἐν Χριστῷ	
2:4			ἐν Χριστῷ	
2:17			ἐν Χριστῷ	
3:14			ἐν Χριστῷ	
3:26			ἐν Χριστῷ	
3:27	βαπτίζω			

Table 4. Galatians *(Continued)*

Gal	Group A	Group B	Group C	Group D
3:28			ἐν Χριστῷ	
5:10			ἐν κυρίῳ	
5:16				τελέω

Table 5. Philippians

Phil	Group A	Group B	Group C	Group D
1:1		ἅγιος		
1:1			ἐν Χριστῷ	
1:13			ἐν Χριστῷ	
1:14			ἐν κυρίῳ	
1:26			ἐν Χριστῷ	
2:1			ἐν Χριστῷ	
2:5			ἐν Χριστῷ	
2:19			ἐν κυρίῳ	
2:24			ἐν κυρίῳ	
2:29			ἐν κυρίῳ	
3:1			ἐν κυρίῳ	
3:3			ἐν Χριστῷ	
3:12				τελειόω
3:14			ἐν Χριστῷ	
3:15				τέλειος
3:19				τέλος
4:1			ἐν κυρίῳ	
4:2			ἐν κυρίῳ	
4:4			ἐν κυρίῳ	
4:7			ἐν Χριστῷ	
4:10			ἐν κυρίῳ	
4:12				μυέω
4:19			ἐν Χριστῷ	
4:21		ἅγιος		
4:22		ἅγιος		

Table 6. 1 Thessalonians

1 Thess	Group A	Group B	Group C	Group D
1:5		ἅγιος		
1:6		ἅγιος		
2:14			ἐν Χριστῷ	
2:16				τέλος
3:8			ἐν κυρίῳ	
3:13		ἁγιωσύνη		
3:13		ἅγιος		
4:1			ἐν κυρίῳ	
4:3		ἁγιασμός		
4:4		ἁγιασμός		
4:7		ἁγιασμός		
4:8		ἅγιος		
4:16			ἐν Χριστῷ	
5:12			ἐν κυρίῳ	
5:18			ἐν Χριστῷ	
5:26		ἅγιος		

Table 7. Philemon

Phm	Group A	Group B	Group C	Group D
5		ἅγιος		
7		ἅγιος		
8			ἐν Χριστῷ	
16			ἐν κυρίῳ	
20			ἐν Χριστῷ	
20			ἐν κυρίῳ	
23			ἐν Χριστῷ	

Bibliography

Agersnap, Søren. *Baptism and the New Life: A Study of Romans 6.1–14*, trans. Christine Crowley and Frederick Crowley. Aarhus: Aarhus University Press, 1999.
Alcock, Susan E., and Robin Osborne, eds. *Placing the Gods: Sanctuaries and Sacred Space in Ancient Greece*. New York: Oxford University Press, 1994.
Alvar, Jaime. *Romanizing Oriental Gods: Myth, Salvation and Ethics in the Cults of Cybele, Isis and Mithras*, translated and edited by Richard Gordon. RGRW 165. Leiden; Boston: Brill, 2008.
Alvar, Jaime. "Social Agentivity in the Eastern Mediterranean Cult of Isis." In *Individuals and Materials in the Greco-Roman Cults of Isis. Agents, Images, and Practices: Proceedings of the VIth International Conference of Isis Studies (Erfurt, May 6–8, 2013 – Liège, September 23–24, 2013)*. Volume 1, edited by Valentino Gasparini and Richard Veymiers, 221–47. Leiden; Boston: Brill, 2018.
Ascough, Richard S. *Paul's Macedonian Associations: The Social Context of Philippians and 1 Thessalonians*. WUNT II/161. Tübingen: Mohr Siebeck, 2003.
Ashton, John. *The Religion of Paul the Apostle*. New Haven: Yale University Press, 2000.
Athanassiadi, Polymnia, and Michael Frede, eds. *Pagan Monotheism in Late Antiquity*. Oxford: Clarendon Press, 1999.
Athanassiadi, Polymnia, and Constantinos Macris. "La philosophisation du religieux." In *Panthée: Religious Transformations in the Graeco-Roman Empire*, edited by Laurent Bricault and Corinne Bonnet, 41–83. Leiden: Brill, 2013.
Auffarth, Christoph. "The Materiality of God's Image: The Olympian Zeus and Ancient Christology." In *The Gods of Ancient Greece: Identities and Transformations*, edited by Jan N. Bremmer and Andrew Erskine, 465–480. Edinburgh: Edinburgh University Press, 2010.
Aune, David E. "Magic in Early Christianity." ANRW 2.23.2 (1980): 1507–57.
Aune, David E. "Human Nature and Ethics in Hellenistic Philosophical Traditions and Paul: Some Issues and Problems." In *Paul in His Hellenistic Context*, edited by Troels Engberg-Pedersen, 291–312. Minneapolis: Fortress, 1995.
Baird, William. *History of New Testament Research, Vol. 2*. Minneapolis: Fortress, 2003.
Balch, David L. "The Suffering of Isis/Io and Paul's Portrait of Christ Crucified (Gal. 3:1): Frescoes in Pompeian and Roman Houses and in the Temple of Isis in Pompeii." *JR* 83 (2003): 24–55.
Balch, David L., Everett Ferguson, and Wayne A. Meeks, eds. *Greeks, Romans, and Christians: Essays in Honor of Abraham J. Malherbe*. Minneapolis: Fortress Press, 1990.
Balch, David L., and Annette Weissenrieder, eds. *Contested Spaces: Houses and Temples in Roman Antiquity and the New Testament*. Tübingen: Mohr Siebeck, 2012.
Ballard, C. Andrew. "The Mysteries of Paideia: 'Mystery' and Education in Plato's *Symposium*, 4QInstruction, and 1 Corinthians." In *Pedagogy in Ancient Judaism and Early Christianity*, edited by Karina Martin Hogan, Matthew Goff, and Emma Wasserman, 243–81. Atlanta: Society of Biblical Literature, 2017.
Barclay, John M. G. *Paul and the Gift*. Grand Rapids: Eerdmans, 2015.
Barr, James. *The Semantics of Biblical Language*. London: Oxford University Press, 1961.
Barrett, C. K. *The Epistle to the Romans*. Rev. ed. Grand Rapids: Baker Academic, 2011.
Barth, Gerhard. *Die Taufe in frühchristlicher Zeit*. 2nd ed. Neukirchen-Vluyn: Neukirchener, 2002.
Bassler, Jouette M. "Paul's Theology: Whence and Whither?" In *Pauline Theology. Volume II: 1 & 2 Corinthians*, edited by David M. Hay, 3–17. Minneapolis: Fortress, 1993.
Beasley-Murray, George Raymond. *Baptism in the New Testament*. New York: St Martin's Press, 1962.

Beker, J. C. *Paul the Apostle: The Triumph of God in Life and Thought*. Philadelphia: Fortress, 1984.
Belayche, Nicole. "Les dévotions à Isis et Sérapis dans la Judée-Palestine Romaine." In *Nile into Tiber. Egypt in the Roman World: Proceedings of the Third International Conference of Isis studies, Faculty of Archaeology, Leiden University, May 11–14 2005*, edited by Laurent Bricault, Miguel John Versluys, and Paul G. P. Meyboom, 448–69. Leiden: Brill, 2007.
Bell, Brigidda. "The Cost of Baptism? The Case for Paul's Ritual Compensation." *JSNT* 42 (2020): 431–52.
Bell, Catherine. "Ritualization of Texts and Textualization of Ritual in the Codification of Taoist Liturgy." *HR* 27 (1988): 366–92.
Bell, Catherine. *Ritual Theory, Ritual Practice*. Oxford: Oxford University Press, 1992.
Bell, Catherine. *Ritual: Perspectives and Dimensions*. New York: Oxford University Press, 1997.
Bell, Catherine. "The Chinese 'Believe' in Spirits: Belief and Believing in the Study of Religion." In *Radical Interpretation in Religion*, edited by N. Frankenberry, 100–6. Cambridge: Cambridge University Press, 2002.
Bell, Catherine. "Belief: A Classificatory Lacuna and Disciplinary 'Problem.'" In *Introducing Religion: Essays in Honor of Jonathan Z. Smith*, edited by Willi Braun and Russell T. McCutcheon, 85–99. London: Equinox, 2008.
Berger, Peter L. and Thomas Luckmann. *The Social Construction of Reality: A Treatise in the Sociology of Knowledge*. New York: Anchor Books, 1967.
Bergman, Jan. "'I Overcome Fate, Fate Harkens to Me.'" In *Fatalistic Beliefs in Religion, Folklore, and Literature: Papers read at the Symposium on Fatalistic Beliefs held at Åbo on the 7th–9th of September, 1964*, edited by Helmer Ringgren, 35–51. Stockholm: Almqvist & Wiksell, 1967.
Bernabé, Alberto, and Ana Isabel Jiménez San Cristóbal, eds. *Instructions for the Netherworld: The Orphic Gold Tablets*. RGRW 162. Leiden: Brill, 2013.
Betz, Hans Dieter. *Nachfolge und Nachahmung Jesu Christi im Neuen Testament*. Tübingen: Mohr, 1967.
Betz, Hans Dieter. *Galatians: A Commentary on Paul's Letters to the Churches in Galatia*. Hermeneia. Philadelphia: Fortress, 1979.
Betz, Hans Dieter. "Transferring a Ritual: Paul's Interpretation of Baptism in Rom 6." In *Paul in His Hellenistic Context*, edited by Troels Engberg-Pedersen, 84–118. Minneapolis: Fortress, 1995.
Betz, Hans Dieter and Edgar W. Smith, Jr. "De Iside et Osiride (Moralia 351C – 384C)." In *Plutarch's Theological Writings and Early Christian Literature*, edited by Hans Dieter Betz, 36–84. Leiden: Brill, 1975.
Bhabha, Homi K. *The Location of Culture*. London; New York: Routledge, 2004.
Bianchi, Ugo, and Maarten J. Vermaseren, eds. *La soteriologia dei culti orientali nell'Imperio Romano: Atti del Colloquio Internazionale su La soteriologia dei culti orientali nell'Impero Romano, Roma 24–28 Settembre 1979*. Leiden: Brill, 1982.
Blakely, Sandra. *Myth, Ritual, and Metallurgy in Ancient Greece and Recent Africa*. New York: Cambridge University Press, 2006.
Blakely, Sandra. "Toward an Archaeology of Secrecy: Power, Paradox, and the Great Gods of Samothrace." *Archaeological Papers of the American Anthropology Association* 21 (2012): 49–71.
Blakely, Sandra. "Daimones in the Thracian Sea: Mysteries, Iron, and Metaphor." *ARG* 14 (2013): 155–82
Blakely, Sandra. "Maritime Risk and Ritual Responses: Sailing with the Gods in the Ancient Mediterranean." In *The Sea in History. The Ancient World*, edited by Philip de Souza, Pascal Arnaud, Christian Buchet, 362–79. Woodbridge, Suffolk: Boydell, 2017.

Blakely, Sandra. "Leukothea's Sash, Lucretius' Magnets, and Samothracian Rings/Maritime Amulets." Unpublished article.
Blegen, Carl W., Hazel Palmer, and Rodney S. Young. *Corinth Vol. XIII: The North Cemetery*. Princeton: American School of Classical Studies at Athens, 1964.
Bockmuehl, Markus N. A. *Revelation and Mystery in Ancient Judaism and Pauline Christianity*. WUNT II/36. Tübingen: Mohr Siebeck, 1990.
Boers, Hendrikus. "The Structure and Meaning of Romans 6:1–14." *CBQ* 63 (2001): 664–82.
Bowden, Hugh. *Mystery Cults of the Ancient World*. Princeton: Princeton University Press, 2010.
Bøgh, Birgitte. "In Life and Death: Choice and Conversion in the Cult of Dionysos." In *Conversion and Initiation in Antiquity: Shifting Identities – Creating Change*, edited by Birgitte Bøgh, 25–46. Frankfurt am Main: Peter Lang, 2014.
Bøgh, Birgitte. "Beyond Nock: From Adhesion to Conversion in the Mystery Cults." *HR* 54 (2015): 260–87.
Bookidis, Nancy. "The Sanctuaries of Corinth." In *Corinth XX: The Centenary*, edited by Charles K. Williams and Nancy Bookidis, 247–59. Princeton: The American School of Classical Studies at Athens, 2003.
Bookidis, Nancy. "Religion in Corinth: 146 B.C.E. to 100 C.E." In *Urban Religion in Roman Corinth: Interdisciplinary Approaches*, edited by Daniel N. Schowalter and Steven J. Friesen, 141–64. Cambridge, MA: Harvard Theological Studies, 2005.
Bookidis, Nancy, and Ronald S. Stroud. *Demeter and Persephone in Ancient Corinth*. Princeton: American School of Classical Studies at Athens, 1987.
Bookidis, Nancy, and Ronald S. Stroud. *Corinth XVIII: The Sanctuary of Demeter and Kore: Topography and Architecture*. Princeton: American School of Classical Studies at Athens, 1997.
Bornkamm, Günter. "Baptism and New Life in Paul (Romans 6)." In *Early Christian Experience*, trans. Paul L. Hammer, 71–86. New York: Harper & Row, 1969.
Bousset, Wilhelm. *Kyrios Christos: A History of the Belief in Christ from the Beginning of Christianity to Irenaeus*, trans. John E. Steely. Waco: Baylor University Press, 2013.
Brandon, S. G. F. "The Historical Element in Primitive Christianity." *Numen* 2 (1955): 156–67.
Bremmer, Jan N. "Greek Maenadism Reconsidered." *ZPE* 55 (1984): 267–86.
Bremmer, Jan N. *Initiation into the Mysteries of the Ancient World*. Berlin: Walter de Gruyter, 2014.
Bremmer, Jan N. "The Construction of an Individual Eschatology: The Case of the Orphic Gold Leaves." In *Burial Rituals, Ideas of Afterlife, and the Individual in the Hellenistic World and the Roman Empire*, edited by Katharina Waldner, Richard Gordon, and Wolfgang Spickermann, 31–51. Stuttgart: Franz Steiner Verlag, 2016.
Brenk, Frederick E. "A Gleaming Ray: Blessed Afterlife in the Mysteries." *ICS* 18 (1993): 147–64.
Brenk, Frederick E. "'Great Royal Spouse Who Protects Her Brother Osiris': Isis in the Iseaum at Pompeii." In *Mystic Cults in Magna Graecia*, edited by Giovanni Casadio and Patricia A. Johnston, 217–34. Austin: University of Texas Press, 2009.
Bricault, Laurent. *Recueil des inscriptions concernant les cultes isiaques*. 3 vols. Paris: Académie des inscriptions et belles-lettres, 2005.
Bricault, Laurent. *Les cultes isiaques dans le monde gréco-romain*. Paris: Les belles lettres, 2013.
Bricault, Laurent. "Les prêtres isiaques du monde romain." In vol. 1, *Individuals and Materials in the Greco-Roman Cults of Isis: Agents, Images, and Practices*, edited by Valentino Gasparini and Richard Veymiers, 155–97. Leiden: Brill, 2018.
Bricault, Laurent, and Corinne Bonnet, eds. *Panthée: Religious Transformations in the Graeco-Roman Empire*. RGRW 177. Leiden: Brill, 2013.

Bricault, Laurent, Miguel John Versluys, and Paul G. P. Meyboom, eds. *Nile into Tiber. Egypt in the Roman World: Proceedings of the Third International Conference of Isis studies, Faculty of Archaeology, Leiden University, May 11 – 14 2005.* RGRW 159. Leiden: Brill, 2007.
Broneer, Oscar. "Paul and the Pagan Cults at Isthmia," *HTR* 64 (1971): 169 – 87.
Brooten, Bernadette J. *Women Leaders in the Ancient Synagogue: Inscriptional Evidence and Background Issues.* Atlanta: Scholars Press, 1982.
Brown, Raymond. "The Semitic Background of the New Testament Mysterion (I)." *Bib* 39 (1958): 426 – 48
Brown, Raymond. "The Semitic Background of the New Testament Mysterion (II)." *Bib* 40 (1959): 70 – 87.
Brown, Raymond. *An Introduction to the New Testament.* New York: Doubleday, 1997.
Bultmann, Rudolf. *Theology of the New Testament*, trans. Kendrick Grobel. Waco: Baylor University Press, 2007.
Bultmann, Rudolf. "Karl Barth, *The Resurrection of the Dead.*" In *Faith and Understanding I*, trans. Louise P. Smith, 66 – 94. London: SCM, 1969.
Burkert, Walter. *Ancient Mystery Cults.* Cambridge: Harvard University Press, 1987.
Burkert, Walter. "Bacchic *Teletai* in the Hellenistic Age." In *Masks of Dionysus*, edited by Thomas H. Carpenter and Christopher A. Faraone, 259 – 75. Ithaca: Cornell University Press, 1993.
Burns Jr., J. Patout. *Romans: Interpreted by Early Christian Commentators.* Grand Rapids: Eerdmans, 2012.
Cabrera, Paloma. "The Gifts of Dionysos." In *Redefining Dionysos*, edited by Alberto Bernabé, Miguel Herrero de Jáuregui, Ana Isabel Jiménez San Cristóbal, and Raquel Martin Hernández, 488 – 503. Berlin: Walter de Gruyter, 2013.
Cameron, Ron, and Merrill P. Miller, eds. *Redescribing Paul and the Corinthians.* Atlanta: Society of Biblical Literature, 2011.
Campbell, Douglas A. *The Deliverance of God: An Apocalyptic Reading of Justification in Paul.* Grand Rapids: Eerdmans, 2009.
Casadesus, Francesc. "The Transformation of the Initiation Language of Mystery Religions into Philosophical Terminology." In *Greek Philosophy and Mystery Cults*, edited by María José Martín-Velasco and María José García Blanco, 1 – 26. Cambridge: Cambridge Scholars, 2016.
Casadio, Giovanni. "Dionysus in Campania: Cumae." In *Mystic Cults in Magna Graecia*, edited by Giovanni Casadio and Patricia A. Johnston, 33 – 45. Austin: University of Texas Press, 2009.
Casadio, Giovanni. "*Religio* versus Religion." In *Myths, Martyrs, and Modernity: Studies in the History of Religions in Honour of Jan N. Bremmer*, edited by Jitse Dijkstra, Justin Kroesen, and Yme Kuiper, 301 – 26. Leiden: Brill, 2010.
Casadio, Giovanni, and Patricia A. Johnston, eds. *Mystic Cults in Magna Graecia.* Austin: University of Texas Press, 2009.
Cassidy, William. "Dionysos, Ecstasy, and The Forbidden." *Historical Reflections / Reflexions Historiques* 17 (1991): 23 – 44.
Casson, Lionel. *Selected Satires of Lucian.* New York: Norton, 1968.
Castelli, Elizabeth. *Imitating Paul: A Discourse of Power.* Louisville: Westminster John Knox, 1991.
Cavallin, Clemens. *Ritualization and Human Interiority.* Copenhagen: Museum Tusculanum Press, 2013.
Černušková, Veronika, Judith L. Kovacs, and Jana Plátová, eds. in cooperation with Vít Hušek. *Clement's Biblical Exegesis: Proceedings of the Second Colloquium on Clement of Alexandria.* Leiden; Boston: Brill, 2017.

Chang, Kai-Hsuan. *The Impact of Bodily Experience on Paul's Resurrection Theology.* LNTS 655. London: T&T Clark, 2022.
Chaniotis, Angelos. "The Ithyphallic Hymn for Demetrios Poliorcetes and Hellenistic Religious Mentality." In *More than Men, Less than Gods. Studies in Royal Cult and Imperial Worship. Proceedings of the International Colloquium Organized by the Belgian School at Athens (1–2 November 2007)*, edited by P. P. Iossif, A. S. Chankowski, and C. C. Lorber, 157–95. Leuven: Peeters, 2011.
Chester, Stephen J. *Conversion at Corinth: Perspectives on Conversion in Paul's Theology and the Corinthian Church.* London; New York: T&T Clark, 2005.
Choi, Mihwa. "Extreme Asceticism: Confucian Practice and Riesebrodt's Religious Virtuoso." *JSSR* 51 (2012): 456–67.
Chrysanthou, Anthi. *Defining Orphism: The Beliefs, the Teletae and the Writings.* Berlin: Walter de Gruyter, 2020.
Clinton, Kevin. "Stages of Initiation in the Eleusinian and Samothracian Mysteries." In *Greek Mysteries: The Archaeology and Ritual of Ancient Greek Secret Cults*, edited by Michael B. Cosmopoulos, 50–78. London; New York: Routledge, 2003.
Cole, Susan Guettel. *Landscapes, Gender, and Ritual Space: The Ancient Greek Experience.* Berkeley: University of California Press, 2004.
Collins, John J. *The Apocalyptic Imagination: An Introduction to Jewish Apocalyptic Literature.* 2nd ed. Grand Rapids: Eerdmans, 1998.
Collins, Raymond F. "'This is the Will of God: Your Sanctification.' (1 Thess 4:3)." In *Studies on the First Letter to the Thessalonians*, 299–325. Leuven: University Press, 1984.
Collins, Raymond F. *First Corinthians.* SP. Collegeville: Liturgical Press, 1999.
Concannon, Cavan W. *"When You Were Gentiles" Specters of Ethnicity in Roman Corinth and Paul's Corinthian Correspondence.* New Haven; London: Yale University Press, 2014.
Conroy, Jr., John T. "Philo's 'Death of the Soul': Is this Only a Metaphor?" *The Studia Philonica Annual* 23 (2011): 23–40.
Conzelmann, Hans. *1 Corinthians: A Commentary on the First Epistle to the Corinthians*, trans. James W. Leitch. Hermeneia. Philadelphia: Fortress, 1975.
Cook, John Granger. "1Cor 15,40–41: Paul and the Heavenly Bodies." *ZNW* 113 (2022): 159–79.
Coote, Robert B. "The Gospel of Mark: Baptism and Passover Initiation." In *Worship, Women and War: Essays in Honor of Susan Niditch*, edited by John J. Collins, T. M. Lemos, and Saul M. Olyan, 63–82. Providence, RI: Brown University, 2015.
Corrington, Gail Paterson. "The Milk of Salvation: Redemption by the Mother in Late Antiquity and Early Christianity." *HTR* 82 (1989): 393–420.
Cosmopoulos, Michael B. ed. *Greek Mysteries: The Archaeology and Ritual of Ancient Greek Secret Cults.* London; New York: Routledge, 2003.
Courtney, Edward. *Musa Lapidaria: A Selection of Latin Verse Inscriptions.* Atlanta: Scholars Press, 1995.
Cranfield, C. E. B. *A Critical and Exegetical Commentary on the Epistle to the Romans.* Vol. 1. ICC. Edinburgh: T&T Clark, 1975.
Croasmun, Matthew. *The Emergence of Sin: The Cosmic Tyrant in Romans.* Oxford: Oxford University Press, 2017.
Cumont, Franz. *Oriental Religions in Roman Paganism*, trans. Grant Showerman. New York: Dover Publications, 1956 (French original:1906 and 1909).
Dahl, Nils Alstrup, and David Hellholm. "Garment-Metaphors: The Old and the New Human Being." In *Antiquity and Humanity: Essays on Ancient Religion and Philosophy Presented to Hans Dieter Betz*

on his 70th Birthday, edited by Adela Yarbro Collins and Margaret M. Mitchell, 139–58. Tübingen: Mohr Siebeck, 2001.

Davies, W. D. *Paul and Rabbinic Judaism: Some Rabbinic Elements in Pauline Theology.* London: S.P.C.K., 1948.

de Boer, Martinus C. *Galatians.* NTL. Louisville: Westminster John Knox, 2011.

de Jáuregui, Miguel Herrero. "'Trust the God': *Tharsein* in Ancient Greek Religion." *HSCP* 108 (2015): 1–52.

de la Fuente, David Hernández. "Parallels between Dionysos and Christ in Late Antiquity: Miraculous Healings in Nonnus' *Dionysiaca.*" In *Redefining Dionysos*, edited by Alberto Bernabé, Miguel Herrero de Jáuregui, Ana Isabel Jiménez San Cristóbal, and Raquel Martin Hernández, 464–87. Berlin: Walter de Gruyter, 2013.

DeMaris, Richard E. "Corinthian Religion and Baptism for the Dead (1 Corinthians 15:29): Insights from Archaeology and Anthropology." *JBL* 114 (1995): 661–82.

DeMaris, Richard E. *The New Testament in its Ritual World.* London; New York: Routledge, 2008.

Dijkstra, Jitse, Justin Kroesen, and Yme Kuiper, eds. *Myths, Martyrs, and Modernity: Studies in the History of Religions in Honour of Jan N. Bremmer.* Leiden: Brill, 2010.

Dillon, John. *The Middle Platonists, 80 B.C. to A.D. 220.* 2nd ed. Ithaca: Cornell University Press, 1996.

Dinkler, Michal Beth. *Literary Theory and the New Testament.* New Haven: Yale University Press, 2019.

Dodds, E. R. *Euripides. Bacchae.* Oxford: Clarendon Press, 1960.

Dodson, Joseph R. *The 'Powers' of Personification: Rhetorical Purpose in the 'Book of Wisdom' and the Letter to the Romans.* BZNW 161. Berlin: Walter de Gruyter, 2008.

Douglas, Mary. *Purity and Danger: An Analysis of Concepts of Pollution and Taboo.* London: Routledge Classics, 1966.

Dunbabin, Katherine. "The Triumph of Dionysus on Mosaics in North Africa." *Papers of the British School at Rome* 39 (1971): 52–65.

Dunn, James D. G. *Baptism in the Holy Spirit: A Re-examination of the New Testament Teaching on the Gift of the Spirit in Relation to Pentecostalism Today.* London: S.C.M., 1970.

Dunn, James D. G. *Romans 1–8.* WBC 38 A. Dallas: Word, 1988.

Dunn, James D. G. *The Theology of Paul the Apostle.* Grand Rapids: Eerdmans, 1997.

Dunn, James D. G. "'Baptized' as Metaphor." In *Baptism, the New Testament and the Church: Historical and Contemporary Studies in Honor of R. E. O. White*, edited by Stanley Porter and Anthony R. Cross, 294–310. Sheffield: Sheffield Academic, 1999.

Eastman, David L. *Paul the Martyr: The Cult of the Apostle in the Latin West.* Atlanta: Society of Biblical Literature, 2011.

Edmonds III, Radcliffe G. "Tearing Apart the Zagreus Myth: A Few Disparaging Remarks on Orphism and Original Sin," *Classical Antiquity* 18 (1999): 35–73.

Edmonds III, Radcliffe G. *Redefining Ancient Orphism: A Study in Greek Religion.* Cambridge: Cambridge University Press, 2013.

Edmonds III, Radcliffe G. *Drawing the Moon: Magic in the Ancient Greco-Roman World.* Princeton: Princeton University Press, 2019.

Edsall, Benjamin A. *The Reception of Paul and Early Christian Initiation: History and Hermeneutics.* Cambridge: Cambridge University Press, 2019.

Edwards, Mark J. "Review of *Pagan Monotheism in Late Antiquity* Edited by Polymnia Athanassiadi and Michael Frede." *JTS* 51 (2000): 339–42.

Elliott, John H. *1 Peter: A New Translation with Introduction and Commentary.* 37B. New York: Doubleday, 2000.

Elliott, Susan M. "Choose Your Mother, Choose Your Master: Galatians 4:21–5:1 in the Shadow of the Anatolian Mother of the Gods." *JBL* 118 (1999): 661–683.
Engberg-Pedersen, Troels. *Cosmology and Self in the Apostle Paul*. Oxford: Oxford University Press, 2010.
Engels, Donald. *Roman Corinth: An Alternative Model for the Classical City*. Chicago: University of Chicago Press, 1990.
Fauconnier, Gilles, and Mark Turner. *The Way We Think: Conceptual Blending and the Mind's Hidden Complexities*. New York: Basic Books, 2002.
Fee, Gordon D. *The First Epistle to the Corinthians*. NICNT. Grand Rapids: Eerdmans, 1987.
Ferguson, Everett. *Baptism in the Early Church: History, Theology, and Liturgy in the First Five Centuries*. Grand Rapids: Eerdmans, 2009.
Fernandez, James W. "Symbolic Consensus in a Fang Reformative Cult." *AA* 67 (1965): 902–29.
Fitzgerald, John T. *Cracks in an Earthen Vessel: An Examination of the Catalogues of Hardships in the Corinthian Correspondence*. Atlanta: Scholars Press, 1988.
Fitzgerald, John T., Thomas H. Olbricht, and L. Michael White, eds. *Early Christianity and Classical Culture: Comparative Studies in Honor of Abraham J. Malherbe*. Leiden: Brill, 2003.
Fitzmyer, Joseph A. *First Corinthians: A New Translation with Introduction and Commentary*. AB 32. New Haven: Yale University Press, 2008.
Foley, Helene P., ed. *The Homeric Hymn to Demeter: Translation, Commentary, and Interpretative Essays*. Princeton: Princeton University Press.
Frankenberry. N., *Radical Interpretation in Religion*. Cambridge: Cambridge University Press, 2002.
Frazer, James G. *The Golden Bough*. 2 vols. London: Macmillan, 1890.
Friesen, Courtney J. P. *Reading Dionysus: Euripides'* Bacchae *and the Cultural Contestations of Greeks, Jews, Romans, and Christians*. Tübingen: Mohr Siebeck, 2015.
Früchtel, Ursula. *Die kosmologischen Vorstellungen bei Philo von Alexandrien: Ein Beitrag zur Geschichte der Genesisexegese*. Leiden: Brill, 1968.
Gager, John G. *Curse Tablets and Binding Spells from the Ancient World*. New York: Oxford University Press, 1999.
Gasparini, Valentino. "Isis and Osiris: Demonology vs. Henotheism?" *Numen* 58 (2011): 697–728.
Gasparini, Valentino. "I will not be thirsty. My lips will not be dry." In *Burial Rituals, Ideas of Afterlife, and the Individual in the Hellenistic World and the Roman Empire*, edited by Katharina Waldner, Richard Gordon, and Wolfgang Spickermann, 125–50. Stuttgart: Franz Steiner Verlag, 2016.
Gasparini, Valentino, and Richard Veymiers, eds. *Individuals and Materials in the Greco-Roman Cults of Isis: Agents, Images, and Practices: Proceedings of the VIth International Conference of Isis Studies (Erfurt, May 6–8, 2013 – Liège, September 23–24, 2013)*. 2 volumes. RGRW 187/I,II. Leiden: Brill, 2018.
Gasparro, Giulia Sfameni. "The Hellenistic Face of Isis: Cosmic and Saviour Goddess." In *Nile into Tiber. Egypt in the Roman World: Proceedings of the Third International Conference of Isis studies, Faculty of Archaeology, Leiden University, May 11–14 2005*, edited by Laurent Bricault, Miguel John Versluys, and Paul G. P. Meyboom, 40–72. Leiden: Brill, 2007.
Gasparro, Giulia Sfameni. "Identités religieuses isiaques: pour la définition de'une catégorie historico-religieuse." In *Individuals and Materials in the Greco-Roman Cults of Isis: Agents, Images, and Practices*. Volume 1, edited by Valentino Gasparini and Richard Veymiers, 74–107. Leiden: Brill, 2018.
Gaventa, Beverly Roberts. "The Cosmic Power of Sin in Paul's Letter to Romans." *Interpretation* 58 (2004): 229–40.

Gebhard, Elizabeth R. "Rites for Melikertes-Palaimon in the Early Roman Corinthia." In *Urban Religion in Roman Corinth: Interdisciplinary Approaches*, edited by Daniel Schowalter and Steven J. Friesen, 165–203. Cambridge: Harvard Theological Studies, 2005.
Geertz, Clifford. "Religion as a Cultural System." In *The Interpretation of Cultures*. 3rd ed., 93–135. New York: Basic Books, 2017 [1973].
Gladd, Benjamin L. *Revealing the Mysterion: The Use of Mystery in Daniel and Second Temple Judaism with its Bearing on First Corinthians*. BZNW 160. Berlin: Walter de Gruyter, 2008.
Goldstein, Ronnie, and Guy G. Stroumsa. "The Greek and Jewish Origins of Docetism: A New Proposal." *ZAC* 10 (2006): 423–41.
Goodenough, Erwin R. *By Light, Light: The Mystic Gospel of Hellenistic Judaism*. New Haven: Yale University Press, 1935.
Goodrich, John K. "'As long as the heir is a child': The Rhetoric of Inheritance in Galatians 4:1–2 and P.Ryl 2.153." *NovT* 55 (2013): 61–76.
Gordon, Richard L. "Mystery Religions, Religious Studies." *RPP* 8:652–53.
Graf, Fritz. "Dionysian and Orphic Eschatology: New Texts and Old Questions." In *Masks of Dionysus*, edited by Thomas H. Carpenter and Christopher A. Faraone, 239–58. Ithaca: Cornell University Press, 1993.
Graf, Fritz. "Theories of Magic in Antiquity." In *Magic and Ritual in the Ancient World*, edited by Paul Mirecki and Marvin Meyer, 93–104. Leiden: Brill, 2001.
Graf, Fritz. "The Blessings of Madness: Dionysos, Madness, and Scholarship." *ARG* 12 (2010): 169–82.
Graf, Fritz. "Theoi Soteres." *ARG* 18–19 (2017): 239–53.
Graf, Fritz, and Sarah Iles Johnston. *Ritual Texts for the Afterlife: Orpheus and the Bacchic Gold Tablets*. 2nd ed. New York: Routledge, 2013.
Grandjean, Yves. *Une nouvelle arétalogie d'Isis à Maronée*. Leiden: Brill, 1975.
Grenfell, Bernard P., and Arthur S. Hunt. *The Oxyrhynchus Papyri. Part XI*. London, 1915.
Griffiths, J. Gwyn. *Apuleius, The Isis-Book*. Leiden: Brill, 1975.
Grimes, Ronald L. *Ritual Criticism: Case Studies in Its Practice, Essays on Its Theory*. Columbia: University of South Carolina Press, 1990.
Grimes, Ronald L. *The Craft of Ritual Studies*. New York: Oxford University Press, 2014.
Gruen, Erich S. *Studies in Greek Culture and Roman Policy*. Leiden; New York: Brill, 1990.
Gupta, Nijay. K. *Worship That Makes Sense to Paul: A New Approach to the Theology and Ethics of Paul's Cultic Metaphors*. BZNW 175. Berlin: Walter de Gruyter, 2010.
Hanges, James C. *Paul, Founder of Churches: A Study in Light of the Evidence for the Role of "Founder-Figures" in the Hellenistic-Roman Period*. WUNT 292. Tübingen: Mohr Siebeck, 2012.
Harland, Philip A. *Associations, Synagogues, and Congregations: Claiming a Place in Ancient Mediterranean Society*. Minneapolis: Fortress, 2003.
Harland, Philip A. "Christ-Bearers and Fellow-Initiates: Local Cultural Life and Christian Identity in Ignatius' Letters." *JECS* 11 (2003): 481–99.
Harland, Philip A. *Greco-Roman Associations: Texts, Translations, and Commentary. Volume II. North Coast of the Black Sea, Asia Minor*. Berlin: Walter de Gruyter, 2014.
Harrill, J. Albert. "Coming of Age and Putting on Christ: The *toga virilis* Ceremony, Its Paraenesis, and Paul's Interpretation of Baptism in Galatians." *NovT* 44 (2002): 252–77.
Harrison, Stephen J. *Apuleius: A Latin Sophist*. Oxford: Oxford University Press, 2000.
Harrison, Thomas. "Review Article: Beyond the *Polis*? New Approaches to Greek Religion." *JHS* 135 (2015): 165–80.
Hays, Richard B. *Echoes of Scripture in the Letters of Paul*. New Haven: Yale University Press, 1989.

Hays, Richard B. *First Corinthians.* Louisville: Westminster John Knox Press, 1997.
Hays, Richard B. *The Faith of Jesus Christ: The Narrative Substructure of Galatians 3:1–4:11.* Grand Rapids: Eerdmans, 2002.
Hellholm, David, Tor Vegge, Øyvind Norderval, and Christer Hellholm, eds. *Ablution, Initiation, and Baptism: Late Antiquity, Early Judaism, and Early Christianity.* 3 vols. Berlin: Walter de Gruyter, 2011.
Henrichs, Albert. "Introduction: What is a Greek Priest?" In *Practitioners of the Divine: Greek Priests and Religious Officials from Homer to Heliodorus*, edited by Beate Dignas and Kai Trampedach, 1–14. Cambridge: Center for Hellenic Studies, 2008.
Herbener, Jens-André P. "On the Term 'Monotheism.'" *Numen* 60 (2013): 61–48.
Hewitt, J. Thomas. *Messiah and Scripture: Paul's "In Christ" Idiom in Its Ancient Jewish Context.* WUNT II/522. Tübingen: Mohr Siebeck, 2020.
Heyob, Sharon Kelly. *The Cult of Isis among Women in the Graeco-Roman World.* Leiden: Brill, 1975.
Hogan, Karina Martin, Matthew Goff, and Emma Wasserman, eds. *Pedagogy in Ancient Judaism and Early Christianity.* Atlanta: Society of Biblical Literature, 2017.
Hofius, Otfried. "The Adam-Christ Antithesis and the Law: Reflections on Romans 5:12–21." In *Paul and the Mosaic Law*, edited by James D. G. Dunn, 165–205. Grand Rapids: Eerdmans, 2001.
Holloway, Paul A. *Philippians: A Commentary.* Hermeneia. Minneapolis: Fortress, 2017.
Hooker, Morna D. "Another Look at πίστις Χριστοῦ." *SJT* 69 (2016): 46–62.
Hope, Valerie M. *Death in Ancient Rome: A Sourcebook.* New York: Routledge, 2007.
Hope, Valerie M. *Roman Death: The Dying and the Death in Ancient Rome.* London; New York: Continuum, 2009.
Hopkins, Keith. "Novel Evidence for Roman Slavery." *PP* 138 (1993): 3–27.
Horrell, David G. *The Social Ethos of the Corinthian Correspondence: Interests and Ideology from 1 Corinthians and 1 Clement.* Edinburgh: T&T Clark, 1996.
Horrell, David G. and Edward Adams. "Introduction: The Scholarly Quest for Paul's Church at Corinth: A Critical Survey." In *Christianity at Corinth: The Quest for the Pauline Church*, edited by Edward Adams and David G. Horrell, 1–43. Louisville: Westminster John Knox, 2004.
Hultgren, Arland J. *Paul's Letter to the Romans: A Commentary.* Grand Rapids: Eerdmans, 2011.
Humphrey, Caroline and James Laidlaw. *The Archetypal Actions of Ritual: A Theory of Ritual Illustrated by the Jain Rite of Worship.* Oxford: Clarendon Press, 1994.
Hunt, Peter. *Slaves, Warfare, and Ideology in the Greek Historians.* New York: Cambridge University Press, 1998.
Hylen, Susan E. "Metaphor Matters: Violence and Ethics." *CBQ* 73 (2011): 777–796.
Hylen, Susan E. *Women in the New Testament World.* New York: Oxford University Press, 2019.
Hylen, Susan E. "Public and Private Space and Action in the Early Roman Period." *NTS* 66 (2020): 534–53.
Ibáñez, Jesús-M. Nieto. "The Sacred Grove of Scythopolis (Flavius Josephus, *Jewish War* II 466–471)." *IEJ* 49 (1999): 260–68.
Isler-Kerényi, Cornelia. *Dionysos in Archaic Greece: An Understanding through Images.* RGRW 181. Leiden: Brill, 2007.
Isler-Kerényi, Cornelia. "New Contributions of Dionysiac Iconography to the History of Religions in Greece and Italy." In *Mystic Cults in Magna Graecia*, edited by Giovanni Casadio and Patricia A. Johnston, 61–72. Austin: University of Texas Press, 2009.
Isler-Kerényi, Cornelia. *Dionysos in Classical Athens: An Understanding through Images.* Leiden: Brill, 2015.

Jaccottet, Anne-Françoise. *Choisir Dionysos: les associations dionysiaques, ou, la face cachée du dionysisme.* Zürich: Akanthvs, 2003.
Jensen, Robin M. *Baptismal Imagery in Early Christianity: Ritual, Visual, and Theological Dimensions.* Grand Rapids: Baker Academic, 2012.
Jeong, Donghyun. "God's Hoplites: Slaves and Warfare in Romans 6:12–23." *KJCS* 105 (2017): 47–72.
Jeong, Donghyun. "1 Corinthians 15:35–58: An Assessment of Stoic Interpretation." *KJCS* 109 (2018): 45–70.
Jeong, Donghyun. "Review of Terri Moore, *The Mysteries, Resurrection, and 1 Corinthians 15.*" *RBL* (2020): 1–4.
Jewett, Robert. *Romans: A Commentary.* Hermeneia. Minneapolis: Fortress, 2007.
Jim, Theodora Suk Fong. *Sharing with the Gods:* Aparchai *and* Dekatai *in Ancient Greece.* Oxford: Oxford University Press, 2014.
Jim, Theodora Suk Fong. "'Salvation' (*Soteria*) and Ancient Mystery Cults." *ARG* 18–19 (2017): 255–82.
Johnson, Luke Timothy. *Reading Romans: A Literary and Theological Commentary.* New York: Crossroad, 1997.
Johnson Hodge, Caroline. *If Sons, Then Heirs: A Study of Kinship and Ethnicity in the Letters of Paul.* Oxford: Oxford University Press, 2007.
Johnston, Sarah Iles. *Restless Dead: Encounters Between the Living and the Dead in Ancient Greece.* Berkeley: University of California Press, 1999.
Johnston, Sarah Iles, and Timothy J. McNiven. "Dionysos and the Underworld in Toledo." *MH* 53 (1996): 25–36.
Käsemann, Ernst. *Leib und Leib Christi.* Tübingen: Mohr, 1933.
Käsemann, Ernst. "The Beginnings of Christian Theology." *JTC* 6 (1969): 162–85.
Käsemann, Ernst. "On Paul's Anthropology." In *Perspectives on Paul*, trans. Margaret Kohl, 1–31. Philadelphia: Fortress Press, 1971.
Käsemann, Ernst. *Commentary on Romans*, trans. Geoffrey W. Bromiley. Grand Rapids: Eerdmans, 1980.
Kearns, Conleth. "The Interpretation of Romans 6,7." In *Studiorum Paulinorum Congressus Internationalis Catholicus 1961: simul Secundus Congressus Internationalis Catholicus de Re Biblica. Completo undevicesimo saeculo post S. Pauli in urbem adventum.* Volume 1. Analecta Biblica 17–18, 303–307. Romae: E Pontificio Instituto Biblico, 1963.
Kennedy, H. A. A. *St. Paul and the Mystery-Religions.* New York; London: Hodder and Stoughton, 1913.
Kim, Seon Yong. *Curse Motifs in Galatians: An Investigation into Paul's Rhetorical Strategies.* WUNT II/531. Tübingen: Mohr Siebeck, 2020.
Kim, Yung Suk. *Christ's Body in Corinth: The Politics of a Metaphor.* Minneapolis: Fortress, 2008.
Kindt, Julia. *Rethinking Greek Religion.* Cambridge: Cambridge University Press, 2012.
King, Charles W. *The Ancient Roman Afterlife:* Di Manes, *Belief, and the Cult of the Dead.* Austin: University of Texas Press, 2020.
Kittel, Gerhard, and Gerhard Friedrich, eds. *Theological Dictionary of the New Testament*, trans. Geoffrey W. Bromiley. 10 vols. Grand Rapids: Eerdmans, 1964–1976.
Klawans, Jonathan. *Impurity and Sin in Ancient Judaism.* Oxford: Oxford University Press, 2000.
Klauck, Hans-Josef. *The Religious Context of Early Christianity: A Guide to Graeco-Roman Religions*, trans. Brian McNeil. Minneapolis: Fortress, 2003.
Klein, Günter. "Paul's Purpose in Writing the Epistle to the Romans." In *The Romans Debate.* Rev. and exp. ed, edited by Karl P. Donfried, 29–43. Peabody: Hendrickson, 1991.

Kloppenborg, John S. "Collegia and *Thiasoi:* Issues in Function, Taxonomy and Membership." In *Voluntary Associations in the Graeco-Roman World*, edited by John S. Kloppenborg and Stephen G. Wilson, 16–30. London; New York: Routledge, 1996.

Kloppenborg, John S. *Christ's Associations: Connecting and Belonging in the Ancient City.* New Haven: Yale University Press, 2019.

Koester, Helmut. "Melikertes at Isthmia: A Roman Mystery Cult." In *Greeks, Romans, and Christians: Essays in Honor of Abraham J. Malherbe*, edited by David L. Balch, Everett Ferguson, and Wayne A. Meeks, 355–66. Minneapolis: Fortress Press, 1990.

Kouremenos, Theokritos, George M. Parássoglou, and K. Tsantsanoglou, eds. *The Derveni Papyrus.* Firenze: Leo S. Olschki Editore, 2006.

Kraemer, Ross S. "Ecstasy and Possession: The Attraction of Women to the Cult of Dionysus." *HTR* 72 (1979): 55–80.

Kraemer, Ross S. *Women's Religions in the Greco-Roman World: A Sourcebook.* Oxford: Oxford University Press, 2004.

Kraftchick, Steven J. "Death in Us, Life in You." In *Pauline Theology. Volume II: 1 & 2 Corinthians*, edited by David M. Hay, 156–81. Minneapolis: Fortress, 1993.

Kraftchick, Steven J. "Recast, Reclaim, Reject: Myth and Validity." In *Myth and Scripture: Contemporary Perspectives on Religion, Language, and Imagination*, edited by Dexter E. Callender, 179–200. Atlanta: Society of Biblical Literature, 2014.

Krauskopf, Ingrid. "Leukothea nach den antiken Quellen." In *Akten des Kolloquiums zum Thema die Göttin von Pyrgi: archäologische, linguistische und religionsgeschichtliche Aspekte (Tübingen, 16–17 Januar 1979)*, 137–48. Florence: Olschki, 1981.

Kreinath, Jens, J. A. M. Snoek, and Michael Stauberg, eds. *Theorizing Rituals: Issues, Topics, Approaches, Concepts.* 2 vols. Leiden: Brill, 2006.

Kuo-Yu Tsui, Teresa. "'Baptized into His Death' (Rom 6,3) and 'Clothed with Christ' (Gal 3,27): The Soteriological Meaning of Baptism in Light of Pauline Apocalyptic." *ETL* 88 (2012): 395–417

Kurtz, Donna C. and John Boardman. *Greek Burial Customs.* Ithaca: Cornell University Press, 1971.

Lambert, David. "'Desire' Enacted in the Wilderness: Problems in the History of the Self and Bible Translation." In *Self, Self-Fashioning, and Individuality in Late Antiquity: New Perspectives*, edited by Maren R. Niehoff and Joshua Levinson, 25–49. Tübingen: Mohr Siebeck, 2019.

Lampe, Peter. *From Paul to Valentinus: Christians at Rome in the First Two Centuries*, trans. Michael Steinhauser, edited by Marshall D. Johnson. Minneapolis: Fortress, 2003.

Lakoff, George and Mark Johnson. *Metaphors We Live By.* Chicago: University of Chicago Press, 1980.

Lancellotti, Maria Grazia. *Attis: Between Myth and History: King, Priest and God.* Leiden: Brill, 2002.

Lang, T. J. *Mystery and the Making of a Christian Historical Consciousness: From Paul to the Second Century.* BZNW 219. Berlin: Walter de Gruyter, 2015.

Lannoy, Annelies. "St Paul in the Early 20th Century History of Religions. 'The Mystic of Tarsus' and the Pagan Mystery Cults after the Correspondence of Franz Cumont and Alfred Loisy." *ZRG* 64 (2012): 222–39.

Last, Richard. *The Pauline Church and the Corinthian Ekklēsia: Greco-Roman Associations in Comparative Context.* Cambridge: Cambridge University Press, 2016.

Lawrence, Jonathan D. *Washing in Water: Trajectories of Ritual Bathing in the Hebrew Bible and Second Temple Literature.* Atlanta: Society of Biblical Literature, 2006.

Lease, Gary. "Jewish Mystery Cults since Goodenough." *Aufstieg und Niedergang der römischen Welt* 20 (1987): 864–71.

Lee, Michelle V. *Paul, the Stoics, and the Body of Christ.* Cambridge: Cambridge University Press, 2006.

Lefkowitz, Mary and Maureen B. Fant. *Women's Lives in Greece and Rome*. 2nd ed. Baltimore: Johns Hopkins University Press, 1992.
Levison, John R. "Adam and Eve in Romans 1.18–25 and the Greek *Life of Adam and Eve*." *NTS* 50 (2004): 519–34.
Levy, Robert I. "The Life and Death of Ritual: Reflections on Some Ethnographic and Historical Phenomena in the Light of Roy Rappaport's Analysis of Ritual." In *Ecology and the Sacred: Engaging the Anthropology of Roy A. Rappaport*, edited by Ellen Messer and Michael Lambek, 145–69. Ann Arbor: The University of Michigan Press, 2001.
Libby, Brigitte B. "Moons, Smoke, and Mirrors in Apuleius' Portrayal of Isis." *AJP* 132 (2011): 301–22.
Lipka, Michael. *Romans Gods: A Conceptual Approach*. Leiden; Boston: Brill, 2009.
Litwa, M. David. *We Are Being Transformed: Deification in Paul's Soteriology*. BZNW 187. Berlin: Walter de Gruyter, 2012.
Lohse, Eduard. "Taufe und Rechtfertigung bei Paulus." *KD* 11 (1965): 308–24.
Loisy, Alfred. "The Christian Mystery." *HJ* 10 (1911): 45–64.
Longenecker, Richard N. *Galatians*. WBC 41. Dallas: Word Books, 1990.
Longenecker, Richard N. *The Epistle to the Romans: A Commentary on the Greek Text*. NIGTC. Grand Rapids: Eerdmans, 2016.
Lüdemann, Gerd. "Die 'Religionsgeschichtliche Schule' und die Neutestamentliche Wissenschaft." In *Die "Religionsgeschichtliche Schule": Facetten eines theologischen Umbruchs*, edited by Gerd Lüdemann, 9–22. Frankfurt am Main; New York: Peter Lang, 1996.
MacDonald, Dennis R. *The Dionysian Gospel: The Fourth Gospel and Euripides*. Minneapolis: Fortress, 2017.
Mack, Burton L. "Rereading the Christ Myth: Paul's Gospel and the Christ Cult Question." In *Redescribing Paul and the Corinthians*, edited by Ron Cameron and Merrill P. Miller, 35–73. Atlanta: Society of Biblical Literature, 2011.
Malherbe, Abraham J. *The Letters to the Thessalonians: A New Translation with Introduction and Commentary*. AB 32B. New York: Doubleday, 2000.
Marshall, Jill E. "Uncovering Traditions in 1 Corinthians 11:2–16." *NovT* 61 (2019): 70–87.
Martín-Velasco, María José and María José García Blanco, eds. *Greek Philosophy and Mystery Cults*. Cambridge: Cambridge Scholars, 2016.
Martin, S. Rebecca. "Ethnicity and Greek Art History in Theory and Practice." In *Theoretical Approaches to the Archaeology of Ancient Greece: Manipulating Material Culture*, edited by Lisa Nevett, 143–63. Ann Arbor: University of Michigan Press, 2017.
Martin, Troy W. "Paul's Pneumatological Statements and Ancient Medical Texts." In *The New Testament and Early Christian Literature in Greco-Roman Context: Studies in Honor of David E. Aune*, edited by John Fotopoulos, 105–26. Leiden: Brill, 2006.
Martyn, J. Louis. *Galatians: A New Translation with Introduction and Commentary*. AB 33 A. New York: Doubleday, 1997.
Martzavou, Paraskevi. "Priests and Priestly Roles in the Isiac Cults: Women as Agents in Religious Change in Late Hellenistic and Roman Athens." In *Ritual Dynamics in the Ancient Mediterranean: Agency, Emotion, Gender, Representation*, edited by Angelos Chaniotis, 61–84. HABES 49. Stuttgart: Franz Steiner Verlag, 2011.
Martzavou, Paraskevi. "What is an Isiac Priest in the Greek World?" In *Individuals and Materials in the Greco-Roman Cults of Isis: Agents, Images, and Practices*, vol. 1, edited by Valentino Gasparini and Richard Veymiers, 127–54. Leiden: Brill, 2018.

McGowan, Andrew Brian. "'Is There A Liturgical Text in This Gospel?': The Institution Narratives and Their Early Interpretative Communities." *JBL* 118 (1999): 73–87.
Meeks, Wayne. "The Image of the Androgyne: Some Uses of a Symbol in Earliest Christianity." *HR* 13 (1974): 165–208.
Merkelbach, Reinhold. "Ein ägyptischer Priestereid." *ZPE* 2 (1968): 7–30.
Merkelbach, Reinhold."Fragment eines satirischen Romans: Aufforderung zur Beichte." *ZPE* 11 (1973): 81–100.
Merkelbach, Reinhold. *Isis regina, Zeus Sarapis: die griechisch-ägyptische Religion nach den Quellen dargestellt.* Stuttgart: B. G. Teubner, 1995.
Messer, Ellen, and Michael Lambek, eds. *Ecology and the Sacred: Engaging the Anthropology of Roy A. Rappaport.* Ann Arbor: The University of Michigan Press, 2001.
Mettinger, Tryggve N. D. "The 'Dying and Rising God': A Survey of Research from Frazer to the Present Day." *SEÅ* 63 (1998): 111–23.
Meyer, Marvin W. "Mysteries Divine." *Numen* 39 (1992): 235–38.
Meyer, Marvin W., ed. *The Ancient Mysteries: A Sourcebook of Sacred Texts.* Philadelphia: University of Pennsylvania Press, 1999.
Mills, Lynn, and Nicholas J. Moore. "One Baptism Once: The Origins of the Unrepeatability of Christian Baptism." *EC* 11 (2020): 206–26.
Mitchell, Margaret M. *Paul and the Rhetoric of Reconciliation: An Exegetical Investigation of the Language and Composition of 1 Corinthians.* Tübingen: J. C. B. Mohr Paul Siebeck, 1991.
Mitchell, Stephen, ed. *One God: Pagan Monotheism in the Roman Empire.* Cambridge: Cambridge University Press, 2010.
Moles, John. "Jesus and Dionysus in The Acts of The Apostles and Early Christianity." *Hermathena* 180 (2006): 65–104.
Moore, George Foot. "Christian Writers on Judaism." *HTR* 14 (1921): 197–254.
Moore, Terri. *The Mysteries, Resurrection, and 1 Corinthians 15: Comparative Methodology and Contextual Exegesis.* Lanham: Lexington/Fortress, 2018.
Morales, Isaac A. "Baptism and Union with Christ." In *"In Christ" in Paul*, edited by M. J. Thate, Kevin J. Vanhoozer, and Constantine R. Campbell, 157–79. Tübigen: Mohr Siebeck, 2014.
Morgan, Teresa. *Roman Faith and Christian Faith:* Pistis *and* Fides *in the Early Roman Empire and Early Churches.* Oxford: Oxford University Press, 2015.
Morgan, Teresa. *Being 'in Christ' in the Letters of Paul: Saved through Christ and in his Hands.* Tübingen: Mohr Siebeck, 2020.
Moss, Candida R. *The Other Christs: Imitating Jesus in Ancient Christian Ideologies of Martyrdom.* New York: Oxford University, 2010.
Murphy-O'Connor, Jerome. "'Baptized for the Dead' (I Cor XV, 29) A Corinthian Slogan?" *RB* 88 (1981): 532–43.
Murphy-O'Connor, Jerome. "The Irrevocable Will (Gal 3:15)." *RB* 106 (1999): 224–35.
Musurillo, Herbert. "Euripides and Dionysiac Piety (Bacchae 370–433)." *TPAPA* 97 (1966): 299–309.
Mylonas, George E. *Eleusis and the Eleusinian Mysteries.* Princeton: Princeton University Press, 1961.
Nasrallah, Laura S. "Grief in Corinth: The Roman City and Paul's Corinthian Correspondence." In *Contested Spaces: Houses and Temples in Roman Antiquity and the New Testament*, edited by David L. Balch and Annette Weissenrieder, 109–39. Tübingen: Mohr Siebeck, 2012.
Nilsson, Martin P. *The Dionysiac Mysteries of the Hellenistic and Roman Age.* New York: Arno Press, 1975.
Nock, Arthur Darby. "Cremation and Burial in the Roman Empire." *HTR* 25 (1932): 321–59.

Nock, Arthur Darby. *Early Gentile Christianity and Its Hellenistic Background.* New York: Harper & Row, 1964.
Novenson, Matthew V. *Christ among the Messiahs: Christ Language in Paul and Messiah Language in Ancient Judaism.* Oxford: Oxford University Press, 2012.
Novenson, Matthew V. *The Grammar of Messianism: An Ancient Jewish Political Idiom and Its Users.* Oxford: Oxford University Press: 2017.
Oakley, John H. "Women in Athenian Ritual and Funerary Art." In *Worshiping Women: Ritual and Reality in Classical Athens*, edited by Nikolaos Kaltsas and Alan Shapiro, 335–41. New York: Alexander S. Onassis Public Benefit Foundation in collaboration with the National Archaeological Museum, Athens, 2008.
Overbeck, Bernhard and Mechtild Overbeck. *Dionysus and His World: The Fascination of Precious Gems.* Athens: Hatzimichalis Estate, 2005.
Ogden, Daniel. *Magic, Witchcraft, and Ghosts in the Greek and Roman Worlds.* Oxford; New York: Oxford University Press, 2002.
O'Neill, Kevin Lewis. "Introduction: Further Explorations in Theory and Practice." *HR* 51 (2012): 291–98.
Osborne, R. "Archaeology, the Salaminioi, and the Politics of Sacred Space in Archaic Attica." In *Placing the Gods: Sanctuaries and Sacred Space in Ancient Greece*, edited by Susan E. Alcock and Robin Osborne, 143–60. New York: Oxford University Press, 1994.
Osann, F. G. *Sylloge inscriptionum antiquarum graecarum et latinarum.* Leipzig: Leske, 1834.
Osiek, Carolyn and Margaret Y. MacDonald, with Janet H. Tulloch. *A Woman's Place: House Churches in Earliest Christianity.* Minneapolis: Augsburg Fortress, 2006.
Otto, Walter F. *Dionysus: Myth and Cult*, trans. Robert B. Palmer. Bloomington: Indiana University Press, 1965.
Pache, Corine Ondine. *Baby and Child Heroes in Ancient Greece.* Urbana; Chicago: University of Illinois Press, 2004.
Pache, Corine Ondine. "Singing Heroes: The Poetics of Hero Cult in the Heroikos." In *Philostratus's Heroikos: Religion and Cultural Identity in the Third Century C.E.*, edited by E. B. Aitken and K. B. Maclean, 3–24. Atlanta: Society of Biblical Literature, 2004.
Pagis, Michal. "Review: *The Promise of Salvation: A Theory of Religion*, by Martin Riesebrodt." *SoR* 72 (2011): 375–77.
Pailler, Jean-Marie. "Les religions orientales, troisieme epoque." *Pallas* 35 (1989): 95–113.
Pakkala, Juha. *Intolerant Monolatry in the Deuteronomistic History.* Helsinki; Göttingen: Vandenhoeck & Ruprecht, 1999.
Pakkala, Juha. "The Monotheism of the Deuteronomistic History." *SJOT* 21 (2007): 159–178.
Parca, Maryline, and Angeliki Tzanetou, ed. *Finding Persephone: Women's Rituals in the Ancient Mediterranean.* Bloomington; Indianapolis: Indiana University Press, 2007.
Parker, Robert. *Miasma: Pollution and Purification in Early Greek Religion.* Oxford: Clarendon Press, 1983.
Parker, Robert. "Religion in the Prose Hymns." In *In Praise of Asclepius: Aelius Aristides, Selected Prose Hymns*, edited by Donald A. Russell, Michael Trapp, and Heinz-Günther Nesselrath, 67–88. Tübingen: Mohr Siebeck, 2016.
Petersen, Anders Klostergaard. "Shedding New Light on Paul's Understanding of Baptism: a Ritual-Theoretical Approach to Romans 6." *ST* 52 (1998): 3–28.
Powell, Mark Allan. *Jesus as a Figure in History: How Modern Historians View the Man from Galilee.* 2nd ed. Louisville: Westminster John Knox, 2013.

Powers, Daniel G. *Salvation through Participation: An Examination of the Notion of the Believers' Corporate Unity with Christ in Early Christian Soteriology*. Leuven: Peeters, 2001.

Peacock, James. "Belief Beheld—Inside and Outside, Insider and Outsider in the Anthropology of Religion." In *Ecology and the Sacred: Engaging the Anthropology of Roy A. Rappaport*, edited by Ellen Messer and Michael Lambek, 207–26. Ann Arbor: The University of Michigan Press, 2001.

Peerbolte, Bert Jan Lietaert. "Paul, Baptism, and Religious Experience." In *Experientia, Volume 2: Linking Text and Experience*, edited by Colleen Shantz and Rodney A. Werline, 181–204. Atlanta: Society of Biblical Literature, 2012.

Rabens, Volker. *Holy Spirit and Ethics in Paul: Transformation and Empowering for Religious-Ethical Life*. Minneapolis: Fortress, 2013.

Ramelli, Ilaria L. E. "The Mysteries of Scripture: Allegorical Exegesis and the Heritage of Stoicism, Philo, and Pantaenus." In *Clement's Biblical Exegesis: Proceedings of the Second Colloquium on Clement of Alexandria*, edited by Veronika Černušková, Judith L. Kovacs, and Jana Plátová in cooperation with Vit Hušek, 80–110. Leiden; Boston: Brill, 2017.

Rappaport, Roy A. *Pigs for Ancestors: Ritual in the Ecology of a New Guinea People*. New Haven: Yale University Press, 1967.

Rappaport, Roy A. *Ritual and Religion in the Making of Humanity*. Cambridge: Cambridge University Press, 1999.

Reitzenstein, Richard. *Hellenistic Mystery-Religions: Their Basic Ideas and Significance*, trans. John E. Steely. Waco: Baylor University Press, 2018.

Rollens, Sarah E. "Inventing Tradition in Thessalonica: The Appropriation of the Past in 1 Thessalonians 2:14–16." *BTB* 46 (2016): 123–32.

Richter, Daniel S. "Plutarch on Isis and Osiris: Text, Cult, and Cultural Appropriation." *TAPA* 131 (2001): 191–216.

Riedweg, Christopher. *Mysterienterminologie bei Platon, Philon und Klemens von Alexandrien*. Berlin: Walter de Gruyter, 1987.

Riesebrodt, Martin. *The Promise of Salvation: A Theory of Religion*, trans. Steven Rendall. Chicago: University of Chicago Press, 2010.

Ringgren, Helmer, ed. *Fatalistic Beliefs in Religion, Folklore, and Literature: Papers read at the Symposium on Fatalistic Beliefs held at Åbo on the 7th–9th of September, 1964*. Stockholm: Almqvist & Wiksell, 1967.

Rives, James. "Religious Choice and Religious Change in Classical and Late Antiquity: Models and Questions." *ARS* 9 (2011): 265–80.

Reynolds, Benjamin E., and Loren T. Stuckenbruck, eds. *The Jewish Apocalyptic Tradition and the Shaping of New Testament Thought*. Minneapolis: Fortress, 2017.

Robbins, Joel. "Ritual Communication and Linguistic Ideology: A Reading and Partial Reformulation of Rappaport's Theory of Ritual." *CA* 42 (2001): 591–99.

Robbins, Vernon K. *The Invention of Christian Discourse*. Blandford Forum: Deo Publishing, 2009.

Roetzel, Calvin J. *The Letters of Paul: Conversations in Context*. 6th ed. Louisville: Westminster John Knox Press, 2015.

Rose, Valentinus. *Aristotelis qui ferebantur librorum fragmenta*. Lepzig: Teubner, 1886.

Rowland, Christopher. *The Open Heaven: A Study of Apocalyptic in Judaism and Early Christianity*. New York: Crossroad, 1982.

Rowland, Christopher, and C. R. A. Morray-Jones. *The Mystery of God: Early Jewish Mysticism and the New Testament*. Leiden; Boston: Brill, 2009.

Rüpke, Jörg. "Theorising Religion for the Individual." In *Individuals and Materials in the Greco-Roman Cults of Isis. Agents, Images, and Practices: Proceedings of the VIth International Conference of Isis Studies (Erfurt, May 6–8, 2013 – Liège, September 23–24, 2013).* Volume 1. Edited by Valentino Gasparini and Richard Veymiers, 61–73. Leiden; Boston: Brill, 2018.

Sabou, Sorin. "A Note on Romans 6:5: The Representation (ὉΜΟΊΩΜΑ) of His Death." *TynBul* 55 (2004): 219–29.

Salvá, Mercedes López. "Dionysos and Dionysism in the Third Book of Maccabees." In *Redefining Dionysos*, edited by Alberto Bernabé, Miguel Herrero de Jáuregui, Ana Isabel Jiménez San Cristóbal, and Raquel Martin Hernández, 452–63. Berlin: Walter de Gruyter, 2013.

Samellas, Antigone. *Death in the Eastern Mediterranean (50–600 A.D.).* Tübingen: Mohr Siebeck, 2002

San Cristóbal, Ana Jiménez. "The Meaning of βάκχος and βακχεύειν in Orphism." In *Mystic Cults in Magna Graecia*, edited by Giovanni Casadio and Patricia A. Johnston, 46–60. Austin: University of Texas Press, 2009.

Sanders, E. P. *Paul and Palestinian Judaism: A Comparison of Patterns of Religion.* Philadelphia: Fortress, 1977.

Santamaría, Marco Antonio. "The Term βάκχος and Dionysos Βάκχιος." In *Redefining Dionysos*, edited by Alberto Bernabé, Miguel Herrero de Jáuregui, Ana Isabel Jiménez San Cristóbal, and Raquel Martin Hernández, 38–57. Berlin: Walter de Gruyter, 2013.

Schäfer, Peter. *The Origins of Jewish Mysticism.* Tübingen: Mohr Siebeck, 2009.

Shantz, Colleen, and Rodney A. Werline, eds. *Experientia, Volume 2: Linking Text and Experience.* Atlanta: Society of Biblical Literature, 2012.

Scheid, John. *An Introduction to Roman Religion.* Bloomington: Indiana University Press, 2003.

Schellenberg, Ryan S. "Does Paul Call Adam a 'Type' of Christ?" *ZNW* 105 (2014): 54–63.

Schellenberg, Ryan S. "οἱ πιστεύοντες: An Early Christ-Group Self-Designation and Paul's Rhetoric of Faith." *NTS* (2019): 33–42.

Schnackenburg, Rudolf. *Baptism in the Thought of St. Paul*, trans. G. R. Beasley-Murray. Oxford: Blackwell, 1964.

Schnelle, Udo. *Apostle Paul: His Life and Theology*, trans. M. Eugene Boring. Grand Rapids: Baker Academic, 2005.

Schnelle, Udo. *Theology of the New Testament*, trans. M. Eugene Boring. Grand Rapids: Baker Academic, 2009.

Schowalter, Daniel, and Steven J. Friesen, eds. *Urban Religion in Roman Corinth: Interdisciplinary Approaches.* Cambridge: Harvard Theological Studies, 2005.

Schrage, Wolfgang. *Der Erste Brief an die Korinther (1Kor 1,1–6,11).* EKK VII/1. Zürich: Benziger Verlag; Neukirchener Verlag, 1991.

Schrage, Wolfgang. *Der Erste Brief an die Korinther (1Kor 6,12–11,16).* EKK VII/2. Zürich: Benziger Verlag; Neukirchener Verlag, 1995.

Schuman, Verne B. "A Second-Century Treatise on Egyptian Priests and Temples." *HTR* 53 (1960): 159–70.

Schowalter, Daniel N., and Steven J. Friesen, eds. *Urban Religion in Roman Corinth: Interdisciplinary Approaches.* Cambridge, MA: Harvard Theological Studies, 2005.

Schweitzer, Albert. *Paul and his Interpreters.* London: Adam and Charles Black, 1912.

Schweitzer, Albert. *The Mysticism of Paul the Apostle*, trans. W. Montgomery. Baltimore: Johns Hopkins University Press, 1998.

Scroggs, Robin. "Paul and Rhetorician: Two Homilies in Romans 1–11." In *Jews, Greeks, and Christians: Religious Cultures in Late Antiquity: Essays in Honor of William David Davies*, edited by Robert Hamerton-Kelly and Robin Scroggs, 271–98. Leiden: Brill, 1976.

Segal, Charles Paul. "The Character and Cults of Dionysus and the Unity of the Frogs." *HSCP* 65 (1961): 207–42.

Sekita, Karolina. *"Orphica non grata?* Underworld Palace Scenes on Apulian Red-Figure Pottery Revisited." In *Greek Art in Motion: Studies in Honor of Sir John Boardman on the Occasion of his 90th Birthday*, edited by Rui Morais, Delfim Leão, Diana Rodríguez Pérez;with Daniela Ferreira, 465–72. Oxford: Archaeopress, 2019.

Sellin, Gerhard. "Mythologeme und mythische Züge in der paulinischen Theologie." In *Mythos und Rationalität*, edited by Hans Heinrich Schmid, 209–23. Gütersloh: Gütersloher Verlagshaus G. Mohn, 1988.

Sharot, Stephen. *A Comparative Sociology of World Religions: Virtuosi, Priests, and Popular Religion.* New York: New York University Press, 2001.

Sharp, Daniel B. "Vicarious Baptism for the Dead: 1 Corinthians 15:29." *SBA* 6 (2014): 36–66.

Sierksma-Agteres, Suzan J. M. "Imitation in Faith: Enacting Paul's Ambiguous *Pistis Christou* formulations on a Greco-Roman Stage." *IJPT* 77 (2016): 119–53.

Siikavirta, Samuli. *Baptism and Cognition in Romans 6–8.* WUNT II/407; Tübingen: Mohr Siebeck, 2015.

Slane, Kathleen W. *Corinth Vol. XXI: Tombs, Burials, and Commemoration in Corinth's Northern Cemetery.* Princeton: American School of Classical Studies at Athens, 2017.

Slater, William J. "Life as a Party: A Pindaric Look at Dionysus in the Underworld." *MA* 17 (2004): 223–29.

Smit, Peter-Ben. "Ritual Failure in Romans 6." *HTS Teologiese Studies/Theological Studies* 72 (2016): 1–13.

Smith, Jonathan Z. *Imagining Religion: From Babylon to Jonestown.* Chicago: The University of Chicago Press, 1982.

Smith, Jonathan Z. *Drudgery Divine: On the Comparison of Early Christianities and the Religions of Late Antiquity.* Chicago: University of Chicago Press, 1990.

Smith, Jonathan Z. "Re: Corinthians." In *Redescribing Paul and the Corinthians*, edited by Ron Cameron and Merrill P. Miller, 17–34. Atlanta: Society of Biblical Literature, 2011.

Snoek, Jan A. M. "Defining 'Rituals.'" In *Theorizing Rituals: Issues, Topics, Approaches, Concepts*, edited by Jens Kreinath, J. A. M. Snoek, and Michael Stauberg, 3–14. Leiden: Brill, 2006.

Snyder, Benjamin J. "Samuli Siikavirta, *Baptism and Cognition in Romans 6–8: Paul's Ethics beyond 'Indicative' and 'Imperative.'*" *TJ* 38 (2017): 103–105.

Staal, Frits. "The Meaninglessness of Ritual." *Numen* 26 (1979): 2–22.

Stone, Michael E. *Secret Groups in Ancient Judaism.* Oxford: Oxford University Press, 2018.

Stafford, Emma. *Worshipping Virtues: Personification and the Divine in Ancient Greece.* London: The Classical Press of Wales, 2000.

Steimle, Christopher. *Religion im römischen Thessaloniki: Sakraltopographie, Kult und Gesellschaft 168 v. Chr.–324 n.Chr.* Tübingen: Mohr Siebeck, 2008.

Sterling, Gregory E. "Deities in Disguise: The Care of Strangers as a Criterion for Discipleship." In *Scripture and Social Justice: Catholic and Ecumenical Essays*, edited by Anathea E. Portier-Young and Gregory E. Sterling, 159–75. Lanham: Lexington Books/Fortress Academic, 2018.

Sterling, Gregory E. "*Imitatio Dei* (Eph 5:1–2): The Soteriological Basis for Ethics." In *Sōtēria: Salvation in Early Christianity and Antiquity: Festschrift in Honour of Cilliers Breytenbach on the

Occasion of his 65th Birthday, edited by David S. du Toit, Christine Gerber, and Christiane Zimmermann, 345–60. Leiden: Brill, 2019.

Still, Todd D. "Interpretative Ambiguities and Scholarly Proclivity in Pauline Studies: A Treatment of Three Texts from 1 Thessalonians 4 as a Test Case." *CBR* 5 (2007): 207–19.

Stowers, Stanley K. "What is 'Pauline Participation in Christ?'" In *Redefining First-Century Jewish and Christian Identities: Essays in Honor of Ed Parish Sanders*, edited by Fabian E. Udoh with Susannah Heschel, Mark Chancey, and Gregory Tatum, 352–71. Notre Dame: University of Notre Dame Press.

Strecker, G. *Theology of the New Testament*. Berlin: Walter de Gruyter, 2000.

Strenski, Ivan. "Martin Riesebrodt, *The Promise of Salvation: A Theory of Religion*." *HR* 53 (2014): 315–16.

Stuhlmacher, Peter. *Paul's Letter to the Romans: A Commentary*, trans. Scott J. Hafemann. Louisville: Westminster John Knox, 1994.

Takács, Sarolta A. *Isis and Sarapis in the Roman World*. Leiden: Brill, 1995.

Tannehill, Robert C. *Dying and Rising with Christ: A Study in Pauline Theology*. Berlin: Verlag Alfred Töpelmann, 1966.

Tappenden, Frederick S. *Resurrection in Paul: Cognition, Metaphor, and Transformation*. Atlanta: SBL, 2016.

Theissen, Gerd. *Sociology of Early Palestinian Christianity*, trans. John Bowden. Philadelphia: Fortress, 1978.

Theissen, Gerd. *Die Religion der ersten Christen: eine Theorie des Urchristentums*. Gütersloh: Kaiser, 2000.

Thiessen, Matthew. *Paul and the Gentile Problem*. New York: Oxford University Press, 2016.

Thiessen, Matthew. "Gentiles as Impure Animals in the Writings of Early Christ Followers." In *Perceiving the Other in Ancient Judaism and Early Christianity*, edited by Michal Bar-Asher Siegal, Wolfgang Grünstäudl, and Matthew Thiessen, 19–32. Tübingen: Mohr Siebeck, 2017.

Thiessen, Matthew. *Jesus and the Forces of Death: The Gospels' Portrayal of Ritual Impurity within First-Century Judaism*. Grand Rapids: Baker Academic, 2020.

Thiselton, Anthony C. *The First Epistle to the Corinthians: A Commentary on the Greek Text*. NIGTC. Grand Rapids: Eerdmans, 2000.

Thom, Johan C. "God the Saviour in Greco-Roman Popular Philosophy." In *Sōtēria: Salvation in Early Christianity and Antiquity: Festschrift in Honour of Cilliers Breytenbach on the Occasion of his 65th Birthday*, edited by David S. du Toit, Christine Gerber, and Christiane Zimmermann, 86–100. Leiden: Brill, 2019.

Tidball, D. *An Introduction to the Sociology of the New Testament*. Exeter: Paternoster, 1983.

Tilg, Stefan. "Aspects of a Literary Rationale of *Metamorphoses* 11." In *Aspects of Apuleius' Golden Ass: The Isis-Book: A Collection of Original Papers*, edited by W. H. Keulen, 132–55. Leiden: Brill, 2011.

Toynbee, J. M. C. *Death and Burial in the Roman World*. London: Thames & Hudson, 1971.

Trendall, A. D. and A. Cambitoglou. *The Red-Figured Vases of Apulia, Volume II*. Oxford: Clarendon Press, 1982.

Trumbower, Jeffrey A. *Rescue for the Dead: The Posthumous Salvation of Non-Christians in Early Christianity*. Oxford: Oxford University Press, 2001.

Turley, Stephen Richard. *The Ritualized Revelation of the Messianic Age: Washings and Meals in Galatia and 1 Corinthians*. New York: T&T Clark, 2015.

Turner, Nigel. *A Grammar of New Testament Greek* by James Hope Moulton. Volume 4. Edinburgh: T.&T. Clark, 1976.

Turner, Victor. *The Forest of Symbols: Aspects of Ndembu Ritual.* Ithaca: Cornell University Press, 1967.
Tzifopoulos, Yannis Z. "The Derveni Papyrus and the Bacchic-Orphic *Epistomia.*" In *Poetry as Initiation: The Center for Hellenic Studies Symposium on the Derveni Papyrus,* edited by Ioanna Papadopoulou and Leonard Muellner, 135–64. Washington D.C.: Center for Hellenic Studies, 2014.
Uro, Risto. *Ritual and Christian Beginnings: A Socio-Cognitive Analysis.* Oxford: Oxford University Press, 2016.
Vanderlip, Vera F. *The Four Greek Hymns of Isidorus and the Cult of Isis.* Toronto: A. M. Hakkert, 1972.
Veymiers, Richard. "Introduction: Agents, Images, Practices." In *Individuals and Materials in the Greco-Roman Cults of Isis. Agents, Images, and Practices: Proceedings of the VIth International Conference of Isis Studies (Erfurt, May 6–8, 2013 – Liège, September 23–24, 2013).* Volume 1, edited by Valentino Gasparini and Richard Veymiers, 1–58. Leiden; Boston: Brill, 2018.
Versluys, Miguel John. "Aegyptiaca Romana: The Widening Debate." In *Nile into Tiber. Egypt in the Roman World: Proceedings of the Third International Conference of Isis studies, Faculty of Archaeology, Leiden University, May 11–14 2005,* edited by Laurent Bricault, Miguel John Versluys, and Paul G. P. Meyboom, 1–14. Leiden: Brill, 2007.
Versnel, H. S. *Ter Unus: Isis, Dionysos, Hermes: Three Studies in Henotheism.* Leiden: Brill, 1990.
Versnel, H. S. *Coping with the Gods: Wayward Readings in Greek Theology.* Leiden: Brill, 2011.
Wagner, Günter. *Pauline Baptism and the Pagan Mysteries: the Problem of the Pauline Doctrine of Baptism in Romans VI.1–11, in the light of its Religio-historical "Parallels,"* trans. J. P. Smith. Edinburgh, London: Oliver & Boyd, 1967 (German original: 1962).
Walbank, Mary E. Hoskins. "Unquiet Graves: Burial Practices of the Roman Corinthians." In *Urban Religion in Roman Corinth: Interdisciplinary Approaches,* edited by Daniel N. Schowalter and Steven J. Friesen, 249–80. Cambridge, MA: Harvard Theological Studies, 2005.
Wallace, Daniel B. *Greek Grammar beyond the Basics: An Exegetical Syntax of the New Testament.* Grand Rapids: Zondervan, 1996.
Walters, Elizabeth J. *Attic Grave Reliefs that Represent Women in the Dress of Isis.* Hesperia Supplement XXII; Princeton: American School of Classical Studies at Athens, 1988.
Walters, James. "Civic Identity in Roman Corinth and its Impact on Early Christians." In *Urban Religion in Roman Corinth: Interdisciplinary Approaches,* edited by Daniel N. Schowalter and Steven J. Friesen, 397–418. Cambridge, MA: Harvard Theological Studies, 2005.
Wasserman, Emma. *The Death of the Soul in Romans 7.* WUNT II/256. Tübingen: Mohr Siebeck, 2008.
Watanabe, John M. and Barbara B. Smuts. "Explaining Religion without Explaining It Away: Trust, Truth, and the Evolution of Cooperation in Roy A. Rappaport's 'The Obvious Aspects of Ritual,'" *AA* 101 (1999): 98–112.
Watson, Francis. *Paul and the Hermeneutics of Faith.* London: T&T Clark, 2004.
Watson, Nathan. "Dreams and Superstition: A Reinterpretation of Satire in Apuleius, *Metamorphoses* 11." *AN* 11 (2014): 133–58.
Watzlawick, Paul. *The Invented Reality: How Do We Know What We Believe We Know? Contributions to Constructivism.* New York: Norton, 1984.
Weber, Max. *Sociology of Religion.* Boston: Beacon, 1963.
Wedderburn, A. J. M. "Paul and the Hellenistic Mystery-Cults: On Posing the Right Questions." In *La soteriologia dei culti orientali nell'Imperio Romano: Atti del Colloquio Internazionale su La soteriologia dei culti orientali nell'Impero Romano, Roma 24–28 Settembre 1979,* edited by Ugo Bianchi and Maarten J. Vermaseren, 817–33. Leiden: Brill, 1982.

Wedderburn, A. J. M. *Baptism and Resurrection: Studies in Pauline Theology against its Graeco-Roman Background.* Tübingen: Mohr Siebeck, 1987.
Wedderburn, A. J. M. "The Soteriology of the Mysteries and Pauline Baptismal Theology." *NovT* 29 (1987): 53–72.
West, M. L. *The Orphic Poems.* Oxford: Oxford University Press, 1983.
White, Joel R. "'Baptized on Account of the Dead': The Meaning of 1 Corinthians 15:29 in Its Context." *JBL* 116 (1997): 487–99.
White, Joel R. "Recent Challenges to the communis opinio on 1 Corinthians 15.29." *CBR* 10 (2012): 379–95.
White, L. Michael, and John T. Fitzgerald. "*Quod Est Comparandum:* The Problem of Parallels." In *Early Christianity and Classical Culture: Comparative Studies in Honor of Abraham J. Malherbe,* edited by John T. Fitzgerald, Thomas Olbricht, and L. Michael White, 13–39. Leiden: Brill, 2003.
Wild, Robert A. *Water in the Cultic Worship of Isis and Sarapis.* Leiden: Brill, 1981.
Wilson, Walter T. *The Mysteries of Righteousness: The Literary Composition and Genre of the* Sentences of Pseudo-Phocylides. Tübingen: J. C. B. Mohr, 1994.
Wilson, Walter T. *The Hope of Glory: Education and Exhortation in the Epistle to the Colossians.* Leiden: Brill, 1997.
Winkle, Jeffrey Thomas. "Daemons, Demiurges, and Dualism: Apuleius' *Metamorphoses* and the Mysticism of Late Antiquity." PhD dissertation. Northwestern University, 2002.
Witherington, Ben. *Conflict and Community in Corinth: A Socio-Rhetorical Commentary on 1 and 2 Corinthians.* Grand Rapids: Eerdmans, 1995.
Witt, R. E. *Isis in the Ancient World.* Baltimore: Johns Hopkins University Press, 1997.
Wolf, Eric R. "Cognizing 'Cognized Models.'" *AA* 101 (1999): 19–22.
Wolfson, Harry A. *Philo: Foundations of Religious Philosophy in Judaism, Christianity and Islam.* 2 vols. Cambridge: Harvard University Press, 1947.
Wolter, Michael. *Paul: An Outline of His Theology,* trans. Robert L. Brawley. Waco: Baylor University Press, 2015.
Wright, N. T. *The Climax of the Covenant: Christ and the Law in Pauline Theology.* Minneapolis: Fortress, 1992.
Yarbro Collins, Adela. *Cosmology and Eschatology in Jewish and Christian Apocalypticism.* Leiden: Brill, 1996.
Yarbro Collins, Adela. "Apocalypse Now: The State of Apocalyptic Studies Near the End of the First Century of the Twenty-First Century." *HTR* 104 (2011): 447–57.
Yuh, Jason N. "Analyzing Paul's Reference to Baptism in Galatians 3.27 through Studies of Memory, Embodiment and Ritual." *JSNT* 41 (2019): 478–500.
Zeller, Dieter. "The Life and Death of the Soul in Philo of Alexandria: The Use and Origin of a Metaphor." *The Studia Philonica Annual* 7 (1995): 19–55.

Index of Names

Adams, Edward   4
Agersnap, Søren   12, 24, 232
Aitken, E. B.   204
Alcock, Susan E.   64
Alvar, Jaime.   33f., 57, 115
Ascough, Richard S.   160
Ashton, John   232, 239, 242, 276, 278
Athanassiadi, Polymnia   9, 33, 65, 183f.
Auffarth, Christoph   184
Aune, David E.   166, 189, 277

Baird, William.   11
Balch, David L.   4, 30f., 238
Ballard, C. Andrew   37
Barclay, John M. G.   137, 270, 277f.
Barr, James.   83, 268
Barrett, C. K.   245
Barth, Gerhard.   194, 247
Bassler, Jouette M.   37
Beasley-Murray, George Raymond   163, 245, 247
Beker, J. C.   242, 247
Belayche, Nicole   109
Bell, Brigidda   162
Bell, Catherine   2f., 39, 41, 63f., 162, 198
Berger, Peter L.   60
Bergman, Jan   118f.
Bernabé, Alberto   34, 67
Betz, Hans Dieter   14, 28, 30, 85, 131, 136, 161f., 228, 230f., 235, 238, 258f., 277
Bhabha, Homi K.   257
Bianchi, Ugo   25, 33
Blakely, Sandra   34, 117, 202, 209
Blanco, María José García   14, 35, 129
Blegen, Carl W.   215, 218
Boardman, John   99, 211, 214, 216
Bockmuehl, Markus N. A.   26
Boers, Hendrikus   239
Bøgh, Birgitte   56–58, 67, 69, 74, 79
Bonnet, Corinne   9, 35
Bookidis, Nancy   31, 141, 213, 220
Bornkamm, Günter   25f., 247

Bousset, Wilhelm   11–13, 15, 20, 32, 198, 242, 248
Bowden, Hugh.   143, 162, 208
Brandon, S. G. F.   254
Braun, Willi   64
Bremmer, Jan N.   1f., 14, 34, 52, 67, 79, 99, 101, 109, 118, 139, 184, 209, 232
Brenk, Frederick E.   125, 128, 130f., 141
Bricault, Laurent   9, 34f., 109f., 118f., 139f., 150
Broneer, Oscar   200, 202f., 205
Brooten, Bernadette J.   114
Brown, Raymond   25, 159, 255
Bultmann, Rudolf   11–13, 15f., 194, 242
Burkert, Walter   1f., 14, 23, 33f., 61, 70, 74f., 77, 87, 115, 122, 129
Burns Jr., J. Patout   277

Cabrera, Paloma   81, 95f.
Callender, Dexter E.   255
Cambitoglou, A.   95
Cameron, Ron   3, 236
Campbell, Douglas A.   267
Carpenter, Thomas H.   70
Casadesus, Francesc   35
Casadio, Giovanni   28, 51f., 94
Cassidy, William   73
Casson, Lionel   162
Castelli, Elizabeth   277
Černušková, Veronika   36
Chang, Kai-Hsuan   56f., 150, 224, 244
Chaniotis, Angelos   75, 132, 150
Chankowski, A. S.   75
Chester, Stephen J.   7
Choi, Mihwa   54
Chrysanthou, Anthi   86
Clinton, Kevin   106f., 143
Cole, Susan Guettel   120
Collins, John J.   26, 255
Collins, Raymond F.   159f., 169, 186
Concannon, Cavan W.   214
Conroy, Jr., John T.   249
Conzelmann, Hans   186, 198f.

https://doi.org/10.1515/9783110791389-013

Cook, John Granger 237
Coote, Robert B. 254
Corrington, Gail Paterson 119
Cosmopoulos, Michael B. 34
Courtney, Edward 81
Cranfield, C. E. B. 245, 248, 256, 259, 269
Croasmun, Matthew 270 f.
Cross, Anthony R. 16, 241
Cumont, Franz 2, 13, 15 – 17, 19 f., 33, 44, 62, 68, 104, 110

Dahl, Nils Alstrup 235
Davies, W. D. 155, 267
de Boer, Martinus C. 229 f.
de Jáuregui, Miguel Herrero 111
de la Fuente, David Hernández 69, 135
de Souza, Philip 34
DeMaris, Richard E. 4, 14, 31, 200, 203, 210 f., 213 – 215, 219, 222, 243
Dignas, Beate 151
Dijkstra, Jitse 52
Dillon, John 260
Dinkler, Michal Beth 38
Dodds, E. R. 84, 98
Dodson, Joseph R. 270
Donald A. Russell 103
Douglas, Mary 41, 195
du Toit, David S. 116
Dunbabin, Katherine 87
Dunn, James D. G. 189, 241 f., 245, 256, 258 f., 263, 265

Eastman, David L. 283
Edmonds III, Radcliffe G. 65
Edsall, Benjamin A. 254
Edwards, Mark J. 184
Eichhorn, Albert 11
Elliott, John H. 179
Elliott, Susan M. 31
Engberg-Pedersen, Troels 28, 189, 237
Engels, Donald 213
Erskine, Andrew 184

Fant, Maureen B. 71
Faraone, Christopher A. 70
Fauconnier, Gilles 222 – 225
Fee, Gordon D. 189, 198

Ferguson, Everett 5
Fernandez, James W. 273
Fitzgerald, John T. 5, 52, 277 f.
Fitzmyer, Joseph A. 163, 165, 169, 171, 175, 179, 186 – 188, 198, 200, 248, 259
Foley, Helene P. 84
Fotopoulos, John 189
Frankenberry, N. 64
Frazer, James G. 12, 15
Frede, Michael 183 f.
Friesen, Courtney J. P. 69, 75 f., 86, 98
Friesen, Steven J. 30 f.
Früchtel, Ursula 36

Gager, John G. 220
Gasparini, Valentino 33, 35, 118, 123, 125, 127, 135, 151
Gasparro, Giulia Sfameni 33, 116 f., 134, 144
Gaventa, Beverly Roberts 247, 270
Gebhard, Elizabeth R. 31, 204 f., 214
Geertz, Clifford 50, 264
Gladd, Benjamin L. 26
Goldstein, Ronnie 259
Goodenough, Erwin R. 35 f.
Goodrich, John K. 231
Gordon, Richard L. 11, 33
Graf, Fritz 66 f., 69, 77 – 82, 93, 101 f., 104, 116, 166
Grandjean, Yves 117
Grenfell, Bernard P. 114, 119
Griffiths, J. Gwyn 112, 119, 137, 140, 146 f.
Grimes, Ronald L. 3, 45, 50 f.
Gruen, Erich S. 76 f.
Gunkel, Hermann 11
Gupta, Nijay. K. 175 f.

Hamerton-Kelly, Robert 267
Hanges, James C. 161
Harland, Philip A. 71, 213, 283
Harrill, J. Albert 234 f.
Harrison, Stephen J. 110
Harrison, Thomas 54
Hay, David M. 37, 279
Hays, Richard B. 165, 180 f., 183, 187, 189 f., 198, 229, 255, 261
Heitmüller, Wilhelm 11, 163
Hellholm, David 235

Henrichs, Albert 151
Herbener, Jens-André P. 183 f.
Hewitt, J. Thomas 155
Heyob, Sharon Kelly 114, 119 f., 139
Hofius, Otfried 256
Hogan, Karina Martin 37
Holloway, Paul A. 259
Hooker, Morna D. 231
Hope, Valerie M. 175, 211, 213, 241
Hopkins, Keith 71, 110, 117, 142, 155
Horrell, David G. 4, 38
Hultgren, Arland J. 21, 259
Hunt, Arthur S. 114, 119
Hunt, Peter. 252
Hylen, Susan E. 114, 249

Ibáñez, Jesús-M. Nieto 68
Iossif, P. P. 75
Isler-Kerényi, Cornelia 35, 68, 73, 88–91, 93

Jaccottet, Anne-Françoise 68, 72, 75, 83, 85, 92
Jensen, Robin M. 6
Jeong, Donghyun 56, 190, 237, 252
Jewett, Robert 244 f., 259, 263 f.
Jim, Theodora Suk Fong 54, 76, 80, 83, 116
Johnson, Luke Timothy 243, 249
Johnson, Mark 249
Johnson Hodge, Caroline 234
Johnston, Patricia A. 28
Johnston, Sarah Iles 66, 80–82, 88, 99–102, 216, 219–222

Kaltsas, Nikolaos 211
Käsemann, Ernst 26, 154 f., 247, 253, 271
Kearns, Conleth 264
Kennedy, H. A. A. 21, 25
Keulen, W. H. 110
Kim, Seon Yong 166
Kim, Yung Suk 160 f.
Kindt, Julia 64
King, Charles W. 22, 64, 124, 157
Klauck, Hans-Josef 1, 27, 68, 142 f., 166
Klawans, Jonathan 160, 195
Klein, Günter 273
Kloppenborg, John S. 3–7, 63, 213
Koester, Helmut 14, 30, 200, 204 f.
Kouremenos, Theokritos 105

Kovacs, Judith L. 74
Kraemer, Ross S. 79, 114, 120
Kraftchick, Steven J. 255, 279
Krauskopf, Ingrid 202
Kreinath, Jens 3
Kuo-Yu Tsui, Teresa 242, 265
Kurtz, Donna C. 211, 214, 216

Lakoff, George 249
Lambek, Michael 44, 48
Lambert, David 128
Lampe, Peter 164, 273
Lancellotti, Maria Grazia 22
Lang, T. J. 11, 37, 56
Lannoy, Annelies 16 f., 19, 62, 104
Last, Richard 35
Lawrence, Jonathan D. 6, 173
Lease, Gary 36
Lee, Michelle V. 187
Lefkowitz, Mary 71
Leipoldt, J. 254
Lemos, T. M. 255
Levinson, Joshua 128 f.
Levison, John R. 257, 261 f.
Levy, Robert I. 44, 46
Libby, Brigitte B. 110
Lietzmann, H. 198, 254
Lipka, Michael 54
Litwa, M. David 5, 75, 232
Lohse, Eduard 156, 269
Loisy, Alfred 13, 15–19, 62, 103 f.
Longenecker, Richard N. 21, 24, 231
Lorber, C. C. 75
Luckmann, Thomas 60
Lüdemann, Gerd 11

MacDonald, Dennis R. 19, 98
MacDonald, Margaret Y. 114
Mack, Burton L. 3 f., 12
Maclean, K. B. 204
Macris, Constantinos 9, 33, 65
Malherbe, Abraham J. 5, 30, 170
Marquardt, Steve 185
Marshall, Jill E. 165, 190
Martin, Dale 237
Martin, S. Rebecca 235
Martin, Troy W. 189

Martín-Velasco, María José   14, 35, 129
Martyn, J. Louis   228–230
Martzavou, Paraskevi   132, 137, 149–151
McCutcheon, Russell T.   52, 64
McGowan, Andrew Brian   228
McNiven, Timothy J.   99–101
Meeks, Wayne A.   228, 234
Merkelbach, Reinhold   110 f., 139, 141, 147, 150
Messer, Ellen   44, 48
Mettinger, Tryggve N. D.   12
Meyboom, Paul G. P.   34
Meyer, Marvin W.   28, 166
Miller, Merrill P.   3, 236
Mills, Lynn   164
Mirecki, Paul   166
Mitchell, Margaret M.   160, 164, 235
Mitchell, Stephen   183
Moles, John   19
Moore, George Foot   27
Moore, Nicholas J.   164
Moore, Terri   14, 31, 56, 196
Morais, Rui   99
Morales, Isaac A.   156, 178, 191, 238, 252, 266
Morgan, Teresa   29, 63, 156, 200, 230, 283–285
Morray-Jones, C. R. A.   26
Moss, Candida R.   283
Muellner, Leonard   104
Murphy-O'Connor, Jerome   200, 229, 255
Musurillo, Herbert   74
Mylonas, George E.   106, 113, 208

Nasrallah, Laura S.   31, 200 f., 214, 221 f.
Nevett, Lisa   235
Niehoff, Maren R.   128 f.
Nilsson, Martin P.   68, 92 f.
Nock, Arthur Darby   21, 57 f., 118, 215
Novenson, Matthew V.   30, 156

Oakley, John H.   211
Ogden, Daniel   220
Olyan, Saul M.   255
O'Neill, Kevin Lewis   64
Osborne, Robin   64
Osiek, Carolyn   114
Ossan, F. G.   124
Otto, Walter F.   88

Overbeck, Bernhard   96
Overbeck, Mechtild   96

Pache, Corine Ondine   201 f., 204, 206–208
Pagis, Michal   59
Pailler, Jean-Marie   33
Pakkala, Juha   184
Palmer, Hazel   88, 215
Papadopoulou, Ioanna   104
Parca, Maryline   120
Parker, Robert   103, 172, 208 f.
Peacock, James   47, 53
Peerbolte, Bert Jan Lietaert   14, 31 f., 37
Petersen, Anders Klostergaard   247, 250, 255 f.
Porter, Stanley   241
Portier-Young, Anathea E.   98
Powell, Mark Allan   13
Powers, Daniel G.   241, 270

Rabens, Volker   189
Ramelli, Ilaria L. E.   36
Rappaport, Roy A.   7 f., 31 f., 38–48, 54, 58 f.,
   62 f., 104, 113, 146, 172, 174, 176 f., 198,
   250–252, 266
Reitzenstein, Richard   13, 15, 18 f., 138, 147,
   198, 242
Reynolds, Benjamin E.   26
Richter, Daniel S.   90, 110
Riedweg, Christopher   36
Riesebrodt, Martin   7 f., 38 f., 46, 48–55, 58 f.,
   63, 106, 246, 250
Ringgren, Helmer   118
Rives, James   57
Robbins, Joel   39
Robbins, Vernon K.   117
Roetzel, Calvin J.   159
Rollens, Sarah E.   169
Rose, Valentinus   105
Rowland, Christopher   26
Rüpke, Jörg   63, 124 f.

Sabou, Sorin   256
Salvá, Mercedes López   68
Samellas, Antigone   221
San Cristóbal, Ana Isabel Jiménez   34, 67, 92
Sanders, E. P.   27, 189, 206, 237, 266
Santamaría, Marco Antonio   67, 80, 88, 92

Schäfer, Peter 23
Scheid, John 47, 111 f., 129, 134
Schellenberg, Ryan S. 4, 271
Schmid, Hans Heinrich 264
Schnackenburg, Rudolf 163, 173, 175, 177, 180, 182, 186, 190, 198 f., 241, 246
Schnelle, Udo 155 f., 158, 168, 195, 242, 248
Schowalter, Daniel N. 30 f.
Schrage, Wolfgang 167, 176, 179, 181 f.
Schuman, Verne B. 150
Schweitzer, Albert 13, 155, 242, 248, 278
Scroggs, Robin 267
Segal, Charles Paul 52, 74
Sekita, Karolina 99 f.
Sellin, Gerhard 264, 266
Shantz, Colleen 32
Shapiro, Alan 211
Sharot, Stephen 253
Sharp, Daniel B. 198
Siegal, Michal Bar-Asher 169
Sierksma-Agteres, Suzan J. M. 230 f., 260
Siikavirta, Samuli 22, 177, 238, 248, 252, 269
Slane, Kathleen W. 211, 215, 217
Slater, William J. 100
Smit, Peter-Ben 251
Smith, Jonathan Z. 2, 22, 25, 27–29, 52 f., 64, 220, 236
Smith, Jr., Edgar W. 131, 136
Smuts, Barbara B. 47
Snoek, Jan A. M. 3
Snyder, Benjamin J. 269
Stafford, Emma 270
Steimle, Christopher 144
Sterling, Gregory E. 98, 260
Still, Todd D. 98, 159, 171, 240
Stone, Michael E. 36
Stowers, Stanley K. 189, 237
Strecker, G. 189
Strenski, Ivan 51–54, 59
Stroud, Ronald S. 141, 220
Stroumsa, Guy G. 259
Stuckenbruck, Loren T. 26
Stuhlmacher, Peter 243, 259

Takács, Sarolta A. 112
Tannehill, Robert C. 239, 241 f., 244, 263 f., 266
Tappenden, Frederick S. 224

Thate, M. J. 156
Theissen, Gerd 55, 162, 243, 249, 254, 263, 278
Thiessen, Matthew 169, 236 f., 252
Thiselton, Anthony C. 164
Thom, Johan C. 116
Tidball, D. 44
Tilg, Stefan 110
Toynbee, J. M. C. 211, 213, 215 f.
Trampedach, Kai 151
Trendall, A. D. 95
Trumbower, Jeffrey A. 219
Tsantsanoglou, K. 105
Tulloch, Janet H. 114
Turley, Stephen Richard 4, 31 f., 41, 174–177, 186 f., 189, 228, 266
Turner, Mark 222–225
Turner, Nigel 175
Turner, Victor 3
Tzanetou, Angeliki 120
Tzifopoulos, Yannis Z. 105

Udoh, Fabian E. 189
Uro, Risto 198, 227

van Gennep, Arnold 250
Vanderlip, Vera F. 116, 119
Vermaseren, Maarten J. 25, 33
Versluys, Miguel John 34, 111
Versnel, H. S. 54, 64, 80, 116, 118, 133, 147, 184
Veymiers, Richard 33, 35, 109, 123

Wagner, Günter 13 f., 22–25, 28, 32 f., 60–62, 109, 113, 140–143, 149, 243, 254, 265
Walbank, Mary E. Hoskins 215
Waldner, Katharina 67
Wallace, Daniel B. 175
Walters, Elizabeth J. 125
Walters, James 214
Wasserman, Emma 249
Watanabe, John M. 47
Watson, Francis 237
Watson, Nathan 130
Watzlawick, Paul 249
Weber, Max 8, 47, 50, 55, 60, 63, 106

Wedderburn, A. J. M. 13, 22–25, 27f., 32f., 138, 242, 244, 265
Weiss, Johannes 11, 198
Weissenrieder, Annette 31
Werline, Rodney A. 32
West, M. L. 19, 48, 85, 283
White, Joel R. 198–200
White, L. Michael 5
Wild, Robert A. 143–145
Williams, Charles K. 141
Wilson, Stephen G. 213
Wilson, Walter T. 36, 241
Winkle, Jeffrey Thomas 130, 140

Witherington, Ben 165, 182
Witt, R. E. 117, 134f., 141
Wolf, Eric R. 45, 47
Wolfson, Harry A. 36
Wolter, Michael 163, 165, 182, 236, 242, 244f., 247f., 257, 260
Wright, N. T. 155

Yarbro Collins, Adela 20, 26, 235
Young, Rodney S. 215
Yuh, Jason N 236

Zeller, Dieter 221, 249

Index of Ancient Names

Aeschylus 105
Albinus 260
Apollodorus 77, 87, 93, 201
Apuleius 23, 57, 109–112, 118–122, 128–132, 136–140, 144–147, 150f., 209, 252, 270, 281
Aretaeus of Cappadocia 78
Aristides 103, 207f.
Aristophanes 74, 81, 83, 121
Aristotle 105, 270
Augustine 128, 186

Cicero 277
Clement of Alexandria 36, 38
Cyril of Jerusalem 254f.

Demosthenes 79

Epictetus 147, 277
Eudorus 260
Euripides 19, 66f., 69, 72, 74–78, 84, 86, 98, 101, 106, 110, 201

Firmicus Maternus 116, 138

Galen 78

Heliodorus 151, 220
Herodian 75
Herodotus 67, 78, 106, 139f., 144, 219, 235
Hesiod 82
Himerius 92f.
Homer 57, 84, 98, 119, 151, 202
Horace 75, 86, 211

Ignatius of Antioch 283

Josephus 68, 232
Juvenal 148

Livy 72, 76
Lucan 220
Lucian 161f., 185

Martial 211

Nonnus of Panopolis 69, 93, 135

Origen 86f., 277
Ovid 98, 119f., 140, 147f., 201f.

Pausanias 79, 87, 141, 144, 201–205, 207
Philo of Alexandria 35f., 75, 160, 230, 237, 249, 260
Philostratus 204–206, 209
Pindar 202
Plato 35–37, 57, 76f., 87, 104, 198, 219, 260, 270
Plutarch 57, 68, 75, 109–111, 128–131, 135, 140f., 144f., 147, 151, 203f., 270
Pseudo-Cyprian 235
Pseudo-Phocylides 36

Rufinus of Aquileia 113

Sophocles 80
Statius 139, 209
Synesius 105, 270

Tacitus 85
Tertullian 11, 164, 199, 235

https://doi.org/10.1515/9783110791389-014

Index of Subjects

Afterlife   17, 79, 80–83, 88, 91–100, 105–108, 114, 121–25, 128–29, 137, 145, 149, 151, 192, 215, 221, 233, 274, 280
Apocalypse/apocalyptic   26, 32, 169, 242, 247, 261, 263–66, 282
Assimilation between the deity and devotees   75, 92–96, 106–107, 125, 127, 258, 260–61, 281
Associations/*collegia*   3–7, 49, 63, 68, 70, 71, 72, 85–86, 91, 106–108, 115, 160, 213, 283

Conceptual blending   197, 222–27, 243–44, 255

Dionysus/Dionysiac mysteries   1, 8, 15, 19, 28, 38, 56, 65, Ch. 3 (66–108), 109, 111–12, 116, 129–31, 135, 138, 144, 146, 149–52, 171, 198, 201, 204, 206, 232, 234, 236, 253, 280–82
Divine-human relationships   8–9, 82, 98, 111, 117, 120, 121, 123, 124, 130, 138, 139, 140, 147, 148, 151, 163, 165, 172, 185, 196, 256–61, 274, 280, 282–85
"Dying and rising" (or "death and resurrection")   6, 11–13, 15, 18–19, 22–24, 32, 86, 136, 138, 140, 194–95, 202, 239, 243, 245, 248–49, 256, 261, 275, 278–79, 282–83

Eleusis/Eleusinian mysteries   15, 17, 22–23, 67–68, 76, 82, 84, 106–109, 113, 117, 121, 134, 140, 143, 149, 161, 208–209, 232, 281
Ethnicity/ethnic   168, 179, 190, 214, 235–36, 282
Experience/experiential   1, 2, 4, 10, 17–18, 23, 31–32, 34, 37, 51, 53, 57, 62–63, 68, 70, 75–77, 79, 87–88, 91, 96, 98–99, 101, 104–108, 121, 125, 128, 130, 135–38, 140, 142–44, 149, 162, 173–74, 181, 183, 186, 188, 190, 204–205, 210, 221, 226, 229, 237–38, 244, 246–47, 249, 253, 257–58, 278–79, 281–82, 285

Funeral/funerary   83, 92, 94, 99, 100–101, 123, 125, 143, 145, 150, 197, 200, 202, 204, 210–23, 225–27, 243, 255

History of religions (school)   11–12, 15–16, 20, 28, 30, 33–34, 36, 111, 266

Intra-human (or social) relationships   8–9, 58, 69–73, 107, 111–15, 151, 162, 167, 190, 196, 216, 274, 280, 284–85
Isis/Isis mysteries   1, 8, 15, 20–23, 29, 31, 38, 57, 65, 96, 103, Ch. 4 (109–52), 171, 181, 201, 209, 232, 234, 236, 238, 252–53, 270, 280–82

Melikertes-Palaimon   30–31, 197, 200, 201–10, 214, 222–26
Mithra/Mithras   15, 17, 20–21
Mysticism/mystical   23, 35, 83, 111, 156, 163, 204, 232, 240, 242, 245, 272, 278–79

"Oriental"/"Oriental religions"   15–16, 18–20, 25, 33, 34, 68, 129, 147

Philosophy/philosophical   9, 14, 33, 35–37, 57, 65, 87, 116, 128–30, 141–42, 144, 147, 189, 200, 248–49, 255, 260, 270, 277
Platonism/Platonic   24, 87, 104, 110, 128–31, 135, 140, 249, 259–61
Purification/purity   1, 5, 23, 76–77, 85, 87, 111, 113, 117, 145, 149, 154, 160, 169, 170, 172–75, 183, 194–95, 208–209, 216, 221, 240, 254, 274

Religious virtuosity   8, 10, 54–56, 60, 66, 103, 106, 108, 146, 148–50, 152, 160, 172, 246, 253, 276–77, 280–81
Resurrection   24, 28, 32, 86, 88, 98, 155, 179, 192–97, 200, 219, 239, 243–50, 253, 256, 259–60, 263, 272, 275–79, 285
Ritual innovation   8, 198, 227, 243, 282

Ritual messages (self-referential and canonical messages)   8, 39–47, 54–65, 280–82, 285; the entire discussion in Chs. 3–7

Samothrace/Samothracian   34, 117, 202
Secret/secrecy   1, 5, 34, 36, 74, 84, 203
Stoicism/Stoic   86, 135, 189–90, 237

Index of Ancient Sources

1 Hebrew Bible/Old Testament

Genesis
1:20 – 26	257
1:26 LXX	261
3:1 – 7	257
3:15	233
12:1 – 3	229
15	237
15:1 – 6	229
15:6	230
15:7 – 8	178
15:10 – 11	178
17	178
18:18	229

Exodus
13	178
20:4	257
23:30	178

Leviticus
11:44 – 45	171 – 72
19:2	171 – 72

Numbers
25:3 LXX	185
27:26	229
28:58	229
30:10	229

Deuteronomy
1:38 – 39	178
4:12	257
4:15	257
4:16	257
4:17	257
4:18	257
4:23	257
4:25	257
5:8	257
32:17	185

Joshua
22:28	257

Judges
8:18	257

1 Samuel
2:20	233
6:5	257
19:20 – 24	232
28:15	220

1 Kings
15:12	157

2 Kings
16:10	257

2 Chronicles
4:3	257

Nehemiah
9:20	186

Psalms
78:24 – 25	186
79:6	170
103 LXX	237
105 LXX	258
106:20 (= 105:20 LXX)	256 – 57
143:12 LXX	257
148:1 – 3	237

Song of Songs
1:11	257

Isaiah
40:18	257
40:19	257

Jeremiah
10:25	170

Ezekiel
1:5	257
1:16	257
1:22	257
1:26	257
1:28	257–58
8:2	257–58
8:3	257
10:1	257
10:8	257
10:10	257
10:21	257
23:15	257

Daniel
3:92 LXX	257

Amos
3:1	265
7:9	157

Habakkuk
2:4	229

2 Apocrypha, Pseudepigrapha, Qumran Texts, Rabbinic Literature, and Other Jewish Writings

2 Baruch
54:19	265

4 Ezra
7:118–119	265

Genesis Rabbah
20.12	265

Josephus
Jewish Antiquities
6.56	232
6.76	232

Life of Adam and Eve (Apocalypse of Moses)
14.2–3	262
20–21	265

1 Maccabees
3:48	257

2 Maccabees
12:43–45	219, 221
12:44	219

3 Maccabees
2:30	68
	157

Pesaḥ
10.5	265

Philo of Alexandria
De Abrahamo (Abr.)
262	230

De migratione Abrahami (Migr.)
44	230

De mutatione nominum (Mut.)
186	230

De praemiis et poenis (Praem.)
28	230

De virtutibus (Virt.)
102–103	160
216	230

Legum allegoriae (Leg.)
3.228	230

Quaestiones et solutiones in Exodum (QG)
4.181	237

Quis rerum divinarum heres sit (Her.)
1	230
86–87	237

Quod Deus sit immutabilis (Deus)
4	230

1QH^a
9.11b–14a	237

Sirach	
34:3	257
38:28	257

Wisdom of Solomon	
2:24	262
12:4	157
14:15	157
14:23	157

3 New Testament

Matthew	
3:11	267
11:28 – 30	121
19:28	94
22:14	104
25:31 – 46	98
28:16 – 20	84
28:19	175, 241
28:19 – 20	253

Mark	
1:4 – 8	240
1:5	173
1:9 – 11	87, 93, 253
10:38 – 40	241

Luke	
3:16	267
9:62	175
11:7	175
14:7	104

John	
1:18	175
3 – 4	240
3:15	175
3:22 – 26	240
4:1 – 2	240
6:39 – 40	170
13:35	7
14:16 – 17	237
15:26	237

Acts	
1:8	237
2:38	173, 175, 240, 241
2:42	240
8:14 – 17	241
8:16	155, 175, 240
10	241
10:44 – 48	241
10:48	175, 240
19:5	155
22:16	154, 174

Romans	
1	261, 268
1 – 4	267, 271
1:1	273
1:2	154, 229
1:4	154
1:7	154, 273
1:15	273
1:18 – 25	257
1:22 – 23	257
1:23	256, 258, 261
1:24	170
2	147, 267 – 68
2 – 3	267
2:27	157
3	267 – 68
3:3 – 4	251
3:24	157
4	267 – 68
4:2	175
4:25	195
5	193, 246, 250, 256, 261, 265, 267 – 69, 271
5 – 6	260 – 62, 265, 267, 269
5 – 7	269 – 70
5 – 8	10, 238, 239, 255, 267 – 72, 276 – 78, 282
5:1 – 11	271
5:3 – 4	277 – 78
5:5	154, 267
5:6	256

5:7	256	6:12	256
5:8	256, 271	6:12–23	252
5:10	256	6:12–14	240, 248
5:12	256, 262	6:12–13	251, 278
5:12–21	256, 262, 264	6:13	251
5:13	262	6:14	251, 256
5:14	256, 258, 262	6:15	256
5:15	256	6:16	256
5:15–17	262	6:17	256
5:16	256, 271	6:18	256
5:17	256, 271	6:19	154, 251, 274
5:18	256, 271	6:20	256
5:18–19	262	6:21	157, 256
5:19	256, 260, 271	6:22	154, 157, 248, 251, 256
5:20	262	6:23	157, 256
5:21	256	7	267, 268
6	11, 13, 19–22, 24, 26, 28–30, 43, 121, 149, 158, 188, 190, 197, 224, 227, 239, 241–54, 256, 260–65, 267–68, 270, 272, 278, 282	7–8	269
		7:6	267
		7:12	154
		8	158, 267–69, 271–72
		8:1	155, 157, 271
		8:2	157, 270, 272, 274
6–8	158, 170, 177, 249, 269, 276	8:3	257–60, 272
6:1–2	240	8:4	270
6:1–11	22	8:5–6	270
6:1–14	11, 19, 158, 239–41, 256	8:6	274
6:1–23	158	8:9	272
6:2	12, 240, 248, 250, 256	8:9–11	270, 274
6:3	11–12, 154, 188, 240–42, 244–45, 248, 250, 256, 260, 272	8:10–11	277–78
		8:11	272
		8:14	270
6:3–6	241	8:18	272
6:3–4	243–45, 262	8:26	270, 272
6:4	154, 239–40, 248, 256, 270, 274, 278	8:27	154
		8:30	175
6:4–5	246–47	8:31–39	272
6:5	239–40, 248, 256–60, 263, 271	8:34	264, 272
		8:39	157
6:6	239, 263–64	9	267–68
6:6–7	240	9–11	263
6:7	248, 256, 264, 272	9:1	154, 157
6:8	240, 248, 256, 263, 272	10	267–68
6:8–11	263	10:4	157–58
6:9	256, 262–63	11	268, 272
6:9–11	240	11:16	154, 194
6:10	249, 256	11:25	157–58
6:11	157, 239, 248, 250, 263	12	158, 268

12:1	154, 278	1:12–13	162–63
12:1–2	278	1:13	154–55, 160, 162, 165, 167, 176, 181
12:2	157, 274		
12:5	157	1:13–17	236
12:10	7	1:14	154, 160
12:13	154	1:14–17	161, 163, 167
13	158, 267–68	1:15	154, 160, 176
13:6	157	1:16	154, 160
13:7	157–58	1:17	154, 160, 167
14	268	1:18	168
14:14	157	1:18–25	168
14:17	154	1:22–23	168
14:20	154	1:24	168, 171
15	158, 268	1:26	168
15:4	229	1:26–31	158, 168–69, 171–72, 178, 274–75
15:13	154		
15:16	154, 252, 278	1:30	154, 157, 168, 171, 192, 194–95, 275
15:17	157		
15:20	273	1:30–31	171, 179, 194
15:25	154	1:31	157
15:26	154	2:1	157
15:31	154	2:4	166
16	158, 268	2:6	157
16:2	154, 157	2:7	157
16:3	155, 157	3:1	157
16:7	157	3:5	164
16:8	157	3:6	162, 164
16:9	157	3:17	154
16:10	157	4:1	157
16:11	157	4:6	164
16:12	157	4:10	157
16:13	157	4:15	157, 162
16:15	154	4:17	157
16:16	154	6	32, 173, 177, 185, 195, 252
16:22	157	6:1	154
16:25	157	6:2	154
		6:8	177
1 Corinthians		6:9	174, 177–78
1	160, 165–67, 185, 192, 194, 274	6:9–10	174, 177, 194
		6:9–11	158, 172, 175–76, 178, 191, 274–75
1:2	154, 157, 165, 177		
1:4	157	6:10	174
1:8	157	6:11	1, 154, 170, 172–73, 175–78, 181, 194–95, 253, 267
1:10	165		
1:10–17	158–61, 166–68, 172, 183, 191, 274–75		
		6:19	154
1:12	164, 181	7:14	154

7:18–19	228	12:13	11, 154, 158, 162–63, 176, 186–90, 237
7:22	157, 228		
7:34	154	13:2	157
7:39	157	13:10	157
8	178	14:2	157
8–10	183, 191, 277	14:20	157
8:1	178	14:33	154
8:4	183–84	15	24, 158, 193, 231, 244, 256, 261
8:4–6	183–84		
8:9–13	183	15:1–3	244
9	178	15:3	241
9:1	157	15:3–4	241, 245
9:2	157	15:3–8	194
9:10	179	15:4	241
10	166, 178–82, 185–87, 189, 191, 232, 274	15:5–8	244
		15:8	244
10:1	179–80, 182	15:9–11	244
10:1–4	183	15:12	192–93
10:1–5	158, 178–79, 181, 185–87, 189, 191–92	15:12–22	192
		15:13	194
10:1–11	182	15:13–15	194
10:1–13	182	15:14	194, 196
10:1–5	274	15:14–15	194
10:2	154, 158, 180–81, 187–90	15:14–19	193
10:2–4	186–88	15:16	194
10:3–4	186	15:16–19	194
10:4	186–88	15:17	194–96
10:5	183	15:17–19	194, 196, 274
10:6	183	15:18	157, 196
10:11	157, 183	15:18–19	158, 192, 274–75
10:16–17	284	15:19	155, 157
10:19–22	185	15:20	157, 193–94
10:20	185	15:20–21	194
11	186	15:20–22	194
11:1	277	15:21	193
11:11	157, 181	15:21–22	193–94
11:17	165	15:24	157
11:23–26	254, 284	15:29	4, 8, 154, 158, 164, 191, 196–201, 204, 208, 210, 219, 221–27, 243–44, 274
11:27–34	275		
12	32, 178, 187, 189, 191, 232, 245–46		
		15:31	157
12–14	73	15:33	174
12:2	1, 174, 194	15:35–58	190
12:3	154	15:47–49	261
12:12	188–89	15:48	171, 172, 194
12:12–13	158, 178, 186–89, 191–92, 273–75	15:51	157
		15:58	157

16:1	154	3	32, 168, 179–80, 227–29, 233, 238, 246, 265, 267, 274–75, 282
16:15	154		
16:19	157		
16:20	154	3–4	270
16:24	157	3:1	4, 31, 238
		3:1–5	229
2 Corinthians		3:1–14	229
1:1	154	3:2	236, 238
2:12	157	3:5	238
2:27	157	3:6–9	229
3:13	157	3:8	238
3:14	157	3:10–12	229
4	159, 244	3:10–29	158
4:7–12	277–78	3:13	171–72, 236, 238
4:10	277–78	3:13–14	229
4:10–11	278	3:14	157, 230, 237, 267
4:11	277	3:15	228–29
4:12	277	3:15–22	229
5:15	264	3:16	180, 229, 233, 275
5:17	157	3:17	230
5:19	157	3:18	229–30
6:2	116	3:19–21	230
6:6	154	3:22	230
7:1	154	3:23	231
8:4	154	3:23–29	234
9:1	154	3:24	231
9:12	154	3:25	231
10:17	157	3:25–29	158, 228, 231, 274–75
11:15	157	3:26	157
12:2	157	3:26–27	13
12:4	123	3:26–29	162, 178
12:9	157	3:27	154, 188, 231–35, 274
12:19	157	3:27–28	155, 228, 235
13:12	154	3:27–29	231
13:13	154	3:28	155, 157, 188, 190, 228, 231, 234–36
Galatians		3:29	180, 230–33
1	166	4:1–2	231
1:2	165	4:4	259
1:22	157	4:11	231, 234
2:4	157	4:21–5:1	31
2:17	155, 157	5:10	157
2:19	276	5:16	157
2:19–21	238	5:19–21	178
2:20	278	5:21	178
		6:7	174

Ephesians	
4:5	154
4:24	234
5:26	154

Philippians	
1:1	154, 157
1:13	157
1:14	157
1:26	157
2	260
2:1	157
2:5	157
2:7	257–59
2:8	260, 271
2:17	278
2:19	157
2:24	157
2:29	157
3:1	157
3:3	157
3:10	276
3:12	157
3:14	157
3:15	157
3:17	277
3:19	157
4:1	157
4:2	157
4:4	157
4:7	157
4:10	157
4:12	157
4:19	157
4:21	154, 157
4:22	154

Colossians	
1:28	157
2:11–13	24
2:12	154, 241
3:10	234
4:12	157

1 Thessalonians	
1:5	155
1:6	155
1:9	160, 164
1:9–10	1, 169
2:14	157, 168–69
2:16	157
3:8	157, 168
3:13	154–55
4	172, 194, 196, 252–53, 270, 274
4:1	157, 168
4:1–8	159–60, 168–70, 183, 274
4:3	154, 159, 170
4:3–7	252
4:4	154, 159
4:5	169–70
4:7	154, 159–60, 170
4:8	155, 170, 232, 267
4:16	157, 168
5:9–10	241, 264
5:12	157, 168
5:18	157, 168, 170
5:18–19	170
5:18–22	170
5:19	170, 267
5:22	170
5:26	155

2 Thessalonians	
2:13	154

1 Timothy	
2	73
2:15	154
3:9	154
4:5	154

2 Timothy	
1:3	154
2:18	24
2:21	154
2:22	154

Titus	
2:14	154
3:5	154

Philemon	
5	155

7	155	6:2	154
8	157	9:10	154
16	157		
20	157	1 Peter	
23	157	1:15 – 26	171
		3:20 – 21	179

Hebrews
2:17   93, 98
2:18   136

Revelation
9:7   258

4 Other Early Christian Texts

Apostolic Tradition
21   234

Cyril of Jerusalem
Catechetical Lectures
3   254
Lectures on the Mysteries
2.4 – 8   254

Didache
7.1   254

Firmicus Maternus
De errore profanarum religionum
22.1   138

Ignatius of Antioch
To the Ephesians (*Eph.*)
12.2   283

Origen
Commentary on Romans
5.8   277
Contra Celsum (*Cels.*)
2.33 – 35   86
3.23   86

Pseudo-Cyprian
De pascha computus
17   235

Rufinus of Aquileia
Church History
11.23   113

Tertullian
Ad nationes
1.8   235
De baptismo
5   11

5 Greek and Latin Texts

Aeschylus
  Agammemnon
  177 – 178   105

Apollodorus
  Library
  1.9.1   201
  1.9.2   201
  3.4.2   201
  3.4.3   202

  3.5.1   77, 87

Apuleius
  Metamorphoses
  1.6 – 7   118
  3.14   118, 136
  3.15   134
  3.22   136
  3.25   146
  3.29 – 4.2   146

5.22–24	136	**Demosthenes**	
6.2–3	134	*On the Crown*	
6.20	136	259	79
7.2	118		
7.15	146	**Dio Cassius**	
7.20	118	*Roman History*	
8	134	50.5.3	75
8.24	118	50.25.2–4	75
9.15	136		
11	109–10, 112–13, 118, 130, 132–33, 140–42, 146, 148–49, 209, 252	**Epictetus** *Diatribai (Dissertationes)* 2.1.39	277
11.1	116	2.19.19	147
11.2	133	3.717	147
11.5	116, 133, 136		
11.6	120–22, 133, 146–47	**Euripides**	
11.9	136	*Bacchae*	
11.10	112	1–5	84
11.11	140, 144–45	20–23	84
11.12	118	43–50	84
11.13	133, 146	53–54	84
11.14	112	67–68	76
11.15	121, 136	72–87	74
11.16	117, 136	84–85	91
11.17	117	135–144	74
11.19	113, 130, 133, 139, 143	157	74
11.20	130	215–262	74
11.23	142	233–238	96
11.24	113	298–301	79
11.25	117	313–318	72
11.30	140	353	103
		370–433	74
Aretaeus of Cappadocia		378	79
Symptoms and Reasons for Chronic Illness		421–423	79
1.6.4	78	443–450	101
		444–450	79
Aristides		477–478	103
Isthmikos		465	98
46.40	207–208	466	98
		471–474	66
Aristophanes		498	98, 102
Frogs		500	98
449–59	121	502	98
		518	98
Cicero		760–764	77
Tusculanae disputationes		1037–1038	77
1.30.74	277	1114–1152	77

1286	77	1.16	86

Cretans, fr. 472   86
  Medea
  1282–1291   201

Heliodorus
  6.12–5   220

Herodian
  Ab excessu divi Marci
  1.3.3   75

Herodotus
  The Persian Wars
  2.171   139
  2.42   144
  2.47–48   144
  4.78–80   78
  4.79   78
  4:80   78

Hesiod
  Theogony
  106   82
  Works and Days
  108   82

Homer
  Iliad
  6.138–40   84
  15.67   119
  16.419–507   119
  23   216
  Odyssey
  5.333–335   202
  11   216–19

Homeric Hymn to Demeter
  473–79   84

Homeric Hymn to Dionysus
  53–57   84

Horace
  Epistles
  1.7   211

Juvenal
  Satires
  6.526–541   148

Livy
  History of Rome
  39.8–9   72, 76

Lucan
  Pharsalia
  6.588–830   220

Lucian
  Alexander the False Prophet
  38   161–62
  Essays in Portraiture Defended
  23   185

Martial
  Epigrams
  1.47   211

Nonnus of Panopolis
  Dionysiaca
  12.171   135

Ovid
  Amores
  2.13   120
  Fasti
  6.501–502   202
  Metamorphoses
  4.416–542   201
  9.685–701   119–20
  9.693   140
  9.696   120

Pausanias
  1.20.3   79
  1.44.8   202
  2.2.1   203
  2.2.6   87
  2.4.6–7   141
  2.7.6   87
  8.37.5   87

8.54.5	144	360D	135
		361D–E	135
Philostratus		361E	135
Heroikos		362B	144
53.4	204, 209	364E	144
		365B	144–45
Pindar		366E–F	141
Isthmian fr. 5	202	*Life of Antony*	
		24.3	75
Plato		60.3	75
Laws		*On the Eating of the Flesh*	
672B	87	1.7	130
790D–E	77	*Table Talk*	
815	77	Question 6	68
Phaedo		*Theseus*	
67E	277	25	203
69D	104		
Phaedrus		Seneca	
244E	76	*Epistles*	
250	260	71.26	277
Republic			
2.362E–367E	219	Sophocles	
2.365 A	219	*Antigone*	
2.366 A	219	963–964	80
Theaetetus			
176 A–B	260	Statius	
		Silvae	
Plutarch		5.3.242–245	139
Isis and Osiris (Is. Os.)		*Thebaid*	
351E	147	6.11	209
351E–F	131		
351E–352 A	131	Synesius	
351F	131	*Dio*	
351F–352 A	141–42	10 (Aristotle, *fr.* 15)	105, 270
352 A	131		
352C	147	Tacitus	
355E	131	*Histories*	
356B	144	4.83	85

6 Inscriptions

CED 120	119	Jaccottet #22	72
CIL 3.686 = CLE 1233	81	Jaccottet #45	72
IG II² 1043	75	Jaccottet #147	72
IG IV 203	204	Jaccottet #149	72
IG X,2 1.83	143	Jaccottet #150	72

Jaccottet #174   72
Jaccottet #180   83, 92
Jaccottet #181   72
Jaccottet #188   72
Jaccottet #98 = AHK 116   75
Jaccottet #37 = AHK 64   75
LSAM 48 = I.Miletos 8   70–71
RICIS 101/502   115
RICIS 105/0895 = SIRIS 62   114
RICIS 113/0301   120
RICIS 113/0537 = IG X,2 1.259   114, 144
RICIS 113/0545 = IG X,2 1.254   132
RICIS 114/0202 = Totti #19   109, 116, 121, 134
RICIS 202/1101 = IG XII,5 14   132
RICIS 202/1801 = IG XII,5 739   137
RICIS 302/0204 = I.Kyme 41   118, 120, 133

RICIS 308/1201   123
RICIS 501/0127 = SIRIS 390   121
RICIS 501/0174   144
RICIS 501/0196 = SIRIS 463 = IG XIV 2098   125, 143
RICIS 504/0208 = SIRIS 487   115
RICIS 504/0701 = SIRIS 501 = CIL X 3759   141
RICIS 603/0101 = SIRIS 761 = CIL II 3386   119
SEG 8, n. 549   119
SEG 17, n. 495 = Jaccottet #146 = AHK 202   85
SEG 17, n. 496 = Jaccottet #147 = AHK 203   72
SEG 31, n. 122 = AHK 9   72
SEG 46, n. 800 = AHK 45   71
Syll.^{3} 3.1012   70
Syll.^{3} 3.1109 = IG II^2 1368 = AHK 7   70, 91
Syll.^{3} 3.1115 = Jaccottet #94 = AHK 115   72

7 Papyri

Derveni Papyrus   105
PGM 36   135
P.Oxy. 1380   114, 119, 134

P.Ryl 2.153   231
Papyrus Washington University inv. 138   150

8 Tablets

Lead tablet from the Sanctuary of Demeter and Kore
Plate 32   220

"Orphic" Gold Tablets
  GJ 1 = OF 474   67, 81–82, 94
  GJ 2 = OF 476   81, 94
  GJ 3 = OF 487   81, 94
  GJ 5 = OF 488   94
  GJ 6 = OF 492   102
  GJ 7 = OF 489   102
  GJ 8 = OF 475   82, 94
  GJ 9 = OF 491   94, 102
  GJ 10   82
  GJ 10–14 = OF 478, 479, 480, 482, 483   94

  GJ 11   82
  GJ 12   82
  GJ 13   82
  GJ 14   82
  GJ 16 = OF 481   82, 94
  GJ 18 = OF 484a   82, 94
  GJ 20 = OF 496e   82
  GJ 25   82
  GJ 26a = OF 485   82, 101
  GJ 26b = OF 486   82, 101
  GJ 27 = OF 493   81, 102
  GJ 28 = OF 493a   82
  GJ 29 = OF 484   82, 94
  GJ 30 = OF 496n   66, 102
  GJ 31 = OF 496b   102